The American Express
International Traveler's Pocket
ITALIAN
Dictionary and Phrase Book

The American Express
International Traveler's Pocket
ITALIAN
Dictionary and Phrase Book

Simon and Schuster
New York

List of abbreviations

abbrev	–	abbreviation	*num*	–	numeral
adj	–	adjective	*pl*	–	plural
adv	–	adverb	*pref*	–	prefix
art	–	article	*prep*	–	preposition
conj	–	conjunction	*pron*	–	pronoun
excl	–	exclamation	*vi*	–	intransitive verb
f	–	feminine noun	*vr*	–	reflexive verb
m	–	masculine noun	*vt*	–	transitive verb
n	–	noun	*vt/i*	–	transitive/intransitive verb

The asterisk * denotes an irregular verb, to which the reader is referred in the list of irregular verbs in the grammar section.

The dash — denotes that the plural is invariable.

Cross-reference letter keys occur in brackets after main section headings. Phrases are numbered in sequence following each main heading. Phrase words are cross-referenced in the English-Italian dictionary section by letter and number to their relevant phrases.

William Collins Sons & Co

Editors
Lorna Sinclair
Nicholas Rollin
with
Andrew Wilkin
Ennio Bilucaglia
Lesley Robertson
Assistant Editors
Susan Dunsmore
Valerie McNulty
Managing Editor
Richard H. Thomas

Mitchell Beazley Publishers

Editors
James Hughes
Christopher McIntosh
Designer
Philip Lord
Executive Art Editor
Douglas Wilson
Production
Julian Deeming

Edited by William Collins Sons & Co. Ltd
and by Mitchell Beazley International Ltd
Designed by Mitchell Beazley International Ltd
14–15 Manette Street
London W1V 5LB
© Mitchell Beazley Publishers 1983
© William Collins Sons & Company Ltd 1983

Published by Simon and Schuster, Inc.
Simon and Schuster Building
Rockefeller Center
1230 Avenue of the Americas
New York, New York 10020

Library of Congress Cataloging in Publication Data

The American Express international traveler's pocket dictionaries and phrase books, English/Italian.

Includes index.
1. Italian language—Conversation and phrase books. 2. Italian language—Dictionaries—English. 3. English language—Dictionaries—Italian. I. American Express Company. II. Mitchell Beazley Ltd.
PC1121.A48 1983   458.3'421   82-19623
ISBN 0-671-47031-0

Typeset by Coats Dataprint Ltd, Inverness

Printed in Great Britain by William Collins Sons & Co Ltd, Glasgow.

Contents

Pronunciation

English spelling gives only an approximate idea of the Italian sounds, which can be learned only by listening to the Italians themselves. However, Italian is a fairly easy language to read. In this guide the words have been split up for greater clarity, but in fact there should be no pause between syllables.

The spellings *c* and *ch* can be confusing, because *c* is sometimes pronounced like English *ch* (see the table), while the Italian *ch* is pronounced like English *k*. Thus *c'è* (there is) is pronounced like English *check* without the final *ck*, while *chi?* (who?) is pronounced *kee*. Also, the spellings *cia*, *cie*, *cio* and *ciu* are pronounced *cha*, *chay*, *cho* and *choo*: the *i* is not pronounced unless it is part of a stressed syllable. The letter *g* behaves in a similar way, as can be seen in the table.

The vowels *a*, *e*, and *o* can be either 'long' or 'short', i.e. pronounced as either *ah* or *a*, *ay* or *e*, *oh* or *o*, depending on the circumstances. These are shown in the accompanying pronunciation scheme.

Sometimes Italian has two distinct vowel sounds next to each other, as in words like *dei*. These sounds merge into each other and should not be separated by a pause.

In English, the letter *r* is often nothing more than a sign to make the vowel sound longer, as in *more*, but in Italian all *r*'s are rolled.

Stress

Longer words are usually stressed on the penultimate (second last) syllable, but in this guide the stressed syllable is indicated each time it appears, and not only in exceptional cases. Any sound not explained here or in the table should be clear from the pronunciation shown beside each word in the dictionary section.

How to Pronounce Italian

Italian spelling	Closest English sound	Shown here by	Example	
a	p*a*t	*a*	quando	**kwan**·doh
	or f*a*ther	*ah*	comprare	kom·**prah**·ray
e	p*e*t	*e*	letto	**let**·toh
	or g*a*te	*ay*	per	payr
i	m*ee*t	*ee*	vino	**vee**·noh
	or *y*et	*y*	fieno	**fye**·noh
o	th*ou*ght	*o*	soldi	**sol**·dee
	or b*o*ne	*oh*	cosa	**koh**·sa
u	b*oo*t	*oo*	luna	**loo**·na
	or *w*on't	*w*	uomo	**wo**·moh
c	before e, i *ch*at	*ch*	centro	**chen**·troh
	before a, o, u *c*at	*k*	cosa	**koh**·sa
ch	*c*at	*k*	chi	kee
g	before e, i *g*in	*j* or *dj*	giorno	**jor**·noh
	before a, h, o, u *g*ot	*g*	regalo	ray·**ga**·loh
gl	mi*lli*on	*ly*	figlio	**feel**·yoh
gn	compa*ni*on	*ny*	bisogno	bee·**zon**·yoh
h	not pronounced		ho	oh
r	ca*rr*ot	*r*	fare	**fah**·ray
s	*s*et	*s*	soldi	**sol**·dee
	or pha*s*e	*z*	caso	**kah**·zoh
sc	before e, i *sh*op	*sh*	uscita	oo·**shee**·ta
	before a, o, u *sc*ar	*sk*	capisco	ka·**pees**·koh
z	ca*ts*	*ts*	senza	**sen**·tsa
	or ro*ds*	*dz*	mezzo	**medz**·dzoh

Introduction

The Italian language

Italian is spoken by some 60 million as their mother tongue. The Swiss
have it as one of their official languages, and it is also the local vernacular
in parts of France and Yugoslavia. Italians speak it with a conscious pride
and brio; it is a language of excitement and rhetoric, expressing joy in
life. It is comparatively easy to speak adequately (though difficult to
achieve excellence in), and with this book you should soon be able to
make your way around.

How the book works

This is a combined phrasebook and dictionary, designed primarily for the
needs of the traveler. It enables you to find easily and quickly just the
phrase you need, whether you are buying a suit or trying to tell a garage
mechanic what is wrong with your car. The Italian is accompanied in all
cases by an instant guide to pronunciation.

Many of the phrases listed consist of a basic group of words which can
be linked up with different subsidiary words to produce variations, in the
way that a power tool can be fitted with extensions. With phrases of this
kind the basic "tool" is shown on one side and the "extension" on the
other, with a dash in between: alternative extensions are either indicated
by an oblique stroke or shown on the line below. A further stock of
extensions is found in the dictionary section at the back of the book, and
this serves also as a cross-reference index to the phrases.

Here is an example. If you look up the word "toll" in the dictionary,
you will find "il pedaggio" and a cross-reference to Section T (Travel).
Here you will see, following the number shown in the cross-reference,
the kind of phrase you might need in using this word.

You will soon be able to express yourself in the language with
flexibility and confidence, and what you learn from this book can open
the door to the whole Italian language.

Understanding what you hear

This book not only tells you what to say but also helps you to interpret
some of the things that will be said to you. For example, the section on
"Finding the way" anticipates the sort of directions you may be given.
Fortunately, Italians usually enunciate very clearly, but it will be
necessary to attune your ear to unfamiliar sounds and intonations.

As you start to hear some of the words you have learned being used by
the Italians themselves, you will be able to adjust your pronunciation
accordingly. Bear in mind that Italian words are heavily stressed. The
stressed syllable is usually the first or second one from the end except
where an accent marks it as coming on the last syllable — for example,
specialità, "specialty". The stressed syllable is marked in the
pronunciation guide by *bold* lettering (*spe·cha·lee·ta*). When speaking,
open your mouth wide and utter the words as fully and roundly as
possible.

So read, listen, learn and practice. Even a limited competence in
Italian will bring you great satisfaction as you travel.
Buon viaggio!

Basic equipment (B)

Here are some of the words and phrases which make up the basic coinage of Italian and which it is useful to have in your pocket for a wide variety of situations. You would be well advised to read through this whole section before starting your trip. If you can memorize any of it, so much the better.

Some essentials

Yes
Sí
see

No
No
no

Please
Per favore
payr fa·voh·re

Thank you
Grazie
gra·tsye

No thank you
No grazie
no gra·tsye

Thank you (in return)
Grazie a Lei
gra·tsye a ley

You're welcome
Prego
pre·go

Please and thank you

Italians have rather more ritualistic conventions of common politeness than do most English speakers. In English one says "Thank you" and there, often, is an end to it; an Italian will almost invariably reply "Prego", which means "You're welcome" or "Not at all". You will show courtesy by doing as much yourself. Again, an Italian will often reply "Prego" to "Mi dispiace" (I'm sorry) or "Mi scusi" (Forgive me).

1 I'm sorry
  Mi dispiace
  mee dee·spyah·che
2 Excuse me/Please let me by
  Permesso
  payr·mays·soh
3 Forgive me
  Mi scusi
  mee skoo·zee

4 It doesn't matter
  Non importa
  nohn eem·por·ta
5 That's all right/That's OK
  Va bene
  va be·ne

Greetings and general exchanges

Italians use the words "Signore", "Signora" and "Signorina" much more frequently than the English use "Sir" or "Madam". It is usual to address any man, woman or girl you do not know or do not know well as "Signore", "Signora" or "Signorina", and if, for instance, you wanted to ask someone the way you would attract his or her attention by saying "Signore" or "Signora" instead of "Excuse me". Again, for example, when confronting an official, you would say "Buona sera, Signore" or "Buona sera, Signora", rather than simply "Buona sera" (Good afternoon).

6 Good morning — Sir
   Buon giorno — Signore
   bwon johr·noh — see·nyoh·re
   — Madam
   — Signora
   — *see·nyoh·ra*
   — Miss
   — Signorina
   — *see·nyoh·ree·na*

7 Good afternoon/evening
Buona sera
bwo·na say·ra

8 Good night
Buona notte
bwo·na not·te

9 Hello (informal)
Ciao
chow

10 Hello (by telephone)
Pronto
prohn·to

11 Goodbye
Arrivederci
ar·ree·ve·dayr·chee

12 Goodbye (informal)
Ciao
chow

13 How do you do?/I'm very glad
to meet you
Piacere/lieto di fare la Sua
conoscenza
*pya·chay·re/lye·to dee fah·ray
la soo·a ko·no·shen·tsa*

14 See you soon/See you later
A presto
a pre·sto

15 What is your name?
Come si chiama Lei?
koh·me see kyah·ma ley

16 My name is . . .
Mi chiamo . . .
mee kyah·mo . . .

17 How are you?
Come sta?
koh·me sta

18 I'm very well/I'm fine, thank
you
Stò bene, grazie
sto be·ne gra·tsye

19 Just a minute
Un momento
oon mo·mayn·toh

20 What did you say?
Come?
koh·me

21 I understand
Capisco
ka·pee·sko

22 I do not understand
Non capisco
nohn ka·pee·sko

23 Do you understand?
Capisce?
ka·pee·she

24 I do not speak Italian
Non parlo italiano
nohn par·lo ee·ta·lyah·no

25 I do not speak Italian
very well
Non parlo bene l'italiano
*nohn par·lo be·ne
lee·ta·lyah·no*

26 Please repeat that
Vuol ripeterlo, per favore
*vwol ree·pe·ter·lo payr
fa·voh·re*

27 Please speak more slowly
Parli piú piano, per favore
*par·lee pyoo pyah·no payr
fa·voh·re*

28 Please write that down for me
Me lo scriva, per favore
may lo skree·va payr fa·voh·re

29 Do you speak English?
Parla inglese?
par·la een·glay·se

30 I am American
Sono americano(a)
*soh·no a·me·ree·
kah·no(a)*

31 Really?
Vero?
vay·ro

32 Agreed
D'accordo
dak·kor·doh

33 Fine
Bene
be·ne

34 You are right
Ha ragione
a ra·joh·ne

Common questions and statements

Many of the things you will need to ask and say will involve the following
groups of words. To most of them you can just add the name of the thing
you need, or the place you are going to, or what you want to do or want
done. Many of them will be enough on their own – "How much?", for
instance.

35   Do I have to — reserve a table?
                Devo — prenotare un tavolo?
                de·vo — pre·no·tah·ray oon tah·vo·loh

36   Do we have to — pay?
             Dobbiamo — pagare?
         dob·byah·mo — pa·gah·ray

37   Do you have — any matches?
                Ha — dei fiammiferi?
             a — dey fyam·mee·fe·ree
                    — the time?
                    — l'ore?
                    — *loh·re*

38 Could you come with me, please?
Potrebbe venire con me, per favore?
po·treb·be ve·nee·re kohn may payr fa·voh·re

39 What's the matter?
Che cosa c'è?
ke ko·sa che

40 I've made a mistake
Ho fatto uno sbaglio
o fat·to oo·no zba·lyoh

41 It's a mistake
È uno sbaglio
e oo·no zba·lyoh

42 What does that mean?
Cosa significa?
ko·sa see·nyee·fee·ka

43 What is this/that?
Cos'è questo/quello?
ko·se kway·sto/kwayl·lo

44 What time is it?
Che ora è?
ke oh·ra e

45 At what time?
A che ora?
a ke oh·ra

46 How much/many?
Quanto/quanti?
kwan·to/kwan·tee

47 How often?
Ogni quanto tempo?
oh·nyee kwan·to tem·poh

48 How long will that take?
Quanto tempo ci vorrà?
kwan·to tem·poh chee vor·ra

49 Where is?
Dov'è?
doh·ve

50 Here it is/Here you are
Eccolo/Eccoti
ek·ko·lo/ek·ko·tee

51 How do you say "..." in Italian?
Come si dice "..." in italiano?
koh·me see dee·che "..." een ee·ta·lyah·no

52 I/We need — something to drink
Ho/abbiamo bisogno di — qualcosa da bere
o/ab·byah·mo bee·zoh·nyoh dee — kwal·ko·sa da bay·re

53 I want — a cup of coffee
Voglio — una tazza di caffè
vo·lyo — oo·na tats·tsa dee kaf·fe
— to go to Florence
— andare a Firenze
— *an·dah·ray a fee·ren·tse*

54 I would like — a glass of wine
Vorrei — un bicchiere di vino
vor·rey — oon beek·kye·re dee vee·noh

55 May I borrow your pen?
Può prestarmi la penna?
pwo pre·star·mee la payn·na

56 Do you mind if — I open the window?
Le dispiace se — apro la finestra?
le dee·spyah·che se — ah·pro la fee·ne·stra

57 Whom should I see about this?
A chi devo rivolgermi per questo?
a kee de·vo ree·vol·jer·mee payr kway·sto

58 Can you — help me?
Può — aiutarmi?
pwo — a·yoo·tar·mee
— tell me the way?
— indicarmi la strada?
— *een·dee·kar·mee la strah·da*

59 Do you know — a good restaurant near here?
Conosce — un buon ristorante qui vicino?
ko·noh·she — oon bwon re·sto·ran·te kwee vee·chee·no
— where the Hotel Ritz is?
— dov'è l'albergo Ritz?
— *doh·ve lal·ber·goh reets*

General problems and requests

60 Can you help me, please?
Può aiutarmi, per favore?
pwo a·yoo·tar·mee payr fa·voh·re

61 We need someone who can speak English
Abbiamo bisogno di qualcuno che parli inglese
ab·byah·mo bee·zoh·nyoh dee kwal·koo·no ke par·lee een·glay·se

62 **Please repeat that**
Vuol ripeterlo, per favore?
vwol ree·pe·ter·lo payr fa·voh·re

63 **We are in a hurry**
Abbiamo fretta
ab·byah·mo frayt·ta

64 **Can you do it for me — at once?**
Me lo può fare — subito?
may lo pwo fah·ray — soo·bee·to

65 **The machine has broken down**
La macchina è guasta
la mak·kee·na e gwa·sta

66   **I have broken — the switch/the glass**
Ho rotto — l'interruttore/il vetro
o roht·to — leen·ter·root·toh·re/eel vay·troh

67   **I have spilled — the water/the wine**
Ho versato — l'acqua/il vino
o ver·sah·to — lak·kwa/eel vee·noh

68   **I have forgotten — my glasses/my key**
Ho dimenticato — gli occhiali/la chiave
o dee·men·tee·kah·to — lyee ok·kyah·lee/la kyah·ve

69   **I have left my bag — in the plane/in the coach**
Ho lasciato la mia borsa — sull'aereo/sul pullman
o la·shah·to la mee·a bohr·sa — sool·la·e·re·o/sool pool·man

70   **I wish to leave a message for — Mr Smith**
Vorrei lasciare un messaggio per — il Signor Smith
vor·rey la·shah·ray oon mes·saj·joh payr — eel see·nyohr smeeth

71 **Is there a message/letter for me?**
C'è un messaggio/una lettera per me?
che oon mes·saj·joh/oo·na let·te·ra payr may

72 **Go away!**
Va' via!
va vee·a

Travel   (T)

General

1   **I am leaving — tomorrow**
Parto — domani
par·to — do·mah·nee
          — on Thursday
          — giovedí
          — jo·ve·dee

2 **How long will the train/flight be delayed?**
Con quanto ritardo partirà il treno/l'aereo?
kohn kwan·to ree·tar·doh par·tee·ra eel tre·noh/la·e·re·oh

3   **I have missed — my train**
Ho perso — il treno
o per·so — eel tre·noh
          — my flight
          — il volo
          — eel voh·loh

4   **At what time is the next — train?**
A che ora è il prossimo — treno?
a ke oh·ra e eel pros·see·mo — tre·noh
          — flight?
          — volo?
          — voh·loh
          — bus?
          — autobus?
          — ow·to·boos

5 I am a member of the American Express party traveling to Milan
Faccio parte del gruppo American Express che va a Milano
fach·cho **par**·te del **groop**·poh a·**me**·ree·kan ek·**spres** ke va a
mee·**lah**·no

6 My party has left without me
Il mio gruppo è partito senza di me
eel **mee**·o **groop**·poh e par·**tee**·to **sen**·tsa dee may

7 I have lost the rest of my party
Ho perso gli altri del mio gruppo
o **per**·so **al**·tree del **mee**·o **groop**·poh

8   Where do I get the
                    connection — for Palermo?
Dove faccio la coincidenza — per Palermo?
doh·ve **fach**·cho la
ko·een·chee·**den**·tsa — payr pa·**ler**·mo

9   Could you — keep my seat for me, please?
Potrebbe — tenermi il posto, per favore?
po·**treb**·be — te·**nayr**·mee eel **poh**·stoh payr
fa·**voh**·re

                    — keep an eye on my luggage
                       for a few moments, please?
— guardarmi un momento i
bagagli, per favore?
— gwar·**dar**·mee oon mo·**mayn**·toh
ee ba·**ga**·lyee payr fa·**voh**·re

Arrival and departure

10   Here is — my passport
Ecco — il mio passaporto
ek·ko — eel **mee**·o pas·sa·**por**·toh
— my driver's license
— la mia patente
— la **mee**·a pa·**ten**·te

11 My wife and I are on a joint passport
Mia moglie è sul mio passaporto
mee·a **moh**·lye e sool **mee**·o pas·sa·**por**·toh

12 Our children are on this passport
I bambini sono su questo passaporto
ee bam·**bee**·nee **soh**·no soo **kway**·sto pas·sa·**por**·toh

13   I am staying — for two weeks
Sto — per due settimane
sto — payr **doo**·e set·tee·**mah**·ne
— at the hotel Gloria
— all'albergo Gloria
— al·lal·**ber**·goh **glo**·rya

14 I have nothing to declare
Non ho niente da dichiarare
nohn o **nyen**·te da dee·kya·**rah**·ray

15 I have the usual allowance of cigarettes and liquor
Ho la quantità permessa di tabacco e di alcool
o la kwan·tee·**ta** payr·**mays**·sa dee ta·**bak**·koh e dee **al**·kol

16 These are for my personal use
Questi sono per il mio uso personale
kway·stee **soh**·no payr eel **mee**·o oo·zoh payr·so·**nah**·le

17 I represent Universal Chemicals
Rappresento la Universal Chemicals
rap·pre·**zen**·to la oo·nee·ver·sal ke·mee·kals

18 I am looking for the representative of Alpha Engineering
Cerco il rappresentante dell'Alpha Engineering
chayr·ko eel rap·pre·zen·**tan**·te del·**lal**·fa en·jee·**nee**·reeng

19 He/she was due to meet me here
Lui/lei doveva incontrarmi qui
loo·ee/lley do·**vay**·va een·kon·**trar**·mee kwee

20 The people I was to meet have not turned up
Le persone che dovevo incontrare non si sono fatte vedere
le per·**soh**·ne ke do·**vay**·vo een·kon·**trah**·ray nohn see **soh**·no
fat·te ve·**day**·re

Luggage

21   **Please take these bags — to platform 9**
       Per favore porti queste
              valigie — al binario nove
       *payr fa·**voh**·re **por**·tee*
          ***kway**·ste va·**lee**·je — al bee·**nah**·ryoh **no**·ve*
                    — to a taxi
                    — ad un tassí
                    *— ad oon tas·**see***

22   **My luggage — has not arrived**
       I miei bagagli — non sono arrivati
       *ee mee·**yay** ba·**ga**·lyee — nohn **soh**·no ar·ree·**vah**·tee*

23   **Where is the luggage from**
                    the flight — from London?
       Dove sono i bagagli del
                    volo — da Londra?
       ***doh**·ve **soh**·no ee ba·**ga**·lyee*
              del **voh**·loh — da **lohn**·dra

24   **Is there a baggage checkroom?**
      C'è un deposito bagagli?
      *che oon de·**po**·zee·toh ba·**ga**·lyee*

25   **Are there any — porters?**
       Ci sono — dei portabagagli?
       *chee **soh**·no — dey por·ta·ba·**ga**·lyee*
                  — luggage carts?
                  — dei carrelli portabagagli?
                  *— dey kar·**rel**·lee por·ta·ba·**ga**·lyee*

26   **That bag is not mine**
      Quella valigia non è mia
      ***kwayl**·la va·**lee**·ja nohn **e mee**·a*

27   **Where is my other bag?**
      Dov'è l'altra mia valigia?
      *doh·ve **lal**·tra **mee**·a va·**lee**·ja*

28   **The contents of that bag are fragile**
      Il contenuto di quella valigia è fragile
      *eel kon·te·**noo**·toh dee **kwayl**·la va·**lee**·ja e **frah**·jee·le*

29   **I wish to have my luggage sent on ahead**
      Vorrei spedire i bagagli in anticipo
      *vor·**rey** spe·**dee**·re ee ba·**ga**·lyee een an·**tee**·chee·poh*

30   **I sent a suitcase in advance. Where do I pick it up?**
      Ho spedito una valigia in anticipo. Dove la posso ritirare?
      *o spe·**dee**·to **oo**·na va·**lee**·ja een an·**tee**·chee·poh **doh**·ve la **pos**·so*
      *ree·tee·**rah**·ray*

31   **That case is specially insured**
      Quella valigia è assicurata particolarmente
      ***kwayl**·la va·**lee**·ja e as·see·koo·**rah**·ta par·tee·ko·lar·**mayn**·te*

32   **I wish to leave these bags in the baggage checkroom**
      Voglio lasciare queste valigie al deposito bagagli
      *vo·lyo la·**shah**·ray **kway**·ste va·**lee**·je al de·**po**·zee·toh ba·**ga**·lyee*

33   **I shall pick them up — this evening/tomorrow**
       Le riprenderò — stasera/domani
       *le ree·pren·de·**ro** — sta·**say**·ra/do·**mah**·nee*

34   **How much is it per suitcase?**
      Quanto costa per valigia?
      ***kwan**·to **ko**·sta payr va·**lee**·ja*

35   **What time do you close?**
      A che ora chiudete?
      *a ke **oh**·ra kyoo·**day**·te*

Airport and flight inquiries

36   **Where do I get the bus — for Leonardo da Vinci**
                                  (Fiumicino) airport?
       Da dove parte il pullman — per l'aeroporto di Fiumicino?
       *da **doh**·ve **par**·te eel **pool**·man — payr la·e·ro·**por**·toh dee*
                                  *fyoo·mee·**chee**·noh*

             Where do I get the bus — for the center of town?
           Da dove parte il pullman — per il centro della città?
      da doh·ve par·te eel pool·man — payr eel chen·troh del·la cheet·ta

37   I wish to check my luggage — to Turin on the Alitalia flight
             Voglio registrare i miei
                    bagagli — per il volo Alitalia per Torino
      vo·lyo re·jee·strah·ray ee
        mee·yay ba·ga·lyee — payr eel voh·loh a·lee·ta·lya
                         payr to·ree·no

38   Where is the arrival/departure board?
     Dov'è la tabella orario degli arrivi/delle partenze?
     doh·ve la ta·bel·la oh·rah·ryoh de·lyee ar·ree·vee/del·le par·ten·tse

39   When will the boarding announcement for the flight be made?
     A che ora sarà annunciato il volo?
     a ke oh·ra sa·ra an·noon·chah·to eel voh·loh

40   Which gate do I go to?
     A quale uscita mi devo dirigere?
     a kwah·le oo·shee·ta mee de·vo dee·ree·je·re

41   Is there a snack bar/duty-free shop in the departure lounge?
     C'è un buffè/duty-free nella sala imbarco?
     che oon boof·fe/dyoo·tee·free nel·la sah·la eem·bar·koh

42   Will a meal be served on the plane?
     Verrà servito un pasto sull'aereo?
     ver·ra ser·vee·to oon pa·stoh sool·la·e·re·oh

43   What are weather conditions like for the flight?
     Che tempo si prevede per il volo?
     ke tem·poh see pre·vay·de payr eel voh·loh
     (for answers see "The weather" under "Making conversation",
     p.65)

44   Can I change my seat?
     Posso cambiare posto?
     pos·so kam·byah·ray poh·stoh

                I should like to be — near the front/the window
                   Vorrei stare — davanti/vicino al finestrino
             vor·rey stah·ray — da·van·tee/vee·chee·no al
                         fee·ne·stree·noh

45   I suffer from airsickness
     Soffro di mal d'aria
     sof·fro dee mal dah·rya

46   I should like to speak to the airport police
     Vorrei parlare con la polizia dell'aeroporto
     vor·rey par·lah·ray kohn la po·lee·tsee·a del·la·e·ro·por·toh

47   I am meeting somebody arriving on a flight from Madrid
     Incontro qualcuno che arriva con il volo da Madrid
     een·kohn·tro kwal·koo·no ke ar·ree·va kohn eel voh·loh da ma·dreed

48   At what time do you expect the flight from Madrid to arrive?
     A che ora è previsto l'arrivo del volo da Madrid?
     a ke oh·ra e pre·vee·sto lar·ree·voh del voh·loh da ma·dreed

---

Trains

The Italian railway system is comprehensive and not expensive, so if you are traveling from town to town it is probably the best way to go — better than by bus, and sometimes even than by car.

Inquiring

Inquiring at large Italian stations is often difficult, with long lines outside the English-speaking Ufficio Informazioni Turistiche. You might be better off to read the timetables (the Italians take a delight in a code of numerous colored symbols) or to go straight to the ticket office. Here are some of the questions you will want to ask. Note that the Italian name of most major Italian (or foreign) cities is not the same as the English one. For numerals and the time, see pp. 68, 69.

49 Where is the ticket office/
   timetable board please?
   Dov'è la biglietteria/tabella
   degli orari per favore?
   *doh·ve la bee·lyayt·te·ree·a/
   ta·bel·la de·lyee oh·rah·ree
   payr fa·voh·re*

50 I want to go to Milan
   Voglio andare a Milano
   vo·lyo an·dah·ray a mee·lah·no

51 What are the times of trains
   between 8 a.m. and noon?
   Qual è l'orario dei treni fra le
   otto e mezzogiorno?
   *kwahl e loh·rah·ryoh dey
   tre·nee fra le ot·to e
   medz·dzo·johr·noh*

52 Which is the fastest train?
   Qual è il treno piú veloce?
   *kwahl e eel tre·noh pyoo
   ve·loh·che*

53 When does the next/last train
   for Genoa leave?
   Quando parte il prossimo/
   l'ultimo treno per Genova?
   *kwan·do par·te eel
   pros·see·mo/lool·tee·mo
   tre·noh payr je·no·va*

54 Is it an express?
   È un rapido?
   e oon ra·pee·doh

55 What time does the train get
   there?
   A che ora ci arriva il treno?
   *a ke oh·ra chee ar·ree·va eel
   tre·noh*

56 Do I have to change?
   Devo cambiare?
   de·vo kam·byah·ray

Tickets and reservations

Between the major cities there are special deluxe, air-conditioned trains,
called *super-rapidi*, which require reservations (for which there is an
extra charge), and in summer you would be advised to book well in
advance. Expresses are called *rapidi*, and are not to be confused with
espressi, which are sometimes not much faster than the *diretti*, while the
locali can be very slow indeed.

Children under ten pay half-fare, and under four travel free. If you
want to travel around you can get a *biglietto chilometrico*, which allows
you to travel at a reduced rate over a specified distance. If you travel at
night you can reserve a sleeper (*vagone letto*) or, more cheaply, a
couchette (*cuccetta*), which is a simple berth with blankets in a
compartment shared by several passengers.

Be warned that there are seldom snack bars on Italian trains. But you
can buy mineral water, wine and sandwiches (at high prices) at any
station of any size.

57   A single — to Mantua
        Uno andata — per Mantova, per favore
        oo·no an·dah·ta — payr man·to·va payr fa·voh·re

58   A round trip — to Florence, please
     Uno andata e ritorno — per Firenze, per favore
        *oo·no an·dah·ta e
        ree·tohr·noh — payr fee·ren·tse payr fa·voh·re*

59   A child's round trip — to Venice
     Uno andata e ritorno
              ridotto — per Venezia
        *oo·no an·dah·ta e
        ree·tohr·noh ree·doht·to — payr ve·nay·tsya*

60 He is under ten
   Ha meno di dieci anni
   a may·no dee dye·chee an·nee

61   A first-class ticket — to Rome, please
     Un biglietto di prima classe — per Roma, per favore
        *oon bee·lyayt·toh dee
        pree·ma klas·se — payr roh·ma payr fa·voh·re*

62   I want to reserve — a seat on the *rapido* to Naples
     Voglio prenotare — un posto sul rapido per Napoli
        *vo·lyo pre·no·tah·ray — oon poh·stoh sool ra·pee·doh payr
        nah·po·lee*
                     — a couchette on the 22:00 to
                       Bologna
                     — una cuccetta sul treno delle
                       ventidue per Bologna
                     *— oo·na koo·chayt·ta sool tre·noh
                       del·le ven·tee·doo·e payr
                       bo·loh·nya*

I want to reserve — two places on the sleeper to Sicily
Voglio prenotare — due posti sul vagone letto per la Sicilia
vo·lyo pre·no·tah·ray — doo·e poh·stee sool va·goh·ne let·to payr la see·chee·lya

63 There are no seats left on that train
Non c'è più nessun posto su quel treno
nohn che pyoo nes·soon poh·stoh soo kwayl tre·noh

64 Very well, when can I book a seat?
Allora, quando posso prenotare un posto?
al·loh·ra kwan·do pos·so pre·no·tah·ray oon poh·stoh

65 Write it down for me, please
Me lo scriva, per favore
may lo skree·va payr fa·voh·re

66 I'll take that, then
Prendo quello, allora
pren·do kwayl·lo al·loh·ra

67 How much does it cost to go to Bologna?
Quanto costa per andare a Bologna?
kwan·to ko·sta payr an·dah·ray a bo·loh·nya

68 I would like a place — by the window
Vorrei un posto — accanto al finestrino
vor·rey oon poh·stoh — ak·kan·to al fee·ne·stree·noh
— in a smoking compartment
— in uno scompartimento per fumatori
— *een oo·no skom·par·tee·mayn·toh payr foo·ma·toh·ree*

Station and journey

69 Which platform do I go to for the Padua train?
A quale binario prendo il treno per Padova?
a kwah·le bee·nah·ryoh pren·do eel tre·noh payr pah·do·va

70 Is this the right platform for Florence?
È questo il binario giusto per Firenze?
e kway·sto eel bee·nah·ryoh joo·sto payr fee·ren·tse

71 Is this the Florence express?
È questo il rapido per Firenze?
e kway·sto eel ra·pee·doh payr fee·ren·tse

72 When do we get to Chiusi?
Quando arriviamo a Chiusi?
kwan·do ar·ree·vyah·mo a kyoo·see

73 Do we stop at Perugia?
Si ferma a Perugia?
see fayr·ma a pe·roo·ja

74 Is this a through train?
È un treno diretto questo?
e oon tre·noh dee·ret·to kway·sto

75 Where do I have to change for Perugia?
Dove devo cambiare per Perugia?
doh·ve de·vo kam·byah·ray payr pe·roo·ja

76 Is this seat taken?
Questo posto è occupato?
kway·sto poh·stoh e ok·koo·pah·to

77 This is my seat
Questo è il mio posto
kway·sto e eel mee·o poh·stoh

78 Can you help me with my bags, please?
Mi può aiutare con le valigie, per favore?
mee pwo a·yoo·tah·ray kohn le va·lee·je payr fa·voh·re

79 May I open/shut the window?
Posso aprire/chiudere il finestrino?
pos·so a·pree·re/kyoo·de·re eel fee·ne·stree·noh

80 This is a nonsmoking compartment
Questo è uno scompartimento per non-fumatori
kway·sto e oo·no skom·par·tee·mayn·toh payr nohn·foo·ma·toh·ree

81 Are we in Arezzo yet?
Siamo già ad Arezzo?
syah·mo ja ad a·rayts·tso

82 Are we on time?
Siamo in orario?
syah·mo een oh·rah·ryoh

83 Is a delay as long as this usual?
È normale un ritardo cosí lungo?
e nor·mah·le oon ree·tar·doh ko·see loon·go

Buses and subways

Italian towns and cities, and to a lesser degree their suburbs, are well served by buses (or, in Venice, by boat-buses, *vaporetti*), supplemented in Rome, Milan and Naples by subway. Usually you are required to buy your (fixed-fare) ticket first and surrender it to the driver or conductor when you get on; if you are using public transportation at all frequently it is well worth buying a strip of these tickets, on sale near the stop at newsstands, cafés or special booths (but sometimes unobtainable at night).

84 One ticket, please
    Un biglietto, per favore
    oon bee·lyayt·toh payr fa·voh·re

85 A strip of ten tickets, please
    Un blocchetto di dieci biglietti, per favore
    oon blok·kayt·toh dee dye·chee bee·lyayt·tee payr fa·voh·re

86   Where can I buy a ticket — for the bus?
            Dove posso comprare dei
                                biglietti — per l'autobus?
        doh·ve pos·so kom·prah·ray
            dey bee·lyayt·tee — payr low·to·boos
                              — for the subway?
                              — per la metropolitana?
                              — *payr la me·tro·po·lee·tah·na*

87   Which bus do I take — for the Piazza Navona?
            Quale autobus devo
                        prendere — per Piazza Navona?
        kwah·le ow·to·boos de·vo
                pren·de·re — payr pyats·tsa na·voh·na

88 Where do I get a bus for — Leonardo da Vinci airport
                                        (Fiumicino)?
    Da dove posso prendere un
                        pullman — per Fiumicino?
        da doh·ve pos·so pren·de·re
            oon pool·man — payr fyoo·mee·chee·no

89   Does this bus go — to the Vatican?
            Questo autobus va — al Vaticano?
        kway·sto ow·to·boos va — al va·tee·kah·no

90   I want to go — to Santa Maria della Salute
            Voglio andare — a Santa Maria della Salute
        vo·lyo an·dah·ray — a san·ta ma·ree·a del·la sa·loo·te

91 Where should I change?
    Dove devo cambiare?
    doh·ve de·vo kam·byah·ray

92 And then, what number do I take?
    E poi, quale numero devo prendere?
    e poy kwah·le noo·me·roh de·vo pren·de·re

93 Can you tell me when to get off?
    Può dirmi quando devo scendere?
    pwo deer·mee kwan·do de·vo shayn·de·re

94 Should I get out at the next stop for the Cathedral?
    Devo scendere alla prossima fermata per il Duomo?
    de·vo shayn·de·re al·la pros·see·ma fer·mah·ta payr eel dwo·moh

95 How long does it take to get to Fiesole?
    Quanto tempo ci vuole per andare a Fiesole?
    kwan·to tem·poh chee vwo·le payr an·dah·ray a fye·so·le

Taxis

Taxis should be picked up at a stand rather than hailed, or they can be telephoned for. Make sure it is a proper taxi with a meter — if it is a gypsy cab you will have to pay a lot more than the going fare. Tell the driver where you want to go just by stating your destination and saying "per favore" (pronounced *payr fa·voh·re* — "please"). The following phrases may also be useful:

96 **Can you order me a taxi?**
Può chiamarmi un tassí?
pwo kya·mar·mee oon tas·see

97 **Where can I get a taxi?**
Dove posso prendere un tassí?
doh·ve pos·so pren·de·re oon tas·see

98   **Please take me — to this address**
Per favore mi porti — a questo indirizzo
payr fa·voh·re mee por·tee — a kway·sto een·dee·reets·tsoh

99   **How much is the fare — to/from the airport?**
Quanto costa andare — all'/dall'aeroporto?
kwan·to ko·sta an·dah·ray — al/dal·la·e·ro·por·toh

100 **Please drive us around the town**
Per favore, ci porti a fare un giro per la città
payr fa·voh·re chee por·tee a fah·ray oon jee·roh payr la cheet·ta

101 **Would you put the luggage in the trunk?**
Può mettere i bagagli nel portabagagli?
pwo mayt·te·re ee ba·ga·lyee nel por·ta·ba·ga·lyee

102 **I'm in a hurry**
Ho fretta
o frayt·ta

103 **Please wait here for a few minutes**
Per favore, aspetti qui un po'
payr fa·voh·re a·spet·tee kwee oon po

104 **Turn left/right, please**
Giri a sinistra/destra, per favore
jee·ree a see·nee·stra/de·stra payr fa·voh·re

105 **Stop here, please**
Si fermi qui, per favore
see fayr·mee kwee payr fa·voh·re

106 **How much is that, please?**
Quant'è, per favore?
kwan·te payr fa·voh·re

107 **Keep the change**
Tenga il resto
ten·ga eel re·stoh

Motoring

There are some disadvantages to motoring in Italy. On the whole, the roads are twisty and narrow and often crowded. Much of the country is mountainous. Some of the expressways, notoriously the *autostrada* from Florence to Bologna, are overused, so that driving on them is unpleasant and nerve-wracking; but others are perfectly all right and the network is fairly complete. In the cities, traffic is dense, jams are frequent and drivers are impatient — the anarchy of the Naples rush-hour is famous. Avoid driving in cities you do not know reasonably well. The Italians have a reputation for bad driving that is not justified — they take a delight in their skill, but this can look risky. Gasoline and car-rental are expensive, even by European standards. On the other hand, there is no better way of seeing the Italian countryside and small towns than by car.

Renting a car

108 **A rental car should be ready for me**
Ci dovrebbe essere pronta una macchina noleggiata per me
chee do·vreb·be es·se·re prohn·ta oo·na mak·kee·na no·lej·jah·ta payr may

109 **I arranged it through the Speed-Link fly-drive service**
L'ho prenotata tramite il servizio "Speed-Link/aereo piú macchina"
lo pre·no·tah·ta trah·mee·te eel sayr·vee·tsyoh speed·link/a·e·re·oh pyoo mak·kee·na

110   **I want to rent a car — to drive myself**
Voglio noleggiare una macchina — da guidare personalmente
vo·lyo no·lej·jah·ray oo·na mak·kee·na — da gwee·dah·ray per·so·nal·mayn·te

— with a chauffeur
— con autista
— *kohn ow·tee·sta*

111   I want it — for five days
La voglio — per cinque giorni
la vo·lyo — payr cheen·kwe johr·nee

112   What is the charge — per day/per week?
Quanto costa — al giorno/alla settimana?
kwan·to ko·sta — al johr·noh/al·la set·tee·mah·na

113 Is the mileage unlimited?
Il chilometraggio è illimitato?
eel kee·lo·me·traj·joh e eel·lee·mee·tah·to

114 Do you have a car that is — larger/cheaper?
Avete una macchina — più grande/meno cara?
a·vay·te oo·na mak·kee·na — pyoo gran·de/may·no kah·ra

115 My wife/my husband will be driving as well
Anche mia moglie/mio marito guiderà
an·ke mee·a moh·lye/mee·o ma·ree·toh gwee·de·ra

116 I should like comprehensive insurance
Vorrei un'assicurazione contro tutti i rischi
vor·rey oo·nas·see·koo·ra·tsyoh·ne kohn·tro toot·tee ee ree·skee

117 Must I return the car here?
Devo riportare la macchina qui?
de·vo ree·por·tah·ray la mak·kee·na kwee

118 I should like to leave the car in Rimini
Vorrei lasciare la macchina a Rimini
vor·rey la·shah·ray la mak·kee·na a ree·mee·nee

119 I should like the car delivered to my hotel
Vorrei che mi consegnano la macchina al mio albergo
vor·rey ke mee kon·se·nya·ste la mak·kee·na al mee·o al·ber·goh

120 Please show me how to operate the controls
Mi faccia vedere come funziona la macchina, per favore
mee fach·cha ve·day·re koh·me foon·tsyoh·na la mak·kee·na payr fa·voh·re

121 Please explain the car documents
Per favore mi spieghi i documenti di noleggio
payr fa·voh·re mee spee·e·gee ee do·koo·mayn·tee dee no·lej·joh

---

Parking

In busy towns parking is usually a headache, and sometimes impossible. Although parking meters have appeared in Italian cities, they have not replaced supervised parking areas, where you must pay the attendant and park where he directs you: these are your best hope, although they are often situated outside the center. Sometimes you will find streets where parking is allowed on one side only on even-numbered dates, on the other side only on odd-numbered dates. There are also disk zones, in which you are required to leave a special disk on your windshield, which shows when you arrived and so by what time you should leave.

122 Where can I park?
Dove posso parcheggiare?
doh·ve pos·so par·kej·jah·ray

123 Can I park here?
Posso parcheggiare qui?
pos·so par·kej·jah·ray kwee

124 Are you leaving?
Va via Lei?
va vee·a ley

125 Is there a parking lot nearby?
C'è un parcheggio qui vicino?
che oon par·kayj·joh kwee vee·chee·no

126 What time does the parking lot close?
A che ora chiude il parcheggio?
a ke oh·ra kyoo·de eel par·kayj·joh

127 How much does it cost per hour?
Quanto costa all'ora?
kwan·to ko·sta al·loh·ra

128 How long can I leave the car here?
Per quanto tempo posso lasciare qui la macchina?
payr kwan·to tem·poh pos·so la·shah·ray kwee la mak·kee·na

129 I will only be a few minutes
Non sarò che qualche minuto
nohn sa·ro ke kwal·ke mee·noo·toh

130 Do I need a parking disk?
È necessario il disco orario?
e ne·ches·sah·ryo eel dee·skoh oh·rah·ryo

131 Where can I get a parking disk?
Dove posso trovare un disco orario?
doh·ve pos·so tro·vah·ray oon dee·skoh oh·rah·ryo

132 Do I need parking lights?
Devo lasciare accesi i fari di posizione?
de·vo la·shah·ray ach·chay·see ee fah·ree dee po·zee·tsyoh·ne

Road conditions

The quickest way of traveling about Italy is by expressway (*autostrada*), on which you will periodically have to stop to pay a toll (*pedaggio*). These *autostrade* usually have two lanes in each direction and the outer (left) lane is very definitely for passing: keep right. The major hazard on expressways is trucks, which sometimes pull out to pass with total disregard for cars coming up behind.

Both on expressways and on ordinary roads traffic may be restricted by men working on the road (see p.18/19 for signs). In the north snow and ice are a seasonal hazard; sometimes roads further south are also slippery in winter. Road borders tend to be ill-defined, and markings are comparatively rare.

In towns, you will need to know exactly where you are going and exactly how you are going to get there through the system of one-way streets. Traffic jams and traffic backups are frequent, not only in the larger cities.

133 Is there a route that avoids the traffic?
C'è un'altra strada per evitare il traffico?
che oo·nal·tra strah·da payr e·vee·tah·ray eel traf·fee·koh

134 Is there a short-cut/detour?
C'è una scorciatoia/deviazione?
che oo·na skor·cha·to·ya/de·vya·tsyoh·ne

135 Is the traffic heavy?
Il traffico è intenso?
eel traf·fee·koh e een·ten·so

136 What is causing this tie-up?
Perché c'è questo ritardo?
payr·kay che kway·sto ree·tar·doh

137 When will the road be clear?
Quando sarà libera la strada?
kwan·do sa·ra lee·be·ra la strah·da

138 What is the speed limit?
Qual è il limite di velocità?
kwahl e eel lee·mee·te dee ve·lo·chee·ta

139 Is there a toll on this highway?
Si paga il pedaggio su quest'autostrada?
see pah·ga eel pe·daj·joh soo kway·stow·to·strah·da

140 Is the road to Geneva snowed in?
La strada per Ginevra è bloccata dalla neve?
la strah·da payr jee·nay·vra e blok·kah·ta dal·la nay·ve

141 Is the pass open?
È aperto il valico?
e a·per·to eel va·lee·koh

142 Do I need studded tires/chains?
Devo usare le gomme chiodate/le catene?
de·vo oo·zah·ray le gohm·me kyo·dah·te/le ka·tay·ne

Road signs

Italy uses International Road Signs, but the following notices often appear without an accompanying image.

143 Alt
Stop

144 Attenzione
Danger

145 Entrata
Entrance

146 Lavori in Corso
Men working on the road

147 Rallentare
Slow

148 Senso Vietato
No Entry

149	Sosta Autorizzata **Parking Permitted** **(within the stated times)**	152	Uscita **Exit**
150	Sosta Vietata **No Parking**	153	Vietato Ingresso Veicoli **No Entry for Vehicles**
151	Svolta **Curve**	154	Vietato Transito Autocarri **Closed to Heavy Traffic**

Fuel

Gasoline (*benzina*) comes in two grades: *normale* (2 star) and the higher-octane and more expensive *super* (4 star). Diesel fuel is also used. See conversion tables (p.72) for fuel quantities and tire pressures.

155   **15 liters of — 2 star**
Quindici litri di — normale
kween·dee·chee lee·tree dee — *nor·**mah**·le*
                 — 4 star
               — super
               — *soo·per*
               — diesel fuel
               — gasolio
               — *ga·**zo**·lyoh*

156 **20,000 lire worth, please (for numerals, see p.68)**
Ventimila lire, per favore
*vayn·tee·**mee**·la **lee**·re payr fa·**voh**·re*

157 **Fill her up, please**
Il pieno, per favore
*eel **pye**·noh payr fa·**voh**·re*

158   **Check — the oil**
Controlli — l'olio
*kon·**trol**·lee* — *lo·lyoh*
               — the water
               — l'acqua
               — *lak·kwa*
               — the tire pressure
               — la pressione delle gomme
               — *la pres·**syoh**·ne **del**·le **gohm**·me*

159 **The pressure is 2.3**
La pressione è due virgola tre
*la pres·**syoh**·ne **doo**·e **veer**·go·la tray*

160 **I want some distilled water**
Ho bisogno di un po' di acqua distillata
*o bee·**zoh**·nyoh dee oon po dee **ak**·kwa dee·steel·**lah**·ta*

161 **Could you clean the windshield?**
Potrebbe pulire il parabrezza?
*po·**treb**·be poo·**lee**·re eel pa·ra·**braydz**·dza*

162 **Could you put some water in the windshield washer?**
Potrebbe mettere dell'acqua nel serbatoio del tergicristalli?
*po·**treb**·be **mayt**·te·re del·**lak**·kwa nel ser·ba·**toh**·yoh dey ter·jee·kree·**stal**·lee*

163 **Can I pay by credit card?**
Posso pagare con una carta di credito?
***pos**·so pa·**gah**·ray kohn **oo**·na **kar**·ta dee **kray**·dee·toh*
            Is there — a lavatory/a telephone here?
C'è — una toilette/un telefono qui?
che — *oo·na twa·**let**/oon te·le·fo·noh kwee*

Breakdowns and repairs

164   **My car — has broken down**
La mia macchina — è guasta
*la **mee**·a **mak**·kee·na* — *e **gwa**·sta*
               — will not start
               — non parte
               — *nohn **par**·te*

165 There is something wrong with my car
C'è qualcosa che non va nella mia macchina
che kwal·ko·sa ke nohn va nel·la mee·a mak·kee·na

166 I would like to telephone for emergency road service
Vorrei telefonare al servizio assistenza stradale
vor·rey te·le·fo·nah·ray al ser·vee·tsyoh as·see·sten·tsa stra·dah·le

167   Can you send — a mechanic?
            Può mandare — un meccanico?
         pwo man·dah·ray — oon mek·ka·nee·koh
                — a tow truck?
                — un carro attrezzi?
                — *oon kar·roh at·trayt·tsee*

168   Can you — take me to the nearest garage?
              Può — portarmi al garage piú vicino?
            pwo — por·tar·mee al ga·rahj pyoo
                  vee·chee·no
              — give me a tow?
              — trainarmi?
              — *tra·ee·nar·mee*
              — give me a push?
              — darmi una spinta?
              — *dar·mee oo·na speen·ta*
              — give me a can of gasoline, please?
              — darmi una tanica di benzina, per
                  favore?
              — *dar·mee oo·na ta·nee·ka dee*
                  ben·dzee·na payr fa·voh·re

169 Can you find the trouble?
Riesce a trovare il guasto?
ree·e·she a tro·vah·ray eel gwa·stoh

170 I have run out of gasoline
Sono rimasto senza benzina
soh·no ree·ma·sto sen·tsa ben·dzee·na

171 This is broken
Questo è rotto
kway·sto e roht·to

172 It is making a funny noise
C'è un rumore strano
che oon roo·moh·re strah·no

173   The brakes — have something wrong with them
            I freni — hanno un difetto
         ee fre·nee — an·no oon dee·fet·toh

174   The windshield wipers — are not working
         I tergicristalli — non funzionano
  ee ter·jee·kree·stal·lee — nohn foon·tsyoh·na·no

175 My windshield has shattered
Il parabrezza è rotto
eel pa·ra·braydz·dza e roht·to

176 I have a flat tire
Ho una gomma sgonfia
o oo·na gohm·ma zgohn·fya

177 The battery is dead
La batteria è scarica
la bat·te·ree·a e skah·ree·ka

178 The engine is overheating
Il motore surriscalda
eel mo·toh·re soor·ree·skal·da

179 There is a leak in the radiator
Il radiatore perde acqua
eel ra·dya·toh·re per·de ak·kwa

180 I have blown a fuse
Ho fuso un fusibile
o foo·zo oon foo·zee·bee·le

181 There is a bad connection
C'è un contatto difettoso
che oon kon·tat·toh dee·fet·toh·so

182 I have lost the ignition key
Ho perso la chiave di accensione
o per·so la kyah·ve dee ach·chen·syoh·ne

183   I need — a new fan belt
             Ho bisogno di — una nuova cinghia per il
                           ventilatore
     o bee·zoh·nyoh dee — oo·na nwo·va cheen·gya payr eel
                      ven·tee·la·toh·re

184   Can you replace — the exhaust pipe?
                Può sostituirmi — il tubo di scappamento?
     pwo so·stee·too·eer·mee — eel too·boh dee skap·pa·mayn·toh

185 Is it serious?
     È una cosa seria?
     e oo·na ko·sa se·rya

186 How long will it take to repair it?
     Quanto tempo ci vorrà per ripararlo?
     kwan·to tem·poh chee vor·ra payr ree·pa·rar·lo

187 Do you have the parts?
     Avete i pezzi di ricambio?
     a·vay·te ee pets·tsee dee ree·kam·byoh

188 Can you repair it for the time being?
     Può sistemarlo per adesso?
     pwo see·ste·mar·lo payr a·des·so

189 Can I have an itemized bill for my insurance company?
     Posso avere un conto dettagliato per la mia compagnia
        di assicurazione?
     pos·so a·vay·re oon kohn·toh det·ta·lyah·to payr la mee·a
        kom·pa·nyee·a dee as·see·koo·ra·tsyoh·ne

Accidents and the police

The police in Italy are on the whole well mannered and helpful, and will naturally tend to be lenient towards foreigners. But that is not something to take for granted, and there is nothing to be gained by being irritable, impatient or in a hurry. Very often the police intervene in the directing of traffic in Italy, and indicate that you should stop if you are moving or move if you are stationary by blowing a whistle as well as or instead of gesturing. For a traffic offense, they have the power to fine you on the spot.

190 I'm very sorry, officer
     Mi dispiace molto, signore
     mee dee·spyah·che mohl·to see·nyoh·re

191 I am a foreigner
     Sono straniero(a)
     soh·no stra·nye·ro(a)

192 I did not see the signal
     Non ho visto il segnale
     nohn o vee·sto eel se·nyah·le

193 I did not know about that regulation
     Non conoscevo quella norma
     nohn ko·no·shay·vo kwayl·la nor·ma

194 I did not understand the sign
     Non ho capito il segnale stradale
     nohn o ka·pee·to eel se·nyah·le stra·dah·le

195   Here is — my driver's license
                    Ecco — la mia patente
                  ek·ko — la mee·a pa·ten·te

196 How much is the fine?
     Quant'è la multa?
     kwan·te la mool·ta

197 I was driving at 80 km/h (50 mph) (see Conversion tables, p.72)
     Stavo guidando ad ottanta chilometri all'ora
     stah·vo gwee·dan·do ad ot·tan·ta kee·lo·me·tree al·loh·ra

198 He/she was too close
     Lui/lei era troppo vicino(a)
     loo·ee/ley e·ra trop·po vee·chee·no(a)

199 I did not see him/her
     Non l'ho visto(a)
     nohn lo vee·sto(a)

200 **He was driving too fast**
Stava guidando troppo forte
stah·va gwee·dan·do trop·po for·te

201 **He did not stop**
Lui non si è fermato
loo·ee nohn see e fer·mah·to

202 **He did not yield**
Lui non ha dato la precedenza
loo·ee nohn a dah·to la pre·che·den·tsa

203 **He stopped very suddenly**
Lui si è fermato all'improvviso
loo·ee see e fer·mah·to al·leem·prov·vee·zo

204 **He swerved**
Ha sbandato
a zban·dah·to

205 **The car turned without signaling**
La macchina ha girato senza mettere la freccia
la mak·kee·na a jee·rah·to sen·tsa mayt·te·re la fraych·cha

206 **He passed on a curve**
Ha sorpassato in curva
a sor·pas·sah·to een koor·va

207 **His license plate number was . . .**
Il suo numero di targa era . . .
eel soo·o noo·me·roh dee tar·ga e·ra . . .

208 **The road was wet**
La strada era bagnata
la strah·da e·ra ba·nyah·ta

209 **I skidded**
Ho slittato
o zleet·tah·to

210 **My brakes failed**
I miei freni non hanno funzionato
ee mee·yay fre·nee nohn an·no foon·tsyoh·nah·to

211 **I could not stop in time**
Non ho potuto fermarmi in tempo
nohn o po·too·to fer·mar·mee een tem·poh

212 **What is your name and address?**
Qual è Suo nome e indirizzo?
kwahl e soo·o noh·me e een·dee·reets·tsoh

213 **What is your insurance company?**
Qual'è la Sua compagnia di assicurazione?
kwah·le la soo·a kom·pa·nyee·a dee as·see·koo·ra·tsyoh·ne

214 **We should call the police**
Dovremmo chiamare la polizia
do·vrem·mo kya·mah·ray la po·lee·tsee·a

215 **Will you please be a witness?**
Mi vuol fare da testimone?
mee vwol fah·ray da te·stee·mo·ne

216 **Do you admit responsibility?**
Ammette di essere responsabile?
am·mayt·te dee es·se·re re·spon·sah·bee·le

217 **Could we settle in cash now?**
Possiamo sistemare la cosa ora, in contanti?
pos·syah·mo see·ste·mah·ray la ko·sa oh·ra een kon·tan·tee

Finding the way (F)

Questions

The simplest way to get directions is just to say where you want to go and add "please", as you would with a taxi driver. For example, "Where is the cathedral?" would be "Il duomo, per favore". Here are some other phrases that you may need.

1 **I have lost my way**
Ho perso la strada
o per·so la strah·da

2 **How do I get to this address?**
Come ci arrivo a questo indirizzo?
koh·me chee ar·ree·vo a kway·sto een·dee·reets·tsoh

3 **Where is — the station/the cathedral?**
Dov'è — la stazione/il duomo?
doh·ve — la sta·tsyoh·ne/eel dwo·moh

4 **I would like to go — to the center of town**
Vorrei andare — al centro della città
vor·rey an·dah·ray — al chen·troh del·la cheet·ta

5 **We are looking for — the Tourist Information Office**
Cerchiamo — l'Ufficio Informazioni Turistiche
cher·kyah·mo — loof·fee·choh een·for·ma·tsyoh·nee too·ree·stee·ke

6   Can you tell me the way — to the castle?
         Può indicarmi la strada — per il castello?
         pwo een·dee·**kar**·mee la
                    strah·da — payr eel ka·**stel**·loh
7   Can you show me on the map?
     Può mostrarmi sulla cartina?
     pwo mo·**strar**·mee **sool**·la kar·**tee**·na
8   Where is the nearest post office?
     Dov'è l'ufficio postale più vicino?
     doh·**ve** loof·**fee**·choh po·**stah**·le **pyoo** vee·**chee**·no
9   Is there a service station — near here?
         C'è una stazione di servizio — qui vicino?
         che oo·na sta·**tsyoh**·ne dee
                    ser·**vee**·tsyoh — kwee vee·**chee**·no
10   Is this the right way — to the museum?
         Va bene questa strada — per il museo?
         va **be**·ne **kway**·sta **strah**·da — payr eel moo·**ze**·oh
11   Is it far — to the Forum?
             È lontano — per il Foro?
             e lon·**tah**·no — payr eel **fo**·roh
12   How far is it — to St Mark's?
         Quant'è distante — San Marco?
         kwan·**te** dee·**stan**·te — san **mar**·ko
13   How long does it take to get there?
     Quanto tempo ci vuole per arrivarci?
     kwan·to **tem**·poh chee **vwo**·le payr ar·ree·**var**·chee
14   Can one walk there?
     Si può andare a piedi?
     see **pwo** an·**dah**·ray a **pye**·dee
15   Is there a bus that goes there?
     C'è un autobus che va la?
     che oon **ow**·to·boos ke va **la**
16   Which way do I take — for Gaeta?
         Quale via devo prendere — per Gaeta?
         kwah·le **vee**·a **de**·vo
                    pren·de·re — payr ga·e·ta
17   Do I turn here — for Perugia?
         Devo girare qui — per Perugia?
         de·vo jee·**rah**·ray kwee — payr pe·**roo**·ja
18   Which is the best route — to Viterbo?
         Qual'è la strada migliore — per Viterbo?
         kwah·le **la** **strah**·da
                    mee·**lyoh**·re — payr vee·**ter**·bo
19   Which is the most scenic route?
     Qual'è la strada più panoramica?
     kwah·le **la** **strah**·da **pyoo** pa·no·**ra**·mee·ka
20   How do I get back on to the expressway?
     Come faccio per rientrare sull'autostrada?
     koh·me **fach**·cho payr ree·en·**trah**·ray sool·low·to·**strah**·da
21   Where does this road go to?
     Dove porta questa strada?
     doh·ve **por**·ta **kway**·sta **strah**·da
22   Will we arrive by this evening?
     Arriveremo entro stasera?
     ar·ree·ve·**ray**·mo **ayn**·tro sta·**say**·ra

Answers

These are the key phrases of the answer you will receive when you ask
for directions. In this case the Italian is given first, with the English
below.

23   Lei va — sempre diritto
                    ley va — **sem**·pre dee·**reet**·to
              You go — straight ahead
                        — a destra
                        — a **de**·stra
                        — right

	Lei va — a sinistra
	ley va — *a see·nee·stra*
	You go — left
	— fino a ...
	— *fee·no a*
	— as far as ...
24	Giri — a destra
	jee·ree — *a de·stra*
	Turn — right
	— a sinistra
	— *a see·nee·stra*
	— left
25	Continui — verso ...
	kon·tee·nwee — **ver·so**
Keep going straight ahead	— towards ...
	— fino a ...
	— *fee·no a*
	— until ...
26	Prenda — la strada per ...
	pren·da — *la **strah·da** payr*
	Take — the road for ...
	— la prima a destra
	— *la **pree·ma** a **de·stra***
	— the first (road) on the right
	— la seconda a sinistra
	— *la se·**kohn·da** a see·nee·stra*
	— the second (road) on the left
27	Attraversi — la strada
	*at·tra·**ver·see*** — *la **strah·da***
	Cross — the street
	— al passaggio a livello
	— *al pas·**saj·**joh a lee·**vel·**loh*
	— at the grade crossing
	— il ponte
	— *eel **pohn·**te*
	— the bridge
	— vicino
	— *vee·**chee·**no*
	— not far from here
	— all'incrocio
	— *al·leen·**kroh·**choh*
	— at the intersection
	— accanto al teatro
	— *ak·**kan·**to al te·**ah·**troh*
	— next to the theater
	— dopo il semaforo
	— ***doh·**po eel se·**mah·**fo·roh*
	— after the traffic lights
	— di fronte alla chiesa
	— *dee **frohn·**te **al·**la **kye·**za*
	— opposite the church
	— lassú
	— *las·**soo***
	— over there
	— dietro l'angolo
	— ***dye·**tro **lan·**go·loh*
	— around the corner

Money   (M)

General

1	How much is that — altogether?
	Quanto costa — in tutto?
	***kwan·**to **ko·**sta — *een **toot·**to*
2	How much is it — to get in?
	Quanto costa — l'ingresso?
	***kwan·**to **ko·**sta — *leen·**gres·**soh*

How much is it — for a child?
Quanto costa — per un bambino?
kwan·to ko·sta — payr oon bam·**bee**·noh
— per person?
— a persona?
— a per·**soh**·na
— per kilo?
— al chilo?
— al **kee**·loh

3 Is there any extra charge?
C'è bisogno di pagare un supplemento?
che bee·**zoh**·nyoh dee pa·**gah**·ray oon soop·ple·**mayn**·toh

4 Is the tip/tax (VAT) included?
È compreso(a) il servizio/l'IVA?
e kom·**pray**·so(a) eel ser·**vee**·tsyoh/**lee**·va

5 Is there a discount for — a group?
Si fa una riduzione per — un gruppo?
see fa **oo**·na
ree·doo·**tsyoh**·ne payr — oon **groop**·poh
— students?
— studenti?
— stoo·**den**·tee
— senior citizens?
— cittadini anziani?
— cheet·ta·**dee**·nee an·**tsyah**·nee

6 How much of a discount can you give me?
Che riduzione mi fa?
ke ree·doo·**tsyoh**·ne mee fa

7 Can you give me a 10 percent discount?
Può farmi una riduzione del dieci per cento?
pwo far·mee **oo**·na ree·doo·**tsyoh**·ne del **dye**·chee payr **chen**·to

8 Can you give me an estimate of the cost?
Può farmi un preventivo del costo?
pwo far·mee oon pre·ven·**tee**·voh del **ko**·stoh

9 Do I have to pay a deposit?
Devo pagare una cauzione?
de·vo pa·**gah**·ray **oo**·na kow·**tsyoh**·ne

10 Do I pay in advance or afterwards?
Pago in anticipo oppure dopo?
pah·go een an·**tee**·chee·po op·**poo**·re **doh**·po

11 Can I pay in installments?
Posso pagare a rate?
pos·so pa·**gah**·ray a **rah**·te

12 Do you accept traveler's checks?
Accettate dei travelers checks?
ach·chet·**tah**·te dey **tra**·vel·lers cheks

13 I wish to pay by credit card
Voglio pagare con una carta di credito
vo·lyo pa·**gah**·ray kohn **oo**·na **kar**·ta dee **kray**·dee·toh

14 May I have — an itemized bill?
Posso avere — un conto dettagliato?
pos·so a·**vay**·re — oon **kohn**·toh det·ta·**lyah**·to
— a receipt?
— una ricevuta?
— **oo**·na ree·che·**voo**·ta

15 You have given me the wrong change
Mi ha dato il resto sbagliato
mee a **dah**·to eel re·stoh zba·**lyah**·to

16 That's too much for me
Per me costa troppo
payr may **ko**·sta **trop**·po

17 I have no money
Non ho soldi
nohn o **sol**·dee

18 I do not have enough money
Non ho abbastanza soldi
nohn o ab·ba·**stan**·tsa **sol**·dee

19 That's all, thank you
Basta così, grazie
ba·sta ko·**see gra**·tsye

20 Can you change a 10,000-lire note into 1,000-lire notes?
   Può cambiarmi diecimila lire in banconote da mille?
   pwo kam·byar·mee dye·chee·mee·la lee·re een ban·ko·no·te·da meel·le

21 Can you give me some small change?
   Mi può dare degli spiccioli?
   mee pwo dah·ray de·lyee speech·cho·lee

Banks and exchange offices

National banks are usually open from 8:30 a.m. to 1:20 p.m, Monday to Friday. Changing money will involve two stages — checking and calculating with a clerk, then collecting the cash from the cashier, at the *cassa*. You can also change money at hotels, large stores and, of course, *uffici di cambio* (exchange offices), but the rate of exchange there tends to be less favorable; this is also true of regional banks, *casse di risparmio*. Exchange offices at airports and major railway stations stay open at night and over the weekend. Remember that you need your passport when changing money. You can change not only traveler's checks but also draw on personal checks with a banker's card from the Eurocheque banks, and on credit cards.

22 Will you change — these traveler's checks?
   Può cambiare — questi travelers checks?
   pwo kam·byah·ray — kway·stee tra·vel·lers cheks
   — these bills?
   — queste banconote?
   — *kway·ste ban·ko·no·te*

23 What is the exchange rate
   for — dollars?
   Quanto è il cambio per — il dollaro?
   kwan·to e eel kam·byoh
   payr — eel dol·la·roh

24 I would like to withdraw 50,000 lire
   Vorrei ritirare cinquantamila lire
   vor·rey ree·tee·rah·ray cheen·kwan·ta·mee·la lee·re

25 I would like to cash a check with my Eurocheque card
   Vorrei riscuotere un assegno con la mia carta Eurocheque
   vor·rey ree·skwo·te·re oon as·say·nyoh kohn la mee·a kar·ta e·oo·ro·chek

26 I would like to obtain a cash advance with my credit card
   Vorrei ottenere un anticipo con la mia carta di credito
   vor·rey ot·te·nay·re oon an·tee·chee·poh kohn la mee·a kar·ta dee kray·dee·toh

27 What is your commission?
   Quanto prendete di commissione?
   kwan·to pren·day·te dee kom·mees·syoh·ne

28 Can you contact my bank to arrange for a transfer of funds?
   Può mettersi in contatto con la mia banca per organizzare un trasferimento di denaro?
   pwo mayt·ter·see een kon·tat·toh kohn la mee·a ban·ka payr or·ga·needz·dzah·ray oon tras·fe·ree·mayn·toh dee·nah·roh

29 I have an account with the Bank of X in London/New York
   Ho un conto aperto con la Banca X di Londra/New York
   o oon kohn·toh a·per·to kohn la ban·ka X dee lohn·dra/New York

30 I have made/I wish to make an arrangement with this bank
   Ho raggiunto/Vorrei raggiungere un accordo con questa banca
   o raj·joon·to/vor·rey raj·joon·je·re oon ak·kor·doh kohn kway·sta ban·ka

31 I would like to speak to the manager
   Vorrei parlare con il direttore
   vor·rey par·lah·ray kohn eel dee·ret·toh·re

Accommodations (A)

Hotel reservations and inquiries

Hotels are officially grouped into categories of 1, 2, 3 and 4 stars, plus a small category of world-class luxury hotels, designated *de luxe*. There are also *pensioni*, which are usually perfectly adequate, if no more than that; they are categorized as first, second or third class. Most hotels can handle a reservation or inquiry in English, but some *pensioni* may not be able to do so, and if you want to take no chances, this section contains some things you might wish to say by letter or telephone, or at the reception desk.

1 Dear Sir
 Egregio Signore
 e·gre·jo see·nyoh·re

2   I wish to stay in Perugia — from... to...
   Vorrei stare a Perugia — dal... al...
   vor·rey stah·ray a pe·roo·ja — *dal... al*
         — with my wife
         — con mia moglie
         — *kohn mee·a moh·lye*
         — with my family
         — con la mia famiglia
         — *kohn la mee·a fa·mee·lya*

3 I wish to stay for three nights
 Vorrei restare per tre notti
 vor·rey re·stah·ray payr tray not·tee

4   Can you provide — a single room with toilet and
           shower/bath?
   Potreste offrire — una camera singola con
           doccia/bagno?
   po·tre·ste of·free·re — *oo·na kah·me·ra seen·go·la kohn*
           dohch·cha/ba·nyoh
         — a room with twin beds?
         — una camera a due letti?
         — *oo·na kah·me·ra a doo·e let·tee*
         — a double room, with a bed for a
          child?
         — una camera matrimoniale, con
          letto aggiunto per un bambino?
         — *oo·na kah·me·ra*
          ma·tree·mo·nyah·le kohn
          let·toh aj·joon·to payr oon
          bam·bee·noh
         — a suite with living room, bedroom,
          bath and toilet?
         — un appartamento con salotto,
          camera da letto e bagno?
         — *oon ap·par·ta·mayn·toh kohn*
          sa·lot·toh kah·me·ra da let·toh e
          ba·nyoh

5   I should like a room — that is quiet
   Vorrei una camera — tranquilla
   vor·rey oo·na kah·me·ra — *tran·kweel·la*
         — with a view
         — con vista
         — *kohn vee·sta*

I should like a room — on the first floor/second floor
Vorrei una camera — al pianterreno/al primo piano
vor·rey oo·na kah·me·ra — al pyan·ter·ray·noh/al pree·mo pyah·noh
— with a TV/radio
— con TV/radio
— *kohn tee·voo/ra·dyoh*

6 Please send me a brochure about your hotel
Vogliate inviarmi un opuscolo del vostro albergo
vo·lyah·te een·vyar·mee oon o·poo·sko·loh del vo·stro al·ber·goh

7 Sincerely yours
Distinti saluti
dee·steen·tee sa·loo·tee

8 How much is the room per night?
Quanto costa la camera per una notte?
kwan·to ko·sta la kah·me·ra payr oo·na not·te

9 Is breakfast/tax (VAT) included?
È compresa la colazione/l'IVA?
e kom·pray·sa la ko·la·tsyoh·ne/lee·va

10 How much is it — with breakfast?
Quanto costa — con la prima colazione?
kwan·to ko·sta — kohn la pree·ma ko·la·tsyoh·ne
— with breakfast and evening meal?
— la mezza pensione?
— *la medz·dza pen·syoh·ne*
— with all meals?
— la pensione completa?
— *la pen·syoh·ne kom·ple·ta*

11 Do you have a swimming pool/sauna?
Avete la piscina/sauna?
a·vay·te la pee·shee·na/sow·na

12 Can you suggest another hotel that might have a vacancy?
Può indicarmi un altro albergo con posti liberi?
pwo een·dee·kar·mee oon al·tro al·ber·goh kohn poh·stee lee·be·ree

Checking in and out

13 I have reserved a room in the name of Smith
Ho prenotato una camera, a nome Smith
o pre·no·tah·to oo·na kah·me·ra a noh·me smeeth

14 Can I see the room, please?
Posso vedere la camera, per favore?
pos·so ve·day·re la kah·me·ra payr fa·voh·re

15 The room is too — small/noisy
La camera è troppo — piccola/rumorosa
la kah·me·ra e trop·po — peek·ko·la/roo·mo·roh·sa

16 When will the room be ready?
Quando sarà pronta la camera?
kwan·do sa·ra prohn·ta la kah·me·ra

17 Where is the bathroom/toilet?
Dov'è il bagno/la toilette?
doh·ve eel ba·nyoh/la twa·let

18 I want to stay an extra night
Vorrei restare un'altra notte
vor·rey re·stah·ray oo·nal·tra not·te

19 We shall be leaving at 9 o'clock tomorrow morning
Partiremo domani mattina alle nove
par·tee·ray·mo do·mah·nee mat·tee·na al·le no·ve

20 By what time do we have to vacate the room?
Per che ora dobbiamo liberare la camera?
payr ke oh·ra dob·byah·mo lee·be·rah·ray la kah·me·ra

21 I would like the bill, please
Il conto, per favore
eel kohn·toh payr fa·voh·re

22 Can I pay by credit card?
Posso pagare con una carta di credito?
pos·so pa·gah·ray kohn oo·na kar·ta dee kray·dee·toh

23   Do you accept — traveler's checks?
                       Accettate — travelers checks?
          ach·chet·tah·te — tra·vel·lers cheks
                                — American Express cards/checks?
                                — carte di credito/assegni
                                   dell'American Express?
                                — *kar·te dee kray·dee·toh/as·say·nyee*
                                   del·la·me·ree·kan ek·spres
24 Could you have my luggage brought down/sent on?
    Può far portare giù/spedire i miei bagagli?
    pwo far por·tah·ray joo/spe·dee·re ee mee·yay ba·ga·lyee
25 Could you have any letters or messages forwarded?
    Può far proseguire la mia posta od eventuali messaggi?
    pwo far pro·se·gwee·re la mee·a po·sta od e·ven·twah·lee mes·saj·jee

---

Service and practical needs

26   What time is — breakfast/lunch?
                       A che ora c'è — la prima colazione/il pranzo?
          a ke oh·ra che — la pree·ma ko·la·tsyoh·ne/eel
                                pran·dzoh
27 Can we have breakfast in our room, please?
    Possiamo prendere la prima colazione in camera, per favore?
    pos·syah·mo pren·de·re la pree·ma ko·la·tsyoh·ne een kah·me·ra
    payr fa·voh·re
28 Where can I park the car?
    Dove posso parcheggiare la macchina?
    doh·ve pos·so par·kej·jah·ray la mak·kee·na
29 What time does the hotel close?
    A che ora chiude l'albergo?
    a ke oh·ra kyoo·de lal·ber·goh
30 Is there an elevator?
    C'è un ascensore?
    che oon a·shen·soh·re
31 Can one drink the tap water?
    L'acqua del rubinetto è potabile?
    lak·kwa del roo·bee·nayt·toh e po·tah·bee·le
32 Please call me at 8 o'clock
    Per favore, chiamatemi alle otto
    payr fa·voh·re kya·mah·te·mee al·le ot·to
33 Can I leave these for safekeeping?
    Posso lasciare queste cose in custodia?
    pos·so la·shah·ray kway·ste ko·se een koo·sto·dya
34 Can I have my things out of the safe?
    Posso avere le cose che avevo lasciato in cassaforte?
    pos·so a·vay·re le ko·se ke a·vay·vo la·shah·to een kas·sa·for·te
35   Can I — make a telephone call from here?
                       Posso — fare una telefonata da qui?
          pos·so — fah·ray oo·na te·le·fo·nah·ta da
                                kwee
                                — send a telex message from here?
                                — mandare un telex da qui?
                                — *man·dah·ray oon te·leks da kwee*
36 Are there any letters/messages for me?
    Ci sono lettere/messaggi per me?
    chee soh·no let·te·re/mes·saj·jee payr may
37 I should like a private room for a conference/cocktail party
    Vorrei una stanza privata per una riunione/un cocktail party
    vor·rey oo·na stan·tsa pree·vah·ta payr oo·na ree·oo·nyoh·ne/oon
    kok·tel par·tee
38 I am expecting a Signor Salutati
    Aspetto un certo Signor Salutati
    a·spet·to oon cher·to see·nyohr sa·loo·tah·tee
39 Could you call me when he arrives?
    Mi può avvisare quando arriva?
    mee pwo av·vee·zah·ray kwan·do ar·ree·va
40 Is the voltage 220 or 110?
    Il voltaggio è duecentoventi o centodieci?
    eel vol·taj·joh e doo·e·chen·to·vayn·tee o chen·to·dye·chee

41   Can I have — my key?
      Posso avere — la mia chiave?
      pos·so a·vay·re — *la mee·a kyah·ve*
      — some soap?
      — del sapone?
      — *del sa·poh·ne*
      — some towels?
      — alcuni asciugamani?
      — *al·koo·nee a·shoo·ga·mah·nee*
      — some notepaper?
      — della carta da scrivere?
      — *del·la kar·ta da skree·ve·re*
      — an ashtray?
      — un portacenere?
      — *oon por·ta·chay·ne·re*
      — another blanket?
      — un'altra coperta?
      — *oo·nal·tra ko·per·ta*
      — another pillow?
      — un altro cuscino?
      — *oon al·tro koo·shee·noh*

42 Where is the outlet for my
    electric razor?
    Dov'è la presa per il mio
    rasoio?
    *doh·ve la pray·sa payr eel
    mee·o ra·soh·yoh*

43 I cannot open the window
    Non riesco ad aprire la finestra
    *nohn ree·e·sko ad a·pree·re la
    fee·ne·stra*

44 The air conditioning/the
    heating is not working
    L'aria condizionata/il
    riscaldamento non funziona
    *lah·rya kon·dee·tsyoh·nah·ta/
    eel ree·skal·da·mayn·toh
    nohn foon·tsyoh·na*

45 I cannot turn the heat off
    Non riesco a spegnere il
    riscaldamento
    *nohn ree·e·sko a spe·nye·re eel
    ree·skal·da·mayn·toh*

46 I want to turn the heat
    up/down
    Voglio alzare/abbassare il
    riscaldamento
    *vo·lyo al·tsah·ray/
    ab·bas·sah·ray eel
    ree·skal·da·mayn·toh*

47 The lock is broken
    La serratura è rotta
    la ser·ra·too·ra e roht·ta

48 There is no hot water
    Non c'è acqua calda
    nohn che ak·kwa kal·da

49 The washbowl is dirty
    Il lavandino è sporco
    eel la·van·dee·noh e spor·ko

50 The plug is broken
    Il tappo è rotto
    eel tap·poh e roht·to

51 There is no toilet paper
    Non c'è carta igienica
    nohn che kar·ta ee·je·nee·ka

52 Do you have a laundry room?
    C'è una lavanderia?
    che oo·na la·van·de·ree·a

53 I want to iron some clothes
    Voglio stirare alcuni vestiti
    *vo·lyo stee·rah·ray al·koo·nee
    ve·stee·tee*

54 I want some clothes ironed
    Vorrei fare stirare alcuni
    vestiti
    *vor·rey fah·ray stee·rah·ray
    al·koo·nee ve·stee·tee*

55 Thank you, we enjoyed our
    stay very much
    Grazie, ci siamo trovati molto
    bene qui
    *gra·tsye chee syah·mo
    tro·vah·tee mohl·to be·ne
    kwee*

Rented houses

56 We have arranged to rent a house through your agency
    Abbiamo preso una casa in affitto tramite la vostra agenzia
    *ab·byah·mo pray·so oo·na kah·sa een af·feet·toh trah·mee·te la
    vo·stra a·jen·tsee·a*

57 Here is our reservation
    Ecco la nostra prenotazione
    ek·ko la no·stra pre·no·ta·tsyoh·ne

58 We need two sets of keys
    Abbiamo bisogno di due mazzi di chiavi
    ab·byah·mo bee·zoh·nyoh dee doo·e mats·tsee dee kyah·vee

59 Will you show us around?
Può farci vedere la casa?
pwo far·chee ve·day·re la kah·sa

60 Which is the key for this door?
Qual'è la chiave di questa porta?
kwah·le la kyah·ve dee kway·sta por·ta

61 Is the cost of electricity included in the rental?
L'elettricità è compresa nell'affitto?
le·let·tree·chee·ta e kom·pray·sa nel·laf·feet·toh

62 Where is the main switch for the electricity?
Dov'è l'interruttore principale dell'elettricità?
doh·ve leen·ter·root·toh·re preen·chee·pah·le del·le·let·tree·chee·ta

63 Where is the main valve for shutting off the water?
Dov'è la valvola principale dell'acqua?
doh·ve la val·vo·la preen·chee·pah·le del·lak·kwa

64 Where is the water heater?
Dov'è lo scaldabagno?
doh·ve lo skal·da·ba·nyoh

65 Please show me how this works
Può farmi vedere come funziona questo?
pwo far·mee ve·day·re koh·me foon·tsyoh·na kway·sto

66 How does the heating work?
Come funziona il riscaldamento?
koh·me foon·tsyoh·na eel ree·skal·da·mayn·toh

67 When does the maid come?
Quando viene la donna delle pulizie?
kwan·do vye·ne la don·na del·le poo·lee·tsee·e

68 Is there any spare bedding?
C'è altra biancheria per il letto?
che al·tra byan·ke·ree·a payr eel let·toh

69 Where can I contact you if there are any problems?
Dove posso mettermi in contatto con voi se ci sono dei problemi?
doh·ve pos·so mayt·ter·mee een kon·tat·toh kohn voy se chee soh·no dey pro·ble·mee

70 The stove does not work
La cucina non funziona
la koo·chee·na nohn foon·tsyoh·na

71 Where are the trashcans?
Dove sono le pattumiere?
doh·ve soh·no le pat·too·mye·re

72 Where can we get logs for the fire?
Dove possiamo trovare dei ceppi per il fuoco?
doh·ve pos·syah·mo tro·vah·ray dey chayp·pee payr eel fwo·koh

73 I can't open the windows
Non riesco ad aprire le finestre
nohn ree·e·sko ad a·pree·re le fee·ne·stre

74 We can't get any water
Non c'è acqua
nohn che ak·kwa

75 The toilet won't flush
Lo sciacquone non funziona
lo sha·kwoh·ne nohn foon·tsyoh·na

76 The pipe is blocked
Il tubo è ostruito
eel too·boh e o·stroo·ee·to

77 A fuse has blown
È saltato un fusibile
e sal·tah·to oon foo·zee·bee·le

78 There is a gas leak
C'è una perdita di gas
che oo·na per·dee·ta dee gas

79 I need somebody to repair this
Ho bisogno di qualcuno per riparare questo
o bee·zoh·nyoh dee kwal·koo·no payr ree·pa·rah·ray kway·sto

Camping

Camping in Italy is a sophisticated activity, with campers bringing lots of home comforts with them. There are many official camping sites, many with excellent facilities. Never camp without permission in fields or on common land, as penalties are severe.

80 Is there anywhere for us to camp near here?
Si può campeggiare qui vicino?
see pwo kam·pej·jah·ray kwee vee·chee·no

81 Have you got a site for our tent?
Avete un posto per la nostra tenda?
a·vay·te oon poh·stoh payr la no·stra ten·da

82 Do you mind if we camp on your land?
Vi dispiace se campeggiamo sul vostro terreno?
*vee dee·**spyah**·che se kam·pej·**jah**·mo sool **vo**·stro ter·**ray**·noh*

83 This site is very muddy
Questo posto è molto fangoso
kway·sto **poh**·stoh e **mohl**·to fan·**goh**·so

84 Could we have a more sheltered site?
Possiamo avere un posto più riparato?
*pos·**syah**·mo a·**vay**·re oon **poh**·stoh **pyoo** ree·pa·**rah**·to*

85 Can we put our trailer here?
Possiamo mettere la nostra roulotte qui?
*pos·**syah**·mo **mayt**·te·re la **no**·stra roo·**lot** kwee*

86 Is there a shop on the site?
C'è un negozio nel camping?
*che oon ne·**go**·tsyoh nel **kam**·peeng*

87 Can I have a shower?
Posso fare una doccia?
pos·so **fah**·ray **oo**·na **dohch**·cha*

88 Where is the drinking water?
Dov'è l'acqua potabile?
doh·ve **lak**·kwa po·**tah**·bee·le*

89 Where are the toilets and washroom?
Dove sono le toilette e il bagno?
doh·ve **soh**·no le twa·**let** e eel **ba**·nyoh*

90 Where can we buy ice?
Dove possiamo comprare del ghiaccio?
doh·ve pos·**syah**·mo kom·**prah**·ray del **gyach**·choh*

91 Where can we wash our dishes/our clothes?
Dove possiamo lavare i piatti/i vestiti?
doh·ve pos·**syah**·mo la·**vah**·ray ee **pyat**·tee/ee ve·**stee**·tee*

92 Is there another camp site near here?
C'è un altro camping qui vicino?
*che oon **al**·tro **kam**·peeng kwee vee·**chee**·noh*

93 Are there any washing machines?
Ci sono lavatrici?
*chee **soh**·no la·va·**tree**·chee*

94 We need to buy a new gas cylinder
Dobbiamo comprare una nuova bombola a gas
*dob·**byah**·mo kom·**prah**·ray **oo**·na **nwo**·va **bohm**·bo·la a gas*

95 I would like to change the position of my tent
Vorrei cambiare posto
*vor·**rey** kam·**byah**·ray **poh**·stoh*

Eating out (E)

Italian food is deceptively simple, and much more varied than people usually believe. Regional traditions of cooking are much stronger, and more authentic, than anywhere else in Europe. Although the Italian attitude is more straightforward than, for instance, the French, it does not prevent them from making imaginative use of local ingredients.

The usual Italian word for restaurant is *trattoria* – which means roughly "eating house". *Ristorante* implies more attention to the surroundings, but this does not mean that *trattorie* are primitive. The words *tavola calda* (literally "hot table") and *pizzeria* (pizza-house) are usually applied to snack bars (see p.39). If you have your family with you, see "Children" p.60.

General

1 Do you know — a good restaurant?
Conosce — un buon ristorante?
*ko·**noh**·she — oon bwon ree·sto·**ran**·te*

2 I would like to reserve a table — for two people
Vorrei prenotare un tavolo — per due persone
*vor·**rey** pre·no·**tah**·ray oon **tah**·vo·loh — payr **doo**·e per·**soh**·ne*
— for 8 o'clock
— per le otto
— payr le **ot**·to

3 I have reserved a table in the name of...
Ho prenotato un tavolo, a nome...
o pre·no·tah·to oon tah·vo·loh a noh·me

4 Do you have a quiet table by the window/on the terrace?
Avete un tavolo tranquillo accanto alla finestra/sulla terrazza?
a·vay·te oon tah·vo·loh tran·kweel·lo ak·kan·to al·la fee·ne·stra/sool·la ter·rats·tsa

5 Is it possible to have a private room?
È possibile avere una stanza privata?
e pos·see·bee·le a·vay·re oo·na stan·tsa pree·vah·ta

6 It is for a business lunch/dinner
È per un pranzo/una cena d'affari
e payr oon pran·dzoh/oo·na chay·na daf·fah·ree

7 Signor Colucci is expecting me
Sono atteso dal Signor Colucci
soh·no at·tay·so dal see·nyohr ko·looch·chee

8 The menu, please
Il menú, per favore
eel me·noo payr fa·voh·re

Menu guide

An Italian menu is usually divided up into courses and into types of fare. You can choose the first course under the heading *antipasti* (hors d'oeuvres), *farinacei* or *paste* (different kinds of pasta) or sometimes *minestre* (soups). The main course will be subdivided into *carne* (meat dishes) and *pesce* (fish dishes), often with *contorni* (vegetables) listed separately. Desserts are sometimes called *postre*. There will normally also be specialties (*specialità*) of the day, listed separately or announced by the waiter or waitress.

There follows an alphabetical list, Italian first, English below. It is intended as a supplement to the dictionary, where basic words for beef, ham, eggs, etc are listed: it explains some of the more common specialty terms you may meet.

Hors d'oeuvres, vegetables and main dishes

Abbacchio Baby lamb

Baccalà alla livornese Salt cod with vegetables and tripe

Bagna calda Literally a "hot bath", made of olive oil, butter, chopped anchovies and garlic, into which you dip raw vegetables

Bistecca alla fiorentina A large charcoal-broiled steak

Bollito misto Mixed boiled meats with a green sauce

Braciolette ripiene Small stuffed veal rolls

Brodetto di pesce Highly seasoned fish soup

Buridda A fish stew (Liguria, Sardinia)

Cacciucco alla livornese Fish stew flavored with sage and garlic

Calamari in umido Squid in oil

Calzone A kind of pizza

Cannelloni Large tubes of pasta, stuffed

Caponata Eggplants, peppers, zucchini, onions, tomatoes, celery, pine nuts, garlic and herbs, cooked in oil

Cappelletti in brodo Pasta stuffed with meat in broth

Cappon magro Fish salad in a garlic and caper sauce

Carpaccio Raw, lean beef in slices

Castrato Mutton

Cima alla genovese Veal with a vegetable and sausage meat stuffing, served cold

Cinghiale in agrodolce Wild boar in a sweet-sour sauce

Cotechino Mild pork salami, served hot in slices

Crostini di fegatini Fried bread with chicken liver pâté

Farsu magru Beef roll stuffed with egg, cheese and salami

Fettuccine Flat strips of egg pasta similar to tagliatelle

Finanziera di pollo Chicken giblet stew

Frittata Omelet

Fritto misto Mixed grill

Fritto misto di mare Mixed fried shellfish

Gnocchi Dumplings of semolina or potato or cornmeal

Granatina A kind of hamburger

Involtini Rolls of veal, with chicken or ham filling

Lasagne A wide flat pasta, often made with spinach (*lasagne verde*)

Macaroni (maccheroni) Tubular pasta

Malfattini in brodo Grains of pasta in broth

Maniche A short tubular pasta

Mazzafegati Liverwurst

Medaglioni alla primavera Medallions of veal with a mushroom sauce

Minestrone (alla genovese) Vegetable soup (flavored with pesto, a cheese and herb mixture)

Noce di vitello arrosto Roast top round of veal

Osso buco Shin of veal cooked in wine

Paglia e fieno Literally "straw and hay", a mixture of white and green tagliatelle with a meat sauce

Panata A kind of pancake in broth

Panzerotti Fried pasta casings, with a filling of mozzarella and ham

Pappardelle con la lepre Wide strips of pasta served in a sauce made from rabbit

Passatelli in brodo A mixture of egg, cheese and breadcrumbs, rolled into dumplings, and cooked in stock

Pasticcio Pasta cooked in a sort of pie

Penne all'arrabbiata "Quills" of pasta with tomato, bacon and red pepper sauce

Peperonata Cold sweet peppers cooked in oil

Piccata di Marsala Thin slices of veal in Marsala wine

Piselli alla toscana Peas with ham

Pizza capricciosa Pizza with whatever filling the cook likes

Pizza rustica A pasta pie, with sausage, egg, cheese and vegetables

Polenta Cornmeal served in various ways

Polpettone Meat roll of ground veal, ham, cheese, etc; or a fish roll

Porchetta Roast suckling pig

Prosciutto di Parma The best cured ham from Parma

Ravioli Pasta casings stuffed with spinach, ricotta and herbs or with meats

Ribollita Soup of navy beans and other vegetables

Risi e bisi A soup with rice and peas in chicken stock

Sa cassola A fish stew (Sardinia)

Saltimbocca Veal with ham and sage

Salume Various types of sausages

Sa merca Rock mullet (Sardinia)

Sartù di riso A rice dish with meat, cheese and vegetables

Scaloppa milanese Thin veal cutlet in breadcrumbs

Scaloppine Thin slices of veal

Spaghetti alla carbonara Spaghetti with chopped bacon and beaten eggs

Stracciatella Consommé with eggs stirred in

Strecchini alla bolognese Fried chicken livers, sweetbreads, etc, skewered with slices of cheese, then cooked in the oven in a white sauce

Strufoli Little onion- and herb-flavored meat pies, deep-fried

Suppli Little balls of cream cheese and rice, covered in egg and breadcrumbs and fried

Taccula Small migrant birds caught and roasted (Sardinia)

Tagliatelle Ribbon-like pasta

Tortelli A kind of ravioli

Tortellini alla bolognese Little coils of egg pasta with a savory filling, topped with either cheese and butter or cream

Trenette al pesto A variety of tagliatelle with a sauce of basil, pine nuts, garlic and pecorino cheese

Trippa alla fiorentina Tripe in tomato sauce, served with Parmesan cheese

Uccelletti di campagna Not "birds" but thin slices of rolled beef

Vermicelli Spaghetti in thin strings

Vincigrassi A pie with lasagne and meat in a smooth sauce

Vitello tonnato Cold veal in tuna sauce

Zampone Stuffed pig's foot

Zuppa alla pavese Fried bread, eggs and Parmesan cheese in broth

Desserts

Castagnaccio   Chestnut-flavored cake

Composta di frutta   Fruit salad

Crostata   Pastry tart

Gelato   Ice cream

Granita   An ice made with fruit syrup and water

Zabaglione   Whipped egg yolks with Marsala wine

Zuppa inglese   Trifle

Cheeses

Mozzarella   A soft, mild, white cheese

Pecorino   A hard cheese made from ewe's milk

Ricotta   A soft white cheese made from ewe's milk

Taleggio   A mild creamy cheese

Wines

It may surprise some readers to know that Italy produces and drinks more wine per capita than any other country in the world. Italian wines come in white (*bianco*), red (*rosso*) and rosé (*rosato*). They have two official categories: DOC (*Denominazione di Origine Controllata*), which implies a certain minimum standard but is in practice erratic; and DOCG (the above with *e garantita* added), which is awarded to only a few top wines and is the real guarantee of quality. The following list includes some of the best-known types of wine as well as a number of terms that you may find useful to know.

Abboccato   Semi-sweet

Amabile   Sweeter than abboccato

Amaro   Bitter

Asti   The sparkling Asti Spumante is well known, but several red and white wines also come from this district

Barbaresco   Dry red wine

Barbera   Grape used for red wine

Barolo   One of the best Italian red wines

Cantina Sociale   Growers' co-operative

Chianti   The famous red wine sometimes sold in a wicker-covered bottle

Chiaretto   Very light red

Classico   Best wines of a region

Colli   Hills (in wine name)

Dolce   Sweet

Est! Est! Est!   A well-known white wine from near Rome

Frascati   A white wine from near Rome. From dry to sweet, depending on the variety

Freisa   A light red wine, sweet, often sparkling

Frizzante   Semi-sparkling

Lacrima Christi del Vesuvio   A full-bodied red wine from Campania; there is also a white

Lambrusco   A slightly sparkling red wine

Liquoroso   Strong and sweet

Malvasia di Lipari   One of the best-known dessert wines

Marsala   Dark dessert wine from Sicily

Merlot del Trentino   A dry red wine

Montepulciano, Vino Nobile di   A red wine from Tuscany that ages well in bottle

Moscato   A dessert wine (strictly a grape variety)

Nebbiolo d'Alba   A light red wine, typically dry

Pinot Bianco   A dry white wine

Riserva   Wine aged in casks

Sangiovese   A good red wine

Savuto   A dry red wine from Calabria

Secco   Dry

Soave   Famous dry white wine from Verona

Spumante   Sparkling

Tocai del Friuli   A dry white wine

Valpolicella   A light red wine

Verdicchio dei Castelli di Iesi   A dry white wine from the Marche

Verduzzo   A dry white wine

Vernaccia   A sweet white wine, served as an aperitif
Vino da pasto   Table wine

Ordering wine

9 May we see the wine list,
   please?
   Possiamo vedere la lista dei
   vini, per favore?
   *pos·syah·mo ve·day·re la
   lee·sta dey vee·nee payr
   fa·voh·re*
10 Can you recommend a good
    local wine?
    Ci può consigliare un buon
    vino locale?
    *chee pwo kon·see·lyah·ray oon
    bwon vee·noh lo·kah·le*
11 A bottle/carafe of house wine
    Una bottiglia/caraffa di vino
    della casa
    *oo·na bot·tee·lya/ka·raf·fa dee
    vee·noh del·la kah·sa*

12 Another bottle/half bottle,
    please
    Un'altra bottiglia/bottiglia da
    mezzo litro, per favore
    *oo·nal·tra bot·tee·lya/
    bot·tee·lya da medz·dzo
    lee·troh payr fa·voh·re*
13 Would you bring another
    glass, please?
    Può portare un altro bicchiere,
    per favore?
    *pwo por·tah·ray oon al·tro
    beek·kye·re payr fa·voh·re*
14 What liqueurs do you have?
    Quali liquori avete?
    kwah·lee lee·kwoh·ree a·vay·te

Ordering the meal and paying

15 Do you have a specialty of the day?
    Avete un menú fisso?
    a·vay·te oon me·noo fees·so
16   I will take today's specialty — at 20,000 lire
             Prendo il menú fisso — a ventimila lire
       pren·do eel me·noo fees·so — a vayn·tee·mee·la lee·re
17 What would you recommend?
    Che cosa ci consigliate?
    ke ko·sa chee kon·see·lyah·te
18 Is this good?
    È buono questo?
    e bwo·no kway·sto
19 How is this dish cooked?
    Qual'è la ricetta per questo piatto?
    kwah·le la ree·chet·ta payr kway·sto pyat·toh
20 Do you have a local specialty?
    Avete delle specialità locali?
    a·vay·te del·le spe·cha·lee·ta lo·kah·lee
21 I'll take that
    Prendo quello
    pren·do kwayl·lo
22   We will begin — with spaghetti with tomato sauce
           Cominceremo — con spaghetti al pomodoro
       ko·meen·che·ray·mo — kohn spa·get·tee al po·mo·do·roh
23   I will have — steak and French fries
             Prendo — una bistecca con patatine fritte
       *pren·do — oo·na bee·stayk·ka kohn
                 pa·ta·tee·ne freet·te*
24   I like steak — very rare
    Mi piace la bistecca — proprio al sangue
       *mee pyah·che la
       bee·stayk·ka — pro·pryo al san·gwe*
                   — rare
                   — al sangue
                   — al san·gwe
                   — medium rare
                   — poco cotta
                   — po·ko kot·ta
                   — well done
                   — ben cotta
                   — ben kot·ta

25 Are vegetables included?
È compreso anche il contorno?
e kom·pray·so an·ke eel kon·tohr·noh

26 Is this cheese very strong?
È molto forte questo formaggio?
e mohl·to for·te kway·sto for·maj·joh

27 This is not what I ordered
Non ho ordinato questo
nohn o or·dee·nah·to kway·sto

28 Does the fish come with anything else?
Servite un contorno con il pesce?
ser·vee·te oon kon·tohr·noh kohn eel pay·she

29   That is for — me
Quello è per — me
kwayl·lo e payr — may
— him/her
— il Signore/la Signora
— *eel see·nyoh·re/la see·nyoh·ra*

30 Some more bread/water, please
Ancora un po' di pane/Ancora dell'acqua, per favore
an·koh·ra oon po dee pah·ne/an·koh·ra del·lak·kwa payr fa·voh·re

31 Could I have some butter?
Posso avere del burro, per favore?
pos·so a·vay·re del boor·roh payr fa·voh·re

32 What is this called?
Come si chiama questo?
koh·me see kyah·ma kway·sto

33 This is very salty
Questo è molto salato
kway·sto e mohl·to sa·lah·to

34 I wanted cheese
Volevo del formaggio
vo·lay·vo del for·maj·joh

35 Have you forgotten the soup?
Avete dimenticato la minestra?
a·vay·te dee·men·tee·kah·to la mee·ne·stra

36 This is cold
Questo è freddo
kway·sto e frayd·do

37 This is very good
Questo è molto buono
kway·sto e mohl·to bwo·no

38 I'll have a dessert
Prenderò il dolce
pren·de·ro eel dohl·che

39 Could I have a salad instead of the cheese course?
Posso avere un'insalata invece del formaggio?
pos·so a·vay·re oo·neen·sa·lah·ta een·vay·che del for·maj·joh

40 What do you have for dessert?
Cosa avete come dolce?
ko·sa a·vay·te koh·me dohl·che

41 Nothing else, thank you — except coffee
Niente altro, grazie — salvo il caffè
nyen·te al·tro gra·tsye — sal·vo eel kaf·fe

42 Waiter, could we have the bill, please?
Cameriere, il conto, per favore
ka·me·rye·re eel kohn·toh payr fa·voh·re

43 We are in a hurry
Abbiamo fretta
ab·byah·mo frayt·ta

44 Is tip included?
Il servizio è compreso?
eel ser·vee·tsyoh e kom·pray·so

45 There seems to be a mistake here
Sembra che ci sia uno sbaglio qui
saym·bra ke chee see·a oo·no zba·lyoh kwee

46 What is this item?
Cos'è questa voce?
ko·se kway·sta voh·che

47 The meal was excellent
Il pasto era ottimo
eel pa·stoh e·ra ot·tee·mo

Phrases you will hear

48 Ha scelto?
a shayl·to
Are you ready to order?

49 Che cosa prende da bere?
ke ko·sa pren·de da bay·re
What would you like to drink?

50 E come secondo?
   e koh·me se·kohn·do
   And to follow?
51 I piatti del giorno sono indicati sul cartello
   ee pyat·tee del johr·noh soh·no een·dee·kah·tee sool kar·tel·loh
   The specialties are on the blackboard
52 È finito
   e fee·nee·to
   That is not available
53 Del formaggio (grattugiato)/pepe (nero)?
   del for·maj·joh (grat·too·jah·to)/pay·pe (nay·ro)
   Some (grated) cheese/(black) pepper?

Cafés and bars

Besides selling drinks, an Italian bar usually offers several other services. In most you will be able to get a snack; in many you will be able to buy cigarettes and stamps and all the usual stock of a *tabaccaio* (see p.51). If you see a yellow and black telephone sign outside you will also be able to make telephone calls (see p.53). In many bars you will have to stand; if you do find somewhere to sit down a waiter will come and take your order, and there will be an additional charge. If you want to drink at the bar you are usually expected to pay first and present your receipt when you order. Public toilets are rare in Italy, but bars usually have toilets available to the public.

Alcohol

---

54 A glass of white/red wine, please
   Un bicchiere di vino bianco/rosso, per favore
   oon beek·kye·re de vee·noh byan·ko/rohs·so payr fa·voh·re
55 A beer
   Una birra
   oo·na beer·ra
56 A whiskey/brandy/gin
   Un whisky/brandy/gin
   oon wee·skee/bran·dee/jeen
57 A Campari and soda
   Un Campari-soda
   oon kam·pah·ree·so·da
58 A Cinzano/Martini/Punt e Mes
   Un Cinzano/Martini/Punt e Mes
   oon cheen·tsah·no/mar·tee·nee/poon·te·mes
59 A Marsala/grappa/sambuca
   Una Marsala/grappa/sambuca
   oo·na mar·sah·la/grap·pa/sam·boo·ka

Cinzano, Martini and Punt e Mes are different varieties of vermouth. Marsala is sweet and heavy like Madeira, but red; *grappa* is a kind of *marc* or brandy; and *sambuca* is a clear, heavy liqueur of some strength, which is often flavored with the oil of roasted coffee beans.

Coffee

If you ask simply for coffee (*caffè*) in Italy you will mostly get *espresso*, a tiny cup of very strong coffee; if you want a larger cup of the same coffee order an *espresso doppio*. If you want something more like the coffee you drink at home, you need to ask for *un caffè normale* (a normal coffee) or *un caffè grande* (a big coffee); it will still be *espresso* but in a bigger cup and with more water). If you ask simply for white coffee or coffee with milk, you will probably get *cappuccino*, coffee with the milk shaken or frothed by aeration (sometimes with shredded chocolate on top – *cioccolato*). If you don't want a *cappuccino* ask for a *caffè macchiato* (literally, "spotted" with milk).

60 Two espressos, please
Due espressi, per favore
*doo·e e·**spres**·see payr fa·**voh**·re*

61 One tea with milk/with lemon
Un tè al latte/al limone
*oon te al **lat**·te/al lee·**moh**·ne*

62 Could I have a glass of water as well, please?
Anche un bicchiere d'acqua, per favore
*an·ke oon beek·**kye**·re dak·kwa payr fa·**voh**·re*

Soft drinks

Bottled soft drinks in Italy are so sweet as to be suitable only for
children, although in many places you will be able to get American soft
drinks as well. Extremely refreshing, however, and widely available, is
fresh orange juice or lemon juice, squeezed for you there and then –
spremuta d'arancia/spremuta di limone. Try it with soda.

63 Two fresh orange juices/lemon juices — with soda
Due spremute di arancia/di limone — con soda
*doo·e spre·**moo**·te dee a·**ran**·cha/dee lee·**moh**·ne — kohn so·da*

64 An orangeade/a lemonade/a limeade
Una aranciata/limonata/cedrata
*oo·na a·ran·**chah**·ta/lee·mo·**nah**·ta/che·**drah**·ta*

65 A raspberry-/strawberry-/mint-flavored cordial
Uno sciroppo di lampone/di fragole/di menta
*oo·no shee·**rop**·poh dee lam·**poh**·ne/dee **frah**·go·le/dee **mayn**·ta*

66 Mineral water
Acqua minerale — this comes in effervescent (*gassata*) and still
(*naturale*) varieties
*ak·kwa mee·ne·**rah**·le*

Snacks

The usual Italian word for a sandwich is *panino*, which is normally in fact
a bun or hard roll. A *tramezzino* is an open sandwich. The question is
academic, however: you are expected to choose from what you see on
display.

67 One of these, please, also one of those
Uno di questi, per favore, anche uno di quelli
*oo·no dee **kway**·stee payr fa·**voh**·re an·ke oo·no dee **kwayl**·lee*

68 A slice of pizza, please
Una porzione di pizza, per favore
*oo·na por·**tsyoh**·ne dee **peets**·tsa payr fa·**voh**·re*

69 A ham/cheese roll
Un panino al prosciutto/al formaggio
*oon pa·**nee**·noh al pro·**shoot**·toh/al for·**maj**·joh*

70 An open sandwich with anchovy paste
Un tramezzino con pasta d'acciuga
*oon tra·medz·**dzee**·noh kohn **pa**·sta dach·**choo**·ga*

71 A toasted sandwich
Un toast
oon tost

72 One of these buns/cakes
Una di queste brioche/paste
*oo·na dee **kway**·ste bree·**osh**/**pa**·ste*

Leisure (L)

Sightseeing

Tourist Information Offices are rare in Italy, but people in hotels, shops
and in the street will readily direct you to the main monuments. Italian
museums are notoriously inconsistent in their opening hours, but are

usually closed one day a week and sometimes in the afternoons.
Churches are open from early in the morning but usually close for three
or four hours at noon.

1 Excuse me, can you tell me please, . . .
  Mi scusi, può dirmi per favore, . . .
  mee skoo·zee pwo deer·mee payr fa·voh·re

2   Where is — the historic center?
                  Dov'è — il centro storico?
                 doh·ve — eel chen·troh sto·ree·ko
                 — the main square?
                 — la piazza principale?
                 — *la pyat·tsa preen·chee·pah·le*
                 — the cathedral?
                 — il duomo?
                 — *eel dwo·moh*
                 — the (municipal) museum?
                 — il museo (comunale)?
                 — *eel moo·ze·oh (ko·moo·nah·le)*

3   Do you have — a guidebook to the town/
                        area (in English)?
         Avete — una guida turistica della
                   città/della zona (in inglese)?
         a·vay·te — oo·na gwee·da too·ree·stee·ka
                   del·la cheet·ta/del·la dzo·na
                   (een een·glay·se)
                 — a map of the town?
                 — una cartina della città?
                 — *oo·na kar·tee·na del·la cheet·ta*
                 — an audio-guide to the museum/
                       church?
                 — una cassetta-guida del museo/
                       della chiesa?
                 — *oo·na kas·sayt·ta·gwee·da del*
                       moo·ze·oh/del·la kye·za

4   Are there any — local festivals?
             Ci sono — delle feste locali?
         chee soh·no — del·le fe·ste lo·kah·lee

5   Is there a guided tour — of the town/castle?
  C'è una gita con guida — della città/del castello?
  che oo·na jee·ta kohn
            gwee·da — del·la cheet·ta/del ka·stel·loh

6   Is there — a one-day excursion to Siena?
                 C'è — una gita a Siena, con ritorno in
                        una giornata?
                 che — oo·na jee·ta a sye·na kohn
                       ree·tohr·noh een oo·na
                       johr·nah·ta

7 When does the tour begin?
  Quando incomincia la gita?
  kwan·do een·ko·meen·cha la jee·ta

8 How long does it last?
  Quanto dura?
  kwan·to doo·ra

9 Where is the point of departure?
  Da dove parte?
  da doh·ve par·te

10 Is there an English-speaking guide?
  C'è una guida che parla inglese?
  che oo·na gwee·da ke par·la een·glay·se

11 What is this building?
  Che cos'è questo edificio?
  ke ko·se kway·sto e·dee·fee·choh

12 What time does the museum/palace open?
  A che ora apre il museo/il palazzo?
  a ke oh·ra a·pre eel moo·ze·oh/eel pa·lats·tsoh

13 What is the admission charge?
  Quanto costa l'ingresso?
  kwan·to ko·sta leen·gres·soh

14 Is one allowed to take photos with a flash/tripod?
   Si possono fare delle fotografie con il flash/treppiedi?
   *see **pos**·so·no **fah**·ray **del**·le fo·to·gra·**fee**·e kohn eel flash/trep·**pye**·dee*
15 **Where can I buy — slides?**
   Dove posso comprare — delle diapositive?
     doh·ve **pos**·so
     kom·**prah**·ray — *del·le dee·a·po·zee·tee·ve*
             — postcards?
             — delle cartoline?
             — *del·le kar·to·lee·ne*

Visiting churches

Sightseeing in Italy will involve visiting not only museums but also churches, which are organized not for sightseeing at all but for worship. Always be tactful, and if there is a service try to come back later. The sacristan is often helpful, and it is usual to tip him.

16   Where is — the sculpture by Michelangelo?
              Dov'è — la scultura di Michelangelo?
             *doh·ve — la skool·**too**·ra dee*
                *mee·ke·**lan**·je·loh*
              — the painting by Titian?
              — il quadro di Tiziano?
              — *eel **kwa**·droh dee tee·**tsyah**·noh*
              — the fresco by Filippo Lippi?
              — l'affresco di Filippo Lippi?
              — *laf·**fray**·skoh dee fee·**leep**·po*
                leep·pee

17 Are you the sacristan?
   È Lei il sagrestano?
   *e ley eel sa·gre·**stah**·noh*
18 Would you open this chapel
   for me, please?
   Potrebbe farmi visitare questa
   cappella, per favore?
   *po·**treb**·be **far**·mee*
   *vee·zee·**tah**·ray **kway**·sta*
   *kap·**pel**·la payr fa·**voh**·re*
19 Could I see the Bellini in the
   sacristy?
   Potrei vedere il Bellini nella
   sagrestia?
   *po·**trey** ve·**day**·re eel*
   *bel·**lee**·nee **nel**·la*
   *sa·gre·**stee**·a*
20 Is it possible to visit the crypt?
   È possibile visitare la cripta?
   *e pos·**see**·bee·le vee·zee·**tah**·ray*
   *la **kreep**·ta*

21 Can we go in?
   Possiamo entrare?
   *pos·**syah**·mo en·**trah**·ray*
22 Can one go to the top?
   Si può andare in cima?
   *see **pwo** an·**dah**·ray een*
   chee·ma*
23 Which way is it to the cloister?
   Per dove si va al chiostro?
   *payr **doh**·ve see va al **kyo**·stroh*
24 Is it closed for restoration?
   È chiuso(a) per restauro?
   *e **kyoo**·so(a) payr re·**stow**·roh*
25 When will the service be over?
   Quando finisce la messa?
   kwan·do fee·**nee**·she la*
   mays·sa*

Beach and sports

Changing rooms as well as beach and sports items can often be rented on the main beaches, although sometimes only in private sections where you have to pay to enter.

26 Is it dangerous to swim here?
   È pericoloso nuotare qui?
   *e pe·ree·ko·**loh**·so nwo·**tah**·ray kwee*
27 Can you recommend a quiet beach?
   Mi può consigliare una spiaggia tranquilla?
   *mee **pwo** kon·see·**lyah**·ray oo·na **spyaj**·ja tran·**kweel**·la*
28 Where can we change?
   Dove sono gli spogliatoi?
   doh·ve **soh**·no lyee spo·lya·**toy**

29   Can I rent — a deckchair?
        Posso prendere in affitto — una sedia a sdraio?
         pos·so **pren**·de·re een
              af·**feet**·toh — oo·na se·dya a **zdra**·yoh
                    — a sunshade?
                    — un ombrellone?
                    — oon om·brel·**loh**·ne
                    — a sailboat?
                    — una barca a vela?
                    — oo·na **bar**·ka a **vay**·la
                    — a rowboat?
                    — una barca a remi?
                    — oo·na **bar**·ka a **re**·mee
                    — a motorboat?
                    — un motoscafo?
                    — oon mo·to·**skah**·foh
                    — scuba equipment?
                    — l'attrezzatura subacquea?
                    — lat·trets·tsa·**too**·ra soob·**a**·kwe·a

30   Is it possible to go — sailing?
                  Si può fare — della vela?
             see **pwo** fah·ray — **del**·la **vay**·la
                    — water skiing?
                    — lo sci nautico?
                    — lo shee **now**·tee·ko

31 What sports can one take part in here?
    Quali sport si possono praticare qui?
    kwah·lee sport see **pos**·so·no pra·tee·**kah**·ray kwee

32 Is there a swimming pool?
    C'è una piscina?
    che oo·na pee·**shee**·na

33   Where can I play — tennis?
                 Dove posso giocare — a tennis?
         doh·ve **pos**·so jo·**kah**·ray — a **ten**·nees
                    — golf?
                    — a golf?
                    — a golf

34   Is it possible to go — gliding?
                 Si può andare — in aliante?
          see **pwo** an·**dah**·ray — een a·**lyan**·te

35 Can I go fishing/riding?
    Posso andare a pescare/a cavallo?
    pos·so an·**dah**·ray a pe·**skah**·ray/a ka·**val**·loh

36 Can I rent the equipment?
    Posso noleggiare le attrezzature?
    pos·so no·lej·**jah**·ray le at·trets·tsa·**too**·re

37 Do you know any interesting walks?
    Conosce delle belle passeggiate?
    ko·**noh**·she **del**·le **bel**·le pas·se·**jah**·te

38 What are the conditions like for skiing/sailing?
    Com'è il tempo per sciare/fare della vela?
    koh·**me** eel **tem**·poh payr shee·**ah**·ray/**fah**·ray **del**·la **vay**·la

39 Are there any picnic areas near here?
    Ci sono qui vicino dei posti per fare picnic?
    chee **soh**·no kwee vee·**chee**·no dey poh·stee payr **fah**·ray peek·neek

40 Is there any interesting wildlife in this area?
    C'è della fauna interessante in questa zona?
    che del·la **fow**·na een·te·res·**san**·te een **kway**·sta dzo·na

41 What is the name of that bird/flower?
    Come si chiama quell'uccello/quel fiore?
    koh·me see **kyah**·ma kwayl·**looch**·**chel**·loh/kwayl **fyoh**·re

Entertainment and night life

42 How can we find out about local entertainment?
    Come possiamo informarci sugli spettacoli locali?
    koh·me pos·**syah**·mo een·for·**mar**·chee soo·lyee spet·**ta**·ko·lee
    lo·**kah**·lee

43   **Where can one go** — **to hear concerts/jazz?**
         Dove si può andare — per ascoltare dei concerti/del jazz?
   doh·ve see **pwo** an·**dah**·ray — payr a·skol·**tah**·ray dey
                      kon·**cher**·teel/del jaz
                — **to dance?**
                — a ballare?
                — a bal·**lah**·ray
                — **to see a floor show?**
                — a vedere il cabaret?
                — a ve·**day**·re eel ka·ba·**re**

44   **Are there any** — **movies in English?**
            Ci sono — dei film in inglese?
       chee **soh**·no — dey feelm een een·**glay**·se
                — **good night clubs/discos?**
                — dei buoni night/delle buone
                    discoteche?
                — dey **bwo**·nee nayt/**del**·le bwo·ne
                    dee·sko·**te**·ke
                — **good concerts?**
                — dei bei concerti in programma?
                — dey bey kon·**cher**·tee een
                    pro·**gram**·ma

45   **Have you any seats** — **for Wednesday evening?**
           Avete dei posti — per mercoledì sera?
       a·**vay**·te dey poh·stee — payr mer·ko·le·**dee** say·ra
46   **I should like to reserve** — **a box**
          Vorrei prenotare — un palco
      vor·**rey** pre·no·**tah**·ray — oon **pal**·koh
                — **two seats in the balcony/**
                    orchestra
                — due posti in galleria/in platea
                — **doo**·e poh·stee een gal·le·**ree**·a/
                    een pla·**te**·a

47 **What is being performed?**
    Che cosa danno?
    ke ko·sa **dan**·no
48 **Who is singing/playing?**
    Chi canta/suona?
    kee **kan**·ta/**swo**·na
49 **How long does the performance last?**
    Quanto dura lo spettacolo?
    kwan·to **doo**·ra lo spet·**ta**·ko·loh
50 **Where can one buy a program?**
    Dove si può comprare il programma?
    doh·ve see pwo kom·**prah**·ray eel pro·**gram**·ma
51   **Is there** — **an intermission?**
                    C'è — un intervallo?
                    che — oon een·ter·**val**·loh
                      — **a snack bar/liquor bar?**
                      — un buffè/un bar?
                      — oon boof·**fe**/oon bar
52 **When does the performance/floor show begin?**
    Quando incomincia la rappresentazione/lo spettacolo?
    kwan·do een·ko·**meen**·cha la rap·pre·zen·ta·**tsyoh**·ne/lo
    spet·**ta**·ko·loh
53 **How much do the drinks cost?**
    Quanto costano le bevande?
    kwan·to ko·**sta**·no le be·**van**·de
54 **Is there a minimum/cover charge?**
    Bisogna pagare un minimo/il coperto?
    bee·**zohn**·ya pa·**gah**·ray oon **mee**·nee·mo/eel ko·**per**·toh

---

Gambling

Without entering in detail into the language of gambling, we include here some of the phrases you might need in a casino. You will also need to recognize the following French phrases which are widely used: "Faites vos jeux" (place your bets, please), and "Les jeux sont faits" (no more bets).

55 What is the minimum/
maximum stake?
Qual'è la posta minima/
massima?
*kwah·le la po·sta
mee·nee·ma/mas·see·ma*

56 Where can I cash my chips?
Dove posso incassare le mie
fiche?
*doh·ve pos·so een·kas·sah·ray
le mee·e feesh*

57 Must one be a member to play
here?
Bisogna essere soci per poter
giocare qui?
*bee·zoh·nya es·se·re so·chee
payr po·tayr jo·kah·ray
kwee*

58 Where is the cashier's
cage?
Dov'è la cassa?
doh·ve la kas·sa

59 Excuse me, you have picked
up my stake/winnings
Scusi, Lei ha preso la mia
puntata/vincita
*skoo·zee ley ha pray·so la
mee·a poon·tah·ta/
veen·chee·ta*

60 You have miscalculated the
odds
Non ha calcolato bene le
probabilità
*nohn a kal·ko·lah·to be·ne le
pro·ba·bee·lee·ta*

61 Do you have a blackjack
table here?
Avete un tavolo di blackjack
qui?
*a·vay·te oon tah·vo·loh dee
blak·jak kwee*

62 I double (in backgammon)
Raddoppio
rad·dohp·pyo

Shopping   (s)

General

1 At what time — do you open?
A che ora — aprite?
a ke oh·ra — a·pree·te
— do you close?
— chiudete?
— *kyoo·day·te*

2 One of these, please
Uno di questi, per favore
oo·no dee kway·stee payr fa·voh·re

3 Two of those, please
Due di quelli, per favore
doo·e dee kwayl·lee payr fa·voh·re

4 How much does that cost?
Quanto costa quello?
kwan·to ko·sta kwayl·lo

5 I am willing to pay up to 50,000 lire
Sono disposto a pagare sino a cinquantamila lire
*soh·no des·spoh·sto a pa·gah·ray see·no a cheen·kwan·ta·mee·la
lee·re*

6 I should like to buy — some presents
Vorrei comprare — dei regali
vor·rey kom·prah·ray — dey re·gah·lee

7 Do you sell — sunglasses?
Vendete — occhiali da sole?
ven·day·te — ok·kyah·lee da soh·le

8 Do you have any — pencils?
Avete — matite?
a·vay·te — ma·tee·te

9 I need — some suntan oil
Ho bisogno di — un olio abbronzante
o bee·zoh·nyoh dee — oon o·lyoh ab·bron·dzan·te

10 Do you sell duty-free goods?
Vendete articoli esenti da dazio?
ven·day·te ar·tee·ko·lee e·zen·te da da·tsyoh

11 Where is — the shoe department?
Dov'è — il reparto scarpe?
doh·ve — eel re·par·toh skar·pe
— the food department?
— il reparto alimentari?
— *eel re·par·toh a·lee·men·tah·ree*

12   Can I see — the hat in the window?
                      Posso vedere — il cappello in vetrina?
                      *pos·so ve·**day**·re — eel kap·**pel**·loh een ve·**tree**·na*
13 No, the other one
   No, quell'altro
   *no kwayl·**lal**·tro*
14   Have you anything — cheaper?
                      Avete qualche cosa — di meno caro?
                      *a·**vay**·te kwal·ke ko·sa — dee **may**·no kah·ro*
                                          — second-hand?
                                          — di seconda mano?
                                          — *dee se·**kohn**·da mah·noh*
15 I need a gadget for . . .
   Ho bisogno di un dispositivo per . . .
   *o bee·**zoh**·nyoh dee oon dee·spo·zee·**tee**·voh payr*
16 Can you show me how it works?
   Può mostrarmi come funziona?
   *pwo mo·**strar**·mee koh·me foon·**tsyoh**·na*
17   Have you got — a larger one?
                      Ne avete — uno piú grande?
                      *nay a·**vay**·te — **oo**·no **pyoo** gran·de*
                                — a smaller one?
                                — uno piú piccolo?
                                — **oo**·no **pyoo** peek·ko·lo
18 I'm just looking
   Sto soltanto guardando
   *sto sol·**tan**·to gwar·**dan**·do*
19   I'm looking for — a blouse
                      Sto cercando — una camicetta
                      *sto cher·**kan**·do — **oo**·na ka·mee·**chayt**·ta*
20 I like this one
   Mi piace questo(a)
   *mee **pyah**·che **kway**·sto(a)*
21 I don't like it
   Non mi piace
   *nohn mee **pyah**·che*
22   I'll take — this one
                      Prendo — questo(a)
                      ***pren**·do — **kway**·sto(a)*
                               — the other one
                               — l'altro(a)
                               — **lal**·tro(a)
23 Please wrap it
   Può incartarlo(a), per favore?
   *pwo een·kar·**tar**·lo(a) payr fa·**voh**·re*
24 There's no need to wrap it, thank you
   Non c'è bisogno di incartarlo(a), grazie
   *nohn che bee·**zoh**·nyoh dee een·kar·**tar**·lo(a) **gra**·tsye*
25 Can I have a plastic bag?
   Un sacchetto di plastica, per favore
   *oon sak·**kayt**·toh dee **pla**·stee·ka payr fa·**voh**·re*
26 How much would it cost to send it to England/America?
   Quanto viene a costare per mandarlo(a) in Inghilterra/America?
   ***kwan**·to **vye**·ne a ko·**stah**·ray payr man·**dar**·lo(a) een een·geel·**ter**·ra/ a·**me**·ree·ka*
27 Please send it to this address
   Lo(a) mandi a questo indirizzo, per favore
   *lo(a) **man**·dee a **kway**·sto een·dee·**reets**·tsoh payr fa·**voh**·re*
28 Please pack it carefully
   Lo(a) impacchetti bene, per favore
   *lo(a) eem·pak·**kayt**·tee be·ne payr fa·**voh**·re*

Food and drink

Italy has countless small, family-run food shops which usually make for better shopping than the new supermarkets. Most are general grocers; others specialize not only in the normal way – as butchers, bakers, chocolate-makers – but also in some specifically Italian ways – in fresh pasta, for instance.

A word about weights. The usual quantities in which the Italians buy and sell are the *etto* (100 grams) and the *chilo* (1000 grams, or a kilogram). Cheese, for instance, will be sold by the *etto*, and you will find it useful to remember that one *etto* is a little less than ¼ lb, two *etti* are just under half a pound (in fact almost exactly 7 oz). If you want a full half-pound ask for two and a half *etti* (*due etti e mezzo*). Fruit, meat and vegetables are sold in units of a *chilo* or half-chilo (*mezzo-chilo*), and a *mezzo-chilo* of tomatoes is just over 1 lb 1 oz.

29		Where can I find — a baker/butcher?
	Dove posso trovare	— un panificio/una macelleria?
	doh·ve **pos**·so tro·**vah**·ray	— oon pah·nee·**fee**·choh/**oo**·na ma·chel·le·**ree**·a
30	What sort of cheese/butter do you have?	
	Che tipo di formaggio/burro avete?	
	ke **tee**·poh dee for·**maj**·joh/**boor**·roh a·**vay**·te	
31		I would like — a kilo of apples
	Vorrei	— un chilo di mele
	vor·**rey**	— oon **kee**·loh dee **may**·le
		— half a kilo of tomatoes
		— mezzo chilo di pomodori
		— **medz**·dzo **kee**·loh dee po·mo·**do**·ree
		— 200 grams of sugar
		— due etti di zucchero
		— **doo**·e **et**·tee dee **tsook**·ke·roh
		— 250 grams of ground coffee
		— due etti e mezzo di caffè macinato
		— **doo**·e **et**·tee e **medz**·dzo dee kaf·**fe** ma·chee·**nah**·to
		— five slices of Parma ham
		— cinque fettine di prosciutto
		— **cheen**·kwe fet·**tee**·ne dee pro·**shoot**·toh
		— half a dozen eggs
		— sei uova
		— sey **wo**·va
32	A package	— of salt, please
	Un pacco	— di sale, per favore
	oon **pak**·koh	— dee **sah**·le payr fa·**voh**·re
33	A can	— of tomatoes
	Una scatola	— di pomodori
	oo·na **skah**·to·la	— dee po·mo·**do**·ree
34	A liter	— of milk
	Un litro	— di latte
	oon **lee**·troh	— dee **lat**·te
35	A bottle	— of wine
	Una bottiglia	— di vino
	oo·na bot·**tee**·lya	— dee **vee**·noh

36 Two pork chops	39 Shall I help myself?
Due braciole di maiale	Devo servirmi?
doo·e bra·**cho**·le de ma·**yah**·le	**de**·vo ser·**veer**·mee
37 A joint of lamb	
Un pezzo di agnello	
oon **pets**·tsoh dee a·**nyel**·loh	
38 I would like enough for two people	
Ne vorrei quanto basta per due	
nay vor·**rey kwan**·to **ba**·sta payr **doo**·e	

Pharmacist

In Italy a pharmacist is just that, and often does not sell toiletries and photographic equipment (see p.47), for which there are special shops. A pharmacy, marked by a red cross, will diagnose minor ailments and sell the appropriate medicines. Many pharmacies sell homeopathic as well as allopathic remedies.

40　　　　　　I want something for — a headache
　　　　Vorrei qualche cosa per — il mal di testa
　　vor·rey kwal·ke ko·sa payr — *eel mal dee te·sta*
　　　　　　　　　　　　　　　　— insect bites
　　　　　　　　　　　　　　　　— le punture di insetti
　　　　　　　　　　　　　　　　— *le poon·too·re dee een·set·tee*
　　　　　　　　　　　　　　　　— a cold
　　　　　　　　　　　　　　　　— il raffreddore
　　　　　　　　　　　　　　　　— *eel raf·fred·doh·re*
　　　　　　　　　　　　　　　　— a cough
　　　　　　　　　　　　　　　　— la tosse
　　　　　　　　　　　　　　　　— *la tohs·se*
　　　　　　　　　　　　　　　　— hay fever
　　　　　　　　　　　　　　　　— la febbre da fieno
　　　　　　　　　　　　　　　　— *la feb·bre da fye·noh*
　　　　　　　　　　　　　　　　— a sore throat
　　　　　　　　　　　　　　　　— il mal di gola
　　　　　　　　　　　　　　　　— *eel mal dee goh·la*
　　　　　　　　　　　　　　　　— sunburn
　　　　　　　　　　　　　　　　— le scottature solari
　　　　　　　　　　　　　　　　— *le skot·ta·too·re so·lah·ree*
　　　　　　　　　　　　　　　　— an upset stomach
　　　　　　　　　　　　　　　　— il mal di stomaco
　　　　　　　　　　　　　　　　— *eel mal dee sto·ma·koh*

41　How many do I take?
　　Quanti(e) ne devo prendere?
　　kwan·tee(·te) nay de·vo pren·de·re

42　How often do I take them?
　　Ogni quanto tempo dovrei prenderli(e)?
　　oh·nyee kwan·to tem·poh do·vrey pren·der·lee(·le)

43　Are they safe for children to take?
　　Vanno bene per bambini?
　　van·no be·ne payr bam·bee·nee

44　Could I see a selection of perfume/toilet water?
　　Mi fa vedere dei profumi/dell'acqua di colonia?
　　mee fa ve·day·re dey pro·foo·mee/del·lak·kwa dee ko·lo·nya

45　I would like something with a floral scent
　　Vorrei qualcosa con profumo di fiori
　　vor·rey kwal·ko·sa kohn pro·foo·moh dee fyoh·ree

46　May I smell/try it, please?
　　Posso odorarlo/provarlo?
　　pos·so o·do·rar·lo/pro·var·lo

Cameras and film

47　　　　　　　I need film — for this camera
　　Ho bisogno di una pellicola — per questa macchina fotografica
　　o bee·zoh·nyoh dee oo·na
　　　　　pel·lee·ko·la — *payr kway·sta mak·kee·na fo·to·gra·fee·ka*
　　　　　　　　　　　　　　— for this cine-camera
　　　　　　　　　　　　　　— per questa cinepresa
　　　　　　　　　　　　　　— *payr kway·sta chee·ne·pray·sa*

48　　　　　　　I want — black-and-white film
　　　　　　Vorrei — una pellicola in bianco e nero
　　　　vor·rey — *oo·na pel·lee·ko·la een byan·ko e nay·ro*
　　　　　　　　— 35mm film
　　　　　　　　— una pellicola di trentacinque millimetri
　　　　　　　　— *oo·na pel·lee·ko·la dee trayn·ta·cheen·kwe meel·lee·me·tree*
　　　　　　　　— fast/slow film
　　　　　　　　— una pellicola per esposizioni brevi/lunghe
　　　　　　　　— *oo·na pel·lee·ko·la payr e·spo·zee·tsyoh·nee bre·vee/loon·ge*

I want — color-print film
Vorrei — una pellicola a colori
*vor·***rey** — *oo·na pel·***lee**·*ko·la a ko·***loh**·*ree*
— color-slide film
— una pellicola a colori per diapositive
— *oo·na pel·***lee**·*ko·la a ko·***loh**·*ree payr dee·a·po·zee·***tee**·*ve*
— batteries for the flash
— delle batterie per il flash
— ***del**·le bat·te·***ree**·*e payr eel flash*

49 Can you develop this film please?
Può sviluppare questa pellicola per favore?
*pwo zvee·loop·***pah**·*ray* **kway**·*sta pel·***lee**·*ko·la payr fa·***voh**·*re*

50 I would like two prints of this one
Vorrei due copie di questo
*vor·***rey** *doo·e ***ko**·*pye dee* **kway**·*sto*

51 When will the photographs be ready?
Quando saranno pronte le foto?
kwan**·*do sa·ran**·*no ***prohn**·*te le ***fo**·*toh*

52 I would like this photograph enlarged
Vorrei un ingrandimento di questa foto
*vor·***rey** *oon een·gran·dee·***mayn**·*toh dee* **kway**·*sta ***fo**·*toh*

53 There is something wrong with my camera
C'è qualcosa che non va nella mia macchina fotografica
*che kwal·***ko**·*sa ke nohn va ***nel**·la ***mee**·a ***mak**·kee·na fo·to·***gra**·fee·ka*

54 The film is jammed
La pellicola è bloccata
*la pel·***lee**·*ko·la e blok·***kah**·*ta*

55 I would like to buy a
camera — with single-lens reflex
Vorrei comprare una
macchina fotografica — con obiettivo semplice reflex
*vor·***rey** *kom·***prah**·*ray
oo·na ***mak**·kee·na
fo·to·***gra**·fee·ka — kohn o·byet·***tee**·voh ***saym**·plee·che ree·fleks*

I would like to buy a
camera — with built-in light meter
Vorrei comprare una
macchina fotografica — con esposimetro incorporato
*vor·***rey** *kom·***prah**·*ray
oo·na ***mak**·kee·na
fo·to·***gra**·fee·ka — kohn e·spo·***zee**·me·troh een·kor·po·***rah**·to*
— with instant developing
— con sviluppo istantaneo
— *kohn zvee·***loop**·poh ee·stan·***tah**·ne·o*
— with flash attachment
— con flash
— *kohn flash*
— with close-up/wide-angle lens
— con obiettivo per primi piani/ obiettivo grandangolare
— *kohn o·byet·***tee**·voh payr ***pree**·mee ***pyah**·nee/o·byet·***tee**·voh gran·dan·go·***lah**·re*
— with a camera case
— con una custodia da macchina fotografica
— *kohn oo·na koo·***sto**·dya da ***mak**·kee·na fo·to·***gra**·fee·ka*

Clothes and shoes

---

56 I am looking for — a dress
Sto cercando — un vestito
*sto cher·***kan**·do — oon ve·***stee**·toh*

57   I would like something — informal
        Vorrei qualcosa — di sportivo
        *vor·**rey** kwal·**ko**·sa — dee spor·**tee**·vo*
                               — for evening wear
                               — da indossare la sera
                               — *da een·dos·**sah**·ray la **say**·ra*

58   Can you please show me
                    some — sun dresses?
        Mi può mostrare, per favore — dei vestiti prendisole?
        *mee **pwo** mo·**strah**·ray payr*
                    *fa·**voh**·re — dey ve·**stee**·tee pren·dee·**soh**·le*
                               — silk shirts?
                               — delle camicie di seta?
                               — *del·le ka·**mee**·che dee **say**·ta*

59   I would like to have a suit/pair of shoes custom-made
     Vorrei farmi fare un completo/un paio di scarpe su misura
     *vor·**rey** far·mee **fah**·ray oon kom·**ple**·toh/oon pa·yoh dee **skar**·pe soo*
     *mee·**zoo**·ra*

60   I would prefer — a dark material/natural fiber
        Preferirei — una stoffa scura/una fibra naturale
        *pre·fe·ree·**rey** — **oo**·na **stof**·fa **skoo**·ra/**oo**·na*
                            ***fee**·bra na·too·**rah**·le*

61   I take a continental size 40
     Porto la misura quaranta
     ***por**·to la mee·**zoo**·ra kwa·**ran**·ta*
62   I take a continental shoe size 40
     Calzo il numero quaranta
     ***kal**·tso eel **noo**·me·roh kwa·**ran**·ta*
63   Can you measure me?
     Può prendermi le misure?
     ***pwo** pren·**der**·mee le mee·**zoo**·re*
64   Do you have this — in blue?
        Avete questo — in blu?
        *a·**vay**·te **kway**·sto — een **bloo***
65   What is the material?
     Che stoffa è?
     *ke **stof**·fa e*
66   I like — this one
                     Mi piace — questo(a)
                     *mee **pyah**·che — **kway**·sto(a)*
                              — that one
                              — quello(a)
                              — ***kwayl**·lo(a)*
                              — the one in the window
                              — quello(a) in vetrina
                              — ***kwayl**·lo(a) een ve·**tree**·na*

67   May I see it in the daylight?   71   I like it
     Posso vederlo alla luce?   Mi piace
     ***pos**·so ve·**dayr**·lo **al**·la **loo**·che   *mee **pyah**·che*
68   May I try it on?   72   I don't like it
     Posso provarlo(a)?   Non mi piace
     ***pos**·so pro·**var**·lo(a)*   *nohn mee **pyah**·che*
69   Where are the dressing rooms?   73   I prefer the blue one
     Dove sono i camerini di   Preferisco quello(a) blu
        prova?   *pre·fe·**ree**·sko **kwayl**·lo(a) bloo*
     *doh·ve **soh**·no ee   74   It does not suit me
        ka·me·**ree**·nee dee pro·va*   Non mi sta bene
70   I would like a mirror   *nohn mee sta **be**·ne*
     Ho bisogno di uno specchio   75   It does not fit
     *o bee·**zoh**·nyoh dee **oo**·no   Non è la mia misura
        spek·kyoh*   *nohn e la **mee**·a mee·**zoo**·ra*

76   It is too — tight
                     È troppo — stretto(a)
                     *e **trohp**·po — **strayt**·to(a)*
                              — big
                              — grande
                              — ***gran**·de*
                              — small
                              — piccolo(a)
                              — ***peek**·ko·lo(a)*

77	Can you —	alter it?
	Potete —	fare delle modifiche?
	po·tay·te —	**fah·**ray *del·*le mo·**dee·**fee·ke
	—	take it in?
	—	restringerlo(a)?
	—	re·**streen·**jer·lo(a)
	—	let it out?
	—	allargarlo(a)?
	—	al·lar·**gar·**lo(a)
78	I'd like one —	with a zipper
	Ne vorrei uno —	con la cerniera
	*nay vor·***rey** *oo·no* —	kohn la cher·**nye·**ra
	—	without a belt
	—	senza cintura
	—	**sen·**tsa cheen·**too·**ra

79 Is this all you have?	82 Will it shrink?
Non ha altro?	Si restringerà?
nohn a **al·***tro*	see re·streen·je·**ra**
80 I'll take it	83 Must it be dry-cleaned?
Lo prendo	Deve essere lavato a secco?
lo **pren·***do*	**de·**ve **es·**se·re la·**vah·**to a
81 Is it washable?	**sayk·**ko
È lavabile?	
*e la·***vah·***bee·le*	

Jewelers, silversmiths and watchmakers

84	Have you any —	antique/modern jewelry?
	Avete —	gioielli antichi/moderni?
	*a·***vay·***te* —	jo·**yel·**lee an·**tee·**kee/mo·**der·**nee
85	I am a collector of —	silverware/brooches
	Sono un collezionista di —	oggetti d'argento/spille
	soh·no oon	oj·**jet·**tee dar·**jen·**toh/**speel·**le
	kol·le·tsyoh·**nee·**sta dee	
86	Could you show me some —	rings/watches?
	Mi può mostrare degli —	anelli/orologi?
	mee **pwo** mo·**strah·**ray	
	de·lyee —	a·**nel·**lee/o·ro·**lo·**jee

87 What precious stone is this?
Che pietra preziosa è questa?
ke **pye·***tra pre·***tsyoh·***sa e* **kway·***sta*

88 Is this solid gold/silver?
Questo è oro/argento massiccio?
kway·sto e o·roh/ar·**jen·**toh mas·**seech·**cho

89 Is it gold-/silver-plated?
È placcato d'oro/d'argento?
e plak·**kah·**to do·roh/dar·**jen·**toh

90	Can you repair —	this watch/necklace?
	Può riparare —	quest'orologio/questa collana?
	*pwo ree·pa·***rah·***ray* —	kway·sto·ro·**lo·**joh/**kway·**sta
		kol·**lah·**na

Books, newspapers, postcards and stationery

If you want a newspaper, you will get it at a newsstand, *un'edicola*, while stationery is generally sold along with books in a *cartoleria*. Some major foreign newspapers are available on the larger stands, sometimes a day or two late. Postcards are sold usually in *edicole* (outside museums or tourist spots), also in *cartolerie*.

91	Do you have any —	English/American newspapers?
	Avete —	dei giornali inglesi/americani?
	*a·***vay·***te* —	dey johr·**nah·**lee een·**glay·**see/
		a·me·ree·**kah·**nee
	—	postcards?
	—	delle cartoline?
	—	**del·**le kar·to·**lee·**ne

92	I would like	— some notepaper
	Vorrei	— della carta da lettere
	*vor·**rey***	— ***del**·la **kar**·ta da **let**·te·re*
		— some envelopes
		— delle buste
		— ***del**·le **boo**·ste*
		— some mailing envelopes
		— delle buste con l'imbottitura
		— ***del**·le **boo**·ste kohn*
		*leem·bot·tee·**too**·ra*
		— a ball-point pen
		— una penna biro
		— *oo·na **payn**·na **bee**·ro*
		— a pencil
		— una matita
		— *oo·na ma·**tee**·ta*
93	I need	— some airmail stickers
	Ho bisogno di	— alcune etichette indicando "Posta Aerea"
	*o bee·**zoh**·nyoh dee*	— *al·**koo**·ne e·tee·**kayt**·te,*
		*een·dee·**kan**·do **po**·sta a·e·re·a*
		— some airmail envelopes
		— alcune buste per la Posta Aerea
		— *al·**koo**·ne **boo**·ste payr la **po**·sta*
		a·e·re·a
		— some Scotch tape
		— un nastro adesivo
		— *oon **na**·stroh a·de·**zee**·vo*
94	Do you sell	— English paperbacks?
	Vendete	— dei tascabili inglesi?
	*ven·**day**·te*	— *dey ta·**skah**·bee·lee een·**glay**·see*
		— street maps?
		— delle piante stradali?
		— ***del**·le **pyan**·te stra·**dah**·lee*

Tobacco shop

There are numerous little shops and stalls whose main business is selling tobacco, stamps, lottery tickets and other state monopolies. They are called *tabaccherie* and are marked with a T (normally a white T on a black background). Similar things are also sold at counters in bars and supermarkets. British and American brands of cigarettes are usually available along with Italian varieties, usually of rougher Turkish or African tobacco.

95	A pack of . . . please
	Un pacchetto di . . . per favore
	*oon pak·**kayt**·toh dee payr fa·**voh**·re*
	— with filter tip
	— con filtro
	— *kohn **feel**·troh*
	— without filter
	— senza filtro
	— ***sen**·tsa **feel**·troh*

96	Do you have any American/ English brands?	98	Some pipe cleaners
	Avete delle marche americane/ inglesi?		Degli scovolini per la pipa
	*a·**vay**·te **del**·le **mar**·ke*		*de·**lyee** sko·vo·**lee**·nee payr la*
	*a·me·ree·**kah**·ne/een·**glay**·see*		***pee**·pa*
97	A package of pipe tobacco	99	A box of matches
	Un pacchetto di tabacco da pipa		Una scatola di fiammiferi
	*oon pak·**kayt**·toh dee*		*oo·na **skah**·to·la dee*
	*ta·**bak**·koh da **pee**·pa*		*fyam·**mee**·fe·ree*

100	A cigar Un sigaro *oon see·ga·roh*	102	A butane refill Una bomboletta di gas *oo·na bom·bo·layt·ta dee gas*
101	A cigarette lighter Un accendino *oon ach·chen·dee·noh*		

Presents and souvenirs

103   I am looking for a present
                  for — my wife/husband
       Sto cercando un regalo per — mia moglie/mio marito
       sto cher·kan·do oon
       re·gah·loh payr — *mee·a moh·lye/mee·o ma·ree·toh*

104 I would like to pay between 10,000 and 20,000 lire
     Vorrei pagare fra le dieci e le ventimila lire
     vor·rey pa·gah·ray fra le dye·chee e le vayn·tee·mee·la lee·re

105 Can you suggest anything?
     Mi può consigliare qualcosa?
     mee pwo kon·see·lyah·ray kwal·ko·sa

106 Have you anything suitable for a ten-year-old girl/boy?
     Avete qualcosa che vada bene per una bambina/un bambino di dieci
     anni?
     a·vay·te kwal·ko·sa ke vah·da be·ne payr oo·na bam·bee·na/oon
     bam·bee·noh dee dye·chee an·nee

107   Do you have anything — made locally?
          Avete degli articoli — locali?
          a·vay·te de·lyee
          ar·tee·ko·lee — *lo·kah·lee*
                          — hand made?
                          — lavorati a mano?
                          — *la·vo·rah·tee a mah·noh*

108 Do you have anything unusual?
     Avete qualcosa di insolito?
     a·vay·te kwal·ko·sa dee een·so·lee·to

Services and everyday needs (Sn)

Post office

Stamps can also be bought in a *tabaccheria*. Mailboxes are red and
marked *poste* or *lettere*. Mail can be addressed general delivery, marked
Fermo Posta, to the central post office of any town, and collected on
payment of a small fee and proof of identity. Allow 7–10 days for mail
from abroad to reach Italy (or vice versa).

1   How much is a letter — to Britain?
          Quanto costa una lettera — per la Gran Bretagna?
          kwan·to ko·sta oo·na
               let·te·ra — *payr la gran bre·ta·nya*
                          — to the United States?
                          — per gli Stati Uniti?
                          — *payr lyee stah·tee oo·nee·tee*

2 I would like six stamps for postcards/letters to Britain/the United
   States
   Vorrei sei francobolli per cartoline/lettere per la Gran Bretagna/gli
   Stati Uniti
   vor·rey sey fran·ko·bohl·lee payr kar·to·lee·ne/let·te·re payr la gran
   bre·ta·nya/lyee stah·tee oo·nee·tee

3   I want to send — this parcel
          Vorrei spedire — questo pacco
          vor·rey spe·dee·re — *kway·sto pak·koh*
                          — a telegram
          Vorrei mandare — un telegramma
          vor·rey man·dah·ray — *oon te·le·gram·ma*

4 A telegram form, please
 Un modulo per telegrammi, per favore
 *oon mo·doo·loh payr te·le·**gram**·mee payr fa·**voh**·re*
5 When will it arrive?
 Quando arriverà?
 *kwan·do ar·ree·ve·**ra***
6 I want to send this by registered mail
 Voglio mandare questo per raccomandata
 *vo·lyo man·**dah**·ray **kway**·sto payr rak·ko·man·**dah**·ta*
7 I am expecting a letter general delivery
 Sto aspettando una lettera fermo posta
 *sto a·spet·**tan**·do oo·na **let**·te·ra **fayr**·mo po·sta*

Telephoning

The simplest but most expensive way to telephone is from your hotel.
The next easiest, if you want to make a long-distance call, is to go to the
post office: the official will tell you (or write down for you) the code you
need and give you a token or a booth-number. You can talk in peace (the
booths are soundproof) and you pay the official after you have finished.

 Otherwise you can use a public telephone (they are comparatively
rare) or a telephone in a bar. Bars with telephones display a yellow disc
with a black telephone dial, but you will only be able to make local calls
unless the sign says explicitly *interurbano* ("between cities", i.e. long-
distance). In these telephones you need to use not coins but *gettoni*,
metal tokens, worth 100 lire. Usually the bartender will be able to
provide some, but unfortunately not always; you can get them at the post
office. One *gettone* is enough for a local call, but for long-distance you
need eight or more. Insert the token or tokens first, then dial. Your
tokens are refunded if you cannot get through. (A token is acceptable
everywhere as a 100-lire coin.) The ringing signal in Italy consists of long
and fairly low bursts separated by short gaps. The busy signal has shorter
bursts. The reply in Italy is invariably *Pronto* (Hello).

 In Italian, telephone numbers are not given as single digits but in pairs,
so that 4321 would be forty-three, twenty-one. (For numerals, see p.68).

Phrases you will use

8 Hello
 Pronto
 prohn·to
9 This is Peter Williams
 Sono Peter Williams
 soh·no Peter Williams
10 Can I speak to Signor Peruzzi?
 Posso parlare col signor Peruzzi?
 *pos·so par·**lah**·ray kol see·**nyohr** pe·**roots**·tsee*
11 I would like to make a phone call to Britain/America
 Voglio fare una telefonata in Gran Bretagna/in America
 *vo·lyo **fah**·ray oo·na te·le·fo·**nah**·ta een gran bre·**ta**·nya/een
 a·**me**·ree·ka*
12 The number I want is . . .
 Voglio telefonare al numero . . .
 *vo·lyo te·le·fo·**nah**·ray al **noo**·me·roh*
13 I wish to make a — collect call
 Voglio fare una — telefonata con la "R"
 *vo·lyo **fah**·ray oo·na — te·le·fo·**nah**·ta kohn la **er**·re*
 — person-to-person call
 — telefonata personale
 — *te·le·fo·**nah**·ta per·so·**nah**·le*
14 What is the area code for Pisa/Los Angeles?
 Qual è il prefisso per Pisa/Los Angeles?
 *kwahl e eel pre·**fees**·soh payr **pee**·sa/los **an**·je·les*
15 Would you write it down for me, please?
 Me lo può scrivere, per favore?
 *may lo **pwo skree**·ve·re payr fa·**voh**·re*

16 **Could you put me through to (international) directory assistance?**
Può mettermi in comunicazione con il Servizio (internazionale)
Informazioni Abbonati?
pwo mayt·ter·mee een ko·moo·nee·ka·tsyoh·ne kohn eel ser·vee·tsyoh
(een·ter·na·tsyoh·nah·le) een·for·ma·tsyoh·nee ab·bo·nah·tee

17 **May I use the phone, please?**
Posso usare il telefono, per favore?
pos·so oo·zah·ray eel te·le·fo·noh payr fa·voh·re

18 **Do I need a token?**
Ho bisogno di un gettone?
o bee·zoh·nyoh dee oon jet·toh·ne

19 **Can I have three tokens, please?**
Posso avere tre gettoni per favore?
pos·so a·vay·re tray jet·toh·nee payr fa·voh·re

20 **We have been cut off**
Ci è stata tolta la comunicazione
chee e stah·ta tol·ta la ko·moo·nee·ka·tsyoh·ne

21 **Is there a cheap rate?**
C'è una tariffa ridotta?
che oo·na ta·reef·fa ree·doht·ta

22 **What is the time now — in Hong Kong?**
Che ora è adesso — a Hong Kong?
ke oh·ra e a·des·so — a hong kong

23 **I cannot get through**
Non riesco a ottenere la comunicazione
nohn ree·e·sko a o·t·te·nay·re la ko·moo·nee·ka·tsyoh·ne

24 **Can I check this number/code?**
Posso controllare questo numero/prefisso?
pos·so kon·trol·lah·ray kwes·to noo·me·roh/pre·fees·soh

25 **Do you have a directory — for Florence?**
Avete l'elenco telefonico — di Firenze?
a·vay·te le·len·koh
te·le·fo·nee·ko — dee fee·ren·tse

Phrases you will hear

26 Chi parla?
kee par·la
Who is speaking?

27 Le passo il signor Peruzzi
le pas·so eel see·nyohr
pe·roots·tsee
I am putting you through to
Signor Peruzzi

28 Resti in linea
re·stee een lee·ne·a
Hold the line

29 Sto cercando di metterLa in
comunicazione
sto cher·kan·do dee mayt·ter·la
een ko·moo·nee·ka·tsyoh·ne
I am trying to connect you

30 La linea è occupata
la lee·ne·a e ok·koo·pah·ta
The line is busy

31 Richiami piú tardi, per favore
ree·kyah·mee pyoo tar·dee
payr fa·voh·re
Please try later

32 Questo numero è bloccato
kway·sto noo·me·roh e
blok·kah·to
This number is out of order

33 Non riesco a ottenere questo
numero
nohn ree·e·sko a o·t·te·nay·re
kway·sto noo·me·roh
I cannot reach this number

34 È in linea — può parlare
e een lee·ne·a pwo par·lah·ray
Please go ahead

The hairdresser

35 **I'd like to make an appointment**
Vorrei un appuntamento
vor·rey oon ap·poon·ta·mayn·toh

36 **I want — a haircut**
Desidero — un taglio di capelli
de·see·de·ro — oon ta·lyoh dee ka·payl·lee
— a trim
— una spuntata
— oo·na spoon·tah·ta

I want — a blow-dry
Desidero — asciugarli col phon
de·see·de·ro — *a·shoo·gar·lee kol fon*

37 I want my hair — fairly short
Voglio i capelli — tagliati piuttosto corti
vo·lyo ee ka·payl·lee — *ta·lyah·tee pyoot·to·sto kohr·tee*
— not too short
— non troppo corti
— *nohn trohp·po kohr·tee*
— short and curly
— corti e ricci
— *kohr·tee e reech·chee*
— layered
— a ciocche
— *a chok·ke*
— in bangs
— con la frangia
— *kohn la fran·ja*

38 Take more off — the front
Li tagli piú corti — davanti
lee ta·lyee pyoo kohr·tee — *da·van·tee*
— the back
— dietro
— *dye·tro*

39 Not too much off — the sides
Non tagli troppo — ai lati
nohn ta·lyee trohp·po — *ay lah·tee*
— the top
— sopra
— *soh·pra*

40 I like a part — in the center
Vorrei la scriminatura — al centro
vor·rey la skree·mee·na·too·ra — *al chen·troh*
— on the left
— a sinistra
— *a see·nee·stra*
— on the right
— a destra
— *a de·stra*

41 I'd like — a perm
Vorrei — una permanente
vor·rey — *oo·na per·ma·nen·te*
— a shampoo and set
— uno sciampo e messa in piega
— *oo·no sham·poh e mays·sa een pye·ga*
— my hair tinted
— farmi la tintura
— *far·mee la teen·too·ra*
— my hair streaked
— farmi le mesti
— *far·mee le me·stee*

42 The water is too hot/cold
L'acqua è troppo calda/fredda
lak·kwa e trohp·po kal·da/frayd·da

43 The dryer is too hot/cold
Il casco è troppo caldo/freddo
eel ka·skoh e trohp·po kal·do/frayd·do

44 I'd like — a conditioner
Vorrei — un balsamo
vor·rey — *oon bal·sa·moh*
— hair spray
— la lacca
— *la lak·ka*

45 That's fine, thank you
Va bene, grazie
va be·ne gra·tsye

Repairs and technical jobs

This section covers household jobs — from plumbing to a faulty switch —
and any other articles that could need repair, such as glasses or shoes
(cars are dealt with on p.19, clothes on p.48).

46 Where can I get this repaired?
Dove posso farlo riparare?
doh·ve pos·so far·lo ree·pa·rah·ray

47   I am having trouble — with my heating/plumbing
           C'è qualcosa che non va — col riscaldamento/coi tubi
        che kwal·ko·sa ke nohn va — *kol ree·skal·da·mayn·toh/koy*
                         too·bee

48   This — is broken
        Questo — è rotto
      kway·sto — *e roht·to*
              — is not working
              — non funziona
              — *nohn foon·tsyoh·na*
              — is damaged
              — è danneggiato
              — *e dan·nej·jah·to*
              — is blocked
              — è ostruito
              — *e o·stroo·ee·to*

49 There is a leak in the pipe/roof
Il tubo/il tetto perde
eel too·boh/eel tayt·toh per·de

50 There is a gas leak
C'è una fuga di gas
che oo·na foo·ga dee gas

51 Would you have a look at this, please?
Può dare un'occhiata a questo, per favore?
pwo dah·ray oo·nok·kyah·ta a kway·sto payr fa·voh·re

52   Can you repair — my suitcase?
         Può ripararmi — la valigia?
      pwo ree·pa·rar·mee — *la va·lee·ja*

53 Can you reheel/resole these
shoes?
Può rifare i tacchi/le suole a
queste scarpe?
*pwo ree·fah·ray ee tak·kee/le
swo·le a kway·ste skar·pe*

54 Have you got a replacement
part?
Ha un pezzo di ricambio?
*a oon pets·tsoh dee
ree·kam·byoh*

55 Can you get it working again?
Lo può riparare?
lo pwo ree·pa·rah·ray

56 When will it be ready?
Quando sarà pronto?
kwan·do sa·ra prohn·to

57 Can you do it quickly?
Può farlo in poco tempo?
pwo far·lo een po·ko tem·poh

58 I would like a duplicate of this
key
Vorrei un doppione di questa
chiave
*vor·rey oon dop·pyoh·ne dee
kway·sta kyah·ve*

59 I have lost my key
Ho perso la chiave
o per·so la kyah·ve

60 I have locked myself out
Mi sono chiuso(a) fuori
mee soh·no kyoo·so(a) fwo·ree

61 Can you open the door?
Può aprire la porta?
pwo a·pree·re la por·ta

62 The fuse for the lights has
blown
È saltata la luce
e sal·tah·ta la loo·che

63 There is a loose connection
C'è un contatto difettoso
*che oon kon·tat·toh
dee·fet·toh·so*

64 Sometimes it works,
sometimes it doesn't
A volte funziona, a volte no
*a vol·te foon·tsyoh·na a vol·te
no*

Laundry, dry cleaners and clothes-mending

A dry cleaner's is called *una lavanderia a secco*; sometimes it is combined with *una lavanderia* (laundry), which will usually provide a fairly quick service. You will also be able to have things mended. A laundromat is *una lavanderia automatica*; even in these you will usually find staff to do your laundry.

65   Will you — clean this skirt?
     Potete — smacchiare questa gonna?
     po·tay·te — zmak·kyah·ray kway·sta gon·na
     — press these trousers?
     — stirare questi pantaloni?
     — stee·rah·ray kway·stee pan·ta·loh·nee
     — wash and iron these shirts?
     — lavare e stirare queste camicie?
     — la·vah·ray e stee·rah·ray kway·ste ka·mee·che
     — wash these clothes?
     — lavare questi vestiti?
     — la·vah·ray kway·stee ve·stee·tee

66 Can you get this stain out?
Potete togliere questa macchia?
po·tay·te to·lye·re kway·sta mak·kya

67   This stain is — grease/ink
     Questa è una macchia — di unto/di inchiostro
     kway·sta e oo·na mak·kya — dee oon·toh/dee een·kyo·stroh

68 This fabric is delicate
Questa stoffa è delicata
kway·sta stof·fa e de·lee·kah·ta

69 When will my things be ready?
Quando saranno pronte le mie robe?
kwan·do sa·ran·no prohn·te le mee·e ro·be

70 I need them in a hurry
Ne ho assoluto bisogno
nay o as·so·loo·to bee·zoh·nyoh

71 Is there a laundromat nearby?
C'è una lavanderia automatica qui vicino?
che oo·na la·van·de·ree·a ow·to·ma·tee·ka kwee vee·chee·no

72 Can I have my laundry done?
Mi potete lavare la biancheria?
mee po·tay·te la·vah·ray la byan·ke·ree·a

73 Where can I get clothes repaired?
Dove posso farmi rammendare degli indumenti?
doh·ve pos·so far·mee ram·men·dah·ray de·lyee een·doo·mayn·tee

74 Can you do invisible mending?
Potete fare un rammendo invisibile?
po·tay·te fah·ray oon ram·men·doh een·vee·zee·bee·le

75 Do you think you could repair this?
Pensate di poterlo rammendare?
pen·sah·te dee po·tayr·lo ram·men·dah·ray

76   Would you — sew this button back on?
     Potreste — ricucire questo bottone?
     po·tray·ste — ree·koo·chee·re kway·sto bot·toh·ne
     — mend this tear?
     — rammendare questo strappo?
     — ram·men·dah·ray kway·sto strap·poh
     — replace this zipper?
     — cambiare questa cerniera?
     — kam·byah·ray kway·sta cher·nye·ra
     — turn up/let down the hem?
     — accorciare/allungare l'orlo?
     — ak·kor·chah·ray/al·loon·gah·ray lohr·loh

Police and legal matters

77 I wish to call the police
   Voglio chiamare la polizia
   vo·lyo kya·mah·ray la po·lee·tsee·a

78 Where is the police station?
   Dov'è il posto di polizia?
   doh·ve eel poh·stoh dee po·lee·tsee·a

79   I should like to report — a theft
            Vorrei denunciare — un furto
   vor·rey de·noon·chah·ray — oon foor·toh
                            — the loss of a camera
                            — la scomparsa di una macchina
                              fotografica
                            — *la skom·par·sa dee oo·na*
                              mak·kee·na
                              fo·to·gra·fee·ka

80   Someone has broken into — my car/my room
            Mi hanno rubato — dalla macchina/in camera
   mee an·no roo·bah·to — dal·la mak·kee·na/een kah·me·ra

81   Someone has stolen — my wallet
            Mi hanno rubato — il portafoglio
   mee an·no roo·bah·to — eel por·ta·fo·lyoh

82   I have lost — my passport
            Ho perso — il passaporto
   o per·so — eel pas·sa·por·toh

83   I wish/I demand — to see a lawyer
            Desidero/Chiedo di — vedere un avvocato
   de·see·de·ro/kye·do dee — ve·day·re oon av·vo·kah·toh

84 My son is lost
   Mio figlio si è perso
   mee·o fee·lyoh see e per·so

85 Where is the British/American Consulate?
   Dov'è il consolato britannico/americano?
   doh·ve eel kon·so·lah·toh bree·tan·nee·ko/a·me·ree·kah·no

Worship

Italy is a Roman Catholic country, but all other main denominations and religions are usually represented in the larger cities.

86   Where is there — a (Catholic) church?
            Dove c'è — una chiesa (cattolica)?
   doh·ve che — oo·na kye·za (kat·to·lee·ka)
                            — a Protestant church?
                            — una chiesa protestante?
                            — *oo·na kye·za pro·te·stan·te*

87 What time is the service?
   A che ora c'è l'ufficio?
   a ke oh·ra che loof·fee·choh

88   I'd like to see — a priest
            Vorrei vedere — un prete
   vor·rey ve·day·re — oon pre·te
                            — a minister
                            — un ministro
                            — *oon mee·nee·stroh*

89   Is there one — who speaks English?
            Ce n'è uno — che parla inglese?
   che ne oo·no — ke par·la een·glay·se

90   Could you hear my
        confession — in English?
            Posso confessarmi — in inglese?
   pos·so kon·fes·sar·mee — een een·glay·se

Business matters (Bm)

Making appointments (see also Telephoning p.53)

1   **My name is George Baker — of Universal Chemicals**
    Mi chiamo George Baker — dell'Universal Chemicals
    mee kyah·mo George Baker — del·loo·nee·ver·sal ke·mee·kals
2   **Here is my card**
    Ecco il mio biglietto da visita
    ek·ko eel mee·o bee·lyayt·toh da vee·zee·ta
3   **Could I see/speak to your — Managing Director/Buyer?**
    Potrei vedere/parlare con il
                        vostro — Amministratore Delegato/
                                Direttore agli acquisti?
    po·trey ve·day·re/par·lah·ray
            kohn eel vo·stro — am·mee·nee·stra·toh·re
                            de·le·gah·to/dee·ret·toh·re a·lyee
                            ak·kwee·stee
4   **He/she is expecting me to telephone**
    Aspetta una mia telefonata
    a·spet·ta oo·na mee·a te·le·fo·nah·ta
5   **Could you put me through to Signor Peruzzi?**
    Mi passa il signor Peruzzi, per favore?
    mee pas·sa eel see·nyohr pe·roots·tsee payr fa·voh·re
6   **Is Signor Peruzzi in?**
    C'è il signor Peruzzi?
    che eel see·nyohr pe·roots·tsee
7   **Is his assistant/secretary there?**
    C'è la sua segretaria personale/la sua segretaria?
    che la soo·a se·gre·tah·rya per·so·nah·le/la soo·a se·gre·tah·rya
8   **When will he/she be back?**
    Quando ritornerà?
    kwan·do ree·tor·ne·ra
9   **I would like to make — an appointment with Signor Peruzzi**
                Vorrei fissare — un appuntamento con il signor Peruzzi
    vor·rey fees·sah·ray — oon ap·poon·ta·mayn·toh kohn eel see·nyohr pe·roots·tsee
10 **I am free on Thursday between 9:00 and 11:00**
    Sono libero giovedì fra le nove e le undici
    soh·no lee·be·ro jo·ve·dee fra le no·ve e le oon·dee·chee

Miscellaneous

11 **I am on a business trip to Italy**
    Sono in viaggio d'affari in Italia
    soh·no een vyaj·joh daf·fah·ree een ee·ta·lya
12   **I wish to hire — a secretary/a typist**
                Vorrei servirmi di — una segretaria/una dattilografa a ore
    vor·rey ser·veer·mee dee — oo·na se·gre·tah·rya/oo·na dat·tee·lo·gra·fa a oh·re
                            — a conference room
    Vorrei prendere in affitto — una sala per conferenze
    vor·rey pren·de·re een af·feet·toh — oo·na sah·la payr kon·fe·ren·tse
13 **Where can I get photocopying done?**
    Dove posso far fare delle fotocopie?
    doh·ve pos·so far fah·ray del·le fo·to·ko·pye
14 **Can I send a telex from here?**
    Posso mandare un telex da qui?
    pos·so man·dah·ray oon te·leks da kwee
15   **My firm specializes in — agricultural equipment**
    La mia ditta è specializzata in — macchine agricole
    la mee·a deet·ta e spe·cha·leedz·dzah·ta een — mak·kee·ne a·gree·ko·le

16   I wish — to carry out a market survey
                 Vorrei — fare una ricerca di mercato
                *vor·**rey** — **fah**·ray oo·na ree·**chayr**·ka dee*
                             *mer·**kah**·toh*
                 — to test the Italian market for this product
                 — sondare il mercato italiano per questo prodotto
                 — *son·**dah**·ray eel mer·**kah**·toh ee·ta·**lyah**·no payr **kway**·sto pro·**doht**·toh*

17 My firm is launching an advertising/sales campaign
    La mia ditta sta lanciando una campagna pubblicitaria/di vendita
    *la **mee**·a **deet**·ta sta lan·**chan**·do oo·na kam·**pa**·nya poob·blee·chee·**tah**·rya/dee **vayn**·dee·ta*

18 Have you seen our catalog?
    Ha visto il nostro catalogo?
    *a **vee**·sto eel **no**·stro ka·**tah**·lo·goh*

19 Can I send our sales representative to see you?
    Posso mandarLe il nostro rappresentante?
    *pos·so man·**dar**·le eel **no**·stro rap·pre·zen·**tan**·te*

20 I will send you a letter/telex with the details
    Le manderò una lettera/un telex con i dettagli
    *le man·de·ro oo·na **let**·te·ra/oon te·leks kohn ee det·**ta**·lyee*

21   Can I see — a sample of your product?
            Posso vedere — un campione del Vostro prodotto?
            *pos·so ve·**day**·re — oon kam·**pyoh**·ne del **vo**·stro pro·**doht**·toh*
                   — a selection of your goods?
                   — un assortimento della Vostra merce?
                   — *oon as·sor·tee·**mayn**·toh **del**·la **vo**·stra **mer**·che*

22 Can I have a copy of this document/brochure?
    Posso avere una copia di questo documento/opuscolo?
    *pos·so a·**vay**·re oo·na **ko**·pya dee **kway**·sto do·koo·**mayn**·toh/o·**poo**·sko·loh*

23 Can you give me an estimate of the cost?
    Può farmi un preventivo del costo?
    *pwo far·mee oon pre·ven·**tee**·voh del **ko**·stoh*

24 What percentage of the cost is for freight and delivery?
    Con quale percentuale incide il trasporto sul costo?
    *kohn **kwah**·le per·chen·**twah**·le een·**chee**·de eel tra·**spor**·toh sool **ko**·stoh*

25 What is the wholesale/retail price?
    Qual è il prezzo all'ingrosso/al dettaglio?
    *kwahl e eel **prets**·tsoh al·leen·**gros**·soh/al det·**ta**·lyoh*

26 What is the rate of inflation in Italy?
    Qual è il tasso d'inflazione in Italia?
    *kwahl e eel **tas**·soh deen·fla·**tsyoh**·ne een ee·**ta**·lya*

27 How high are current rates of interest?
    Quali sono gli attuali tassi d'interesse?
    *kwah·lee soh·no lyee at·**twah**·lee tas·see deen·te·**res**·se*

28 It's a pleasure to do business with you
    È un piacere trattare affari con Lei
    *e oon pya·**chay**·re trat·**tah**·ray af·**fah**·ree kohn ley*

Children (C)

1   Do you have — a special menu for children?
                 Avete — un menú per bambini?
              *a·**vay**·te — oon me·**noo** payr bam·**bee**·nee*
                   — half portions for children?
                Servite — mezze porzioni per bambini?
             *ser·**vee**·te — **medz**·dze por·**tsyoh**·nee payr bam·**bee**·nee*

2 Can you warm this bottle for me?
  Potete riscaldarmi questo biberon?
  *po·**tay**·te ree·skal·**dar**·mee kway·sto bee·be·**ron***

3 Do you have a highchair?
  Avete un seggiolone?
  *a·**vay**·te oon sej·jo·**loh**·ne*

4 Do you operate — a baby-sitting service?
  Avete — un servizio baby-sitter?
  *a·**vay**·te — oon ser·**vee**·tsyoh **ba**·by·seet·ter*
  — a day nursery?
  — un asilo-nido?
  — *oon a·**zee**·loh·nee·doh*

5 Do you know anyone who will baby-sit for us?
  Conoscete qualcuno che ci potrebbe fare da baby-sitter?
  *ko·no·**shay**·te kwal·**koo**·no ke chee po·**treb**·be **fah**·ray da
  ba·by·seet·ter*

6 We shall be back at 11
  Torneremo alle undici
  *tor·ne·**ray**·mo **al**·le **oon**·dee·chee*

7 She/he goes to bed at 8
  Va a letto alle otto
  *va a **let**·toh **al**·le ot·to*

8 Are there any organized activities for the children?
  Ci sono delle attività organizzate per i bambini?
  *chee **soh**·no **del**·le at·tee·vee·**ta** or·ga·needz·**dzah**·te payr
  ee bam·**bee**·nee*

9 Is there — a wading pool?
  C'è — una piscina per bambini?
  *che — **oo**·na pee·**shee**·na payr
      bam·**bee**·nee*
  — a playground?
  — un campo-giochi?
  — *oon **kam**·poh·**jo**·kee*
  — an amusement park?
  — un luna-park?
  — *oon loo·na·**park***
  — a zoo nearby?
  — uno zoo qui vicino?
  — *oo·no dzo·oh kwee vee·**chee**·no*

10 My son has hurt himself
   Mio figlio si è fatto male
   *mee·o **fee**·lyoh see e **fat**·to **mah**·le*

11 My daughter is ill
   Mia figlia non sta bene
   *mee·a **fee**·lya nohn sta **be**·ne*

12 Do you have a crib for our baby?
   Avete un lettino per il bambino?
   *a·**vay**·te oon let·**tee**·noh payr eel bam·**bee**·noh*

13 Can my son sleep in our room?
   Mio figlio può dormire in camera nostra?
   *mee·o **fee**·lyoh pwo dor·**mee**·re een **kah**·me·ra **no**·stra*

14 Are there any other children in the hotel?
   Ci sono altri bambini nell'albergo?
   *chee **soh**·no **al**·tree bam·**bee**·nee nel·lal·**ber**·goh*

15 How old are your children?
   Quanti anni hanno i Suoi bambini?
   ***kwan**·tee **an**·nee **an**·no ee swoy bam·**bee**·nee*

16 My son is 9 years old
   Mio figlio ha nove anni
   *mee·o **fee**·lyoh a **no**·ve **an**·nee*

17 My daughter is 15 months
   Mia figlia ha quindici mesi
   *mee·a **fee**·lya a **kween**·dee·chee **may**·see*

18 Where can I feed my baby?
   Dove posso allattare il bambino?
   ***doh**·ve **pos**·so al·lat·**tah**·ray eel bam·**bee**·noh*

19 I need some disposable diapers
   Ho bisogno di pannolini da buttar via
   *o bee·**zoh**·nyoh dee pan·no·**lee**·nee da boot·**tar** vee·a*

Illness and disability (1)

The disabled

1   I suffer from — **a weak heart**
                    Ho — il cuore debole
                    o — eel kwo·re day·bo·le
                             — **asthma**
                Soffro — di asma
                sof·fro — dee az·ma

2   Do you have — **facilities for the disabled?**
                Avete — servizi per gli handicappati fisici?
              a·vay·te — ser·vee·tsee payr lyee
                          an·dee·kap·pah·tee fee·zee·chee
                             — **a toilet for the disabled?**
                           — una toilette per gli
                                  handicappati fisici?
                           oo·na twa·let payr lyee
                             an·dee·kap·pah·tee fee·zee·chee

3 Is there a reduced rate for disabled people?
   C'è una riduzione per gli handicappati fisici?
   che oo·na ree·doo·tsyoh·ne payr lyee an·dee·kap·pah·tee fee·zee·chee

4   I am unable to — **climb stairs**
              Non posso — salire le scale
            nohn pos·so — sa·lee·re le skah·le
                        — **walk very far**
                        — camminare a lungo
                        — kam·mee·nah·ray a loon·go

5 Can you supply a wheelchair?
   Avete una sedia a rotelle?
   a·vay·te oo·na se·dya a ro·tel·le

Doctors and hospitals

If a visit to a doctor is necessary, you will have to pay on the spot. Proper accident and medical insurance is still advisable. It is important to make these arrangements with your own insurance company before going abroad, to ensure complete coverage. A pharmacy (see p.46) will both prescribe and provide something for a minor ailment; for something more serious, go in the first instance to a doctor rather than a hospital. In an emergency, ambulances (which also have to be paid for) can be called by dialling 113.

Preliminary

6 I need a doctor
   Ho bisogno di un dottore
   o bee·zoh·nyoh dee oon dot·toh·re

7 I feel ill
   Mi sento male
   mee sen·to mah·le

8 Can I have an appointment with the doctor?
   Posso fissare un appuntamento con il dottore?
   pos·so fees·sah·ray oon ap·poon·ta·mayn·toh kohn eel dot·toh·re

9 I would like a general checkup
   Vorrei fare una visita generale
   vor·rey fah·ray oo·na vee·zee·ta je·ne·rah·le

10   I would like to see — **a skin specialist**
           Vorrei vedere — un dermatologo
          vor·rey ve·day·re — oon der·ma·to·lo·goh
                      — **an eye specialist**
                      — un oculista
                      — oon o·koo·lee·sta

In the event of an accident

11 **There has been an accident**
C'è stato un incidente
che stah·to oon een·chee·den·te

12 **Call an ambulance**
Chiamate un'ambulanza
kya·mah·te oo·nam·boo·lan·tsa

13 **Get a doctor**
Chiamate un dottore
kya·mah·te oon dot·toh·re

14 **He is unconscious**
Ha perso conoscenza
a per·so ko·no·shen·tsa

15 **He is in pain**
Soffre dolore
sof·fre do·loh·re

16 **He/she has been seriously injured**
È ferito(a) gravemente
e fe·ree·to(a) grah·ve·mayn·te

17 **I have cut myself**
Mi sono tagliato(a)
mee soh·no ta·lyah·to(a)

18 **He/she has burnt himself/herself**
Si è bruciato(a)
see e broo·chah·to(a)

19 **I have had a fall**
Sono caduto(a)
soh·no ka·doo·to(a)

20 **She has been bitten**
È stata morsa
e stah·ta mor·sa

21 **I have hurt my arm/my leg**
Mi sono fatto(a) male ad un braccio/ad una gamba
mee soh·no fat·to(a) mah·le ad oon brach·choh/ad oo·na gam·ba

22 **I have broken my arm**
Mi sono rotto(a) il braccio
mee soh·no roht·to(a) eel brach·choh

23 **He has dislocated his shoulder**
Si è slogato una spalla
see e zlo·gah·to oo·na spal·la

24 **She has sprained her ankle**
Ha preso una storta alla caviglia
a pray·so oo·na stor·ta al·la ka·vee·lya

25 **I have pulled a muscle**
Ho uno stiramento
o oo·no stee·ra·mayn·toh

Symptoms, conditions and treatment

26 **There is a swelling here**
C'è un gonfiore qui
che oon gon·fyoh·re kwee

27 **It is inflamed here**
È infiammato qui
e een·fyam·mah·to kwee

28 **I have a pain here**
Mi fa male qui
mee fa mah·le kwee

29 **I find it painful to walk/ breathe**
Mi fa male quando cammino/ respiro
mee fa mah·le kwan·do kam·mee·no/re·spee·ro

30 **I have a headache/a sore throat**
Ho mal di testa/mal di gola
o mal dee te·sta/mal dee goh·la

31 **I have a high temperature**
Ho la febbre alta
o la feb·bre al·ta

32 **I can't sleep**
Non riesco a dormire
nohn ree·e·sko a dor·mee·re

33 **I have sunstroke**
Ho preso un'insolazione
o pray·so oo·neen·so·la·tsyoh·ne

34 **My stomach is upset**
Ho dei disturbi di stomaco
o dey dee·stoor·bee dee sto·ma·koh

35 **I feel nauseated**
Ho la nausea
o la now·ze·a

36 **I think I have food poisoning**
Penso di avere un'intossicazione da cibo
pen·so dee a·vay·re oo·neen·tos·see·ka·tsyoh·ne da chee·boh

37 **I have vomited**
Ho vomitato
o vo·mee·tah·to

38 **I have diarrhea**
Ho la diarrea
o la dee·ar·re·a

39 **I am constipated**
Sono stitico(a)
soh·no stee·tee·ko(a)

40 **I feel faint**
Mi sento svenire
mee sen·to zve·nee·re

41 **I am allergic to penicillin/ to cortisone**
Sono allergico(a) alla penicillina/ al cortisone
soh·no al·ler·jee·ko(a) al·la pe·nee·cheel·lee·na/ al kor·tee·zoh·ne

42 **I have high blood pressure**
Ho la pressione alta
o la pres·syoh·ne al·ta

43 **I am a diabetic**
Sono diabetico(a)
soh·no dya·be·tee·ko(a)

44 **I am taking these drugs**
Sto prendendo queste medicine
sto pren·den·do kway·ste me·dee·chee·ne

45 Can you give me an Italian
   prescription for them?
   Può farmi una ricetta italiana
   per questa medicina?
   *pwo far·mee oo·na ree·chet·ta
   ee·ta·lyah·na payr kway·sta
   me·dee·chee·na*

46 I am pregnant
   Sono incinta
   soh·no een·cheen·ta

47 I am on the pill
   Sto prendendo la pillola
   sto pren·den·do la peel·lo·la

48 My blood group is . . .
   Il mio gruppo sanguigno è . . .
   *eel mee·o groop·poh
   san·gwee·nyo e*

49 I don't know my blood group
   Non conosco il mio gruppo
   sanguigno
   *nohn ko·noh·sko eel mee·o
   groop·poh san·gwee·nyo*

50 Must I stay in bed?
   Devo stare a letto?
   de·vo stah·ray a let·toh

51 Will I be able to go out
   tomorrow?
   Potrò uscire domani?
   po·tro oo·shee·re do·mah·nee

52 Will I have to go to the
   hospital?
   Devo andare in ospedale?
   *de·vo an·dah·ray een
   o·spe·dah·le*

53 How do I get reimbursed?
   Come posso essere
   rimborsato(a)?
   *koh·me pos·so es·se·re
   reem·bohr·sah·to(a)*

Dentists

54 I need to see the dentist
   Devo vedere il dentista
   de·vo ve·day·re eel den·tee·sta

55 I have a toothache
   Ho mal di denti
   o mal dee den·tee

56 It's this one
   È questo
   e kway·sto

57 I've broken a tooth
   Mi sono spezzato(a) un dente
   *mee soh·no spets·tsah·to(a)
   oon den·te*

58 The filling has come out
   È uscita l'otturazione
   e oo·shee·ta lot·too·ra·tsyoh·ne

59 Will you have to take it out?
   Bisogna toglierlo?
   bee·zoh·nya to·lyer·lo

60 Are you going to fill it?
   Farà un'otturazione?
   fa·ra oo·not·too·ra·tsyoh·ne

61 That hurt
   M'ha fatto male
   ma fat·to mah·le

62 Please give me an anesthetic
   Mi faccia un'iniezione, per
   favore
   *mee fach·cha
   oo·neen·ye·tsyoh·ne payr
   fa·voh·re*

63 My gums hurt
   Mi fanno male le gengive
   mee fan·no mah·le le jen·jee·ve

64 My dentures are broken
   La mia dentiera si è rotta
   *la mee·a den·tye·ra see e
   roht·ta*

65 Can you repair them?
   Può ripararla?
   pwo ree·pa·rar·la

Emergencies and accidents (Ea)

Hopefully you will not need the following phrases, but it is better to
know them, as they could make a difference in a critical situation. For a
medical emergency, see also p.63.

1 Help!
   Aiuto!
   a·yoo·toh

2 Stop thief!
   Alt al ladro!
   alt al la·droh

3 There has been an accident
   C'è stato un incidente
   che stah·to oon een·chee·den·te

4 A fire has broken out
   È scoppiato un incendio
   e skop·pyah·to oon een·chen·dyoh

5   I have been — robbed/attacked
                      Mi hanno — derubato/assalito
                      *mee **an**·no — de·roo·**bah**·to/as·sa·**lee**·to*

6 Where is the nearest telephone/hospital?
Dov'è il telefono/l'ospedale piú vicino?
*doh·ve eel te·**le**·fo·noh/lo·spe·**dah**·le pyoo vee·**chee**·no*

7   Call — a doctor
                      Chiamate — un medico
                      *kya·**mah**·te — oon **me**·dee·koh*

                              — the police
                              — la polizia
                              — *la po·lee·**tsee**·a*

                              — an ambulance
                              — un'ambulanza
                              — *oo·nam·boo·**lan**·tsa*

                              — the fire department
                              — i pompieri
                              — *ee pom·**pye**·ree*

8 This is an emergency
È un caso di emergenza
*e oon **kah**·zoh dee e·mer·**jen**·tsa*

9 It is urgent
È urgente
*e oor·**jen**·te*

10 Please hurry
Fate presto, per favore
***fah**·te **pre**·sto payr fa·**voh**·re*

11 My address is . . .
Il mio indirizzo è . . .
*eel **mee**·o een·dee·**reets**·tsoh e*

Making conversation   (Mc)

Topics

The weather

Italians do not talk about the weather as much as, for example, the Americans and the English do, but there are occasions when you will find the following useful.

1 It's a lovely day
È una bella giornata
*e **oo**·na **bel**·la johr·**nah**·ta*

2 It's hot/cold
Fa caldo/freddo
*fa **kal**·do/**frayd**·do*

3 It's raining
Piove
***pyo**·ve*

4 It's windy
Tira vento
***tee**·ra **ven**·toh*

5 It's snowing
Nevica
***nay**·vee·ka*

6 It's foggy/misty
C'è nebbia/bruma
*che **nayb**·bya/**broo**·ma*

7 Is it going to be a nice day?
Sarà una bella giornata?
*sa·**ra oo**·na **bel**·la johr·**nah**·ta*

8 Is it going to rain?
Pioverà?
*pyo·ve·**ra***

9 What is the temperature?
Quanti gradi ci sono?
***kwan**·tee **grah**·dee chee **soh**·no*

10 Is the water warm?
È calda l'acqua?
*e **kal**·da **lak**·kwa*

11 It's a clear night
È una notte serena
*e **oo**·na **not**·te se·**ray**·na*

National and regional characteristics

This is an endlessly fruitful source of material for conversation, and the main form of Italian small talk. It is an aspect of *campanilismo*, loyalty to the belfry, that is, to one's own village, town or region. Here are some points that might be raised.

12 **Where do you come from?**
Da dove viene?
da **doh**·ve vye·ne

13 **Do you know the country around Florence?**
Conosce i dintorni di Firenze?
ko·**noh**·she ee deen·**tohr**·nee dee fee·**ren**·tse

14 **The wine from Orvieto/Treviso is wonderful**
Il vino di Orvieto/Treviso è ottimo
eel **vee**·noh dee or·**vye**·to/tre·**vee**·zo e ot·**tee**·mo

15 **Florence is a beautiful city**
Firenze è una bella città
fee·**ren**·tse e oo·na **bel**·la cheet·ta

16 **Have you ever been to Venice?**
È mai stato(a) a Venezia?
e my **stah**·to(a) a ve·**nay**·tsya

17 **The best time to go to Venice is in the spring**
Il periodo migliore per andare a Venezia è in primavera
eel pe·**ree**·o·doh mee·**lyoh**·re par an·**dah**·ray a ve·**nay**·tsya e een
pree·ma·**ve**·ra

18 **What are the people like in . . . ?**
Com'è la gente a . . . ?
koh·**me** la **jen**·te a

19 **Where did you spend your vacation last year?**
Dove ha passato le Sue vacanze l'anno scorso?
doh·ve a pas·**sah**·to le **soo**·e va·**kan**·tse lan·noh **skohr**·so

20 **Did you like it there?**
Le è piaciuto?
le e pya·**choo**·to

21 **What are the main industries of the region?**
Quali sono le industrie principali della regione?
kwah·lee **soh**·no le een·**doo**·strye preen·chee·**pah**·lee **del**·la re·**joh**·ne

22 **Is it prosperous?**
È ricca?
e **reek**·ka

23 **Does it remain unspoiled?**
Il paesaggio è intatto?
eel pa·e·**zaj**·joh e een·**tat**·to

24 **What sports are popular in Italy?**
Quali sport sono popolari in Italia?
kwah·lee sport **soh**·no po·po·**lah**·ree een ee·**ta**·lya

Breaking the ice

Here are a few stock questions and answers that tend to be exchanged by people who meet casually.

25 **Do you mind if — I sit here?**
Le dispiace se — mi siedo qui?
le dee·**spyah**·che say — mee **sye**·do kwee
— I smoke?
— fumo?
— **foo**·mo

26 **Can I — offer you a cigarette?**
Gradisce — una sigaretta?
gra·**dee**·she — **oo**·na see·ga·**rayt**·ta
— buy you a drink?
— qualcosa da bere?
— kwal·**ko**·sa da **bay**·re

27 **May I introduce myself?**
Permetta che mi presenti
per·**mayt**·ta ke mee pre·**zen**·tee

28 **Are you Italian? Where do you come from?**
È italiano(a)? Da dove viene?
e ee·ta·**lyah**·no(a) da **doh**·ve vye·ne

29 **I am American/English**
Sono americano(a)/inglese
soh·no a·me·**ree**·**kah**·no(a)/een·**glay**·se

30 I live in New York/London
Abito a New York/Londra
ah·bee·to a new york/lohn·dra

31 Is this your first visit to Rome?
È questa la prima volta che viene a Roma?
e kway·sta la pree·ma vol·ta ke vye·ne a roh·ma

32 This is my third visit
Questa è la mia terza visita
kway·sta e la mee·a ter·tsa vee·zee·ta

33 Have you been here long?
È qui da molto?
e kwee da mohl·to

34 I have been here two days
Sono qui da due giorni
soh·no kwee da doo·e johr·nee

35 Are you staying long?
Si fermerà per molto?
see fer·me·ra payr mohl·to

36 I am staying for two weeks
Mi fermerò per due settimane
mee fer·me·ro payr doo·e set·tee·mah·ne

37 Where are you staying?
Dove alloggia?
doh·ve al·loj·ja

38 I am staying at the Hotel Gloria
Alloggio all'albergo Gloria
al·loj·jo al·lal·ber·goh glo·rya

39 What is your job?
Che lavoro fa?
ke la·voh·roh fa

40 Have you visited England/America?
Ha visitato l'Inghilterra/l'America?
a vee·zee·tah·to leen·geel·ter·ra/la·me·ree·ka

41   What do you think — of the people?
Cosa ne pensa — della gente?
ko·sa nay pen·sa   — del·la jen·te
                   — the food?
                   — del cibo?
                   — del chee·boh
                   — the country?
                   — del paese?
                   — del pa·ay·ze

42 Are you married?
È sposato(a)?
e spo·zah·to(a)

43 Do you have any children?
Ha bambini?
a bam·bee·nee

44   Would you like — a cup of coffee/a drink?
Gradisce — un caffè/qualcosa da bere?
gra·dee·she   — oon kaf·fe/kwal·ko·sa da bay·re
             — to show me something of your city?
Le dispiacerebbe — mostrarmi qualcosa della Sua città?
le dee·spyah·che·reb·be   — mo·strar·mee kwal·ko·sa del·la soo·a cheet·ta
             — to have dinner/lunch with me?
Le farebbe piacere — cenare/pranzare con me?
le fa·reb·be pya·chay·re   — che·nah·ray/pran·dzah·ray kohn may
             — to go to the movies/theater with me?
             — andare al cinema/a teatro con me?
             — an·dah·ray al chee·ne·ma/a te·ah·troh kohn may
             — to go out with me this evening?
             — uscire insieme stasera?
             — oo·shee·re een·sye·me sta·say·ra

Reference (R)

The alphabet

The Italian alphabet is the standard European one, although native
Italian words lack J, K, W, X and Y. In the following table the names of
the letters are given phonetically, and each letter (except for the five
mentioned above) forms the initial of the word on the right. This is a
standard system for classification, which might be used, for example,
when a word is being spelled out over the telephone.

A	for	Ancona	N	for	Napoli
a		*an·koh·na*	*en·ne*		*nah·po·lee*
B		Bari	O		Otranto
bee		*bah·ree*	*o*		*o·tran·to*
C		Como	P		Palermo
chee		*ko·mo*	*pee*		*pa·ler·mo*
D		Domodossola	Q		quarto
dee		*do·mo·dos·so·la*	*koo*		*kwar·to*
E		Empoli	R		Roma
ay		*aym·po·lee*	*er·re*		*roh·ma*
F		Firenze	S		Savona
ef·fe		*fee·ren·tse*	*es·se*		*sa·voh·na*
G		Genova	T		Torino
jee		*je·no·va*	*tee*		*to·ree·no*
H		Hotel	U		Udine
ak·ka		*o·tel*	*oo*		*oo·dee·ne*
I		Imperia	V		Venezia
ee		*eem·pe·rya*	*voo*		*ve·nay·tsya*
J			W		
ee loon·goh			*voo·dohp·pyo*		
K			X		
kap·pa			*eeks*		
L		Livorno	Y		
el·le		*lee·vohr·no*	*ee gre·ko*		
M		Milano	Z		zebra
em·me		*mee·lah·no*	*dze·ta*		*dze·bra*

Numbers

Cardinal numbers

0 zero	11 undici	22 ventidue
dze·ro	*oon·dee·chee*	*ven·tee·doo·e*
1 uno, una	12 dodici	23 ventitré
oo·noh, oo·na	*doh·dee·chee*	*ven·tee·tray*
2 due	13 tredici	30 trenta
doo·e	*tray·dee·chee*	*trayn·ta*
3 tre	14 quattordici	31 trentuno
tray	*kwat·tohr·dee·chee*	*tren·too·no*
4 quattro	15 quindici	40 quaranta
kwat·tro	*kween·dee·chee*	*kwa·ran·ta*
5 cinque	16 sedici	50 cinquanta
cheen·kwe	*say·dee·chee*	*cheen·kwan·ta*
6 sei	17 diciassette	60 sessanta
say	*dee·chas·set·te*	*ses·san·ta*
7 sette	18 diciotto	70 settanta
set·te	*dee·chot·to*	*set·tan·ta*
8 otto	19 diciannove	80 ottanta
ot·to	*dee·chan·no·ve*	*ot·tan·ta*
9 nove	20 venti	90 novanta
no·ve	*vayn·tee*	*no·van·ta*
10 dieci	21 ventuno	100 cento
dye·chee	*ven·too·no*	*chen·to*

101 centuno	300	2,000
*chen·**too**·no*	trecento	duemila
110 centodieci	*tray·**chen**·to*	1,000,000
*chen·toh·**dye**·chee*	1,000	*doo·e·**mee**·la*
200 duecento	mille	1,000,000
*doo·e·**chen**·to*	**meel·**le	un milione
		*oon mee·**lyoh**·ne*

Ordinal numbers

1st	11th	20th
primo/prima	undicesimo(a)	ventesimo(a)
pree·mo/**pree·**ma	*oon·dee·**che·**zee·mo(a)*	*ven·**te·**zee·mo(a)*
2nd	12th	21st
secondo/seconda	dodicesimo(a)	ventunesimo(a)
*se·**kohn·**do/*	*do·dee·**che·**zee·mo(a)*	*ven·too·**ne·**zee·mo(a)*
*se·**kohn·**da*	13th	22nd
3rd	tredicesimo(a)	ventiduesimo(a)
terzo(a)	*tre·dee·**che·**zee·mo(a)*	*ven·tee·*
ter·tso(a)	14th	*doo·e·zee·mo(a)*
4th	quattordicesimo(a)	23rd
quarto(a)	kwat·tor·	ventitreesimo(a)
kwar·to(a)	dee·**che·**zee·mo(a)	*ven·tee·*
5th	15th	*tre·e·zee·mo(a)*
quinto(a)	quindicesimo(a)	30th
kween·to(a)	kween·	trentesimo(a)
6th	dee·**che·**zee·mo(a)	*tren·**te·**zee·mo(a)*
sesto(a)	16th	40th
*se·**sto(a)*	sedicesimo(a)	quarantesimo(a)
7th	*se·dee·**che·**zee·mo(a)*	*kwa·ran·**te·**zee·mo(a)*
settimo(a)	17th	50th
set·tee·mo(a)	diciassettesimo(a)	cinquantesimo(a)
8th	dee·chas·	*cheen·kwan·*
ottavo(a)	set·**te·**zee·mo(a)	*te·zee·mo(a)*
*ot·**tah·**vo(a)*	18th	100th
9th	diciottesimo(a)	centesimo(a)
nono(a)	dee·chot·**te·**zee·mo(a)	*chen·**te·**zee·mo(a)*
no·no(a)	19th	1,000th
10th	diciannovesimo(a)	millesimo(a)
decimo(a)	dee·chan·	*meel·**le·**zee·mo(a)*
de·chee·mo(a)	no·**ve·**zee·mo(a)	

Other numerical terms

a half	10 percent	five times
la metà	dieci per cento	cinque volte
*la me·**ta***	*dye·chee payr **chen·**to*	*cheen·kwe **vol·**te*
a quarter	a dozen	the last (one)
*oon **kwar·**to*	una dozzina	l'ultimo(a)
a third	*oo·na dodz·**dzee·**na*	*lool·tee·mo(a)*
un terzo	half a dozen	
*oon **ter·**tso*	una mezza dozzina	
	*oo·na **medz·**dza*	
	*dodz·**dzee·**na*	

The time

In reply to the question "che ore sono?" (what time is it?) you will hear
"sono" (it is), followed by the number. The 24-hour clock is often used.
Otherwise one says "di mattina" (a.m.) or "di sera" (p.m.). Here are
some examples.

9:00 — le nove
— *le **no·**ve*
9:05 — le nove e cinque
— *le **no·**ve ay **cheen·**kwe*
9:15 — le nove e un quarto
— *le **no·**ve ay oon **kwar·**to*

9:25	— le nove e venticinque	
	— *le* ***no***·*ve ay ven*·*tee*·***cheen***·*kwe*	
9:30	— le nove e mezza	
	— *le* ***no***·*ve ay* ***medz***·*dza*	
9:35	— le dieci meno venticinque	
	— *le* ***dye***·*chee* ***may***·*no*	
	ven·*tee*·***cheen***·*kwe*	
10:45	— le undici meno un quarto	
	— *le* ***oon***·*dee*·*chee* ***may***·*no oon*	
	kwar·*to*	

Here are some other useful phrases connected with time.

tonight	**before midnight**	**in an hour's time**
stasera	prima di mezzanotte	fra un'ora
sta·***say***·*ra*	***pree***·*ma dee*	*fra oo*·***noh***·*ra*
at night	*medz*·*dza*·***not***·*te*	**two hours ago**
di notte	**after 3 o'clock**	due ore fa
dee ***not***·*te*	dopo le tre	***doo***·*e oh*·*re fa*
the morning	***doh***·*po le tray*	**in half an hour**
la mattina	**at half past 6**	fra mezz'ora
la mat·***tee***·*na*	alle sei e mezza	*fra medz*·***dzoh***·*ra*
this afternoon	*al*·*le say ay* ***medz***·*dza*	**soon**
questo pomeriggio	**nearly 5 o'clock**	fra poco
kway·*sto*	quasi le cinque	*fra* ***po***·*ko*
po·*me*·***reej***·*joh*	***kwah***·*zee le* ***cheen***·*kwe*	**early**
at midday	**at about 1 o'clock**	presto
a mezzogiorno	circa l'una	***pre***·*sto*
a medz·*dzo*·***johr***·*noh*	***cheer***·*ka* ***loo***·*na*	**late**
		tardi
		tar·*dee*

The calendar

Sunday	**tomorrow**	**June**
domenica	domani	giugno
do·***may***·*nee*·*ka*	*do*·***mah***·*nee*	***joo***·*nyo*
Monday	**spring**	**July**
lunedí	la primavera	luglio
loo·*ne*·***dee***	*la pree*·*ma*·***ve***·*ra*	***loo***·*lyo*
Tuesday	**summer**	**August**
martedí	l'estate	agosto
mar·*te*·***dee***	*le*·***stah***·*te*	*a*·***goh***·*sto*
Wednesday	**autumn (fall)**	**September**
mercoledí	l'autunno	settembre
mer·*ko*·*le*·***dee***	*low*·***toon***·*noh*	*set*·***tem***·*bre*
Thursday	**winter**	**October**
giovedí	l'inverno	ottobre
joh·*ve*·***dee***	*leen*·***ver***·*noh*	*ot*·***toh***·*bre*
Friday	**in spring**	**November**
venerdí	in primavera	novembre
ve·*ner*·***dee***	*een pree*·*ma*·***ve***·*ra*	*no*·***vem***·*bre*
Saturday	**in summer**	**December**
sabato	d'estate	dicembre
sa·***ba***·*to*	*de*·***stah***·*te*	*dee*·***chem***·*bre*
on Friday	**January**	**in June**
venerdí	gennaio	in giugno
ve·*ner*·***dee***	*jen*·***na***·*yo*	*een* ***joo***·*nyo*
next Tuesday	**February**	**July 6**
martedí prossimo	febbraio	il sei luglio
mar·*te*·***dee***	*feb*·***bra***·*yo*	*eel say* ***loo***·*lyo*
pros·*see*·*mo*	**March**	**next week**
yesterday	marzo	la settimana prossima
ieri	***mar***·*tso*	*la set*·*tee*·***mah***·*na*
ye·*ree*	**April**	***pros***·*see*·*ma*
today	aprile	**last month**
oggi	*a*·***pree***·*le*	il mese scorso
oj·*jee*	**May**	*eel* ***may***·*se* ***skohr***·*so*
	maggio	
	maj·*jo*	

Public holidays

New Year's Day	January 1
Easter Monday	
Liberation Day	April 25
Labor Day	May 1
Assumption	August 15
All Saints' Day	November 1
Immaculate Conception	December 8
Christmas Day	December 25
St Stephen's Day	December 26

Abbreviations

ACI	Automobile Club d'Italia (Italian Motoring Organisation)
CEE	Comunità Economica Europea (Common Market)
CIT	Compagnia Italiana del Turismo
ENIT	Ente Nazionale Italiano per il Turismo (Italian Tourist Authorities)
FS	Ferrovie dello Stato (Railways)
IVA	Imposta sul Valore Aggiunto (Value Added Tax)
PT	Poste e Telecomunicazioni (Post Office)
RAI	Radio Audizioni Italiane (Italian Radio & Television)
SIP	Società Italiana per l'esercizio telefonico (Italian Telephone Company)
TCI	Touring Club Italiano (Italian Touring Club)

Signs and notices (see also Road signs, p.18)

Ai treni **To the trains**	Ingresso gratuito *or* libero **Admission free**	Signori **Gentlemen**
Al completo **Full**	In restauro **Undergoing restoration**	Si prega di attendere **Please wait**
Alt **Stop**	Lavori in Corso **Men at work**	Sottopassaggio **Underpass**
Aperto **Open**	Libero **Vacant**	Spingere **Push**
Ascensore **Elevator**	Non toccare **Do not touch**	Suonare **Ring**
Attenzione **Danger**	Occupato **Occupied**	Tirare **Pull**
Avanti **Cross now**	Pericoloso sporgersi **Do not lean out**	Uomini **Gentlemen**
Cassa (in shop) **Cashier's desk**	Polizia **Police**	Uscita **Exit**
Chiuso **Closed**	Saldi **Sale**	Vernice fresca **Wet paint**
Degustazione **Sampling**	Servizio compreso **Tip included**	Vietato il bagno **No swimming**
Donne **Ladies**	Servizio escluso **Tip not included**	Vietato calpestare le aiuole **Keep off the grass**
Fermata **Bus stop**	Signore **Ladies**	Vietato fumare **No smoking**
Guasto **Out of order**		

Conversion tables

In the tables for weight and length, the central figure may be read as either a metric or a traditional measurement. So to convert from pounds to kilos you look at the figure on the right, and for kilos to pounds you want the figure on the left.

feet		meters	inches			cm	lbs		kg
3.3	1	0.3	0.39		1	2.54	2.2	1	0.45
6.6	2	0.61	0.79		2	5.08	4.4	2	0.91
9.9	3	0.91	1.18		3	7.62	6.6	3	1.4
13.1	4	1.22	1.57		4	10.6	8.8	4	1.8
16.4	5	1.52	1.97		5	12.7	11	5	2.2
19.7	6	1.83	2.36		6	15.2	13.2	6	2.7
23	7	2.13	2.76		7	17.8	15.4	7	3.2
26.2	8	2.44	3.15		8	20.3	17.6	8	3.6
29.5	9	2.74	3.54		9	22.9	19.8	9	4.1
32.9	10	3.05	3.9		10	25.4	22	10	4.5
			4.3		11	27.9			
			4.7		12	30.1			

°C	0	5	10	15	17	20	22	24	26	28	30	35	37	38	40	50	100
°F	32	41	50	59	63	68	72	75	79	82	86	95	98.4	100	104	122	212

Km	10	20	30	40	50	60	70	80	90	100	110	120
Miles	6.2	12.4	18.6	24.9	31	37.3	43.5	49.7	56	62	68.3	74.6

Tire pressures

lb/sq in	15	18	20	22	24	26	28	30	33	35
kg/sq cm	1.1	1.3	1.4	1.5	1.7	1.8	2	2.1	2.3	2.5

Fuel

UK gallons	1.1	2.2	3.3	4.4	5.5	6.6	7.7	8.8
liters	5	10	15	20	25	30	35	40
US gallons	1.3	2.6	3.9	5.2	6.5	7.8	9.1	10.4

Basic Italian Grammar

NOUNS AND ARTICLES

Gender

This is one of the basic differences between Italian and English. In English, we say 'the knife' and 'the fork', but in Italian it is '*il coltello*' and '*la forchetta*', reflecting the fact that '*coltello*' is masculine and '*forchetta*' feminine. Equally, when using the indefinite article ('a', 'an' in English) it is '*un coltello*' but '*una forchetta*'.

While gender must be learned along with each new word you acquire, a useful guide is that:

(i) most masculine nouns end in -*o* in the singular which changes to -*i* in the plural e.g. *libro/libri*

(ii) most feminine nouns end in -*a* in the singular which changes to -*e* in the plural e.g. *casa/case*

(iii) nouns ending in -*e* in the singular can be *either* masculine *or* feminine; the -*e* becomes -*i* in the plural e.g. *padre* (*m*)/*padri*, *madre* (*f*)/*madri*

(iv) most masculine nouns ending in -*a* in the singular end in -*i* in the plural e.g. *macchinista/macchinisti*

(v) many nouns ending in -*a* in the singular can be *either* masculine *or* feminine; the -*a* becomes -*i* for the masculine plural and -*e* for the feminine plural e.g. *artista/artisti/artiste*

(vi) most masculine nouns ending in -*co* or -*go* in the singular end in -*chi* or -*ghi* in the plural; but nouns of more than two syllables where -*co* or -*go* is preceded by a vowel, end in -*ci* or -*gi* in the plural e.g. *fuoco/fuochi*, *albergo/alberghi*; *amico/amici*, *psicologo/psicologi*

(vii) nouns ending in -*ca* or -*ga* in the singular end in -*che* or -*ghe* in the plural if they are feminine and in -*chi* or -*ghi* if they are masculine e.g. *mosca/mosche*, *collega/colleghi*

(viii) most feminine nouns ending in -*cia* or -*gia* in the singular end in -*cie* or -*gie* in the plural when the *i* is stressed, and in -*ce* or -*ge* when it is not e.g. *bugia/bugie*; *provincia/province*

(ix) most masculine nouns ending in *-io* in the singular end in *-ii* in the plural
    when the *i* is stressed, and in *i* when it is not e.g. *zio/zii*; *studio/studi*
Any exceptions are clearly shown in the Italian-English dictionary section.

In Italian, the article must agree in gender (i.e. masculine or feminine) and
number (i.e. singular or plural) with the noun it accompanies. The following
table outlines the variation in article. The bracketed form is the one used with a
masculine noun beginning with *z*, *gn*, *pn*, *ps*, *x*, or *s* + consonant. See below for
examples.

	Definite article singular	**Definite article plural**	**Indefinite article**
masculine	*il (lo)*	*i (gli)*	*un (uno)*
	l' (before a vowel)	*gli* (before a vowel)	
feminine	*la*	*le*	*una*
	l' (before a vowel)		*un'* (before a vowel)
Thus:	*il libro*	*i libri*	*un libro*
	lo gnomo	*gli gnomi*	*uno gnomo*
	lo psicologo	*gli psicologi*	*uno psicologo*
	lo sportello	*gli sportelli*	*uno sportello* .
	l'anello	*gli anelli*	*un anello*
	la casa	*le case*	*una casa*
	l'entrata	*le entrate*	*un'entrata*

Use of articles
1) In almost all cases where 'the' is not used in English, the article must be used
in Italian. For instance:
    apples are good for you   *le mele fanno bene*
    meat is expensive   *la carne è cara*
    France is beautiful   *la Francia è bella*
    he likes ice cream   *gli piace il gelato*
2) *a + il*, *da + il*, *su + il*, *in + il* etc
When the articles '*il*', '*lo*', '*gli*', *etc* are preceded by the prepositions *a* (at; to),
da (by; from), *su* (on) and *in* (in; into), they are contracted thus:

a + il = al	*da + il = dal*	*su + il = sul*	*in + il = nel*
a + lo = allo	*da + lo = dallo*	*su + lo = sullo*	*in + lo = nello*
a + l' = all'	*da + l' = dall'*	*su + l' = sull'*	*in + l' = nell'*
a + la = alla	*da + la = dalla*	*su + la = sulla*	*in + la = nella*
a + i = ai	*da + i = dai*	*su + i = sui*	*in + i = nei*
a + gli = agli	*da + gli = dagli*	*su + gli = sugli*	*in + gli = negli*
a + le = alle	*da + le = dalle*	*su + le = sulle*	*in + le = nelle*

Thus: *alla casa* to the house   *dai ragazzi* from the boys
        sul tavolo on the table   *nello specchio* in the mirror
3) *di + il* etc
When the articles '*il*', '*lo*', '*gli*' etc are preceded by the preposition *di* (of), they
are contracted thus:
    di + il = del   *di + l' = dell'*   *di + i = dei*   *di + le = delle*
    di + lo = dello   *di + la = della*   *di + gli = degli*
NB The above forms also have the meaning 'some/any' and you should avoid
confusing this meaning with the '*of*' meaning
Thus:
voglio del pane*   I want *some* bread
but   *il titolo del libro*   the title *of the* book
*Note, however, that in a negative sentence, there is no article:
non voglio pane   I don't want (any) bread
4) *con + il/i*
When the articles '*il*' and '*i*' are preceded by *con* (with), they are contracted
thus:
    con + il = col   *con + i = coi*
    Thus: *col maestro* with the teacher   *coi ragazzi* with the boys

ADJECTIVES

Position
Adjectives generally *follow* the noun in Italian:
    una gonna rossa   a *red* skirt
    la risposta sbagliata   the *wrong* answer
Among those which often *precede* the noun are some very common adjectives:
    *grande (big)   *giovane* (young)   *buono (good)
    piccolo (small)   *vecchio* (old)   *cattivo* (bad)
    lungo (long)   *bello (beautiful)   *nuovo* (new)
    breve (short)   *brutto* (ugly)
*NB *Grande* becomes *gran* before a singular noun beginning with a consonant
other than z, *gn* etc, and *grand'* before a noun beginning with a vowel
    e.g. *un gran libro*   *una gran donna*   *un grand'uomo*
When placed before the noun, *bello* takes a form corresponding to *di + il* etc
contracted (see p.73) e.g. *un bel libro*, *un bello specchio* etc, while the singular

forms of *buono* correspond to those of the indefinite article (see p.73) e.g. *un buon libro, un buono sconto* etc

Agreement

In Italian, the adjective has to 'agree' in number and in gender with its noun. There are two types of adjectives: those ending in *-o* in the masculine singular and *-a* in the feminine singular, and those ending in *-e* in both the masculine and feminine singular. In the plural, as is the case for regular nouns, the *-o* becomes *-i*, the *-a* becomes *-e*, and the *-e* becomes *-i*.

Some examples:

Masculine singular	Feminine singular	Masculine plural	Feminine plural
il libro *rosso*	la porta *rossa*	i libri *rossi*	le porte *rosse*
il *piccolo* albero	la *piccola* casa	i *piccoli* alberi	le *piccole* case
il *giovane* ragazzo	la *giovane* ragazza	i *giovani* ragazzi	le *giovani* ragazze
l'uomo *inglese*	la donna *inglese*	gli uomini *inglesi*	le donne *inglesi*

Adjectives ending in *-co*, *-go*, *etc* follow the same pattern as the nouns (see notes iv to ix in the first section)

Possessive Adjectives

Unlike English, the possessive varies in Italian according to the gender and number of the noun it qualifies. Whether the owner is male or female, it is *il suo libro* (= *his* or *her* book), *la sua valigia* (= *his* or *her* case), *i suoi libri* (= *his* or *her* books), *le sue valigie* (= *his* or *her* cases).

There are few possessive adjectives and they can be easily summarized in, and learned from, a table:

	SINGULAR		PLURAL	
	Masculine	Feminine	Masculine	Feminine
my	il mio	la mia	i miei	le mie
your (*familiar*)	il tuo	la tua	i tuoi	le tue
(*polite*)	il Suo	la Sua	i Suoi	le Sue
his/her/its	il suo	la sua	i suoi	le sue
our	il nostro	la nostra	i nostri	le nostre
your (*plural*)	il vostro	la vostra	i vostri	le vostre
(*polite*)	il loro	la loro	i loro	le loro
their	il loro	la loro	i loro	le loro

Notes

1) The '*il vostro*' form is now widely accepted as the plural form for both the '*il tuo*' and '*il Suo*' forms.

2) The definite article is omitted when any possessive (*except* **loro**) precedes a word in the singular indicating family relationship

e.g. *mio padre* my father   **but**   *il loro padre* their father
       nostra madre our mother   *la loro madre* their mother

Demonstrative Adjectives

The word for 'this' — *questo* — follows the same pattern as adjectives ending in *-o*, thus:

questo libro	this book	*questi* libri	these books
questa tazza	this cup	*queste* tazze	these cups

In addition, before a singular word beginning with a vowel, *questo* and *questa* become *quest'*:

quest'albergo	this hotel	*quest'arancia*	this orange

The word for 'that' — *quello* — follows the same pattern as the definite article (p.73):

quel libro	that book	*quei* libri	those books
quello sportello	that door	*quegli* sportelli	those doors
quell'anello	that ring	*quegli* anelli	those rings
quella casa	that house	*quelle* case	those houses
quell'entrata	that entrance	*quelle* entrate	those entrances

PRONOUNS

Personal Pronouns

Subject	Direct Object	Indirect Object	In stressed position	Reflexive
SINGULAR				
1st person				
io (I)	mi (me)	mi; me* (to me)	me (me)	mi
2nd person				
tu (you: familiar)	ti (you)	ti; te* (to you)	te (you)	ti
3rd person (m)				
lui, egli (he)	lo, l' (him/it)	gli; glie* (to him/it)	lui (him)	si
esso (it)			esso (it)	

Subject	Direct Object	Indirect Object	In stressed position	Re- flexive
3rd person (*f*)				
lei, ella (she)	*la, l'* (her/it)	*le; glie** (to her/it)	*lei* (her)	*si*
essa (it)			*essa* (it)	
3rd person (*m/f*)				
lei (you: polite)	*la* (you)	*le; glie** (to you)	*lei* (you)	*si*
PLURAL				
1st person				
noi (we)	*ci* (us)	*ci; ce** (to us)	*noi* (us)	*ci*
2nd person				
voi (you)	*vi* (you)	*vi; ve** (to you)	*voi* (you)	*vi*
3rd person (*m*)				
loro (they)	*li* (them)	*loro* (to them)	*loro* (them)	*si*
essi (they: people/ things)			*essi* (them)	
3rd person (*f*)				
loro (they)	*le* (them)	*loro* (to them)	*loro* (them)	*si*
esse (they: people/ things)			*esse* (them)	
3rd person (*m/f*)				
loro (you: polite)	*li* (*m*) (you) *le* (*f*)	*loro* (to you)	*loro* (you)	*si*

*See note 2 under heading 'Order of Pronouns'.

Notes
1) The polite forms of the word 'you' are *lei* (singular) and *loro* (plural),
which take the third person of the verb. You should use the familiar form of
tu only with someone you know very well, with young children, or when
invited to do so. The *voi* form is now widely accepted as the plural form for
both *tu* and *lei*.
2) The form *l'* (2nd column) is used when the following word begins with a
vowel or an 'h'.
3) The forms shown in the 4th column ('in stressed position') are used
following prepositions e.g. *per me* for me, *con lei* with her
4) In Italian, the subject pronouns are often omitted before verbs, since the
verb ending generally distinguishes the person (see p.77). They are included,
however, when required for emphasis or clarity.
5) Reflexive pronouns are used with reflexive verbs (i.e. those ending in -*si*),
having the value of 'oneself', e.g.:
lavarsi
mi lavo   I wash myself
ti lavi   you wash yourself (*familiar*)
si lava   he/she washes himself/herself; you wash yourself (*polite*)
ci laviamo   we wash ourselves
vi lavate   you wash yourselves
si lavano   they wash themselves; you wash yourselves (*polite*)
Occasionally the value of 'oneself' is not reflected in the English, but if the
Italian verb is reflexive, you must use the appropriate form of the pronoun,
e.g.:

sedersi	to sit down	*mi siedo**	I sit down
muoversi	to move	*si muove**	it moves

*For appropriate forms of the verb, see the section on verb conjugations
Order of Pronouns
1) Direct and indirect object pronouns usually *precede* the verb:
lo vedo   I see him
gli legge una storia   she is reading him a story
Exception: *loro* which always *follows* the verb:
scriverò *loro*   I shall write to them/you
However, used with an infinitive, the pronoun follows and is attached to the
infinitive minus its final '*e*' (with the exception of *loro* which remains
unattached).
Thus: *voglio sentirlo*   I want to hear it
        non vuole parlargli   she doesn't want to speak to him
but: *voglio dare loro il libro*   I want to give them/you the book
Similarly, the pronoun follows and is attached to the present participle (for
formation see p.76) e.g. *vedendolo* on seeing him
The object pronoun also follows the verb and is written as one word with it, in
commands of the type 'sell it', 'bring me . . .' given to people *other* than those
addressed as *lei* or *loro* (i.e. polite forms), in which case the pronoun *precedes*
the verb.
Thus: *vendilo* (*tu*), *vendetelo* (*voi*)
but: *lo venda* (*lei*), *lo vendano* (*loro*)   sell it

portami (tu), portatemi (voi)

mi porti (lei), mi portino (loro)   bring me ...

2) When both a direct and indirect object pronoun are used with the same verb, the indirect object pronouns **mi**, **ti**, **ci** and **vi** become **me**, **te**, **ce** and **ve** when followed by **lo**, **la**, **li** or **le**. Similarly the indirect object pronouns **gli** and **le** become **glie**, and combine with **lo**, **la**, **li** and **le** to become one single word: **glielo**, **gliela**, **glieli** and **gliele** (see table p. 74/75). With the exception of **loro**, which always *follows* the verb, the indirect object pronoun always *precedes* the direct.

Thus: **mi** *parla*   he talks to me
    me li dà   he gives them to me
    gli *scrivo*   I write to him
    glielo *mando*   I send it to him/her
    glieli *dia* (**lei**)
    date**glieli** (**voi**)   give them to him/her
    mostrando**melo**   on showing it to me
    *voglio vender***glielo**   I want to sell it to him/her
    but
    lo *manderò* **loro**   I shall send it to them/you
    lo *dia* **loro**   give it to them

Demonstrative Pronouns

To translate 'this (one)', 'these'/'that (one)', 'those', Italian uses *'questo'*/*'quello'* respectively, varying the endings to indicate the gender and number of the object(s) referred to, thus:

    questo/*quest***a** this (one)   *quello*/*quell***a** that (one)
    questi/*queste* these   *quelli*/*quelle* those

'*Quello*' etc has the additional meaning of 'the one' etc as in:

    the one in the window   *quello*/*quella in vetrina*
    the ones on the shelf   *quelli*/*quelle sullo scaffale*

Possessive Pronouns

Used to translate 'mine', 'his' etc, they also depend on the number and gender of the noun described (and not on the sex of the 'possessor' — cf the possessive adjectives, above):

	with a masculine noun	with a feminine noun	with a masculine plural noun	with a feminine plural noun
mine	il mio	la mia	i miei	le mie
yours (*familiar*)	il tuo	la tua	i tuoi	le tue
(*polite*)	il Suo	la Sua	i Suoi	le Sue
his/hers/its	il suo	la sua	i suoi	le sue
ours	il nostro	la nostra	i nostri	le nostre
yours (*plural*)	il vostro	la vostra	i vostri	le vostre
(*polite*)	il loro	la loro	i loro	le loro
theirs	il loro	la loro	i loro	le loro

VERBS

Verb conjugations

The verb tables below will give you the ending patterns for the 'regular' verbs, and in a separate list you will find patterns to help you with all the irregular verbs marked with an asterisk in the dictionary section of this book. We only. set out the forms of four tenses in this short grammar section, as the present, the imperfect, the future and the perfect will cater to most of your needs.

Tenses

1) As in English, an action in the present is expressed by the **present** tense. Hence: *parto* = I leave OR I am leaving

When the English has the sense of 'being in the process of doing' (rendered by the 'progressive' -*ing* form e.g. I am read*ing*), the present tense of '*stare*' (see present list, p.79) is used in conjunction with the present participle. To form the present participle, the infinitive endings -**are**, -**ere** and -**ire** are dropped and replaced by -**ando** for -**are** verbs and -**endo** for -**ere** and -**ire** verbs. Thus:

    *stiamo mangi***ando**   we're eat*ing*
    *sto legg***endo**   I'm read*ing*
    *il treno sta part***endo**   the train is leav*ing*

2) Past actions are shown by the **perfect** or **imperfect** tense in Italian. The latter is a simple tense, whereby endings are added to the verb stem (see table). The perfect is formed by the use of **avere** ('to have') plus the past participle (see table)

    e.g. *parl***avo**   I was speaking   **ho** *parl***ato**   I spoke

Some verbs expressing the concepts of 'motion' or 'becoming' take **essere** instead of **avere** in the perfect tense. The main ones are: *andare, arrivare, cadere, divenire, diventare, entrare, essere, morire, nascere, partire, restare, rimanere, salire, scendere, stare, tornare, uscire, venire.*

Similarly, all reflexive verbs in Italian are conjugated with **essere**

    e.g. *lavarsi* ('to wash'): *mi sono lavato* ('I washed')

For actions in the past which happened at a specific point in time, Italian always uses the **perfect** tense, which corresponds to our structure 'to have done'. This applies even when in English we would use a simple past tense:

> I **did** it yesterday   l'**ho fatto** ieri (literally: I *have* done it . . .)
> we **saw** him   l'**abbiamo visto** (literally: we *have* seen him)

The Italian perfect is also used where this tense is used in English:

> I **have seen** him   l'**ho visto**   we **have done** it   l'**abbiamo fatto**

The **imperfect** tense in Italian is used only for an action or state in the past without definite limits in time, or for habitual actions in the past

> e.g.
>
> **era** malata   she *was* ill
>
> **abitavamo** a Londra durante la guerra   we *lived* in London during the war
>
> **andavo** in ufficio alle nove   I *went* (= used to go) to the office at nine o'clock

3) Largely used as its English counterpart, the **future** tense endings (see table) are added to the stem (for exceptions, see the table of irregular verbs). One particular point to note is that after **quando** ('when') and **se** ('if'), the future is used in Italian, where we use the present tense to describe a future action:

> when he goes to Rome   quando **andrà** a Roma
>
> if he comes   se **verrà**

Regular verb conjugations

The table below shows you how to conjugate regular verbs ending in -**are**, -**ere** and -**ire*** in the infinitive (the form given in the dictionary), in all the tenses you will need for basic communication. For all other regular verbs with these endings (i.e. those NOT marked with an asterisk in the dictionary) remove the infinitive ending and add the endings shown. Since the subject pronouns are often omitted in Italian unless required for clarity or emphasis, they have been shown in brackets.

*You will note that 2 examples of the -**ire** verbs have been given, since this conjugation is divided into 2 distinct groups: those which, like **dormire**, form their present tense by removing the infinitive ending and adding the endings -**o**, -**i**, -**e**, -**iamo**, -**ite**, -**ono**; and those which, like **finire**, form their present tense by removing the infinitive ending and adding the endings -**isco**, -**isci**, -**isce**, -**iamo**, -**ite**, -**iscono**

INFINITIVE:	parl*are*	vend*ere*	dorm*ire*	fin*ire*

PRESENT

(io)	parl*o*	vend*o*	dorm*o*	fin*isco*
(tu)	parl*i*	vend*i*	dorm*i*	fin*isci*
(lui/lei)	parl*a*	vend*e*	dorm*e*	fin*isce*
(noi)	parl*iamo*	vend*iamo*	dorm*iamo*	fin*iamo*
(voi)	parl*ate*	vend*ete*	dorm*ite*	fin*ite*
(loro)	parl*ono*	vend*ono*	dorm*ono*	fin*iscono*

FUTURE

(io)	parl*erò*	vend*erò*	dorm*irò*	fin*irò*
(tu)	parl*erai*	vend*erai*	dorm*irai*	fin*irai*
(lui/lei)	parl*erà*	vend*erà*	dorm*irà*	fin*irà*
(noi)	parl*eremo*	vend*eremo*	dorm*iremo*	fin*iremo*
(voi)	parl*erete*	vend*erete*	dorm*irete*	fin*irete*
(loro)	parl*eranno*	vend*eranno*	dorm*iranno*	fin*iranno*

IMPERFECT

(io)	parl*avo*	vend*evo*	dorm*ivo*	fin*ivo*
(tu)	parl*avi*	vend*evi*	dorm*ivi*	fin*ivi*
(lui/lei)	parl*ava*	vend*eva*	dorm*iva*	fin*iva*
(noi)	parl*avamo*	vend*evamo*	dorm*ivamo*	fin*ivamo*
(voi)	parl*avate*	vend*evate*	dorm*ivate*	fin*ivate*
(loro)	parl*avano*	vend*evano*	dorm*ivano*	fin*ivano*

PERFECT*

(io)	ho parl*ato*	ho vend*uto*	ho dorm*ito*	ho fin*ito*
(tu)	hai parl*ato*	hai vend*uto*	hai dorm*ito*	hai fin*ito*
(lui/lei)	ha parl*ato*	ha vend*uto*	ha dorm*ito*	ha fin*ito*
(noi)	abbiamo parl*ato*	abbiamo vend*uto*	abbiamo dorm*ito*	abbiamo fin*ito*
(voi)	avete parl*ato*	avete vend*uto*	avete dorm*ito*	avete fin*ito*
(loro)	hanno parl*ato*	hanno vend*uto*	hanno dorm*ito*	hanno fin*ito*

*If a verb takes **essere** in the perfect instead of **avere** as shown here, the relevant part of **essere** (see p.78) replaces that of **avere**, and the past participle agrees in number and gender with its subject:

> sono *andato*/*andata*   siamo *partiti*/*partite*

Irregular Verb Forms

To identify the pattern of a verb marked with an asterisk in the dictionary and not shown here, refer to the verb with the identical ending. This may take the form of the whole word (e.g. for **promettere** see **mettere**, for **supporre** see *porre*) or only part of the word (e.g. for *ardere* see *prendere*, for *scegliere* see *cogliere*).

The irregular forms shown below are: 1) the present tense in full 2) the first person of the future tense 3) the first person of the imperfect tense 4) the past participle used with '*avere*' or '*essere*' to give the perfect tense 5) the present participle where irregular. For the future and imperfect tenses use the form shown but alternate the endings as in the table of regular verbs with the first person ending given here.

aggiungere	1) aggiungo, aggiungi, aggiunge, aggiungiamo, aggiungete, aggiungono 2) aggiungerò 3) aggiungevo 4) aggiunto
andare	1) vado, vai, va, andiamo, andate, vanno 2) andrò 3) andavo 4) andato
apparire	1) appaio, appari/apparisci, appare/apparisce, appariamo, apparite, appaiono/appariscono 2) apparirò 3) apparivo 4) apparso
aprire	1) apro, apri, apre, apriamo, aprite, aprono 2) aprirò 3) aprivo 4) aperto
assistere	1) assisto, assisti, assiste, assistiamo, assistete, assistono 2) assisterò 3) assistevo 4) assistito
assumere	1) assumo, assumi, assume, assumiamo, assumete, assumono 2) assumerò 3) assumevo 4) assunto
avere	1) ho, hai, ha, abbiamo, avete, hanno 2) avrò 3) avevo 4) avuto
bere	1) bevo, bevi, beve, beviamo, bevete, bevono 2) berrò 3) bevevo 4) bevuto 5) bevendo
cadere	1) cado, cadi, cade, cadiamo, cadete, cadono 2) cadrò 3) cadevo 4) caduto
chiedere	1) chiedo, chiedi, chiede, chiediamo, chiedete, chiedono 2) chiederò 3) chiedevo 4) chiesto
cogliere	1) colgo, cogli, coglie, cogliamo, cogliete, colgono 2) coglierò 3) coglievo 4) colto
conoscere	1) conosco, conosci, conosce, conosciamo, conoscete, conoscono 2) conoscerò 3) conoscevo 4) conosciuto
correre	1) corro, corri, corre, corriamo, correte, corrono 2) correrò 3) correvo 4) corso
costruire	1) costruisco, costruisci, costruisce, costruiamo, costruite, costruiscono 2) costruirò 3) costruivo 4) costruito/costrutto
crescere	1) cresco, cresci, cresce, cresciamo, crescete, crescono 2) crescerò 3) crescevo 4) cresciuto
cuocere	1) cuocio, cuoci, cuoce, cociamo, cocete, cuociono 2) cuocerò 3) cuocevo 4) cotto
dare	1) do, dai, dà, diamo, date, danno 2) darò 3) davo 4) dato
dipingere	1) dipingo, dipingi, dipinge, dipingiamo, dipingete, dipingono 2) dipingerò 3) dipingevo 4) dipinto
dire	1) dico, dici, dice, diciamo, dite, dicono 2) dirò 3) dicevo 4) detto 5) dicendo
dirigere	1) dirigo, dirigi, dirige, dirigiamo, dirigete, dirigono 2) dirigerò 3) dirigevo 4) diretto
discutere	1) discuto, discuti, discute, discutiamo, discutete, discutono 2) discuterò 3) discutevo 4) discusso
distinguere	1) distinguo, distingui, distingue, distinguiamo, distinguete, distinguono 2) distinguerò 3) distinguevo 4) distinto
dolere	1) dolgo, duoli, duole, doliamo, dolete, dolgono 2) dorrò 3) dolevo 4) doluto
dovere	1) devo/debbo, devi, deve, dobbiamo, dovete, devono/debbono 2) dovrò 3) dovevo 4) dovuto
esigere	1) esigo, esigi, esige, esigiamo, esigete, esigono 2) esigerò 3) esigevo 4) esatto
esprimere	1) esprimo, esprimi, esprime, esprimiamo, esprimete, esprimono 2) esprimerò 3) esprimevo 4) espresso
essere	1) sono, sei, è, siamo, siete, sono 2) sarò 3) ero, eri, era, eravamo, eravate, erano 4) stato
fare	1) faccio, fai, fa, facciamo, fate, fanno 2) farò 3) facevo 4) fatto 5) facendo
fondere	1) fondo, fondi, fonde, fondiamo, fondete, fondono 2) fonderò 3) fondevo 4) fuso
immergere	1) immergo, immergi, immerge, immergiamo, immergete, immergono 2) immergerò 3) immergevo 4) immerso
leggere	1) leggo, leggi, legge, leggiamo, leggete, leggono 2) leggerò 3) leggevo 4) letto
mentire	1) mento/mentisco, menti/mentisci, mente/mentisce, mentiamo, mentite, mentono/mentiscono 2) mentirò 3) mentivo 4) mentito
mettere	1) metto, metti, mette, mettiamo, mettete, mettono 2) metterò 3) mettevo 4) messo
morire	1) muoio, muori, muore, moriamo, morite, muoiono 2) morirò/morrò 3) morivo 4) morto

muovere 1) muovo, muovi, muove, moviamo, movete, muovono
2) muoverò 3) muovevo 4) mosso

nascere 1) nasco, nasci, nasce, nasciamo, nascete, nascono 2) nascerò
3) nascevo 4) nato

nascondere 1) nascondo, nascondi, nasconde, nascondiamo, nascondete,
nascondono 2) nasconderò 3) nascondevo 4) nascosto

offrire 1) offro, offri, offre, offriamo, offrite, offrono 2) offrirò
3) offrivo 4) offerto

parere 1) paio, pari, pare, paiamo, parete, paiono 2) parrò 3) parevo
4) parso

perdere 1) perdo, perdi, perde, perdiamo, perdete, perdono 2) perderò
3) perdevo 4) perso/perduto

piacere 1) piaccio, piaci, piace, piacciamo, piacete, piacciono 2) piacerò
3) piacevo 4) piaciuto

piovere 1) piove 2) pioverà 3) pioveva 4) piovuto (used in 3rd person
singular only)

porre 1) pongo, poni, pone, poniamo, ponete, pongono 2) porrò
3) ponevo 4) posto 5) ponendo

potere 1) posso, puoi, può, possiamo, potete, possono 2) potrò
3) potevo 4) potuto

prendere 1) prendo, prendi, prende, prendiamo, prendete, prendono
2) prenderò 3) prendevo 4) preso

prudere like *vendere*, but defective: no past participle

ridurre 1) riduco, riduci, riduce, riduciamo, riducete, riducono
2) ridurrò 3) riducevo 4) ridotto 5) riducendo

riempire 1) riempio, riempi, riempie, riempiamo, riempite, riempiono
2) riempirò 3) riempivo 4) riempito 5) riempiendo

riflettere 1) rifletto, rifletti, riflette, riflettiamo, riflettete, riflettono
2) rifletterò 3) riflettevo 4) riflettuto/riflesso

rimanere 1) rimango, rimani, rimane, rimaniamo, rimanete, rimangono
2) rimarrò 3) rimanevo 4) rimasto

risolvere 1) risolvo, risolvi, risolve, risolviamo, risolvete, risolvono
2) risolverò 3) risolvevo 4) risolto

rispondere 1) rispondo, rispondi, risponde, rispondiamo, rispondete,
rispondono 2) risponderò 3) rispondevo 4) risposto

rompere 1) rompo, rompi, rompe, rompiamo, rompete, rompono
2) romperò 3) rompevo 4) rotto

salire 1) salgo, sali, sale, saliamo, salite, salgono 2) salirò 3) salivo
4) salito

sapere 1) so, sai, sa, sappiamo, sapete, sanno 2) saprò 3) sapevo
4) saputo

scrivere 1) scrivo, scrivi, scrive, scriviamo, scrivete, scrivono 2) scriverò
3) scrivevo 4) scritto

scuotere 1) scuoto, scuoti, scuote, scotiamo, scotete, scuotono 2) scoterò
3) scotevo 4) scosso 5) scotendo

sedere 1) siedo/seggo, siedi, siede, sediamo, sedete, siedono/seggono
2) sederò 3) sedevo 4) seduto

spargere 1) spargo, spargi, sparge, spargiamo, spargete, spargono
2) spargerò 3) spargevo 4) sparso

sparire 1) sparisco, sparisci, sparisce, spariamo, sparite, spariscono
2) sparirò 3) sparivo 4) sparito

spegnere 1) spengo, spegni, spegne, spegniamo, spegnete, spengono
2) spegnerò 3) spegnevo 4) spento

stare 1) sto, stai, sta, stiamo, state, stanno 2) starò 3) stavo 4) stato

stringere 1) stringo, stringi, stringe, stringiamo, stringete, stringono
2) stringerò 3) stringevo 4) stretto

succedere 1) succedo, succedi, succede, succediamo, succedete, succedono
2) succederò 3) succedevo 4) successo

tenere 1) tengo, tieni, tiene, teniamo, tenete, tengono 2) terrò 3) tenevo
4) tenuto

trarre 1) traggo, trai, trae, traiamo, traete, traggono 2) trarrò 3) travo
4) tratto 5) traendo

uscire 1) esco, esci, esce, usciamo, uscite, escono 2) uscirò 3) uscivo
4) uscito

valere 1) valgo, vali, vale, valiamo, valete, valgono 2) varrò 3) valevo
4) valso

vedere 1) vedo/veggo, vedi, vede, vediamo, vedete, vedono/veggono
2) vedrò 3) vedevo 4) visto/veduto

venire 1) vengo, vieni, viene, veniamo, venite, vengono 2) verrò
3) venivo 4) venuto

vincere 1) vinco, vinci, vince, vinciamo, vincete, vincono 2) vincerò
3) vincevo 4) vinto

vivere 1) vivo, vivi, vive, viviamo, vivete, vivono 2) vivrò 3) vivevo
4) vissuto

volere 1) voglio, vuoi, vuole, vogliamo, volete, vogliono 2) vorrò
3) volevo 4) voluto

ITALIAN–ENGLISH DICTIONARY

a *a prep* at; in; to; **a scuola** *a skwo·la* at/to school; **a Londra** *a lohn·dra* at/in/to London; **alla stazione** *al·la sta·tsyoh·ne* at/to the station; **alla televisione** *al·la te·le·vee·zee·oh·ne* on television; **alla parete** *al·la pa·ray·te* on the wall; **a sinistra/destra** *a see·nee·stra/de·stra* on/to the left/right; **alle 4** *al·le 4* at 4 o'clock; **a 30 chilometri** *a 30 kee·lo·me·tree* 30 kilometers away; **da lunedì a venerdì** *da loo·ne·dee a ve·ner·dee* Monday through Friday; **due volte al giorno** *doo·ay vol·tay al jor·noh* twice a day; **uno a uno** *oo·no a oo·no* one by one

abbagliare *ab·bal·yah·ray vt* dazzle

abbaiare *ab·ba·yah·ray vi* bark

abbandonare *ab·ban·do·nah·ray vt* abandon

abbassare *ab·bas·sah·ray vt* lower; turn down; dim (*headlights*)

abbastanza *ab·ba·stan·tsa adv* enough; quite; **ce ne sono abbastanza** *che nay soh·no ab·ba·stan·tsa* there are quite a few; **abbastanza tempo/libri** *ab·ba·stan·tsa tem·poh/lee·bree* enough time/books; **abbastanza grande** *ab·ba·stan·tsa gran·de* big enough

abbattere *ab·bat·te·re vt* knock down

abbazia *ab·ba·tsee·a f* abbey

abbigliamento *ab·beel·ya·mayn·toh m* clothes; **l'abbigliamento per uomo** *ab·beel·ya·mayn·toh payr wo·moh* menswear

abbonamento *ab·bo·na·mayn·toh m* subscription (*to periodical*); season ticket

abbonarsi a *ab·bo·nar·see a vr* subscribe to (*periodical*)

abbonato(a) *ab·bo·nah·to(a) m/f* subscriber

abbozzare *ab·bots·tsah·ray vt* sketch

abbozzo *ab·bots·tsoh m* sketch; draft (*rough outline*)

abbracciare *ab·brach·chah·ray vt* embrace; cuddle; hug

abbreviazione *ab·bre·vya·tsyoh·ne f* abbreviation

abbronzarsi *ab·bron·dzar·see vr* tan

abbronzato(a) *ab·bron·dzah·to(a) adj* sun-tanned

abbronzatura *ab·bron·dza·too·ra f* suntan

abete *a·bay·te m* fir (tree)

abilità *a·bee·lee·ta f —* ability; cleverness; skill

abitante *a·bee·tan·te m/f* inhabitant

abitare *a·bee·tah·ray vi* live (*reside*) □ *vt* live in

abito *ah·bee·toh m* dress; suit (*man's*); **l'abito da sposa** *ah·bee·toh da spo·za* wedding dress; **l'abito da sera** *ah·bee·toh da say·ra* evening dress (*woman's*)

abituale *a·bee·too·ah·le adj* usual

abituarsi a *a·bee·twar·see a vr* get used to

abitudine *a·bee·too·dee·ne f* habit

abolire *a·bo·lee·re vt* abolish

aborto *a·bor·toh m* miscarriage; abortion

accademia *ak·ka·de·mya f* academy

accadere *ak·ka·day·re vi* happen

accamparsi *ak·kam·pahr·see vr* camp

accanto *ak·kan·to adv* nearby; **accanto a** *ak·kan·to a* beside

accappatoio *ak·kap·pa·toh·yoh m* bathrobe

accarezzare *ak·ka·rets·tsah·ray vt* stroke

accasciarsi *ak·ka·shar·see vr* collapse (*person*)

accelerare *ach·che·le·rah·ray vt/i* accelerate; speed up

acceleratore *ach·che·le·ra·toh·re m* accelerator

accendere* *ach·chen·de·re vt* turn on; light (*fire, cigarette*); switch on; **accendere* un fiammifero** *ach·chen·de·re oon fyam·mee·fe·roh* to strike a match; **mi fa accendere?** *mee fa ach·chen·de·re* have you got a light?

accendino *ach·chen·dee·noh m* cigarette lighter

accenditore *ach·chen·dee·toh·re m* pilot light (*gas*)

accensione *ach·chen·syoh·ne f* ignition (*car*)

accento *ach·chen·toh m* accent; stress; **l'accento acuto** *ach·chen·toh a·koo·to* acute (accent); **l'accento grave** *ach·chen·toh grah·vay* grave (accent)

accentuare *ach·chen·too·ah·ray vt* emphasize (*syllable etc*)

acceso(a) *ach·chay·so(a) adj* on (*light, radio*)

accessibile *ach·ches·see·bee·le adj* accessible

accesso *ach·ches·soh m* access; fit

accessori *ach·ches·so·ree mpl* accessories

accettare *ach·chet·tah·ray vt* accept

accettazione *ach·chet·ta·tsyoh·ne f* acceptance

acchiappare *ak·kyap·pah·ray vt* catch

acciaio *ach·cha·yoh m* steel

accidentale *ach·chee·den·tah·le adj* accidental

acciuga *ach·choo·ga f* anchovy

accoglienza *ak·kol·yen·tsa f* welcome

accogliere* *ak·kol·ye·ray vt* receive (*guest*); welcome

accomodarsi *ak·ko·mo·dar·see vr* make oneself comfortable; **si accomodi** *see ak·ko·mo·dee* take a seat

accompagnare *ak·kom·pan·yah·ray vt* escort; accompany; **accompagnare qualcuno a casa** *ak·kom·pan·yah·ray kwal·koo·no a kah·sa* to see someone home; **accompagnare qualcuno alla porta** *ak·kom·pan·yah·ray kwal·koo·no al·la por·ta* to show someone out

accompagnatore *ak·kom·pan·ya·toh·re m* escort

acconciatura *ak·kon·cha·too·ra f* hairstyle

acconto *ak·kohn·toh m* down payment

accorciare *ak·kor·chah·ray vt* shorten

accordare *ak·kor·dah·ray vt* tune (*instrument*); grant (*wish*)

accordo *ak·kor·doh m* agreement; **l'accordo globale** *ak·kor·doh glo·bah·le* package deal; **essere* d'accordo con qualcuno** *es·se·re dak·kor·doh kon kwal·koo·no* to agree with somebody; **mettersi d'accordo su** *mayt·ter·see dak·kor·doh soo* to agree on

accreditare *ak·kre·dee·tah·ray vt* credit

accrescimento *ak·kre·shee·mayn·toh m* increase (*in size*)

accumularsi *ak·koo·moo·lar·see vr* accumulate

accusa *ak·koo·za f* charge (*accusation*)

accusare *ak·koo·zah·ray vt* accuse

acerbo(a) *a·cher·bo(a) adj* unripe; sour (*sharp*)

aceto *a·chay·toh m* vinegar

acido *ah·chee·doh m* acid □ *adj* acido(a) *ah·chee·do(a)* sour (*milk*)

acne *ak·ne f* acne

acqua *ak·kwa f* water; l'acqua corrente *ak·kwa kor·ren·te* running water; l'acqua potabile *ak·kwa po·tah·bee·le* drinking water; l'acqua distillata *ak·kwa dee·steel·lah·ta* distilled water; l'acqua minerale *ak·kwa mee·ne·rah·lay* mineral water; l'acqua tonica *ak·kwa to·nee·ka* tonic water; l'acqua di Colonia *ak·kwa dee ko·lon·ya* cologne; fare* acqua *fah·ray ak·kwa* to leak (*boat*)

acquaio *ak·kwa·yoh m* sink (*basin*)

acquario *ak·kwah·ryoh m* aquarium

acquazzone *ak·kwats·tsoh·ne m* shower (*rain*)

acquirente *ak·kwee·ren·te m/f* buyer (*customer*)

acquisizione *ak·kwee·zee·tsyoh·ne f* acquisition

acquistare *ak·kwee·stah·ray vt* acquire

acquisti *ak·kwee·stee mpl* shopping

acquisto *ak·kwee·stoh m* purchase

acrilico(a) *a·kree·lee·ko(a) adj* acrylic

acuto(a) *a·koo·to(a) adj* sharp; acute

adattare *a·dat·tah·ray vt* adapt

adatto(a) *a·dat·to(a) adj* suitable

addebitare *ad·day·bee·tah·ray vt* debit; lo addebiti al mio conto *loh ad·de·bee·tee al mee·oh kohn·toh* charge it to my account

addebito *ad·day·bee·toh m* debit

addestrare *ad·de·strah·ray vt* train

addizione *ad·dee·tsyoh·ne f* addition

addobbi *ad·dob·bee mpl* decorations

addome *ad·do·me m* abdomen

addormentato(a) *ad·dor·men·tah·to(a) adj* asleep; essere* profondamente addormentato(a) *es·se·re pro·fohn·da·mayn·te ad·dor·men·tah·to(a)* to be fast asleep

adolescente *a·do·le·shen·te m/f* teenager

adottare *a·dot·tah·ray vt* adopt

Adriatico *a·dree·a·tee·koh m* Adriatic (Sea)

adulto *a·dool·toh m* adult □ *adj* adulto(a) *a·dool·to(a)* adult; grown-up

aereo *a·e·re·oh m* plane; aircraft; in aereo *een a·e·re·oh* by plane

aereo(a) *a·e·re·o(a) adj* air; per via aerea *payr vee·a a·e·re·a* by air

aerobus *a·e·ro·boos m* air bus

aerodinamico(a) *a·e·ro·dee·na·mee·ko(a) adj* streamlined (*car*)

aeroplano *a·e·ro·plah·noh m* airplane

aeroporto *a·e·ro·por·toh m* airport

affamato(a) *af·fa·mah·to(a) adj* starving

affare *af·fah·re m* affair (*matter*); deal; per affari *payr af·fah·ree* on business; fare* affari con qualcuno *fah·ray af·fah·ree kohn kwal·koo·no* to do business with someone

affari *af·fah·ree mpl* business (*dealings, work*); affairs

affascinante *af·fa·shee·nan·te adj* fascinating; glamorous

affatto *af·fat·to adv* at all

afferrare *af·fer·rah·ray vt* seize; grab

affettare *af·fayt·tah·ray vt* slice

affetto *af·fet·toh m* affection

affettuosamente *af·fet·too·oh·sa·mayn·te adv* love from (*on letter*)

affettuoso(a) *af·fet·twoh·so(a) adj* affectionate

affidabilità *af·fee·da·bee·lee·ta f* reliability (*of car*)

affievolirsi *af·fye·vo·leer·see vr* grow weak; fade

affiggere* *af·feej·je·re vt* put up (*notice*)

affilato(a) *af·fee·lah·to(a) adj* sharp (*knife*)

affiliato(a) *af·fee·lyah·to(a) adj* subsidiary

affittare *af·feet·tah·ray vt* rent (*house etc*); let (*rent out*)

affittasi *af·feet·ta·see* to let (*house etc*)

affitto *af·feet·toh m* lease; rent

affogato(a) *af·fo·gah·to(a) adj* drowned; poached

affollato(a) *af·fol·lah·toh(a) adj* crowded

affondare *af·fohn·dah·ray vt/i* sink (*in water*)

affrancare *af·fran·kah·ray vt* stamp (*letter*)

affrettarsi *af·fret·tar·see vr* hurry

affrontare *af·fron·tah·ray vt* tackle (*problem*)

affumicato(a) *af·foo·mee·kah·to(a) adj* smoked (*salmon etc*)

afoso(a) *a·foh·soh(a) adj* close (*stuffy*)

Africa *a·free·ka f* Africa

africano(a) *a·free·kah·no(a) adj* African

agenda *a·jen·da f* diary

agente *a·jen·te m* agent; broker; l'agente marittimo *a·jen·te ma·reet·tee·mo* shipping agent; l'agente di viaggi *a·jen·te dee vee·aj·jee* travel agent; l'agente immobiliare *a·jen·te eem·mo·beel·yah·ray* realtor; l'agente di polizia *a·jen·te dee po·lee·tsee·a* officer (*police*); l'agente di cambio *a·jen·te dee kam·byoh* stockbroker

agenzia *a·jen·tsee·a f* agency (*office*); l'agenzia pubblicitaria *a·jen·tsee·a poob·blee·chee·tah·rya* advertising agency; l'agenzia di viaggi *a·jen·tsee·a dee vee·aj·jee* travel agency

aggiornare *aj·johr·nah·ray vt* update

aggiungere* *aj·joon·je·re vt* add

aggiustare *aj·joo·stah·ray vt* adjust

aggressivo(a) *ag·gres·see·vo(a) adj* aggressive

aggrovigliare *ag·gro·veel·yah·ray vt* tangle

agile *ah·jee·le adj* agile

agire *a·jee·re vi* act; work

agitare *a·jee·tah·ray vt* shake; agitare la mano *a·jee·tah·ray la mah·noh* to wave

agitato(a) *a·jee·tah·to(a) adj* rough (*sea*); restless; upset

agli = a + gli

aglio *al·yoh m* garlic

agnello *an·yel·loh m* lamb

ago *ah·goh m* needle

agosto *a·goh·sto m* August

agricolo(a) *a·gree·ko·lo(a) adj* agricultural

agricoltore *a·gree·kol·toh·re m* farmer

agricoltura *a·gree·kol·too·ra f* agriculture

ai = a + i

aia *a·ya f* farmyard

aiuola *a·yoo·wo·la f* flowerbed

aiutare *a·yoo·tah·ray vt* help; mi può

aiutare? *mee pwo a·yoo·tah·ray* can you help me?

aiuto *a·yoo·toh* m help; aiuto! *a·yoo·toh* help!

ala *ah·la* f ali wing

alba *al·ba* f dawn

albergo *al·ber·goh* m hotel

albero *al·be·roh* m tree; mast (*ship's*); l'albero di Natale *al·be·roh dee na·tah·lay* Christmas tree; l'albero a camme *al·be·roh a kam* camshaft

albicocca *al·bee·kok·ka* f apricot

album *al·boom* m album (*for photos etc*)

alcol *al·kol* m alcohol

alcolici *al·ko·lee·chee* mpl liquor

alcolico *al·ko·lee·koh* m alcoholic drink □ *adj* alcolico(a) *al·ko·lee·ko(a)* alcoholic (*drink*)

alcolizzato(a) *al·ko·leedz·dzah·to(a)* m/f alcoholic

alcool *al·kol* m alcohol; l'alcool denaturato *al·kol day·na·too·rah·toh* methylated spirits

alcova *al·ko·va* f alcove

alcuni(e) *al·koo·nee(·ne)* adj pron some

alcuno(a) *al·koo·no(a)* adj any

alfabeto *al·fa·be·toh* m alphabet

Algeri *al·je·ree* f Algiers

Algeria *al·je·ree·a* f Algeria

algerino(a) *al·je·ree·no(a)* adj Algerian

alghe *al·ge* fpl seaweed

aliante *a·lee·an·tay* m glider

allacciare *al·lach·chah·ray* vt fasten

Allah *al·la* m Allah

allarmare *al·lar·mah·ray* vt alarm

allarmarsi *al·lar·mar·see* vr panic

allarme *al·lar·me* m alarm (*signal, apparatus*); l'allarme antincendio *al·lar·me an·teen·chen·dyoh* fire alarm

alleanza *al·le·an·tsa* f alliance

allegato *al·le·gah·toh* m enclosure (*in letter*)

allegro(a) *al·lay·groh(a)* adj cheerful

allenamento *al·le·na·mayn·toh* m training (*for sports*)

allenarsi *al·le·nar·see* vr train (*athlete*)

allenatore *al·le·na·toh·ray* m coach (*instructor*)

allergia *al·ler·jee·a* f allergy

allergico(a) a *al·ler·jee·ko(a)* adj allergic to

allevare *al·le·vah·ray* vt raise (*family*); rear (*children, cattle*)

alleviare *al·le·vyah·ray* vt ease (*pain*)

alloggiare *al·loj·jah·ray* vt put up (*accommodate*) □ *vi* live (*reside*)

alloggio *al·loj·joh* m lodgings; accommodations

allora *al·loh·ra* adv then; d'allora in poi *dal·loh·ra een poy* from then on; da allora è sempre lì *da al·loh·ra e sempre lee* he's been there ever since

alludere* a *al·loo·de·ray* a vi refer to (*allude to*)

alluminio *al·loo·mee·nyoh* m aluminum

allungare *al·loon·gah·ray* vt lengthen

almeno *al·may·no* adv at least

Alpi *al·pee* fpl Alps

alpinismo *al·pee·nee·zmoh* m mountaineering; fare* dell'alpinismo *fah·ray del·lal·pe·nee·zmoh* to go mountaineering

alpino(a) *al·pee·no(a)* adj alpine

altalena *al·ta·lay·na* f swing; seesaw

altare *al·tah·re* m altar

alterare *al·te·rah·ray* vt alter

alternatore *al·ter·na·toh·re* m alternator (*in car*)

altezza *al·tayts·tsa* f height

altitudine *al·tee·too·dee·ne* f altitude

alto *al·to* adv high; aloud; in alto *een al·to* high; up, upward(s)

alto(a) *al·to(a)* adj high; tall; alto(a) 6 metri *al·to(a) 6 me·tree* 6 meters high; quanto è alto lei? *kwan·to e al·to ley* how tall are you?

altoparlante *al·to·par·lan·te* m loudspeaker

altrimenti *al·tree·mayn·tee* adv otherwise

altro(a) *al·tro(a)* adj other □ *pron* l'altro(a) *lal·tro(a)* the other; l'altro sesso *lal·tro ses·soh* the opposite sex; l'altro giorno *lal·tro johr·noh* the other day

altrove *al·troh·ve* adv somewhere else

alunno(a) *a·loon·no(a)* m/f pupil

alzare *al·tsah·ray* vt raise; turn up (*heat*)

alzarsi *al·tsahr·see* vr get up; stand up; rise

amaca *a·mah·ka* f hammock

amante *a·man·tay* m/f lover; mistress

amare *a·mah·ray* vt love

amaro(a) *a·mah·ro(a)* adj bitter

ambasciata *am·ba·shah·ta* f embassy

ambasciatore *am·ba·sha·toh·re* m ambassador

ambedue *am·be·doo·e* adj, pron both

ambiente *am·byen·te* m environment

ambizione *am·bee·tsyoh·ne* f ambition

ambizioso(a) *am·bee·tsyoh·so(a)* adj ambitious

ambulanza *am·boo·lan·tsa* f ambulance

ambulatorio *am·boo·la·to·ree·oh* m consulting room

America *a·me·ree·ka* f America; l'America del Sud *la·me·ree·ka del sood* South America; l'America del Nord *a·me·ree·ka del nord* North America

America Latina *a·me·ree·ka la·tee·na* f Latin America

americano(a) *a·me·ree·kah·no(a)* adj American

ametista *a·me·tee·sta* f amethyst

amianto *a·myan·toh* m asbestos

amichevole *a·mee·kay·vo·le* adj friendly

amico(a) *a·mee·ko(a)* m/f friend

amido *ah·mee·doh* m starch

ammaccatura *am·mak·ka·too·ra* f dent; bruise

ammaestrare *am·ma·e·strah·ray* vt train (*animal*)

ammettere* *am·met·te·ray* vt admit

amministrazione *am·mee·nee·stra·tsyoh·nay* f administration; l'amministrazione statale *am·mee·nee·stra·tsyoh·nay sta·tah·lay* civil service

ammirare *am·mee·rah·ray* vt admire

ammobiliare *am·mo·bee·lyah·ray* vt furnish (*room etc*)

ammontare a *am·mohn·tah·ray* a vi amount to

ammortizzare *am·mor·teedz·dzah·ray* vt absorb (*shock*)

ammortizzatore *am·mor·teedz·dza·toh·re* m shock absorber

ammucchiare *am·mook·kyah·ray* vt pile up

amo *ah·moh* m hook (*fishing*)

amore *a·moh·re* m love

ampère *am·pehr* m amp

ampio(a) *am·pyo(a)* adj loose (*clothing*)

amplificatore *am·plee·fee·ka·toh·re* m amplifier

analcolico(a) *a·nal·ko·lee·koh(a)* adj nonalcoholic; soft (*drink*)

analisi *a·nah·lee·see* f — analysis

analista-programmatore *a·na·lee·sta· pro·gram·ma·toh·re* m systems analyst

analizzare *a·na·leedz·dzah·ray* vt analyze

ananas *a·na·nas* m — pineapple

anatra *ah·na·tra* f duck

anca *an·ka* f hip

anche *an·ke* adv too; also; even

ancora *an·koh·ra* adv still (*up to this time*); yet; again; c'è ancora minestra? che *an·koh·ra mee·ne·stra* is there any more soup?; ancor piú veloce *an·kohr pyoo ve·loh·che* even faster; ancora del formaggio *an·koh· ra del for·maj·joh* more cheese; gradirei ancora un po' *gra·dee·ray an· koh·ra oon po* I'd like (some) more; ancora una birra, per favore! *an·koh· ra oo·na beer·ra payr fa·voh·re* another beer please!

ancora *an·ko·ra* f anchor

andare* *a·dah·ray* vi go; andiamo *an· dyah·mo* let's go; andiamo alla spiaggia *an·dyah·mo al·la spyaj·ja* we are going to the beach; va bene *va be·ne* O.K., okay (*agreement*); it's OK; il mio orologio va avanti *eel meo o·ro·lo·joh va a·van·tee* my watch is fast; andare* in macchina *an·dah·ray een mak·kee·na* to drive; andare* via *an·dah·ray vee·a* to go away; andare* in bicicletta *an·dah·ray een bee· klayt·ta* to cycle; andare* alla deriva *an·dah·ray al·la de·ree·va* to drift (*boat*); andarsene* *an·dar·se·ne* to go away

anello *a·nel·loh* m ring (*on finger*); l'anello di fidanzamento *a·nel·loh dee fee·dan·tsa·mayn·toh* engagement ring

anemico(a) *a·ne·mee·ko(a)* adj anemic

anestetico *a·ne·ste·tee·koh* m anesthetic

angelo *an·je·loh* m angel

angolo *an·go·loh* m corner; angle; è dietro l'angolo *e dye·tro lan·go·loh* it's round the corner

angora *an·go·ra* f angora (*fabric*)

angoscia *an·go·sha* f distress

anguille *an·gweel·lay* fpl eels

anguria *an·goo·ree·a* f watermelon

anima *ah·nee·ma* f soul

animale *a·nee·mah·le* m animal; l'animale domestico *a·nee·mah·le do·me· stee·ko* pet

animato(a) *a·nee·mah·to(a)* adj busy (*place*)

annata *an·nah·ta* f vintage; year (*as duration*)

annegare *an·ne·gah·ray* vi drown

anniversario *an·nee·ver·sah·ryoh* m anniversary

anno *an·noh* m year; quanti anni ha? *kwan·tee an·nee a* how old are you?; all'anno *al·lan·noh* per annum

annodare *an·no·dah·ray* vt tie (*string, ribbon*); knot

annoiare *an·no·yah·ray* vt bore; annoy

annotare *an·no·tah·ray* vt write down

annuale *an·noo·ah·le* adj annual; yearly

annualmente *an·noo·al·mayn·te* adv yearly

annullare *an·nool·lah·ray* vt cancel

annuncio *an·noon·choh* m announcement

annunziare *an·noon·tsyah·ray* vt announce

ansia *an·see·a* f concern (*anxiety*)

ansimare *an·see·mah·ray* vi pant

Antartide *an·tar·tee·de* f Antarctic

antenato(a) *an·te·nah·to(a)* m/f ancestor

antenna *an·tayn·na* f aerial; antenna; l'antenna trasmittente *an·tayn·na tras·meet·ten·tay* mast (*radio*)

anteprima *an·te·pree·ma* f preview

anteriore *an·te·ryoh·re* adj front

antiappannante *an·tee·ap·pan·nan·te* m defroster

antibiotico *an·tee·bee·o·tee·koh* m antibiotic

antichità *an·tee·kee·ta* f — antique; antiquity

anticipare *an·tee·chee·pah·ray* vt advance (*money*)

anticipo *an·tee·chee·poh* m advance (*loan*); Lei è in anticipo *Lay e een an· tee·chee·poh* you're early; in anticipo *een an·tee·chee·poh* in advance

antico(a) *an·tee·ko(a)* adj antique; ancient

anticoncezionale *an·tee·kon·che·tsyoh· nah·lay* m contraceptive

anticongelante *an·tee·kon·je·lan·te* m antifreeze

antieconomico(a) *an·tee·e·ko·no·mee· ko(a)* adj uneconomic

antipasto *an·tee·pa·stoh* m hors d'œuvre

antiquario *an·tee·kwah·ryoh* m antique dealer

antiquato(a) *an·tee·kwa·to(a)* adj out of date; old-fashioned

antisettico *an·tee·set·tee·koh* m antiseptic

antistaminico *an·tee·sta·mee·nee·koh* m antihistamine

ape *ah·pe* f bee

aperitivo *a·pe·ree·tee·voh* m aperitif

aperto(a) *a·per·to(a)* adj on (*water supply*); open; all'aperto *al·la·per·to* in the open (air); open-air

apparecchiare *ap·pa·rek·kyah·ray* vt lay (*table*)

apparecchio *ap·pa·rayk·kyoh* m appliance; l'apparecchio acustico *ap· pa·rayk·kyoh a·koo·stee·ko* hearing aid

apparentemente *ap·pa·ren·te·mayn·te* adv apparently

apparire* *ap·pa·ree·re* vi appear

appartamento *ap·par·ta·mayn·toh* m apartment

appartenere* a *ap·par·te·nay·re a* vi belong to

appena *ap·pay·na* adv scarcely; è appena partito *e ap·pay·na par·tee·to* he's just left

appendere* *ap·pen·de·re* vt hang

appendicite *ap·pen·dee·chee·te* f appendicitis

appetito *ap·pe·tee·toh* m appetite

appezzamento *ap·pets·tsa·mayn·toh* m plot (*of land*)

appiccicoso(a) *ap·peech·chee·koh· so(a)* adj sticky

applaudire *ap·plow·dee·ray* vt/i clap; cheer

applausi *ap·plow·zee* mpl applause

appoggiarsi a *ap·poj·jar·see a* vr lean against

apposta *ap·po·sta* adv on purpose; deliberately

apprendista *ap·pren·dee·sta* m/f apprentice; trainee

apprezzare *ap·prets·tsah·ray* vt appreciate

appropriato(a) *ap·pro·pree·ah·to(a)* adj suitable (*fitting*)

approssimativamente *ap·pros·see·ma·tee·va·mayn·tay* adv roughly (*approximately*)

approssimativo(a) *ap·pros·see·ma·tee·vo(a)* adj approximate

approvare *ap·pro·vah·ray* vt approve of

approvazione *ap·pro·vah·tsyoh·ne* f approval

appuntamento *ap·poon·ta·mayn·toh* m appointment (*rendezvous*); date

apribottiglie *ah·pree·bot·teel·ye* m — bottle opener

aprile *a·pree·le* m April

aprire* *a·pree·re* vt open; turn on □ vi open (*store, bank*); aprire* con chiave *a·pree·re kohn kyah·ve* to unlock

apriscatole *ah·pree·skah·to·lay* m — can-opener

aquila *ah·kwee·la* f eagle

aquilone *a·kwee·loh·ne* m kite

arabo(a) *a·ra·bo(a)* m/f Arab □ adj Arabic □ m l'arabo *a·ra·bo* Arabic

arachide *a·ra·kee·de* f peanut

aragosta *a·ra·goh·sta* f lobster

arancia *a·ran·cha* f orange

aranciata *a·ran·chah·ta* f orangeade

arancione *a·ran·choh·ne* adj orange

aratro *a·ra·troh* m plow

arbitro *ahr·bee·troh* m umpire; referee (*sports*)

arbusto *ar·boo·stoh* m shrub

architetto *ar·kee·tayt·toh* m architect

architettura *ar·kee·tet·too·ra* f architecture

archivio *ar·kee·vyoh* m file (*dossier*); filing cabinet; l'archivio di dati *ar·kee·vyoh dee dah·tee* data file

arco *ar·koh* m arch

arcobaleno *ar·ko·ba·lay·noh* m rainbow

ardere* *ar·de·re* vi burn

ardesia *ar·de·zya* f slate

area *ah·re·a* f area; l'area di servizio *ah·re·a dee ser·vee·tsyoh* service area

argenteria *ar·jen·te·ree·a* f silver (*ware*)

Argentina *ar·jen·tee·na* f Argentina

argentino(a) *ar·jen·tee·no(a)* adj Argentine

argento *ar·jen·toh* m silver (*metal*); un braccialetto d'argento *oon brach·cha·layt·toh dar·jen·toh* a silver bracelet

argilla *ahr·jeel·la* f clay

argomento *ar·go·mayn·toh* m topic

aria *ah·rya* f air; tune; con aria condizionata *kohn ah·rya kon·dee·tsyoh·nah·ta* air-conditioned; all'aria aperta *al·lah·rya a·per·ta* in the open (air); outdoor

arieggiare *a·ree·ej·jah·ray* vt air (*room*)

aringa *a·reen·ga* f herring

aritmetica *a·reet·me·tee·ka* f arithmetic

arma *ar·ma* f —i weapon; l'arma da fuoco *ar·ma da fwo·koh* firearm

armadietto *ar·mah·dyayt·toh* m locker

armadio *ahr·mah·dyoh* m cupboard; wardrobe (*furniture*)

armi *ar·mee* fpl arms

armonioso(a) *ar·mo·nyoh·so(a)* adj harmonious

arnese *ar·nay·se* m tool

arpa *ar·pa* f harp

arrabbiato(a) *ar·rab·byah·to(a)* adj angry (*person*)

arrampicarsi su *ar·ram·pee·kahr·see soo* vr climb (*tree, wall*)

arrangiarsi *ar·ran·jahr·see* vr manage

arrestare *ar·re·stah·ray* vt arrest

arretrati *ar·re·trah·tee* mpl arrears

arrivare *ar·ree·vah·ray* vi arrive; arrivare a *ar·ree·vah·ray a* to reach; come ci si arriva? *koh·may chee see ar·ree·va* how do we get there?; arrivare a casa *ar·ree·vah·ray a kah·sa* to get home

arrivederci *ar·ree·ve·dayr·chee* excl goodbye

arrivo *ar·ree·voh* m arrival

arrossire *ar·ros·see·re* vi blush

arrostire *ar·ro·stee·ray* vt roast

arrosto *ar·ro·stoh* m roast meat

arrotolare *ar·ro·to·lah·ray* vt roll up (*newspaper etc*)

arruffato(a) *ar·roof·fah·to(a)* adj untidy (*hair*)

arrugginirsi *ar·rooj·jee·neer·see* vr rust

arrugginito(a) *ar·rooj·jee·nee·to(a)* adj rusty

arte *ar·te* f art; craft

arteria *ar·te·ree·a* f artery

Artico *ar·tee·koh* m Arctic

articolo *ar·tee·ko·loh* m article; gli articoli di vetro *ar·tee·ko·lee dee vay·troh* glass (*glassware*); gli articoli da toeletta *ar·tee·ko·lee da to·e·let·ta* toiletries

artificiale *ar·tee·fee·chah·le* adj artificial; man-made

artigiano *ahr·tee·jah·noh* m craftsman

artista *ar·tee·sta* m/f artist

artrite *ar·tree·te* f arthritis

ascensore *a·shen·soh·re* m elevator

ascesso *a·shays·soh* m abscess

asciugacapelli *a·shoo·ga·ka·payl·lee* m — hair-drier

asciugamano *a·shoo·ga·mah·noh* m towel

asciugare *a·shoo·gah·ray* vt dry; wipe

asciutto(a) *a·shoot·to(a)* adj dry

ascoltare *a·skol·tah·ray* vi listen □ vt listen to

Asia *ah·zee·a* f Asia

asiatico(a) *a·zee·a·tee·ko(a)* adj Asian

asilo d'infanzia *a·zee·loh deen·fan·tsya* m nursery school

asino *ah·see·noh* m donkey

asma *az·ma* f asthma

asparago *a·spa·ra·goh* m asparagus

aspettare *a·spet·tah·ray* vt wait for; expect □ vi wait; fare* aspettare qualcuno *fah·ray a·spet·tah·ray kwal·koo·no* to keep someone waiting; aspetti! *a·spet·tee* hang on! (*on phone*)

aspetto *a·spet·toh* m look (*appearance*)

aspirapolvere *a·spee·ra·pohl·ve·re* m — vacuum cleaner

aspirina *a·spee·ree·na* f aspirin

assaggiare *as·saj·jah·ray* vt taste (*try*)

assalire* *as·sa·lee·ray* vt attack

assassinare *as·sas·see·nah·ray* vt murder

assassino *as·sas·see·noh* m killer

asse *as·se* m axle □ f board (*of wood*)

assecondare *as·se·kon·dah·ray* vt back (*support*)

assegnare *as·sen·yah·ray* vt allocate

assegno *as·sayn·yoh* m check (*banking*); allowance (*state payment*); l'assegno per viaggiatori *as·sayn·yoh payr vyaj·ja·toh·ree* traveler's check

assente *as·sen·te* adj absent

assenteismo *as·sen·te·ee·zmoh* m absenteeism

assetato(a) *as·se·tah·to(a)* adj thirsty

assicurare *as·see·koo·rah·ray* vt underwrite; insure

assicurarsi *as·see·koo·rar·see* vr insure oneself

assicurato(a) *as·see·koo·rah·to(a) adj* insured

assicuratore *as·see·koo·ra·toh·ray* m underwriter

assicurazione *as·see·koo·ra·tsyoh·ne* f insurance; **l'assicurazione contro terzi** *as·see·koo·ra·tsyoh·ne kohn·tro ter·tsee* third party insurance; **l'assicurazione contro tutti i rischi** *as·see·koo·ra·tsyoh·ne kohn·troh toot·tee ee ree·skee* comprehensive insurance

assistente *as·see·sten·te* m/f assistant; **l'assistente sociale** *as·see·sten·te so·chah·le* social worker

assistere* *as·see·ste·re* vt assist; **assistere* a** *as·see·ste·re a* to attend *(meeting etc)*

asso *as·soh* m ace *(cards)*

associazione *as·so·cha·tsyoh·ne* f society; association

assoluto(a) *as·so·loo·to(a) adj* absolute

assomigliare a *as·so·meel·yah·ray a* vi resemble

assorbente *as·sor·ben·te adj* absorbent □ m **l'assorbente igienico** *as·sor·ben·te ee·je·nee·ko* sanitary napkin

assorbire *as·sor·bee·re* vt absorb *(fluid)*

assortito(a) *as·sor·tee·to(a) adj* assorted

assumere* *as·soo·me·ray* vt recruit *(personnel)*; **assumere* il controllo di una ditta** *as·soo·me·ray eel kon·trol·loh dee oo·na deet·ta* to take over a firm

assurdo(a) *as·soor·do(a) adj* absurd

asta *a·sta* f auction; **l'asta dell'olio** *a·sta del·lol·yoh* dipstick

astenersi* *a·ste·nayr·see* vr abstain

astratto(a) *a·strat·to(a) adj* abstract

astronave *a·stro·nah·ve* f spacecraft

astuccio *a·stooch·choh* m case *(for jewelry etc)*

astuto(a) *a·stoo·to(a) adj* shrewd

Atene *a·te·ne* f Athens

atlante *at·lan·te* m atlas

Atlantico *at·lan·tee·ko* m Atlantic Ocean

atleta *at·le·ta* m/f athlete

atout *a·too* m trump *(cards)*

attaccapanni *at·tak·ka·pan·nee* m — peg *(for coat)*; hat stand; coat hanger

attaccare *at·tak·kah·ray* vt attach; attack; fasten; **attaccare un cane ad un palo** *at·tak·kah·ray oon kah·ne ad oon pah·loh* to tie a dog to a post

attacco *at·tak·koh* m raid *(military)*; attack; **l'attacco cardiaco** *at·tak·koh kar·dee·a·ko* heart attack

atteggiamento *at·tej·ja·mayn·toh* m attitude

attendere* *at·ten·de·re* vt wait for

attenzione *at·ten·tsyoh·nay* f attention; **attenzione allo scalino** *at·ten·tsyoh·nay al·loh ska·lee·noh* mind the step; **attenzione!** *at·ten·tsyoh·nay* look out!

atterraggio *at·ter·raj·joh* m landing *(of plane)*; **l'atterraggio di emergenza** *at·ter·raj·joh dee e·mer·jen·tsa* emergency landing; **l'atterraggio di fortuna** *at·ter·raj·joh dee for·too·na* crash-landing

atterrare *at·ter·rah·ray* vi land *(plane)*

attico *at·tee·koh* m attic; penthouse

attività *at·tee·vee·ta* f activity

attivo(a) *at·tee·vo(a) adj* active □ m **l'attivo** *at·tee·voh* asset *(financial)*

atto *at·toh* m act; action; deed; **l'atto di nascita** *at·toh dee na·shee·ta* birth certificate

attore *at·toh·re* m actor

attraversamento pedonale *at·tra·vayr·sa·mayn·toh pe·do·nah·lay* m crosswalk

attraversare *at·tra·ver·sah·ray* vt cross *(road, sea)*; **attraversare la Manica a nuoto** *at·tra·ver·sah·ray la mah·nee·ka a nwo·toh* to swim the Channel; **abbiamo attraversato la Francia in macchina** *ab·byah·mo at·tra·ver·sah·to la fran·cha een mak·kee·na* we drove across France

attraverso *at·tra·ver·so prep* through

attrezzatura *at·trets·tsa·too·ra* f tackle *(gear)*

attrice *at·tree·che* f actress

attuale *at·twah·le adj* present

audace *ow·dah·che adj* bold

audioguida *ow·dyo·gwee·da* f audioguide

audiovisivo(a) *ow·dyo·vee·zee·vo(a) adj* audio-visual

auguri *ow·goo·ree mpl* wishes

aumentare *ow·men·tah·ray* vt increase; turn up *(volume)* □ vi increase; **aumentare di valore** *ow·men·tah·ray de va·loh·re* to appreciate *(in value)*

aumento *ow·mayn·toh* m increase *(in number)*; raise; growth *(in amount etc)*

Australia *ow·strah·lya* f Australia

australiano(a) *ow·stra·lyah·no(a) adj* Australian

Austria *ow·strya* f Austria

austriaco(a) *ow·stree·a·ko(a) adj* Austrian

autentico(a) *ow·ten·tee·koh(a) adj* genuine

autista *ow·tees·ta* m chauffeur

autobus *ow·to·boos* m — bus

autogrú *ow·to·groo* f tow truck

automaticamente *ow·to·ma·tee·ka·mayn·te adv* automatically

automatico(a) *ow·to·ma·tee·ko(a) adj* automatic; **la macchina automatica** *mak·kee·na ow·to·ma·tee·ka* automatic *(car)*

automatizzare *ow·to·ma·teedz·dzah·ray* vt computerize *(system)*

automazione *ow·to·ma·tsyoh·ne* f automation

automobile *ow·to·mo·bee·lay* f car; **l'automobile decappottabile** *ow·to·mo·bee·lay de·kap·pot·tah·bee·lay* convertible

automobilista *ow·to·mo·bee·lee·sta* m/f motorist

autonomo(a) *ow·to·no·mo(a) adj* self-employed

autopompa *ow·to·pohm·pa* f fire engine

autore *ow·toh·re* m author

autorimessa *ow·toh·ree·mes·sa* f garage *(for parking)*

autostop *ow·to·stop* m hitchhiking; **fare* l'autostop** *fah·ray low·to·stop* to hitchhike

autostoppista *ow·to·stop·pee·sta* m/f hitchhiker

autostrada *ow·to·strah·da* f expressway; freeway; **l'autostrada a pedaggio** *ow·to·strah·da a pe·daj·joh* turnpike

autunno *ow·toon·noh* m fall

avanti *a·van·te adv* in front; forward(s); **il sedile è troppo in avanti**

eel se·dee·le e trop·po een a·van·tee
the seat is too far forward
avanzare *a·van·tsah·ray vi* remain (*be left over*); advance; ci avanza un po' di panna *chee a·van·tsa oon po dee pan·na* there's some cream left
avaria *a·va·ree·a f* breakdown (*of car*); failure (*mechanical*)
avena *a·vay·na f* oats
avere* *a·vay·re vt* have; non abbiamo pane *nohn ab·byah·mo pah·ne* we haven't any bread; ha del pane? *a del pah·ne* have you any bread?; ho fame *o fah·me* I am hungry; ha quarant'anni *a kwa·ran·tan·nee* he's forty
aviazione *a·vya·tsyoh·ne f* air force; aviation
aviogetto *a·vyo·jet·toh m* jet (*plane*)
avocado *a·vo·kah·doh m* avocado
avorio *a·vo·ryoh m* ivory
avvenimento *av·ve·nee·mayn·toh m* event
avventura *av·ven·too·ra f* adventure
avvertire *av·vayr·tee·re vt* warn
avviarsi *av·vee·ar·see vr* set off
avvicinarsi *av·vee·chee·nar·see vr* approach; avvicinarsi ad un luogo *av·vee·chee·nar·see ad oon lwo·goh* to approach a place
avvisare *av·vee·zah·ray vt* inform; warn
avviso *av·vee·zoh m* warning; announcement; advertisement; notice
avvocato *av·vo·kah·toh m* counselor; lawyer; attorney
avvolgere* *av·vol·je·re vt* wind; wrap
azione *a·tsyoh·ne f* action (*movement*); share (*finance*); le azioni privilegiate *a·tsyoh·nee pree·vee·le·jah·te* preferred stock
azionista *a·tsyoh·nee·sta m/f* investor; stockholder
azzurro(a) *adz·dzoor·ro(a) adj* blue

B

babysitter *bay·bee·see·ter f* baby-sitter
bacca *bak·ka f* berry
baccarà *bak·ka·ra m* baccarat
baciare *ba·chah·ray vt* kiss
baciarsi *ba·char·see vr* kiss (each other)
bacino *ba·chee·noh m* dock; pond (*artificial*)
bacio *bah·choh m* kiss
badare a *bah·dah·ray a vi* look after; pay attention to
baffi *baf·fee mpl* moustache
bagagli *ba·gal·yee mpl* luggage
bagagliaio *ba·gal·ya·yoh m* trunk (*of car*); baggage car
bagaglio a mano *ba·gal·yoh a mah·noh m* hand-luggage
bagliore *bal·yoh·re m* flash (*of light*)
bagnare *ban·yah·ray vt* wet
bagnarsi *ban·yar·see vr* get wet; bathe
bagnato(a) *ban·yah·to(a) adj* wet
bagnino *ban·yee·noh m* lifeguard
bagno *ban·yoh m* bathroom (*lavatory*); bath
baia *ba·ya f* bay (*on coast*)
balcone *bal·koh·ne m* balcony
balena *ba·lay·na f* whale
balenare *ba·le·nah·ray vi* flash (*light*)
ballare *bal·lah·ray vi* dance
balletto *bal·layt·toh m* ballet
ballo *bal·loh m* ball; dance
balsamo *bal·sa·moh m* conditioner (*for hair*)

bambinaia *bam·bee·na·ya f* nurse(maid)
bambino(a) *bam·bee·noh(a) m/f* child; baby
bambola *bam·bo·la f* doll
bambú *bam·boo m* bamboo
banana *ba·nah·na f* banana
banca *ban·ka f* bank (*finance*); la banca dei dati *ban·ka de·ee dah·tee* data bank, data base
bancarella *ban·ka·rel·la f* stall; stand
bancarotta *ban·ka·roht·ta f* bankruptcy
banchetto *ban·kayt·toh m* banquet
banchiere *ban·kye·re m* banker
banchina *ban·kee·na f* platform (*in station*); quay; quayside
banco *ban·koh m* bar (*counter*); bench (*seat, work table*); counter (*in shop*); il banco di sabbia *ban·koh dee sab·bya* sandbank
banconota *ban·ko·no·ta f* bank note
banda *ban·da f* gang; band (*musical*)
bandiera *ban·dye·ra f* banner; flag
bandito *ban·dee·toh m* gunman
bar *bar m* — bar; pub
bara *bah·ra f* coffin
barattolo *ba·rat·to·loh m* can; jar
barba *bar·ba f* beard
barbabietola *bar·ba·bye·to·la f* beet
barbecue *bar·bee·kyoo m* barbecue
barbiere *bar·bye·re m* barber
barca *bar·ka f* boat
barcollare *bar·kol·lah·ray vi* stagger; sway
barella *ba·rel·la f* stretcher
barile *ba·ree·le m* barrel
barista *ba·ree·sta m/f* barman; barmaid
barra *bar·ra f* rod
barricata *bar·ree·kah·ta f* barricade
barriera *bar·rye·ra f* barrier
basare *ba·zah·ray vt* base
base *bah·ze f* base; basis; di base *dee bah·ze* basic
baseball *bays·bol m* baseball
basso(a) *bas·so(a) adj* low; short (*person*); in basso *een bas·so* downward(s)
bastare *ba·stah·ray vi* be enough; grazie, basta così *gra·tsye ba·sta ko·see* thank you, that's plenty; basta così? *ba·sta ko·see* will it do?
bastoncini *ba·ston·chee·nee mpl* chopsticks
bastone *ba·stoh·ne m* stick; walking stick; il bastone da passeggio *ba·stoh·ne da pas·sayj·joh* walking stick
battaglia *bat·tal·ya f* battle
battello *bat·tel·loh m* boat; il battello da diporto *bat·tel·loh da dee·por·toh* pleasure boat; il battello di salvataggio *bat·tel·loh dee sal·va·taj·joh* lifeboat
battere *bat·te·re vt* hit; beat; break (*record*) □ *vi* beat (*heart*); l'orologio ha battuto le tre *lo·ro·lo·joh a bat·too·to le tray* the clock struck three; battere le palpebre *bat·te·re le pal·pe·bre* to blink
batteria *bat·te·ree·a f* battery (*in car*); heat (*sports*)
battersi *bat·ter·see vr* fight; battersi la testa *bat·ter·see la te·sta* to bang one's head
battesimo *bat·tay·zee·moh m* baptism
baule *ba·oo·le m* trunk
bazar *ba·dzar m* — bazaar
beccare *bek·kah·ray vt* peck
beige *bayzh adj* beige
bellezza *bel·layts·tsa f* beauty
bello(a) *bel·lo(a) adj* beautiful; hand-

botteghino

some; lovely; fine (*weather*); **fa bello**
fa bel·lo the weather's fine

benché *ben·ke conj* although

benda *ben·da f* blindfold; bandage

bene *be·ne adv* well; all right; **stare***
bene *stah·ray be·ne* to be well; **il latte**
ti fa bene *eel lat·te tee fa be·ne* milk is
good for you; **molto bene!** *mohl·to*
be·ne (that's) fine!; **va bene** *va be·ne*
all right

benedire* *be·ne·dee·re vt* bless

beneficiario *be·ne·fee·chah·ryoh m*
payee

Benelux *be·ne·looks m* Benelux

beni *be·nee mpl* goods; property

benvenuto(a) *ben·ve·noo·to(a) adj* welcome

benzina *ben·dzee·na f* gas(oline)

bere* *bay·re vt* drink; **prenda qualcosa**
da bere! *pren·da kwal·ko·sa da bay·re*
have a drink!

berlina *ber·lee·na f* sedan (*car*)

bernoccolo *ber·nok·ko·loh m* bump
(*lump*)

berretto *ber·rayt·toh m* cap (*hat*)

bersaglio *ber·sal·yoh m* target

bestemmiare *be·stem·myah·ray vi*
swear (*curse*)

bestiame *be·stee·ah·may m* cattle

betulla *be·tool·la f* birch (*tree*)

bevanda *be·van·da f* drink

biancheria *byan·ke·ree·a f* linen (*for
beds, table*); **la biancheria da letto**
byan·ke·ree·a da let·toh bedding; **la**
biancheria intima *byan·ke·ree·a een·*
tee·ma underwear

bianchetti *byan·kayt·tee mpl* whitebait

bianco(a) *byan·ko(a) adj* white; blank;
l'assegno in bianco *as·sayn·yoh een*
byan·ko blank check; **lasciate in**
bianco per favore *la·shah·te een byan·*
ko payr fa·voh·re please leave blank

Bibbia *beeb·bya f* Bible

biberon *be·be·ron m* bottle (*baby's*)

bibita *bee·bee·ta f* soft drink

biblioteca *bee·blee·o·te·ka f* library;
bookcase

bicchiere *beek·kye·re m* glass (*tumbler*); **il bicchiere da vino** *beek·kye·re*
da vee·noh wineglass

bicicletta *bee·chee·klayt·ta f* bicycle;
andare* in bicicletta *an·dah·ray een*
bee·chee·klayt·ta to cycle

bidone *bee·doh·ne m* ashcan

bigliettaio *beel·yet·ta·yoh m* conductor
(*on bus*)

biglietteria *beel·yet·te·ree·a f* ticket office

biglietto *beel·yayt·toh m* note (*letter*);
ticket; card; **il biglietto di abbona-**
mento *beel·yayt·toh dee ab·bon·a·*
mayn·toh commutation ticket; **il bi-**
glietto di andata e ritorno *beel·yayt·*
toh dee an·dah·ta e ree·tohr·noh
round trip ticket; **il biglietto di solo**
andata *beel·yayt·toh dee soh·lo an·*
dah·ta one-way ticket

bigodino *bee·go·dee·noh m* curler (*for
hair*)

bikini *bee·kee·nee m* — bikini

bilancia *bee·lan·cha f* scales (*for
weighing*); **la bilancia dei pagamenti**
bee·lan·cha de·ee pa·ga·mayn·tee balance of payments; **la bilancia com-**
merciale *bee·lan·cha kom·mer·chah·*
le balance of trade

bilanciare *bee·lan·chah·ray vt* balance

bilancio *bee·lan·choh m* balance sheet;
il bilancio preventivo *bee·lan·choh*
pre·ven·tee·vo budget

bilia *beel·ya f* marble (*ball*)

biliardo *bee·lyar·doh m* billiards

bilingue *bee·leen·gwe adj* bilingual

binario *bee·nah·ryoh m* track (*for
trains*); line; platform

binocolo *bee·no·ko·loh m* binoculars

biologia *bee·o·lo·jee·a f* biology

biondo(a) *byon·do(a) adj* blond(e);
fair

birra *beer·ra f* beer; **la birra con limo-**
nata *beer·ra kohn lee·mo·nah·ta*
shandygaff; **la birra alla spina** *beer·ra*
al·la spee·na draft beer; **la birra**
chiara *beer·ra kyah·ra* lager

birreria *beer·re·ree·a f* brewery

bis *bees m* — encore; **bis!** *bees* encore!

biscotto *bee·skot·toh m* cookie

bisognare *bee·zohn·yah·ray vi* to have
to

bisogno *bee·zohn·yoh m* need; **avere***
bisogno di *a·vay·ray bee·zohn·yoh*
dee to need

bistecca *bee·stayk·ka f* steak; **la bi-**
stecca di filetto *bee·stayk·ka dee fee·*
layt·toh fillet steak

bivio *bee·vyoh m* fork (*in road*)

bloccare *blok·kah·ray vt* block; **bloc-**
care un assegno *blok·kah·ray oon as·*
sayn·yoh to stop a check

bloccarsi *blok·kar·see vr* jam
(*machine*)

blocco *blok·koh m* block (*of stone*);
pad (*notepaper*); **il blocco dei salari**
blok·koh de·ee sa·lah·ree wage freeze

blu marina *bloo ma·ree·na adj* navy
blue

blue-jeans *bloo·jeenz mpl* jeans

blusa *bloo·za f* smock

boa *bo·a f* buoy

bocca *bohk·ka f* mouth

bocciolo *boch·cho·loh m* bud

boccone *bok·koh·ne m* bite (*of food*)

boicottare *boy·kot·tah·ray vt* boycott

bolla *bol·la f* bubble; blister

bollettino *bol·let·tee·noh m* bulletin

bollicina *bol·lee·chee·na f* pimple

bollire *bol·lee·re vi* boil; **fare* bollire**
fah·ray bol·lee·re to boil (*water*)

bollitore *bol·lee·toh·re m* kettle

bomba *bohm·ba f* bomb

bombetta *bom·bayt·ta f* derby

bombola *bohm·bo·la f* cylinder (*for
gas*); **la bombola spray** *bohm·bo·la*
spray spray (*container*)

bombolone *bom·bo·loh·ne m* doughnut

boom *boom m* boom (*economic*)

bordo *bohr·doh m* border; edge; **il**
bordo del marciapiede *bohr·doh del*
mar·cha·pye·de curb; **a bordo** *a bohr·*
doh on board (*ship, plane*); **salire* a**
bordo *sa·lee·re a bohr·doh* to go
aboard; **a bordo della nave** *a bohr·*
doh del·la nah·ve aboard the ship

borghese *bor·gay·say adj* middle-class

borgo *bohr·goh m* district

borsa *bohr·sa f* handbag; carryall; bag;
briefcase; **la borsa dell'acqua calda**
bohr·sa del·lak·kwa kal·da hot-water
bottle; **la borsa per la spesa** *bohr·sa*
payr la spay·sa shopping bag; **la**
borsa di studio *bohr·sa dee stoo·dee·*
oh grant (*to student*); **la Borsa** *bohr·*
sa stock market; stock exchange; **la**
borsa nera *bohr·sa nay·ra* black market

borsellino *bor·sel·lee·noh m* purse (*for
money*)

borsetta *bor·sayt·ta f* handbag

bosco *bo·skoh m* wood (*forest*)

bottega *bot·te·ga f* shop

botteghino *bot·te·gee·noh m* box office

bottiglia *bot·teel·ya f* bottle
bottoncino *bot·ton·chee·noh m* stud (*for collar*)
bottone *bot·toh·ne m* button; **il bottone automatico** *bot·toh·ne ow·to·ma·tee·ko* snap fastener
boutique *boo·teek f* boutique
box *boks m* playpen
bozzetto *bots·tsayt·toh m* sketch (*drawing*)
braccialetto *brach·cha·layt·toh m* bracelet
bracciata *brach·chah·ta f* stroke (*swimming*)
braccio *brach·choh m* —a arm (*of person*)
braciola *bra·cho·la f* chop (*food*)
a brandelli *a bran·del·lee adv* ragged (*clothes*)
brandina *bran·dee·na f* cot
brandy *bran·dee m* brandy
brano *bra·no m* passage (*from book*)
bretelle *bre·tel·le fpl* suspenders
breve *bre·ve adj* brief
brevetto *bre·vayt·toh m* patent
brezza *bredz·dza f* breeze
briciola *bree·cho·la f* crumb
bridge *breej m* bridge (*game*)
briglia *breel·ya f* rein; bridle
brillare *breel·lah·ray vi* shine
brindare a *breen·dah·ray a vi* toast (*drink to*)
brindisi *breen·dee·zee m* — toast (*drink, speech*)
britannico(a) *bree·tan·nee·ko(a) adj* British
brocca *brok·ka f* jug
broccoli *brok·ko·lee mpl* broccoli
brodo *bro·doh m* stock (*for soup etc*)
bronchite *bron·kee·te f* bronchitis
brontolare *bron·to·lah·ray vi* grumble
bronzo *brohn·dzoh m* bronze
bruciare *broo·chah·ray vt/i* burn; **mi sono bruciato il braccio** *mee soh·no broo·chah·to eel brach·choh* I've burned my arm
bruciore di stomaco *broo·choh·re dee sto·ma·koh m* heartburn
bruno(a) *broo·no(a) adj* brown; dark
brusco(a) *broo·sko(a) adj* abrupt; sharp (*bend*)
brutto(a) *broot·toh(a) adj* ugly
Bruxelles *brook·sel f* Brussels
buca *boo·ka f* hole; **la buca per le lettere** *boo·ka payr le let·te·re* letter box
bucato *boo·kah·toh m* washing; laundry; **fare* il bucato** *fah·ray eel boo·kah·toh* to do the washing
buccia *booch·cha f* peel, skin
buco *boo·koh m* hole; **il buco della serratura** *boo·koh del·la ser·ra·too·ra* keyhole
bufera *boo·fe·ra f* storm; **la bufera di neve** *boo·fe·ra dee nay·ve* blizzard
bugia *boo·jee·a f* lie (*untruth*)
buio(a) *boo·yo(a) adj* dark
bulbo *bool·boh m* bulb
bulldozer *bool·do·zer m* bulldozer
bulletta *bool·layt·ta f* tack (*nail*)
buongustaio *bwon·goos·ta·ee·yoh m* gourmet
buono *bwo·noh m* voucher; coupon; token; **il buono premio** *bwo·noh pre·myoh* trading stamp
buono(a) *bwo·noh(a) adj* good; **buon giorno!** *bwon johr·noh* good morning/afternoon!; **buona sera!** *bwo·na say·ra* good evening!; **buona notte!** *bwo·na not·tay* good night!; **a buon mercato** *a bwon mer·kah·toh* cheap

buono-regalo *bwo·noh·re·gah·loh m* gift token
burrasca *boor·ra·ska f* storm
burrascoso(a) *boor·ras·koh·so(a) adj* gusty (*wind*); rough (*weather*)
burro *boor·roh m* butter
bussare *boos·sah·ray vi* knock
bussola *boos·so·la f* compass
busta *boo·sta f* envelope
bustina *boo·stee·na f* sachet; **la bustina di tè** *boo·stee·na dee te* tea bag
busto *boo·stoh m* bust
butano *boo·tah·noh m* butane
buttare via *boot·tah·ray vee·a vt* throw away

C

cabaret *ka·ba·ray m* cabaret
cabina *ka·bee·na f* cabin (*in ship*); cubicle; **la cabina telefonica** *ka·bee·na te·le·fo·nee·ka* telephone booth
cabinato *ka·bee·nah·toh m* cabin cruiser
cacao *ka·kow m* cocoa
caccia *kach·chah f* hunting; shooting
cacciagione *kach·cha·joh·nay f* game (*hunting*)
cacciare *kach·chah·ray vt* hunt; chase away
cacciavite *kach·cha·vee·te m* — screwdriver
cachemire *kash·meer m* cashmere
cacto *kak·toh m* cactus
cadavere *ka·dah·ve·re m* body (*corpse*)
caddie *kad·dee m* caddie
cadere* *ka·day·re vi* fall; fall over; fall down; drop; **fare* cadere** *fah·ray ka·day·re* to knock over; **lasciare cadere** *la·shah·ray ka·day·re* to drop (*let fall*)
caduta *ka·doo·ta f* fall
caffè *kaf·fe m* — café; coffee; **il caffè nero** *kaf·fe nay·roh* black coffee
caffellatte *kaf·fel·lat·tay m* — coffee with milk
caffettiera *kaf·fet·tye·ra f* coffeepot
calamita *ka·la·mee·ta f* magnet
calare *ka·lah·ray vi* fall
calcestruzzo *kal·che·stroots·tsoh m* concrete
calciare *kal·chah·ray vt* kick (*ball*)
calcio *kal·choh m* kick; football (*soccer*); calcium; **dare* un calcio a** *dah·ray oon kal·choh a* to kick
calcolare *kal·ko·lah·ray vt* calculate; **calcoli 10 minuti per arrivarci** *kal·ko·lee 10 mee·noo·tee payr ar·ree·var·chee* allow 10 minutes to get there
calcolatrice *kal·ko·la·tree·chay f* calculator
calcolo *kal·ko·loh m* calculation; un **calcolo approssimativo** *oon kal·ko·loh ap·pros·see·ma·tee·vo* a rough estimate
caldo(a) *kal·do(a) adj* hot; **fa caldo oggi** *fa kal·do oj·jee* it's warm/hot today; **ho caldo** *o kal·do* I'm warm/hot
calendario *ka·len·dah·ree·oh m* calendar
callo *kal·loh m* corn (*on foot*)
calma *kal·ma f* peace (*calm*)
calmante *kal·man·te m* painkiller
calmarsi *kal·mar·see vr* to calm down
calmo(a) *kal·moh(a) adj* calm
calore *ka·loh·re m* warmth; heat
caloria *ka·lo·ree·a f* calorie
calpestare *kal·pes·tah·ray vt* tread on
calvo(a) *kal·vo(a) adj* bald
calza *kal·tsa f* stocking; sock

calzatura *kal·tsa·too·ra* f footwear
calzino *kal·tsee·noh* m sock
calzoncini *kal·tson·chee·nee* mpl shorts
calzoni *kal·tsoh·nee* mpl slacks
cambiale *kam·bee·ah·le* f draft (*financial*)
cambiamento *kam·bya·mayn·toh* m change; **un cambiamento del tempo** *oon kam·bya·mayn·toh del tem·poh* a change in the weather
cambiare *kam·byah·ray* vi change □ vt change; exchange; **cambiare treno a Marsiglia** *kam·byah·ray tre·noh a Mahr·seel·ya* to change trains at Marseilles; **cambiare casa** *kam·byah·ray kah·sa* to move (*change residence*); **cambiare qualcosa per qualcos'altro** *kam·byah·ray kwal·ko·sa payr kwal·ko·sal·tro* to exchange something for something; **cambiare marcia** *kam·byah·ray mar·cha* to shift gear
cambiarsi *kam·bee·ahr·see* vr change one's clothes
cambio *kam·byoh* m change; exchange; rate of exchange; gears; **il cambio sincronizzato** *kam·byoh seen·kro·needz·dzah·to* synchromesh
camera *kah·me·ra* f room; la camera (da letto) *kah·me·ra (da let·toh)* bedroom; **una camera singola** *oo·na kah·me·ra seen·go·la* a single room; **la camera matrimoniale** *kah·me·ra ma·tree·mo·nyah·le* double room; **la camera blindata** *kah·me·ra bleen·dah·ta* strongroom; **la camera dei bambini** *kah·me·ra dey bam·bee·nee* nursery; **la camera degli ospiti** *kah·me·ra del·yee o·spee·tee* guest-room; **la camera di commercio** *kah·me·ra dee kom·mer·choh* Chamber of Commerce; **la camera libera** *kah·me·ra lee·be·ra* vacancy (*in hotel etc*)
cameriera *ka·me·rye·ra* f waitress; chambermaid; **la cameriera al banco** *ka·me·rye·ra al ban·koh* barmaid
cameriere *ka·me·rye·re* m waiter; **il cameriere di bordo** *ka·me·rye·re dee bohr·doh* steward
camicetta *ka·mee·chayt·ta* f blouse
camicia *ka·mee·cha* f shirt; **la camicia da notte** *ka·mee·cha da not·tay* nightgown
caminetto *ka·mee·nayt·toh* m mantelpiece
camino *ka·mee·noh* m chimney; fireplace
camion *ka·myon* m — truck; **il camion di traslochi** *ka·myon dee tra·zlo·kee* moving van; **il camion cisterna** *ka·myon chee·ster·na* tanker (*truck*)
camionista *ka·myo·nee·sta* m truck driver
cammello *kam·mel·loh* m camel
camminare *kam·mee·nah·ray* vi walk
campagna *kam·pan·ya* f country; countryside; campaign; **la campagna di pubblicità** *kam·pan·ya dee poob·blee·chee·ta* publicity campaign; **la campagna giornalistica** *kam·pan·ya johr·na·lee·stee·ka* press-campaign; **in campagna** *een kam·pan·ya* in the country
campana *kam·pah·na* f bell
campanello *kam·pa·nel·loh* m bell; doorbell
campeggio *kam·payj·joh* m camping; camp(ing) site; **fare* del campeggio** *fah·ray del kam·payj·joh* to go camping

campione *kam·pyoh·ne* m sample (*of goods*); specimen; champion
campo *kam·poh* m field; **il campo da gioco** *kam·poh da jo·koh* playing field; **il campo di golf** *kam·poh dee golf* golf course; **il campo della fiera** *kam·poh del·la fye·ra* fairground; **il campo da tennis** *kam·poh da ten·nees* tennis court
camposanto *kam·po·san·toh* m graveyard; churchyard
Canadà *ka·na·da* m Canada
canadese *ka·na·day·say* adj Canadian
canale *ka·nah·lay* m canal
canasta *ka·na·sta* f canasta
cancellare *kan·chel·lah·ray* vt rub out; cancel; **cancellare un debito** *kan·chel·lah·ray oon de·bee·toh* to write off a debt
cancellata *kan·chel·lah·ta* f railings
cancelleria *kan·chel·le·ree·a* f stationery
cancelliere *kan·chel·lyay·ray* m chancellor
cancello *kan·chel·loh* m gate (*of garden*)
cancro *kan·kroh* m cancer
candela *kan·day·la* f spark plug; candle
candidato(a) *kan·dee·da·toh(a)* m/f candidate
cane *kah·nay* m dog; **il cane per ciechi** *kah·nay payr che·kee* guide dog
canestro *ka·ne·stroh* m basket
canna da pesca *kan·na da pay·ska* f fishing rod
cannella *kan·nel·la* f cinnamon
cannone *kan·noh·nay* m gun; cannon
canoa *ka·no·a* f canoe; **fare* della canoa** *fah·ray del·la ka·no·a* to go canoeing
canottaggio *ka·not·taj·joh* m rowing (*sport*)
canottiera *ka·not·tye·ra* f undershirt
canovaccio *ka·no·vach·choh* m dishtowel
cantare *kan·tah·ray* vt/i sing
cantiere *kan·tye·re* m building site; **il cantiere navale** *kan·tye·re na·vah·le* shipyard
cantilena *kan·tee·le·na* f jingle (*advertising*)
cantina *kan·tee·na* f cellar; wine cellar
canto *kan·toh* m song; singing; **il canto di Natale** *kan·toh dee na·ta·lay* carol; **il canto folcloristico** *kan·toh fol·klo·ree·stee·ko* folk song
canzone *kan·tsoh·ne* f song
capace *ka·pah·chay* adj capable
capacità *ka·pa·chee·ta* f ability
capanna *ka·pan·na* f hut (*shed*)
capelli *ka·payl·lee* mpl hair
capello *ka·payl·loh* m hair (*single strand*)
capezzale *ka·pets·tsah·le* m bolster
capire *ka·pee·ray* vt understand
capitale *ka·pee·tah·lay* f capital (*city*) □ m capital (*finance*); **il capitale d'esercizio** *ka·pee·tah·lay de·zer·chee·tsyoh* working capital
capitalismo *ka·pee·ta·lee·zmoh* m capitalism
capitalista *ka·pee·ta·lee·sta* m/f capitalist
capitano *ka·pee·tah·noh* m captain; **il capitano di porto** *ka·pee·tah·noh dee por·toh* harbor master
capitolo *ka·pee·to·loh* m chapter
capo *kah·poh* m head; leader; boss
capocuoco *ka·po·kwo·koh* m chef
Capodanno *kah·po·dan·noh* m New Year's Day

capolavoro *kah·po·la·voh·roh m* masterpiece

capolinea *kah·po·lee·ne·a m* terminal (buses)

caposquadra *kah·po·skwa·dra m* foreman

capotreno *kah·po·tre·noh m* conductor (on train)

cappa *kap·pa f* cape

cappella *kap·pel·la f* chapel

cappello *kap·pel·loh m* hat; **il cappello da sole** *kap·pel·loh da soh·le* sun-hat; **il cappello a cilindro** *kap·pel·loh a chee·leen·droh* top hat

cappio *kap·pyoh m* loop

cappotto *kap·pot·toh m* overcoat

cappuccino *kap·pooch·chee·no m* frothy white coffee

cappuccio *kap·pooch·choh m* hood

capra *kah·pra f* goat

capretto *ka·prayt·toh m* kid

capsula *kap·soo·la f* capsule

caraffa *ka·raf·fa f* decanter; carafe

caramella *ka·ra·mel·la f* candy; toffee; **la caramella alla menta** *ka·ra·mel·la al·la maynt·ta* mint

caramello *ka·ra·mel·loh m* caramel

carato *ka·ra·toh m* carat

carattere *ka·rat·te·ray m* character

carbone *kahr·boh·nay m* coal

carbonio *kar·boh·nyoh m* carbon

carburante *kar·boo·ran·te m* fuel; **la pompa del carburante** *pom·pa del kar·boo·ran·te* fuel pump

carburatore *kar·boo·ra·toh·ray m* carburetor

carcere *kar·che·re m* prison

carciofo *kar·cho·foh m* artichoke

cardigan *kahr·dee·gan m* — cardigan

cardinale *kar·dee·nah·le m* cardinal

cardio *kahr·dee·oh m* cockle

carenza *ka·ren·tsa f* shortage

carezzare *ka·rets·tsah·ray vt* pat; caress

caricare *ka·ree·kah·ray vt* load; **caricare un orologio** *ka·ree·kah·ray oon o·ro·lo·joh* to wind up a clock

carico *kah·ree·koh m* shipment; cargo; load

carino(a) *ka·ree·no(a) adj* lovely; pretty; nice

carnagione *kahr·na·joh·nay f* complexion

carne *kar·nay f* meat; flesh; **la carne di maiale** *kar·nay dee ma·yah·le* pork; **la carne di manzo** *kar·nay dee man·dzoh* beef; **la carne di cervo** *kar·nay dee cher·voh* venison; **la carne tritata** *kar·nay tree·tah·ta* ground beef; **la carne di montone** *kar·nay dee mon·toh·nay* mutton

carnevale *kahr·ne·vah·lay m* carnival

caro(a) *kah·ro(a) adj* dear □ *m/f* darling

carota *ka·ro·ta f* carrot

carreggiata doppia *kar·rej·jah·ta dop·pya f* divided highway

carrello *kar·rel·loh m* cart; **il carrello per bagagli** *kar·rel·loh payr ba·gal·yee* luggage cart

carriera *kar·ree·e·ra f* career

carriola *kar·ryo·la f* wheelbarrow

carro *kar·roh m* wagon; **il carro armato** *kar·roh ar·mah·to* tank (military)

carrozzina *kar·rots·tsee·na f* baby buggy, baby carriage

carta *kar·ta f* paper; card; **alla carta** *al·la kar·ta* à la carte; **la carta di credito** *kar·ta dee kray·dee·toh* credit card; **la carta d'identità** *kar·ta dee·den·tee·ta* identity card; **la carta d'imbarco**

karta *deem·bar·koh* boarding pass; **la carta carbone** *kar·ta kar·boh·nay* carbon paper; **la carta velina** *kar·ta ve·lee·na* tissue paper; **la carta da gioco** *kar·ta da jo·koh* playing card; **la carta verde** *kar·ta vayr·day* green card; **la carta geografica** *kar·ta jay·oh·gra·fee·ka* map (of country); **la carta nautica** *kar·ta now·tee·ka* chart (map); **la carta stradale** *kar·ta stra·dah·le* road map; **la carta d'imballaggio** *kar·ta deem·bal·laj·joh* wrapping paper; **la carta da parati** *kar·ta da pa·rah·tee* wallpaper; **la carta increspata** *kar·ta een·kre·spah·ta* corrugated paper; **la carta da lettere** *kar·ta da let·te·ray* notepaper; **la carta da scrivere** *kar·ta da skree·ve·re* writing paper; **la carta igienica** *kar·ta ee·je·nee·ka* toilet paper

cartella *kar·tel·la f* folder; briefcase; schoolbag

cartello *kahr·tel·loh m* sign; signpost; cartel

cartoleria *kar·to·le·ree·a f* stationer's (shop)

cartolina *kar·to·lee·na f* postcard; greeting card; **la cartolina di Natale** *kar·to·lee·na dee na·tah·lay* Christmas card

cartone *kahr·to·nay m* cardboard; **il cartone animato** *kahr·to·nay a·nee·mah·toh* cartoon (animated)

cartuccia *kahr·tooch·cha f* cartridge

casa *kah·sa f* house; home; **a casa** *kah·sa* at home; **andare* a casa** *an·dah·ray a kah·sa* to go home; **a casa mia** *a kah·sa mee·a* at my house; **offerto(a) dalla casa** *of·fer·to(a) dal·la kah·sa* on the house; **la casa di cura** *kah·sa dee koo·ra* nursing home; **la casa colonica** *kah·sa ko·lo·nee·ka* farmhouse; **la casa dello studente** *kah·sa del·lo stoo·den·te* dormitory; **la Casa Bianca** *kah·sa byan·ka* White House; **l'indirizzo di casa** *een·dee·reets·tsoh dee kah·sa* home address

casalinga *ka·sa·leen·ga f* housewife

casamento *ka·sa·mayn·toh m* apartment block

cascata *ka·skah·ta f* waterfall

casco *ka·skoh m* helmet; crash helmet

casella postale *ka·sel·la po·stah·le f* post-office box

caserma *ka·ser·ma f* barracks; **la caserma dei pompieri** *ka·ser·ma dey pom·pye·ree* fire station

casinò *ka·see·noh m* — casino

caso *kah·zoh m* case (instance); **nel caso che** *nel kah·zoh kay* in case; **in caso di** *een kah·zoh dee* in case of; **a caso** *a kah·zoh* at random; **per caso** *payr kah·zoh* by accident; by chance

cassa *kas·sa f* cashdesk; till (cash register); checkout (in store); crate; **la cassa di pensionamento** *kas·sa dee pen·syoh·na·mayn·toh* pension fund; **la cassa di risparmio** *kas·sa dee ree·spar·myoh* savings bank; **la cassa da imballaggio** *kas·sa da eem·bal·laj·joh* packing case

cassaforte *kas·sa·for·te f* **casseforti** strongbox; safe

casseruola *kas·ser·wo·la f* saucepan; casserole (dish)

cassetta *kas·sayt·ta f* box; cartridge (of tape); cassette; **la cassetta di pronto soccorso** *kas·sayt·ta dee prohn·to sok·kohr·soh* first-aid kit; **la cassetta per le lettere** *kas·sayt·ta payr le let·te·re* post-box

cassetto *kas·sayt·toh* m drawer

cassiere(a) *kas·sye·ray(a)* m/f cashier; teller

castagna *ka·stan·ya* f chestnut

castano(a) *ka·stah·no(a)* adj brown (hair)

castello *ka·stel·loh* m castle

casuale *ka·zoo·ah·le* adj chance

catalogo *ka·tah·lo·goh* m catalog

catarifrangente *ka·ta·ree·fran·jen·tay* m reflector (on cycle, car)

catena *ka·tay·na* f chain; range (of mountains); **la catena di montaggio** *ka·tay·na dee mon·taj·joh* assembly line

catrame *ka·trah·me* m tar

cattedrale *ka·te·drah·lay* f cathedral

cattivo(a) *kat·tee·vo(a)* adj bad; nasty; evil; naughty

cattolico(a) *kat·to·lee·ko(a)* adj Roman Catholic

catturare *kat·too·rah·ray* vt capture

causa *kow·za* f cause; case (lawsuit); **a causa di** *a kow·za dee* because of

causare *kow·zah·ray* vt cause

cauzione *kow·tsyoh·ne* f security (for loan); bail (for prisoner); deposit (for key etc); **su cauzione** *soo kow·tsyoh·ne* on bail

cava *kah·va* f quarry

cavalcare *ka·val·kah·ray* vt/i ride

cavalcata *ka·val·kah·ta* f ride (on horse); riding

cavalcavia *ka·val·ka·vee·a* m — flyover (road)

cavaliere *ka·va·lye·re* m partner (dancing)

cavalletto per il bucato *ka·val·layt·toh payr eel boo·kah·toh* m clotheshorse

cavallo *ka·val·loh* m horse; **il cavallo da corsa** *ka·val·loh da kohr·sa* racehorse

cavare *ka·vah·ray* vt take out; **cavarsela** *ka·var·se·la* to manage

cavatappi *ka·va·tap·pee* m — corkscrew

caverna *ka·ver·na* f cave

caviale *ka·vee·ah·lay* m caviar(e)

caviglia *ka·veel·ya* f ankle

cavo *kah·voh* m cable

cavo(a) *ka·vo(a)* adj hollow

cavolfiore *ka·vol·fyoh·ray* m cauliflower

cavolini di Bruxelles *kah·vo·lee·nee dee brook·sel* mpl Brussels sprouts

cavolo *kah·vo·loh* m cabbage; **il cavolo rapa** *kah·vo·loh rah·pa* kohlrabi

c'è *che* there is

ce *che* pron, adv before **lo, la, li, le, ne** = **ci**

Cecoslovacchia *che·ko·slo·vak·kya* f Czechoslovakia

cecoslovacco(a) *che·ko·slo·vak·koh(a)* adj Czech(oslovakian)

cedere *che·de·ray* vi give in (yield)

cedro *chay·droh* m cedar; lime (fruit); **il succo di cedro** *sook·koh dee chay·droh* lime juice

C.E.E. *che·e* f E.E.C.

celebrare *che·le·brah·ray* vt celebrate

celibe *che·lee·be* adj single (not married: man)

cella *chel·la* f cell (in prison)

cellofan *chel·lo·fan* m cellophane

Celsius *chel·syoos* adj Celsius

cemento *che·mayn·toh* m cement

cena *chay·na* f dinner; supper; dinner party

cenere *chay·ne·re* f ash (cinders)

cenno *chen·no* m sign; nod; wave

centenario *chen·te·na·ree·oh* m centenary

centesimo *chen·te·zee·moh* m cent
□ adj **centesimo(a)** *chen·te·zee·mo(a)* hundredth

centigrado *chen·tee·gra·doh* adj centigrade

centilitro *chen·tee·lee·troh* m centiliter

centimetro *chen·tee·me·troh* m centimeter

centinaio *chen·tee·na·yoh* m a hundred; about a hundred; **centinaia di libri** *chen·tee·na·ya dee lee·bree* hundreds of books

cento *chen·to* num hundred; **cento persone** *chen·to per·soh·ne* a hundred people

centrale *chen·trah·le* adj central □ f **la centrale** *chen·trah·le* exchange (telephone); **la centrale telefonica** *chen·trah·le te·le·fo·nee·ka* telephone exchange

centralinista *chen·tra·lee·nee·sta* m/f switchboard operator

centralino *chen·tra·lee·noh* m switchboard

centro *chen·troh* m center; **il centro commerciale** *chen·troh kom·mer·chah·le* shopping center; **il centro di Chicago** *chen·troh dee shee·kah·go* downtown Chicago; **il centro della città** *chen·troh del·la cheet·ta* city center; **il centro per il giardinaggio** *chen·troh payr eel jar·dee·naj·joh* garden center

ceppo *chayp·poh* m log (of wood); **il ceppo del freno** *chayp·poh del fre·noh* shoe (of brake)

cera *chay·ra* f wax; polish (for floor)

ceramica *che·ra·mee·ka* f pottery; **la fabbrica di ceramiche** *fab·bree·ka dee che·ra·mee·ke* pottery (workshop)

cercare *cher·kah·ray* vt look for; look up (word); **cercare di fare qualcosa** *cher·kah·ray dee fah·ray kwal·ko·sa* to try to do something

cerchio *chayr·kyoh* m ring; hoop; circle

cereale *che·re·ah·lay* m cereal

cerimonia *che·ree·mo·nee·a* f ceremony

cerniera lampo *cher·nye·ra lam·poh* f zipper

cerotto *che·rot·toh* m sticking-plaster; bandaid

certamente *cher·ta·mayn·tay* adv definitely; certainly

certificato *cher·tee·fee·kah·toh* m certificate; **il certificato di morte** *cher·tee·fee·kah·toh dee mor·te* death certificate

certo(a) *cher·toh(a)* adj certain; sure; definite

cerume *che·roo·me* m wax (in ear)

cervello *cher·vel·loh* m brain; brains (as food)

cervo *cher·voh* m deer

cespuglio *che·spool·yoh* m bush

cesta *chay·sta* f hamper

cestino *che·stee·noh* m waste paper basket

cetriolino *che·tree·oh·lee·noh* m gherkin

cetriolo *che·tree·o·loh* m cucumber

chalet *sha·le* m — chalet

che *ke* conj that; than □ pron who; whom; which; that; what; **l'uomo che...** *lwo·moh ke* the man who...; **l'uomo che vede** *lwo·moh ke ve·de* the man whom you see; **il libro, che è lungo** *eel lee·broh ke e loon·go* the book, which is long; la mela che ha mangiato *la may·la ke a man·jah·to* the apple which you ate; la foto che Le ho dato *la fo·to ke le o dah·to* the photo that I gave you; dopo di che *doh·po dee ke* after which; che c'è? *ke che* what's wrong?; che cos'è successo? *ke ko·se sooch·ches·so* what's happened?; che disordine! *ke dee·zohr·dee·ne* what a mess!; spero che... *spe·ro ke* I hope that...; non era che un errore *nohn e·ra ke oon er·roh·re* it was just a mistake

cherosene *ke·ro·ze·ne* m kerosene

chi *kee pron* who; whom; di chi è questo libro? *dee kee e kway·sto lee·broh* whose book is this?; io so di chi è *ee·o so dee kee e* I know whose it is; chi di voi? *kee dee voy* which one of you?; chi è? *kee e* who's that?

chiacchiera *kya·kye·ra* f gossip (*chatter*)

chiacchierare *kya·kye·rah·ray* vi chat; gossip

chiamare *kya·mah·ray* vt call; fare* chiamare *fah·ray kya·mah·ray* to page

chiamarsi *kya·mar·see* vr to be called; come Si chiama? *koh·may see kya·ma* what is your name?; mi chiamo Paul *mee kya·moh Paul* my name is Paul

chiamata *kya·mah·ta* f call (*on phone*); una chiamata urbana *oo·na kya·mah·ta oor·bah·na* a local call

chiaretto *kya·rayt·toh* m claret

chiaro(a) *kyah·roh(a)* adj clear; light (*bright, pale*)

chiatta *kyat·ta* f barge

chiave *kyah·ve* f key; wrench; la chiave dell'accensione *kyah·ve del·lach·chen·syoh·ne* ignition key

chiavistello *kya·vee·stel·loh* m bolt; chiudere* a chiavistello *kyoo·de·re a kya·vee·stel·loh* to bolt (*door, gate*)

chiedere* *kyay·de·re* vt ask; ask for; chiedere* l'ora a qualcuno *kyay·de·re loh·ra a kwal·koo·no* to ask someone the time

chiesa *kye·za* f church

chile *kee·lay* m chili

chilo *kee·loh* m kilo

chilogrammo *kee·lo·gram·moh* m kilogram

chilometraggio *kee·lo·me·traj·joh* m ≈ mileage

chilometro *kee·lo·me·troh* m kilometer

chilowatt *kee·lo·vat* m kilowatt

chimica *kee·mee·ka* f chemistry

chimico(a) *kee·mee·koh(a)* adj chemical

chinarsi *kee·nar·see* vr bend (*person*)

chiocciola *kyoch·cho·la* f snail

chiodo *kyo·do* m nail (*metal*); stud; il chiodo di garofano *kyo·do dee ga·ro·fa·noh* clove

chiosco *kyo·sko* m kiosk

chip *cheep* m chip (*electronics*)

chirurgia *kee·roor·jee·a* f surgery (*operation*); la chirurgia estetica *kee·roor·jee·a e·ste·tee·ka* cosmetic surgery; la chirurgia plastica *kee·roor·jee·a pla·stee·ka* plastic surgery

chirurgo *kee·roor·goh* m surgeon

chitarra *kee·tar·ra* f guitar

chiudere* *kyoo·de·re* vt shut; close; turn off; chiudere* l'elettricità/l'acqua al contatore *kyoo·de·re le·let·tree·chee·ta/lak·kwa al kon·ta·toh·re* to turn the electricity/water off at

the main; chiudere* a chiave *kyoo·de·re a kyah·ve* to lock

chiudersi* *kyoo·der·see* vr shut; la porta si chiuse *la por·ta see kyoo·say* the door closed; a che ora si chiudono i negozi? *a kay oh·ra see kyoo·do·no ee ne·go·tsee* when do the shops close?

chiunque *kee·oon·kwe* pron whoever; anybody

chiusa *kyoo·sa* f lock (*in canal*)

chiuso(a) *kyoo·so(a)* adj shut; off (*tap, light etc*)

ci *chee* pron us; to us; ourselves; one another; ci sono *chee soh·no* there are; ci è andato *chee e an·dah·to* he went there

cialda *chal·da* f waffle

ciao *chow* excl hello; goodbye

ciascuno(a) *cha·skoo·no(a)* adj, pron each

cibo *chee·boh* m food; i cibi naturali *chee·bee na·too·rah·lee* health foods

cicatrice *chee·ka·tree·che* f scar

ciclismo *chee·klee·zmoh* m cycling; fare* del ciclismo *fah·ray del chee·klee·zmoh* to go cycling

ciclista *chee·klee·sta* m/f cyclist

ciclomotore *chee·klo·mo·toh·ray* m moped

cicoria *chee·ko·rya* f endive; chicory

cieco(a) *che·ko(a)* adj blind

cielo *che·loh* m sky

cifra *chee·fra* f figure (*number*); la cifra tonda *chee·fra tohn·da* round figure/number

ciglio *cheel·yoh* m —a eyelash

cigno *cheen·yoh* m swan

ciliegia *chee·lee·ay·jah* f cherry

ciliegio *chee·lee·ay·joh* m cherry (*tree*)

cilindro *chee·leen·droh* m cylinder

cima *chee·ma* f peak (*of mountain*); top (*of mountain, ladder*)

cimice *chee·mee·che* f bug (*insect*)

cimitero *chee·mee·te·roh* m cemetery

Cina *chee·na* f China

cincin *cheen·cheen* excl cheers!

cinema *chee·ne·ma* m — cinema

cinepresa *chee·ne·pray·sa* f movie camera

cinese *chee·nay·say* adj Chinese □ m il cinese *chee·nay·say* Chinese

cinghia *cheen·gya* f strap; la cinghia della ventola *cheen·gya del·la ven·to·la* fanbelt

cinquanta *cheen·kwan·ta* num fifty

cinque *cheen·kwe* num five

cintura *cheen·too·ra* f belt (*for waist*); la cintura di sicurezza *cheen·too·ra dee see·koo·rayts·tsa* seat belt; safety belt; la cintura di salvataggio *cheen·too·ra dee sal·va·taj·joh* lifebelt

cinturato(a) *cheen·too·rah·to(a)* adj radial ply

ciò *cho* pron this; that; ciò che *cho ke* what

cioccolata *chok·ko·lah·ta* f chocolate

cioccolato *chok·ko·lah·toh* m chocolate; il cioccolato scuro *chok·ko·lah·toh skoo·ro* plain chocolate

cioè *cho·e* adv that is (to say)...

ciottolo *chot·to·loh* m pebble

cipolla *chee·pohl·la* f onion

cipollina *chee·pol·lee·na* f spring onion

cipria *chee·prya* f powder (*cosmetic*)

Cipro *chee·proh* m Cyprus

circa *cheer·ka* adv, prep about

circo *cheer·koh* m circus

circolare *cheer·ko·lah·ray* vi move (*traffic*)

circolo *cheer·ko·loh* m circle; il circolo

della gioventú *cheer·ko·loh del·la jo·ven·too* youth club; **il circolo ricreativo** *cheer·ko·loh ree·kre·a·tee·vo* leisure center

circondare *cheer·kon·dah·ray* vt surround

circonvallazione *cheer·kon·val·la·tsyoh·nay* f beltway; bypass

circoscrizione *cheer·ko·skree·tsyoh·ne* f district (administrative); precinct

circostanze *cheer·ko·stan·tsay* fpl circumstances

circuito *cheer·koo·ee·toh* m circuit (electric)

citare *chee·tah·ray* vt quote (passage); sue

citazione *chee·ta·tsyoh·ne* f quotation (passage); summons

citofono *chee·to·foh·noh* m intercom

città *cheet·ta* f — town; city; **andare* in città** *an·dah·ray een cheet·ta* to go to town

civilizzazione *chee·vee·leed·za·tsee·oh·nay* f civilization

clacson *klak·son* m — horn (of car)

classe *klas·say* f grade; class; **la classe alta** *klas·say al·ta* the upper class; **la classe turistica** *klas·say too·ree·stee·ka* tourist class

classico(a) *klas·see·koh(a)* adj classical

clausola *klow·zo·la* f clause (in contract)

cliente *klee·en·tay* m/f customer; guest (at hotel); client

clima *klee·ma* m climate

clinica *klee·nee·ka* f clinic

club *kloob* m — club (society); **il club di golf** *kloob dee golf* golf club

cocco *kok·koh* m coconut

coccodrillo *kok·koh·dreel·loh* m crocodile

cocktail *kok·tail* m cocktail (drink)

cocomero *ko·koh·me·roh* m watermelon

coda *koh·da* f tail; line; train (of dress); **fare* la coda** *fah·ray la koh·da* to stand in line

codeina *ko·de·ee·na* f codeine

codice *ko·dee·che* m code; **il codice postale** *ko·dee·che po·stah·le* postcode; zip code; **il codice stradale** *ko·dee·che stra·dah·le* Highway Code

cofano *ko·fa·noh* m hood (of car)

cogliere* *kol·ye·re* vt pick (flower)

cognac *kon·yak* m cognac

cognata *kon·yah·ta* f sister-in-law

cognato *kon·yah·toh* m brother-in-law

cognome *kon·yoh·me* m surname; **il cognome da nubile** *kon·yoh·me da noo·bee·lay* maiden name

coincidenza *ko·een·chee·den·tsa* f connection (train etc); coincidence; **questo treno fa coincidenza con quelle delle 16.45** *kway·stoh tre·noh fa ko·een·chee·den·tsa kohn kwayl·lay del·lay 16.45* this train connects with the 16:45

coincidere* *koh·een·chee·de·ray* vi coincide

colapasta *koh·la·pa·sta* m — colander

colare *ko·lah·ray* vt strain (tea etc)

colazione *ko·la·tsyoh·ne* f breakfast

colesterina *koh·lay·stay·ree·na* f cholesterol

colica *ko·lee·ka* f colic

colino *ko·lee·noh* m strainer; **il colino da tè** *ko·lee·noh da te* tea strainer

colla *kol·la* f glue; paste

collaborare *kol·la·bo·rah·ray* vi collaborate

collana *kol·lah·na* f necklace

collant *ko·loñ* m tights; panty hose

collare *kol·lah·ray* m collar (for dog)

collaudare *kol·low·dah·ray* vt test (product)

collega *kol·le·ga* m/f colleague

collegio *kol·le·joh* m college

collera *kol·le·ra* f anger; **andare* in collera** *an·dah·ray een kol·le·ra* to lose one's temper

colletto *kol·layt·toh* m collar

collezionare *kol·le·tsyo·nah·ray* vt collect (stamps etc)

collezione *kol·le·tsyoh·ne* f collection

collina *kol·lee·na* f hill

collinoso(a) *kol·lee·noh·so(a)* adj hilly

collo *kol·loh* m neck; **il collo alto** *kol·loh al·to* polo neck; **il collo a V** *kol·loh a vee* V-neck

collocare *kol·lo·kah·ray* vt place

colloquio *kol·lo·kwee·oh* m interview (for job)

colmo *kol·mo* adj full up

colomba *ko·lohm·ba* f dove

colonia *ko·lo·nee·a* f colony; holiday camp

colonna *ko·lohn·na* f column; **la colonna sonora** *ko·lohn·na so·no·ra* sound track; **la colonna dello sterzo** *ko·lohn·na del·lo ster·tsoh* steering column

colore *ko·loh·ray* m color; color turchese *ko·lohr toor·kay·se* turquoise

colpa *kohl·pa* f fault (blame); **di chi è la colpa?** *dee kee e la kohl·pa* whose fault is it?; **non è colpa mia** *nohn e kohl·pa mee·a* it's not my fault

colpevole *kol·pay·vo·lay* adj guilty; **essere* colpevole** *es·se·re kol·pay·vo·lay* to be to blame

colpevolezza *kol·pay·vo·layts·tsa* f guilt

colpire *kol·pee·re* vt hit; beat; strike; knock

colpo *kohl·poh* m knock; blow; hit; shot (from gun); stroke; bang (of gun etc); thump (noise); **il colpo di stato** *kohl·poh dee stah·toh* coup d'état

coltello *kol·tel·loh* m knife

coltivare *kol·tee·vah·ray* vt grow (plants); cultivate

coma *ko·ma* m coma

comandante *ko·man·dan·tay* m captain

comandi *ko·man·dee* mpl controls

combattimento *kom·bat·tee·mayn·toh* m fight

combustibile *kom·boo·stee·bee·le* m fuel

come *koh·me* adv, conj like; as; how; come? *koh·me* pardon?; **com'è?** *kohm·e* what's it like?; **come è andato?** *koh·me e an·dah·toh* how did it go?; **come va?** *koh·me va* how are you getting on?; **come si chiama?** *koh·me see kyah·ma* what's it called?; **come si dice "dog" in italiano?** *koh·me see dee·che dog een ee·ta·lyah·no* what's the Italian for "dog"?; **faccia come le dico io** *fach·cha koh·me le dee·ko ee·o* do as I say; **come se** *koh·me say* as if, as though

comico *ko·mee·koh* m comedian

cominciare *ko·meen·chah·ray* vt/i start; begin

comitato *ko·mee·tah·toh* m committee

commedia *kom·me·dya* f comedy; play

commento *kom·mayn·toh* m comment

commerciale *kom·mer·chah·lay* adj commercial

commercializzato(a) *kom·mer·cha·leedz·dzah·to(a)* adj commercialized

commerciante *kom·mayr·chan·te* m/f dealer; trader

commerciare in *kom·mayr·chah·ray een* vi deal in

commercio *kom·mer·choh* m commerce; trade

commesso(a) *kom·mays·so(a)* m/f sales assistant; clerk (*in store*); **il commesso viaggiatore** *kom·mays·so vyaj·ja·toh·re* salesman (*rep*)

commettere* *kom·mayt·te·ray* vt commit (*crime*)

commissariato *kom·mees·sa·ryah·toh* m police station

commissione *kom·mees·syoh·ne* f errand; commission; **fare* una commissione** *fah·ray oo·na kom·mees·syoh·ne* to run an errand

commosso(a) *kom·mos·so(a)* adj excited

comodità *ko·mo·dee·ta* fpl amenities

comodo(a) *ko·mo·doh(a)* adj comfortable

compagnia *kom·pan·yee·a* f company; **la compagnia aerea** *kom·pan·yee·a a·e·re·a* airline; **la compagnia di navigazione** *kom·pan·yee·a dee na·vee·ga·tsyoh·ne* shipping company

compartecipazione agli utili *kom·par·te·chee·pa·tsyoh·ne al·yee oo·tee·lee* f profit-sharing

compassione *kom·pas·syoh·ne* f pity; sympathy

compensato *kom·pen·sah·toh* m plywood

competente *kom·pe·ten·tay* adj competent

competizione *kom·pe·tee·tsyoh·nay* f competition

compiti *kohm·pee·tee* mpl homework

compito *kohm·pee·toh* m job; duty; task

compleanno *kom·ple·an·noh* m birthday

complesso pop *kom·ples·soh pop* m pop group

completamente *kom·ple·ta·mayn·tay* adv completely

completare *kom·ple·tah·ray* vt complete

completo *kom·ple·toh* m suit; outfit; two-piece □ adj **completo(a)** *kom·ple·toh(a)* complete; full up (*bus etc*); **al completo** *al kom·ple·toh* full; no vacancies

complicato(a) *kom·plee·kah·toh(a)* adj complex; elaborate; complicated

complimento *kom·plee·mayn·toh* m compliment; **complimenti!** *kom·plee·mayn·tee* congratulations!

comporre* *kom·pohr·re* vt dial (*number*)

comportamento *kom·por·ta·mayn·toh* m behavior

comportarsi *kom·por·tar·see* vr behave; act; **comportati bene!** *kom·por·ta·tee be·ne* behave yourself!

compositore *kom·po·zee·toh·ray* m composer

comprare *kom·prah·ray* vt buy; purchase; **comprare qualcosa per corrispondenza** *kom·prah·ray kwal·ko·sa payr kor·ree·spon·den·tsa* to buy something by mail order

compratore *kom·pra·toh·re* m buyer

compratrice *kom·pra·tree·che* f buyer

comprensione *kom·pren·syoh·nay* f understanding

comprensivo(a) *kom·pren·see·vo(a)* adj understanding

compreso(a) *kom·pray·so(a)* adj including; **servizio compreso** *ser·vee·tsyoh kom·pray·so* inclusive of tip; **... non compreso(a)** *nohn kom·pray·so(a)* exclusive of...

comproprietà *kom·pro·pree·e·ta* f joint ownership

computer *kom·pyoo·ta* m — computer

comune *ko·moo·nay* adj common

comunicare *ko·moo·nee·kah·ray* vi communicate

comunicazione *ko·moo·nee·ka·tsyoh·ne* f communication; **la comunicazione telefonica** *ko·moo·nee·ka·tsyoh·ne te·le·fo·nee·ka* telephone call; **non sono riuscito ad ottenere la comunicazione** *nohn soh·no ree·oo·shee·to ad ot·te·nay·re la ko·moo·nee·ka·tsyoh·ne* I couldn't get through (*on phone*)

comunista *ko·moo·nee·sta* m/f Communist □ adj Communist

comunque *ko·moon·kwe* adv in any case; nevertheless □ conj however

con *kohn* prep with

concernere *kon·cher·ne·re* vt concern

concerto *kon·cher·toh* m concert; **il concerto pop** *kon·cher·toh pop* pop concert

concessionario *kon·ches·syoh·nah·ryoh* m agent; dealer

conchiglia *kon·keel·ya* f shell

conciliatore *kon·chee·lya·toh·re* m trouble-shooter (*political*)

concorrente *kon·kor·ren·tay* adj rival □ m/f il/la **concorrente** *kon·kor·ren·tay* competitor; contestant

concorrenza *kon·kor·ren·tsa* f competition

concorso *kon·kohr·soh* m contest (*competition*)

condannare *kon·dan·nah·ray* vt sentence; condemn

condimenti *kon·dee·mayn·tee* mpl condiments

condimento *kon·dee·mayn·toh* m dressing; seasoning; **il condimento per l'insalata** *kon·dee·mayn·toh payr leen·sa·lah·ta* salad dressing

condizionamento dell'aria *kon·dee·tsyoh·na·mayn·toh del·lah·rya* m air-conditioning

condizione *kon·dee·tsyoh·nay* f condition; proviso; **a condizione che... a** *kon·dee·tsyoh·nay kay* on condition that...

condizioni *kon·dee·tsyoh·nee* fpl terms (*of contract*)

conducente *kon·doo·chen·te* m driver (*of taxi, bus*)

condurre* *kon·door·re* vt/i lead

conduttori elettrici *kon·doot·toh·ree e·let·tree·chee* mpl jumper cables

confarsi* a *kon·far·see a* vr suit; agree with

conferenza *kon·fe·ren·tsa* f lecture; conference

confermare *kon·fer·mah·ray* vt confirm

confessare *kon·fes·sah·ray* vt confess

confessarsi *kon·fes·sahr·see* vr confess

confessione *kon·fes·syoh·nay* f confession

confezionato(a) *kon·fe·tsyoh·nah·to(a)* adj ready-made (*clothes*)

confidenza *kon·fee·den·tsa* f confidence

confidenziale *kon·fee·den·tsyah·lay* adj confidential; private

confine *kon·fee·ne* m boundary; border

conflitto *kon·fleet·toh* m dispute (*industrial*)

confondere* *kon·fohn·de·ray* vt mix up; confuse; confondere* una cosa con un'altra *kon·fohn·de·ray oo·na ko·sa kohn oo·nal·tra* to confuse one thing with another

conforto *kon·for·toh* m comfort

confrontare *kon·fron·tah·ray* vt compare

confuso(a) *kon·foo·zoh(a)* adj confused

congedo *kon·je·doh* m leave (*holiday*); in congedo *een kon·je·doh* on leave

congelare *kon·je·lah·ray* vt freeze (*food*)

congelato(a) *kon·je·lah·to(a)* adj frozen (*food*)

congelatore *kon·je·la·toh·re* m deep-freeze; freezer

congetturare *kon·jet·too·rah·ray* vi guess

congratularsi con *kon·gra·too·lahr·see kohn* vr congratulate; congratularsi con qualcuno per qualcosa *kon·gra·too·lahr·see kohn kwal·koo·noh payr kwal·ko·sa* to congratulate someone on something

coniglio *ko·neel·yoh* m rabbit

connazionale *kon·na·tsyoh·nah·le* m/f fellow countryman/woman

cono *ko·noh* m cone

conoscenza *ko·no·shen·tsa* f acquaintance; knowledge; fare* la conoscenza di *fah·ray la ko·no·shen·tsa dee* to meet (*make acquaintance of*)

conoscere* *ko·nóh·she·re* vt know; conoscere* bene qualcosa *ko·nóh·she·re be·ne kwal·ko·sa* to be familiar with something

conoscersi* *ko·nóh·sher·see* vr meet

conoscitore *ko·no·shee·toh·ray* m connoisseur

consegna *kon·sayn·ya* f delivery; consignment

consegnare *kon·sen·yah·ray* vt deliver (*goods*)

conseguenza *kon·se·gwen·tsa* f consequence (*result*)

conservarsi *kon·ser·var·see* vr keep

conservatore *kon·sayr·va·toh·ray* adj conservative

conservatorio *kon·ser·va·to·ryoh* m academy of music

conservatrice *kon·sayr·va·tree·chay* adj conservative

considerare *kon·see·de·rah·ray* vt consider

consigliare *kon·seel·yah·ray* vt advise; consigliare a qualcuno di fare qualcosa *kon·seel·yah·ray a kwal·koo·no dee fah·ray kwal·ko·sa* to advise someone to do something

consiglio *kon·seel·yoh* m advice; il consiglio comunale *kon·seel·yoh ko·moo·nah·lay* corporation (*of town*); council; il consiglio d'amministrazione *kon·seel·yoh dam·mee·nee·stra·tsyoh·ne* board (*of directors*)

consistere* in *kon·see·ste·ray een* vi consist of

consolato *kon·so·lah·toh* m consulate

console *kon·so·lay* m consul

consommé *kon·som·may* m consommé

consulente *kon·soo·len·tay* m consultant

consultare *kon·sool·tah·ray* vt consult; refer to

consumatore *kon·soo·ma·toh·ray* m consumer

contachilometri *kon·ta·kee·lo·me·tree* m odometer

contagioso(a) *kon·ta·joh·soh(a)* adj infectious; contagious

container *kon·tay·ner* m container (*for shipping etc*)

contante *kon·tan·te* m cash; pagare qualcosa in contanti *pa·gah·ray kwal·ko·sa een kon·tan·tee* to pay cash for something

contare *kon·tah·ray* vt/i count; contare su *kon·tah·ray soo* to rely on (*person*); contare fino a 10 *kon·tah·ray fee·no a 10* to count up to 10

contatore *kon·ta·toh·ray* m meter

contattare *kon·tat·tah·ray* vt reach (*contact*)

contatto *kon·tat·toh* m contact; mettersi* in contatto con *mayt·ter·see een kon·tat·toh kohn* to contact

contea *kon·te·a* f county

contemporaneo(a) *kon·tem·po·rah·ne·oh(a)* adj contemporary

contenere* *kon·te·nay·re* vt hold; contain

contento(a) *kon·tayn·to(a)* adj happy; pleased; content(ed)

contenuto *kon·te·noo·toh* m contents

contestare *kon·te·stah·ray* vt dispute

continentale *kon·tee·nen·tah·lay* adj continental

continente *kon·tee·nen·tay* m mainland; continent

continuamente *kon·tee·noo·a·men·tay* adv continuously

continuare *kon·tee·noo·ah·ray* vt/i continue; continuare a fare *kon·tee·noo·ah·ray a fah·ray* to continue to do

continuo(a) *kon·tee·nwoh(a)* adj continuous; continual

conto *kohn·toh* m check; bill; account; il conto per favore *eel kohn·toh payr fa·voh·ray* can I have the check please?; il conto deposito *kohn·toh de·po·zee·toh* savings account; il conto corrente *kohn·toh kor·ren·tay* checking account; il conto bancario *kohn·toh ban·kah·ryo* bank account; per conto di *payr kohn·toh dee* on behalf of

contrabbandare *kon·trab·ban·dah·ray* vt smuggle

contrabbando *kon·trab·ban·doh* m contraband

contrario *kon·trah·ryoh* m opposite; al contrario *al kon·trah·ryoh* on the contrary

contrattazione *kon·trat·ta·tsyoh·ne* f bargaining (*negotiation*)

contratto *kon·trat·toh* m contract

contravvenzione *kon·trav·ven·tsyoh·ne* f fine

contribuire *kon·tree·boo·ee·ray* vi contribute

contro *kohn·tro* prep against; versus

controllare *kon·trol·lah·ray* vt check; control

controllo *kon·trol·loh* m check; control; il controllo improvviso *kon·trol·loh eem·prov·vee·zo* spot check

contusione *kon·too·zyoh·ne* f bruise

convalescenza *kon·va·le·shen·tsa* f convalescence

conveniente *kon·ve·nyen·te* adj convenient

convenire *kon·ve·nee·re* vi be suitable; Le conviene giovedì? *le kon·vye·ne jo·ve·dee* does Thursday suit you?

convento *kon·ven·toh m* monastery; convent

conversazione *kon·ver·sa·tsyoh·ne f* talk; conversation

convincere* *kon·veen·che·ray vt* convince

cooperativa *koh·o·pay·ra·tee·va f* cooperative

coperchio *ko·per·kyoh m* cover; lid

coperta *ko·per·ta f* cover; blanket; la coperta elettrica *ko·per·ta e·let·tree·ka* electric blanket

coperte *ko·per·te fpl* bedclothes

copertina *ko·payr·tee·na f* cover (*of book*)

coperto *ko·per·toh m* place setting; al coperto *al ko·per·toh* indoor (*games*)

copia *ko·pya f* copy; print (*photographic*); la copia carbone *ko·pya kar·boh·nay* carbon copy

copiare *ko·pyah·ray vt* copy

coppa *kop·pa f* cup (*trophy*)

coppia *kop·pya f* pair (*of people*); couple

coprire* *ko·pree·ray vt* cover

copyright *ko·pee·rite m* copyright

coraggio *ko·raj·joh m* nerve; courage

coraggioso(a) *ko·raj·joh·so(a) adj* brave

corallo *ko·ral·loh m* coral

corda *kor·da f* cord (*twine*); rope; string

cordiale *kor·dyah·lay m* cordial

cordialmente *kor·dyal·mayn·te adv* yours sincerely

cornamusa *kor·na·moo·za f* (bag)pipes

cornetto *kor·nayt·toh m* cornet (*of ice cream*)

cornice *kor·nee·che f* frame (*of picture*)

corno *kor·noh m* horn

coro *koh·roh m* choir

corona *ko·roh·na f* crown

corpo *kor·poh m* body

correggere* *kor·rej·je·ray vt* correct

corrente *kor·ren·te f* power (*electricity*); current; la corrente d'aria *kor·ren·te dah·ree·a* draft (*wind*)

correntemente *kor·ren·te·mayn·te adv* fluently

correre* *kohr·re·re vi* run (*person, animal*); correre* dietro a qualcuno *kohr·re·re dye·tro a kwal·koo·no* run after someone

correttamente *kor·ret·ta·mayn·te adv* properly

corretto(a) *kor·rayt·to(a) adj* right; correct; proper

correzione *kor·re·tsyoh·nay f* correction

corrida *kor·ree·da f* bullfight

corridoio *kor·ree·doh·yoh m* corridor

corrimano *kor·ree·mah·noh m* handrail (*on stairs*); rail

corrispondente *kor·ree·spon·den·te m/f* correspondent; pen pal

corrispondenza *kor·ree·spon·den·tsa f* correspondence

corrispondere* *kor·ree·spohn·de·re vi* correspond

corrodere* *kor·roh·de·ray vt* corrode

corrompere* *kor·rohm·pe·re vt* corrupt; bribe

corrotto(a) *kor·ro·toh(a) adj* corrupt

corruzione *kor·roo·tsee·oh·nay f* corruption

corsa *kohr·sa f* race (*sport*); le corse ippiche *kohr·se eep·pee·ke* horse-racing

corsetto *kor·sayt·toh m* girdle; corset

corsia *kor·see·a f* lane; ward (*in hospital*); la corsia di emergenza *kor·see·a*

dee e·mer·jen·tsa* berm; la corsia di sorpasso *la kor·see·a dee sor·pas·soh* the outside lane (*in road*)

Corsica *kor·see·ka f* Corsica

corso *kohr·soh m* course; il corso intensivo *kohr·soh een·ten·see·voh* crash course; il corso per corrispondenza *kohr·soh payr kor·ree·spon·den·tsa* correspondence course

corso del cambio *kohr·soh del kam·byoh m* exchange rate

corteccia *kor·taych·cha f* bark (*of tree*)

corteo *kor·te·oh m* parade

cortile *kor·tee·lay m* courtyard; yard; playground

corto(a) *kohr·to(a) adj* short; essere* a corto di qualcosa *es·se·re a kohr·to dee kwal·ko·sa* to be short of something

cosa *ko·sa f* thing; cosa vuole? *ko·sa vwo·le* what do you want?

coscia *ko·sha f* thigh; drumstick (*of chicken*); la coscia di pollo *ko·sha dee pohl·loh* chicken leg

coscienza *ko·shen·tsa f* conscience

coscienzioso(a) *ko·shen·tsyoh·zo(a) adj* conscientious; thorough (*work*)

cosciotto *ko·shot·toh m* leg; il cosciotto d'agnello *ko·shot·toh dan·yel·loh* leg of lamb

così *ko·see adv* so; thus (*in this way*); così contento(a) che... *ko·see kon·ten·to(a) ke* so pleased that...; e così siamo partiti *e ko·see syah·mo par·tee·tee* and so we left; così grande come *ko·see gran·de koh·me* as big as

cosmetici *koz·me·tee·chee mpl* cosmetics

cosmopolita *koz·mo·po·lee·ta adj* cosmopolitan

cospargere* di *ko·spar·je·re dee vt* sprinkle with

costa *ko·sta f* coast

Costa Azzurra *ko·sta adz·dzoor·ra f* Riviera

costare *ko·stah·ray vt* cost; costare il doppio *ko·stah·ray eel dop·pyoh* to cost double; quanto costa? *kwan·to ko·sta* how much is it?

costo *ko·stoh m* cost; il costo della vita *ko·stoh del·la vee·ta* cost of living; il costo di esercizio *ko·stoh dee e·zayr·chee·tsyoh* running costs

costola *ko·sto·la f* rib

costoso(a) *ko·stoh·so(a) adj* expensive; poco costoso(a) *po·ko ko·stoh·so(a)* inexpensive

costringere* *ko·streen·je·re vt* force (*compel*)

costruire* *ko·stroo·ee·re vt* build; construct

costruzione *ko·stroo·tsyoh·ne f* construction; la costruzione navale *ko·stroo·tsyoh·ne na·vah·le* shipbuilding

costume *ko·stoo·may m* custom; fancy dress; costume; il costume da bagno *ko·stoo·may da ban·yoh* swimsuit; swimming trunks; il costume nazionale *ko·stoo·may na·tsyoh·nah·lay* national dress

costura *ko·stoo·ra f* seam

cotoletta *ko·to·layt·ta f* cutlet

cotone *ko·toh·nay m* cotton (*fabric*); il cotone idrofilo *ko·toh·nay ee·dro·fee·lo* absorbent cotton

cotto(a) *ko·to(a) adj* done (*cooked*); insufficientemente cotto(a) *een·soof·fee·chen·te·mayn·tay kot·to(a)* undercooked; underdone

cottura *kot·too·ra f* cooking; baking

coupé *koo·pay m* — coupé (*car*)

cozza *kots·tsa f* mussel

crampo *kram·poh m* cramp

cravatta *kra·vat·ta f* tie; necktie; la cravatta a farfalla *kra·vat·ta a far·fal·la* bow tie

crawl *krol m* crawl (*swimming*)

creare *kray·ah·ray vt* create

credenza *kre·den·tsa f* sideboard; belief (*tenet*)

credere *kray·de·re vt/i* believe; credere a *kray·de·re a* to believe in; credo di sì *kre·do dee see* I think so; I expect so

credito *kray·dee·toh m* credit; a credito *a kray·dee·toh* on credit; fare* credito a qualcuno *fah·ray kray·dee·toh a kwal·koo·noh* to give somebody credit

creditore *kray·dee·toh·ray m* creditor

creditrice *kray·dee·tree·chay f* creditor

crema *kre·ma adj* cream □ *f* la crema *kre·ma* cream (*cosmetic*); custard; la crema per il viso *kre·ma payr eel vee·zoh* face cream; la crema per le mani *kre·ma payr le mah·nee* hand cream; la crema per barba *kre·ma payr bar·ba* shaving cream

crepuscolo *kre·poo·sko·lo m* dusk

crescere* *kre·she·ray vi* grow; grow up

crescione *kre·shoh·nay m* cress

crescita *kray·shee·ta f* growth

crespo di cotone *kray·spoh dee ko·toh·ne m* seersucker

Creta *kray·ta f* Crete

cric *kreek m* — jack (*for car*)

criminale *kree·mee·nah·lay adj, m/f* criminal

crimine *kree·mee·ne m* crime

crisantemo *kree·zan·te·moh m* chrysanthemum

crisi *kree·zee f* — crisis

cristallo *kree·stal·loh m* crystal (*glass*)

cristiano(a) *kree·stee·ah·noh(a) m/f* Christian

criticare *kree·tee·kah·ray vt* criticize

croccante *krok·kan·tay adj* crisp

crocchetta *krok·kayt·ta f* croquette

croce *kroh·chay f* cross

crocevia *kroh·chay·vee·a m* — crossroads

crociera *kro·che·ra f* cruise; fare* una crociera *fah·ray oo·na kro·che·ra* to go on a cruise

croco *kroh·koh m* crocus

croissant *krwah·soñ m* croissant

crollare *krol·lah·ray vi* collapse; slump

crollo *krol·loh m* collapse; slump

cromo *kro·moh m* chrome

cronaca *kro·na·ka f* news

cronista *kro·nee·sta m/f* reporter (*press*)

cronometro *kro·no·me·troh m* stop watch

crosta *kro·sta f* crust; scab

crostacei *kros·ta·che·ee mpl* shellfish

crostino *kro·stee·noh m* crouton

croupier *kroo·pyay m* croupier

crudele *kroo·de·lay adj* cruel

crudo(a) *kroo·do(a) adj* raw (*uncooked*)

crumiro *kroo·mee·roh m* strikebreaker

cruscotto *kroos·kot·toh m* dash(board)

cubetto di ghiaccio *koo·bayt·toh dee gyach·choh m* ice cube

cubo *koo·boh m* cube

cuccetta *koo·chayt·ta f* couchette; berth; bunk

cucchiaia *kook·kee·a·ya f* tablespoon

cucchiaiata *kook·kee·a·yah·ta f* tablespoon (*measure*); spoonful

cucchiaino *kook·kya·ee·noh m* teaspoon

cucchiaio *kook·kee·a·yoh m* spoon; dessertspoon

cucina *koo·chee·na f* kitchen; cooker; stove; cuisine; cooking; la cucina a gas *koo·chee·na a gas* gas stove

cucinare *koo·chee·nah·ray vt* cook

cucire *koo·chee·re vt* sew

cucitrice *koo·chee·tree·che f* stapler

cuffia *koof·fya f* headphones; la cuffia da bagno *koof·fya da ban·yoh* bathing cap

cugino(a) *koo·jee·noh(a) m/f* cousin

cui *koo·ee pron* that, which; whose; il ragazzo con cui... *eel ra·gats·tsoh kohn koo·ee* the boy with whom...; l'uomo, il cui figlio *lwo·moh, eel koo·ee feel·yoh* the man, whose son; il giorno in cui noi... *eel johr·noh een koo·ee noy* the day when we...

culla *kool·la f* cradle

cullare *kool·lah·ray vt* rock

cultura *kool·too·ra f* culture; la cultura generale *kool·too·ra je·ne·rah·lay* general knowledge

cumulo *koo·moo·loh m* pile; il cumulo di neve *koo·moo·loh dee nay·ve* snowdrift

cunetta *koo·nayt·ta f* gutter (*in street*)

cuocere* *kwo·che·re vt/i* cook; cuocere* al forno *kwo·che·re al fohr·noh* to bake; cuocere* ai ferri *kwo·che·re ai fer·ree* to grill

cuoco(a) *kwo·koh(a) m/f* cook

cuoio *kwo·yoh m* leather; il cuoio verniciato *kwo·yoh ver·nee·chah·to* patent leather; il cuoio capelluto *kwo·yoh ka·pel·loo·to* scalp

cuore *kwo·ray m* heart; nel cuore della notte *nel kwo·ray del·la not·tay* in the middle of the night

cuori *kwo·ree mpl* hearts (*cards*)

cura *koo·ra f* care; treatment (*medical*)

curare *koo·rah·ray vt* treat; cure; look after; nurse; take care of

curato *koo·rah·toh m* vicar

curioso(a) *koo·ree·oh·soh(a) adj* curious; funny; quaint

curva *koor·va f* bend; corner; curve; prendere* la curva *pren·de·ray la koor·va* to corner; la curva a gomito *koor·va a goh·mee·toh* hairpin curve; la curva senza visibilità *koor·va sen·tsa vee·zee·bee·lee·ta* blind corner

curvare *koor·vah·ray vt/i* bend

cuscinetti *koo·shee·nayt·tee mpl* bearings (*in car*)

cuscino *koo·shee·noh m* cushion

custode *koo·sto·day m* caretaker

custodire *koo·sto·dee·ray vt* guard (*prisoner*)

D

da *da prep* from; by; since; cadere* da un muro *ka·day·re da oon moo·roh* to fall off a wall; vado dal giornalaio *va·do dal johr·na·la·yoh* I'm going to the newsdealer's; l'uomo dal cappello grigio *lwo·moh dal cap·pel·loh gree·joh* the man with the grey hat; da quando siamo arrivati *da kwan·do syah·mo ar·ree·vah·tee* since we arrived

dadi *dah·dee mpl* dice

dagli = da + gli, dai = da + i

dama *dah·ma f* checkers; partner (*dancing*)

danese *da·nay·se adj* Danish □ *m* il danese *da·nay·se* Danish

Danimarca *da·nee·mar·ka f* Denmark

danneggiare *dan·nej·jah·ray vt* spoil; damage

danni *dan·nee mpl* damages

danno *dan·noh m* damage; harm

dappertutto *dap·per·toot·to adv* everywhere

dapprima *dap·pree·ma adv* at first

dardo *dar·doh m* dart (*to throw*); il gioco dei dardi *jo·koh de·ee dar·dee* game of darts

dare* *dah·ray vt* give; dare* qualcosa a qualcuno *dah·ray kwal·koh·sa a kwal·koo·no* to give someone something; me lo dia *me lo dee·a* give it to me; glielo dia *lye·lo dee·a* give it to him/her; dare* la precedenza *dah·ray la pre·che·den·tsa* to yield (*to traffic*); dare* un passaggio a qualcuno *dah·ray oon pas·saj·joh a kwal·koo·no* to give somebody a ride; dare* una festa *dah·ray oo·na fes·ta* to give a party; questa porta dà sul giardino *kway·sta por·ta da sool jar·dee·noh* this door leads into the garden; dare* uno sguardo a *dah·ray oo·no zgwar·doh a* to glance at; dare* un esame *dah·ray oon e·zah·me* to take an exam

data *dah·ta f* date (*day*)

dati *dah·tee mpl* data

datore di lavoro *da·toh·re dee la·voh·roh m* employer

dattero *dat·te·roh m* date (*fruit*)

dattilografo(a) *dat·tee·lo·gra·fo(a) m/f* typist

dattiloscritto(a) *dat·tee·lo·skreet·to(a) adj* typewritten

dattiloscrivere* *dat·tee·lo·skree·ve·re vt* type (*letter*)

davanti *da·van·tee adv* in front; opposite; davanti a *da·van·tee a* in front of; opposite; davanti agli altri *da·van·tee al·yee al·tree* ahead of the others

dazio *da·tsyoh m* customs duty

debito *day·bee·toh m* debt; debit; un debito insolvibile *oon day·bee·toh een·sol·vee·bee·le* a bad debt; avere* dei debiti *a·vay·re de·ee day·bee·tee* to be in debt

debole *day·bo·le adj* weak; dim (*light*); faint (*sound etc*)

decaffeinizzato(a) *de·kaf·fe·ee·needz·dzah·to(a) adj* decaffeinated

decennio *de·chen·nyoh m* decade

decente *de·chen·te adj* decent

decidere* *de·chee·de·re vi* decide; decidere* di fare qualcosa *de·chee·de·re dee fah·ray kwal·ko·sa* to decide to do something

decidersi* *de·chee·der·see vr* make up one's mind; decide

decimale *de·chee·mah·le adj* decimal □ *m* il decimale *de·chee·mah·le* decimal

decimo(a) *de·chee·mo(a) adj* tenth

decisione *de·chee·zyoh·nay f* decision

deciso(a) *de·chee·zo(a) adj* determined; essere* deciso a fare qualcosa *es·se·re de·chee·zo a fah·ray kwal·ko·sa* to be determined to do something

decollare *de·kol·lah·ray vi* take off (*plane*)

decollo *de·kol·loh m* takeoff (*of plane*)

decorare *de·ko·rah·ray vt* decorate

decoratore *de·ko·ra·toh·re m* painter (*decorator*)

deficienza *de·fee·chen·tsa f* shortage

deficit *de·fee·cheet m* — deficit

deflazione *de·fla·tsyoh·ne f* deflation

deforme *de·fohr·me adj* deformed

degli = di + gli

degustare *de·goo·stah·ray vt* sample (*wine*)

dei = di + i, del = di + il

delegare *de·le·gah·ray vt* delegate

delegazione *de·le·ga·tsyoh·nay f* delegation

deliberatamente *de·lee·be·ra·ta·mayn·te adv* deliberately

delicato(a) *de·lee·kah·to(a) adj* delicate; dainty

delitto *de·leet·toh m* crime

delizioso(a) *de·lee·tsyoh·so(a) adj* delightful; delicious

deludere* *de·loo·de·re vt* disappoint

deluso(a) *de·loo·zo(a) adj* disappointed

denaro *de·nah·roh m* money

denso(a) *den·so(a) adj* thick; dense

dente *den·te m* tooth; il mal di denti *mal dee den·tee* toothache; avere* il mal di denti *a·vay·re eel mal dee den·tee* to have a toothache

dentiera *den·tye·ra f* false teeth; dentures

dentifricio *den·tee·free·choh m* toothpaste

dentista *den·tee·sta m/f* dentist

dentro *dayn·tro adv, prep* in; inside; stare*/andare* dentro *stah·ray/an·dah·ray dayn·tro* to be/go inside

deodorante *de·o·do·ran·te m* deodorant

deporre* *de·pohr·re vt* lay down; put down; deporre* il ricevitore *de·pohr·re eel ree·che·vee·toh·re* to hang up (*phone*)

depositare *de·po·zee·tah·ray vi* settle (*wine*) □ *vt* deposit; bank

deposito *de·po·zee·toh m* deposit; il deposito bagagli *de·po·zee·toh ba·gal·yee* baggage checkroom

derubare *de·roo·bah·ray vt* rob (*person*)

descrivere* *de·skree·ve·re vt* describe

descrizione *de·skree·tsyoh·ne f* description

deserto *de·zer·toh m* desert

desiderare *de·see·de·rah·ray vt* wish for; desire

desiderio *de·see·de·ryoh m* wish; desire

desideroso(a) *de·see·de·roh·so(a) adj* eager

destinare *de·stee·nah·ray vt* intend

destinazione *de·stee·na·tsyoh·ne f* destination; con destinazione per *kohn de·stee·na·tsyoh·nay payr* bound for (*ship*)

destra *de·stra f* right (*right-hand side*); a destra *a de·stra* on/to the right; girare a destra *jee·rah·ray a de·stra* to turn right

destro(a) *de·stro(a) adj* right (*not left*)

detersivo *de·ter·see·voh m* soap powder; detergent

detrarre* *de·trar·re vt* deduct

dettagliante *det·tal·yan·te m* retailer

dettagliatamente *det·tal·yah·ta·mayn·tay adv* in detail

dettagliato(a) *det·tal·yah·to(a) adj* detailed; itemized (*bill etc*)

dettaglio *det·tal·yoh m* detail

dettare *det·tah·ray vt* dictate

deviare *de·vee·ah·ray vt* reroute; divert □ *vi* swerve

deviazione *de·vee·a·tsyoh·ne f* detour; fare* una deviazione *fah·ray oo·na de·vee·a·tsyoh·ne* to make a detour

di *dee prep* of; l'acqua di rubinetto *ak·*

kwa dee roo·bee·nayt·toh water from the faucet; tre di loro tray dee loh·ro 3 of them; di pietra dee pye·tra made of stone; di giorno/notte dee johr·noh/not·tay by day/night; meglio di lui mel·yo dee loo·ee better than him; L.20000 di benzina L20000 dee ben·dzee·na L.20000 worth of gas; del pane del pah·ne some bread; dei soldi de·ee sol·dee some money

diabete dee·a·be·te m diabetes
diabetico(a) dee·a·be·tee·ko(a) m/f diabetic
diagnosi dee·an·yo·zee f diagnosis
diagonale dee·a·go·nah·le adj diagonal
diagramma dee·a·gram·ma m diagram
dialetto dee·a·let·toh m dialect
diamante dee·a·man·te m diamond
diametro dee·a·me·troh m diameter
diapositiva dee·a·po·zee·tee·va f slide (photo)
diarrea dee·ar·re·a f diarrhea
dibattito dee·bat·tee·toh m debate
dicembre dee·chem·bre m December
dichiarare dee·kya·rah·ray vt declare; state; niente da dichiarare nyen·te da dee·kya·rah·ray nothing to declare
dichiarazione dee·kya·ra·tsyoh·ne f declaration; statement
diciannove dee·chan·no·vay num nineteen
diciassette dee·chas·set·te num seventeen
diciassettesimo(a) dee·chas·set·te·zee·mo(a) adj seventeenth
diciotto dee·chot·toh num eighteen
dieci dye·chee num ten
diesel dee·zel m diesel
dieta dee·e·ta f diet (slimming); stare* a dieta stah·ray a dee·e·ta to be on a diet
dietro dye·tro adv behind □ prep behind; after
difendere* dee·fen·de·re vt defend
difesa dee·fay·sa f defense
difetto dee·fet·toh m defect; fault
difettoso(a) dee·fet·toh·so(a) adj defective; faulty; imperfect
differente deef·fe·ren·te adj different
differenza deef·fe·ren·tsa f difference
difficile deef·fee·chee·le adj difficult; hard
difficoltà deef·fee·kol·ta f — difficulty
diffondere* deef·fohn·de·re vt spread (news)
diga dee·ga f dam; dike
digitale dee·jee·tah·le adj digital
dilatare dee·la·tah·ray vt expand
dilatarsi dee·la·tar·see vr expand
dilettante dee·let·tan·te m amateur
diluire dee·loo·ee·re vt dilute
dimagrire dee·ma·gree·ray vi lose weight
dimenare dee·me·nah·ray vt wave; wag (tail)
dimensioni dee·men·syoh·nee fpl size; dimensions
dimenticare dee·men·tee·kah·ray vt forget; ho dimenticato di fare... o dee·men·tee·kah·to dee fah·ray I forgot to do...
dimettersi* dee·mayt·ter·see vr resign
diminuire dee·mee·noo·ee·re vt reduce; diminish
diminuzione dee·mee·noo·tsyoñ·ne f fall (decrease)
dimissioni dee·mees·syoh·nee fpl resignation
dimostrazione dee·mo·stra·tsyoh·ne f demonstration

dinamico(a) dee·na·mee·ko(a) adj dynamic
dinamo dee·na·mo f — dynamo
dinghy din·gee m — dinghy
dintorni deen·tohr·nee mpl surroundings
di nuovo dee nwo·vo adv again
dio dee·oh m dei god; Dio dee·oh God
dipendere* da dee·pen·de·re da vi depend on; dipende dee·pen·de it depends
dipingere* dee·peen·je·re vt/i paint
diploma dee·plo·ma m diploma
diplomatico dee·plo·ma·tee·koh m diplomat
dire* dee·re vt tell (fact, news); say; dire* qualcosa a qualcuno dee·re kwal·ko·sa a kwal·koo·no to tell someone something; dire* a qualcuno di fare qualcosa dee·re a kwal·koo·no dee fah·ray kwal·ko·sa to tell someone to do something; dire* sciocchezze dee·re shok·kayts·tse to talk nonsense; si dice che... see dee·che ke... they say that... (people in general)
direttamente dee·ret·ta·mayn·te adv straight
diretto(a) dee·ret·to(a) adj direct; il treno diretto tre·noh dee·ret·to through train
direttore dee·ret·toh·re m conductor (of orchestra); governor (of institution); manager; president (of company); director (of firm); il direttore di banca dee·ret·toh·re dee ban·ka bank manager; il direttore del personale dee·ret·toh·re del per·so·nah·le personnel manager; il direttore di marketing dee·ret·toh·re dee mahr·ke·ting marketing manager; il direttore delle vendite dee·ret·toh·re del·le vayn·dee·te sales manager; il direttore generale dee·ret·toh·re je·ne·rah·lay managing director, M.D.
direttrice dee·ret·tree·chay f manageress
direzione dee·rets·yo·nay f management; direction
dirigere dee·ree·je·ray vt manage (business); run (a business, country); direct
dirimpetto dee·reem·pet·to adv opposite
diritto dee·reet·toh m right (entitlement); right side (of cloth etc) □ adv straight □ adj diritto(a) dee·ret·to(a) straight
dirottare dee·rot·tah·ray vt hijack
dirottatore dee·rot·ta·toh·re m hijacker
disapprovare dee·zap·pro·vah·ray vt disapprove of
disarcionare dee·zar·cho·nah·ray vt throw (rider)
disarmato(a) dee·zar·mah·toh(a) adj unarmed (person)
disastro dee·za·stroh m disaster
discesa dee·shay·sa f descent; in discesa een dee·shay·sa downhill
disciplina dee·shee·plee·na f discipline
disc-jockey deesk·jok·kee m disc jockey
disco dee·sko m disk; record; il disco orario dee·sko o·rah·ryo parking disk
discorso dee·skohr·soh m speech (oration)
discoteca dee·sko·te·ka f disco(thèque)
discreto(a) dee·skray·to(a) adj discreet; fair
discriminazione dee·skree·mee·na·tsyoh·ne f discrimination
discussione dee·skoos·syoh·ne f dis-

cussion; **fuori discussione** *fwo·ree dee·skoos·syoh·ne* out of the question

discutere* *dee·skoo·te·re* vt discuss

disdire* *dees·dee·re* vt cancel

disegnare *dee·sen·yah·ray* vt draw; design

disegnatore *dee·sen·ya·toh·re* m designer; draftsman

disegno *dee·sayn·yoh* m plan; design; pattern; drawing

disfare* *dee·sfah·ray* vt unpack (*case*); undo; unwrap

disgelare *dee·zje·lah·ray* vt/i defrost; thaw; **fare* disgelare** *fah·ray dee·zje·lah·ray* to thaw (*food*)

disgusto *dee·zgoo·stoh* m disgust

disinfettante *dee·zeen·fet·tan·te* m disinfectant

disinfettare *dee·zeen·fet·tah·ray* vt disinfect

disinteressare *dee·zeen·te·res·sah·ray* vt buy out (*partner etc*)

disoccupati *dee·zok·koo·pah·tee* mpl the unemployed

disoccupato(a) *dee·zok·koo·pah·to(a)* adj unemployed

disoccupazione *dee·zok·koo·pa·tsyoh·nay* f unemployment

disonesto(a) *dee·zo·ne·sto(a)* adj dishonest

disordinato(a) *dee·zor·dee·nah·to(a)* adj untidy

disordine *dee·zohr·dee·nay* m mess; **in disordine** *een dee·zohr·dee·nay* in a muddle

dispari *dee·spa·ree* adj odd (*number*)

dispensa *dee·spen·sa* f larder

disperato(a) *dee·spe·rah·to(a)* adj desperate

disperso(a) *dee·spayr·soh(a)* adj missing (*person*)

dispetto *dee·spet·toh* m spite

dispiacere* a *dee·spya·che·re a* vi displease; **non mi dispiace il caldo** *nohn mee dee·spyah·chee eel kal·doh* I don't mind the heat; **mi dispiace** *mee dee·spyah·che* (I'm) sorry; **mi dispiace ma non posso farlo** *mee dee·spyah·che ma nohn pos·so far·lo* I'm afraid I can't do it

disponibile *dee·spo·nee·bee·le* adj available

disporre* *dee·spohr·re* vt arrange (*flowers, furniture*)

dispositivo *dees·po·see·tee·vo* m gadget

disposto(a) *dee·spoh·sto(a)* adj willing

disputa *dee·spoo·ta* f dispute

dissenso *dees·sen·soh* m disagreement

distante *dee·stan·te* adj distant

distanza *dee·stan·tsa* f distance; **a poca distanza dal mare** *a po·ka dee·stan·tsa dal mah·re* within easy reach of the sea

distilleria *dee·steel·le·ree·a* f distillery

distinguere* *dee·steen·gwe·re* vt distinguish; **non posso distinguere* tra di loro** *nohn pos·so dee·steen·gwe·re tra dee loh·ro* I can't tell the difference between them

distintivo *dee·steen·tee·voh* m badge

distinto(a) *dee·steen·to(a)* adj distinct

distorsione *dee·stor·syoh·ne* f sprain

distrarre* *dee·strar·re* vt distract

distretto postale *dee·strayt·toh po·stah·le* m postal district

distribuire *dee·stree·boo·ee·re* vt tribute; deliver (*mail*)

distributore *dee·stree·boo·toh·re* m distributor; **il distributore di benzina** *dee·stree·boo·toh·re dee ben·dzee·na*

gas pump; **il distributore automatico** *dee·stree·boo·toh·re ow·to·ma·tee·ko* slot machine; vending machine

distribuzione *dee·stree·boo·tsyoh·ne* f distribution; delivery (*of mail*)

distruggere* *dee·strooj·je·re* vt destroy

disturbare *dee·stoor·bah·ray* vt disturb; **pregasi non disturbare** *pre·ga·see nohn dee·stoor·bah·ray* do not disturb

disturbarsi *dee·stoor·bar·see* vr put oneself out; **non si disturbi per favore** *nohn see dee·stoor·bee payr fa·vor·re* please don't bother

disturbo *dee·stoor·boh* m trouble; **i disturbi allo stomaco** *dee·stoor·bee al·lo sto·ma·koh* stomach trouble

disubbidiente *dee·zoob·bee·dyen·te* adj disobedient

disubbidire *dee·zoob·bee·dee·re* vi disobey

dito *dee·toh* m —a finger; **il dito del piede** *dee·toh del pye·de* toe

ditta *deet·ta* f business; firm; company

divano *dee·va·noh* m couch; sofa; divan

diventare *dee·ven·tah·ray* vi become; **diventare professionista** *dee·ven·tah·ray pro·fes·syoh·nee·sta* to turn professional

diversi(e) *dee·ver·see(·se)* adj several

diversificare *dee·ver·see·fee·kah·ray* vt diversify

diverso(a) *dee·ver·so(a)* adj different

divertente *dee·ver·ten·te* adj funny (*amusing*)

divertire *dee·ver·tee·re* vt amuse

divertirsi *dee·ver·teer·see* vr enjoy oneself; have a good time

dividendo *dee·vee·den·doh* m dividend

dividere* *dee·vee·de·re* vt divide; share; split

**divieto di … ** *dee·vye·toh dee* no …, … prohibited

divisa *dee·vee·za* f uniform; **la divisa estera** *dee·vee·za e·ste·ra* foreign currency

divo(a) *dee·vo(a)* m/f star (*celebrity*)

divorziato(a) *dee·vor·tsyah·to(a)* adj divorced

divorzio *dee·vor·tsyoh* m divorce

dizionario *dee·tsyoh·nah·ree·oh* m dictionary

doccia *dohch·cha* f shower (*bath*); **fare* una doccia** *fah·ray oo·na dohch·cha* to have a shower

documentazione *do·koo·men·ta·tsyoh·nay* f record (*register*)

documenti *do·koo·mayn·tee* mpl papers (*passport etc*)

documento *do·koo·mayn·toh* m document

dodicesimo(a) *do·dee·che·zee·mo(a)* adj twelfth

dodici *doh·dee·chee* num twelve

dogana *do·gah·na* f customs; **esente da dogana** *e·zen·te da do·gah·na* duty-free

doganiere *do·ga·nye·ray* m customs officer

dolce *dohl·che* m dessert; cake □ adj sweet; mild

dolciumi *dol·choo·mee* mpl candy

dolere* *do·lay·re* vi hurt

dollaro *dol·la·roh* m dollar

dolore *do·loh·re* m ache; grief; pain

doloroso(a) *do·lo·roh·so(a)* adj sore; painful

domanda *do·man·da* f question; demand; application (*for job*); **fare* una domanda** *fah·ray oo·na do·man·*

da to ask a question; **fare* domanda per** *fah·ray do·man·da payr* to apply for

domandare *do·man·dah·ray vt* ask; ask for; demand

domandarsi *do·man·dar·see vr* wonder

domani *do·mah·nee adv* tomorrow

domattina *do·mat·tee·na adv* tomorrow morning

domenica *do·me·nee·ka f* Sunday

domestico(a) *do·me·stee·ko(a) adj* domestic □ *m/f* il/la domestico(a) *do·me·stee·ko(a)* servant

dominare *do·mee·nah·ray vt* dominate; control

donare *do·nah·ray vt* donate

dondolare *don·do·lah·ray vi* swing

donna *don·na f* woman; **la donna delle pulizie** *don·na del·lay poo·lee·tsee·ay* cleaner (*of house etc*); **la donna poliziotto** *don·na po·lee·tsyot·toh* policewoman; **la donna d'affari** *don·na daf·fah·ree* businesswoman

dono *doh·noh m* gift; donation

dopo *doh·po prep* after □ *adv* afterward(s); **4 anni dopo** *4 an·nee doh·po* 4 years later; **dopo che fummo partiti** *doh·po ke foom·mo par·tee·tee* after we had left

dopobarba *doh·po·bar·ba m* — aftershave (lotion)

dopodomani *doh·po·do·mah·nee adv* the day after tomorrow

doppio(a) *dop·pyo(a) adj* double

dorato(a) *do·rah·toh(a) adj* golden

dormire *dor·mee·re vi* sleep

dormitorio *dor·mee·to·ryoh m* dormitory (*room*)

dosaggio *do·zaj·joh m* dosage

dose *do·ze f* dose; **la dose eccessiva** *do·ze ech·ches·see·va* overdose

dotato(a) *do·tah·toh(a) adj* gifted

dottore *dot·toh·re m* doctor

dove *doh·ve adv* where; **di dove è?** *dee doh·ve e* where are you from?

dovere *do·vay·re m* duty (*obligation*)

dovere* *do·vay·re vt* owe □ *vi* to have to; **mi deve L.50000** *me de·ve L50000* he owes me L.50000; **deve farlo** *de·ve far·lo* she has to do it; **devo andare** *de·voh an·dah·ray* I must go; **dovrebbe vincere** *do·vreb·be veen·che·re* he ought to win; **dovremmo comprarlo** *do·vrem·mo kom·prar·lo* we should buy it

dovunque *do·voon·kwe* wherever; everywhere; **la porterò dovunque voglia** *la por·te·ro do·voon·kwe vol·yah* I'll take you anywhere you like

dozzina *dodz·dzee·na f* dozen; **4 dozzine di uova** *4 dodz·dzee·nee dee wo·va* 4 dozen eggs

dramma *dram·ma m* drama; play (*theatrical*)

drammatico(a) *dram·ma·tee·ko(a) adj* dramatic

drastico(a) *dra·stee·ko(a) adj* drastic

droga *dro·ga f* drug (*narcotic*)

drogheria *dro·ge·ree·a f* grocery shop

droghiere *dro·gye·ray m* grocer

dubbio *doob·byoh m* doubt; **senza dubbio** *sen·tsa doob·byoh* no doubt; **senza alcun dubbio** *sen·tsa al·koon doob·byoh* without (a) doubt

dubitare *doo·bee·tah·ray vi* doubt; **ne dubito** *ne doo·bee·to* I doubt it

duca *doo·ka m* duke

due *doo·e num* two; **tutte e due le ragazze** *toot·te e doo·e le ra·gats·tse* both girls; **tutti(e) e due** *toot·tee(·te) e doo·e* both

dumping *dum·peeng m* dumping (*of goods*)

duna *doo·na f* dune

dunque *doon·kwe conj* so

durante *doo·ran·te prep* during; **durante tutto l'anno** *doo·ran·te toot·to lan·noh* (all) through the year

durare *doo·rah·ray vi* last; **quanto dura il programma?** *kwan·to doo·ra eel pro·gram·ma* how long is the program?

duro(a) *doo·ro(a) adj* hard; tough (*meat etc*)

E

e *ay conj* and

ebreo *e·bre·oh m* Jew □ *adj* ebreo(a) *e·bre·o(a)* Jewish

ecc *ech·che·te·ra abbrev* etc

eccedente *ech·che·den·te adj* excess

eccedenza *ech·che·den·tsa f* excess; surplus; **in eccedenza** *een ech·che·den·tsa* overweight (*baggage*)

eccellente *ech·chel·len·te adj* excellent

eccentrico(a) *ech·chen·tree·ko(a) adj* eccentric

eccesso *ech·ches·soh m* excess; **l'eccesso di velocità** *ech·ches·soh dee ve·lo·chee·ta* speeding (*in car*)

eccezionale *ech·che·tsyoh·nah·le adj* exceptional

eccezione *ech·che·tsyoh·ne f* exception

eccitazione *ech·chee·ta·tsyoh·ne f* excitement

ecco *ek·ko adv* here is/are; **ecco mia sorella** *ek·ko mee·a so·rel·la* here's my sister; **eccola che viene** *ek·ko·la ke vye·ne* here she comes; **eccolo** *ek·ko·lo* here/there he/it is; **eccola** *ek·ko·la* here/there she/it is; **eccoli(gli)** *ek·ko·lee(·le)* here/there they are

eco *e·koh m/f* echo

economia *e·ko·no·mee·a f* economy; economics

economico(a) *e·ko·no·mee·ko(a) adj* economic; economical (*use, method*)

economista *e·ko·no·mee·sta m/f* economist

eczema *ek·ze·ma m* eczema

edicola *e·dee·ko·la f* newsstand

edificio *e·dee·fee·choh m* building

editore *e·dee·toh·re m* publisher

editrice *e·dee·tree·che f* publisher

edizione *e·dee·tsyoh·ne f* edition

educato(a) *e·doo·kah·toh(a) adj* well-mannered

effetto *ef·fet·toh m* effect; **avere* effetto** *a·vay·re ef·fet·toh* to take effect; **gli effetti personali** *ef·fet·tee per·so·nah·lee* belongings

efficace *ef·fee·kah·che adj* effective (*remedy etc*)

efficiente *ef·fee·chen·te adj* efficient

Egitto *e·jeet·toh m* Egypt

egiziano(a) *e·jee·tsyah·no(a) adj* Egyptian

egli *ayl·yee pron* he; **egli stesso** *ayl·yee stays·so* (he) himself

egoistico(a) *e·go·ee·stee·ko(a) adj* selfish

egregio(a) *e·gre·jo(a) adj* distinguished; **Egregio Signor Smith** *e·gre·joh seen·yohr smith* Dear Mr. Smith

elaborazione dei dati *e·la·bo·ra·tsyoh·nay de·ee dah·tee f* data processing

elastico(a) *e·la·stee·koh m* elastic; elastic band

elefante *e·le·fan·te m* elephant

elegante *e·le·gan·te adj* stylish; elegant; smart

eleggere* *e·lej·je·re vt* elect

elementare *e·le·men·tah·ray adj* junior (*class, pupil*)

elemento *e·le·mayn·toh m* unit (*of machinery, furniture*); element

elencare *e·len·kah·ray vt* list

elenco *e·len·koh m* list; **l'elenco di indirizzi** *e·len·koh dee een·dee·ree·tsee* mailing list; **l'elenco telefonico** *e·len·koh te·le·fo·nee·ko* telephone directory

elettricista *e·let·tree·chee·sta m* electrician

elettricità *e·let·tree·chee·ta f* electricity

elettrico(a) *e·let·tree·ko(a) adj* electric(al)

elettronica *e·let·tro·nee·ka f* electronics

elettronico(a) *e·let·tro·nee·ko(a) adj* electronic

elevare *e·le·vah·ray vt* raise

elevatore *e·le·va·toh·ray m* ramp (*in garage*)

elezione *e·le·tsyoh·ne f* election; **le elezioni politiche** *e·le·tsyoh·nee po·lee·tee·kay* general election

elicottero *e·lee·kot·te·roh m* helicopter

eliminato(a) *e·lee·mee·nah·to(a) adj* out (*team, player*)

ella *ayl·la pron* she; you

embargo *em·bar·goh m* embargo

emergenza *e·mer·jen·tsa f* emergency

emicrania *e·mee·krah·nee·a f* migraine

emigrare *e·mee·grah·ray vi* emigrate

emissione *e·mees·syoh·ne f* issue

emorragia nasale *e·mor·ra·jee·a na·sah·lay f* nosebleed

emorroidi *e·mor·roy·dee fpl* hemorrhoids

emozionante *e·mo·tsyoh·nan·te adj* exciting

emozione *e·mo·tsyoh·ne f* emotion

enciclopedia *en·chee·klo·pe·dee·a f* encyclop(a)edia

energia *e·ner·jee·a f* energy

energico(a) *e·ner·jee·ko(a) adj* energetic

enfasi *en·fa·zee f* stress; emphasis; **l'enfasi su qualcosa** *len·fa·zee soo kwal·ko·sa* emphasis on something

enorme *e·nor·me adj* enormous

entrambi(e) *en·tram·bee(·be) adj, pron* both

entrare *en·trah·ray vi* come in; enter; go in; **entrare in** *en·trah·ray een* to enter (*room*)

entrata *en·trah·ta f* entrance; admission

entrate *en·trah·te fpl* takings; income

entusiasmo *en·too·zee·a·zmoh m* enthusiasm

entusiasta *en·too·zee·a·sta adj* enthusiastic

epidemia *e·pee·de·mee·a f* epidemic

epilessia *e·pee·les·see·a f* epilepsy

epoca *e·po·ka f* age (*era*)

eppure *ep·poo·re conj* and yet

equatore *e·kwa·toh·re m* equator

equilibrio *e·kwe·lee·bree·oh m* balance; **perdere* l'equilibrio** *per·de·re le·kwe·lee·bree·oh* to lose one's balance; **l'equilibrio politico** *e·kwe·lee·bree·oh po·lee·tee·ko* balance of power

equipaggiamento *e·kwe·paj·ja·mayn·toh m* equipment; gear

equipaggio *e·kwe·paj·joh m* crew (*of ship, plane*)

equitazione *e·kwe·ta·tsyoh·ne f* horseback riding; **fare* dell'equitazione** *fah·ray del·le·kwe·ta·tsyoh·ne* to go horseback riding

equivalente *e·kwee·va·len·te adj* equivalent

erba *er·ba f* grass

erbaccia *er·bach·cha f* weed

erbe *er·be fpl* herbs

ereditare *e·re·dee·tah·ray vt* inherit

ermetico(a) *er·me·tee·ko(a) adj* airtight

ernia *er·nee·a f* hernia; **l'ernia al disco** *er·nee·a al dee·sko* slipped disk

erotico(a) *e·ro·tee·ko(a) adj* erotic

erpese zoster *er·pe·te zo·ster m* shingles (*illness*)

errare *er·rah·ray vi* wander

errore *er·roh·re m* error; **l'errore di stampa** *er·roh·re dee stam·pa* misprint

eruzione *e·roo·tsyoh·nay f* rash

esagerare *e·za·je·rah·ray vt* exaggerate

esagerazione *e·za·je·ra·tsyoh·ne f* exaggeration

esame *e·zah·me m* examination; exam; **l'esame di guida** *e·zah·me dee gwee·da* test (*driving test*)

esaminare *e·za·mee·nah·ray vt* examine; test (*sight, hearing*)

esatto(a) *e·zat·toh(a) adj* exact (*time etc*); accurate

esaurimento *e·zow·ree·mayn·toh m* exhaustion; **l'esaurimento nervoso** *e·zow·ree·mayn·toh ner·voh·so* nervous breakdown

esaurito(a) *e·zow·ree·to(a) adj* exhausted; out of print; sold out

esausto(a) *e·zow·sto(a) adj* exhausted

esca *ay·ska f* bait

esclamare *e·skla·mah·ray vi* exclaim

escludere* *e·skloo·de·re vt* exclude

esclusiva *e·skloo·zee·va f* exclusive rights

esclusivo(a) *e·skloo·zee·vo(a) adj* exclusive (*club, shop*)

escrescenza *es·kre·shen·tsa f* growth (*anatomical*)

escursione *e·skoor·syoh·ne f* excursion; **l'escursione a piedi** *e·skoor·syoh·ne a pye·dee* hike

eseguire *e·ze·gwee·ray vt* carry out (*order*)

esempio *e·zem·pyoh m* example; **per esempio** *payr e·zem·pyoh* for example

esente *e·zen·te adj* exempt; **esente da tasse** *e·zen·te da tas·se* tax-free

esercitarsi *e·zer·chee·tar·see vr* practice; **esercitarsi nel correre** *e·zer·chee·tar·see nel kohr·re·re* to practice running; **esercitarsi al pianoforte** *e·zer·chee·tar·see al pya·no·for·te* to practice the piano

esercito *e·zer·chee·toh m* army

esercizio *e·zer·chee·tsyoh m* exercise

esigenza *e·ze·jen·tsa f* requirement

esigere* *e·zee·je·re vt* demand

esistenza *e·zee·sten·tsa f* existence

esistere* *e·zee·ste·re vi* exist

esitare *e·zee·tah·ray vi* hesitate; **esitare a fare qualcosa** *e·zee·tah·ray a fah·ray kwal·ko·sa* to hesitate to do something

esito *e·zee·toh m* result; **avere* buon esito** *a·vay·re bwon e·zee·toh* to be successful

esotico(a) *e·zo·tee·ko(a) adj* exotic

esperanto *e·spe·ran·toh m* Esperanto

esperienza *e·spe·ree·en·tsa f* experience

esperimento *e·spe·ree·mayn·toh m* experiment

esperto *e·sper·toh m* expert □ *adj*

esperto(a) *e·sper·to(a) adj* expert; experienced

esplodere* *e·splo·de·re vi* explode

esplorare *e·splo·rah·ray vt* explore

esplosione *e·splo·zyoh·ne f* explosion

esporre* *es·pohr·re vt* expose; explain; display

esportare *e·spor·tah·ray vt* export

esportatore *e·spor·ta·toh·re m* exporter

esportazione *e·spor·ta·tsyoh·ne f* export

esposto(a) *e·spo·sto(a) adj* exposed; **esposto(a) a nord** *e·spo·sto(a) a nord* facing north

espressione *e·spres·syoh·ne f* expression

espresso *e·spres·soh m* express letter; express train; espresso (coffee)

esprimere* *e·spree·me·re vt* express

essenziale *es·sen·tsyah·le adj* essential (*necessary*)

essere* *es·se·re vi* be; sono *soh·no* I am; è *e* you are; he/she/it is; siamo *syah·mo* we are; siete *sye·te* you are; sono *soh·no* they are; è medico e medee·koh he is a doctor; sono 5 chilometri *soh·no 5 kee·lo·me·tree* it's 5 kilometers; sono le 4 *soh·no le 4* it's 4 o'clock; sono qui dalle 4 *soh·no kwee dal·le 4* I've been here since 4 o'clock; sono io *soh·no ee·o* it's me; che c'è? *ke che* what's the matter?; non c'è di che! *nohn che dee ke* don't mention it

essi(e) *es·see(·se) pron* they; them

esso(a) *es·so(a) pron* it

est *est m* east; **ad est** *ad est* east

estate *e·stah·te f* summer

esterno *e·ster·noh m* outside □ *adj* **esterno(a)** *e·ster·no(a)* exterior; external

estero(a) *e·ste·ro(a) adj* foreign; **all'estero** *al·le·ste·roh* abroad

estintore *e·steen·toh·re m* fire extinguisher

estremamente *e·stre·ma·mayn·te adv* extremely

estremo(a) *e·stre·mo(a) adj* extreme

Estremo Oriente *e·stre·mo o·ryen·te m* the Far East

età *e·ta f* age (*of person*)

etichetta *e·tee·kayt·ta f* etiquette; tag; label

etichettare *e·tee·ket·tah·ray vt* label

etico(a) *e·tee·ko(a) adj* ethical

etnico(a) *et·nee·ko(a) adj* ethnic

Europa *e·oo·ro·pa f* Europe; **l'Europa continentale** *e·oo·ro·pa kon·tee·nen·tah·lay* the Continent

europeo(a) *e·oo·ro·pe·o(a) adj* European

evaporare *e·va·po·rah·ray vi* evaporate

eventuale *e·ven·too·ah·le adj* possible

evitare *e·vee·tah·ray vt* avoid

evoluzione *e·vo·loo·tsyoh·ne f* evolution

ex- *eks pref* ex-

eye-liner *eye·line·er m* eyeliner

F

fa *fa adv* ago

fabbrica *fab·bree·ka f* factory

fabbricante *fab·bree·kan·tay m* manufacturer

fabbricare *fab·bree·kah·ray vt* manufacture; **fabbricare in serie** *fab·bree·kah·ray een ser·ye* to mass-produce

fabbricazione *fab·bree·ka·tsyo·nay f* manufacturing

facchino *fak·kee·noh m* porter (*for luggage*)

faccia *fach·cha f* face

facile *fah·chee·le adj* easy

facilmente *fah·cheel·mayn·te adv* easily

facoltà *fa·kol·ta f* — faculty

faggio *faj·joh m* beech

fagiano *fa·jah·noh m* pheasant

fagioli *fa·jo·lee mpl* beans

fagiolini *fa·jo·lee·nee mpl* runner beans

falciare *fal·chah·ray vt* mow

falciatrice *fal·cha·tree·che f* lawn mower

falegname *fa·len·yah·may m* carpenter; joiner

falena *fa·le·na f* moth

fallimento *fal·lee·mayn·toh m* failure; bankruptcy

fallire *fal·lee·re vi* fail; go bankrupt

fallito(a) *fal·lee·to(a) m/f* failure (*person*) □ *adj* bankrupt

fallo *fal·loh m* error; **senza fallo** *sen·tsa fal·loh* without fail

falò *fa·lo m* — bonfire

falsificazione *fal·see·fee·ka·tsyoh·ne f* forgery

falso(a) *fal·so(a) adj* false; fake

fama *fah·ma f* fame; reputation

fame *fah·me f* hunger; **avere* fame** *a·vay·re fah·me* to be hungry

famiglia *fa·meel·ya f* family; household

famoso(a) *fa·moh·so(a) adj* famous

fanale *fa·nah·lay m* light (*on car*); **i fanali di posizione** *fa·nah·lee dee po·zee·tsyoh·ne* parking lights; sidelights; **i fanali dei freni** *fa·nah·lee dey fre·nee* stoplights

fango *fan·goh m* mud

fangoso(a) *fan·goh·soh(a) adj* muddy

fantascienza *fan·ta·shen·tsa f* science fiction

fantasma *fan·taz·ma m* ghost

fante *fan·te m* jack (*cards*)

fantino *fan·tee·noh m* jockey

farcito(a) *far·chee·to(a) adj* stuffed (*chicken*)

fare* *fah·ray vt* do; make; **dovremo fare a meno del latte** *do·vray·moh fah·ray a may·noh del lat·tay* we will have to go without milk; **gli spinaci fanno bene alla salute** *lyee spee·nah·chee fan·no be·nay al·la sa·loo·tay* spinach is good for you; **le farà bene** *lay fa·ra be·nay* it'll do you good; **ce la fa?** *chay la fa* can you manage?; **faccia pure!** *fach·cha poo·ray* go ahead!; **fa caldo** *fa kal·do* it is warm/hot; **fare* 10 km a piedi** *fah·ray 10 km a pye·dee* to walk 10 km; **fare* fare qualcosa a qualcuno** *far fah·ray kwal·koh·sa a kwal·koo·noh* to make someone do something; **far* fare qualcosa** *far fah·ray kwal·ko·sa* to have something done; **fare* da** *fah·ray da* to act as; **non fa niente** *nohn fa nyen·tay* it doesn't matter

farfalla *far·fal·la f* butterfly

farina *fa·ree·na f* flour; **la farina di granturco** *fa·ree·na dee gran·toor·koh* cornstarch

farmacia *far·ma·chee·a f* drugstore; pharmacy; chemist's shop

farmacista *far·ma·chee·sta m/f* pharmacist; druggist

faro *fah·roh m* headlight; lighthouse

farsa *far·sa f* farce

fascino *fa·shee·noh m* charm

fascio *fa·shoh m* bundle

fastidio *fa·stee·dyoh m* bother; **dare* fastidio a** *dah·ray fa·stee·dyoh a* to annoy

fata *fah·ta f* fairy

fatale *fa·tah·le adj* fatal

fatelo da voi *fah·te·lo da voy* m do-it-yourself

fattezze *fat·tayts·tse* fpl features

fattibilità *fat·tee·bee·lee·ta* f feasibility

fatto *fat·toh* m fact

fattore *fat·toh·re* m factor

fattoria *fat·to·ree·a* f farm

fattorino d'albergo *fat·to·ree·noh dal·ber·goh* m bellboy

fattura *fat·too·ra* f invoice

favore *fa·voh·re* m favor; **per favore** *payr fa·voh·re* please; **fare* un favore a qualcuno** *fah·ray oon fa·voh·re a kwal·koo·no* to do someone a favor; **non sono a favore di quell'idea** *non soh·no a fa·voh·re dee kwayl·lee·de·a* I'm not in favor of that idea

favorito(a) *fa·vo·ree·to(a)* adj favorite

fazzolettino di carta *fats·tso·let·tee·noh dee kar·ta* m tissue (*handkerchief*)

fazzoletto *fats·tso·layt·toh* m handkerchief; scarf (*head*)

febbraio *feb·bra·yoh* m February

febbre *feb·bre* f fever; **avere* la febbre** *a·vay·re la feb·bre* to have a temperature; **la febbre da fieno** *feb·bre da fye·noh* hay fever

fede *fay·de* f faith; belief; wedding ring

fedeltà *fe·del·ta* f faithfulness; **ad alta fedeltà** *ad al·ta fe·del·ta* hi-fi

federa *fe·de·ra* f pillowcase, pillowslip

federale *fe·de·rah·le* adj federal

feed-back *feed·bak* m feedback

fegato *fay·ga·toh* m liver

felce *fayl·che* f fern; bracken

felice *fe·lee·chay* adj glad

felicissimo(a) *fe·lee·chees·see·mo(a)* adj delighted

felicità *fe·lee·chee·ta* f happiness

felicitazioni *fe·lee·chee·ta·tsyoh·nee* fpl congratulations; **felicitazioni!** *fe·lee·chee·ta·tsyoh·nee* congratulations!

feltro *fayl·troh* m felt (*cloth*)

femmina *faym·mee·na* adj female (*animal*)

femminile *fem·mee·nee·le* adj feminine; **il sesso femminile** *eel ses·soh fem·mee·nee·le* the female sex

feriale *fe·ree·ah·le* adj work, week

ferie *fay·ree·ay* fpl vacation

ferire *fe·ree·re* vt injure; wound

ferita *fe·ree·ta* f wound; injury; cut

ferito(a) *fe·ree·to(a)* adj injured

fermare *fer·mah·ray* vt stop

fermarsi *fer·mar·see* vr stop; stall (*car engine*)

fermata *fer·mah·ta* f stop; **la fermata autobus** *fer·mah·ta ow·to·boos* bus stop; **la fermata facoltativa** *fer·mah·ta fa·kol·ta·tee·va* flag stop

fermo(a) *fayr·mo(a)* adj firm; steady; stationary; off (*machine*)

feroce *fe·roh·che* adj fierce

ferramenta *fer·ra·mayn·ta* fpl hardware

ferro *fer·roh* m iron (*material, golf club*); **il ferro da calza** *fer·roh da kal·tsa* knitting needle; **il ferro da stiro** *fer·roh da stee·roh* iron (*for clothes*)

ferrovia *fer·ro·vee·a* f railroad; per ferrovia *payr fer·ro·vee·a* by rail

fertile *fer·tee·le* adj fertile (*land*)

fessura *fes·soo·ra* f slot; crack (*split*)

festa *fes·ta* f party (*celebration*); holiday (*day*); **fare* festa** *fah·ray fe·sta* to celebrate

festeggiare *fes·tej·jah·ray* vt celebrate

festival *fe·stee·val* m — festival

fetta *fayt·ta* f slice

fiacco(a) *fyak·ko(a)* adj slack (*business*)

fiamma *fyam·ma* f flame; la casa è in

fiamme *la kah·sa e een fyam·me* the house is on fire

fiammifero *fyam·mee·fe·roh* m match

fiammingo(a) *fyam·meen·go(a)* adj Flemish □ m il fiammingo *fyam·meen·goh* Flemish

fiato *fyah·toh* m breath

fibbia *feeb·bya* f clasp; buckle

fibra *fee·bra* f fiber

fico *fee·koh* m fig

fidanzamento *fee·dan·tsa·mayn·toh* m engagement (*betrothal*)

fidanzato(a) *fee·dan·tsah·to(a)* m/f fiancé(e) □ adj engaged (*betrothed*)

fidarsi di *fee·dar·see dee* vr trust

fidato(a) *fee·dah·to(a)* adj reliable (*person*)

fiducia *fee·doo·cha* f confidence (*trust*)

fiducioso(a) *fee·doo·choh·so(a)* adj confident

fieno *fye·noh* m hay

fiera *fye·ra* f fair

fiero(a) *fye·ro(a)* adj proud

figlia *feel·ya* f daughter

figliastra *feel·ya·stra* f stepdaughter

figliastro *feel·ya·stroh* m stepson

figlio *feel·yoh* m son

figura *fee·goo·ra* f figure (*of human*); face card

fila *fee·la* f row; line

filare *fee·lah·ray* vt spin (*wool*)

filetto *fee·layt·toh* m fillet (*of meat, fish*)

filiale *fee·lyah·le* f branch; subsidiary (*company*)

film m — film; movie; **il film d'orrore** *feelm dor·roh·re* horror movie

filo *fee·loh* m thread; lead (*electrical*); edge (*of blade*); **il filo elettrico** *fee·loh el·let·tree·ko* wire (*electrical*); **il filo di cotone** *fee·loh dee ko·toh·nay* cotton (*thread*)

filo di ferro *fee·loh dee fer·roh* m wire; **il filo di ferro spinato** *fee·loh dee fer·roh spee·nah·to* barbed wire

filtrare *feel·trah·ray* vt filter

filtro *feel·troh* m filter; **con filtro** *kohn feel·troh* filter-tip (*cigarettes*); **il filtro dell'olio** *feel·troh del·lol·yoh* oil filter; **il filtro dell'aria** *feel·troh del·lah·rya* air filter

finale *fee·nah·le* f finals (*sports*) □ adj final

finalmente *fee·nal·mayn·te* adv finally

finanza *fee·nan·tsa* f finance

finanziare *fee·nan·tsyah·ray* vt finance; back

finanziario(a) *fee·nan·tsy·ah·ryo(a)* adj financial

finanziatore *fee·nan·tsya·toh·re* m backer

finché *feen·kay* conj as long as; until; **finché egli verrà** *feen·kay el·yee ver·ra* until he comes

fine *fee·ne* f end □ m aim (*purpose*) □ adj fine; **alla fine** *al·la fee·ne* at last; eventually; **il/la fine settimana** *fee·ne set·tee·mah·na* weekend

finestra *fee·ne·stra* f window (*in house*)

finestrino *fee·ne·stree·noh* m window (*in car, train*)

fingere* *feen·je·re* vt pretend; **fingere* di fare qualcosa** *feen·je·re dee fah·ray kwal·ko·sa* to pretend to do something

finimenti *fee·nee·mayn·tee* mpl harness

finire *fee·nee·re* vi/vt finish; **la partita è finita** *la par·tee·ta e fee·nee·ta* the match is over; **è finito tutto il nostro denaro** *e fee·nee·toh toot·toh*

eel no·stroh de·nah·roh all our money's gone
finlandese *feen·lan·day·se adj* Finnish
Finlandia *feen·lan·dya f* Finland
fino *fee·no adv* even; **fino a** *fee·no a* until; as far as; **fino a 6** *fee·no a 6* up to 6
fino(a) *fee·no(a) adj* fine
finora *fee·noh·ra adv* up till now
fiocco *fyok·koh m* flake (of snow); **i fiocchi di granturco** *fyok·kee dee gran·toor·koh* cornflakes
fioraio(a) *fyoh·ra·yo(a) m/f* florist
fiore *fyoh·re m* flower
fiori *fyoh·ree mpl* clubs (in cards)
fiorire *fyo·ree·re vi* bloom
firma *feer·ma f* signature
firmare *feer·mah·ray vt* sign (document)
fiscale *fee·skah·le adj* fiscal
fischiare *fee·skyah·ray vt/i* whistle
fischietto *fee·skyayt·toh m* whistle (object)
fischio *fee·skyoh m* whistle (sound)
fisco *fee·skoh m* Internal Revenue
fisica *fee·zee·ka f* physics
fisico(a) *fee·zee·ko(a) adj* physical
fissare *fees·sah·ray vt* stare at; fix; arrange (meeting)
fitta *feet·ta f* stitch (pain)
fitto(a) *feet·to(a) adj* dense (fog etc)
fiume *fyoo·me m* river
flash *flash m* — flashbulb; flash (on camera)
flatulenza *fla·too·len·tsa f* wind (in stomach)
flauto *flow·toh m* flute
flessibile *fles·see·bee·le adj* flexible
flipper *fleep·per m* pinball
flirtare *fleer·tah·ray vi* flirt
flotta *flot·ta f* fleet
fluido *floo·ee·doh m* fluid
fluoro *floo·o·roh m* fluorine
flusso *floos·soh m* flow; **il flusso di capitale** *floos·soh dee ka·pee·tah·lay* cash flow
focolare *fo·ko·lah·re m* hearth; fireplace
fodera *fo·de·ra f* lining
foglia *fol·ya f* leaf
foglio *fol·yoh m* sheet (of paper)
fogna *fohn·ya f* drain
folla *fol·la f* crowd
folle *fol·lay adj* mad; **in folle** *een fol·lay* in neutral
fondamentalmente *fon·da·mayn·tal·mayn·te adv* basically
fondare *fon·dah·ray vt* establish (business)
fondere* *fohn·de·ray vt* melt
fondersi* *fohn·der·see vr* melt; merge
fondi *fohn·dee mpl* funds
fondo *fohn·doh m* back (of hall, room); bottom; **i fondi di caffè** *fohn·dee dee kaf·fe* grounds (of coffee)
fontana *fon·tah·na f* fountain
fontanella *fon·ta·nel·la f* fountain (for drinking)
fonte *fohn·te f* source
footing *foo·teeng m* jogging; **fare* del footing** *fah·ray del foo·teeng* to go jogging
forare *fo·rah·ray vt* pierce; punch (ticket etc)
foratura *fo·ra·too·ra f* blow-out; puncture
forbici *for·bee·chee fpl* scissors
forchetta *for·kayt·ta f* fork
forcina *for·chee·na f* bobby pin; hairpin
foresta *fo·re·sta f* forest

forfora *fohr·fo·ra f* dandruff
forma *fohr·ma f* form; shape; **in forma** *een fohr·ma* in good form; fit (strong, healthy)
formaggio *for·maj·joh m* cheese
formale *for·mah·le adj* formal
formazione *for·ma·tsyoh·ne f* training (for job)
formica *for·mee·ka f* ant
fornaio *for·na·yoh m* baker
fornire *for·nee·re vt* provide; supply; **fornire del capitale** *for·nee·re del ka·pee·tah·le* to put up capital; **fornire qualcosa a qualcuno** *for·nee·re kwal·ko·sa a kwal·koo·no* to supply someone with something
forno *fohr·noh m* oven; **il forno a microonde** *fohr·noh a mee·kro·ohn·day* microwave oven
forse *fohr·se adv* perhaps; possibly
forte *for·te adj* strong; loud; **essere* forte nel golf** *es·se·ray for·te nel golf* to be good at golf
fortemente *for·te·mayn·te adv* loudly
fortuna *for·too·na f* fortune (wealth); luck; **buona fortuna!** *bwo·na for·too·na* good luck!
foruncolo *fo·roon·ko·loh m* boil (on skin)
forza *for·tsa f* strength; force
foschia *fo·skee·a f* mist
fossa *fos·sa f* pit
fossato *fos·sah·toh m* ditch
foto *fo·toh f* — photo
fotocopia *fo·to·ko·pya f* photocopy
fotocopiare *fo·to·ko·pyah·ray vt* photocopy
fotografare *fo·to·gra·fah·ray vt* photograph
fotografia *fo·to·gra·fee·a f* photography; photograph
fotografo *fo·to·gra·foh m* photographer
fotometro *fo·to·me·troh m* light meter
fra *fra prep* between; among; **tornerà fra 2 giorni** *tor·ne·ra fra 2 johr·nee* he'll be back in 2 days
fracasso *fra·kas·soh m* crash (noise)
fragile *frah·jee·le adj* fragile
fragola *frah·go·la f* strawberry
fragore *fra·goh·ray m* noise (loud)
fragrante *fra·gran·te adj* sweet (smell)
frana *frah·na f* landslide
francese *fran·chay·ze adj* French □ *m* il francese *fran·chay·ze* French
Francia *fran·cha f* France
francobollo *fran·ko·bohl·loh m* stamp (postage)
frangia *fran·ja f* fringe
frantumare *fran·too·mah·ray vt* smash
frase *frah·ze f* phrase; sentence
frassino *fras·see·noh m* ash (tree)
fratellastro *fra·tel·la·stroh m* stepbrother
fratello *fra·tel·loh m* brother
frattura *frat·too·ra f* fracture (of arm etc)
freccia *fraych·cha f* arrow; indicator (of car)
freddo(a) *frayd·doh(a) adj* cold; **ho freddo** *o frayd·doh* I'm cold
fregare *fre·gah·ray vt* rub
frenare *fre·nah·ray vt/i* brake
freno *fray·noh m* brake; **il freno a mano** *fray·noh a mah·noh* handbrake; **il freno a pedale** *fray·noh a pe·dah·le* footbrake; **i freni a disco** *fray·nee a dee·sko* disc brakes
frequente *fre·kwen·te adj* frequent
fresco(a) *fray·skoh(a) adj* cool; fresh; wet (paint)

fretta *frayt·ta* f rush; haste; **avere* fretta** *a·vay·re frayt·ta* to be in a hurry

friggere* *freej·je·re* vt fry

frigo *free·goh* m fridge

frigorifero *free·go·ree·fe·roh* m refrigerator

frittata *freet·tah·ta* f omelet

frittella *freet·tel·la* f fritter; pancake

fritto(a) *freet·to(a)* adj fried

frizione *free·tsyoh·nay* f clutch (of car)

frontale *fron·tah·le* adj head-on

fronte *frohn·te* f forehead; **di fronte** *dee frohn·te* facing; **la casa di fronte la kah·sa dee frohn·te** the house opposite; **di fronte a** *dee frohn·te a* opposite; facing

frontiera *fron·tye·ra* f frontier; border (of country)

frullato *frool·lah·toh* m milkshake

frullatore *frool·la·toh·ray* m mixer

frullino *frool·lee·noh* m whisk

frumento *froo·mayn·toh* m wheat

frusta *froo·sta* f whip

frustino *froo·stee·noh* m crop (whip)

frutta *froot·ta* f fruit

frutteto *froot·tay·toh* m orchard

frutto *froot·toh* m fruit; **i frutti di mare** *froot·tee dee mah·re* seafood

fu *foo* adj late

fucile *foo·chee·le* m rifle; gun

fuga *foo·ga* f leak (gas)

fuggire *fooj·jee·re* vi run away; get away (escape)

fulvo(a) *fool·vo(a)* adj fawn

fumare *foo·mah·ray* vt/i smoke; **lei fuma?** *ley foo·ma* do you smoke?

fumatore *foo·ma·toh·re* m smoker (person)

fumo *foo·moh* m smoke

funerale *foo·ne·rah·le* m funeral

fungere* *da foon·je·re da* vi act as

fungo *foon·goh* m mushroom

funzionare *foon·tsyoh·nah·ray* vi work (clock, mechanism); **questa macchina funziona a nafta** *kway·sta mak·kee·na foon·tsyoh·na a naf·ta* this car runs on diesel; **fare* funzionare** *fah·ray foon·tsyoh·nah·ray* to operate (machine)

funzionario(a) statale *foon·tsyo·nah·ree·oh(a) sta·tah·lay* m/f civil servant

fuoco *fwo·koh* m fire; focus; **appiccare il fuoco a** *ap·pee·kah·ray eel fwo·koh a* to set fire to; **i fuochi d'artificio** *fwo·kee dar·tee·fee·choh* fireworks; **mettere* a fuoco** *mayt·te·re a fwo·koh* to focus

fuori *fwo·ree* adv outside; out (not at home); **fuori la mia portata** *fwo·ree la mee·a por·tah·ta* beyond my reach; **fuori di** *fwo·ree dee* out of (outside); **fuori della strada principale** *fwo·ree del·la strah·da preen·chee·pah·le* off the main road; **fuori della casa** *fwo·ree del·la kah·sa* outside the house; **fuori di casa** *fwo·ree dee kah·sa* away from home

fuoribordo *fwo·ree·bohr·doh* m — speedboat □ adj outboard

furgone *foor·goh·nay* m van

furioso(a) *foo·ree·oh·soh(a)* adj mad (angry)

furto *foor·toh* m robbery

fusibile *foo·zee·bee·le* m fuse

fusione *foo·zyoh·ne* f amalgamation; merger

fuso orario *foo·soh o·rah·ryoh* m time zone

futuro *foo·too·roh* m future; **pensare al**

futuro *pen·sah·ray al foo·too·roh* to think ahead

G

gabbia *gab·bya* f cage; crate

gabinetto *ga·bee·nayt·toh* m toilet (lavatory); **il gabinetto medico** *ga·bee·nayt·toh me·dee·ko* doctor's office

gaio(a) *ga·yoh(a)* adj merry

gala *gah·la* f gala

galleggiante *gal·lej·jan·te* m float (for swimming, fishing)

galleggiare *gal·lej·jah·ray* vi float

galleria *gal·le·ree·a* f tunnel; gallery; circle (in theater); arcade; **la prima galleria** *pree·ma gal·le·ree·a* dress circle; **la galleria d'arte** *gal·le·ree·a dar·te* art gallery

Galles *gal·les* m Wales

gallese *gal·lay·se* adj Welsh □ m **il gallese** *gal·lay·se* Welsh

gallina *gal·lee·na* f hen; **la gallina faraona** *gal·lee·na fa·ra·oh·na* guinea fowl

gallo *gal·loh* m cock(erel)

gallone *gal·loh·nay* m gallon

galoppare *ga·lop·pah·ray* vi gallop

galoppo *ga·lop·poh* m gallop; **andare* al galoppo** *an·dah·ray al ga·lop·poh* to go at a gallop

gamba *gam·ba* f leg (of person)

gamberetto *gam·be·rayt·toh* m shrimp; prawn

gambero *gam·be·roh* m crawfish, crayfish

gamma *gam·ma* f range; **la gamma di prezzi** *gam·ma dee prets·tsee* price range

gancio *gan·choh* m hook; **il gancio ad occhiello** *gan·choh ad ok·kyel·loh* hook and eye; **il gancio per rimorchio** *gan·choh payr ree·mor·kyoh* tow-bar (on car)

gangster *gang·ster* m gangster

garage *ga·raj* m garage (service station)

garantire *ga·ran·tee·ray* vt guarantee

garanzia *ga·ran·tsee·a* f guarantee; warrant(y)

garofano *ga·ro·fa·noh* m carnation

garza *gar·dza* f gauze; lint

gas *gas* m gas; **il gas di scappamento** *gas dee skap·pa·mayn·toh* exhaust (fumes)

gassoso(a) *gas·soh·so(a)* adj fizzy

gatto *gat·toh* m cat

gelare *je·lah·ray* vt/i freeze

gelateria *je·lah·te·ree·a* f ice cream shop

gelato *je·lah·toh* m ice cream; **il gelato alla vaniglia** *je·lah·toh al·la va·neel·ya* vanilla ice cream

gelo *je·loh* m frost

geloso(a) *je·loh·so(a)* adj jealous

gemelli *je·mel·lee* mpl twins

gemello *je·mel·loh* m cuff link

gemere *je·me·ray* vi groan; moan

gemito *je·me·toh* m groan; moan

gemma *jem·ma* f gem

generale *je·ne·rah·lay* adj general □ m **il generale** *je·ne·rah·lay* general (soldier); **in generale** *een je·ne·rah·lay* in general

generalmente *je·ne·rahl·mayn·tay* adv generally

generatore *je·ne·ra·toh·ray* m generator (electrical)

generazione *je·ne·ra·tsee·oh·nay* f generation

genere *je·ne·re* m kind (type); gender

generi alimentari *je·ne·ree a·lee·men·tah·ree mpl* foodstuffs

genero *je·ne·roh m* son-in-law

generoso(a) *je·ne·roh·soh(a) adj* generous

gengiva *jen·jee·va f* gum (*of teeth*)

genitori *je·nee·toh·ree mpl* parents

gennaio *jen·na·yoh m* January

gente *jen·te f* people

gentile *jen·tee·le adj* kind; polite

geografia *jay·oh·gra·fee·a f* geography

geologia *jay·oh·loh·jee·a f* geology

geometra *je·o·me·tra m* surveyor (*of land*)

geometria *jay·oh·me·tree·a f* geometry

geranio *je·rah·nee·oh m* geranium

gergo *jer·goh m* slang

Germania *jer·mah·nya f* Germany

Germania Occidentale *jer·mah·nya och·chee·den·tah·le f* West Germany

Germania Orientale *jer·mah·nya o·ree·en·tah·le f* East Germany

gesso *jes·soh m* chalk; plaster cast (*for limb*); plaster of Paris

gesto *jes·toh m* gesture

gettare *jet·tah·ray vt* throw; **gettare via** *jet·tah·ray vee·a* to throw away

gettone *jet·toh·ne m* token (*for machine*); chip (*in gambling*); counter

ghetto *get·toh m* ghetto

ghiacciaia *gyach·cha·ya f* icebox

ghiaccio *gyach·choh m* ice

ghiacciolo *gyach·cho·loh m* popsicle

ghiaia *gee·a·ya f* gravel

ghianda *gyan·da f* acorn

ghiandola *gee·an·doh·la f* gland

ghisa *gee·za f* cast iron

già *ja adv* already

giacca *jak·ka f* jacket; **la giacca a vento** *jak·ka a ven·toh* anorak; **la giacca di salvataggio** *jak·ka de sal·va·taj·joh* life jacket; **la giacca sportiva** *jak·ka spor·tee·va* sport coat, sport jacket

giacere* *ja·chay·re vi* lie

giallo *jal·loh m* yellow; thriller (*book*) □ *adj* **giallo(a)** *jal·lo(a)* yellow

Giappone *jap·poh·ne m* Japan

giapponese *jap·po·nay·se adj* Japanese □ *m* **il giapponese** *jap·po·nay·se* Japanese

giardinetta *jar·dee·nayt·ta f* station wagon

giardiniere *jar·dee·nye·ray m* gardener

giardino *jar·dee·noh m* garden; **il giardino botanico** *jar·dee·noh bo·ta·nee·ko* botanical gardens

gigante *jee·gan·tay m* giant

giglio *jeel·yoh m* lily

gin *jeen m* gin (*drink*)

Ginevra *jee·ne·vra f* Geneva

ginnastica *jeen·nas·tee·ka f* gymnastics

ginocchio *jee·nok·kyoh m* —**chi**, —**chia** knee; **mettersi* in ginocchio** *mayt·ter·see een jee·nok·kyoh* to kneel down

giocare *jo·kah·ray vt* play □ *vi* play; gamble; **giocare al calcio** *jo·kah·ray al kal·choh* to play football; **giocare a carte** *jo·kah·ray a kahr·tay* to play cards; **giocare con** *jo·kah·ray kohn* to play with

giocatore *jo·ka·toh·ray m* player (*in sport*); **il giocatore di golf** *jo·ka·toh·ray dee golf* golfer; **il giocatore d'azzardo** *jo·ka·toh·ray dadz·dzar·doh* gambler

giocatrice *jo·ka·tree·che f* player (*in sport*)

giocattolo *jo·kat·to·loh m* toy

gioco *jo·ko m* game; **essere* in gioco**

es·se·re een jo·ko to be at stake; **il gioco della dama** *jo·ko del·la dah·ma* checkers; **il gioco del ventuno** *jo·ko del ven·too·no* blackjack; **il gioco d'azzardo** *jo·ko dadz·dzar·doh* gambling; **il gioco di carte** *jo·ko dee kahr·tay* card game

giogo *joh·goh m* ridge

gioia *jo·ya f* joy

gioielli *jo·yel·lee mpl* jewelry

gioielliere *jo·yel·lye·re m* jeweler

gioiello *jo·yel·loh m* jewel; **i gioielli di fantasia** *jo·yel·lee dee fan·ta·zee·a* costume jewelry

giornalaio *johr·na·la·yoh m* newsdealer

giornale *johr·nah·lay m* newspaper; **il giornale della sera** *johr·nah·lay del·la say·ra* evening paper; **il giornale a fumetti** *johr·nah·lay a foo·mayt·tee* comic

giornalista *johr·na·lee·sta m/f* journalist

giornata *johr·nah·ta f* day (*length of time*); **tutta la giornata** *toot·ta la johr·nah·ta* all day long

giorno *johr·noh m* day; **di giorno in giorno** *dee johr·noh een johr·noh* day by day; **il giorno festivo** *johr·noh fe·stee·vo* holiday; **il giorno feriale** *johr·noh fe·ree·ah·le* weekday; **il giorno di mercato** *johr·noh dee mayr·kah·toh* market-day

giostra *jo·stra f* merry-go-round

giovane *jo·va·ne adj* young

giovedì *jo·ve·dee m* — Thursday

gioventù *jo·ven·too f* youth (*period*)

giradischi *jee·ra·dee·skee m* — recordplayer

girare *jee·rah·ray vi* turn (*person, car*); spin (*rotate*) □ *vt* turn; **girare qualcosa** *jee·rah·ray kwal·ko·sa* to turn something round

giro *jee·roh m* tour; turn; rev (*in engine*); lap (*of track*); round (*of golf*); **fare* un giro in macchina** *fah·ray oon jee·roh een mak·kee·na* to go for a drive; **il giro d'affari** *jee·roh daf·fah·ree* turnover (*money*)

gita *jee·ta f* trip; excursion; run; outing; **fare* una gita** *fah·ray oo·na gee·ta* to go on an excursion

gittata *jeet·tah·ta f* range (*of missile*)

giù *joo adv* down; downstairs

giubileo *joo·bee·le·oh m* jubilee

giudicare *joo·dee·kah·ray vt* judge

giudice *joo·dee·che m* judge

giugno *joon·yoh m* June

giuncata *joon·kah·ta f* junket

giuntura *joon·too·ra f* joint (*of body etc*)

giurare *joo·rah·ray vt/i* swear

giustizia *joo·stee·tsya f* justice

giustiziare *joo·stee·tsyah·ray vt* execute (*kill*)

giusto(a) *joo·sto(a) adj* right (*morally good*); fair (*just*); sì, giusto *see joo·sto* yes, that's right

glassa *glas·sa f* icing (*on cake*)

gli *lyee art* the □ *pron* to him/it; **glielo dia** *lye·lo dee·a* give it to him/her

glicerina *glee·che·ree·na f* glycerin(e)

globale *glo·bah·le adj* inclusive (*costs*); global

globo *glo·boh m* globe

goccia *gohch·cha f* drop (*of liquid*); drip

gocciolare *goch·cho·lah·ray vi* drip

goffo(a) *gof·foh(a) adj* clumsy (*person*)

gola *goh·la f* throat

golf *golf m* — golf; cardigan

goloso(a) go·loh·soh(a) adj greedy

gomito goh·mee·toh m elbow

gomitolo go·mee·to·loh m ball (of string, wool)

gomma gohm·ma f rubber; tire; **la gomma per cancellare** gohm·ma payr kan·chel·lah·ray eraser; **la gomma da masticare** gohm·ma da ma·stee·kah·ray chewing gum

gommone gom·moh·ne m dinghy (inflatable)

gonfiabile gon·fyah·bee·le adj inflatable

gonfiare gon·fee·ah·re vt inflate

gonfiarsi gon·fyar·see vr swell (up) (limb etc)

gonfio(a) gohn·fyo(a) adj swollen

gonfiore gon·fyoh·re m lump (on skin)

gonna gon·na f skirt

governante go·ver·nan·te f housekeeper

governare go·vayr·nah·ray vt govern (country); rule; steer (boat)

governatore go·vayr·na·toh·ray m governor (of colony)

governo go·vayr·noh m government

gradevole gra·day·vo·le adj pleasant

gradino gra·dee·noh m step; stair; **il gradino della porta** gra·dee·noh del·la por·ta doorstep

gradire gra·dee·re vt accept; like; **gradirei un gelato** gra·dee·re·ee oon je·lah·toh I'd like an ice cream

grado grah·doh m grade; standard; degree; **a 2 gradi sotto zero** a 2 grah·dee soht·toh dze·roh at minus 2 degrees; **un whisky di 40 gradi** oon wee·skee dee 40 grah·dee a 70° proof whiskey

graduale gra·dwa·lay adj gradual

gradualmente gra·doo·al·men·tay adv gradually

graffetta graf·fayt·ta f paper clip; staple

graffiare graf·fyah·ray vt scratch

grafico gra·fee·koh m graph; chart (diagram, table)

grammatica gram·ma·tee·ka f grammar

grammo gram·moh m gram

granaio gra·na·yoh m barn

Gran Bretagna gran bre·tan·ya f Great Britain

granchio gran·kyoh m crab

grande gran·day adj great; large; big; **di gran lunga** dee gran loon·ga by far

grandinare gran·dee·nah·ray vi hail

grandine gran·dee·ne f hail

graniglia gra·neel·ya f grit

granita gra·nee·ta f sherbet

grano grah·noh m grain

granturco gran·toor·koh m corn

grasso gras·soh m fat; grease □ adj

grasso(a) gras·so(a) fat (person); greasy

grassoccio(a) gras·soch·cho(a) adj plump

grata grah·ta f grating

grato(a) grah·toh(a) adj grateful

grattacielo grat·ta·che·loh m skyscraper

grattugia grat·too·jah f grater

grattugiare grat·too·jah·ray vt grate (food)

gratuito(a) gra·too·ee·to(a) adj free (costing nothing)

gravida gra·vee·da adj pregnant

grazie gra·tsye excl thank you; **grazie a** gra·tsye a thanks to

grazioso(a) gra·tsyoh·so(a) adj charming; sweet (cute, pretty); graceful

Grecia gray·cha f Greece

greco(a) gre·koh(a) adj Greek □ m **il greco** gre·koh Greek

gregge grayj·je m flock

grembiule grem·byoo·le m apron

grembo grem·boh m lap (of person)

grezzo(a) graydz·dzo(a) adj raw (unprocessed); crude (oil etc)

gridare gree·dah·ray vt/i shout

grido gree·doh m cry; shout

grigio(a) gree·joh(a) adj gray

griglia greel·ya f grill (gridiron)

grondaia gron·da·ya f gutter (on building)

groppa grop·pa f back (of animal)

grossa gros·sa f gross

grossista gros·sees·ta m/f wholesaler

grosso(a) gros·so(a) adj big; thick

grossolano(a) gros·so·lah·no(a) adj rude

grottesco(a) grot·tay·skoh(a) adj grotesque

gru groo f — crane

gruccia grooch·cha f crutch; coat hanger

grugnire groon·yee·ray vi grunt

grumo groo·moh m lump (in sauce)

gruppo groop·poh m group; **il gruppo sanguigno** groop·poh san·gween·yo blood group; **il gruppo di pressione** groop·poh dee pres·syoh·ne pressure group

guadagnare gwa·dan·yah·ray vt earn; gain (obtain)

guadagno gwa·dan·yoh m earnings; return (profit)

guado gwah·doh m ford

guai gwy mpl trouble (problems); **essere* nei guai** es·se·re nay gwy to be in trouble

guancia gwan·cha f cheek

guanciale gwan·chah·le m pillow

guanto gwan·toh m glove

guardacoste gwahr·da·ko·stay m — coastguard

guardare gwar·dah·ray vt watch; look at □ vi look

guardaroba gwar·da·ro·ba m — wardrobe (furniture); cloakroom

guardia gwar·dya f guard (soldiers); **la guardia del corpo** gwar·dya del kor·poh bodyguard (person)

guardiano gwar·dee·ah·noh m warder; caretaker

guarire gwa·ree·re vt cure; heal □ vi recover; heal

guarnizione gwar·nee·tsee·oh·nay f gasket

guastarsi gwa·star·see vr go bad (food); fail (brakes); break down (car etc)

guasto(a) gwa·sto(a) adj out of order (machine) □ m **il guasto** gwa·stoh failure (mechanical); **il guasto al motore** gwa·stoh al mo·toh·re engine trouble

guerra gwer·ra f war; **la guerra civile** gwer·ra chee·vee·lay civil war; **la guerra mondiale** gwer·ra mon·dee·ah·le world war

guida gwee·da f directory; courier; guide; guidebook; **la guida a sinistra** gwee·da a se·nee·stra left-hand drive

guidare gwee·dah·ray vt drive (car etc); steer (car); **sa guidare?** sa gwee·dah·ray do you drive?

guidatore gwee·da·toh·re m driver (of car); **il guidatore principiante** gwee·da·toh·re preen·chee·pyan·te student driver

guinzaglio gween·tsal·yoh m lead (dog's); leash

impresa

gulasch *goo·lash* m goulash
guscio *goo·shoh* m shell (*of egg*)
gustare *goo·stah·ray* vt taste; enjoy (*concert, outing*)
gusto *goo·stoh* m taste; di cattivo/buon gusto *dee kat·tee·vo/bwon goo·stoh* in poor/good taste

H

hamburger *ham·bur·gur* m — hamburger
handicap *han·dee·kap* m — handicap (*sports*)
hardware *hard·wer* m hardware (*computing*)
hockey *ho·kee* m hockey; l'hockey su ghiaccio *ho·kee soo gyach·choh* ice hockey
hostess *ho·stess* f — flight attendant; stewardess
hot-dog *hot·dog* m — hot dog
hovercraft *ho·ver·kraft* m hovercraft

I

i *ee* art the
idea *ee·de·a* f idea; cambiare idea *kam·byah·ray ee·de·a* to change one's mind
ideale *ee·de·ah·le* adj ideal
identico(a) *ee·den·tee·ko(a)* adj identical
identificare *ee·den·tee·fee·kah·ray* vt identify
identità *ee·den·tee·ta* f — identity
idiota *ee·dyo·ta* m/f idiot
idraulico *ee·drow·lee·koh* m plumber
ieri *ye·ree* adv yesterday
igienico(a) *ee·je·nee·ko(a)* adj hygienic
ignorante *een·yo·ran·te* adj ignorant
ignorare *een·yo·rah·ray* vt ignore (*person*)
il *eel* art the
illegale *eel·le·gah·le* adj illegal
illegittimo(a) *eel·lay·jeet·tee·moh(a)* adj illegitimate
illimitato(a) *eel·lee·mee·tah·to(a)* adj unlimited
illuminato(a) *eel·loo·mee·nah·to(a)* adj floodlit
illuminazione *eel·loo·mee·na·tsyoh·ne* f lighting; illumination; l'illuminazione al neon *eel·loo·mee·na·tsyoh·ne al ne·on* strip-lighting
illustrazione *eel·loo·stra·tsyoh·ne* f illustration
imballaggio *eem·bal·laj·joh* m packing
imballare *eem·bal·lah·ray* vt pack (*goods*); wrap up (*parcel*); rev
imbarazzato(a) *eem·ba·rats·tsah·to(a)* adj embarrassed
imbarcarsi *eem·bar·kar·see* vr embark
imbattibile *eem·bat·tee·bee·lay* adj unbeatable (*offer*)
imbottito(a) *eem·bot·tee·to(a)* adj stuffed (*cushion etc*)
imbrogliare *eem·brol·yah·ray* vt mix up; cheat
imbucare *eem·boo·kah·ray* vt post
imitare *ee·mee·tah·ray* vt imitate
immagazzinare *eem·ma·gadz·dzee·nah·ray* vt store
immaginare *eem·ma·jee·nah·ray* vt imagine
immaginazione *eem·ma·jee·na·tsee·oh·nay* f imagination
immangiabile *eem·man·jah·bee·le* adj inedible
immediato(a) *eem·me·dyah·to(a)* adj immediate; instant

immergere* *eem·mer·je·re* vt dip (*into liquid*)
immigrante *eem·mee·gran·te* m/f immigrant
immobile *eem·mo·bee·le* adj still (*motionless*)
immondizie *eem·mon·dee·tsye* fpl trash; garbage
immutato(a) *eem·moo·tah·toh(a)* adj unchanged
imparare *eem·pa·rah·ray* vt learn
imparziale *eem·par·tsee·ah·lay* adj unbiased
impasto *eem·pa·stoh* m mixture
impaziente *eem·pa·tsyen·te* adj impatient; essere* impaziente di fare qualcosa *es·se·re eem·pa·tsyen·te dee fah·ray kwal·ko·sa* to be eager to do something
impedire *eem·pe·dee·re* vt hinder; impedire a qualcuno di fare qualcosa *eem·pe·dee·re a kwal·koo·no dee fah·ray kwal·ko·sa* to stop someone doing something
impegnarsi a *eem·pen·yar·see a* vr undertake
impegnativo(a) *eem·pen·ya·tee·vo(a)* adj demanding (*work*)
impegno *eem·payn·yoh* m undertaking; commitment
imperatore *eem·pe·ra·toh·re* m emperor
impermeabile *eem·payr·me·ah·bee·le* adj waterproof □ m l'impermeabile *eem·payr·me·ah·bee·le* raincoat
impero *eem·pe·roh* m empire
impersonale *eem·per·so·nah·le* adj impersonal
impiccare *eem·peek·kah·ray* vt hang (*criminal*)
impiegare *eem·pye·gah·ray* vt employ; spend
impiegato(a) *eem·pye·gah·to(a)* m/f employee; clerk (*in office*); l'impiegato(a) d'ufficio *eem·pye·gah·to(a) doof·fee·choh* office worker
impiego *eem·pye·goh* m employment; job; occupation
imponibile *eem·po·nee·bee·le* adj taxable
imporre* *eem·pohr·re* vt impose
importante *eem·por·tan·te* adj important
importanza *eem·por·tan·tsa* f importance
importare *eem·por·tah·ray* vt import □ vi matter; non importa *nohn eem·por·tah* it doesn't matter; non me ne importa *nohn me ne eem·por·tah* I don't care
importatore *eem·por·ta·toh·re* m importer
importazione *eem·por·ta·tsyoh·ne* f import
importo *eem·por·toh* m amount (*total*)
impossibile *eem·pos·see·bee·le* adj impossible
imposta *eem·poh·sta* f tax (*on income*); shutter (*on window*); l'imposta sul reddito *eem·poh·sta sool red·dee·toh* income tax; le imposte sul consumo *eem·poh·ste sool kon·soo·moh* excise duties; l'imposta sul valore aggiunto *eem·poh·sta sool va·loh·ray aj·joon·toh* value-added tax
imprenditore *eem·pren·dee·toh·ray* m contractor
impresa *eem·pray·sa* f venture; enterprise; undertaking; l'impresa privata *eem·pray·sa pree·vah·ta* private enterprise

impressionabile *eem·pres·syoh·nah· bee·le adj* emotional (*person*)

impressionante *eem·pres·syoh·nan·te adj* impressive

impressionare *eem·pres·syoh·nah·ray vt* impress (*win approval*)

impressione *eem·pres·syoh·ne f* impression

improbabile *eem·pro·bah·bee·lay adj* unlikely

improvvisamente *eem·prov·vee·za· mayn·te adv* suddenly

improvviso(a) *eem·prov·vee·zo(a) adj* sudden

in *prep* in; to; into; in Francia *een fran·cha* in/to France; lo metta nella scatola *lo mayt·ta nel·la skah·to·la* put it in the box; in maggio *een maj· joh* in May; in treno/macchina *een tre·noh/mak·kee·na* by train/car; in marmo *een mahr·moh* made of marble; siamo in quattro *syah·mo een kwat·troh* there are four of us

inadatto(a) *een·a·dat·to(a) adj* unsuitable

incantevole *een·kan·tay·vo·lay adj* charming

incaricarsi di *een·ka·ree·kar·see dee vr* take charge of

incendio *een·chen·dyoh m* fire; blaze

inceneritore *een·che·ne·ree·toh·re m* incinerator

incentivo *een·chen·tee·voh m* incentive

incerto(a) *een·cher·toh(a) adj* uncertain; doubtful

inchinarsi *een·kee·nar·see vr* bow

inchino *een·kee·noh m* bow

inchiodare *een·kyo·dah·ray vt* nail

inchiostro *een·kyo·stroh m* ink

inciampare *een·cham·pah·ray vi* trip (*stumble*)

incidente *een·chee·den·te m* accident

incinta *een·cheen·ta adj* pregnant

inclinare *een·klee·nah·ray vt* tip (*tilt*)

includere* *een·kloo·de·re vt* include

incluso(a) *een·kloo·zo(a) adj* included; enclosed; dal 6 al 12 incluso *dal 6 al 12 een·kloo·zo* from 6th to 12th inclusive

incollare *een·kol·lah·ray vt* glue

incolpare *een·kol·pah·ray vt* blame

incompleto(a) *een·kom·play·toh(a) adj* incomplete

incondizionato(a) *een·kon·dee·tsyoh· nah·toh(a) adj* unconditional

incontrare *een·kon·trah·ray vt* meet (*encounter*)

incoronazione *een·ko·ro·na·tsyoh·nay f* coronation

incredibile *een·kre·dee·bee·le adj* incredible

incrinarsi *een·kree·nar·see vr* crack

incrocio *een·kroh·choh m* crossroads; l'incrocio a T *een·kroh·choh a tee* T-junction (*on road*)

incubo *een·koo·boh m* nightmare

indecente *een·day·chen·tay adj* indecent

India *een·dee·a f* India

indiano(a) *een·dee·ah·no(a) adj* Indian □ *m/f* l'indiano(a) *een·dee·ah·no(a)* Indian

indicare *een·dee·kah·ray vt* show; point to

indicatore *een·dee·ka·toh·ray m* gauge (*device*)

indicazione *een·dee·ka·tsyoh·ne f* indication

indicazioni *een·dee·ka·tsyoh·nee fpl* directions

indice *een·dee·che m* index; contents (*table in book*)

indietro *een·dye·tro adv* backwards; back; il mio orologio va indietro *eel mee·o o·ro·lo·joh va een·dye·tro* my watch is slow; fare* marcia indietro *fah·ray mar·cha een·dye·tro* to back the car; guardare indietro *gwar·dah· ray een·dye·tro* to look behind

indigestione *een·dee·je·styoh·ne f* indigestion

indigesto(a) *een·dee·je·sto(a) adj* indigestible

indipendente *een·dee·pen·den·te adj* independent

indipendenza *een·dee·pen·den·tsa f* independence

indiretto(a) *een·dee·ret·to(a) adj* indirect

indirizzare *een·dee·reets·tsah·ray vt* send; address (*letter*)

indirizzo *een·dee·reets·tsoh m* address

indivia *een·dee·vya f* endive

individuale *een·dee·vee·doo·ah·le adj* individual

indomani *een·do·mah·nee m* the next day

indossare *een·dos·sah·ray vt* put on (*clothes*)

indossatrice *een·dos·sa·tree·chay f* model (*mannequin*)

indovinare *een·do·vee·nah·ray vt* guess

indumento *een·doo·mayn·toh m* garment; gli indumenti da sport *een· doo·mayn·tee da sport* sportswear

industria *een·doo·stree·a f* industry; l'industria leggera *een·doo·stree·a lej· je·ra* light industry

industriale *een·doo·stree·ah·le adj* industrial

industria terziaria *een·doo·stree·a ter· tsyah·rya f* service industry

inefficiente *een·ef·fee·chen·te adj* inefficient

inevitabile *een·e·vee·tah·bee·lay adj* unavoidable; inevitable

infangato(a) *een·fan·gah·toh(a) adj* muddy (*clothes*)

infatti *een·fat·tee adv* in fact; actually

infelice *een·fe·lee·chay adj* miserable; unhappy

inferiore *een·fe·ryoh·re adj* inferior; lower

infermiera *een·fayr·mye·ra f* nurse

infettivo(a) *een·fet·tee·vo(a) adj* infectious

infezione *een·fe·tsyoh·ne f* infection

infiammabile *een·fyam·mah·bee·le adj* flammable

infiammazione *een·fyam·ma·tsyoh·ne f* inflammation

inflazione *een·fla·tsyoh·ne f* inflation (*economic*)

influenza *een·floo·en·tsa f* influence; flu

influire su *een·floo·ee·re soo vi* influence

informale *een·for·mah·le adj* informal

informare *een·for·mah·ray vt* inform; informarsi (di) *een·for·mar·see (dee)* to inquire (about)

informazioni *een·for·ma·tsyoh·nee fpl* information

infrangibile *een·fran·jee·bee·lay adj* unbreakable

ingannare *een·gan·nah·ray vt* trick; deceive

inganno *een·gan·noh m* trick (*malicious*)

ingegnere *een·jen·ye·re m* engineer

ingegnoso(a) *een·jen·yoh·soh(a) adj* clever (*plan*)

Inghilterra *een·geel·ter·ra f* England

inghiottire *een·gyot·tee·re vt* swallow

inginocchiarsi *een·jee·nok·kyar·see vr* kneel

ingiusto(a) *een·joo·sto(a) adj* unfair

inglese *een·glay·se adj* English □ *m* l'inglese *een·glay·se* English

ingorgo *een·gohr·goh m* tie-up (*traffic*); bottleneck; l'ingorgo stradale *een·gohr·goh stra·dah·le* traffic jam

ingrandire *een·gran·dee·re vt* enlarge

ingredienti *een·gre·dyen·tee mpl* ingredients

ingresso *een·gres·soh m* entry (*way in*); entrance; il prezzo d'ingresso *prets·tsoh deen·gres·soh* admission fee

all'ingrosso *al·leen·gros·soh adv* wholesale

iniezione *een·ye·tsyoh·ne f* injection

iniziali *ee·nee·tsyah·lee fpl* initials

inizio *ee·nee·tsyoh m* start (*beginning*)

innamorarsi *een·na·mo·rar·see vr* fall in love

innamorato(a) *een·na·mo·rah·to(a) adj* in love

innestato(a) *een·ne·stah·toh(a) adj* in gear

inno *een·noh m* hymn; l'inno nazionale *een·noh na·tsyoh·nah·lay* national anthem

innocente *een·no·chen·te adj* innocent

innocuo(a) *een·no·kwo(a) adj* harmless

inoltre *een·ohl·tre adv* besides (*moreover*)

inondazione *een·on·da·tsyoh·ne f* flood

inossidabile *een·os·see·dah·bee·lay adj* rustproof; stainless (*steel*)

input *een·poot m* input (*computing*)

inquilino(a) *een·kwee·lee·no(a) m/f* tenant; lodger

inquinamento *een·kwee·na·mayn·toh m* pollution

insalata *een·sa·lah·ta f* salad; l'insalata verde *een·sa·lah·ta vayr·day* green salad

insegna *een·sayn·ya f* sign (*notice*)

insegnante *een·sen·yan·te m/f* teacher

insegnare *een·sen·yah·ray vt* teach; insegnare qualcosa a qualcuno *een·sen·yah·ray kwal·ko·sa a kwal·koo·no* to teach someone something

inseguire *een·say·gwee·ray vt* chase

inserzione *een·sayr·tsyoh·ne f* advertisement

insetticida *een·set·tee·foo·goh m* insect repellent

insetto *een·set·toh m* insect

insieme *een·sye·me m* ensemble (*clothes*) □ *adv* together

insignificante *een·seen·yee·fee·kan·te adj* insignificant; trivial

insistere *een·see·ste·re vi* insist; insistere su qualcosa *een·see·ste·re soo kwal·ko·sa* to insist on something

insolazione *een·so·la·tsyoh·ne f* sunstroke

insolente *een·so·len·te adj* insolent

insolito(a) *een·so·lee·to(a) adj* unusual

insopportabile *een·sop·por·tah·bee·lay adj* unbearable

installarsi *een·stal·lar·see vr* settle in

insuccesso *een·sooch·ches·soh m* failure

insulina *een·soo·lee·na f* insulin

insultare *een·sool·tah·ray vt* insult

insulto *een·sool·toh m* insult

intanto *een·tan·toh adv* meanwhile

intelligente *een·tel·lee·jen·te adj* bright; smart; intelligent; clever

intelligenza *een·tel·lee·jen·tsa f* intelligence

intenzionale *een·ten·tsyoh·nah·le adj* deliberate

intenzione *een·ten·tsyoh·ne f* intention; avere* l'intenzione di fare qualcosa *a·vay·re leen·ten·tsyoh·ne dee fah·ray kwal·ko·sa* to intend to do something

interessante *een·te·res·san·te adj* interesting

interessare *een·te·res·sah·ray vt* interest; concern (*be important to*)

interessarsi *a een·te·res·sar·see a vr* be interested in

interessato(a) *een·te·res·sah·to(a) adj* interested

interesse *een·te·res·se m* interest; l'interesse composto *een·te·res·se kom·poh·sto* compound interest

interiore *een·te·ryoh·re adj* interior

internazionale *een·ter·na·tsyoh·nah·le adj* international

interno(a) *een·ter·no(a) adj* internal □ *m* l'interno *een·ter·noh* inside

intero(a) *een·te·ro(a) adj* whole

interpretare *een·ter·pre·tah·ray vt* interpret

interpretazione *een·ter·pre·ta·tsyoh·ne f* interpretation; performance (*of actor*)

interprete *een·ter·pre·te m/f* interpreter; fare* da interprete *fah·ray da een·ter·pre·te* to interpret

interrompere* *een·ter·rohm·pe·re vt* interrupt

interruttore *een·ter·root·toh·re m* switch; l'interruttore degli anabbaglianti *een·ter·root·toh·re del·yee an·ab·bal·yan·tee* dimmer

interurbano(a) *een·tayr·oor·bah·no(a) adj* long-distance (*phone call*)

intervallo *een·ter·val·loh m* half-time; intermission (*in performance*)

intervento *een·tayr·ven·toh m* intervention; operation (*medical*)

intervista *een·ter·vee·sta f* interview

intesa *een·tay·sa f* understanding (*agreement*)

intirizzito(a) *een·tee·reedz·dzee·toh(a) adj* numb (*with cold*)

intonaco *een·to·na·koh m* plaster (*for wall*)

intonarsi *een·to·nahr·see vr* match; questo s'intona con il Suo vestito *kwes·toh seen·toh·na kon eel soo·oh ves·tee·toh* this goes with your dress

intorno *een·tohr·no adv* round; intorno a *een·tohr·no a* round; guardarsi intorno *gwar·dar·see een·tohr·no* to look around

intossicazione alimentare *een·tos·see·ka·tsyoh·ne a·lee·men·tah·re f* food poisoning

intraprendere* *een·tra·pren·de·ray vt* undertake

intrattenere* *een·trat·te·nay·re vt* entertain (*amuse*)

introdurre* *een·tro·door·re vt* introduce

introduzione *een·tro·doo·tsyoh·ne f* introduction (*in book*)

introiti *een·tro·ee·tee mpl* income; revenue

intromettersi* *een·tro·mayt·ter·see vr* interfere

inutile *ee·noo·tee·lay adj* unnecessary; useless

invalido(a) *een·va·lee·do(a) adj* disabled; invalid (*contract*) □ *m* l'invalido *een·va·lee·doh* invalid

invano *een·vah·no adv* in vain

invece *een·vay·che adv* instead; invece di *een·vay·che dee* instead of

inventare *een·ven·tah·ray vt* invent

inventario *een·ven·tah·ryoh m* inventory

invenzione *een·ven·tsyoh·ne f* invention

inverno *een·ver·noh m* winter

inversione *een·vayr·syoh·nay f* U-turn (*in car*)

investigatore *een·ve·stee·ga·toh·ray m* detective

investimento *een·ve·stee·mayn·toh m* investment

investire *een·ve·stee·ray vt* run down; invest

invidia *een·vee·dya f* envy

invidiare *een·vee·dyah·ray vt* envy

invidioso(a) *een·vee·dyoh·so(a) adj* envious

invisibile *een·vee·zee·bee·lay adj* invisible

invitare *een·vee·tah·ray vt* invite

invito *een·vee·toh m* invitation

io *ee·o pron* I; sono io *so·noh ee·o* it's me; io stesso(a) *ee·o stays·so(a)* (I) myself

iodio *ee·oh·dee·oh m* iodine

iogurt *yo·goort m* yogurt

ipermercato *ee·per·mer·kah·toh m* superstore

ipoteca *ee·po·te·ka f* mortgage

ipotecare *ee·po·te·kah·ray vt* mortgage

ippodromo *eep·po·dro·moh m* racecourse

Irak *ee·rak m* Iraq

Iran *ee·ran m* Iran

Irlanda *eer·lan·da f* Ireland

irlandese *eer·lan·day·se adj* Irish

irragionevole *eer·ra·joh·nay·vo·le adj* unreasonable

irruzione *eer·roo·tsyoh·nay f* raid (*by police*)

iscritto *ee·skreet·to m* member; per iscritto *payr ee·skreet·to* in writing

Islanda *ee·slan·da f* Iceland

isola *ee·zo·la f* island; l'isola pedonale *ee·zo·la pe·do·nah·le* pedestrian precinct

isolato(a) *ee·zo·lah·to(a) adj* isolated

ispettore *ee·spet·toh·re m* inspector (*of building*); l'ispettore di polizia *ee·spet·toh·re dee po·lee·tsee·a* police inspector

ispezionare *ee·spe·tsyoh·nah·ray vt* examine; inspect

ispezione *ee·spe·tsyoh·ne f* examination (*inspection*)

Israele *ee·zra·e·le m* Israel

istante *ee·stan·te m* instant

isterico(a) *ee·ste·ree·ko(a) adj* hysterical

istituto *ee·stee·too·toh m* institute

istruire *ee·stroo·ee·re vt* educate

istruttore *ee·stroot·toh·re m* instructor

istruttrice *ee·stroot·tree·chay f* instructress

istruzione *ee·stroo·tsyoh·ne f* education

istruzioni *ee·stroo·tsyoh·nee fpl* instructions; directions

Italia *ee·ta·lya f* Italy

italiano(a) *ee·ta·lyah·no(a) adj* Italian □ *m* l'italiano *ee·ta·lyah·noh* Italian

itinerario *ee·tee·ne·rah·ryoh m* route; l'itinerario turistico *ee·tee·ne·rah·ryoh too·ree·stee·ko* scenic route

Iugoslavia *yoo·go·slah·vya f* Yugoslavia

iugoslavo(a) *yoo·go·slah·vo(a) adj* Yugoslav(ian)

J

jazz *jazz m* jazz

jeep *jeep f* jeep

jersey *jer·zee m* jersey (*fabric*)

jolly *jol·lee m* joker (*cards*)

judo *joo·doh m* judo

juke-box *jook·boks m* — jukebox

jumbo *joom·boh m* jumbo jet

K

karatè *ka·rah·te m* karate

kebab *ke·bab m* kebab

Kenia *ken·ya m* Kenya

ketchup *ke·chup m* ketchup

kirsch *keersh m* kirsch

L

la *la art* the □ *pron* her; it; you; la donna *la don·na* the woman

là *la adv* there; per di là *payr dee la* that way

labbro *lab·broh m* —a lip

laboratorio *la·bo·ra·to·ryoh m* laboratory; il laboratorio linguistico *la·bo·ra·to·ryoh leen·gwee·stee·ko* language laboratory

lacca *lak·ka f* hair spray

laccio *lach·choh m* lace (*of shoe*)

lacerare *la·che·rah·ray vt* split (*tear*)

lacrima *la·kree·ma f* tear; in lacrime *een la·kree·me* in tears

ladro *la·droh m* thief

laggiù *laj·joo adv* down there; over there

lagnarsi *lan·yahr·see vr* complain

lago *lah·goh m* lake

lama *lah·ma f* blade (*of knife*)

lamentarsi (di) *la·men·tahr·see (dee) vr* complain (about)

lametta *la·met·ta f* razor blade

lamiera *la·mye·ra f* sheet metal; la lamiera di ferro ondulata *la·mye·ra dee fer·roh on·doo·lah·ta* corrugated iron

lampada *lam·pa·da f* lamp; la lampada a raggi ultravioletti *lam·pa·da a raj·jee ool·tra·vyo·layt·tee* sunlamp; la lampada a stelo *lam·pa·da a ste·loh* floor lamp

lampadina *lam·pa·dee·na f* light bulb; la lampadina tascabile *lam·pa·dee·na ta·skah·bee·le* flashlight

lampione *lam·pyoh·ne m* streetlamp; lamppost

lampo *lam·poh m* lightning

lampone *lam·poh·nay m* raspberry

lana *lah·na f* wool; di lana *dee lah·na* woolen; la lana d'agnello *lah·na dan·yel·loh* lambswool; la lana di vetro *lah·na dee vay·troh* fiberglass

lancetta *lan·chayt·ta f* needle (*on dial*); hand (*of clock*)

lanciare *lan·chah·ray vt* throw; launch

lanolina *la·no·lee·na f* lanolin

lardo *lar·doh m* lard

larghezza *lar·gayts·tsa f* width; breadth

largo(a) *lar·go(a) adj* wide; broad; largo(a) 4 cm. *lar·go(a) 4 cm.* 4 cm. wide; al largo *al lar·go* offshore

laringite *la·reen·jee·te f* laryngitis

lasciare *la·shah·ray vt* leave; let go of; let (*allow*); lo hanno lasciato andare *lo an·no la·shah·to an·dah·ray* they let him go; lasci fare a me *la·shee fah·ray a may* leave it to me; mi lasci entrare *mee la·shee en·trah·ray* let me in

lassativo *las·sa·tee·voh m* laxative

lassù *las·soo adv* up there

lastra *la·stra f* slab; plate *(of glass, metal)*

lastricato *la·stree·kah·toh m* pavement *(roadway)*

latino *la·tee·noh m* Latin □ *adj* latino(a) *la·tee·no(a)* Latin

latinoamericano(a) *la·tee·no·a·me·ree·kah·no(a) adj* Latin American

lato *lah·toh m* side; a tutti e due i lati *a toot·tee e doo·e ee lah·tee* on either side

latrato *la·trah·toh m* bark *(of dog)*

latta *lat·ta f* can

lattaio *lat·ta·yoh m* milkman

latte *lat·tay m* milk; il latte condensato *lat·tay kon·den·sah·toh* condensed milk; il latte scremato *lat·tay skre·mah·to* skim milk; il latte evaporato *lat·tay e·va·po·rah·to* evaporated milk; il latte in polvere *lat·tay een pohl·ve·re* dried milk

latteria *lat·te·ree·a f* dairy store

lattuga *lat·too·ga f* lettuce

laurea *low·re·a f* degree *(university)*

laurearsi *low·ray·ar·see vr* graduate *(from university)*

laureato(a) *low·ray·ah·toh(a) m/f* graduate *(from university)*

lavabile *la·vah·bee·le adj* washable

lavabo *la·vah·boh m* washbasin, wash-bowl

lavacristallo *la·va·kree·stal·loh m* windshield washer

lavanderia *la·van·de·ree·a f* laundry *(place)*; la lavanderia automatica *la·van·de·ree·a ow·to·ma·tee·ka* laundromat

lavandino *la·van·dee·noh m* sink

lavare *la·vah·ray vt* wash; lavare a secco *la·vah·ray a sayk·ko* to dry-clean

lavarsi *la·var·see vr* wash (oneself), wash up; mi sono lavato(a) *mee so·noh la·vah·toh(a)* I washed myself

lavastoviglie *la·va·sto·veel·ye m* — dishwasher

lavatrice *la·va·tree·che f* washing machine

lavorare *la·vo·rah·ray vi* work

lavoratore *la·vo·ra·toh·re m* worker

lavoratrice *la·vo·ra·tree·che f* worker

lavoro *la·voh·roh m* work; un buon lavoro *oon bwon la·voh·roh* a good piece of work; il lavoro manuale *la·voh·roh ma·nwah·le* unskilled labor; il lavoro domestico *la·voh·roh do·me·stee·ko* housework; il lavoro a cottimo *la·voh·roh a kot·tee·moh* piece-work; i lavori stradali *la·voh·ree stra·dah·lee* road works

le *le art* the □ *pron* them; to her/it; to you

lecca-lecca *layk·ka·layk·ka m* — lolli-pop

leccare *lek·kah·ray vt* lick

lega *lay·ga f* alloy

legale *le·gah·le adj* legal

legare *le·gah·ray vt* bind *(tie)*; legare un pacco *le·gah·ray oon pak·koh* to tie up a parcel

legge *layj·je f* law

leggere* *lej·je·re vt/i* read

leggero(a) *lej·je·ro(a) adj* light *(not heavy)*; weak *(tea)*; mild *(cigarette)*; slight; minor *(injury)*

legno *lay·nyoh m* wood *(material)*; di legno *dee layn·yoh* wooden

lei *lay pron* she; her; you; Lei *lay* you; lei stessa *lay stays·sa* (she) herself; lei

stesso(a) *lay stays·so(a)* (you) yourself

lente *len·te f* lens *(of glasses)*; le lenti a contatto *len·tee a kon·tat·toh* contact lenses

lenticchie *len·teek·kye fpl* lentils

lento(a) *len·to(a) adj* slow; slack *(loose)*

lenzuolo *len·tswo·loh m* sheet

leone *le·oh·ne m* lion

lepre *le·pray f* hare

lettera *let·te·ra f* letter; la lettera di accompagnamento *let·te·ra dee ak·kom·pan·ya·mayn·toh* covering letter; la lettera raccomandata *let·te·ra rak·ko·man·dah·ta* registered letter; la lettera per via aerea *let·te·ra payr vee·a a·e·re·a* air letter

letteratura *let·te·ra·too·ra f* literature

lettino *let·tee·noh m* crib *(baby's)*; il lettino portatile *let·tee·noh por·tah·tee·lay* portable crib

letto *let·toh m* bed; a letto *a let·toh* in bed; andare* a letto *an·dah·ray a let·toh* to go to bed; un letto a una piazza *oon let·toh a oo·na pyats·tsa* a single bed; il letto matrimoniale *let·toh ma·tree·mo·nyah·le* double bed; il letto a castello *let·toh a ka·stel·loh* bunk beds; i letti gemelli *let·tee je·mel·lee* twin beds

lettura *let·too·ra f* reading

leva *le·va f* lever

levare *le·vah·ray vt* remove; take away; take off

levata *le·vah·ta f* collection *(of mail)*

levatrice *le·va·tree·chay f* midwife

lezione *le·tsyoh·ne f* lesson; lecture

li *lee pron* them

lì *lee adv* there

libbra *leeb·bra f* pound *(weight)*

liberare *lee·be·rah·ray vt* release

libero(a) *lee·be·ro(a) adj* free; clear *(not blocked)*; vacant *(seat, toilet)*; un giorno libero *oon johr·noh lee·be·ro* a day off

Libia *lee·bya f* Libya

libretto *lee·brayt·toh m* booklet; il libretto di circolazione *lee·brayt·toh dee cheer·ko·la·tsyoh·ne* logbook *(of car)*; il libretto di assegni *lee·brayt·toh dee as·sayn·yee* checkbook; il libretto di banca *lee·brayt·toh dee ban·ka* bankbook

libro *lee·broh m* book; il libro di testo *lee·broh dee te·stoh* textbook; il libro di fraseologia *lee·broh dee fra·ze·o·lo·jee·a* phrase book; il libro di grammatica *lee·broh dee gram·ma·tee·ka* grammar (book); il libro tascabile *lee·broh ta·skah·bee·le* paperback; il libro paga *lee·broh pah·ga* payroll

licenziare *lee·chen·tsyah·ray vt* dismiss *(from job)*; lay off *(workers)*

licenziato(a) *lee·chen·tsyah·to(a) adj* redundant *(worker)*

liceo *lee·che·oh m* high school *(for 14- to 19-year-olds)*

Liechtenstein *leekh·ten·shtine m* Liechtenstein

lieto(a) *lee·yay·to(a) adj* glad

lievito *lye·vee·toh m* yeast

lima *lee·ma f* file *(tool)*

limetta *lee·mayt·ta f* nailfile; la limetta di carta smerigliata *lee·mayt·ta dee kar·ta zme·reel·yah·ta* emery board

limitare *lee·mee·tah·ray vt* restrict

limite *lee·mee·te m* limit; boundary; oltre i limiti *ohl·tre ee lee·mee·tee* out of bounds; il limite di velocità *lee·mee·te dee ve·lo·chee·ta* speed limit

limonata *lee·mo·na·ta* f lemonade
limone *lee·moh·ne* m lemon
limousine *lee·moo·zeen* f limousine
linea *lee·ne·a* f line; la linea punteggiata *lee·ne·a poon·tej·jah·ta* dotted line
lingua *leen·gwa* f language; tongue
linguaggio *leen·gwaj·joh* m language (*way one speaks*)
lino *lee·noh* m linen (*cloth*)
linoleum *lee·no·le·oom* m linoleum
liquidazione *lee·kwee·da·tsyoh·ne* f liquidation; andare* in liquidazione *an·dah·ray een lee·kwee·da·tsyoh·ne* to go into liquidation
liquidità *lee·kwee·dee·ta* f liquid assets
liquido *lee·kwee·doh* m liquid □ adj liquido(a) *lee·kwee·do(a)* liquid
liquirizia *lee·kwee·ree·tsya* f licorice
liquore *lee·kwoh·re* m liquor
liquori *lee·kwoh·ree* mpl spirits (*alcohol*)
liscio(a) *lee·sho(a)* adj smooth; straight (*hair*); neat (*liquor*)
lista *lee·sta* f list; la lista dei vini *lee·sta de·ee ve·nee* wine list; la lista d'attesa *lee·sta dat·tay·sa* waiting list
listino prezzi *lee·stee·noh prets·tsee* m price list
lite *lee·te* f argument; quarrel
litigare *lee·tee·gah·ray* vi argue; quarrel
litro *lee·troh* m liter
livello *lee·vel·loh* m level; il livello del mare *lee·vel·loh del mah·re* sea level
lo *lo* art the □ pron him; it
locale *lo·kah·le* adj local
locanda *lo·kan·da* f inn
locomotiva *lo·ko·mo·tee·va* f engine (*of train*)
loggione *loj·joh·nay* m gallery (*in theater*)
logoramento *lo·go·ra·mayn·toh* m wear and tear
logorare *lo·go·rah·ray* vt wear out
logorarsi *lo·go·rar·see* vr wear out
logoro(a) *loh·go·ro(a)* adj worn; worn-out (*object*)
Londra *lohn·dra* f London
longplaying *long·ple·eeng* m — LP
lontananza *lon·ta·nan·tsa* f distance; in lontananza *een lon·ta·nan·tsa* in the distance
lontano *lon·tah·no* adv far; è lontano e *lon·tah·no* it's a long way; più lontano *pyoo lon·tah·no* farther
lordo(a) *lohr·doh(a)* adj gross; pretax (*profit*)
loro *loh·ro* pron they; them; to them; you; to you; Loro *loh·ro* you; to you; il loro padre *eel loh·ro pah·dre* their/your father; la loro madre *la loh·ro mah·dre* their/your mother; i loro fratelli/le loro sorelle *ee loh·ro fra·tel·lee/le loh·ro so·rel·le* their/your brothers/sisters; il/la loro *eel/la loh·ro* theirs; yours; i/le loro *ee/le loh·ro* theirs; yours; l'hanno fatto loro stessi(e) *lan·no fat·to loh·ro stays·see (·se)* they did it themselves; you did it yourselves
lotta *lot·ta* f struggle; wrestling
lottare *lot·tah·ray* vi struggle; fight
lotteria *lot·te·ree·a* f lottery
lotto *lot·toh* m lottery; lot (*at auction*)
lozione *lo·tsyoh·ne* f lotion
lubrificante *loo·bree·fee·kan·tay* m lubricant
lucchetto *look·kayt·toh* m padlock
luce *loo·che* f light; la luce rossa *loo·che rohs·sa* red light (*traffic light*)

lucidare *loo·chee·dah·ray* vt polish
lucido *loo·chee·doh* m polish (*for shoes*)
luglio *lool·yoh* m July
lui *loo·ee* pron he; him; lui stesso *loo·ee stays·so* (he) himself
luna *loo·na* f moon; la luna di miele *loo·na dee mye·le* honeymoon
luna-park *loo·na·park* m — amusement park
lunedì *loo·ne·dee* m — Monday
lunghezza *loon·gayts·tsa* f length
lungo(a) *loon·go(a)* adj long; lungo la strada *loon·go la strah·da* along the street; quant'è lungo il fiume? *kwan·te loon·go eel fyoo·me* how long is the river?; lungo(a) 6 metri *loon·go(a) 6 me·tree* 6 meters long; a lungo a *loon·go* for a long time
lungomare *loon·go·mah·re* m promenade (*by sea*); seafront
lungometraggio *loon·go·me·traj·joh* m feature film
luogo *lwo·goh* m place; in qualche luogo *een kwal·ke lwo·goh* somewhere; in nessun luogo *een nes·soon lwo·goh* nowhere; sul luogo *sool lwo·goh* on the spot
lupo *loo·poh* m wolf
Lussemburgo *loos·sem·boor·goh* m Luxembourg
lusso *loos·so* m luxury; di lusso *dee loos·so* de luxe; luxury (*car, hotel*)

M

ma *ma* conj but
macadam *ma·ka·dam* m tarmac
maccheroni *mak·ke·roh·nee* mpl macaroni
macchia *mak·kya* f spot; stain; blot
macchiare *mak·kyah·ray* vt stain; mark
macchina *mak·kee·na* f car; machine; la macchina da scrivere *mak·kee·na da skree·ve·re* typewriter; la macchina per cucire *mak·kee·na payr koo·chee·re* sewing machine; la macchina fotografica *mak·kee·na fo·to·gra·fee·ka* camera; la macchina mangiasoldi *mak·kee·na man·ja·sol·dee* one-armed bandit; la macchina della polizia *mak·kee·na del·la po·lee·tsee·a* police car; la macchina sportiva *mak·kee·na spor·tee·va* sport(s) car; la macchina noleggiata *mak·kee·na no·lej·jah·ta* rental car
macchinario *mak·kee·nah·ryoh* m plant (*equipment*); machinery
macchinetta per il caffè *mak·kee·nayt·ta payr eel kaf·fe* f percolator
macedonia *ma·che·don·ya* f fruit salad
macellaio *ma·chel·la·yoh* m butcher
macelleria *ma·chel·le·ree·a* f butcher's (*shop*)
macinare *ma·chee·nah·ray* vt mill; grind
macinato(a) *ma·chee·nah·toh(a)* adj ground (*coffee*)
macinino *ma·chee·nee·noh* m mill (*for coffee, pepper*)
madera *ma·de·ra* m Madeira (*wine*)
madre *mah·dray* f mother
Madrid *ma·dreed* f Madrid
madrina *ma·dree·na* f godmother
maestra *ma·ay·stra* f teacher (*primary school*)
maestro *ma·ay·stroh* m master; teacher (*primary school*)
magazzino *ma·gadz·dzee·noh* m store (*big shop*); store room; warehouse; in magazzino *een ma·gadz·dzee·noh*

in stock; **il grande magazzino** *gran·de ma·gadz·dzee·noh* department store

maggio *maj·joh* m May

maggiorana *maj·jo·rah·na* f marjoram

maggioranza *maj·jo·ran·tsa* f majority; **eletto(a) con una maggioranza di 5 voti** *e·let·toh(a) kon oo·na maj·jo·ran·tsa de 5 voh·tee* elected by a majority of 5

maggiore *maj·joh·re* adj larger; greater; largest; greatest; elder; eldest; **il/la maggiore** *maj·joh·re* elder; eldest; **ne ha la maggior parte** *nay a la maj·johr pahr·tay* he has the most

magia *ma·jee·a* f magic

magico(a) *ma·jee·koh(a)* adj magic

maglia *mal·ya* f jersey (*sweater*); **lavorare a maglia** *la·vo·rah·ray a mal·ya* to knit

maglieria *mal·ye·ree·a* f knitwear

maglietta *mal·yayt·ta* f T-shirt

maglio *mal·yo* m mallet

maglione *mal·yoh·ne* m sweater

magnate *man·yah·te* m tycoon

magnetofono *man·ye·to·fo·noh* m tape recorder; **il magnetofono a cassetta** *man·ye·to·fo·noh a kas·sayt·ta* cassette-recorder

magnifico(a) *ma·nyee·fee·koh(a)* adj great (*excellent*); magnificent; grand

magro(a) *ma·gro(a)* adj thin (*person*); lean (*meat*)

mai *ma·ee* adv never; **egli non viene mai** *el·yee nohn vye·nay ma·ee* he never comes; **è mai stato a Londra?** *e ma·ee stah·to a lohn·dra* have you ever been to London?

maiale *ma·yah·le* m pig; pork

maionese *ma·yo·nay·say* f mayonnaise

mais *ma·ees* m corn (*cereal crop*)

maiuscola *ma·yoos·ko·la* f capital letter; **A maiuscola** *a ma·yoos·ko·la* capital A

malato(a) *ma·lah·to(a)* adj ill; sick

malattia *ma·lat·tee·a* f illness; disease

male *mah·le* adv badly (*not well*) □ m il male *mah·le* pain; ache; **fare* male** *fah·ray mah·le* to hurt; **Si è fatto male** *see e fat·to mah·le* you've hurt yourself; **quello fa male!** *kwayl·lo fa mah·le* that hurts!

malgrado *mal·grah·do* prep in spite of; despite

Malta *mal·ta* f Malta

malto *mal·toh* m malt

malva *mal·va* adj mauve

malvagio(a) *mal·va·jo(a)* adj wicked

mamma *mam·ma* f mom(my)

mancanza *man·kan·tsa* f lack; shortage

mancare *man·kah·ray* vt miss (*target*); **è mancato per poco** *e man·kah·to payr po·ko* it only just missed; **mancano alcune pagine** *man·ka·noh al·koo·nay pah·jee·nay* some pages are missing

mancia *man·cha* f tip (*money given*)

mancino(a) *man·chee·no(a)* adj left-handed

mandare *man·dah·ray* vt send

mandarino *man·da·ree·noh* m tangerine

mandorla *man·dor·la* f almond

manette *ma·nayt·te* fpl handcuffs

mangiare *man·jah·ray* vt eat

manica *mah·nee·ka* f sleeve

Manica *mah·nee·ka* f Channel

manico *mah·nee·koh* m handle (*of brush, knife*)

manicure *ma·nee·koo·ray* f manicure

maniere *man·ye·ray* fpl manners

manifestazione *ma·nee·fe·sta·tsyoh·ne* f demonstration (*political*); rally

manifesto *ma·nee·fe·stoh* m poster

maniglia *ma·neel·ya* f door handle, doorknob

mano *mah·noh* f —i hand; trick (*in cards*); **a mano** *a mah·noh* by hand; **fatto(a) a mano** *fat·to(a) a mah·noh* handmade

manodopera *mah·no·do·pe·ra* f labor; manpower; work force

manopola *ma·no·po·la* f knob (*on radio etc*); mitt(en); **la manopola di spugna** *ma·no·po·la dee spoon·ya* facecloth

manovale *ma·no·vah·le* m laborer

manovella *ma·no·vel·la* f handle (*for winding*)

mantello *man·tel·loh* m cloak; coat; **il mantello di visone** *man·tel·loh dee vee·zoh·nay* mink coat

mantenere* *man·te·nay·re* vt support (*financially*); keep (*feed and clothe*)

manuale *ma·nwah·lay* adj manual □ m il manuale *ma·nwah·lay* manual; handbook

manubrio *ma·noo·bryoh* m handlebar(s)

manutenzione *ma·noo·ten·tsyoh·nay* f upkeep; maintenance

manzo *man·dzoh* m beef

marca *mar·ka* f brand (*of product*); brand name

marchio *mar·kyoh* m hallmark; **il marchio di fabbrica** *mar·kyoh dee fab·bree·ka* trademark; **il marchio depositato** *mar·kyoh de·po·zee·tah·to* registered trademark

marciapiede *mar·cha·pye·de* m pavement; sidewalk; **il marciapiede a rulli** *mar·cha·pye·de a rool·lee* moving walkway

marciare *mar·chah·ray* vi march

marcio(a) *mar·cho(a)* adj rotten (*wood etc*)

marcire *mar·chee·ray* vi rot; go bad

marco *mahr·koh* m mark (*currency*)

Mar dei Caraibi *mahr de·ee ka·ra·ee·bee* m Caribbean (*Sea*)

mare *mah·re* m sea; seaside; **avere* mal di mare** *a·vay·re mal dee mah·re* to be seasick

marea *ma·re·a* f tide; **la bassa marea** *bas·sa ma·re·a* low tide; **c'è alta/bassa marea** *che al·ta/bas·sa ma·re·a* the tide is in/out

Mare del Nord *mah·ray del nord* m North Sea

margarina *mahr·ga·ree·na* f margarine

margine *mar·jee·ne* m margin (*on page*); **il margine di profitto** *mar·jee·ne dee pro·feet·toh* profit margin

marina *ma·ree·na* f navy

marinaio *ma·ree·na·yoh* m sailor

marito *ma·ree·toh* m husband

marketing *mahr·ke·ting* m marketing

marmellata *mar·mel·lah·ta* f jam; **la marmellata d'arance** *mar·mel·lah·ta da·ran·chay* marmalade

marmitta *mar·meet·ta* f muffler (*on car*)

marmo *mahr·moh* m marble (*material*)

marocchino(a) *ma·rok·kee·noh(a)* adj Moroccan

Marocco *ma·rok·koh* m Morocco

marrone *mar·roh·ne* adj brown; marrone rossiccio *mar·roh·ne ros·seech· cho* tan

marsina *mar·see·na* f tailcoat

martedì *mar·te·dee* m — Tuesday

martedì grasso *mar·te·dee gras·so* m Shrove Tuesday

martello *mar·tel·loh* m hammer

marzapane *mahr·tsa·pah·nay* m marzipan

marzo *mahr·tsoh* m March

mascara *mas·ka·ra* m mascara

mascella *ma·shel·la* f jaw

maschera *mas·ke·ra* f mask; usherette

mascherare *mas·ke·rah·ray* vt mask

maschile *mas·kee·lay* adj masculine

maschio *mask·yo* adj male

massa *mas·sa* f mass

massaggiare *mas·saj·jah·ray* vt massage

massaggiatore *mas·saj·ja·toh·re* m masseur

massaggiatrice *mas·saj·ja·tree·chay* f masseuse

massaggio *mas·saj·joh* m massage

massiccio(a) *mas·see·choh(a)* adj massive

massimo *mas·see·moh* m maximum □ adj massimo(a) *mas·see·moh(a)* maximum; al massimo al *mas·see· moh* at the most; sfruttare al massimo *sfroot·tah·ray* al *mas·see·moh* to make the most of

mass media *mass mee·dee·a* mpl media

masticare *ma·stee·kah·ray* vt chew

mastro *ma·stroh* m ledger

matematica *ma·te·ma·tee·ka* f mathematics

materasso *ma·te·ras·soh* m mattress; il materasso pneumatico *ma·te·ras·soh pne·oo·ma·te·ko* air-mattress; air bed

materia *ma·te·ree·a* f subject (*in school*); le materie prime *ma·te·ree·e pree·me* raw materials

materiale *ma·te·ryah·lay* m material

maternità *ma·tayr·nee·ta* f maternity hospital

matita *ma·tee·ta* f pencil

matrice *ma·tree·che* f stub (*of check*)

matrigna *ma·treen·ya* f stepmother

matrimonio *ma·tree·mo·nyoh* m wedding; marriage

matterello *mat·te·rel·loh* m rolling pin

mattina *mat·tee·na* f morning

mattino *mat·tee·noh* m morning

mattone *mat·toh·ne* m brick

maturarsi *ma·too·rar·see* vr ripen; accrue

maturo(a) *ma·too·ro(a)* adj ripe (*fruit*); mature

mazza *mats·tsa* f club; bat

mazziere *mats·tsye·re* m dealer (*cards*)

mazzo *mats·tsoh* m pack (*of cards*); bunch

me *may* pron me

meccanico *mek·kan·ee·koh* m mechanic

meccanismo *mek·ka·nee·zmoh* m mechanism; works

media *me·dya* f average

medicina *me·dee·chee·na* f medicine

medicinale *me·dee·chee·nah·le* m drug (*medicine*)

medico(a) *me·dee·koh(a)* adj medical □ m il medico *me·dee·koh* doctor; il medico generico *me·dee·koh je·ne· ree·koh* general practitioner, G.P.

medio(a) *me·dee·o(a)* adj medium; average

mediocre *me·dee·o·kre* adj poor (*mediocre*)

Medio Oriente *med·yoh o·ree·en·tay* m Middle East

mediterraneo(a) *me·dee·ter·rah·nay· oh(a)* adj Mediterranean □ m il Mediterraneo *me·dee·ter·rah·nay·oh* the Mediterranean (Sea)

medusa *me·doo·za* f jellyfish

meglio *mel·yo* adv, adj better; best; canta meglio di te *kan·ta mel·yo dee te* he sings better than you; sempre meglio *sem·pre mel·yo* better and better

mela *may·la* f apple

melagrana *me·la·grah·na* f pomegranate

melanzana *me·lan·dzah·na* f eggplant

melassa *me·las·sa* f treacle; molasses; la melassa raffinata *me·las·sa raf·fee· nah·ta* (golden) syrup

melo *may·loh* m apple tree

melone *me·loh·nay* m melon

membro *mem·broh* m member

memoria *me·mo·ree·a* f memory; a memoria *a me·mo·ree·a* by heart

mendicante *men·dee·kan·te* m/f beggar

mendicare *men·dee·kah·ray* vi beg

meno *may·no* adv less; minus; a meno che noi non veniamo *a may·no ke noy nohn ve·nya·mo* unless we come; il meno caro *eel may·no kah· ro* the least expensive; il meno denaro *eel may·no de·nah·roh* the least money; ha il meno *a eel may·no* he has the least; meno carne *may·no kar·ne* less meat; meno errori *may·no er·roh·ree* fewer errors; meno rapidamente *may·no ra·pee·da·mayn·te* less quickly; meno di may·no dee less than; meno di un chilometro *may·no dee oon kee·lo·me·troh* under a kilometer

mensa *men·sa* f canteen

mensile *men·see·lay* adj monthly □ m il mensile *men·see·lay* monthly

menta *mayn·ta* f mint (*herb*); la menta peperita *mayn·ta pe·pe·ree·ta* peppermint (*plant*)

mente *mayn·tay* f mind

mentire* *men·tee·re* vi lie (*tell a lie*)

mento *mayn·toh* m chin

mentre *mayn·tre* conj while; whereas; è arrivato mentre stavamo partendo *e ar·ree·vah·to mayn·tre sta·vah·mo par·ten·do* he arrived as we left

menù *me·noo* m — menu

menzionare *men·tsyo·nah·ray* vt mention

menzione *men·tsyoh·nay* f reference (*mention*)

meraviglioso(a) *me·ra·veel·yoh·so(a)* adj wonderful; marvelous

mercante *mayr·kan·tay* m merchant

mercato *mer·kah·toh* m market; il mercato delle valute estere *mer·kah· toh del·le va·loo·te e·ste·re* foreign exchange market; il mercato delle pulci *mer·kah·toh del·le pool·chee* flea market

Mercato Comune *mer·kah·toh ko· moo·nay* m Common Market

merceria *mayr·che·ree·a* f notions

merci *mayr·chee* fpl freight; goods

mercoledì *mayr·ko·le·dee* m — Wednesday

merenda *me·ren·da* f snack

meridionale *me·ree·dyo·nah·le* adj southern

meringa *me·reen·ga* f meringue

meritare *me·ree·tah·ray* vt deserve

merlano *mayr·lah·noh* m whiting

merlo *mer·loh* m blackbird

merluzzo *mayr·loots·tsoh m* cod

meschino(a) *mes·kee·noh(a) adj* mean (*unkind*)

mescolanza *me·sko·lan·tsa f* mixture

mescolare *me·sko·lah·ray vt* blend; mix

mescolarsi *me·sko·lahr·see vr* mix

mese *may·say m* month

messa *mes·sa f* mass (*church*)

messaggero *mes·saj·je·roh m* messenger

messaggio *mes·saj·joh m* message

messicano(a) *mes·see·ka·noh(a) adj* Mexican

Messico *mes·see·koh m* Mexico

mestiere *may·stee·ay·ray m* job; trade

mestruazioni *me·stroo·a·tsyoh·nee fpl* period (*menstruation*)

metà *me·ta f* — half; a metà *a me·ta* half; a metà prezzo *a me·ta prets·tsoh* half-price; a metà strada *a me·ta strah·da* halfway; dividere* a metà *dee·vee·de·re a me·ta* to halve (*divide in two*); ridurre* di metà *ree·door·re dee me·ta* to halve (*reduce by half*)

metallo *me·tal·loh m* metal

metodo *me·to·doh m* method

metrico(a) *met·ree·koh(a) adj* metric

metro *me·troh m* meter (*measure*); il metro a nastro *me·troh a na·stroh* tape measure

metropolitana *me·tro·po·lee·tah·na f* subway; underground railway

mettere* *mayt·te·re vt* put; put on (*clothes*); mettere* qualcuno in comunicazione *mayt·te·re kwal·koo·no een ko·moo·nee·ka·tsyoh·ne* to put someone through (*on phone*)

mezzanotte *medz·dza·not·tay f* midnight

mezzi *medz·dzee mpl* means

mezzo(a) *medz·dzoh(a) adj* half □ m il mezzo *medz·dzoh* half; middle; nel bel mezzo *nel bel medz·dzoh* right in the middle; due e mezzo *doo·e ay medz·dzoh* two and a half; tre chilometri e mezzo *tray kee·lo·me·tree ay medz·dzoh* three and a half kilometers; per mezzo di *payr medz·dzoh dee* by means of; di mezza età *dee medz·dza ay·ta* middle-aged; una mezza dozzina *oo·na medz·dza dodz·dzee·na* a half dozen

mezzogiorno *medz·dzo·johr·noh m* midday; noon

mezz'ora *medz·dzoh·ra f* half-hour

mi *mee pron* me; to me; myself

mia *mee·a adj* my □ pron mine

microbo *mee·kro·boh m* germ

microchip *mee·kro·chip m* — microchip

microcomputer *mee·kro·kom·poo·tayr m* — microcomputer

microfilm *mee·kro·feelm m* — microfilm

microfono *mee·kro·fo·noh m* microphone

microprocessor *mee·kro·pro·ches·sohr m* — microprocessor

microscheda *mee·kro·ske·da f* microfiche

mie *mee·ay adj* my □ pron mine

miei *mee·ay·ee adj* my □ pron mine

miele *mye·le m* honey

mietere *mye·te·re vt* harvest (*grain*)

miglio *meel·yoh m* —a mile

miglioramento *meel·yo·ra·mayn·toh m* improvement

migliorare *meel·yo·rah·ray vt/i* improve

migliore *meel·yoh·re adj* better; best;

il/la migliore *eel/la meel·yoh·re* the best

miliardo *mee·lyar·doh m* billion

milionario *mee·lee·o·nah·ree·oh m* millionaire

milione *mee·lee·oh·nay m* million

milionesimo(a) *mee·lee·o·ne·zee·moh(a) adj* millionth

militare *mee·lee·tah·ray adj* military

mille *meel·le num* thousand

millesimo(a) *meel·le·zee·mo(a) adj* thousandth

milligrammo *mee·lee·gram·moh m* milligram

millilitro *meel·lee·lee·troh m* milliliter

millimetro *meel·lee·me·troh m* millimeter

mina *mee·na f* lead (*in pencil*)

minaccia *mee·nach·cha f* threat

minacciare *mee·nach·chah·ray vt* threaten

minatore *mee·na·toh·ray m* miner

minestrone *mee·ne·stroh·nay m* minestrone (soup)

minicomputer *mee·nee·kom·poo·ter m* minicomputer

miniera *mee·nye·rah f* mine (*for coal etc*)

minigonna *mee·nee·gohn·na f* miniskirt

minimo *mee·nee·moh m* minimum □ adj minimo(a) *mee·nee·moh(a)* minimum

ministero *mee·nee·ste·roh m* ministry; il Ministero del Tesoro *mee·nee·ste·roh del te·zo·roh* Treasury

ministro *mee·nee·stroh m* minister; il Ministro delle Finanze *mee·nee·stroh del·le fee·nan·tse* Finance Minister; il primo ministro *pree·mo mee·nee·stroh* prime minister, P.M.

minoranza *mee·no·ran·tsa f* minority

minore *mee·noh·re adj* less; smaller; lower; younger

minorenne *mee·no·ren·ne adj* under age

minuto *mee·noo·toh m* minute

mio *mee·oh adj* my □ pron mine; un mio amico *oon mee·oh a·mee·koh* a friend of mine

miope *mee·o·pe adj* nearsighted

mira *mee·ra f* aim; prendere* la mira *pren·de·re la mee·ra* to aim

mirtillo *meer·teel·loh m* cranberry

miscela *mee·she·la f* blend

mistero *mee·ster·oh m* mystery

misto(a) *mee·stoh(a) adj* mixed

misura *mee·zoo·ra f* measure; measurement; prendere* le misure per fare qualcosa *pren·de·re le mee·zoo·re payr fah·ray kwal·ko·sa* to take steps to do something; fatto(a) su misura *fat·toh(a) soo mee·zoo·ra* custom-made

misurare *mee·zoo·rah·ray vt/i* measure

mite *mee·tay adj* mild; gentle

mittente *meet·ten·te m/f* sender

mobile *mo·bee·le m* piece of furniture

mobili *mo·bee·lee mpl* furniture

mochetta *mo·kayt·ta f* wall-to-wall carpet(ing)

moda *mo·da f* fashion; l'ultima moda *lool·tee·ma mo·da* the latest fashions; di moda *dee mo·da* fashionable

modellista *mo·del·lee·sta m/f* designer

modello *mo·del·loh m* model

modernizzare *mo·der·needz·dzah·ray vt* modernize

moderno(a) *mo·der·noh(a) adj* modern

modesto(a) *mo·de·stoh(a) adj* modest

modifica *mo·dee·fee·ka f* modification

modificare mo·dee·fee·kah·ray vt modify

modo mo·doh m way; manner; **ad ogni modo** ad ohn·yee mo·doh in any case; **in tutti i modi** een toot·tee ee mo·dee at all costs; **in qualche modo** een kwal·kay mo·doh somehow

modulo mo·doo·loh m form (document); **il modulo d'ordinazione** mo·doo·loh dor·dee·na·tsyoh·ne order-form

mogano mo·ga·noh m mahogany

moglie mohl·ye f wife

mohair mo·er m mohair

molecola mo·le·ko·la f molecule

molla mol·la f spring (coil)

molletta mol·layt·ta f clothespin

molo mo·loh m pier

molti(e) mohl·tee(·te) adj, pron many

moltiplicare mol·tee·plee·kah·ray vt multiply

moltiplicazione mol·tee·plee·kats·yoh·nay f multiplication

molto mohl·to adv a lot; much; very; **mi piace molto** mee pyah·che mohl·to I like it very much; **molto meglio** mohl·to mel·yoh much better

molto(a) mohl·to(a) adj, pron much; **molto latte** mohl·to lat·te a lot of milk; **molta gente** mohl·ta jen·te lots of people

momento mo·mayn·toh m moment; **un momento** oon mo·mayn·toh just a minute; **in questo momento** een kway·stoh mo·mayn·toh at the moment; at present; **per il momento** payr eel mo·mayn·toh for the time being

monaca mo·na·ka f nun

monaco mo·na·koh m monk

Monaco mo·na·koh f Monaco

Monaco di Baviera mo·na·koh dee Ba·vye·ra f Munich

monastero mo·na·ste·roh m monastery

mondo mohn·doh m world

moneta mo·nay·ta f coin

monetario(a) mo·ne·tah·ree·oh(a) adj monetary

monitore mo·nee·toh·ray m monitor (TV)

mono mo·noh adj mono

monopolio mo·no·po·lyo m monopoly

monorotaia mo·no·ro·ta·ya f monorail

montagna mon·tan·ya f mountain

montare mon·tah·ray vt go up; assemble (parts of machine); whip (cream, eggs)

montatura mon·ta·too·ra f frames (of eyeglasses)

monumento mo·noo·mayn·toh m monument

mora mo·ra f blackberry

morbido(a) mor·bee·do(a) adj soft (not hard)

morbillo mor·beel·loh m measles

mordere mor·de·re vt bite

morire mo·ree·re vi die

morso mor·soh m bite (by animal)

morte mor·te f death

morto(a) mor·to(a) adj dead

mosca mo·ska f fly

Mosca moh·ska f Moscow

moscerino mo·she·ree·noh m gnat

moschea mo·skay·a f mosque

mosella mo·zel·la m moselle (wine)

mostarda mo·stahr·da f mustard

mostra moh·stra f show; exhibition

mostrare mo·strah·ray vt show

mostro mo·stroh m monster

motel mo·tel m — motel

moto mo·toh m motion

motocicletta mo·to·chee·klayt·ta f motorbike

motociclista mo·to·chee·klee·sta m/f motorcyclist

motolancia mo·to·lan·cha f launch

motore mo·toh·re m engine; motor; **il motore diesel** mo·toh·re dee·zel diesel engine

motorino d'avviamento mo·to·ree·noh dav·vya·mayn·toh m starter (in car)

motoscafo mo·to·skah·foh m motorboat

mousse moos f mousse

movimento mo·vee·mayn·toh m motion; movement; **il movimento delle merci** mo·vee·mayn·toh del·le mer·chee turnover (in goods)

mucchio mook·kyoh m pile; heap

mulino moo·lee·noh m mill; **il mulino a vento** moo·lee·noh a ven·toh windmill

multa mool·ta f fine; **la multa per sosta vietata** mool·ta payr so·sta vye·tah·ta parking-ticket

multilingue mool·tee·leen·gway adj multilingual

multinazionale mool·tee·nats·yo·nah·lay adj multinational

municipale moo·nee·chee·pah·lay adj municipal

municipio moo·nee·chee·pyoh m town hall; city hall

muovere mwo·ve·ray vt move

muoversi mwo·ver·see vr move

muro moo·roh m wall

muscolo moos·ko·loh m muscle

museo moo·ze·oh m museum

musica moo·ze·ka f music; **la musica leggera** moo·zee·ka lej·je·ra light music

musicista moo·zee·chee·sta m/f musician

musulmano(a) moo·sool·mah·noh(a) adj Muslim □ m/f il/la **musulmano(a)** moo·sool·mah·noh(a) Muslim

mutande moo·tan·day fpl underpants

mutandine moo·tan·dee·ne fpl panties; pants

muto(a) moo·to(a) adj dumb

N

nafta naf·ta f diesel oil

nailon nai·lon m nylon

narrativa nar·ra·tee·va f fiction

nascere na·she·re vi be born

nascita na·shee·ta f birth

nascondere na·skohn·de·re vt hide

nascondersi na·skohn·der·see vr hide

naso nah·soh m nose

nastro na·stroh m ribbon; tape; **il nastro adesivo** na·stroh a·de·zee·vo Scotch tape; **il nastro magnetico** na·stroh man·ye·tee·koh magnetic tape

Natale na·tah·lay m Christmas; **il giorno di Natale** johr·noh dee na·tah·lay Christmas Day

nativo(a) na·tee·voh(a) adj native

nato(a) nah·to(a) adj born

natura na·too·ra f nature

naturale na·too·rah·lay adj natural

naturalizzato(a) na·too·ra·leedz·dzah·toh(a) adj naturalized

naturalmente na·too·ral·mayn·te adv of course; naturally

naufragare now·fra·gah·ray vi be wrecked (ship)

naufragio now·frah·joh m shipwreck

nausea now·ze·a f sickness; nausea

navata na·vah·ta f nave

nave *nah·ve f* ship; **la nave cisterna** *nah·ve chee·ster·na* tanker (*ship*)

nave-traghetto *nah·ve·tra·gayt·toh f* ferry

navigare *na·vee·gah·ray vi* sail

navigazione *na·vee·ga·tsyoh·ne f* navigation

nazionale *na·tsyoh·nah·lay adj* national

nazionalità *na·tsyoh·na·lee·ta f —* nationality

nazionalizzare *na·tsyoh·na·leedz·dzah·ray vt* nationalize

nazione *na·tsyoh·nay f* nation

Nazioni Unite *na·tsyoh·nee oo·nee·tay fpl* United Nations Organization, UN, UNO

ne *nay pron* of him/her/it/them; some; **non ne abbiamo** *nohn nay ab·byah·mo* we haven't any; **ne avanza un po'** *nay a·van·tsah·va oon po* some (of it) was left

né .... né *nay ... nay* neither ... nor; **né l'uno né l'altro** *nay loo·noh nay lal·troh* neither

neanche *nay·an·ke adv, conj* not even; neither

nebbia *nayb·bya f* fog; **c'è della nebbia che** *del·la nayb·bya* it's foggy

nebbioso(a) *neb·byoh·so(a) adj* foggy

necessario(a) *ne·ches·sah·ree·oh(a) adj* necessary

negare *ne·gah·ray vt* deny

negativa *ne·ga·tee·va f* negative (*of photo*)

negli = in + gli

negoziabile *ne·go·tsyah·bee·lay adj* negotiable

negoziante *ne·go·tsyan·tay m* shopkeeper

negoziare *ne·go·tsyah·ray vi* negotiate

negozio *ne·go·tsyoh m* shop; **fare* un giro dei negozi** *fah·ray oon jee·roh de·ee ne·go·tsee* to go round the shops; **il negozio di calzature** *ne·go·tsyoh dee kal·tsa·too·re* shoeshop; **il negozio a catena** *ne·go·tsyoh a ka·tay·na* chain store; **il negozio di giocattoli** *ne·go·tsyoh dee jo·kat·to·lee* toyshop

nei = in + i, nel = in + il

nemico *ne·mee·koh m* enemy

nemmeno *nem·may·noh adv, conj* not even; **io non c'ero e nemmeno lui** *ee·o nohn che·ro e nem·may·noh loo·ee* I wasn't there and neither was he

nero(a) *nay·ro(a) adj* black

nervo *ner·voh m* nerve

nervoso(a) *ner·voh·soh(a) adj* nervous

nessuno(a) *nes·soo·no(a) adj* no; any □ *pron* nobody; none; anybody; **non vedo nessuno** *nohn vay·do nes·soo·no* I can't see anybody; **non lo vedo in nessun luogo** *nohn lo vay·do een nes·soon lwo·goh* I can't see it anywhere

netto(a) *nayt·toh(a) adj* net (*income, price*)

neutrale *ne·oo·trah·lay adj* neutral

neve *nay·ve f* snow

nevicare *ne·vee·kah·ray vi* snow; **nevica** *nay·vee·ka* it's snowing

nevischio *ne·vee·skyoh m* sleet

nido *nee·doh m* nest; **il nido d'infanzia** *nee·doh deen·fan·tsya* day nursery; crèche

niente *nyen·te pron* nothing; anything; □ *m* nothing; **non vedo niente** *nohn vay·do nyen·te* I can't see anything

night-club *nait·kloob m* night club

nipote *nee·poh·tay m* grandson; nephew □ *f* granddaughter; niece

nipotino(a) *nee·po·tee·noh(a) m/f* grandchild

no *no adv* no (*as answer*)

nocca *nok·ka f* knuckle

nocciolo *noch·cho·loh m* stone (*in fruit*)

noce *noh·che f* walnut

nocivo(a) *no·chee·vo(a) adj* harmful

nodo *no·doh m* knot; bow (*ribbon*); **fare* un nodo** *fah·ray oon no·doh* to tie a knot; **il nodo ferroviario** *no·doh fer·ro·vee·ah·ree·oh* junction (*railway*)

noi *noy pron* we; us; **siamo noi** *syah·mo noy* it's us; **noi stessi(e)** *noy stays·see('se)* (we) ourselves

noioso(a) *no·yoh·so(a) adj* dull; boring; annoying

noleggiare *no·lej·jah·ray vt* hire; rent; charter (*plane, bus*)

noleggio *no·layj·joh m* hire; rental

nome *noh·may m* name; first name; **a nome di** *a noh·may dee* on behalf of; **il nome di battesimo** *noh·may dee bat·tay·zee·moh* Christian name

nomina *no·mee·na f* appointment (*to job*)

nominare *no·mee·nah·ray vt* appoint

non *nohn adv* not □ *pref* non- *nohn·* non-

nondimeno *nohn·dee·may·no conj* all the same

non-fumatore *nohn·foo·ma·toh·ray m* nonsmoker (*person*)

nonna *non·na f* grandmother

nonno *non·noh m* grandfather

nono(a) *no·noh(a) adj* ninth

nord *nord m* north; **a nord** *a nord* north

nord-est *nord·est m* northeast

nord-ovest *nord·o·vest m* northwest

norma *nor·ma f* norm; par (*golf*)

normale *nor·mah·lay adj* normal; regular

normalmente *nor·mal·mayn·tay adv* normally

nostalgia *no·stal·jee·a f* homesickness; nostalgia

nostro(a) *no·stroh(a) adj* our □ *pron* nostro *no·stroh pah·dray* ours; nostri(e) *no·streel'(shee)* our; ours

nota *no·ta f* note; memo(randum)

notare *no·tah·ray vt* notice

notevole *no·tay·vo·lay adj* remarkable

notizie *no·tee·tsye fpl* news

notte *not·tay f* night

novanta *no·van·ta num* ninety

nove *no·vay num* nine

novembre *no·vem·bre m* November

novità *no·vee·ta f —* novelty; news

nubile *noo·bee·le* single (*unmarried: woman*)

nucleare *noo·klay·ah·ray adj* nuclear

nudo(a) *noo·doh(a) adj* naked; nude; bare

nullo(a) *nool·loh(a) adj* void (*contract*); nullo(a) e di nessun effetto *nool·loh(a) e dee nes·soon ef·fet·toh* null and void

numero *noo·me·roh m* number (*figure*); act (*at circus etc*); issue (*of magazine*); size (*of shoes*); **il numero telefonico** *noo·me·roh te·le·fo·nee·ko* telephone number; **il numero di immatricolazione** *noo·me·roh dee eem·ma·tree·ko·la·tsyoh·nay* license number (*on car*)

nuora *nwoh·ra f* daughter-in-law

nuotare *nwo·tah·ray vi* swim

nuoto *nwo·toh m* swimming

nuovo(a) *nwo·voh(a) adj* new

nutrire *noo·tree·re* vt feed
nuvola *noo·vo·la* f cloud
nuvoloso(a) *noo·vo·loh·soh(a)* adj
cloudy

O

o *o* conj or; o... o o... *o* either... or...
obbediente *ob·be·dyen·te* adj obedient
obbligo *ob·blee·goh* m obligation
obiettare a *o·byet·tah·ray a vi* object to
obiettivo *o·byet·tee·voh* m lens (*of camera*); target; objective; l'obiettivo grandangolare *o·byet·tee·voh gran·dan·goh·lah·re* wide-angle lens
oblò *o·blo* m porthole
oblungo(a) *o·bloon·go(a)* adj oblong
oca *o·ka* f goose
occasione *ok·ka·zee·oh·ne* f opportunity; occasion; bargain (*cheap buy*)
occhiali *ok·kyah·lee* mpl glasses; goggles; eyeglasses; gli occhiali da sole *ok·kyah·lee da soh·le* sunglasses; shades
occhio *ok·kyoh* m eye; l'occhio nero *ok·kyoh nay·ro* black eye; strizzare l'occhio *streets·tsah·ray lok·kyoh* to wink
occidentale *och·chee·den·tah·le* adj western
Occidente *och·chee·den·te* m the West
occorrere* *ok·kohr·re·re* vi be necessary; non occorre che lei venga *nohn ok·kohr·ray kay le·ee ven·ga* you don't need to come
occuparsi *ok·koo·par·see* vr occupy oneself; occuparsi di qualcosa *ok·koo·par·see dee kwal·ko·sa* to see to something
occupato(a) *ok·koo·pah·to(a)* adj busy; engaged
oceano *o·che·a·noh* m ocean
Oceano Pacifico *o·che·a·noh pa·chee·fee·ko* m Pacific Ocean
odiare *o·dyah·ray* vt hate
odio *o·dyoh* m hatred
odore *o·doh·re* m smell; scent; ha un odore forte *a oon o·doh·re for·te* it has a strong smell
offendere* *of·fen·de·re* vt offend
offerente *of·fe·ren·te* m/f bidder
offerta *of·fer·ta* f bid; offer; l'offerta e la domanda *lof·fer·ta e la do·man·da* supply and demand; l'offerta di acquisto *of·fer·ta dee ak·kwee·stoh* take-over bid; fare* un'offerta per qualcosa *fah·ray oo·nof·fer·ta payr kwal·ko·sa* to bid for something
officina *of·fee·chee·na* f workshop
offrire* *of·free·re* vt offer; bid (*amount*); offrire di fare qualcosa *of·free·re dee fah·ray kwal·ko·sa* to offer to do something; Le offrirò un gelato *lay of·free·ro oon je·lah·toh* I'll treat you to an ice cream cone
oggetto *oj·jet·toh* m object; l'oggetto d'antiquariato *oj·jet·toh dan·tee·kwa·ree·ah·toh* antique
oggi *oj·jee* adv today; quanti ne abbiamo oggi? *kwan·tee ne ab·byah·mo oj·jee* what's the date today?
oggigiorno *oj·jee·johr·noh* adv nowadays
ogni *ohn·yee* adj every; each; ogni due giorni *ohn·yee doo·e johr·nee* every other day; ogni sei giorni *ohn·yee se·ee johr·nee* every 6th day
ognuno *o·nyoo·noh* pron everyone
Olanda *o·lan·da* f Holland
olandese *o·lan·day·se* adj Dutch □ m l'olandese *o·lan·day·se* Dutch

oleodotto *o·le·o·doht·toh* m pipeline
olio *o·lyoh* m oil; l'olio solare *o·lyoh so·lah·re* suntan oil; la coppa dell'olio *kop·pa del·lo·lyoh* oil pan (*in car*); l'olio di ricino *o·lyoh dee ree·chee·noh* castor oil; l'olio d'oliva *o·lyoh do·lee·va* olive oil
oliva *o·lee·va* f olive
olmo *ohl·moh* m elm
oltre *ohl·tre* prep beyond; oltre a lui *ohl·tre a loo·ee* besides him
oltremare *ol·tre·mah·re* adv overseas; d'oltremare *dol·tre·mah·re* overseas (*market*)
ombra *ohm·bra* f shadow; shade
ombrello *om·brel·loh* m umbrella
ombrellone *om·brel·loh·ne* m sunshade (*over table*)
ombretto *om·brayt·toh* m eyeshadow
omettere* *o·mayt·te·re* vt leave out (*omit*); miss out
omicidio *o·mee·chee·dee·oh* m murder
omogeneizzato(a) *o·mo·je·ne·eedz·dzah·to(a)* adj homogenized
oncia *ohn·cha* f ounce
onda *ohn·da* f wave; le onde medie *ohn·day me·dee·ay* medium wave; le onde corte *ohn·day kohr·tay* short wave; le onde lunghe *ohn·day loon·ge* long wave
ondulato(a) *on·doo·lah·to(a)* adj wavy
onesto(a) *o·ne·sto(a)* adj decent (*respectable*); honest
onorario *o·no·rah·ryoh* m fee
OPEC *oh·pek* f OPEC
opera *o·pe·ra* f work (*art, literature*); opera; l'opera d'arte *o·pe·ra dar·te* work of art
operaio(a) *o·pe·ra·yo(a)* adj working-class □ m l'operaio *o·pe·ra·yoh* workman
operazione *o·pe·ra·tsyoh·ne* f operation
opinione *o·pee·nyoh·ne* f opinion
opuscolo *o·poo·sko·loh* m brochure
opzione *op·tsyoh·ne* f option
ora *oh·ra* f hour □ adv now; ogni ora *ohn·yee oh·ra* hourly; è arrivato proprio ora *e ar·ree·vah·to pro·pree·o oh·ra* he arrived just now; l'ora di punta *oh·ra dee poon·ta* rush hour; le ore di punta *oh·re dee poon·ta* peak hours; le ore d'ufficio *oh·re doof·fee·choh* office hours; che ora è? *ke oh·ra e* what's the time?; 100 chilometri all'ora *100 kee·lo·me·tree al·loh·ra* 100 km per hour; l'ora di pranzo *oh·ra dee pran·dzoh* lunch hour; le ore di lavoro *oh·re dee la·voh·roh* working hours; le ore straordinarie *oh·re stra·or·dee·nah·ree·e* overtime
orario *o·rah·ryoh* m timetable; schedule; in orario *een o·rah·ryoh* punctual; on schedule; l'orario delle partenze *o·rah·ryoh del·le par·ten·tse* departure timetable
orchestra *or·ke·stra* f orchestra
ordinare *or·dee·nah·ray* vt order (*goods, meal*)
ordinario(a) *or·dee·nah·ryo(a)* adj ordinary
ordinato(a) *or·dee·nah·toh(a)* adj neat; tidy
ordinazione *or·dee·na·tsyoh·ne* f order (*for goods*)
ordine *or·dee·ne* m command; order; l'ordine pubblico *or·dee·ne poob·blee·ko* law and order; l'ordine successivo *or·dee·ne soo·ches·see·vo* repeat order; l'ordine del giorno *ohr·dee·ne del johr·noh* agenda; di

prim'ordine *dee pree·mohr·dee·ne* high-class

orecchino *o·rek·kee·noh* m earring

orecchio *o·rayk·kyoh* m ear; **il mal d'orecchi** *mal do·rayk·kee* earache; **avere* mal d'orecchi** *a·vay·re mal do·rayk·kee* to have an earache

orecchioni *o·rek·kyoh·nee* mpl mumps

orfano(a) *or·fa·no(a)* m/f orphan

organigramma *or·ga·nee·gram·ma* m flow chart

organizzare *or·ga·needz·dzah·ray* vt organize

organizzazione *or·ga·needz·dza·tsyoh·ne* f organization

organo *or·ga·noh* m organ (*instrument*)

orgoglio *or·gohl·yoh* m pride

orgoglioso(a) *or·goh·lyoh·so(a)* adj proud

orientale *o·ree·en·tah·le* adj oriental; eastern

orientarsi *o·ree·en·tar·see* vr take one's bearings

Oriente *o·ree·en·te* m the East

originale *o·ree·jee·nah·le* adj original □ m **l'originale** *o·ree·jee·nah·le* original

originariamente *o·ree·jee·nah·rya·mayn·te* adv originally (*at first*)

origine *o·ree·jee·ne* f origin

orizzontale *o·reedz·dzon·tah·le* adj level; horizontal

orizzonte *o·reedz·dzohn·te* m horizon

orlo *ohr·loh* m hem; verge

ormeggiare *or·mej·jah·ray* vt moor

ornamento *or·na·mayn·toh* m ornament

ornare *or·nah·ray* vt decorate

oro *o·roh* m gold; **in oro massiccio** *een o·roh mas·seech·cho* in solid gold; **d'oro** *do·roh* gold; **placcato d'oro** *plak·kah·toh do·roh* gold-plated

orologio *o·ro·lo·joh* m watch; clock; **l'orologio a pendolo** *o·ro·lo·joh a pen·do·loh* grandfather clock

orribile *or·ree·bee·le* adj horrible

orso *ohr·soh* m bear

ortaggi *or·taj·jee* mpl vegetables

osare *o·zah·ray* vt/i dare

oscillare *o·sheel·lah·ray* vi sway (*building, bridge*)

oscuro(a) *o·skoo·ro(a)* adj dim; obscure

ospedale *o·spe·dah·le* m hospital; **l'ospedale psichiatrico** *o·spe·dah·le psee·kee·a·tree·koh* mental hospital

ospitalità *o·spee·ta·lee·ta* f hospitality

ospite *o·spee·tay* m/f guest; host; hostess; **l'ospite pagante** *o·spee·tay pa·gan·te* paying guest

osservazione *os·sayr·va·tsyoh·nay* f remark

ossessione *os·ses·syoh·ne* f obsession

ossigeno *os·see·je·noh* m oxygen

osso *os·soh* m bone

ostacolare *o·sta·ko·lah·ray* vt obstruct; hinder

ostacolo *o·sta·ko·loh* m obstacle

ostaggio *o·staj·joh* m hostage; **prendere* qualcuno come ostaggio** *pren·de·re kwal·koo·no koh·me o·staj·joh* to take someone hostage

ostello *o·stel·loh* m hostel; **l'ostello della gioventù** *o·stel·loh del·la jo·ven·too* youth hostel

ostrica *o·stree·ka* f oyster

ostruzione *o·stroo·tsyoh·ne* f blockage

ottanta *ot·tan·ta* num eighty; **gli anni ottanta** *an·nee ot·tan·ta* eighties (*decade*)

ottavo(a) *ot·tah·vo(a)* adj eighth

ottenere* *ot·te·nay·re* vt obtain; get; win (*contract*); **ottenere* la linea** *ot·te·nay·re la lee·nay·a* to get through (*on phone*)

ottico *ot·tee·koh* m optician

ottimista *ot·tee·mee·sta* adj optimistic

otto *ot·to* num eight

ottobre *ot·toh·bre* m October

ottone *ot·toh·ne* m brass

otturatore *ot·too·ra·toh·re* m shutter (*in camera*)

otturazione *ot·too·ra·tsyoh·ne* f filling (*in tooth*)

ovale *o·vah·le* adj oval

ovatta *o·vat·ta* f cotton batting

overdrive *oh·ver·draiv* m overdrive

ovest *o·vest* m west; **all'ovest** *al·lo·vest* west

ovviamente *ov·vya·mayn·te* adv obviously

ovvio(a) *ov·vyo(a)* adj obvious

ozio *o·tsyoh* m leisure

P

pacchetto *pak·kayt·toh* m pack; packet

pacco *pak·koh* m package; parcel

pace *pah·che* f peace

pachistano(a) *pa·kee·stah·no(a)* adj Pakistani

padella *pa·del·la* f skillet; fry(ing) pan

padre *pah·dre* m father

padrino *pa·dree·noh* m godfather

padrona *pa·droh·na* f landlady

padrone *pa·droh·ne* m landlord

paesaggio *pa·e·zaj·joh* m scenery; countryside

paese *pa·ay·zay* m country; land

Paesi Bassi *pa·ay·zee bas·see* mpl Low Countries

paesino *pa·e·zee·noh* m village

paga *pah·ga* f pay

pagabile *pa·gah·bee·le* adj payable

pagaia *pa·ga·ya* f paddle (*oar*)

pagamento *pa·ga·mayn·toh* m payment; **pagamento alla consegna** *pa·ga·mayn·toh al·la kon·sayn·ya* cash on delivery; **come pagamento parziale** *koh·me pa·ga·mayn·toh par·tsyah·le* as a trade-in

pagare *pa·gah·ray* vt pay; pay for; **pagare il conto** *pa·gah·ray eel kohn·toh* to check out; **fare* pagare qualcosa** *fah·ray pa·gah·ray kwal·ko·sa* to make a charge for something; **da pagarsi** *da pa·gar·see* due (*owing*)

pagato(a) *pa·gah·to(a)* adj paid; **mal pagato(a)** *mal pa·gah·to(a)* underpaid; **non pagato(a)** *nohn pa·gah·to(a)* unpaid (*debt*)

paggio *paj·joh* m pageboy

pagina *pah·jee·na* f page

paglia *pal·ya* f straw

pagliaccio *pal·yach·choh* m clown

pagnotta *pan·yot·ta* f round loaf

paio *pa·yoh* m —a pair; **paio di scarpe** *pa·yoh dee skar·pe* pair of shoes; **un paio di** *oon pa·yoh dee* a couple of (*a few*)

Pakistan *pa·kee·stan* m Pakistan

pala *pah·la* f shovel

palazzo *pa·lats·tsoh* m mansion; palace; **il palazzo di uffici** *pa·lats·tsoh dee oof·fee·chee* office-block

palco *pal·koh* m platform

palcoscenico *pal·ko·she·nee·koh* m stage

Palestina *pa·le·stee·na* f Palestine

palestinese *pa·le·stee·nay·se* adj Palestinian

palestra *pa·le·stra* f gym(nasium)

paletta *pa·layt·ta f* dustpan

palla *pal·la f* ball; **la palla da golf** *pal·la da golf* golf ball; **la palla di neve** *pal·la dee nay·ve* snowball

pallacanestro *pal·la·ka·ne·stroh f* basketball

pallavolo *pal·la·voh·loh f* volleyball

pallido(a) *pal·lee·do(a) adj* pale

pallone *pal·loh·ne m* balloon; football (*ball*)

pallottola *pal·lot·to·la f* bullet

palma *pal·ma f* palm-tree

palmo *pal·moh m* palm (*of hand*)

palo *pah·loh m* pole (*wooden*); post; **il palo da tenda** *pah·loh da ten·da* tent pole; **il palo indicatore** *pah·loh een·dee·ka·toh·re* signpost

palpebra *pal·pe·bra f* eyelid

palude *pa·loo·de f* swamp; bog

panca *pan·ka f* bench

pancetta *pan·chayt·ta f* bacon

panciotto *pan·chot·toh m* vest

pane *pah·ne m* bread; loaf (of bread); **il pane integrale** *pah·ne een·te·grah·le* wholewheat bread; **il pan di Spagna** *pan dee span·ya* sponge (*cake*); **il pane di segale** *pah·ne dee say·ga·le* rye bread; **il pane tostato** *pah·ne to·stah·to* toast

panico *pa·nee·koh m* panic; **preso(a) dal panico** *pray·so(a) dal pa·nee·koh* in a panic

paniere *pa·nye·re m* basket; hamper

panificio *pah·nee·fee·choh m* bakery

panino *pa·nee·noh m* roll (*bread*); bun; **il panino imbottito** *pa·nee·noh eem·bot·tee·to* sandwich; **un panino al prosciutto** *oon pa·nee·noh al pro·shoot·toh* a ham sandwich

panna *pan·na f* cream; **la panna montata** *pan·na mon·tah·ta* whipped cream; **la panna agra** *pan·na a·gra* sour cream

panno *pan·noh m* cloth (*cleaning*)

pannocchia *pan·nok·kya f* corn-on-the-cob

pannolino *pan·no·lee·noh m* diaper

pantaloni *pan·ta·loh·nee mpl* pants; trousers; pair of trousers; **i pantaloni da sci** *pan·ta·loh·nee da shee* ski pants

pantofola *pan·to·fo·la f* slipper

papa *pah·pa m* pope

papà *pa·pa m* dad(dy)

paprica *pa·pree·ka f* paprika

parabrezza *pa·ra·brayts·tsa m —* windshield

paracadute *pa·ra·ka·doo·te m* parachute

parafango *pa·ra·fan·goh m* mudguard

paraffina *pa·raf·fee·na f* kerosene

paragrafo *pa·ra·gra·foh m* paragraph

paralizzato(a) *pa·ra·leedz·dzah·to(a) adj* paralyzed

parallelo(a) *pa·ral·le·lo(a) adj* parallel

paralume *pa·ra·loo·me m* lampshade

parasole *pa·ra·soh·le m —* parasol

paraspruzzi *pa·ra·sproots·tsee m —* mud-flap

paraurti *pa·ra·oor·tee m —* bumper (*on car*); fender

paravento *pa·ra·ven·toh m* screen (*partition*)

parcheggiare *par·kej·jah·ray vt/i* park; **posso parcheggiare qui?** *pos·so par·kej·jah·ray kwee* can I park here?

parcheggio *par·kayj·joh m* parking lot

parchimetro *par·kee·me·troh m* parking meter

parco *par·koh m* park; **il parco mac-**

chine *par·koh mak·kee·ne* fleet of vehicles

parecchi(ie) *pa·rayk·kee(·kye) adj* several; **parecchi di noi** *pa·rayk·kee dee noy* several of us

pareggiare *pa·rej·jah·ray vt* balance (*accounts*); **pareggiare i costi** *pa·rej·jah·ray ee ko·stee* to break even

parente *pa·ren·te m/f* relation; relative; **il parente stretto** *pa·ren·te strayt·toh* next of kin

parentesi *pa·ren·te·zee f —* bracket

parere* *pa·ray·ray vi* seem, appear □ **m il parere** *pa·ray·ray* view (*opinion*); **pare che... pah·re ke** it appears that...; **a mio parere** *a mee·o pa·ray·ray* in my opinion

parete *pa·ray·te f* wall

pari *pah·ree f* par (*business*); **un numero pari** *oon noo·me·roh pah·ree* an even number; **sopra la pari** *soh·pra la pah·ree* above par

Parigi *pa·ree·jee f* Paris

parlamento *par·la·mayn·toh m* parliament

parlare *par·lah·ray vt/i* talk; speak; **parlare di qualcosa** *par·lah·ray dee kwal·ko·sa* to talk about something; **parlare a qualcuno di qualcosa** *par·lah·ray a kwal·koo·no dee kwal·ko·sa* to talk to someone about something; **parla inglese?** *par·la en·glay·se* do you speak English?

parmigiano *par·mee·jah·noh m* Parmesan

parola *pa·ro·la f* word; **parola per parola** *pa·ro·la payr pa·ro·la* word for word

parrucca *par·rook·ka f* wig

parrucchiere *par·rook·kye·re m* hairdresser

parte *par·te f* share; part; **la parte anteriore** *par·te an·te·ryoh·re* front (*foremost part*); **l'ho visto dall'altra parte della strada** *lo vee·sto dal·lal·tra par·te del·la strah·da* I saw him from across the road; **in parte** *een par·te* partly; **a parte** *a par·te* apart (*separately*)

partecipare *par·te·chee·pah·ray vi* participate

partecipazione *par·te·chee·pa·tsyoh·ne f* participation

partenza *par·ten·tsa f* departure

particolare *par·tee·ko·lah·re adj* particular □ **m il particolare** *par·tee·ko·lah·re* detail; **in particolare** *een par·tee·ko·lah·re* in particular

particolarmente *par·tee·ko·lar·mayn·te adv* particularly

partire *par·tee·ray vi* go; leave; **i treni partono ogni ora** *ee tre·nee par·to·no ohn·yee oh·ra* the trains run every hour; **è partito per una settimana** *e par·tee·to payr oo·na set·tee·mah·na* he's away for a week

partita *par·tee·ta f* match (*sport*); round (*in competition*); **una partita di tennis** *oo·na par·tee·ta dee ten·nees* a game of tennis

partito *par·tee·toh m* party (*political*)

Pasqua *pa·skwa f* Easter

passaggio *pas·saj·joh m* passage; gangway; **il passaggio a livello** *pas·saj·joh a lee·vel·loh* grade crossing; **dare* un passaggio in città a qualcuno** *dah·ray oon pas·saj·joh een cheet·ta a kwal·koo·noh* to give someone a ride into town; **il passaggio pedonale** *pas·saj·joh pe·do·nah·le* pedestrian crossing

passaporto *pas·sa·por·toh m* passport

passare *pas·sah·ray* vt pass (*place*); pass (*hand on: object*); **la strada passa davanti alla casa** *la strah·da pas·sa da·van·tee al·la kah·sa* the road runs past the house; **è passato un aereo** *e pas·sah·to oon a·e·reh·o* a plane flew by; **mi passi il Signor X** *mee pas·see eel seen·yohr X* put me through to Mr X (*on phone*); **passare correndo** *pas·sah·ray kor·ren·do* to run past; **mi ha passato di corsa** *mee a pas·sah·to dee kohr·sa* he ran past me; **mi passa lo zucchero per favore** *mee pas·sa lo tsook·ke·roh payr fa·voh·re* please pass the sugar

passatempo *pas·sa·tem·poh* m interest; hobby

passato(a) *pas·sah·to(a)* adj past; bad (*meat*) □ m il passato *pas·sah·toh* past

passeggero(a) *pas·sej·je·ro(a)* m/f passenger

passeggiare *pas·sej·jah·ray* vi walk (*for pleasure, exercise*)

passeggiata *pas·sej·jah·ta* f walk; **fare* una passeggiata** *fah·ray oo·na pas·sej·jah·ta* to go for a walk

passeggiatina *pas·sej·ja·tee·na* f stroll

passeggino *pas·sej·jee·noh* m stroller

passe-partout *pas·par·too* m — master key

passera *pas·se·ra* f plaice

passerella *pas·se·rel·la* f gangway (*bridge*)

passero *pas·se·roh* m sparrow

passione *pas·syoh·ne* f passion

passivo *pas·see·voh* m liabilities (*on balance sheet*)

passo *pas·soh* m pace; step; pass (*in mountains*); **fare* quattro passi** *fah·ray kwat·tro pas·see* to go for a stroll; **tenere* il passo di** *te·nay·re eel pas·soh dee* to keep pace with

pasta *pa·sta* f pastry; pasta; dough; **la pasta di mandorla** *pa·sta dee man·dor·la* almond paste

pastella *pa·stel·la* f batter (*for frying*)

pastello *pa·stel·loh* m crayon

pasticceria *pa·steech·che·ree·a* f cake shop

pasticciere *pa·steech·che·ray* m confectioner

pasticcio *pa·steech·choh* m muddle; pie (*meat*)

pastiglia *pa·steel·ya* f tablet (*medicine*); pastille; **le pastiglie per la tosse** *pa·steel·yay payr la tohs·say* cough drops

pastinaca *pa·stee·nah·ka* f parsnip

pasto *pas·toh* m meal

pastore *pa·stoh·ray* m minister (*of religion*)

pastorizzato(a) *pa·sto·reedz·dzah·to(a)* adj pasteurized

patata *pa·tah·ta* f potato; **la patata dolce** *pa·tah·ta dohl·che* sweet potato

patatine *pa·ta·tee·nay* fpl chips; **le patatine fritte** *pa·ta·tee·nay freet·tay* french fried potatoes, french fries

pâté *pa·tay* m pâté

patente *pa·ten·te* f license; **la patente di guida** *pa·ten·te dee gwee·da* license (*for driving*)

patio *pa·tyoh* m patio

patrigno *pa·treen·yoh* m stepfather

patrimonio *pa·tree·mo·nyoh* m property (*estate*)

patron *pa·tron* m pattern (*dressmaking*)

patta *pat·ta* f flap

pattinare *pat·tee·nah·ray* vi skate

pattino *pat·tee·noh* m skate (*for ice*); **il pattino a pedali** *pat·tee·noh a pe·dah·lee* pedalo; **i pattini a rotelle** *pat·tee·nee a ro·tel·le* roller skates

pattumiera *pat·too·mye·ra* f trash can; garbage can

paura *pa·oo·ra* f fear; **avere* paura di qualcosa** *a·vay·re pa·oo·ra dee kwal·ko·sa* to be afraid of something

pausa *pow·za* f pause; break; **la pausa per il caffè** *pow·za payr eel kaf·fe* coffee break; **la pausa per il tè** *pow·za payr eel te* tea-break; **fare* una pausa** *fah·roo·na pow·za* to pause

pavimento *pa·vee·mayn·toh* m floor

paziente *pa·tsyen·te* adj patient □ m/f il/la paziente *pa·tsyen·te* patient

pazienza *pa·tsyen·tsa* f patience

pazzo(a) *pats·tsoh(a)* adj mad (*insane*); crazy

peccato *pek·kah·toh* m sin; **che peccato!** *ke pek·kah·toh* what a shame!

pecora *pe·ko·ra* f sheep

pedaggio *pe·daj·joh* m toll (*on road etc*)

pedale *pe·dah·le* m pedal

pediatra *pe·dya·tra* m/f pediatrician

pedicure *pay·dee·koo·ray* m podiatrist

pedone *pe·doh·ne* m pedestrian

peggio *pej·jo* adv worse; **fare* qualcosa di peggio** *fah·ray kwal·ko·sa dee pej·jo* to do something worse; **l'ha fatto il peggio** *la fat·to eel pej·jo* he did it worst

peggiore *pej·joh·re* adj worse; **il peggiore libro** *eel pej·joh·re lee·broh* the worst book; **è peggiore (dell'altro)** *e pej·joh·re (del·lal·tro)* it's worse (than the other)

pelle *pel·le* f skin; hide (*leather*); **la pelle di montone** *pel·le dee mon·toh·ne* sheepskin; **la pelle scamosciata** *pel·le ska·mo·shah·ta* suede; **la pelle di cinghiale** *pel·le dee cheen·gyah·le* pigskin

pelliccia *pel·leech·cha* f fur coat; **la pelliccia di ermellino** *pel·leech·cha dee er·mel·lee·noh* ermine (*fur*)

pellicola *pel·lee·ko·la* f film (*for camera*)

pelo *pay·loh* m hair; fur

pena *pay·na* f sentence; sorrow; **darsi* pena di fare qualcosa** *dar·see pay·na dee fah·ray kwal·ko·sa* to go to the trouble of doing something

pendenza *pen·den·tsa* f slope

pendere *pen·de·re* vi hang; lean

pendio *pen·dee·oh* m hill; slope (*sloping ground*)

pendolare *pen·do·lah·ray* m commuter

pene *pe·ne* m penis

penetrare *pe·ne·trah·ray* vt penetrate

penicillina *pe·nee·cheel·lee·na* f penicillin

penna *payn·na* f pen; **la penna stilografica** *payn·na stee·lo·gra·fee·ka* fountain pen

pennarello *pen·na·rel·loh* m felt-tip pen

pennello *pen·nel·loh* m brush; **il pennello da barba** *pen·nel·loh da bar·ba* shaving brush

pensare *pen·sah·ray* vt/i think; **penso che... pen·so ke** I feel that...; **pensare a qualcosa** *pen·sah·ray a kwal·ko·sa* to think of something; **pensare a qualcuno** *pen·sah·ray a kwal·koo·no* to think about someone

pensiero *pen·sye·roh* m thought

pensionato(a) *pen·syoh·nah·to(a)* m/f pensioner; retiree

pensione *pen·syoh·ne* f boarding house; pension; superannuation; guest-house; **andare* in pensione** *an·dah·ray een pen·syoh·ne* to retire

Pentecoste *pen·te·ko·ste* f Whitsun; Whitsunday

pentola *payn·to·la* f pot; saucepan; **la pentola a pressione** *payn·to·la a pres·syoh·ne* pressure cooker

pepaiola *pe·pa·yo·la* f pepper pot

pepato(a) *pe·pah·to(a)* adj peppery

pepe *pay·pe* m pepper

peperone *pe·pe·roh·ne* m pepper (*capsicum*); **il peperone verde/rosso** *pe·pe·roh·ne vayr·de/rohs·so* green/red pepper

per *payr* prep for; per; **per fare qualcosa** *payr fah·ray kwal·ko·sa* in order to do something; **per sempre** *payr sem·pre* forever; **fa caldo per marzo** *fa kal·do payr mar·tsoh* it's warm for March; **vendere qualcosa per $5000** *vayn·de·re kwal·ko·sa payr $5000* to sell something for $5000; **partire per Londra** *par·tee·re payr lohn·dra* to leave for London; **saremo lì per le 4** *sa·ray·mo lee payr le 4* we'll be there by 4 o'clock; **3 metri per 3** *3 me·tree payr 3* 3 meters square; **per via aerea** *payr vee·a a·e·re·a* by air; **per me** *payr may* for my sake; **per persona** *payr per·soh·na* per person; **20 per cento** *20 payr chen·to* 20 per cent

pera *pay·ra* f pear

percallina a quadretti *payr·kal·lee·na a kwa·dret·tee* f gingham

percentuale *per·chen·too·ah·le* f percentage

perché *payr·kay* adv why □ conj because; **l'ha fatto perché io andassi** *la fat·to payr·kay ee·oh an·das·see* he did it so that I would go

percorrere* *per·kohr·re·re* vt travel (*a distance*)

percorso *payr·kohr·soh* m ride (*in vehicle*); **non è che un breve percorso** *nohn e ke oon bre·ve payr·kohr·soh* it's only a short ride

perdere* *per·de·re* vt lose; miss (*train*); **perdere* tempo** *per·de·re tem·poh* to waste one's time

perdita *per·dee·ta* f leak; loss

perdonare *per·do·nah·ray* vt forgive

perfetto(a) *per·fet·to(a)* adj perfect

perforare *payr·fo·rah·ray* vt drill (*hole*)

pericolo *pe·ree·ko·loh* m danger; **una nave in pericolo** *oo·na nah·ve een pe·ree·ko·loh* a ship in distress

pericoloso(a) *pe·ree·ko·loh·so(a)* adj dangerous

periferia *pe·ree·fe·ree·a* f outskirts; the suburbs

periodo *pe·ree·o·doh* m period (*of time*); **durante il suo periodo di carica** *doo·ran·te eel soo·o pe·ree·o·doh dee kah·ree·ka* during his term of office

perito *pe·ree·toh* m expert; surveyor

perizia *pe·ree·tsya* f survey (*of building*)

perla *per·la* f pearl; bead

permanente *per·ma·nen·te* adj permanent □ f la permanente *per·ma·nen·te* perm

permanentemente *per·ma·nen·te·mayn·te* adv permanently

permesso *per·mays·soh* m permission; permit; **il permesso di soggiorno** *per·mays·soh dee soj·johr·noh* residence permit; **il permesso di uscita** *per·mays·soh dee oo·shee·ta* exit permit

permettere* *per·mayt·te·re* vt permit; **permettere* a qualcuno di partire** *per·mayt·te·re a kwal·koo·no dee par·tee·re* to allow someone to go; **permettere* a qualcuno di fare qualcosa** *per·mayt·te·re a kwal·koo·no dee fah·ray kwal·ko·sa* to permit someone to do something; **non me lo posso permettere** *nohn may lo pos·so per·mayt·te·re* I can't afford it

pernice *per·nee·che* f partridge

pernottare *per·not·tah·ray* vi stay the night

perquisire *payr·kwee·zee·re* vt search

persiana *per·syah·na* f shutter

persiano(a) *per·syah·no(a)* adj Persian

persona *per·soh·na* f person; **di persona** *dee per·soh·na* in person

personale *per·so·nah·le* adj personal □ m il personale *per·so·nah·le* staff; personnel

personalità *per·so·na·lee·ta* f personality

personalmente *per·so·nal·mayn·te* adv personally

persuadere* *per·swa·day·re* vt persuade; **persuadere* qualcuno a fare qualcosa** *per·swa·day·re kwal·koo·no a fah·ray kwal·ko·sa* to persuade someone to do something

pertinente a *payr·tee·nen·te a* adj relevant to

pertosse *payr·tohs·se* f whooping cough

p. es. *payr e·zaym·pyoh* abbrev e.g.

pesante *pe·san·te* adj heavy; rich (*food*); **troppo pesante** *trop·po pe·san·te* overweight (*person*)

pesare *pe·sah·ray* vt/i weigh

pesca *pe·ska* f angling; fishing; peach; **andare* a pesca** *an·dah·ray a pay·ska* to go fishing

pescatore *pe·ska·toh·re* m angler

pesce *pay·she* m fish; **il pesce rosso** *pay·she rohs·soh* goldfish

pescecane *pe·she·kah·ne* m shark

pescivendolo *pe·shee·vayn·do·loh* m fishmonger

peso *pay·soh* m weight; **il peso netto** *pay·soh nayt·toh* net weight

pessimista *pes·see·me·sta* adj pessimistic

pessimo(a) *pes·see·moh(a)* adj awful

petardo *pe·tahr·doh* m cracker (*paper toy*)

petroliera *pe·tro·lye·ra* f oil tanker

petrolio *pe·tro·lyoh* m oil (*petroleum*)

pettinare *pet·tee·nah·ray* vt comb

pettine *pet·tee·nay* m comb; scallop

petto *pet·toh* m breast (*chest, of poultry*); chest (*of body*)

pezza *pets·tsa* f patch (*of material*)

pezzettino *pets·tset·tee·noh* m scrap (*bit*)

pezzo *pets·tsoh* m piece; cut (*of meat*); component (*for car etc*); **il pezzo di ricambio** *pets·tsoh dee ree·kam·byoh* spare (part); **un pezzo di** *oon pets·tsoh dee* a bit of

pezzuola *pets·tswo·la* f cloth; rag

piacere* *pya·chay·re* vi please □ m il piacere *pya·chay·re* enjoyment; pleasure; **piacere* a** *pya·chay·re a* to like; **piacere* molto a qualcuno fare qualcosa** *pya·chay·re mohl·to a kwal·koo·no fah·ray kwal·ko·sa* to love doing something; **mi piacerebbe andare** *mee pya·che·reb·be an·dah·ray* I'd love to go; I'd like to go

piacevole *pya·chay·vo·le* adj pleasant

pialla *pyal·la* f plane (*tool*)

pianerottolo *pya·ne·rot·to·loh* m landing (*on stairs*)

pianeta *pya·nay·ta* m planet

piangere* *pyan·je·ray* vi cry

pianificazione *pya·nee·fee·ka·tsyoh·ne* f planning (*economic*)

piano(a) *pyah·no(a)* adj level (*surface*) □ adv quietly (*speak*) □ m il piano *pyah·noh* story (*of building*); piano; a piú piani *a pyoo pyah·nee* multilevel; il primo piano *pree·mo pyah·noh* 1st floor (*Brit*), 2nd floor (*US*)

pianoforte a coda *pya·no·for·tay a koh·da* m grand piano

pianta *pyan·ta* f sole (*of foot*); map (*of town*); plan; plant

piantare *pyan·tah·ray* vt plant; pitch (*tent*)

pianterreno *pyan·ter·ray·noh* m first floor; ground floor

pianura *pya·noo·ra* f plain

piastra riscaldante *pya·stra ree·skal·dan·te* f hotplate

piastrella *pya·strel·la* f tile

piattaforma *pyat·ta·fohr·ma* f platform; la piattaforma petroliera *pyat·ta·fohr·ma pe·tro·lye·ra* oil-rig

piattino *pyat·tee·noh* m saucer

piatto(a) *pyat·to(a)* adj flat □ m il piatto *pyat·toh* dish; course (*of meal*); plate; il primo piatto *pree·mo pyat·toh* entrée

piazza *pyats·tsa* f square (*in town*); la piazza del mercato *pyats·tsa del mayr·kah·toh* market-place

piazzola *pyats·tso·la* f (*roadside*) stopping place

piccante *peek·kan·te* adj spicy; hot

picche *peek·ke* fpl spades (*cards*)

picchetto *peek·kayt·toh* m peg; picket; tent stake

picchiare *peek·kyah·ray* vt hit □ vi knock (*engine*)

piccione *peech·choh·ne* m pigeon

piccolo(a) *peek·ko·lo(a)* adj little; small

piccone *peek·koh·ne* m pick; pickaxe

picnic *peek·neek* m picnic; andare* a fare un picnic *an·dah·ray a fah·ray oon peek·neek* to go on a picnic

pidocchio *pee·dok·kyoh* m louse

piede *pye·de* m foot (*of person, measurement*); bottom (*of page, list*)

piega *pye·ga* f crease; farsi* fare la messa in piega *far·see* fah·ray la mays·sa een pye·ga* to have one's hair set

piegare *pye·gah·ray* vt fold; bend

pieghettato(a) *pye·get·tah·to(a)* adj pleated

pieno(a) *pye·no(a)* adj full; il pieno, per favore! *eel pye·noh pear fa·voh·re* fill it up! (*car*); pieno(a) di *pye·no(a) dee* full of; a tempo pieno *a tem·po pye·noh* full-time

pietra *pye·tra* f stone; la pietra focaia *pye·tra fo·ka·ya* flint (*in lighter*)

piffero *peef·fe·roh* m pipe (*musical*)

pigiama *pee·jah·ma* m pajamas

pigro(a) *pee·gro(a)* adj lazy

pila *pee·la* f battery (*for radio etc*)

pilastro *pee·la·stroh* m pillar

pillola *peel·lo·la* f pill; prendere* la pillola *pren·de·re la peel·lo·la* to be on the pill

pilota *pee·lo·ta* m pilot

pince *pañs* f dart (*on clothes*)

ping-pong *peeng·pong* m ping-pong

pinne *peen·ne* fpl flippers (*for swimming*)

pino *pee·noh* m pine

pinze *peen·tse* fpl pliers

pinzette *peen·tsayt·te* fpl tweezers

pioggia *pyoj·jah* f rain

piombo *pyohm·boh* m lead

pioppo *pyop·poh* m poplar

piovere* *pyo·ve·re* vi rain; piove *pyo·ve* it's raining

piovigine *pyo·veej·jee·ne* f drizzle

piovoso(a) *pyo·voh·so(a)* adj rainy; wet (*weather, day*)

pipa *pee·pa* f pipe (*for smoking*)

pipistrello *pee·pee·strel·loh* m bat (*animal*)

piramide *pee·ra·mee·de* f pyramid

Pirenei *pee·re·ne·ee* mpl Pyrenees

piroscafo *pee·ro·ska·foh* m steamer (*ship*)

piscina *pee·shee·na* f swimming pool; la piscina per bambini *pee·shee·na payr bam·bee·nee* wading pool

piselli *pee·sel·lee* mpl peas

pista *pee·sta* f track (*sports*); race track; la pista d'atterraggio *pee·sta dat·ter·raj·joh* runway; la pista di pattinaggio *pee·sta de pat·tee·naj·joh* skating rink; la pista da ballo *pee·sta da bal·loh* dance floor; la pista da sci *pee·sta da shee* ski run

pistone *pee·stoh·ne* m piston

pittore *peet·toh·re* m painter

piú *pyoo* adv more; most; plus □ mpl i piú *ee pyoo* most people; pesa piú di un chilo *pay·sa pyoo dee oon kee·loh* it weighs over a kilo; piú le spese postali *pyoo le spay·se po·stah·lee* postage extra; in piú *een pyoo* extra; piú di 10 *pyoo dee 10* more than 10; il/la piú bello(a) *eel/la pyoo bel·loh(a)* the most beautiful; piú gente *pyoo jen·tay* more people; piú pericoloso che *pyoo pe·ree·ko·loh·soh kay* more dangerous than; piú o meno *pyoo o may·noh* more or less; sono piú ricchi di noi *soh·no pyoo reek·kee dee noy* they are better off than us (*richer*); il piú grande numero di macchine *eel pyoo gran·day noo·me·roh dee mak·kee·nay* the most cars

piuma *pyoo·ma* f feather; down (*fluff*)

piumino *pyoo·mee·noh* m comforter; eiderdown

piuttosto *pyoot·to·sto* adv quite; fairly; rather

pizza *peets·tsa* f pizza

pizzicare *peets·tsee·kah·ray* vt pinch

pizzico *peets·tsee·koh* m pinch; sting

pizzo *peets·tsoh* m lace

placcare *plak·kah·ray* vt tackle (*in sports*)

placcato(a) di *plak·kah·to(a) dee* adj plated (*with metals*)

plaid *plahd* m plaid

planetario *pla·ne·tah·ryoh* m planetarium

plastica *pla·stee·ka* f plastic; in plastica *een pla·stee·ka* plastic

platano *pla·ta·noh* m plane (*tree*)

platea *pla·te·a* f orchestra (*in theater*)

platino *pla·tee·noh* m platinum

plexiglas *plek·see·glas* m plexiglas

plico *plee·koh* m parcel; bundle; in plico a parte *een plee·koh a par·te* under separate cover

pneumatico *pne·oo·ma·tee·koh* m tire; lo pneumatico rimodellato *pne·oo·ma·tee·koh ree·mo·del·lah·toh* retread

po' *see* poco(a)

pochi(e) *po·kee(·ke)* adj few; pochi libri *po·kee lee·bree* a few books

poco(a) *po·ko(a)* adj little □ adv poco

po·ko little □ *pron* little, not much; **un po'** *oon po* a little; **un po' di X** *oon po dee X* a small amount of X; **poco sopra il gomito** *po·ko soh·pra eel go·mee·toh* just above the elbow; **fra poco** *fra po·ko* shortly (*soon*)
poesia *po·e·zee·a f* poem; poetry
poggiatesta *poj·ja·te·sta m* headrest
poi *poy adv* then
poiché *poy·kay conj* because; **poiché è malato** *poy·kay e ma·lah·to* since he's ill
poker *po·ker m* poker (*card game*)
polacco(a) *po·lak·ko(a) adj* Polish □ *m/f* il/la **polacco(a)** *po·lak·ko(a)* Pole □ *m* il **polacco** *po·lak·koh* Polish
polaroid *po·la·royd adj* Polaroid
poliestere *po·lee·e·ste·re m* polyester
polietilene *po·lee·e·tee·le·ne m* polyethylene
polio *po·lyoh f* polio
politica *po·lee·tee·ka f* policy; politics; **la politica estera** *po·lee·tee·ka e·ste·ra* foreign policy
politico(a) *po·lee·tee·ko(a) adj* political; **l'uomo politico** *wo·moh po·lee·tee·ko* politician
polizia *po·lee·tsee·a f* police
poliziotto *po·lee·tsyot·toh m* policeman
polizza *po·leets·tsa f* policy; **la polizza di assicurazione** *po·leets·tsa dee as·see·koo·ra·tsyoh·ne* insurance policy
pollame *pol·lah·me m* poultry
pollice *pol·lee·che m* thumb
pollo *pohl·loh m* chicken
polmone *pol·moh·ne m* lung
polmonite *pol·mo·nee·te f* pneumonia
polo *po·loh m* polo; terminal (*electricity*)
Polonia *po·lo·nya f* Poland
Polo Nord *po·loh nord m* North Pole
Polo Sud *po·loh sud m* South Pole
polsino *pol·see·noh m* cuff (*of shirt*)
polso *pohl·soh m* wrist
poltrona *pol·troh·na f* armchair
polvere *pohl·ve·re f* dust; powder
polveroso(a) *pol·ve·roh·so(a) adj* dusty
pomeriggio *po·me·reej·joh m* afternoon
pomo *poh·moh m* knob (*on door*)
pomodoro *po·mo·do·roh m* tomato
pompa *pohm·pa f* pump
pompare *pohm·pah·ray vt* pump
pompelmo *pom·pel·moh m* grapefruit
pompiere *pom·pye·re m* fireman
ponce *pon·che m* punch (*drink*)
ponte *pohn·te m* bridge; deck (*of ship*); **il ponte a pedaggio** *pohn·te a pe·daj·joh* toll bridge; **fare* il ponte** *fah·ray eel pohn·te* to take an extra day's holiday
pontile *pon·tee·le m* jetty
pony *poh·nee m* pony
pop *pop adj* pop (*music, art*)
popeline *po·pe·leen f* poplin
popolare *po·po·lah·ray adj* popular
popolazione *po·po·la·tsyoh·ne f* population
popolo *po·po·loh m* people
porcellana *por·chel·lah·na f* china; porcelain
porpora *por·po·ra f* purple
porre* *pohr·re vt* put
porro *por·roh m* leek
porta *por·ta f* door; goal; gate (*of building*)
portabagagli *por·ta·ba·gal·yee m —* luggage rack (*in train*); roof rack
portabottiglie *por·ta·bot·teel·yay m —* rack (*for wine*)

portacenere *por·ta·chay·ne·re m —* ashtray
portachiavi *por·ta·kyah·vee m —* key ring
portafogli *por·ta·fol·yee m —* wallet; pocketbook
portafoglio *por·ta·fol·yoh m* portfolio
portaombrelli *por·ta·om·brel·lee m —* umbrella stand
portare *por·ta·ray vt* carry; bring; wear (*clothes*); **da portar via** *da por·tar vee·a* carry-out (*food*); portare qualcuno a teatro *por·tah·ray kwal·koo·no a te·ah·troh* to take someone out to the theater; **portare qualcuno alla stazione** *por·tah·ray kwal·koo·no al·la sta·tsyoh·ne* to take someone to the station; **porti questo alla posta** *por·tee kway·sto al·la po·sta* take this to the post office; **portare al limite massimo** *por·tah·ray al lee·mee·tay mas·see·moh* to maximize
portasigarette *por·ta·see·ga·rayt·tay m* cigarette case
portata *por·tah·ta f* range; capacity; **fuori portata** *fwo·ree por·tah·ta* out of reach
portatile *por·tah·tee·le adj* portable
portauovo *por·ta·wo·voh m —* egg cup
portavoce *por·ta·voh·che m —* spokesman
portellone posteriore *por·tel·loh·ne po·ste·ryoh·re m* tailgate (*of car*)
porticciolo *por·teech·cho·loh m* marina
portico *por·tee·koh m* porch
portiera *por·tye·ra f* door
portiere *por·tye·re m* porter (*doorkeeper*); janitor; **il portiere di notte** *por·tye·re dee not·tay* night porter
porto *por·toh m* port; harbor
Portogallo *por·to·gal·loh m* Portugal
portoghese *por·to·gay·se adj* Portuguese □ *m* il **portoghese** *por·to·gay·se* Portuguese
porzione *por·tsyoh·ne f* portion; helping
posare *po·sah·ray vt* put down; lay
posateria *po·sah·te·ree·a f* cutlery
positivo(a) *po·zee·tee·vo(a) adj* positive
posizione *po·zee·tsyoh·ne f* position
posporre* *pos·pohr·re vt* postpone
possedere* *pos·se·day·re vt* own (*possess*)
possibile *pos·see·bee·le adj* possible; **fare* tutto il possibile** *fah·ray toot·to eel pos·see·bee·le* to do all one possibly can
possibilità *pos·see·bee·lee·ta f* possibility; **entro le possibilità di** *ayn·tro le pos·see·bee·lee·ta dee* within the scope of; **egli ha delle buone possibilità di...** *ay·lyee a del·lay bwo·nay pos·see·bee·lee·ta dee* he has a good chance of...
posta *po·sta f* mail; stake (*in gambling*); odds (*in betting*); **per posta aerea** *por po·sta a·e·re·a* by air mail; **la posta raccomandata** *po·sta rak·ko·man·dah·ta* certified mail; **fermo posta** *fayr·mo po·sta* general delivery; **per posta** *payr po·sta* by post
postale *po·stah·le adj* postal
postdatare *post·da·tah·ray vt* postdate
Poste *po·ste fpl* the Post Office
posteggio *po·stayj·joh m* parking lot; **il posteggio per tassi** *po·stayj·joh payr tas·see* taxi stand
posteriore *po·ste·ryoh·ray adj* rear; later (*date etc*)

postino *po·stee·noh* m mailman; postman

posto *poh·stoh* m place; position (*place, job*); seat; **a posto** *a poh·stoh* in place; **fuori posto** *fwo·ree poh·stoh* out of place (*object*); **il posto vacante** *poh·stoh va·kan·tay* vacancy (*job*)

potabile *po·tah·bee·lay* adj drinking; drinkable

potare *po·tah·ray* vt trim (*hedge*)

potente *po·ten·te* adj powerful

potenza *po·ten·tsa* f power (*of machine*)

potere* *po·tay·re* vi can □ m **il potere** *po·tay·re* power (*authority*); **lo potremmo fare** *loh po·trem·moh fah·ray* we could do it; **potrei avere… po·tre·ee a·vay·ray** could I have…; **potere* fare qualcosa** *po·tay·re fah·ray kwal·ko·sa* to be able to do something; **non potere* fare qualcosa** *nohn po·tay·re fah·ray kwal·ko·sa* to be unable to do something; **posso entrare?** *pos·soh en·trah·ray* may I come in?; **potrà piovere** *po·tra pyo·ve·ray* it may rain; **potrebbe piovere** *po·treb·bay pyo·ve·ray* it might rain; **non posso farci nulla** *nohn pos·so far·chee nool·la* I can't help it; **il potere mondiale** *po·tay·re mon·dee·ah·le* world power

povero(a) *po·ve·ro(a)* adj poor

pozzanghera *pots·tsan·ge·ra* f puddle; pool

pozzo *pohts·tsoh* m well

Praga *prah·ga* f Prague

pranzo *pran·dzoh* m lunch

prassi *pras·see* f normal procedure

pratica *pra·tee·ka* f practical experience

pratico(a) *pra·tee·ko(a)* adj practical; handy (*convenient*); **poco pratico(a)** *po·ko pra·tee·ko(a)* inconvenient

prato rasato *prah·toh ra·sah·to* m lawn

precedente *pre·che·den·te* adj previous; earlier

precedenza *pre·che·den·tsa* f right of way (*on road*); **dare* la precedenza** *dah·ray la pre·che·den·tsa* to yield (*to traffic*)

precipitarsi *pre·chee·pee·tar·see* vr rush

precisamente *pre·chee·za·mayn·te* adv exactly

precisione *pre·chee·zyoh·ne* f precision

preciso(a) *pre·chee·zo(a)* adj precise; exact; accurate

precotto(a) *pre·kot·to(a)* adj ready-cooked

predire* *pre·dee·re* vt predict

predizione *pre·dee·tsyoh·ne* f prediction

preferire *pre·fe·ree·re* vt prefer; **preferirei andare al cinema** *pre·fe·ree·ray an·dah·ray al chee·ne·ma* I'd rather go to the movies

pregare *pre·gah·ray* vt pray

preghiera *pre·gye·ra* f prayer

pregiudizio *pre·joo·dee·tsyoh* m prejudice

prego *pre·go* excl don't mention it!; after you!

preliminare *pre·lee·mee·nah·re* adj preliminary

preludio *pre·loo·dee·oh* m overture

pré-maman *pray·ma·man* m maternity dress

premere *pre·me·re* vt push; press

premio *pre·myoh* m bonus (*on salary*); premium; prize; **il Gran Premio** *gran pre·myoh* Grand Prix

prendere* *pren·de·re* vt take; get

(*fetch*); catch (*train, illness*); **andare* a prendere un amico** *an·dah·ray a pren·de·re oon a·mee·koh* to pick up a friend; **me lo ha preso** *me lo a pray·so* he took it from me; **andare* a prendere** *an·dah·ray a pren·de·re* to fetch; **prendere* freddo** *pren·de·re frayd·doh* to catch cold

prenotare *pre·no·tah·ray* vt reserve (*tickets*); book (*seat*)

prenotazione *pre·no·ta·tsyoh·ne* f reservation (*of seats, rooms etc*); **la prenotazione a gruppo** *pre·no·ta·tsyoh·ne a groop·poh* group reservation

preoccupato(a) *pre·ok·koo·pah·to(a)* adj worried

preoccupazione *pre·ok·koo·pa·tsyoh·ne* f worry

prepagato(a) *pre·pa·gah·to(a)* adj prepaid

preparare *pre·pa·rah·ray* vt prepare; **preparare il fuoco** *pre·pa·rah·ray eel fwo·koh* to lay the fire

prepararsi *pre·pa·rahr·see* vr get ready; **si prepara a partire** *see pre·pah·ra a par·tee·re* he's preparing to leave

preparativi *pre·pa·ra·tee·vee* mpl preparations (*for trip*)

preparazione *pre·pa·ra·tsyoh·ne* f preparation

presa *pray·sa* f outlet (*electric*)

presbite *prez·bee·te* adj far-sighted

presbiteriano(a) *prez·bee·te·ree·ah·no(a)* adj Presbyterian

presentare *pre·zen·tah·ray* vt introduce (*person*)

presentarsi *pre·zen·tahr·see* vr report; check in (*at airport*)

presentazione *pre·zen·ta·tsyoh·ne* f introduction (*social*); presentation

presente *pre·zen·te* adj present

preservativo *pre·ser·va·tee·voh* m prophylactic (*contraceptive*)

preside *pre·see·de* m/f headmaster; headmistress

presidente *pre·see·den·te* m president; chairman

pressione *pres·syoh·ne* f pressure; **la pressione sanguigna** *pres·syoh·ne san·gween·ya* blood pressure

presso *pres·soh* prep near; care of, c/o

prestare *pre·stah·ray* vt lend; loan

prestigiatore *pre·stee·ja·toh·re* m conjuror

prestigio *pre·stee·joh* m prestige

prestito *pre·stee·toh* m loan; **il prestito bancario** *pre·stee·toh ban·kah·ryo* bank loan; **prendere* in prestito** *pren·de·re een pre·stee·toh* to borrow; **prendere* qualcosa in prestito da qualcuno** *pren·de·re kwal·ko·sa een pre·stee·toh da kwal·koo·no* to borrow something from someone

presto *pre·sto* adv early; soon; **faccia presto!** *fach·cha pre·sto* hurry up!

prete *pre·te* m priest

previsione *pre·vee·zyoh·ne* f forecast; **le previsioni del tempo** *pre·vee·zyoh·nee del tem·poh* weather forecast

prezioso(a) *pre·tsyoh·so(a)* adj precious (*jewel etc*)

prezzemolo *prets·tsay·mo·loh* m parsley

prezzo *prets·tsoh* m price; **il prezzo minimo** *prets·tsoh mee·nee·mo* upset price; **il prezzo del coperto** *prets·tsoh del ko·per·toh* cover charge; **comprare qualcosa a prezzo di costo** *kom·prah·ray kwal·ko·sa a prets·tsoh dee*

ko·stoh to buy something at cost; **il prezzo della corsa** *prets·tsoh del·la kohr·sa* fare (*in taxi*); **il prezzo fisso** *prets·tsoh fees·so* flat rate; **il prezzo di catalogo** *prets·tsoh dee ka·tah·lo·goh* list price; **il prezzo al minuto** *prets·tsoh al mee·noo·toh* retail price; **comprare qualcosa a prezzo ridotto** *kom·prah·ray kwal·ko·sa a prets·tsoh ree·doht·to* to buy something at a reduction; **il prezzo d'ingresso** *prets·tsoh deen·gres·soh* entrance fee; **il prezzo unitario** *prets·tsoh oo·nee·tah·ree·oh* unit price

prigione *pree·joh·ne f* prison; jail; **la prigione sotterranea** *pree·joh·ne sot·ter·rah·ne·a* a dungeon; **in prigione** *een pree·joh·ne* in prison

prigioniero(a) *pree·joh·nye·ro(a) m/f* prisoner

prima *pree·ma adv* before; first; earlier □ *f* **la prima** *pree·ma* première; **prima che** *pree·ma ke* before; **prima di mezzogiorno** *pree·ma dee medz·dzo·johr·noh* before noon

primario(a) *pree·mah·ryo(a) adj* primary (*education*)

primato *pree·mah·toh m* record (*in sports*)

primavera *pree·ma·ve·ra f* spring (*season*)

primo(a) *pree·mo(a) adj* first; top (*in rank*); early; **di prima classe** *dee pree·ma klas·se* first-class (*work etc*); **viaggiare in prima classe** *vyaj·jah·ray een pree·ma klas·se* to travel first class; **in prima** *een pree·ma* in first (*gear*); **il primo piano** *pree·mo pyah·noh* second floor

principale *preen·chee·pah·lay adj* major; main

principalmente *preen·chee·pal·mayn·tay adv* mainly

principe *preen·chee·pe m* prince

principessa *preen·chee·pays·sa f* princess

principiante *preen·chee·pyan·te m/f* beginner

privato(a) *pree·vah·to(a) adj* private; personal (*private*); **in privato** *een pree·vah·to* in private

privo(a) di *pree·vo(a) dee adj* lacking

probabile *pro·bah·bee·le adj* probable; likely; **è probabile che venga** *e pro·bah·bee·le ke ven·ga* he's likely to come

probabilmente *pro·ba·beel·mayn·te adv* probably

problema *pro·ble·ma m* problem

procedimento *pro·che·dee·mayn·toh m* procedure; process (*method*)

processare *pro·ches·sah·ray vt* try (*in law*)

processo *pro·ches·soh m* trial (*in law*); process

prodotti *pro·doht·tee mpl* produce (*products*)

prodotto *pro·doht·toh m* product; commodity; **il prodotto nazionale lordo** *pro·doht·toh na·tsyoh·nah·le lohr·do* gross national product

produrre *pro·door·re vt* produce; bring in (*profit*)

produttività *pro·doot·tee·vee·ta f* productivity

produttore *pro·doot·toh·re m* producer

produzione *pro·doo·tsyoh·ne f* production; output; **la produzione in serie** *pro·doo·tsyoh·ne een ser·ye* mass production

professionale *pro·fes·syoh·nah·le adj* professional

professione *pro·fes·syoh·ne f* profession

professore *pro·fes·soh·re m* professor; teacher (*secondary school*)

professoressa *pro·fes·sor·res·sa f* teacher (*secondary school*)

profiterole *pro·fee·te·rohl f* profiterole

profitto *pro·feet·toh m* profit

profondità *pro·fohn·dee·ta f* depth

profondo(a) *pro·fohn·do(a) adj* deep (*water, hole*); **poco profondo(a)** *po·ko pro·fohn·do(a)* shallow

profumo *pro·foo·moh m* scent; perfume

progettare *pro·jet·tah·ray vt* plan

progetto *pro·jet·toh m* plan; project; blueprint; scheme; **fare* dei progetti in anticipo** *fah·ray de·ee pro·jet·tee een an·tee·chee·po* to plan ahead

programma *pro·gram·ma m* syllabus; schedule; program

programmare *pro·gram·mah·ray vt* program

programmatore *pro·gram·ma·toh·re m* programmer (*person*)

programmatrice *pro·gram·ma·tree·che f* programmer (*person*)

programmazione *pro·gram·ma·tsyoh·nay f* computer programming

progresso *pro·gres·soh m* progress; **fare* progressi** *fah·ray pro·gres·see* to make progress

proibire *pro·ee·bee·re vt* ban; prohibit; **proibire a qualcuno di fare qualcosa** *pro·ee·bee·re a kwal·koo·no dee fah·ray kwal·ko·sa* to forbid someone to do something

proibizione *pro·ee·bee·tsyoh·ne f* ban

proiettare *pro·yet·tah·ray vt* show (*movie*)

proiettore *pro·yet·toh·re m* headlight; projector; **il proiettore fendinebbia** *pro·yet·toh·re fen·dee·nayb·bya* fog light

promessa *pro·mays·sa f* promise

promettere* *pro·mayt·te·re vt* promise

promosso(a) *pro·mos·so(a) adj* promoted; **essere* promosso(a)** *es·se·re pro·mos·so(a)* to pass (*exam*)

promozione *pro·mo·tsyoh·ne f* promotion

promuovere* *pro·mwo·ve·re vt* promote

pronostico *pro·no·stee·koh m* forecast

pronto(a) *prohn·to(a) adj* ready; **il pronto soccorso** *prohn·to sok·kohr·soh* first aid; **pronto!** *prohn·to!* hello! (*on telephone*)

pronuncia *pro·noon·cha f* pronunciation

pronunciare *pro·noon·chah·ray vt* pronounce

proporre* *pro·pohr·re vt* propose (*suggest*)

proposito *pro·po·see·to m* intention; **a proposito** *a pro·po·see·to* by the way

proposta *pro·poh·sta f* proposal (*suggestion*)

proprietà *pro·pree·e·ta f* ownership; property; land; **la proprietà fondiaria** *pro·pree·e·ta fon·dee·ah·ree·a* real estate

proprietario(a) *pro·pree·e·tah·ree·o(a) m/f* owner

proprio *pro·pree·o adv* just; really

proprio(a) *pro·pree·o(a) adj* own

prosciugare *pro·shoo·gah·ray vt* drain (*land*)

prosciutto *pro·shoot·toh m* ham

proseguire *pro·se·gwee·ray* vt continue; **fare* proseguire** *fah·ray pro·se·gwee·ray* to readdress

prospero(a) *pro·spe·ro(a)* adj prosperous; successful (*businessman*)

prospettiva *pro·spet·tee·va* f prospect; outlook

prospetto *pro·spet·toh* m prospectus

prossimo(a) *pros·see·moh(a)* adj next (*stop, station, week*)

proteggere* *pro·tej·je·re* vt protect; guard

proteina *pro·te·e·na* f protein

protesta *pro·te·sta* f protest

protestante *pro·te·stan·te* adj Protestant

protestare *pro·te·stah·ray* vt/i protest

protezione *pro·te·tsyoh·ne* f protection

prototipo *pro·to·tee·poh* m prototype

prova *pro·va* f proof; evidence; rehearsal; test; **la prova su strada** *pro·va soo strah·da* road test; **mettere* alla prova** *mayt·te·re al·la pro·va* to test (*ability*); **in prova** *een pro·va* on approval

provare *pro·vah·ray* vt prove; try; **provare un vestito** *pro·vah·ray oon ve·stee·toh* to try on a dress; **provare una macchina su strada** *pro·vah·ray oo·na mak·kee·na soo strah·da* to test-drive a car

provincia *pro·veen·cha* f province (*region*)

provinciale *pro·veen·chah·le* adj provincial

provvedere* a *prov·ve·day·re a* vi provide for

provvisorio(a) *prov·vee·zo·ryo(a)* adj temporary

provvista *prov·vee·sta* f supply; store (*stock*)

prudente *proo·den·te* adj wise (*decision*); careful (*cautious*)

prudere* *proo·de·re* vi itch

prugna *proon·ya* f plum

prurito *proo·ree·toh* m itch

P.S. *pee·es·se* abbrev P.S.

psichiatra *psee·kee·a·tra* m/f psychiatrist

psichiatrico(a) *psee·kee·a·tree·ko(a)* adj psychiatric

psicologia *psee·ko·lo·jee·a* f psychology

psicologico(a) *psee·ko·lo·jee·ko(a)* adj psychological

psicologo(a) *psee·ko·lo·go(a)* m/f psychologist

pubblicare *poob·blee·kah·ray* vt publish

pubblicità *poob·blee·chee·ta* f publicity; advertising; **fare* pubblicità a** *fah·ray poob·blee·chee·ta a* to advertise (*product*)

pubblico(a) *poob·blee·ko(a)* adj public □ m **il pubblico** *poob·blee·koh* public; audience; **in pubblico** *een poob·blee·koh* in public

pugilato *poo·jee·lah·toh* m boxing

pugnalare *poon·ya·lah·ray* vt stab

pugnale *poon·yah·le* m dagger

pugno *poon·yoh* m fist; punch (*blow*); **dare* un pugno a** *dah·ray oon poon·yoh a* to punch

pulire *poo·lee·ray* vt clean; **fare* pulire un vestito** *fah·ray poo·lee·ray oon ve·stee·toh* to have a suit cleaned

pulito(a) *poo·lee·toh(a)* adj clean

pullman *pool·man* m bus (*long distance*)

pullmino *pool·mee·noh* m minibus

pullover *pool·lo·ver* m — pullover

pungere* *poon·je·re* vt prick; sting

punire *poo·nee·re* vt punish

punizione *poo·nee·tsyoh·ne* f punishment

punta *poon·ta* f point; tip

puntare *poon·tah·ray* vt point; aim (*gun etc*); **puntare su** *poon·tah·ray soo* to back (*bet on*); **puntare un fucile contro qualcuno** *poon·tah·ray oon foo·chee·le kohn·tro kwal·koo·no* to aim a gun at someone

punteggio *poon·tayj·joh* m score

puntina *poon·tee·na* f drawing pin; thumbtack

punto *poon·toh* m point; spot (*dot*); period (*punctuation*); stitch (*sewing*); **il punto di vista** *poon·toh dee vee·sta* point of view; **il punto di riferimento** *poon·toh dee ree·fe·ree·mayn·toh* landmark; **il punto interrogativo** *poon·toh een·ter·ro·ga·tee·vo* question mark; **gli ha risposto punto per punto** *lyee a ree·spoh·sto poon·toh payr poon·toh* he answered him point by point

puntuale *poon·too·ah·le* adj punctual

puntualmente *poon·too·al·mayn·te* adv on time

puntura *poon·too·ra* f bite; sting

pupazzo *poo·pats·tsoh* m puppet

purché *poor·kay* conj as long as (*provided that*); provided; providing; **purché venga** *poor·kay ven·ga* provided (that) he comes

purè *poo·re* m — purée; **il purè di patate** *poo·re dee pa·tah·tay* mashed potatoes

puro(a) *poo·ro(a)* adj pure

purpureo(a) *poor·poo·re·o(a)* adj purple

pustola *poo·sto·la* f spot (*pimple*)

puzzle *puz·zuhl* m jigsaw (*puzzle*)

Q

qua *kwa* adv here; **di qua, per favore** *dee kwa payr fa·voh·re* this way please

quaderno *kwa·der·noh* m exercise book

quadrato(a) *kwa·drah·to(a)* adj square □ m **il quadrato** *kwa·drah·toh* square; **un metro quadrato** *oon me·troh kwa·drah·to* a square meter

a quadretti *a kwa·drayt·tee* adv check(er)ed (*patterned*)

quadri *kwa·dree* mpl diamonds (*cards*)

quadro *kwa·droh* m picture; painting; **i quadri medi** *kwa·dree me·dee* middle management

quaglia *kwal·ya* f quail

qualche *kwal·kay* adj some; **qualche volta** *kwal·kay vol·ta* sometimes

qualcosa *kwal·ko·sa* pron something; **qualcosa di piú grande** *kwal·ko·sa dee pyoo gran·de* something bigger; **può vedere qualcosa?** *pwo ve·day·re kwal·ko·sa* can you see anything?

qualcuno *kwal·koo·no* pron somebody, someone; **qualcuno di voi sa cantare?** *kwal·koo·no dee voy sa kan·tah·ray* can any of you sing?; **può vedere qualcuno?** *pwo ve·day·re kwal·koo·no* can you see anybody?; **qualcun altro** *kwal·koon al·troh* someone else

quale *kwah·le* adj what; which □ pron which one; **qual libro?** *kwahl lee·broh* what book?; **non so quale prendere** *nohn so kwah·le pren·de·re* I don't know which to take; **quali lin-**

gue? *kwah·lee leen·gwe* which languages?

qualificarsi per *kwa·lee·fee·kar see payr vr* qualify for (*in sports*)

qualificato(a) *kwa·lee·fee·kah·to(a) adj* qualified

qualità *kwa·lee·ta f* — quality; gli articoli di qualità *ar·tee·ko·lee dee kwa·lee·ta* quality goods

qualsiasi *kwal·see·a·see adj* any

qualunque *kwa·loon·kwe adj* any

quando *kwan·do conj* when; di quando in quando *dee kwan·do een kwan·do* occasionally

quantità *kwan·tee·ta f* — quantity

quanto(a) *kwan·to(a) adj* how much; quanto tempo? *kwan·to tem·po* how long?; quanti(e)? *kwan·tee(·te) how many?; quante persone? *kwan·te per·soh·ne* how many people?; quanto latte? *kwan·to lat·te* how much milk?; quanto dista da qui a…? *kwan·to dee·sta da kwee a* how far is it to…?; quanto a questo *kwan·to a kway·sto* as for this

quaranta *kwa·ran·ta num* forty

quarantena *kwa·ran·te·na f* quarantine

quartiere *kwar·tye·re m* district (*of town*); il quartiere luce rossa *kwar·tye·re loo·che rohs·sa* red light district

quarto *kwar·toh m* quarter □ *adj* quarto(a) *kwar·to(a)* fourth; un quarto d'ora *oon kwar·toh doh·ra* a quarter of an hour

quarzo *kwar·tsoh m* quartz

quasi *kwah·zee adv* nearly; almost

quattordici *kwat·tor·dee·chee num* fourteen

quattro *kwat·troh num* four

quei *kway adj* those

quel(la) *kwayl(·la) adj* that

quelli(e) *kwayl·lee(·le) adj* those □ *pron* those; ecco quelli(e) che voglio *ek·ko kwayl·lee(·le) ke vol·yo* those are what I want; quelle donne *kwayl·le don·ne* those women

quello *kwayl·lo pron* that; quello(a) lì *kwayl·lo(a) lee* that one; ho visto quello che è successo *o vee·sto kwayl·lo ke e sooch·ches·so* I saw what happened; quello(a) sulla tavola *kwayl·lo(a) sool·la tah·vo·la* the one on the table; ecco quello che voglio *ek·ko kwayl·lo ke vol·yo* this is what I want; che cos'è quello? *ke ko·se kwayl·lo* what's that?

quercia *kwer·cha f* oak

questi(e) *kway·stee(·ste) adj, pron* these

questionario *kwe·styoh·nah·ryoh m* questionnaire

questione *kwe·styoh·ne f* issue; question; è questione di *e kwe·styoh·ne dee* it's a question of

questo(a) *kway·sto(a) adj* this □ *pron* this one

qui *kwee adv* here; venga qui *ven·ga kwee* come over here; è qui in vacanza e *kwee een va·kan·tsa* he's over here on holiday; proprio qui *pro·pree·o kwee* just here

quiche *keesh f* quiche

quindi *kween·dee adv* then

quindici *kween·dee·chee num* fifteen

quindicina di giorni *kween·dee·chee·na dee johr·nee f* fortnight

quinto(a) *kween·to(a) adj* fifth

quota *kwo·ta f* subscription; quota

quotare *kwo·tah·ray vt* quote (*price*)

quotazione *kwo·ta·tsyoh·ne f* quotation (*price*)

quotidiano(a) *kwo·tee·dee·ah·no(a) adj* daily □ *m* il quotidiano *kwo·tee·dee·ah·noh* daily (*newspaper*)

R

rabarbaro *ra·bar·ba·roh m* rhubarb

rabbia *rab·bya f* anger; rabies

rabbino *rab·bee·noh m* rabbi

rabbrividire *rab·bree·vee·dee·re vi* shiver

racchetta *rak·kayt·ta f* racket (*tennis*); paddle (*table tennis*)

raccogliere* *rak·kol·ye·ray vt* gather (*assemble*); collect; pick up (*object*)

raccolto *rak·kol·toh m* crop; harvest

raccomandare *rak·ko·man·dah·ray vt* recommend

raccontare *rak·kon·tah·ray vt* tell (*story*)

raccordo *rak·kor·doh m* adapter, adaptor (*electrical*)

radar *ra·dar m* radar; il controllo radar *kon·trol·loh ra·dar* radar trap

raddoppiare *rad·dop·pyah·ray vt/i* double

radersi* *rah·der·see vr* shave

radiatore *ra·dya·toh·ray m* radiator

radice *ra·dee·chay f* root

radio *ra·dyoh f* — radio; alla radio *al·la ra·dyoh* on the radio

radiografare *ra·dyo·gra·fah·ray vt* X-ray

radiografia *ra·dyo·gra·fee·a f* X-ray (*photo*)

radunarsi *ra·doo·nahr·see vr* gather (*crowd*)

raffermo(a) *raf·fayr·mo(a) adj* stale (*bread*)

raffica *raf·fee·ka f* squall; gust

raffinare *raf·fee·nah·ray vt* refine

raffineria *raf·fee·ne·ree·a f* refinery

raffreddamento *raf·fred·da·men·toh m* cooling

raffreddare *raf·fred·dah·ray vt* chill (*wine, food*)

raffreddore *raf·frayd·doh·ray m* cold (*illness*)

ragazza *ra·gats·tsa f* girl (*young woman*); girlfriend; la ragazza squillo *ra·gats·tsa skwee·loh* call girl

ragazzo *ra·gats·tsoh m* boy; boyfriend

raggio *raj·joh m* beam (*of light*); ray

raggiungere* *raj·joon·je·ray vt* reach

ragione *ra·jo·nay f* reason

ragioneria *ra·jo·ne·ree·a f* accountancy

ragionevole *ra·jo·nay·vo·le adj* sensible; reasonable

ragioniere *ra·jo·nye·re m* accountant; il ragioniere diplomato *ra·jo·nye·re dee·plo·mah·toh* certified public accountant

ragno *ran·yoh m* spider

rallentare *ral·len·tah·ray vt/i* to slow down *or* up

rally *ral·lee m* rally (*sporting*)

ramaiolo *ra·ma·yo·loh m* ladle

rame *rah·may m* copper (*metal*)

rammendare *ram·men·dah·ray vt* darn

ramo *rah·moh m* branch (*of tree*)

ramoscello *ra·mo·shel·loh m* twig

rampa *ram·pa f* ramp (*slope*)

rana *rah·na f* frog

rango *ran·goh m* rank (*status*)

rapa *ra·pa f* rutabaga; la rapa svedese *ra·pa zve·day·se* swede

rapidamente *ra·pee·da·mayn·te adv* quickly

rapido(a) *ra·pee·do(a) adj* high-speed;

quick □ *m* il rapido *ra·pee·doh* express train

rapire *ra·pee·re* vt kidnap

rapporto *rap·por·toh* m ratio; report; relationship; **i rapporti interrazziali** *rap·por·tee een·tayr·rats·tsyah·lee* race relations; **i rapporti sessuali** *rap·por·tee ses·soo·ah·lee* sexual intercourse

rappresentante *rap·pre·zen·tan·te* m/f representative; **il rappresentante sindacale** *rap·pre·zen·tan·te seen·da·kah·le* shop steward

rappresentare *rap·pre·zen·tah·ray* vt represent

rappresentazione *rap·pre·zen·ta·tsyoh·ne* f performance (*of play*); production

raramente *rah·ra·mayn·te* adv seldom

raro(a) *rah·ro(a)* adj rare; scarce

raso *rah·soh* m satin

rasoio *ra·soh·yo* m razor; **il rasoio elettrico** *ra·soh·yo e·let·tree·ko* shaver

rassomigliare *ras·so·meel·yah·ray* vi look like; resemble; **rassomiglia a suo padre** *ras·so·meel·ya a soo·o pah·dre* he resembles his father

rastrello *ra·strel·loh* m rake

rata *rah·ta* f instalment

rateizzare *ra·te·eedz·dzah·ray* vt spread (*payments*)

ratto *rat·toh* m rat

rattristare *rat·tree·stah·ray* vt sadden

ravanello *ra·va·nel·loh* m radish

ravioli *ra·vee·o·lee* mpl ravioli

razionalizzare *ra·tsyoh·na·leedz·dzah·ray* vt rationalize

razionalizzazione *ra·tsyoh·na·leedz·dza·tsyoh·nay* f rationalization

razza *rats·tsa* f race; breed

razzia *rats·tsee·a* f raid

razziale *rats·tsyah·lay* adj racial

razzo *radz·dzoh* m rocket

re *ray* m king

reale *re·ah·le* adj royal

realizzare *re·a·leedz·dzah·ray* vt carry out; realize (*assets*)

realmente *re·al·mayn·tay* adv in real terms

reattore *re·at·toh·ray* m reactor

reazione *re·a·tsyoh·nay* f reaction; backlash

recapito *re·ka·pee·toh* m address; delivery; **il recapito dei bagagli** *re·ka·pee·toh de·ee ba·gal·yee* baggage claim

recensione *re·chen·syoh·nay* f review (*of book etc*)

recente *re·chen·tay* adj recent

recentemente *re·chen·te·mayn·te* adv lately; recently

recessione *re·ches·syoh·nay* f recession

recinto *re·cheen·toh* m fence

recipiente *re·chee·pyen·tay* m container

réclame *ray·klam* f commercial; advertisement

reclamo *re·klah·moh* m complaint (*dissatisfaction*)

recluta *re·kloo·ta* f recruit

reclutamento *re·kloo·ta·mayn·toh* m recruitment

redditizio(a) *red·dee·tee·tsyo(a)* adj profitable

reddito *red·dee·toh* m income; yield (*financial*)

redigere* *re·dee·je·re* vt draw up (*document*)

referenze *re·fe·ren·tse* fpl reference (*testimonial*)

regalare *ray·ga·lah·ray* vt give away; present

regalo *re·gah·loh* m present; gift; **il regalo di nozze** *re·gah·loh dee nots·tse* wedding present

regata *re·gah·ta* f regatta

reggere* *rej·je·re* vt support (*hold up*)

reggiseno *rej·jee·say·noh* m bra

regina *re·jee·na* f queen

regione *re·joh·nay* f region; district (*in country*); area

regista *re·jee·sta* m/f producer (*of play*); director (*of film*)

registrare *re·jee·strah·ray* vt tape record; register; record

registrarsi *re·jee·strahr·see* vr check in (*at hotel*)

registro *re·jee·stroh* m register

Regno Unito *rayn·yoh oo·nee·to* m United Kingdom, U.K.

regola *re·go·la* f rule (*regulation*)

regolamento *re·go·la·mayn·toh* m regulation (*rule*)

regolare *re·go·lah·ray* adj regular; steady (*pace*) □ vt settle (*argument*)

regolo *re·go·loh* m ruler (*for measuring*); **il regolo calcolatore** *re·go·loh kal·ko·la·toh·re* slide rule

relativo(a) *re·la·tee·vo(a)* adj relevant; relative

relazione *re·la·tsyoh·nay* f relationship; report; **le pubbliche relazioni** *poob·blee·ke re·la·tsyoh·nee* public relations

religione *re·lee·joh·nay* f religion

religioso(a) *re·lee·joh·so(a)* adj religious

remare *re·mah·ray* vi row (*sport*)

remo *re·moh* m oar

rendere* *ren·de·re* vt yield (*investment*); **rendersi conto di** *ren·der·see kohn·toh dee* to realize

rendimento *ren·dee·mayn·toh* m performance (*of car*); profitability; output

rendita *ren·dee·ta* f unearned income; revenue; **la rendita vitalizia** *ren·dee·ta vee·ta·lee·tsya* annuity

rene *re·ne* m kidney (*of person*)

Reno *re·no* m Rhine

reparto *re·par·toh* m department (*in store*); unit

repubblica *re·poob·blee·ka* f republic

repubblicano(a) *re·poob·blee·kah·no(a)* adj republican

residenza *re·see·den·tsa* f residence

residenziale *re·see·den·tsyah·le* adj residential (*area*)

resistente *re·see·sten·te* adj hard-wearing; durable (*fabric, article*); tough (*material*)

resistenza *re·see·sten·tsa* f resistance (*to illness*); strength (*of girder, rope etc*)

resistere* *re·see·ste·ray* vi resist

respingere* *re·speen·je·ray* vt reject

respirare *re·spee·rah·ray* vt/i breathe

responsabile *re·spon·sah·bee·lay* adj responsible; **è lui il responsabile del dipartimento** *e loo·ee eel re·spon·sah·bee·lay del dee·par·tee·mayn·toh* he's responsible for the department; **essere* responsabile per** *es·se·ray re·spon·sah·bee·lay payr* to be in charge of

responsabilità *re·spon·sa·bee·lee·ta* f responsibility; **questo è di Sua responsabilità** *kway·stoh e dee soo·a re·spon·sa·bee·lee·ta* this is your responsibility

restare *res·tah·ray* vi remain; **le uova mi restano sullo stomaco** *le wo·va* *mee re·sta·no sool·lo sto·ma·koh* eggs disagree with me

restituire *re·stee·too·ee·ray* vt return *(give back)*

resto *re·sto* m remainder; change

restringersi* *re·streen·jer·see* vr shrink

restrizione *re·stree·tsyoh·nay* f restriction; **la restrizione del credito** *re·stree·tsyoh·nay del kray·dee·toh* credit squeeze; **la restrizione economica** *re·stree·tsyoh·nay e·ko·no·mee·ka* squeeze *(financial)*

rete *ray·tay* f goal *(sport)*; net; string bag

retro *re·troh* m back; Vedi retro P.T.O.

retrodatare *re·tro·da·tah·ray* vt backdate *(letter)*

retromarcia *re·tro·mar·cha* f reverse *(gear)*; **in retromarcia** *een re·tro·mar·cha* in reverse (gear); **entrare nel garage in retromarcia** *en·trah·ray nel ga·raj een re·tro·mar·cha* to back into the garage

retrospettivamente *re·tro·spet·tee·va·mayn·tay* adv in retrospect

reumatismo *re·oo·ma·tee·zmoh* m rheumatism

revisione *re·vee·zee·oh·nay* f review; service *(for car)*

revisore dei conti *re·vee·zoh·re de·ee kohn·tee* m auditor

riaddestramento *ree·ad·de·stra·mayn·toh* m retraining

riaddestrare *ree·ad·de·strah·ray* vt retrain

riaddestrarsi *ree·ad·de·strar·see* vr retrain

rialzare *ree·al·tsah·ray* vt raise *(price)*

rialzo *ree·al·tso* m upturn *(in business)*; rise *(in prices, wages)*; **in rialzo** *een ree·al·tso* buoyant *(market)*

rianimare *ree·a·nee·mah·ray* vt revive *(person)*

riattaccare *ree·at·tak·kah·ray* vt reattach; **riattaccare il telefono** *ree·at·tak·kah·ray eel te·le·fo·no* to hang up

ribassare *ree·bas·sah·ray* vi fall *(prices etc)*

ribasso *ree·bas·soh* m reduction *(in price)*

ribes *ree·bes* m black currant; **il ribes rosso** *ree·bes rohs·so* red currant

ricamato(a) *ree·ka·mah·to(a)* adj embroidered

ricamo *ree·kah·moh* m embroidery

ricchezza *reek·kayts·tsa* f wealth

ricciolo *reech·cho·loh* m curl

ricciuto(a) *reech·choo·toh(a)* adj curly

ricco(a) *reek·ko(a)* adj wealthy; rich

ricerca *ree·chayr·ka* f research; **la ricerca di mercato** *ree·chayr·ka dee mayr·kah·toh* market research

ricetta *ree·chet·ta* f prescription; recipe

ricevere *ree·chay·ve·re* vt entertain *(give hospitality)*; receive *(letter)*

ricevimento *ree·che·vee·mayn·toh* m reception; reception desk

ricevitore *ree·che·vee·toh·ray* m receiver *(phone)*

ricevuta *ree·che·voo·ta* f receipt; **accusare ricevuta di** *ak·koo·zah·ray ree·che·voo·ta dee* to acknowledge *(letter)*; **con ricevuta di ritorno** *kohn ree·che·voo·ta dee ree·tohr·noh* by registered mail

richiesta *ree·kye·sta* f request

ricompensa *ree·kom·pen·sa* f reward

riconoscere* *ree·ko·noh·she·ray* vt recognize

ricordare *ree·kor·dah·ray* vt remind;

ricordare qualcosa a qualcuno *ree·kor·dah·ray kwal·ko·sa a kwal·koo·no* to remind someone of something; **ricordarsi di** *ree·kor·dar·see dee* to remember

ricordo *ree·kor·doh* m souvenir; **un mio ricordo** *oon mee·oh ree·kor·doh* one of my memories

ricorrere* a *ree·kohr·re·ray a* vi resort to

ricuperare *ree·koo·pe·rah·ray* vt recover; retrieve *(data)*

ridere* *ree·de·re* vi laugh; **ridere* di qualcuno** *ree·de·re dee kwal·koo·no* to laugh at somebody

ridicolo(a) *ree·dee·ko·lo(a)* adj ridiculous

ridistribuire *ree·dee·stree·boo·ee·ray* vt redistribute

ridistribuzione *ree·dee·stree·boo·tsyoh·nay* f redistribution

ridurre* *ree·door·re* vt turn down *(heat)*; reduce

riduzione *ree·doo·tsyoh·nay* f reduction

riempire* *ree·em·pee·re* vt fill; fill in/out/up

riesaminare *ree·e·za·mee·nah·ray* vt review

rifare* *ree·fah·ray* vt do again; repair; **rifare* i letti** *ree·fah·ray ee let·tee* to make the beds

riferimento *ree·fe·ree·mayn·toh* m reference

rifiutare *ree·fyoo·tah·ray* vt refuse; reject; **rifiutarsi di fare qualcosa** *ree·fyoo·tar·see dee far·ray kwal·ko·sa* to refuse to do something

rifiuti *ree·fyoo·tee* mpl rubbish; waste

rifiuto *ree·fyoo·toh* m refusal

riflettere* *ree·flet·te·re* vt reflect; **riflettere* su qualcosa** *ree·flet·te·re soo kwal·ko·sa* to think something over

riflettore *ree·flet·toh·re* m spotlight; floodlight

rifugio *ree·foo·joh* m refuge; shelter

rigido(a) *ree·jee·do(a)* adj stiff

riguardare *ree·gwar·dah·ray* vt concern; **ciò non la riguarda** *cho nohn la ree·gwahr·da* that doesn't concern you

riguardo *ree·gwar·do* m care; respect; **senza riguardo a** *sen·tsa ree·gwar·do* a regardless of

rilassarsi *ree·las·sar·see* vr relax

rilievo *ree·lye·voh* m survey *(of land)*

rimandare *ree·man·dah·ray* vt send back; postpone

rimanere* *ree·ma·nay·re* vi stay; remain

rimbalzare *reem·bal·tsah·ray* vi bounce *(ball)*

rimbombare *reem·bom·bah·ray* vi roar *(engine)*

rimborsare *reem·bohr·sah·ray* vt repay; refund

rimborso *reem·bohr·soh* m refund

rimedio *ree·me·dyoh* m remedy

rimescolare *ree·me·sko·lah·ray* vt shuffle *(cards)*; stir

rimessa *ree·mays·sa* f remittance; garage

rimettere* *ree·mayt·te·ray* vt replace *(put back)*

rimettersi* *ree·mayt·ter·see* vr recover *(from illness)*

rimorchiare *ree·mor·kyah·ray* vt tow

rimorchio *ree·mor·kyoh* m trailer *(for goods)*; **a rimorchio** *a ree·mor·kyoh* in tow

rinchiudere* *reen·kyoo·de·re* vt shut up

rincrescere* *reen·kray·she·ray* vi regret

rinforzare *reen·for·tsah·ray* vt strengthen

rinfreschi *reen·fray·skee* mpl refreshments

ringhiare *reen·gyah·ray* vi growl

ringhiera *reen·gye·ra* f rail (on bridge, balcony)

ringraziare *reen·gra·tsyah·ray* vt thank

rinnovare *reen·no·vah·ray* vt renew (subscription, passport)

rinunciare *ree·noon·chah·ray* vi quit (give up)

rinviare *reen·vyah·ray* vt shelve (project); return (send back); delay (postpone); **rinviare la seduta** *reen·vyah·ray la se·doo·ta* to adjourn the meeting

rinvio *reen·vee·oh* m adjournment; return

riordinare *ree·or·dee·nah·ray* vt reorder (goods)

riorganizzare *ree·or·ga·needz·dzah·ray* vt reorganize

riorganizzazione *ree·or·ga·needz·dza·tsyoh·nay* f reorganization

ripagare *ree·pa·gah·ray* vt repay

riparare *ree·pa·rah·ray* vt mend; repair

ripararsi *ree·pa·rar·see* vr shelter (from rain etc)

riparazione *ree·pa·ra·tsyoh·nay* f repair

ripassare *ree·pas·sah·ray* vt revise

ripetere* *ree·pe·te·re* vt repeat; **può ripetere quello?** *pwo ree·pe·te·re kwayl·lo* could you say that again?

ripetizione *ree·pe·tee·tsyoh·nay* f repetition

ripido(a) *ree·pee·do(a)* adj abrupt; steep

ripieno *ree·pye·noh* m stuffing (in chicken etc)

riportare *ree·por·tah·ray* vt report

riposarsi *ree·po·sar·see* vr rest

riposo *ree·po·soh* m rest

riprendere* *ree·pren·de·re* vt take back; resume; **riprendere* i sensi** *ree·pren·de·re ee sen·see* to come around (recover)

risa *ree·sa* fpl laughter

risarcimento *ree·sar·chee·mayn·toh* m compensation

riscaldamento *ree·skal·da·mayn·toh* m heating; **il riscaldamento centrale** *ree·skal·da·mayn·toh chen·trah·lay* central heating

riscaldatore *ree·skal·da·toh·re* m heater

rischiare *ree·skyah·ray* vt risk

rischio *ree·skyoh* m risk

risciacquare *ree·shak·kwah·ray* vt rinse

riscuotere* *ree·skwo·te·ray* vt cash (check)

riserva *ree·ser·va* f reserve (for game); stock (supply); reservation (doubt)

riservare *ree·ser·vah·ray* vt reserve (seat, room)

riserve *ree·ser·ve* fpl reserves

riso *ree·soh* m laugh; rice

risolvere* *ree·sol·ve·re* vt solve; work out

risorse *ree·sohr·se* fpl resources

risotto *ree·sot·toh* m risotto

risparmiare *ree·spar·myah·ray* vt save

rispettabile *ree·spet·tah·bee·lay* adj respectable

rispettare *ree·spet·tah·ray* vt respect

rispetto *ree·spet·toh* m respect

risplendere* *ree·splen·de·re* vi blaze (lights)

rispondere* *ree·spohn·de·ray* vi reply

□ vt/i answer; **rispondere* a una domanda** *ree·spohn·de·ray a oo·na do·man·da* to reply to a question; **rispondere* al telefono** *ree·spohn·de·ray al te·le·fo·noh* to answer the phone; **rispondere* a** *ree·spon·de·ray* to meet (demand)

risposta *ree·spoh·sta* f reply; answer

ristabilirsi *ree·sta·bee·leer·see* vr recover; get well; **si ristabilisca presto** *see ree·sta·bee·lee·ska pre·sto* get well soon

ristorante *ree·sto·ran·te* m restaurant

risultato *ree·sool·tah·toh* m result

ritardare *ree·tar·dah·ray* vt delay □ vi be late; lose (clock, watch)

ritardo *ree·tar·doh* m delay; **essere* in ritardo** *es·se·re een ree·tar·doh* to be late; **il treno ha un ritardo** *eel tre·no a oon ree·tar·doh* the train has been delayed

ritelefonare *ree·te·le·fo·nah·ray* vt call back

ritenere* *ree·te·nay·re* vt hold back; consider; **lo si ritiene un ingegnere** *lo see ree·tye·ne oon een·jen·ye·re* he's supposed to be an engineer

ritirare *ree·tee·rah·ray* vt withdraw

ritirarsi *ree·tee·rar·see* vr withdraw; retire; **ritirarsi da un affare** *ree·tee·rar·see da oon af·fah·re* to pull out of a deal

ritiro *ree·tee·ro* m retirement; withdrawal

ritmo *reet·moh* m rhythm; **al ritmo di** *al reet·moh dee* at the rate of

ritorno *ree·tohr·noh* m return

riunione *ree·oon·yoh·nay* f meeting; conference

riuscire* *ree·oo·shee·re* vi succeed; **è riuscito a farlo** *e ree·oo·shee·to a far·lo* he succeeded in doing it; **riuscire* a fare qualcosa** *ree·oo·shee·re a fah·ray kwal·ko·sa* to manage to do something; **ci sono appena riuscito** *chee so·no ap·pay·na ree·oo·shee·to* I just managed it; **non riuscire*** *nohn ree·oo·shee·re* to fail (person)

riva *ree·va* f bank (of river, lake)

rivale *ree·vah·le* m/f rival

rivedere* *ree·ve·day·re* vt revise (estimate etc)

rivendere *ree·vayn·de·ray* vt resell

rivendita *ree·vayn·dee·ta* f resale; retailer's shop; **rivendita proibita** *ree·vayn·dee·ta pro·ee·bee·ta* not for resale

rivista *ree·vee·sta* f magazine (journal); revue

rivoltare *ree·vol·tah·ray* vt turn over; turn inside out

rivoluzione *ree·vo·loo·tsyoh·nay* f revolution

roba *ro·ba* f stuff (things)

robot *ro·bot* m robot

roccia *roch·cha* f rock

rodare *ro·dah·ray* vt break in (car)

rognone *ron·yoh·ne* m kidney

rollino *rol·lee·noh* m spool, cartridge (for camera)

Roma *roh·ma* f Rome

Romania *ro·ma·nee·a* f Romania

romano(a) *ro·mah·no(a)* adj Roman

romantico(a) *ro·man·tee·ko(a)* adj romantic

romanzo *ro·man·dzoh* m novel (book)

rombare *rom·bah·ray* vi rumble

rombo *rohm·boh* m turbot; roar (of engine); rumble

romeno(a) *ro·me·no(a)* adj Romanian
□ m il romeno *ro·me·noh* Romanian

rompere* *rohm·pe·re* vt break

rompersi* *rohm·per·see* vr break; **rompersi il braccio** *rohm·per·see eel brach·choh* to break one's arm

rompicapo *rom·pee·kah·poh* m puzzle; worry

rosa *ro·za* adj — pink □ f **la rosa** *ro·za* rose

rosé *ro·zay* m rosé

rossetto *ros·sayt·toh* m lipstick

rosso(a) *rohs·so(a)* adj red; **dai capelli rossi** *dai ka·pel·lee rohs·see* red-haired; **passare con il rosso** *pas·sah·ray kohn eel rohs·soh* to go through a red light

rosticceria *ro·steech·che·ree·a* f grill-room

rotaie *ro·ta·ye* fpl rails (*for train*)

rotolare *ro·to·lah·ray* vi roll; **fare* rotolare** *fah·ray ro·to·lah·ray* to roll (*on wheels*)

rotolo *ro·to·loh* m roll

rotonda *ro·tohn·da* f traffic circle

rotondo(a) *ro·tohn·do(a)* adj round

roulette *roo·let* f roulette

roulotte *roo·lot* f trailer (*home on wheels*)

routine *roo·teen* f routine

rovesciare *ro·ve·shah·ray* vt pour; spill; **rovesciare qualcosa** *ro·ve·shah·ray kwal·ko·sa* to turn something upside down; to turn something over

rovesciarsi *ro·ve·shar·see* vr spill

rovescio *ro·ve·shoh* m back (*reverse side*); the wrong side

rovina *ro·vee·na* f ruin

rovinare *ro·vee·nah·ray* vt wreck (*plans*); ruin

rovine *ro·vee·ne* fpl ruins

R.S.V.P. abbrev R.S.V.P.

rubare *roo·bah·ray* vt steal; **rubare qualcosa a qualcuno** *roo·bah·ray kwal·ko·sa a kwal·koo·no* to steal something from someone

rubinetto *roo·bee·nayt·toh* m faucet; **il rubinetto di arresto** *roo·bee·nayt·toh dee ar·re·stoh* stopcock

rubino *roo·bee·noh* m ruby

rudemente *roo·de·mayn·tay* adv roughly

ruga *roo·ga* f wrinkle

rugby *roog·bee* m rugby

ruggine *rooj·jee·ne* f rust

ruggire *rooj·jee·ray* vi roar

ruggito *rooj·jee·toh* m roar

rum *room* m rum

rumore *roo·moh·ray* m noise

rumoroso(a) *roo·mo·roh·soh(a)* adj noisy

ruota *rwo·ta* f wheel; **la ruota di scorta** *rwo·ta dee skor·ta* spare wheel

rurale *roo·rah·le* adj rural

ruscello *roo·shel·loh* m stream

russare *roos·sah·ray* vi snore

Russia *roos·sya* f Russia

russo(a) *roos·so(a)* adj Russian □ m **il russo** *roos·soh* Russian

ruvido(a) *roo·vee·do(a)* adj rough; coarse (*texture, material*)

S

sabato *sah·ba·toh* m Saturday

sabbia *sab·bya* f sand

sabbioso(a) *sab·byoh·so(a)* adj sandy (*beach*)

saccarina *sak·ka·ree·na* f saccharin

sacchetto *sak·kayt·toh* m bag (*of paper*); **il sacchetto di plastica** *sak·kayt·toh dee pla·stee·ka* polyethylene bag

sacco *sak·koh* m bag; sack; **il sacco a pelo** *sak·koh a pay·loh* sleeping bag; **il sacco in plastica** *sak·koh een pla·stee·ka* plastic bag

saggio(a) *saj·jo(a)* adj wise □ m **il saggio** *saj·joh* essay

saia *sa·ya* f twill

sala *sah·la* f hall (*room*); auditorium; **la sala d'aspetto** *sah·la da·spet·toh* waiting room (*at station*); lounge (*at airport*); **la sala d'esposizione** *sah·la de·spo·zee·tsyoh·ne* showroom; **la sala da pranzo** *sah·la da pran·dzoh* dining room; **la sala di partenza** *sah·la dee par·ten·tsa* departure lounge

salame *sa·lah·me* m salami; **il salame all'aglio** *sa·lah·me al·lal·yoh* garlic sausage

salariato *sa·la·ree·ah·toh* m wage earner

salario *sa·lah·ryoh* m wage, wages

salato(a) *sa·lah·to(a)* adj salted; salty; savory (*not sweet*); **non salato(a)** *nohn sa·lah·to(a)* unsalted

saldare *sal·dah·ray* vt settle (*bill*); weld

saldi *sal·dee* mpl sales (*cheap prices*)

saldo *sal·doh* m balance (*remainder owed*); **il saldo bancario** *sal·doh ban·kah·ryo* bank balance

sale *sah·le* m salt

saliera *sa·lye·ra* f salt cellar

salire* *sa·lee·ray* vi rise □ vt/i go up; **salire* su una collina** *sa·lee·ray soo oo·na kol·lee·na* to go up a hill; **salire* su** *sa·lee·ray soo* to board (*train, bus*)

saliscendi *sa·lee·shayn·dee* m — latch

saliva *sa·lee·va* f saliva

salmone *sal·moh·ne* m salmon

salone *sa·loh·ne* m lounge (*in hotel*); **il salone dell'automobile** *sa·loh·ne del·low·to·mo·bee·lay* auto show

salotto *sa·lot·toh* m living room; sitting room

salsa *sal·sa* f gravy; sauce; **la salsa vinaigrette** *sal·sa vee·nay·gret* vinaigrette (*sauce*); **la salsa di pomodoro** *sal·sa dee po·mo·do·roh* tomato sauce; **la salsa tartara** *sal·sa tar·ta·ra* tartar sauce

salsiccia *sal·seech·cha* f sausage

saltare *sal·tah·ray* vi blow (*fuse*) □ vt/i jump; **saltare un muricciolo** *sal·tah·ray oon moo·reech·cho·loh* to jump (over) a wall

saltato(a) *sal·tah·to(a)* adj sauté

salumeria *sa·loo·me·ree·a* f delicatessen

salutare *sa·loo·tah·ray* vt greet

salute *sa·loo·te* f health

saluto *sa·loo·toh* m greeting; **distinti saluti** *dee·steen·tee sa·loo·tee* sincerely yours

salvagente pedonale *sal·va·jen·te pe·do·nah·le* m island (*traffic*)

salvaguardia *sal·va·gwar·dya* f safeguard

salvare *sal·vah·ray* vt save; rescue

salvataggio *sal·va·taj·joh* m rescue

salvia *sal·vya* f sage (*herb*)

salvo(a) *sal·vo(a)* adj safe

sanatorio *sa·na·to·ryoh* m sanitarium

sandalo *san·da·loh* m sandal

sangue *san·gwe* m blood; **al sangue** *al san·gwe* rare (*steak*)

sanguinare *san·gwee·nah·ray* vi bleed

sano(a) *sah·no(a)* adj healthy

santo(a) *san·to(a)* adj holy □ m/f **il/la santo(a)** *san·to(a)* saint

sanzioni *san·tsyoh·nee* fpl sanctions

sapere* *sa·pay·re* vt know (*fact, sub-*

ject); **sa di pesce** *sa dee pay·she* it tastes of fish; **sapere* di aglio** *sa·pay·re dee al·yoh* to smell of garlic; **sapere* fare qualcosa** *sa·pay·re fah·ray kwal·ko·sa* to know how to do something; **per quanto io sappia** *per kwan·to ee·o sap·pya* as far as I know

sapone *sa·poh·ne* m soap; **il sapone in scaglie** *sa·poh·ne een skal·ye* soap-flakes; **il sapone da barba** *sa·poh·ne da bar·ba* shaving soap

saponetta *sa·po·nayt·ta* f bar of soap

sapore *sa·poh·re* m flavor; taste

sarcastico(a) *sar·ka·stee·ko(a)* adj sarcastic

Sardegna *sar·dayn·ya* f Sardinia

sardella *sar·del·la* f pilchard

sardina *sar·dee·na* f sardine

sarto *sar·toh* m tailor

sassoso(a) *sas·soh·so(a)* adj stony

satellite *sa·tel·lee·te* m satellite

satira *sa·tee·ra* f satire (play)

saturare *sa·too·rah·ray* vt saturate

sauna *sow·na* f sauna

sbadigliare *zba·deel·yah·ray* vi yawn

sbagliarsi *zbal·yahr·see* vr make a mistake

sbagliato(a) *zbal·ya·toh(a)* adj incorrect; wrong

sbaglio *zbal·yoh* m mistake; **per sbaglio** *payr zbal·yoh* by mistake; in error

sbalordire *zba·lor·dee·re* vt amaze

sbandare *zban·dah·ray* vi swerve

sbarcare *zbar·kah·ray* vi land

sbarra *zbar·ra* f bar (metal)

sbattere *zbat·te·re* vt slam; beat (cream, eggs) □ m lo sbattere *zbat·te·re* bang (of door)

sbiadire *zbee·a·dee·re* vi fade

sbloccare *zblok·kah·ray* vt clear

sbornia *zbor·nya* f drunkenness; **avere* mal di testa dopo una sbornia** *a·vay·re mal dee te·sta doh·po oo·na zbor·nya* to have a hangover

sbrinare *zbree·nah·ray* vt defrost (refrigerator)

sbucciare *zbooch·chah·ray* vt peel

scacchi *skak·kee* mpl chess

scadenza *ska·den·tsa* f maturity; **a lunga scadenza** *a loon·ga ska·den·tsa* long-term

scadere* *ska·day·re* vi expire

scaduto(a) *ska·doo·to(a)* adj out-of-date (passport, ticket)

scaffale *skaf·fah·le* m shelf

scaglia *skal·ya* f scale (of fish); flake

scala *skah·la* f ladder; staircase; scale; **la scala portatile** *skah·la por·tah·tee·le* stepladder; **la scala mobile** *skah·la mo·bee·le* escalator

scaldabagno *skal·da·ban·yoh* m immersion heater; water heater

scaldare *skal·dah·ray* vt warm

scale *skah·le* fpl stairs

scalfire *skal·fee·ray* vt graze; scratch

scalfittura *skal·feet·too·ra* f graze

scalinata *ska·lee·nah·ta* f flight of steps

scalino *ska·lee·noh* m step

scalo *skah·loh* m stopover (air travel)

scalogno *ska·lohn·yoh* m scallion

scaloppina *ska·lop·pee·na* f escalope

scalzo(a) *skal·tsoh(a)* adj barefoot

scamiciato *ska·mee·chah·toh* m jumper (dress)

scampi *skam·pee* mpl scampi

Scandinavia *skan·dee·nah·vya* f Scandinavia

scandinavo(a) *skan·dee·nah·vo(a)* adj Scandinavian

scantinato *skan·tee·nah·toh* m cellar

scapolo *skah·po·loh* m bachelor

scappare *skap·pah·ray* vi escape

scarafaggio *ska·ra·faj·joh* m beetle

scaricare *ska·ree·kah·ray* vt unload

scaricato(a) *ska·ree·kah·to(a)* adj dead (battery)

scarico(a) *skah·ree·ko(a)* adj flat (battery); **il luogo di scarico** *lwo·go dee skah·ree·ko* dump (for rubbish)

scarlatto(a) *skar·lat·to(a)* adj scarlet

scarpa *skar·pa* f shoe

scarpetta da tennis *skar·payt·ta da ten·nees* f tennis shoe

scarpette *skar·payt·te* fpl sneakers

scarpone da sci *skar·poh·ne da shee* m ski boot

scassinatore *skas·see·na·toh·re* m burglar

scatola *skah·to·la* f box; carton; in scatola *een skah·to·la* canned; **la scatola di fiammiferi** *skah·to·la dee fyam·mee·fe·ree* matchbox; **la scatola del cambio** *skah·to·la del kam·byoh* gearbox; **la scatola di cartone** *skah·to·la dee kar·toh·ne* box (cardboard)

scattare *skat·tah·ray* vt take (photograph)

scavalcare *ska·val·kah·ray* vt climb over

scavare *ska·vah·ray* vt dig (hole); dig up

scegliere* *shayl·ye·ray* vt choose; pick

scelta *shayl·ta* f range (variety); selection; choice

scena *she·na* f scene; **mettere* in scena** *mayt·te·re een she·na* to produce (play)

scendere* *shayn·de·ray* vt/i go down □ vi go downhill

sceriffo *she·reef·foh* m sheriff

scheda *ske·da* f slip (of paper)

schedario *ske·dah·ree·oh* m card index; file

scheggia *skayj·ja* f splinter (wood)

schermo *skayr·moh* m screen (TV, movie)

scherzo *skayr·tsoh* m joke

schiacciare *skya·chah·ray* vt crush; squash; mash

schiaffeggiare *skyaf·fej·jah·ray* vt smack; slap

schiaffo *skyaf·foh* m smack

schiamazzo *skya·mats·tsoh* m row (noise)

schiantarsi *skyan·tar·see* vr shatter

schiavo(a) *skyah·vo(a)* m/f slave

schiena *skye·na* f back (of person); **il mal di schiena** *mal dee skye·na* backache

schienale *skye·nah·le* m back (of chair)

schiocco *skee·ok·koh* m crack (noise)

schiuma *skyoo·ma* f foam

schizzare *skeets·tsah·ray* vt/i splash

sci *shee* m ski; skiing; **lo sci nautico** *shee now·tee·ko* water-skiing; **fare* dello sci nautico** *fah·ray del·lo shee now·tee·ko* to go water-skiing; **fare* dello sci** *fah·ray del·lo shee* to go skiing

scialbo(a) *shal·bo(a)* adj drab

scialle *shal·le* m shawl; wrap

scialuppa di salvataggio *sha·loop·pa dee sal·va·taj·joh* f lifeboat (on ship)

sciampagna *sham·pan·ya* m champagne

sciampo *sham·poh* m shampoo

sciare *shee·ah·ray* vi ski

sciarpa *shar·pa* f scarf

sciatore *shee·a·toh·re* m skier

sciatrice *shee·a·tree·che* f skier

scientifico(a) *shen·tee·fee·ko(a)* adj scientific

scienza *shen·tsa* f science

scienziato(a) *shen·tsyah·to(a)* m/f scientist

scimmia *sheem·mya* f ape; monkey

scintilla *sheen·teel·la* f spark

scintillare *sheen·teel·lah·ray* vi sparkle

sciocchezze *shok·kayts·tse* fpl nonsense; rubbish

sciogliere *shol·ye·re* vt untie; dissolve

sciogliersi *shol·yer·see* vr dissolve; melt

sciolto(a) *shol·to(a)* adj loose

scioperante *sho·pe·ran·te* m/f striker

scioperare *sho·pe·rah·ray* vi strike (workers)

sciopero *sho·pe·roh* m walkout; strike (industrial); lo sciopero bianco *sho·pe·roh byan·koh* slowdown; lo sciopero non ufficiale *sho·pe·roh nohn oof·fee·chah·lay* unofficial strike; in sciopero *een sho·pe·roh* on strike; paralizzato(a) da uno sciopero *pa·ra·leedz·dzah·to(a) da oo·no sho·pe·roh* strikebound

sciorinare *sho·ree·nah·ray* vt air (clothes)

sciovia *shee·o·vee·a* f ski lift

sciroppo *shee·rop·poh* m syrup; lo sciroppo per la tosse *shee·rop·poh payr la tos·say* cough medicine

sciupato(a) *shoo·pah·to(a)* adj ruined; spoiled; shopworn

scivolare *shee·vo·lah·ray* vi slip; slide; glide

scodella *sko·del·la* f bowl; basin

scogliera *skol·ye·ra* f cliff

scoiattolo *sko·yat·to·loh* m squirrel

scolapiatti *sko·la·pyat·tee* m — drainboard

scolare *sko·lah·ray* vt drain

scommessa *skom·mays·sa* f bet

scommettere* *skom·mayt·te·re* vt bet

scomodo(a) *sko·mo·doh(a)* adj uncomfortable; inconvenient (time, place)

scompartimento *skom·par·tee·mayn·toh* m compartment (on train); lo scompartimento per non-fumatori *skom·par·tee·mayn·toh payr nohn·foo·ma·toh·ree* nonsmoker (compartment); lo scompartimento per fumatori *skom·par·tee·mayn·toh payr foo·ma·toh·ree* smoker

sconfiggere* *skon·feej·je·re* vt defeat

sconfitta *skon·feet·ta* f defeat

sconosciuto(a) *sko·no·shoo·to(a)* adj unknown □ m/f lo/la sconosciuto(a) *sko·no·shoo·to(a)* stranger

sconto *skohn·toh* m discount; sconto del 3% *skohn·toh del 3%* 3% off; con uno sconto *kohn oo·no skohn·toh* at a discount

scontrarsi *skon·trahr·see* vr collide

scontrino *skon·tree·noh* m ticket

scontro *skohn·troh* m collision; crash; avere* uno scontro con la macchina *a·vay·ray oo·noh skohn·troh kohn la mak·kee·na* to crash one's car

sconveniente *skon·ve·nyen·te* adj improper

scooter *skoo·ter* m scooter

scopa *skoh·pa* f broom

scopare *sko·pah·ray* vt sweep (floor)

scoperto *sko·per·toh* m overdraft

scopo *sko·poh* m aim; goal; purpose

scoppiare *skop·pyah·ray* vi burst; fare* scoppiare *fah·ray skop·pyah·ray* to burst

scoppio *skop·pyoh* m blast (explosion)

scoprire* *sko·pree·re* vt discover; find out; uncover

scoraggiato(a) *sko·raj·jah·to(a)* adj discouraged

scorciatoia *skor·cha·toh·ya* f shortcut

scorrere* *skohr·re·re* vi flow; pour

scortese *skor·tay·zay* adj unkind; rude

scossa *skos·sa* f shock

scottarsi *skot·tar·see* vr scald

scottato(a) *skot·tah·to(a)* adj sunburned (painfully)

scottatura *skot·ta·too·ra* f burn; sunburn (painful)

Scozia *sko·tsya* f Scotland

scozzese *skots·tsay·se* adj Scottish □ m/f lo/la scozzese *skots·tsay·se* Scot

scriminatura *skree·mee·na·too·ra* f part (in hair)

scrittore *skreet·toh·re* m writer

scrittrice *skreet·tree·che* f writer

scrittura *skreet·too·ra* f writing

scrivania *skree·va·nee·a* f desk

scrivere* *skree·ve·re* vt/i write; spell; scrivere* a stampatello *skree·ve·re a stam·pa·tel·loh* to print (write in block letters)

scrutinio *skroo·tee·nyoh* m ballot

scultura *skool·too·ra* f sculpture

scuola *skwo·la* f school; la scuola elementare *skwo·la e·le·men·tah·ray* grade school; la scuola serale *skwo·la se·rah·lay* night school; la scuola privata *skwo·la pree·vah·ta* private school; la scuola statale *skwo·la sta·tah·le* public school; la scuola media *skwo·la me·dya* secondary school

scuotere* *skwo·te·re* vt shake

scure *skoo·re* f ax

scuro(a) *skoo·ro(a)* adj dark (color)

scusa *skoo·za* f excuse (pretext)

scusare *skoo·zah·ray* vt excuse; mi scusi *mee skoo·zee* excuse me

scusarsi *skoo·zar·see* vr apologize

scusate *skoo·zah·te* excl pardon

sdraiarsi *zdra·yar·see* vr lie down

sdrucciolevole *zdrooch·cho·lay·vo·le* adj slippery

se *say* conj whether; if

sé *say* pron himself; herself; itself; oneself; themselves; in sé *een say* conscious; l'ha fatto da sé *la fat·to da say* he did it on his own; se stesso(a) *say stays·so(a)* oneself

sebbene *seb·be·ne* conj though

seccare *sek·kah·ray* vt bother (annoy)

seccarsi *sek·kahr·see* vr dry up

seccatura *sek·ka·too·ra* f nuisance; bother

secchio *sayk·kyoh* m pail; bucket

secco(a) *sayk·ko(a)* adj dried (fruit, beans); dry

secolo *se·ko·loh* m century

secondario(a) *se·kon·dah·ryo(a)* adj secondary; minor (road)

secondo(a) *se·kohn·do(a)* adj second □ prep according to □ m il secondo *se·kohn·doh* second (time); di secondo *se·kohn·doh* second (time); di seconda mano *dee se·kohn·da mah·noh* secondhand (car etc); di seconda classe *se·kohn·da klas·se* second-class

sedano *se·da·noh* m celery

sedativo *se·da·tee·voh* m sedative

sede *se·de* f seat; head office

sedere *se·day·re* m bottom (of person)

sedere* *se·day·re* vi sit, be seated

sedersi *se·dayr·see* vr sit down

sedia *se·dya* f chair; la sedia a rotelle *se·dya a ro·tel·le* wheelchair; la sedia a sdraio *se·dya a zdra·yo* deckchair; la sedia pieghevole *se·dya pye·gay·vo·le* folding chair

sedicesimo(a) *say·dee·che·zee·mo(a)* adj sixteenth

sedici *say·dee·chee* num sixteen

sedile *se·dee·le* m bench; **il sedile del passeggero** *se·dee·le del pas·sej·je·roh* passenger seat

seduto(a) *se·doo·toh(a)* adj sitting

segale *say·ga·le* f rye

seggio *sej·jo* m seat

seggiolone *sej·jo·loh·ne* m highchair

seggiovia *sej·jo·vee·a* f chair-lift

segnale *sen·yah·le* m signal; road sign; **il segnale di linea libera** *sen·yah·le dee·lee·nay·a lee·bay·ra* dial tone; **il segnale "occupato"** *sen·yah·le ok·koo·pah·to* busy signal; **il segnale di soccorso** *sen·yah·le dee sok·kohr·soh* distress signal; **il segnale d'allarme** *sen·yah·le dal·lahr·may* alarm signal

segnare *sen·yah·ray* vt mark; score (goal)

segno *sayn·yoh* m sign; mark

segretario(a) *se·gre·tah·ryo(a)* m/f secretary; **il/la segretario(a) particolare** *se·gre·tah·ryo(a) par·tee·ko·lah·re* personal secretary

Segretario di Stato *se·gre·tah·ryo dee stah·toh* m secretary of state

segreto(a) *se·gray·to(a)* adj secret □ m **il segreto** *se·gray·toh* secret

seguente *se·gwen·te* adj following

seguire *se·gwee·re* vt follow □ vi follow; continue; **seguire qualcuno/qualcosa** *se·gwee·re kwal·koo·no/kwal·ko·sa* to come after someone/something

sei *sey* num six

sella *sel·la* f saddle

selvaggina *sel·vaj·jee·na* f game (hunting)

selvaggio(a) *sel·vaj·jo(a)* adj wild (animal, tribe)

selvatico(a) *sel·va·tee·ko(a)* adj wild (flower)

selz *selts* m soda water

semaforo *se·mah·fo·roh* m traffic lights

sembrare *sem·brah·ray* vi look; seem; **sembra malato** *saym·bra ma·lah·to* he appears to be ill

seme *say·me* m suit (cards); seed

semiaperto(a) *se·mee·a·per·to(a)* adj half open

semifinale *se·mee·fee·nah·le* f semifinal

seminterrato *se·meen·ter·rah·toh* m basement

semispecializzato(a) *se·mee·spe·cha·leedz·dzah·to(a)* adj semiskilled

semplice *saym·plee·che* adj plain; simple

sempre *sem·pre* adv always; ever; **sempre meno** *sem·pre may·noh* less and less

senape *say·na·pe* f mustard

senato *se·nah·toh* m senate

senatore *se·na·toh·re* m senator

seno *say·noh* m breast

sensibilità *sen·see·bee·lee·ta* f — feeling

senso *sen·soh* m sense; **avere* senso** *a·vay·re sen·soh* to make sense; **la strada a senso unico** *strah·da a sen·soh oo·nee·ko* one-way street; **il senso comune** *sen·soh ko·moo·ne* sense (common sense)

sentiero *sen·tye·roh* m path; footpath

sentinella *sen·tee·nel·la* f guard (sentry)

sentire *sen·tee·re* vt smell □ vt/i hear; **sento la mancanza di Londra** *sen·to la man·kan·tsa dee lohn·dra* I miss London; **non sento l'aglio** *nohn sen·to lal·yoh* I can't taste the garlic; non

La sento *nohn la sen·to* I can't hear (you); **mi sento meglio** *mee sen·to mel·yoh* I feel better; **mi sento male** *mee sen·to mah·le* I feel sick; **mi sento venir meno** *mee sen·to ve·neer may·no* I feel faint

senza *sen·tsa* prep without; **rimanere* senza benzina** *ree·ma·nay·re sen·tsa ben·dzee·na* to be out of gasoline; **siamo rimasti senza latte** *syah·mo ree·ma·stee sen·tsa lat·te* we've run out of milk

separare *se·pa·rah·ray* vt divide (separate)

separato(a) *se·pa·rah·to(a)* adj separate

seppellire *sep·pel·lee·re* vt bury

sera *say·ra* f evening; **di sera** *dee say·ra* p.m.; **la sera** *la say·ra* in the evening

serbatoio *ser·ba·toh·yoh* m tank (of car)

serie *se·ree·e* f series; round (of talks)

serietà *se·ree·e·ta* f seriousness; reliability (of person)

serio(a) *se·ryo(a)* adj serious; reliable

serpeggiare *ser·pej·jah·ray* vi twist (road)

serpente *ser·pen·te* m snake

serra *ser·ra* f greenhouse

serratura *ser·ra·too·ra* f lock

servire *ser·vee·re* vt attend to; serve; **non ci serve** *nohn chee ser·ve* it's of no benefit (to us); **a che serve?** *a ke ser·ve* what's the point?; **si serva** *see ser·va* help yourself

servizi *ser·vee·tsee* mpl facilities

servizio *ser·vee·tsyoh* m service charge; service; report (in press); **il servizio della domestica** *ser·vee·tsyoh del·la do·mes·tee·ka* maid service; **il servizio di camera** *ser·vee·tsyoh dee kah·me·ra* room service; **in servizio** *een ser·vee·tsyoh* on duty (doctor); **fuori servizio** *fwo·ree ser·vee·tsyoh* off duty; **il servizio sanitario** *ser·vee·tsyoh sa·nee·tah·ryo* health service; **i servizi sociali** *ser·vee·tsee so·chah·lee* social services; **il servizio di spola** *ser·vee·tsyoh dee spo·la* shuttle (service) (airline); **il servizio autobus** *ser·vee·tsyoh ow·to·boos* bus service

sessanta *ses·san·ta* num sixty

sesso *ses·soh* m sex

sesto(a) *se·sto(a)* adj sixth

seta *say·ta* f silk; **un vestito di seta** *oon ve·stee·toh de say·ta* a silk dress

setacciare *se·tach·chah·ray* vt sieve; sift

setaccio *se·tach·choh* m sieve

sete *say·te* f thirst; **avere* sete** *a·vay·re say·te* to be thirsty

settanta *set·tan·ta* num seventy

sette *set·te* num seven

settembre *set·tem·bre* m September

settentrionale *set·ten·tree·o·nah·lay* adj northern

setticemia *set·tee·che·mee·a* f blood poisoning

settimana *set·tee·mah·na* f week; **la settimana scorsa** *la set·tee·mah·na skohr·sa* last week; **$40 la settimana** *$40 la set·tee·mah·na* $40 a week

settimanale *set·tee·ma·nah·le* adj weekly □ m **il settimanale** *set·tee·ma·nah·le* weekly (periodical)

settimanalmente *set·tee·mah·nal·mayn·te* adv weekly

settimo(a) *set·tee·mo(a)* adj seventh

settore *set·toh·re* m sector; **il settore privato** *set·toh·re pree·vah·to* private sector; **il settore pubblico** *set·toh·re poob·blee·ko* public sector

severo(a) *se·ve·ro(a)* adj harsh; strict

sfacciataggine *sfach·cha·taj·jee·nay* f cheek (*impudence*)

sfacciato(a) *sfach·chah·to(a)* adj familiar (*impertinent*); cheeky

sfinito(a) *sfee·nee·to(a)* adj worn-out

sfoderato(a) *sfo·de·rah·to(a)* adj unlined (*clothes*)

sfondo *sfohn·doh* m background

sfortuna *sfor·too·na* f bad luck

sfortunatamente *sfor·too·nah·ta·mayn·tay* adv unfortunately

sfortunato(a) *sfor·too·nah·to(a)* adj unfortunate; unlucky

sforzare *sfor·tsah·ray* vt force; **sforzarsi di fare qualcosa** *sfor·tsar·see dee fah·ray kwal·ko·sa* to struggle to do something

sforzo *sfor·tsoh* m effort

sfuso(a) *sfoo·zo(a)* adj in bulk (*unpackaged*)

sgabello *zga·bel·loh* m stool

sgelare *zje·lah·ray* vi thaw

sghiacciare *zgyach·chah·ray* vt de-ice

sgombro *zgom·bro* m mackerel

sgonfio(a) *zgohn·fyo(a)* adj flat (*deflated*)

sgradevole *zgra·day·vo·le* adj unpleasant

sgualcito(a) *zgwal·chee·toh(a)* adj creased

sguardo *zgwar·doh* m look; glance

squazzare *zgwats·tsah·ray* vi splash; paddle

shock *shok* m shock

si *see* pron himself; herself; oneself; each other; themselves; **si lavano** *see lah·va·no* they wash themselves

si *see* adv yes

siccità *seech·chee·ta* f drought

Sicilia *see·chee·lya* f Sicily

sicuramente *see·koo·ra·mayn·te* adv surely; **verrà sicuramente** *ver·ra see·koo·ra·mayn·te* he's sure to come

sicurezza *see·koo·rayts·tsa* f safety; security (*at airport*); **la sicurezza sociale** *see·koo·rayts·tsa so·chah·le* social security

sicuro(a) *see·koo·ro(a)* adj safe; sure; **sicuro che funzionerà** *see·koo·ro ke foon·tsyoh·ne·ra* it's sure to work

sidro *see·droh* m cider

siepe *sye·pe* f hedge

siesta *sye·sta* f siesta

sigaretta *see·ga·rayt·ta* f cigarette

sigaro *see·ga·roh* m cigar

significare *seen·yee·fee·kah·ray* vt mean (*signify*)

significato *seen·yee·fee·kah·toh* m meaning

Signor *seen·yohr* m Mr

signora *seen·yoh·ra* f lady; madam; **Signora** *seen·yoh·ra* Mrs; **Gentile Signora** *jen·tee·le seen·yoh·ra* Dear Madam

signore *seen·yoh·ray* m sir; gentleman; **Egregio Signore** *e·gre·joh seen·yoh·ray* Dear Sir

Signorina *seen·yo·ree·na* f Miss; Ms

silenzio *see·len·tsyoh* m silence

silenziosamente *see·len·tsyoh·sa·mayn·te* adv quietly (*walk, work*)

silenzioso(a) *see·len·tsyoh·so(a)* adj silent

sillaba *seel·la·ba* f syllable

simbolico(a) *seem·bo·lee·koh(a)* adj nominal (*fee*)

simbolo *seem·bo·loh* m symbol

simile *see·mee·le* adj similar; alike

simmetrico(a) *seem·me·tree·ko(a)* adj symmetrical

simpatico(a) *seem·pa·tee·ko(a)* adj pleasant; nice (*person*)

simposio *seem·po·zyoh* m symposium

sinagoga *see·na·go·ga* f synagogue

sincero(a) *seen·che·ro(a)* adj sincere

sindacato *seen·da·kah·toh* m syndicate; labor union

sindaco *seen·da·koh* m mayor

sinfonia *seen·fo·nee·a* f symphony

singhiozzo *seen·gyots·tsoh* m sob; hiccup; **avere* il singhiozzo** *a·vay·re eel seen·gyots·tsoh* to have (the) hiccups

singolarmente *seen·go·lar·mayn·te* adv individually

singolo(a) *seen·go·lo(a)* adj single

sinistra *see·nee·stra* f the left; **girare a sinistra** *jee·rah·ray a see·nee·stra* to turn left

sinistro *see·nee·stroh* m accident

sinistro(a) *see·nee·stro(a)* adj left; **il lato sinistro** *lah·to see·nee·stro* the left side

sintetico(a) *seen·te·tee·ko(a)* adj synthetic

sintomo *seen·to·moh* m symptom

sirena *see·re·na* f siren

Siria *see·rya* f Syria

siriano(a) *see·ryah·no(a)* adj Syrian

sistema *see·ste·ma* m system; **il sistema hi-fi** *see·ste·ma hi·fi* hi-fi

sistematico(a) *see·ste·ma·tee·ko(a)* adj systematic

sito *see·toh* m site

situazione *see·too·a·tsyoh·ne* f situation

slacciare *zlach·chah·ray* vt unfasten; undo

slavo(a) *zlah·vo(a)* m/f Slav

sleale *zle·ah·lay* adj unfair

slegare *zle·gah·ray* vt untie

slip *zleep* m — briefs

slitta *zleet·ta* f sled(ge); sleigh

slittamento *zleet·ta·mayn·toh* m skid

slittare *zleet·tah·ray* vi skid

slogan *zlo·gan* m slogan

slogare *zlo·gah·ray* vt dislocate; **slogarsi la caviglia** *zlo·gar·see la ka·veel·ya* to sprain one's ankle

smagliatura *zmal·ya·too·ra* f run (in stocking)

smalto *zmal·toh* m nail polish; enamel

smarrirsi *zmar·reer·see* vr lose one's way

smarrito(a) *zmar·ree·toh(a)* adj missing (*object*)

smeraldo *zme·ral·doh* m emerald

smettere* *zmayt·te·ray* vi stop; cease; **smettere* di fare qualcosa** *zmayt·te·ray dee fah·ray kwal·ko·sa* to stop doing something; **smettere* di fumare** *zmayt·te·ray dee foo·mah·ray* to give up smoking

smoking *smo·keeng* m tuxedo; evening dress (*man's*)

smorfia *zmor·fee·a* f grimace

smussato(a) *zmoos·sah·to(a)* adj blunt (*knife*)

snack-bar *znak·bar* m snack bar

snello(a) *znel·lo(a)* adj slim

snobistico(a) *zno·bee·stee·ko(a)* adj snobbish

sobbollire *sob·bol·lee·re* vi simmer

sobborgo *sob·bohr·goh* m suburb

sociale *so·chah·le* adj social

socialismo *so·cha·lee·zmoh* m socialism

socialista *so·cha·lee·sta* adj socialist
□ m/f **il/la socialista** *so·cha·lee·sta* socialist

società *so·che·ta* f society; corporation (firm); la società a responsabilità limitata *so·che·ta a re·spon·sa·bee·lee·ta lee·mee·tah·ta* incorporated company; la società immobiliare *so·che·ta eem·mo·beel·yah·re* savings and loan association; la società per azioni *so·che·ta payr a·tsyoh·nee* joint-stock company

socio(a) *so·cho(a)* m/f associate □ m il socio *so·cho* member; diventare socio di *dee·ven·tah·ray so·cho dee* to join (club)

soda *so·da* f soda

soddisfacente *sod·dee·sfa·chen·te* adj satisfactory

soddisfare* *sod·dee·sfah·ray* vt satisfy

sodo *so·do* adv hard □ adj sodo(a) *so·do(a)* hard-boiled (egg)

soffiare *sof·fyah·ray* vt blow; soffiarsi il naso *sof·fyar·see eel nah·soh* to blow one's nose

soffice *sof·fee·che* adj soft

soffitta *sof·feet·ta* f loft; attic

soffitto *sof·feet·toh* m ceiling

soffocante *sof·fo·kan·te* adj stuffy

soffrire* *sof·free·re* vt/i suffer

sofisticato(a) *so·fee·stee·kah·to(a)* adj sophisticated

soggetto(a) *a soj·jet·to(a) a* adj subject to

soggiorno *soj·johr·noh* m visit; stay

sogliola *sol·yo·la* f lemon sole

sognare *son·yah·ray* vt/i dream; sognare di *son·yah·ray dee* to dream about

sogno *sohn·yoh* m dream

soia *so·ya* f soy bean

solamente *soh·la·mayn·te* adv only

solare *so·lah·re* adj solar

solco *sohl·koh* m track (on record)

soldato *sol·dah·toh* m soldier

soldi *sol·dee* mpl money; fare* soldi *fah·ray sol·dee* to make money

sole *soh·le* m sunshine; sun; fare* un bagno di sole *fah·ray oon ban·yoh dee soh·le* to sunbathe

soleggiato(a) *soh·lej·jah·to(a)* adj sunny

solido(a) *so·lee·do(a)* adj strong (structure, material); solid; fast (dye)

solitario(a) *so·lee·tah·ryo(a)* adj lonely

solito(a) *so·lee·to(a)* adj usual; di solito *dee so·lee·to* usually

solleticare *sol·le·tee·kah·ray* vt tickle

sollevare *sol·le·vah·ray* vt raise; lift; relieve

sollievo *sol·lye·voh* m relief (from pain, anxiety)

solo *soh·lo* adv only □ adj solo(a) *soh·lo(a)* alone; lonely

solubile *so·loo·bee·le* adj soluble; il caffè solubile *kaf·fe so·loo·bee·le* instant coffee

soluzione *so·loo·tsyoh·ne* f solution

somigliare a *so·meel·yah·ray a* vi be like; look like

somma *sohm·ma* f sum; la somma totale *sohm·ma to·tah·le* sum total

sommare *som·mah·ray* vt add (up) (numbers)

sommario *som·mah·ryoh* m summary; outline

sommelier *so·muh·lyay* m wine waiter

sommergibile *som·mer·jee·bee·le* m submarine

sonnecchiare *son·nek·kyah·ray* vi doze

sonnellino *son·nel·lee·noh* m nap (sleep)

sonnifero *son·nee·fe·roh* m sleeping pill

sonno *sohn·noh* m sleep

sontuoso(a) *son·too·oh·so(a)* adj luxurious

sopportare *sop·por·tah·ray* vt bear (endure); stand

sopra *soh·pra* prep on; above; over □ adv on top; above; di sopra *dee soh·pra* upstairs

sopracciglio *so·prach·cheel·yoh* m —a eyebrow

soprattassa *soh·prat·tas·sa* f surcharge

sopravvivere* *soh·prav·vee·ve·re* vt/i survive

sordo(a) *sohr·do(a)* adj deaf

sorella *so·rel·la* f sister

sorellastra *so·rel·la·stra* f stepsister

sorgente *sor·jen·te* f spring (of water)

sorgere* *sohr·je·re* vi rise (sun) □ m il sorgere del sole *sohr·je·re del soh·le* sunrise

sorpassare *sor·pas·sah·ray* vt pass (car)

sorprendere* *sor·pren·de·re* vt surprise

sorpresa *sor·pray·sa* f surprise

sorpreso(a) *sor·pray·so(a)* adj surprised; sorpreso(a) da *sor·pray·so(a) da* surprised at

sorreggere* *sor·rej·je·re* vt bear (weight)

sorridere* *sor·ree·de·re* vi smile

sorriso *sor·ree·soh* m smile

sorvegliante *sor·vel·yan·te* m/f supervisor

sorvegliare *sor·vel·yah·ray* vt watch; supervise

S.O.S. *es·se·o·es·se* m SOS

sospendere* *so·spen·de·re* vt suspend (worker)

sospensione *so·spen·syoh·ne* f suspension

sospirare *so·spee·rah·ray* vi sigh

sosta *so·sta* f stop

sostanza *so·stan·tsa* f substance; stuff

sostanzioso(a) *so·stan·tsyoh·so(a)* adj filling (food)

sostegno *so·stayn·yoh* m backing; support (moral, financial)

sostenere* *so·ste·nay·re* vt support

sostentamento *so·sten·ta·mayn·toh* m maintenance

sostituire *so·stee·too·ee·ray* vt replace (substitute); sostituire qualcosa a qualcos'altro *so·stee·too·ee·ray kwal·ko·sa a kwal·ko·sal·tro* to substitute something for something else

sostituto *so·stee·too·toh* m substitute

sostituzione *so·stee·too·tsyoh·nay* f replacement

sottaceti *sot·ta·chay·tee* mpl pickles

sottana *sot·tah·na* f slip (underskirt)

sotterraneo(a) *soht·ter·rah·ne·oh(a)* adj underground (pipe etc)

sottile *sot·tee·le* adj sheer (stockings); thin; subtle

sotto *soht·toh* prep underneath; under; below □ adv underneath; below; di sotto *dee soht·toh* downstairs; sta di sotto *sta dee soht·toh* it's underneath; sotto Natale *soht·toh na·tah·lay* near (to) Christmas

sottobicchiere *sot·toh·beek·kye·ray* m mat (under a glass)

sottocommissione *soht·to·kom·mees·syoh·ne* f subcommittee

sottoesposto(a) *soht·to·e·spoh·stoh(a)* adj underexposed

sottolineare *soht·to·lee·ne·ah·ray* vt emphasize; underline

sottopassaggio *soht·to·pas·saj·joh* m underpass (for pedestrians)

sottopiatto *soht·to·pyat·toh* m place mat; table-mat

sottoporre* soht·to·pohr·re vt submit (proposal)

sottosopra soht·to·soh·pra adv upside down

sottosviluppato(a) soht·to·zvee·loop·pah·toh(a) adj underdeveloped (country)

sottotitolo soht·to·tee·to·loh m subtitle (of movie)

sottovalutare soht·to·va·loo·tah·ray vt undervalue

sottoveste soht·to·ve·ste f petticoat

sottovia soht·to·vee·a f underpass (for cars)

sottrarre* soht·trar·re vt subtract

soufflé soo·flay m soufflé

sovietico(a) so·vye·tee·ko(a) adj Soviet

sovraesposto(a) soh·vra·e·spoh·sto(a) adj overexposed (photo)

sovvenzionare sov·ven·tsyoh·nah·ray vt subsidize

sovvenzione sov·ven·tsyoh·ne f subsidy; grant (to institution)

spaccatura spak·ka·too·ra f split (tear)

spada spah·da f sword

spaghetti spa·gayt·tee mpl spaghetti

Spagna spah·nya f Spain

spagnolo span·yo·loh m Spanish □ spagnolo(a) span·yo·lo(a) m/f Spaniard □ adj Spanish

spago spah·goh m string

spalla spal·la f shoulder

spallina spal·lee·na f strap (of dress etc)

spalmare spal·mah·ray vt spread (butter)

sparare spa·rah·ray vt fire □ vi fire; shoot

sparire* spa·ree·re vi disappear

spartitraffico spar·tee·traf·fee·koh m — median strip

spatola spa·to·la f spatula

spaventare spa·ven·tah·ray vt frighten

spazio spa·tsyoh m space; room

spazzaneve spats·tsa·nay·ve m — snowplow

spazzola spats·tso·la f brush (for cleaning); la spazzola per capelli spats·tso·la payr ka·payl·lee hairbrush

spazzolare spats·tso·lah·ray vt brush

spazzolino spats·tso·lee·noh m brush; lo spazzolino da unghie spats·tso·lee·noh da oon·gyay nailbrush; lo spazzolino da denti spats·tso·lee·noh da den·tee toothbrush

specchietto retrovisore spek·kyayt·toh re·tro·vee·zoh·ray m rear view mirror

specchio spek·kyoh m mirror

speciale spe·chah·le adj special

specialista spe·cha·lee·sta m/f specialist

specialità spe·cha·lee·ta f — speciality

specializzarsi spe·cha·leedz·dzar·see vr specialize

specializzato(a) spe·cha·leedz·dzah·to(a) adj skilled (workers)

specialmente spe·chal·mayn·te adv especially

specie spe·che f — kind

specificare spe·chee·fee·kah·ray vt specify

specificazioni spe·chee·fee·ka·tsyoh·nee fpl specifications

specifico(a) spe·chee·fee·ko(a) adj specific

spedire spe·dee·re vt send; dispatch; ship (goods); spedire qualcosa per posta ordinaria spe·dee·re kwal·ko·sa payr po·sta or·dee·nah·rya to send something surface mail

spedizione spe·dee·tsyoh·ne f expedition

spegnere* spen·ye·re vt turn off; switch off; put out

spellarsi spel·lar·see vr peel

spendere* spen·de·re vt spend (money)

spento(a) spen·to(a) adj off (radio, light)

speranza spe·ran·tsa f hope

sperare spe·rah·ray vt/i hope; spero di sì/no spe·ro dee see/no I hope so/not

spesa spay·sa f expense (cost); fare* la spesa fah·ray la spay·sa to go shopping; le spese postali spay·se po·stah·lee postage; le spese generali spay·se je·ne·rah·lee overhead; le spese di rappresentanza spay·se dee rap·pre·zen·tan·tsa business expenses; le spese bancarie spay·se ban·kah·rye bank charges

spese spay·se fpl expenditure; expenses; costs (of production etc)

spesso spays·so adv often

spesso(a) spays·so(a) adj thick; spesso(a) 3 metri spays·so(a) 3 me·tree 3 meters thick

spettacolo spet·ta·ko·loh m show (in theater); lo spettacolo di varietà spet·ta·ko·loh dee va·ree·e·ta variety show; lo spettacolo di suoni e luci spet·ta·ko·loh dee swo·nee e loo·chee son et lumière

spezie spe·tsye fpl spices

spezzarsi spets·tsar·see vr snap (break)

spezzatino spets·tsa·tee·noh m stew

spia spee·a f spy

spiacente spya·chen·te adj sorry

spiacere* spya·chay·re vi to be sorry; le spiace se…? le spyah·chay se do you mind if…?

spiacevole spya·chay·vo·le adj unpleasant

spiaggia spyaj·ja f beach; shore

spiccare speek·kah·ray vi stand out

spicchio d'aglio speek·kyoh dal·yoh m clove of garlic

spiccioli speech·cho·lee mpl change (money)

spiedino spye·dee·noh m skewer

spiedo spye·doh m spit (for roasting)

spiegare spee·e·gah·ray vt explain; unfold; spread out

spiegazione spye·ga·tsyoh·ne f explanation

spilla speel·la f brooch

spillo speel·loh m pin; lo spillo di sicurezza speel·loh dee see·koo·rayts·tsa safety pin

spina spee·na f bone (of fish); plug (electric); la spina dorsale spee·na dor·sah·le spine (backbone)

spinaci spee·nah·chee mpl spinach

spingere* speen·je·re vt push

spirito spee·ree·toh m spirit; giù di spirito joo dee spee·ree·toh depressed (person)

splendente splen·den·te adj shiny

splendere splen·de·re vi shine (sun etc)

splendido(a) splen·dee·doh(a) adj splendid

spogliarellista spol·ya·rel·lee·sta f stripper

spogliarello spol·ya·rel·loh m striptease

spogliarsi spol·yar·see vr undress

spogliatoio spol·ya·to·yo m dressing room

spolverare spol·ve·rah·ray vt dust (furniture)

sporcizia spor·chee·tsya f dirt

sporco(a) spor·ko(a) adj dirty

sport sport m — sport(s); gli sport in-

vernali *sport een·ver·nah·lee* winter sports

sposa *spo·za* f bride

sposare *spo·zah·ray* vt marry

sposarsi *spo·zahr·see* vr marry; **si sono sposati ieri** *see so·noh spo·zah·tee ye·ree* they were married yesterday

sposato(a) *spo·zah·toh(a)* adj married

sposo *spo·zoh* m bridegroom

spostare *spo·stah·ray* vt move

sprecare *spre·kah·ray* vt waste

spreco *spre·koh* m waste

spremere *spre·me·re* vt squeeze (*lemon*)

spremilimoni *spre·mee·lee·moh·nee* m — lemon-squeezer

spremuta *spray·moo·ta* f fresh juice

spruzzare *sproots·tsah·ray* vt spray (*liquid*); **spruzzare con acqua** *sproots·tsah·ray kohn ak·kwa* to sprinkle with water

spruzzo *sproots·tsoh* m spray (*of liquid*)

spugna *spoon·ya* f sponge

spumante *spoo·man·te* adj sparkling (*wine*)

spuntare *spoon·tah·ray* vt trim (*hair*)

spuntino *spoon·tee·noh* m snack

sputare *spoo·tah·ray* vi spit

squadra *skwa·dra* f team

squalificare *skwa·lee·fee·kah·ray* vt disqualify

squash *skwosh* m squash (*sport*)

squattrinato(a) *skwat·tree·nah·to(a)* adj broke (*penniless*)

squillare *skweel·lah·ray* vi ring

S.r.l. *es·se·er·el·le abbrev* Ltd

stabile *stah·bee·le* adj stable; firm (*object, material*) □ m lo **stabile** *stah·bee·le* building

stabilimento *sta·bee·lee·mayn·toh* m plant (*factory*)

stabilire *sta·bee·lee·re* vt establish

staccarsi *stak·kahr·see* vr come off

stadio *sta·dyoh* m stadium

stagionato(a) *sta·joh·nah·to(a)* adj ripe (*cheese*); mature

stagione *sta·joh·ne* f season; la **stagione di villeggiatura** *la sta·joh·ne dee vel·lej·ja·too·ra* the vacation season; di **bassa stagione** *dee bas·sa sta·joh·ne* off-season

stagno *stan·yoh* m tin (*substance*); pond (*natural*)

stagnola *stan·yo·la* f tin foil

stalla *stal·la* f stable

stampa *stam·pa* f print; press (*newspapers, journalists*)

stampare *stam·pah·ray* vt print (*book, newspaper*)

stampatello *stam·pa·tel·loh* m block letters

stampato *stam·pah·toh* m printout

stancarsi *stan·kahr·see* vr get tired

stanco(a) *stan·ko(a)* adj tired

standard *stan·dard* adj standard

stanotte *sta·not·te adv* tonight; last night

stantio(a) *stan·tee·o(a)* adj stale; flat (*beer*)

stanza *stan·tsa* f room (*in house*); la **stanza da letto** *stan·tsa da let·toh* bedroom; la **stanza da bagno** *stan·tsa da ban·yoh* bathroom

stare* *stah·ray* vi stay; be; **stare* per fare qualcosa** *stah·ray payr fah·ray kwal·ko·sa* to be about to do something; **stare* in piedi** *stah·ray een pye·dee* to stand; **mi sta bene** *mee sta be·ne* it fits (me); **quel cappello ti sta bene** *kwayl kap·pel·loh tee sta be·ne*

that hat suits you; **non ci sta** *nohn chee sta* it won't go in; **come sta?** *koh·me sta* how are you?; **sta bene** *sta be·ne* he's all right (*safe, fit*)

starnutire *star·noo·tee·re* vi sneeze

starnuto *star·noo·toh* m sneeze

stasera *sta·say·ra adv* tonight

statistica *sta·tee·stee·ka* f statistics; statistic

statistico(a) *sta·tee·stee·ko(a)* adj statistical

Stati Uniti (d'America) *stah·tee oo·nee·tee (da·me·ree·ka)* mpl United States (of America), US(A)

stato *stah·toh* m state (*condition*); lo **Stato** *stah·toh* the State

statua *sta·too·a* f statue

statura *sta·too·ra* f height (*of person*)

stazionario(a) *sta·tsyoh·nah·ryo(a)* adj stationary; unchanged

stazione *sta·tsyoh·ne* f station; resort; la **stazione di servizio** *la sta·tsyoh·ne dee ser·vee·tsyoh* gas station; service station; la **stazione balneare** *sta·tsyoh·ne bal·ne·ah·re* seaside resort; la **stazione autobus** *sta·tsyoh·ne ow·to·boos* bus depot; la **stazione radio** *sta·tsyoh·ne ra·dyoh* station (*radio*); la **stazione termale** *sta·tsyoh·ne ter·mah·le* spa

stecca *stayk·ka* f splint; carton

stella *stayl·la* f star

stelo *ste·loh* m stem

stendere* *sten·de·re* vt stretch; spread; hang out; lay down

stendersi* *sten·der·see* vr lie down

stenodattilografo(a) *ste·no·dat·tee·lo·gra·fo(a)* m/f stenographer

stenografia *ste·no·gra·fee·a* f shorthand

stereo *ste·re·oh* m stereo(phonic)

stereofonico(a) *ste·re·o·fo·nee·ko(a)* adj stereo(phonic)

sterile *ste·ree·le* adj sterile

sterilizzare *ste·ree·leedz·dzah·ray* vt sterilize (*disinfect*)

sterlina *ster·lee·na* f sterling; pound

sterzo *ster·tsoh* m steering wheel; steering (*in car*)

stesso(a) *stays·so(a)* adj same □ pron lo/la **stesso(a)** *lo/la stays·so(a)* the same (one); **lo stesso, per favore** *lo stays·so payr fa·voh·re* (the) same again please!; **l'ho fatto io stesso** *loh fat·toh ee·oh stays·so* I did it myself

stile *stee·le* m style

stima *stee·ma* f estimate

stimare *stee·mah·ray* vt estimate

stinco *steen·koh* m shin

stipendio *stee·pen·dyoh* m salary; lo **stipendio netto** *stee·pen·dyoh nayt·toh* take-home pay

stipula *stee·poo·la* f stipulation

stipulare *stee·poo·lah·ray* vt stipulate

stirare *stee·rah·ray* vt press; iron

stirarsi *stee·rar·see* vr strain (*muscle*); stretch

stitico(a) *stee·tee·koh(a)* adj constipated

stivale *stee·vah·le* m boot

stivalone di gomma *stee·va·loh·ne dee gohm·ma* m wellington boot

stock *stok* m stock (*in shop*)

stoffa *stof·fa* f material (*fabric*)

stola *sto·la* f stole (*wrap*)

stomaco *sto·ma·koh* m stomach; il **mal di stomaco** *mal dee sto·ma·koh* stomach ache; **ho mal di stomaco** o *mal dee sto·ma·koh* I have (a) stomach ache

stoppino *stop·pee·noh* m wick

storcere* *stor·che·re* vt twist

stordire *stor·dee·re* vt stun

storia *sto·ree·a* f history; story; fare* delle storie *fah·ray del·le sto·ree·e* to make a fuss

storto(a) *stor·toh(a)* adj crooked

stoviglie *sto·veel·ye* fpl crockery

straccio *strach·choh* m rag; cloth

strada *strah·da* f road; street; la strada secondaria *strah·da se·kohn·dah·rya* side-street; la strada statale *strah·da sta·tah·le* highway; strada facendo *strah·da fa·chen·do* on the way

strangolare *stran·go·lah·ray* vt strangle

straniero(a) *stran·ye·ro(a)* adj foreign; overseas (*visitor*) □ m/f lo/la straniero(a) *stran·ye·ro(a)* foreigner

strano(a) *strah·no(a)* adj strange; odd

straordinario(a) *stra·or·dee·nah·ree·o(a)* adj extraordinary; fare* dello straordinario *fah·ray del·lo stra·or·dee·nah·ree·o* to work overtime

strappare *strap·pah·ray* vt tear; rip; pull off

strapparsi *strap·par·see* vr rip; split

strappo *strap·poh* m tear

strascico *stra·shee·koh* m train (*on dress*)

strato *strah·toh* m layer

stravagante *stra·va·gan·te* adj extravagant; odd (*peculiar*)

strega *stray·ga* f witch

strettamente *strayt·ta·mayn·te* adv tightly

stretto(a) *strayt·toh(a)* adj narrow; tight (*clothes*)

strillare *streel·lah·ray* vi scream

strillo *streel·loh* m scream

stringa *streen·ga* f shoelace

stringere* *streen·je·re* vt squeeze (*hand*); stringere* la mano a qualcuno *streen·je·re la mah·noh a kwal·koo·no* to shake hands with someone

stringersi* nelle spalle *streen·jer·see nel·le spal·le* vr shrug

striscia *stree·sha* f strip; stripe; strisciare *stree·shah·ray* vt scrape □ vi crawl

strizzare *streets·tsah·ray* vt wring (*clothes*)

strofinaccio *stro·fee·nach·choh* m duster (*cloth*); lo strofinaccio per i piatti *stro·fee·nach·choh payr ee pyat·tee* dishcloth

strofinare *stro·fee·nah·ray* vt rub

strumento *stroo·mayn·toh* m instrument

struttura *stroot·too·ra* f structure

stucchevole *stook·kay·vo·le* adj nauseating

studente *stoo·den·te* m student

studentessa *stoo·den·tays·sa* f student

studiare *stoo·dyah·ray* vt/i study

studio *stoo·dyoh* m study; studio; lo studio della fattibilità *stoo·dyoh del·la fat·tee·bee·lee·ta* feasibility study

stufa *stoo·fa* f stove

stufato *stoo·fah·toh* m stew □ adj stufato(a) *stoo·fah·to(a)* braised

stufo(a) *stoo·fo(a)* adj fed up

stuoia *stoo·oy·a* f mat

stupido(a) *stoo·pee·do(a)* adj stupid; dumb; silly

stupore *stoo·poh·re* m amazement

su *soo* prep on; onto; about □ adv up; in su *een soo* upwards; uphill; sulla tavola *sool·la tah·vo·la* on the table; sul treno *sool tre·noh* on the train

sua *soo·a* adj his; her; its; your □ pron his; hers; its; yours; Sua *soo·a* your; yours

subappaltatore *soo·bap·pal·ta·toh·re* m subcontractor

subappalto *soo·bap·pal·toh* m subcontract

subire *soo·bee·re* vt suffer

subito *soo·bee·to* adv at once; immediately; straight away

subordinato(a) *soo·bor·dee·nah·to(a)* adj subordinate □ m/f il/la subordinato(a) *soo·bor·dee·nah·to(a)* subordinate

subtotale *soob·to·tah·le* m subtotal

suburbano(a) *soo·boor·bah·no(a)* adj suburban

succedere* *sooch·che·de·re* vi happen; che cosa gli è successo? *ke ko·sa lyee e sooch·ches·so* what happened to him?

successo *sooch·ches·soh* m success

succhiare *sook·kyah·ray* vt suck

succhietto *sook·kyayt·toh* m pacifier (*baby's*)

succo *sook·koh* m juice; il succo di limone *sook·koh dee lee·moh·ne* lemon juice; il succo di pompelmo *sook·koh dee pom·pel·moh* grapefruit juice

succoso(a) *sook·koh·so(a)* adj juicy

succursale *sook·koor·sah·le* f branch (*of store, bank etc*)

sud *sood* m south; al sud *al sood* south

Sud-Africa *soo·da·free·ka* m South Africa

sudafricano(a) *soo·da·free·kah·no(a)* adj South African

sudamericano(a) *soo·da·me·ree·kah·no(a)* adj South American

sudare *soo·dah·ray* vi sweat

suddito(a) *sood·dee·to(a)* m/f subject (*person*)

sud-est *soo·dest* m southeast

sudicio(a) *soo·dee·choh(a)* adj filthy

sudiciume *soo·dee·choo·me* m filth

sudore *soo·doh·re* m sweat

sud-ovest *soo·do·vest* m southwest

sue *soo·e* adj his; her; its; your □ pron his; hers; its; yours; Sue *soo·e* your; yours

sufficiente *soof·fee·chen·te* adj sufficient

suggerimento *sooj·je·ree·mayn·toh* m suggestion

suggerire *sooj·je·ree·re* vt suggest

sughero *soo·ge·roh* m cork

sugli = su + gli

sugna *soon·ya* f suet

sui = su + i

suicidio *soo·ee·chee·dyoh* m suicide

suo *soo·o* adj his; her; its; your □ pron his; hers; its; yours; Suo *soo·o* your; yours

suocera *swo·che·ra* f mother-in-law

suocero *swo·che·roh* m father-in-law

suoi *swoy* adj his; her; its; your □ pron his; hers; its; yours; Suoi *swoy* your; yours

suola *swo·la* f sole (*of shoe*)

suolo *swo·loh* m soil

suonare *swo·nah·ray* vi ring; ring the (door)bell; suonare il violino *swo·nah·ray eel vee·o·lee·noh* to play the violin; suonare il clacson *swo·nah·ray eel klak·son* to sound one's horn

suono *swo·noh* m sound

superare *soo·pe·rah·ray* vt exceed; get through (*exam*); pass (*car*)

superbo(a) *soo·per·boh(a)* adj proud; superb

superficie *soo·per·fee·che* f surface

superiore *soo·pe·ryoh·re* adj upper; senior (*in rank*); superior (*quality*)

□ *m* il superiore *soo·pe·ryoh·re* superior

supermercato *soo·per·mer·kah·toh m* supermarket

superpetroliera *soo·per·pe·tro·lye·ra f* supertanker

superstizione *soo·per·stee·tsyoh·ne f* superstition

supplementare *soop·ple·men·tah·re adj* extra

supplente *soop·plen·te adj* temporary; acting

supporre* *soop·pohr·re vt* suppose; figure; assume; **suppongo che verrà** *soop·pohn·go ke ver·ra* I expect he'll come

supposta *soop·poh·sta f* suppository

surfing *soor·feeng m* surfing; **fare* del surfing** *fah·ray del soor·feeng* to go surfing; **il surfing a vela** *soor·feeng a vay·la* windsurfing

surriscaldarsi *soor·ree·skal·dahr·see vr* overheat (*engine*)

susina *soo·see·na f* plum

sussidio *soos·see·dyoh m* subsidy; **i sussidi visivi** *soos·see·dee vee·zee·vee* visual aids

sussurrare *soos·soor·rah·ray vi* whisper

svago *zva·goh m* relaxation; pastime

svaligiare *zva·lee·jah·ray vt* rob (*bank*)

svalutare *zva·loo·tah·ray vt* devalue (*currency*)

svalutazione *zva·loo·ta·tsyoh·ne f* devaluation

svantaggiato(a) *zvan·taj·jah·to(a) adj* at a disadvantage

svantaggio *zvan·taj·joh m* disadvantage; handicap

svedese *zve·day·se adj* Swedish □ *m/f* lo/la **svedese** *zve·day·se* Swede □ *m* lo **svedese** *zve·day·se* Swedish

sveglia *zvayl·ya f* alarm (clock)

svegliare *zvel·yah·ray vt* wake; **mi svegli alle 7 di mattina** *mee zvayl·yee al·lay 7 dee mat·tee·na* call me at 7 a.m. (in hotel etc)

svegliarsi *zvel·yar·see vr* wake up

sveglio(a) *zvayl·yo(a) adj* awake; sharp (intelligent)

svelto(a) *zvel·toh(a) adj* quick

svenire* *zve·nee·re vi* faint

sventolare *zven·to·lah·ray vi* flap (sail)

svestire *zve·stee·ray vt* undress

svestirsi *zve·steer·see vr* undress

Svezia *zve·tsya f* Sweden

sviluppare *zvee·loop·pah·ray vt* develop; expand (business)

svilupparsi *zvee·loop·par·see vr* expand (business); develop

sviluppo *zvee·loop·poh m* development

svincolo *zveen·ko·loh m* entrance/exit ramp

svitare *zvee·tah·ray vt* unscrew

Svizzera *zveets·tse·ra f* Switzerland

svizzero(a) *zveets·tse·ro(a) adj* Swiss

svolta *zvol·ta f* turn

svuotare *zvwo·tah·ray vt* empty; drain (sump, pool)

T

tabaccaio(a) *ta·bak·ka·yoh(a) m/f* tobacconist

tabaccheria *ta·bak·ke·ree·a f* tobacconist's (shop)

tabacco *ta·bak·koh m* tobacco; **il tabacco da fiuto** *ta·bak·koh da fyoo·toh* snuff

tabella *ta·bel·la f* table (list)

tabellone *ta·bel·loh·nay m* bulletin board

taccheggio *tak·kayj·joh m* shoplifting

tacchino *tak·kee·noh m* turkey

tacco *tak·koh m* heel (of shoe); **i tacchi a spillo** *tak·kee a speel·loh* stiletto heels

tachimetro *ta·kee·me·troh m* speedometer

tafano *ta·fah·noh m* horsefly

taglia *tal·ya f* size (of clothes); **di taglia grande** *dee tal·ya gran·de* outsize (clothes)

tagliare *tal·yah·ray vt* cut; **farsi* tagliare i capelli** *far·see tal·yah·ray ee ka·pel·lee* to get one's hair cut; **tagliare qualcosa in due** *tal·yah·ray kwal·ko·sa een doo·e* to cut something in half

tagliarsi *tal·yahr·see vr* cut oneself

taglierini *tal·ye·ree·nee mpl* noodles

taglio *tal·yoh m* cut; **il taglio dei capelli** *tal·yoh dey ka·payl·lee* haircut (style)

tailleur *tye·yur m* suit (women's)

tailleur-pantalone *tye·yur·pan·ta·loh·ne m* pant(s) suit

talco *tal·koh m* talc(um powder)

tale *tah·le adj* such; **un tale libro** *oon tah·le lee·broh* such a book; **tali libri** *tah·lee lee·bree* such books

talento *ta·len·toh m* gift (ability); talent

talloncino *tal·lon·chee·noh m* counterfoil

tallone *tal·loh·ne m* heel

tamburo *tam·boo·roh m* drum

tampone assorbente *tam·poh·ne as·sor·ben·te m* tampon

tango *tan·goh m* tango

tanti(e) *tan·tee(·te) adj* so many

tanto(a) *tan·to(a) adj* so much □ *adv* **tanto** *tan·to* so; so much; **tanto(a) quanto(a)** *tan·to(a) kwan·to(a) as* much/many as; **ogni tanto** *on·yee tan·to* now and then, now and again; **di tanto in tanto** *dee tan·to een tan·to* from time to time

tappa *tap·pa f* stage (point); **a tappe** *a tap·pe* in stages

tappare *tap·pah·ray vt* plug

tappetino *tap·pe·tee·noh m* rug

tappeto *tap·pay·toh m* carpet

tappezzare *tap·pets·tsah·ray vt* paper (wall)

tappo *tap·poh m* top (of bottle); cork; stopper; plug (for basin etc); **i tappi per gli orecchi** *tap·pee payr lyee o·rayk·kee* earplugs

tardi *tar·dee adv* late; late in the day; **più tardi** *pyoo tar·dee* later

tardivo(a) *tar·dee·vo(a) adj* backward (child)

targa d'immatricolazione *tar·ga deem·ma·tree·ko·la·tsyoh·ne f* license plate

tariffa *ta·reef·fa f* tariff (list of charges); rate (price); **la tariffa ridotta** *ta·reef·fa ree·doht·ta* half-fare; **la tariffa doganale** *ta·reef·fa do·ga·nah·le* customs tariff

tartufo *tar·too·foh m* truffle (fungus)

tasca *ta·ska f* pocket

tassa *tas·sa f* tax; **le tasse comunali** *tas·se ko·moo·nah·lee* rates (local tax); **la tassa industriale** *tas·sa een·doo·stryah·lay* corporation tax

tassare *tas·sah·ray vt* tax

tassazione *tas·sa·tsyoh·ne f* taxation

tassì *tas·see m* — taxi

tasso *tas·soh m* rate; **il tasso d'interesse** *tas·soh deen·te·res·se* interest rate; **il tasso di cambio** *tas·soh dee kam·byoh* exchange rate

tasso d'inflazione *tas·soh deen·fla·tsyoh·ne* m rate of inflation

tasto *ta·stoh* m key (of piano, typewriter)

tattica *tat·tee·ka* f tactics

tavola *tah·vo·la* f table; plank; **la tavola reale** *tah·vo·la re·ah·le* backgammon; **la tavola da surfing** *tah·vo·la da soor·feeng* surf board; **la tavola da toeletta** *tah·vo·la da to·e·let·ta* dressing table; **tavola calda** *tah·vo·la kal·da* snack bar

tavoletta *tah·vo·layt·ta* f bar

tazza *tats·tsa* f mug; cup; **la tazza da tè** *tats·tsa da te* teacup; **la tazza da caffè** *tats·tsa da kaf·fe* coffee cup

tè *te* m — tea; **il tè alla menta** *te al·la mayn·ta* mint tea

te *tay* pron you; **te stesso(a)** *tay stays·so(a)* (you) yourself

teatro *te·ah·troh* m theater; drama (art)

tecnica *tek·nee·ka* f technique

tecnico(a) *tek·nee·ko(a)* adj technical □ m/f il/la **tecnico(a)** *tek·nee·ko(a)* technician

tecnologia *tek·no·lo·jee·a* f technology

tecnologico(a) *tek·no·lo·jee·ko(a)* adj technological

tedesco(a) *te·day·skoh(a)* adj German □ m il **tedesco** *te·day·skoh* German

tee *tee* m — tee (in golf)

tegame *te·gah·me* m pan (saucepan)

tegola *tay·go·la* f tile (on roof)

teiera *te·ye·ra* f teapot

tela *tay·la* f cloth; canvas; **la tela di blue-jeans** *tay·la de bloo·jeens* denim; **la tela impermeabile** *tay·la eem·payr·may·ah·bee·lay* groundcloth

telaio *te·la·yoh* m chassis

telecamera *te·le·kah·me·ra* f camera (TV)

telecomando *te·le·ko·man·doh* m remote control

telecomunicazioni *te·le·ko·moo·nee·ka·tsyoh·nee* fpl telecommunications

telefonare *te·le·fo·nah·ray* vt/i telephone; **telefonare ad onere del destinatario** *te·le·fo·nah·ray ad o·ne·re del de·stee·na·tah·ree·oh* to make a collect call; **sta telefonando** *sta te·le·fo·nan·do* he's on the phone

telefonata *te·le·fo·nah·ta* f phone-call; **la telefonata con la R** *te·le·fo·nah·ta kohn la e·rre* collect call; **la telefonata personale** *te·le·fo·nah·ta per·so·nah·le* person-to-person call

telefonista *te·le·fo·nee·sta* m/f telephone operator; operator

telefono *te·le·fo·noh* m telephone; **il telefono interno** *te·le·fo·noh een·ter·no* extension; **essere* al telefono** *es·se·re al te·le·fo·noh* to be on the telephone; **per telefono** *payr te·le·fo·noh* by telephone

telegrafare *te·le·gra·fah·ray* vt/i telegraph

telegramma *te·le·gram·ma* m telegram; wire

telemetro *te·le·me·troh* m range finder (on camera)

teleobiettivo *te·le·o·byet·tee·voh* m telephoto lens

telescopio *te·le·sko·pyoh* m telescope

teletrasmettere* *te·le·tra·zmayt·te·re* vt televise

televisione *te·le·vee·zyoh·ne* f television; **la televisione a circuito chiuso** *te·le·vee·zyoh·ne a cheer·koo·ee·toh kyoo·soh* closed circuit television; **la televisione a colori** *te·le·vee·zyoh·ne a*

ko·loh·ree color TV; **alla televisione** *al·la te·le·vee·zyoh·ne* on television

televisore *te·le·vee·zoh·re* m television (set)

telex *te·lex* m — telex

temere *te·may·ray* vt/i fear; dread; **temo di no** *te·mo dee no* I'm afraid not

temperatura *tem·pe·ra·too·ra* f temperature; **prendere* la temperatura a qualcuno** *pren·de·re la tem·pe·ra·too·ra a kwal·koo·no* to take someone's temperature

temperino *tem·pe·ree·noh* m penknife; pocketknife

tempesta *tem·pe·sta* f storm

tempestoso(a) *tem·pe·stoh·so(a)* adj stormy

tempio *tem·pyoh* m temple (building)

tempo *tem·poh* m weather; time; **a tempo parziale** *a tem·poh par·tsyah·le* part-time; **poco/molto tempo** *po·ko/mohl·to tem·poh* a short/long time; **nei tempi passati** *nay tem·pee pas·sah·tee* in times past; **il tempo libero** *tem·poh lee·be·ro* spare time; **non prenderò molto tempo** *nohn pren·de·ro mohl·to tem·poh* I shan't be long; **giusto in tempo** *joo·sto een tem·poh* just in time

temporale *tem·po·rah·le* m thunderstorm

tenda *ten·da* f curtain; drape; tent

tendenza *ten·den·tsa* f trend; tendency

tendere* *ten·de·re* vt stretch; hold out; **tendere* a fare qualcosa** *ten·de·re a fah·ray kwal·ko·sa* to tend to do something

tendina *ten·dee·na* f blind; window shade

tenere* *te·nay·re* vt keep; hold; lo **tenga fermo** *lo ten·ga fayr·mo* hold him still; **tenga il resto!** *ten·ga eel re·stoh* keep the change!; **tenere* qualcosa per più tardi** *te·nay·re kwal·ko·sa payr pyoo tar·dee* to keep something till later; **tenere* qualcosa in ordine** *te·nay·re kwal·ko·sa een ohr·dee·ne* to keep something tidy

tenero(a) *te·ne·ro(a)* adj tender

tennis *ten·nees* m tennis; **il tennis da tavolo** *ten·nees da tah·vo·loh* table tennis; **il tennis su erba** *ten·nees soo er·ba* lawn tennis

tenore di vita *te·noh·re dee vee·ta* m standard of living

tensione *ten·syoh·nay* f voltage; tension

tentare *ten·tah·ray* vt attempt; tempt

tentativo *ten·ta·tee·voh* m attempt

tenuta *te·noo·ta* f estate (property)

teoria *te·o·ree·a* f theory

teppista *tep·pee·sta* m vandal

tergicristallo *ter·jee·kree·stal·loh* m windshield wiper

terilene *te·ree·le·ne* m dacron

terminal *ter·mee·nal* m terminal

terminare *ter·mee·nah·ray* vt/i end

termine *ter·mee·ne* m term; **a breve termine** *a bre·ve ter·mee·ne* short term

termometro *ter·mo·me·troh* m thermometer

termos *ter·mos* m — Thermos

terra *ter·ra* f ground; earth; soil; land (opposed to sea); **a terra** *a ter·ra* ashore

terrapieno *ter·ra·pye·noh* m embankment

terrazza *ter·rats·tsa* f terrace

terremoto *ter·re·mo·toh* m earthquake

terreni *ter·ray·nee* mpl grounds (*land*)
terribile *ter·ree·bee·le* adj awful; terrible
territorio *ter·ree·to·ryoh* m territory
terrorismo *ter·ro·ree·zmoh* m terrorism
terrorista *ter·ro·ree·sta* m/f terrorist
terzino *ter·tsee·noh* m back (*in sports*)
terzo(a) *ter·tso(a)* adj third; **la terza (marcia)** *ter·tsa (mar·cha)* third (gear)
Terzo Mondo *ter·tso mohn·doh* m Third World
teschio *te·skyoh* m skull
teso(a) *tay·so(a)* adj tight (*rope*); tense
tesoro *te·zo·roh* m treasure
tessere *tes·se·re* vt weave
tessili *tes·see·lee* mpl textiles
tessitura *tes·see·too·ra* f texture
tessuto *tes·soo·toh* m fabric
testa *te·sta* f head; **il mal di testa** *mal dee te·sta* headache; **avere* mal di testa** *a·vay·re mal dee te·sta* to have a headache; **essere* in testa** *es·se·re een te·sta* to lead (*in contest*)
testamento *te·sta·mayn·toh* m will (*testament*)
testardo(a) *te·star·do(a)* adj stubborn
testimone *te·stee·mo·ne* m witness; **il testimone dello sposo** *te·stee·mo·ne del·lo spo·zoh* best man
testimonianza *te·stee·mo·nyan·tsa* f evidence (*of witness*)
testo *te·stoh* m text
tetraone *te·tra·oh·nay* m grouse (*bird*)
tettarella *tet·ta·rel·la* f teat (*for bottle*); pacifier
tetto *tayt·toh* m roof; **il tetto mobile** *tayt·toh mo·bee·le* sunroof
tettoia *tet·toh·ya* f shelter
thermos *ter·mos* m — flask
thriller *threel·ler* m thriller (*film*)
ti *tee* pron you; to you; yourself
tifoso *tee·foh·soh* m fan (*supporter*)
tigre *tee·gre* f tiger
timbro *teem·broh* m stamp (*rubber*)
timido(a) *tee·mee·do(a)* adj shy
timo *tee·moh* m thyme
timone *tee·moh·nay* m rudder
tingere* *teen·je·re* vt dye
tinta *teen·ta* f dye
tintoria *teen·to·ree·a* f dry-cleaner's
tintura *teen·too·ra* f dye; rinse (*for hair*)
tipico(a) *tee·pee·ko(a)* adj typical
tipo *tee·poh* m type (*sort*)
tipografo *tee·po·gra·foh* m printer
tirare *tee·rah·ray* vt pull; **tirare lo sciacquone** *tee·rah·ray lo shak·kwoh·ne* to flush the toilet
tirchio(a) *teer·kyoh(a)* adj mean (*miserly*)
titoli *tee·to·lee* mpl stocks (*financial*)
titolo *tee·to·loh* m headline; qualification (*diploma etc*); title
tizio *tee·tsyoh* m fellow
toboga *to·bo·ga* m — toboggan
toccare *tok·kah·ray* vt touch; feel; handle; **tocca a Lei** *tok·ka a lay* it's your turn
toeletta *to·e·let·ta* f dressing-table; toilet
toga *to·ga* f gown (*academic*)
togliere* *tol·ye·re* vt remove; take away; **farsi* togliere un dente** *far·see tol·ye·re oon den·te* to have a tooth taken out
togliersi* *tol·yer·see* vr take off (*clothes*)
tomba *tohm·ba* f grave
tonfo *tohn·foh* m splash; thud
tonico *to·nee·koh* m tonic (*medicine*)

tonnellata *ton·nel·lah·ta* f ton
tonno *tohn·noh* m tuna fish
tono *to·noh* m tone
tonsillite *ton·seel·lee·te* f tonsillitis
topinambur *to·pee·nam·boor* m Jerusalem artichoke
topo *to·poh* m mouse
torace *to·ra·che* m chest
torcere* *tor·che·re* vt twist
torcicollo *tor·chee·kol·loh* m a stiff neck
tornare *tor·nah·ray* vi return; come/go back; **tornare sui propri passi** *tor·nah·ray soo·ee pro·pree pas·see* to turn back
toro *to·roh* m bull
torre *tohr·re* f tower; **la torre di controllo** *tohr·re dee kon·trol·loh* control tower
torrone *tor·roh·nay* m nougat
torta *tohr·ta* f cake; tart; pie
torto *tor·toh* m wrong (*injustice*); **ha torto** *a tor·toh* you're wrong
tosse *tohs·say* f cough
tossicomane *tos·see·ko·ma·ne* m/f addict
tossire *tos·see·ray* vi cough
tostapane *to·sta·pah·ne* m — toaster
totale *to·tah·le* m total ◻ adj total
tovaglia *to·val·ya* f tablecloth
tovagliolo *to·val·yo·loh* m serviette; napkin
tra *tra* prep between; among; in
traccia *trach·cha* f trace (*mark*); track
tradizione *tra·dee·tsyoh·ne* f tradition
tradurre* *tra·door·re* vt translate
traduzione *tra·doo·tsyoh·ne* f translation
traffico *traf·fee·koh* m traffic
trafiggere* *tra·feej·je·re* vt pierce
traghetto *tra·gayt·toh* m ferry; **il traghetto per auto** *tra·gayt·toh payr ow·toh* car-ferry
tram *tram* m — streetcar
trama *trah·ma* f plot (*in play*)
tramezzino *tra·medz·dzee·noh* m sandwich
tramezzo *tra·medz·dzoh* m partition (*wall*)
tramonto *tra·mohn·toh* m sunset
trampolino *tram·po·lee·noh* m diving-board
tranne *tran·ne* prep except (for), except(ing); **tutti tranne lui** *toot·tee tran·ne loo·ee* all but him
tranquillante *tran·kweel·lan·te* m tranquilizer
tranquillo(a) *tran·kweel·lo(a)* adj quiet; calm; peaceful
transatlantico(a) *tran·sat·lan·tee·ko(a)* adj transatlantic ◻ m **il transatlantico** *trans·at·lan·tee·koh* liner (*ship*)
transazione *tran·sa·tsyoh·ne* f transaction
transistore *tran·see·stoh·re* m transistor
transito *tran·see·toh* m transit
trapano *tra·pa·noh* m drill (*tool*)
trappola *trap·po·la* f trap
trapunta *tra·poon·ta* f quilt
trascinare *tra·shee·nah·ray* vt drag
trascorrere* *tra·skohr·re·re* vt pass (*time*); spend
trasferire *tras·fe·ree·re* vt transfer
trasferirsi *tra·sfe·reer·see* vr move
traslocarsi *traz·lo·kahr·see* vr move (*change residence*)
trasmettere* *tra·zmayt·te·re* vt broadcast
trasmettitore *tra·zmet·tee·toh·re* m transmitter

trasmissione *tra·zmees·syoh·ne f* broadcast; transmission

trasparente *tra·spa·ren·te adj* transparent; clear

traspirare *tra·spee·rah·ray vi* perspire

trasportare *tra·spor·tah·ray vt* carry; transport

trasporto *tra·spor·toh m* transport; **il trasporto aereo** *tra·spor·toh a·e·re·o* air freight

tratta *trat·ta f* bank bill

trattamento *trat·ta·mayn·toh m* treatment

trattare *trat·tah·ray vt* treat; handle (*deal with*); process

trattative *trat·ta·tee·ve fpl* talks; negotiations

trattenere* *trat·te·nay·re vt* hold up (*delay*)

trattino *trat·tee·noh m* dash (*in writing*); hyphen

trattore *trat·toh·re m* tractor

trave *trah·ve f* beam

traversata *tra·vayr·sah·ta f* crossing (*voyage*)

travestimento *tra·ve·stee·mayn·toh m* disguise

travestito(a) *tra·ve·stee·to(a) adj* in disguise

trazione anteriore *tra·tsyoh·ne an·te·ryoh·re f* front-wheel drive

tre *tray num* three

treccia *traych·cha f* plait (*of hair etc*)

tredicesimo(a) *tre·dee·che·zee·mo(a) adj* thirteenth

tredici *tray·dee·chee num* thirteen

tremare *tre·mah·ray vi* shake

treno *tre·noh m* train; **il treno merci** *tre·noh mayr·chee* freight train

trenta *trayn·ta num* thirty

trentesimo(a) *tren·te·zee·mo(a) adj* thirtieth

treppiede *trep·pye·de m* tripod

triangolo *tree·an·go·loh m* triangle

tribù *tree·boo f —* tribe

tribunale *tree·boo·nah·lay m* court (*law*)

trimestre *tree·me·stre m* term (*of school etc*)

trinciare *treen·chah·ray vt* carve (*meat*)

trippa *treep·pa f* tripe

triste *tree·ste adj* sad

tritacarne *tree·ta·kahr·nay m —* mincer

tritare *tree·tah·ray vt* mince; chop

tromba *trohm·ba f* trumpet

trombone *trohm·boh·ne m* trombone; daffodil

tronco *trohn·koh m* trunk (*of tree*)

tropicale *tro·pee·kah·le adj* tropical

tropici *tro·pee·chee mpl* tropics

troppo *trop·po adv* too much; too

troppo(a) *trop·po(a) adj, pron* too much; **troppi(e)** *trop·pee(·pe)* too many

trota *tro·ta f* trout

trottare *trot·tah·ray vi* trot (*horse*)

trovare *tro·vah·ray vt* find

truccarsi *trook·kahr·see vr* make (oneself) up

trucco *trook·koh m* trick (*clever act*); make-up

truppa *troop·pa f* troop

trust *trust m* trust (*company*)

tu *too pron* you; **tu stesso(a)** *too stays·so(a)* (you) yourself

tua *too·a adj* your □ *pron* yours

tubo *too·boh m* pipe; tube; **il tubo fluorescente** *too·boh floo·o·re·shen·te* fluorescent light; **il tubo flessibile** *too·boh fles·see·bee·le* hose (*pipe*); **il tubo di respirazione** *too·boh dee re-*

spee·ra·tsyoh·ne snorkel; **il tubo di scolo** *too·boh dee skoh·loh* drain-pipe; **il tubo di scappamento** *too·boh dee skap·pa·mayn·toh* exhaust

tue *too·e adj* your □ *pron* yours

tuffarsi *toof·far·see vr* dive

tuffo *toof·foh m* dive

tulipano *too·lee·pah·noh m* tulip

tumefazione *too·me·fa·tsyoh·ne f* swelling (*lump*)

tumulto *too·mool·toh m* riot

tunica *too·nee·ka f* tunic (*of uniform*)

Tunisia *too·nee·see·a f* Tunisia

tuo *too·o adj* your □ *pron* yours

tuoi *twoy adj* your □ *pron* yours

tuono *two·noh m* thunder

turbine *toor·bee·ne m* whirlwind

Turchia *toor·kee·a f* Turkey

turco(a) *toor·ko(a) adj* Turkish □ *m* **il turco** *toor·ko* Turkish

turismo *too·ree·zmoh m* tourism

turista *too·ree·sta m/f* tourist

turno *toor·noh m* turn; shift (*of workmen*)

tuta *too·ta f* overall; dungarees; suit (*astronaut, diver*); track suit; **la tuta da lavoro** *too·ta da la·voh·roh* overalls

tutore *too·toh·ray m* guardian

tutrice *too·tree·chay f* guardian

tuttavia *toot·ta·vee·a conj* still (*nevertheless*); however

tutti *toot·tee pron* everybody, everyone; **sanno tutti che...** *san·no toot·tee ke* all of them know that...

tutti(e) *toot·tee(·te) adj* all

tutto *toot·toh pron* everything; del **tutto** *del toot·toh* quite (*absolutely*); **tutto ciò di cui ha bisogno** *toot·toh cho dee koo·ee a bee·zohn·yoh* all you need

tutto(a) *toot·to(a) adj* all; **tutta la giornata** *toot·ta la johr·nah·ta* all day; **tutto il pane** *toot·to eel pah·ne* all the bread

TV *tee·voo f* TV

U

ubbidire *oob·bee·dee·re vi* obey; **ubbidire a qualcuno** *oob·bee·dee·re a kwal·koo·no* to obey someone

ubicazione *oo·bee·ka·tsyoh·ne f* situation (*place*)

ubriaco(a) *oo·bree·ah·ko(a) adj* drunk

uccello *ooch·chel·loh m* bird

uccidere* *ooch·chee·de·re vt* kill

ufficiale *oof·fee·chah·le m* officer (*in army etc*) □ *adj* official

ufficio *oof·fee·choh m* bureau; office; service (*in church*); **l'ufficio informazioni** *oof·fee·choh een·for·ma·tsyoh·nee* information desk/office; **l'ufficio del personale** *oof·fee·choh del per·so·nah·le* personnel department; **l'ufficio turistico** *oof·fee·choh too·ree·stee·ko* tourist office; **l'ufficio postale** *oof·fee·choh po·stah·le* post office

ufficioso(a) *oof·fee·choh·so(a) adj* unofficial

uggioso(a) *ooj·joh·so(a) adj* dull (*day, weather*)

uguale *oo·gwah·le adj* equal; even

ulcera *ool·che·ra f* ulcer

ultimatum *ool·tee·mah·toom m —* ultimatum

ultimissimo *ool·tee·mees·see·mo m* the very last

ultimo(a) *ool·tee·mo(a) adj* last; **in ultimo** *een ool·tee·mo* in the last resort; **per ultimo** *payr ool·tee·mo* last; **le ul-**

time notizie ool·tee·me no·tee·tsye the latest news

umano(a) oo·mah·no(a) adj human

umido(a) oo·mee·do(a) adj wet; damp

umore oo·moh·ray m mood; **di buon umore** dee bwon oo·moh·ray in a good mood; in good spirits; **di cattivo umore** dee kat·tee·vo oo·moh·ray in a bad mood

un oon art a; an; one

unanime oo·nah·nee·may adj unanimous (decision)

uncino oon·chee·noh m hook

undicesimo(a) oon·dee·che·zee·mo(a) adj eleventh

undici oon·dee·chee num eleven

UNESCO oo·ne·sko f UNESCO

ungherese oon·ge·ray·se adj Hungarian □ m **l'ungherese** oon·ge·ray·se Hungarian

Ungheria oon·ge·ree·a f Hungary

unghia oon·gya f nail (human); **il nécessaire per unghie** nay·ses·sayr payr oon·gye manicure set

unguento oon·gwen·toh m ointment

unico(a) oo·nee·ko(a) adj unique; **l'unica donna là** loo·nee·ka don·na la the only woman there; **un figlio unico** oon feel·yoh oo·nee·ko an only child

unilaterale oo·nee·la·te·rah·lay adj unilateral

unione oo·nyoh·nay f union

Unione Sovietica oo·nyoh·ne so·vye·tee·ka f Soviet Union

unire oo·nee·re vt join; unite; connect

unisex oo·nee·sex adj unisex

unità oo·nee·ta f — unit

unito(a) oo·nee·to(a) adj united; plain (not patterned)

universale oo·nee·vayr·sah·lay adj universal

università oo·nee·ver·see·ta f — university

universo oo·nee·ver·soh m universe

uno(a) oo·no(a) adj, num a, an; one; o **l'uno o l'altro di voi** o loo·no o lal·troh dee voy either of you; quale? - o l'uno o l'altro kwah·le - o loo·no o lal·troh which one? - either; **l'un l'altro** loon lal·tro one another; **uno dovrebbe...** oo·no do·vreb·be one should...

uomo wo·moh m **uomini** man; **l'uomo d'affari** wo·moh daf·fah·ree businessman

uovo wo·voh m **—a** egg; **l'uovo di Pasqua** wo·voh dee pa·skwa Easter egg; **un uovo à la coque** oon wo·voh a la kok a boiled egg

uragano oo·ra·gah·noh m hurricane

urbano(a) oor·bah·no(a) adj urban

urgente oor·jen·te adj urgent

urgentemente oor·jen·te·mayn·te adv urgently

urlare oor·lah·ray vi roar (person)

urlo oor·loh m roar (of person)

U.R.S.S. oo·erre·esse·esse f U.S.S.R.

urtare oor·tah·ray vt bump; hit (with car)

urto oor·toh m bump (knock)

usare oo·zah·ray vt use

usato(a) oo·za·toh(a) adj used

uscire* oo·shee·ray vi come out (person, sun); go out; **uscire* con qualcuno** oo·shee·ray kon kwal·koo·noh to go out with somebody; **uscire* da** oo·shee·ray da to leave; **è uscito di corsa dalla casa e** oo·shee·to dee kohr·sa dal·la kah·sa he ran out of

the house; **fare* uscire** fah·ray oo·shee·ray to release (book, film)

uscita oo·shee·ta f exit; **l'uscita di sicurezza** oo·shee·ta dee see·koo·rayts·tsa emergency exit; fire escape

uso oo·zo m use; **in uso** een oo·zo in use

utero oo·te·roh m womb

utile oo·tee·lay adj useful

uva oo·va f grapes; **l'uva passa** oo·va pas·sa currants; raisins; **l'uva sultanina** oo·va sool·ta·nee·na sultanas; **l'uva spina** oo·va spee·na gooseberry

V

vacante va·kan·te adj vacant

vacanza va·kan·tsa f vacation; **in vacanza** een va·kan·tsa on vacation

vacanze va·kan·tse fpl holiday (period); vacation

vacca vak·ka f cow

vaccinazione vach·chee·na·tsyoh·nay f vaccination; inoculation

vagabondo(a) va·ga·bohn·doh(a) m/f tramp

vaglia val·ya m — postal order; money order

vago(a) va·go(a) adj vague

vagone va·goh·nay m car (of train); **il vagone letto** va·goh·nay let·to sleeping car; **il vagone ristorante** va·goh·nay ree·sto·ran·te club car

vaiolo va·yo·loh m smallpox

valanga va·lan·ga f avalanche

valere* va·lay·re vt be worth □ vi be valid; **vale la pena** vah·le la pay·na it's worth it; **tanto vale che andiamo** tan·toh vah·le kay an·dya·moh we might as well go

valido(a) vah·lee·do(a) adj valid

valigetta va·lee·jayt·ta f grip (case)

valigia va·lee·ja f suitcase; **fare* la valigia** fah·ray la va·lee·ja to pack one's suitcase

valle val·le f valley; **a valle** a val·le downstream

valore va·loh·ray m value; **il valore di mercato** va·loh·ray dee mayr·kah·toh market value; **di gran valore** dee gran va·loh·ray valuable; **gli oggetti di valore** oj·jet·tee dee va·loh·ray valuables

valuta va·loo·ta f currency

valutare va·loo·tah·ray vt value

valvola val·vo·la f valve

valzer val·tser m — waltz

vanga van·ga f spade

vangare van·gah·ray vt dig (ground)

vaniglia va·neel·ya f vanilla

vanitoso(a) va·nee·toh·soh(a) adj conceited; vain

vano vah·noh m room

vantaggio van·taj·joh m benefit; advantage

vantaggioso(a) van·taj·joh·so(a) adj profitable

vantarsi van·tar·see vr boast

vapore va·poh·re m steam; **cuocere* a vapore** kwo·che·re a va·poh·re to steam (food)

varare va·rah·ray vt launch (ship)

variabile va·ree·ah·bee·lay adj variable □ f **la variabile** va·ree·ah·bee·lay variable

variare va·ree·ah·ray vt/i vary

variazione va·ree·a·tsyoh·nay f variation

varicella va·ree·chel·la f chicken pox

varietà va·ree·e·ta f — variety

vario(a) vah·ree·oh(a) adj various

Varsavia *var·sah·vya* f Warsaw
vasca da bagno *va·ska da ban·yoh* f bath (*tub*)
vaselina *va·ze·lee·na* f petroleum jelly; vaseline
vasellame *va·zel·la·me* m crockery, china
vasino *va·zee·noh* m pot(ty)
vaso *vah·zoh* m vase; pot
vassoio *vas·soh·yoh* m tray
Vaticano *va·tee·kah·noh* m Vatican
ve *ve* pron, adv before lo, la, li, le, ne = **vi**
vecchio(a) *vayk·kyo(a)* adj old
vedere *ve·day·re* vt/i see; non vedere* l'ora di *nohn ve·day·re loh·ra dee* to look forward to
vedersi *ve·dayr·see* vr meet; show (be visible)
vedova *vay·do·va* f widow
vedovo *vay·do·voh* m widower
veduta *ve·doo·ta* f scene (sight)
vegetariano(a) *ve·je·ta·ree·ah·no(a)* adj vegetarian
vegliare *vel·yah·ray* vi stay up (at night)
veicolo *ve·ee·ko·loh* m vehicle
vela *vay·la* f sail; sailing
veleggiare *ve·lej·jah·ray* vi sail
veleno *ve·lay·noh* m poison
velenoso(a) *ve·le·noh·so(a)* adj poisonous
veliero *ve·lye·roh* m sailboat
velina *ve·lee·na* f tissue paper
vellutato(a) *vel·loo·tah·to(a)* adj creamy (texture)
velluto *vel·loo·toh* m velvet; il velluto a coste *vel·loo·toh a ko·stay* corduroy
velo *vay·loh* m veil
veloce *ve·loh·che* adj fast (speedy)
velocemente *ve·loh·che·mayn·te* adv fast
velocità *ve·lo·chee·ta* f speed
vena *vay·na* f vein
venatura *vay·na·too·ra* f grain (in wood)
vendemmia *ven·daym·mya* f harvest (of grapes); fare* la vendemmia di *fah·ray la ven·daym·mya de* to harvest (grapes)
vendere *vayn·de·re* vt sell; da vendere o rimandare *da vayn·de·re o ree·man·dah·ray* on sale or return; vendere al minuto *vayn·de·re al mee·noo·toh* to retail
vendita *vayn·dee·ta* f sale; la vendita al minuto *vayn·dee·ta al mee·noo·toh* retail; la vendita all'ingrosso *vayn·dee·ta al·leen·gros·soh* wholesale; la vendita all'asta *vayn·dee·ta al·la·sta* auction; la vendita a rate *vayn·dee·ta a rah·te* instalment plan
venditore *ven·dee·toh·ray* m vendor; il venditore a domicilio *ven·dee·toh·ray a do·mee·cheel·yoh* door-to-door salesman
venerdì *ve·ner·dee* m — Friday; venerdì santo *ve·ner·dee san·toh* Good Friday; di venerdì *dee ve·ner·dee* on Fridays
Venezia *ve·ne·tsya* f Venice
venire* *ve·nee·re* vi come (arrive); veniamo domani? *ve·nyah·mo do·mah·nee* shall we come tomorrow?; ella verrebbe se... *ayl·la ver·reb·be* say she would come if...; venire* incontro a qualcuno *ve·nee·re een·kohn·tro a kwal·koo·no* to come towards someone; verrò a prenderla alla stazione *ver·roh a pren·dayr·la al·la sta·tsyoh·nay* I'll meet you at the sta-

tion; venga a casa nostra *ven·ga a kah·sa no·stra* come back to our place; venire* giù *ve·nee·re joo* to come down
ventaglio *ven·tal·yoh* m fan (folding)
venti *vayn·tee* num twenty
ventilatore *ven·tee·la·toh·re* m fan (electric); ventilator
vento *ven·toh* m wind (breeze); tira vento *tee·ra ven·toh* it's windy
ventola *ven·to·la* f fan
ventuno *ven·too·noh* num twenty one
veramente *ve·ra·mayn·tay* adv really
veranda *ve·ran·da* f veranda
verbale *vayr·bah·lay* adj verbal
verde *vayr·day* adj green
verdetto *vayr·dayt·toh* m verdict
verdura *vayr·doo·ra* f vegetables
vergogna *ver·gohn·ya* f shame
vergognarsi (di) *ver·gon·yar·see* (dee) vr be ashamed (of)
verificare *ve·ree·fee·kah·ray* vt check (train time etc); audit
verità *ve·ree·ta* f truth
verme *ver·me* m worm
vermut *ver·moot* m vermouth
vernice *vayr·nee·chay* f varnish; paint
verniciare *vayr·nee·chah·ray* vt paint; varnish
vero(a) *vay·ro(a)* adj true; real; lo conosce, non è vero? *lo ko·no·she, nohn e vay·ro* you know him, don't you?; non è venuto, vero? *nohn e ve·noo·to, vay·ro* he didn't come, did he?; è un vero problema *e oon vay·ro pro·ble·ma* it's a real problem
verruca *ver·roo·ka* f wart
versamento *ver·sa·mayn·toh* m payment; deposit
versare *ver·sah·ray* vt pour (tea, milk)
versione *ver·syoh·nay* f version
verso *ver·so* prep toward(s)
verticale *vayr·tee·kah·lay* adj vertical
vertigine *ver·tee·jee·ne* f dizziness; preso(a) da vertigine *pray·so(a) da ver·tee·jee·ne* dizzy (person)
vescica *ve·shee·ka* f bladder
vescichetta *ve·shee·kayt·ta* f blister (on skin)
vescovo *vay·sko·voh* m bishop
vespa *ve·spa* f wasp
vestaglia *ve·stal·ya* f housecoat; dressing gown
veste *ves·tay* f gown (dress)
vestiario *ve·stee·ah·ree·oh* m wardrobe
vestibolo *ve·stee·bo·loh* m hall; lobby
vestire *ve·stee·re* vt dress (child)
vestirsi *ve·steer·see* vr dress (oneself)
vestiti *ve·stee·tee* mpl clothes; i vestiti sportivi *ve·stee·tee spor·tee·vee* casual clothes, casual wear
vestito *ve·stee·toh* m dress; suit (man's); il vestito da spiaggia *ve·stee·toh da spyaj·ja* sun dress
veterinario(a) *ve·te·ree·nah·ryoh(a)* m/f vet(erinary surgeon)
veto *ve·toh* m veto; mettere* il veto a *mayt·te·ray eel ve·toh a* to veto
vetrata *ve·trah·ta* f glass door/window; la vetrata dipinta *ve·trah·ta dee·peen·ta* stained glass window
vetrina *ve·tree·na* f shop window
vetro *vay·troh* m pane; glass
vettura *vet·too·ra* f coach (of train)
V.H.F. *voo·akka·effe* abbrev V.H.F.
vi *vee* pron you; to you; yourselves; each other □ adv there; here
via *vee·a* f street □ prep via; passare via Londra *pas·sah·ray vee·a lohn·dra* to go via London

viadotto *vee·a·doht·toh m* overpass; viaduct

viaggi *vee·aj·jee mpl* travel

viaggiare *vyaj·jah·ray vi* travel; **viaggiare in prima classe** *vyaj·jah·ray een pree·ma klas·say* to travel first class

viaggiatore *vyaj·ja·toh·re m* traveler

viaggio *vyaj·joh m* journey; trip; drive; **il viaggio organizzato** *vyaj·joh or·ga·needz·dzah·to* package holiday; **siamo in viaggio di nozze** *syah·mo een vyaj·joh dee nots·tse* we're on our honeymoon; **il viaggio d'affari** *vyaj·joh daf·fah·ree* business trip; **il viaggio di andata e ritorno** *vyaj·joh dee an·dah·ta e ree·tohr·noh* round trip; **il viaggio aereo** *vyaj·joh a·e·re·o* air travel

viale *vyah·le m* avenue

vice- *vee·che pref* deputy (*second-in-command*)

vicenda *vee·chen·da f* event; **a vicenda** *a vee·chen·da* in turn

vicepresidente *vee·che·pre·se·den·te m* vice chairman; vice president

viceversa *vee·che·ver·sa adv* vice versa

vicinato *vee·chee·nah·toh m* neighborhood

vicino *vee·chee·noh adv* near; close by □ *m/f* il/la **vicino(a)** *vee·chee·noh(a)* neighbor; **vicino a** *vee·chee·noh a* close to; **vicino alla casa** *vee·chee·noh al·la kah·sa* near (to) the house; **vicino(a) ai negozi** *vee·chee·noh(a) a·ee ne·go·tsee* convenient to stores; **qui vicino** *kwee vee·chee·noh* nearby

vicolo *vee·ko·loh m* alley; lane; **il vicolo cieco** *vee·ko·loh che·ko* blind alley; dead end

video *vee·de·oh m* video

videocassetta *vee·de·o·kas·sayt·ta f* videocassette

videonastro *vee·de·o·na·stroh m* videotape

videoregistratore a cassetta *vee·de·o·re·jee·stra·toh·ray a kas·sayt·ta m* videocassette recorder

Vienna *vee·en·na f* Vienna

vietare *vee·e·tah·ray vt* forbid; **è vietato(a)** *e vee·e·tah·to(a)* it is forbidden

vigile *vee·jee·le m* policeman; **i vigili del fuoco** *vee·jee·lee del fwo·koh* fire department; **il vigile urbano** *vee·jee·le oor·bah·no* traffic policeman

vigilia *vee·jeel·ya f* eve; **la vigilia di Capodanno** *vee·jeel·ya dee kah·po·dan·noh* New Year's Eve; **la vigilia di Natale** *vee·jeel·ya dee na·tah·lay* Christmas Eve

vigliacco *veel·yak·koh m* coward

vigna *veen·ya f* vineyard

vignetta umoristica *veen·yayt·ta oo·mo·ree·stee·ka f* cartoon

villa *veel·la f* detached house; villa

villeggiante *veel·lej·jan·te m/f* vacationer

vimine *vee·mee·ne m* wicker

vincere* *veen·che·re vi* win □ *vt* win; defeat

vincitore *veen·chee·toh·re m* winner

vincitrice *veen·chee·tree·che f* winner

vinile *vee·nee·le m* vinyl

vino *vee·noh m* wine; **un vino di qualità** *oon vee·noh dee kwa·lee·ta* quality wine; **il vino del Reno** *vee·noh del re·noh* Rhine (wine)

violento(a) *vee·o·len·to(a) adj* violent

violenza *vee·o·len·tsa f* violence

violino *vee·o·lee·noh m* violin

violoncello *vee·o·lon·chel·loh m* cello

viottolo *vee·ot·to·loh m* lane (*in country*)

V.I.P. *voo·ee·pee m* V.I.P.

vipera *vee·pe·ra f* adder (*snake*)

virare di bordo *vee·rah·ray dee bohr·doh vi* tack (*sailing*)

virgola *veer·go·la f* comma; **la virgola decimale** *veer·go·la de·chee·mah·le* decimal point; **3 virgola 4** *3 veer·go·la 4* 3 point 4

visibile *vee·zee·bee·lay adj* visible

visiera *vee·zye·ra f* sun visor (*in car*); peak (*of cap*)

visione *vee·zee·oh·ne f* vision; **quando è in visione il film?** *kwan·do é een vee·zee·oh·ne eel feelm* when is the movie on?

visita *vee·zee·ta f* visit; examination (*medical*); **la visita con guida** *vee·zee·ta kohn gwee·da* guided tour

visitare *vee·zee·tah·ray vt* visit; tour

visitatore *vee·zee·ta·toh·ray m* visitor

visitatrice *vee·zee·ta·tree·chay f* visitor

viso *vee·zoh m* face

visone *vee·zoh·nay m* mink (*fur*)

vista *vee·sta f* eyesight; view; **avere*** **la vista debole** *a·vay·re la vee·sta day·bo·le* to have poor sight; **una bella vista** *oo·na bel·la vee·sta* a lovely sight

vistare *vee·stah·ray vt* visa

visto *vee·stoh m* visa, visé; **il visto di transito** *eel vee·stoh dee tran·see·toh* transit visa

vita *vee·ta f* life; waist; **guadagnarsi la vita** *gwa·dan·yar·see la vee·ta* to earn one's living; **l'assicurazione sulla vita** *as·see·koo·ra·tsyoh·ne sool·la vee·ta* life insurance; **a vita** *a vee·ta* for life

vitale *vee·tah·lay adj* vital (*essential*)

vitamina *vee·ta·mee·na f* vitamin

vite *vee·te f* vine; screw

vitello *vee·tel·loh m* veal; calf

vittima *veet·tee·ma f* victim

vittoria *veet·to·ree·a f* victory

vivace *vee·vah·che adj* lively

vivere* *vee·ve·re vi* live

vivo(a) *vee·vo(a) adj* live; alive

viziare *vee·tsyah·ray vt* spoil (*child*)

vocabolario *vo·ka·bo·lah·ree·oh m* vocabulary; dictionary

voce *voh·che f* voice; **ad alta voce** *ad al·ta voh·che* aloud

vodka *vod·ka f* vodka

voi *voy pron* you; **l'avete fatto voi stessi(e)** *la·vay·te fat·to voy stays·see(·se)* you did it yourselves

volano *vo·lah·noh m* badminton

volante *vo·lan·te m* steering wheel

volare *vo·lah·ray vi* fly □ *m* il **volare** *vo·lah·ray* flying

volere* *vo·lay·re vt* want (*wish for*); **vuole partire** *vwo·le par·tee·re* he wants to leave; **vorrei potere…** *vor·re·e po·tay·re* I wish I could…; **ci vuole un grande sforzo/un'ora** *chee vwo·le oon gran·de sfor·tsoh/oo·noh·ra* it takes a lot of effort/an hour; **che cosa vorrebbe?** *ke ko·sa vor·reb·be* what would you like?; **volere*** **fare qualcosa** *vo·lay·re fah·ray kwal·ko·sa* to want to do something

volo *voh·loh m* flight; **il volo a vela** *voh·loh a vay·la* gliding (*sport*); **il volo charter** *voh·loh char·ter* charter flight; **prendere*** **un volo diretto per Venezia** *pren·de·re oon voh·loh dee·ret·to payr ve·ne·tsya* to fly to Venice direct; **il volo di linea** *voh·loh dee lee·ne·a* scheduled flight

volpe *vohl·pe f* fox

volta *vol·ta* f time; **qualche volta** *kwal·ke vol·ta* sometimes; **una volta** *oo·na vol·ta* once; **ancora una volta** *an·koh·ra oo·na vol·ta* once more; **due volte** *doo·e vol·te* twice; **la prima volta** *la pree·ma vol·ta* the first time; **quante volte?** *kwan·te vol·te* how many times?

voltare *vol·tah·ray* vt turn

voltarsi *vol·tar·see* vr turn around; turn over

volume *vo·loo·me* m volume

vomitare *vo·mee·tah·ray* vt vomit

vortice *vor·tee·che* m whirlpool

vostri(e) *vo·stree(·stre)* adj your □ *pron* yours

vostro(a) *vo·stro(a)* adj your □ *pron* yours

votare *vo·tah·ray* vi vote

voto *voh·toh* m vote; mark (*in school*)

vulcano *vool·kah·noh* m volcano

vuotare *vwo·tah·ray* vt empty

vuoto(a) *vwo·to(a)* adj empty

W

wafer *va·fer* m wafer

watt *vat* m watt

week-end *week·end* m weekend

western *wes·tern* m western (*movie*)

whisky *wee·skee* m whiskey; **il whisky scozzese** *wee·skee skots·tsay·se* Scotch (*liquor*); **un whisky con selz** *oon wee·skee kohn selts* a whiskey and soda; **il whisky americano** *wee·skee a·me·ree·kah·no* bourbon; **il whisky di segale** *wee·skee dee say·ga·le* rye (whiskey)

X

xerocopia *kse·ro·ko·pya* f Xerox

Y

yacht *yot* m yacht

yachting *yo·teeng* m yachting; **fare*** **dello yachting** *fah·ray del·lo yo·teeng* to go yachting

yoga *yo·ga* m yoga

yogurt *yo·goort* m yogurt

Z

zaino *dza·ee·noh* m rucksack; back pack

zampa *tsam·pa* f leg (*of animal*); paw; foot

zanzara *dzan·dzah·ra* f mosquito

zanzariera *dzan·dza·ree·e·ra* f mosquito net

zebra *dze·bra* f zebra

zenzero *tsen·tse·roh* m ginger

zerbino *dzer·bee·noh* m doormat

zero *dze·roh* m nil; zero

zia *tsee·a* f aunt(ie)

zinco *tseen·koh* m zinc

zingaro *tseen·ga·roh* m gypsy

zio *tsee·oh* m uncle

zitto(a) *tseet·to(a)* excl be quiet!

zolletta *tsol·layt·ta* f cube; **la zolletta di zucchero** *tsol·layt·ta dee tsook·ke·roh* lump of sugar

zona *dzo·na* f zone; **la zona residenziale** *dzo·na re·see·den·tsyah·le* development (*housing*); **la zona industriale** *dzo·na een·doo·stryah·le* industrial area; **la zona di concentramento** *dzo·na dee kon·chen·tra·men·toh* conurbation

zoo *dzo* m zoo

zoom *zoom* m zoom lens

zoppicare *tsop·pee·kah·ray* vi limp

zoppo(a) *tsop·poh(a)* m/f cripple

zucca *tsook·ka* f pumpkin; squash (*gourd*); marrow (*vegetable*)

zuccheriera *tsook·ke·rye·ra* f sugar bowl

zucchero *tsook·ke·roh* m sugar

zucchini *tsook·kee·nee* mpl zucchini

zuppa *tsoop·pa* f soup; **la zuppa inglese** *tsoop·pa een·glay·se* trifle (*dessert*); **la zuppa di tartaruga** *tsoop·pa dee tar·ta·roo·ga* turtle soup

ENGLISH–ITALIAN DICTIONARY

a *art* un(a) *oon(a)*; **twice a day** due volte al giorno *doo·ay vol·tay al jor·noh*; **$40 a week** $40 la settimana *$40 la se·tee·mah·na*

abbey *n* l'abbazia (f) *ab·ba·tsee·a*

abbreviation *n* l'abbreviazione (f) *ab·bre·vya·tsyoh·ne*

abdomen *n* l'addome (m) *ad·do·me*

ability *n* la capacità *ka·pa·chee·ta*

able *adj* □ **to be able to do something** potere* fare qualcosa *po·tay·re fah·ray kwal·ko·sa*

aboard *adv* □ **to go aboard** salire* a bordo *sa·lee·re a bohr·doh* □ *prep* **aboard the ship** a bordo della nave *a bohr·doh del·la nah·ve*

abolish *vt* abolire *a·bo·lee·re*

about *prep* □ **about $10** circa $10 *cheer·ka $10*; **about here** qui intorno *kwee·een·tohr·no*; **to talk about something** parlare di qualcosa *par·lah·ray dee kwal·ko·sa* □ *adv* **things lying about** cose lasciate in giro *ko·se la·shah·te een jee·roh*; **to look about** guardarsi intorno *gwar·dar·see een·tohr·no*; **to be about to do something** stare* per fare qualcosa *stah·ray payr fah·ray kwal·ko·sa*

above *prep, adv* sopra *soh·pra*

abroad *adv* all'estero *al·le·ste·roh*

abrupt *adj* (*person*) brusco(a) *broo·sko(a)*; (*slope*) ripido(a) *ree·pee·do(a)*

abscess *n* l'ascesso (m) *a·shays·soh*

absent *adj* assente *as·sen·te*

absenteeism *n* l'assenteismo (m) *as·sen·te·e·zmoh*

absolute *adj* assoluto(a) *as·so·loo·to(a)*

absorb *vt* (*fluid*) assorbire *as·sor·bee·re*; (*shock*) ammortizzare *am·mor·teedz·dzah·ray*

absorbent *adj* assorbente *as·sor·ben·te*

absorbent cotton *n* il cotone idrofilo *ko·toh·ne ee·dro·fee·lo*

abstain *vi* (*in voting*) astenersi* *a·ste·nayr·see*

abstract *adj* astratto(a) *a·strat·to(a)*

absurd *adj* assurdo(a) *as·soor·do(a)*

academy *n* □ **academy of music** il conservatorio *kon·ser·va·to·ryoh*; **military academy** l'accademia militare (f) *ak·ka·de·mya mee·lee·tah·re*

accelerate *vi* accelerare *ach·che·le·rah·ray*

accelerator *n* l'acceleratore (m) *ach·che·le·ra·toh·re*

accent *n* l'accento (m) *ach·chen·toh*

accept *vt* accettare *ach·chet·tah·ray*

acceptance *n* l'accettazione (f) *ach·chet·ta·tsyoh·ne*

access *n* l'accesso (m) *ach·ches·soh*

accessible *adj* accessibile *ach·ches·see·bee·le*

accessories *pl* gli accessori *ach·ches·so·ree*

accident *n* l'incidente (m) *een·chee·den·te*; **by accident** per caso *payr kah·zoh* I11, Ea2

accidental *adj* accidentale *ach·chee·den·tah·le*

accommodations *n* l'alloggio (m) *al·loj·joh* A4

accompany *vt* (*go with*) accompagnare *ak·kom·pan·yah·ray*

according to *prep* secondo *se·kohn·do*

account *n* il conto *kohn·toh* M29

accountancy *n* la ragioneria *ra·jo·ne·ree·a*

accountant *n* il ragioniere *ra·jo·nye·re*

accrue *vi* maturarsi *ma·too·rar·see*

accumulate *vi* accumularsi *ak·koo·moo·lar·see*

accurate *adj* preciso(a) *pre·chee·zo(a)*

accuse *vt* accusare *ak·koo·zah·ray*

ace *n* (*cards*) l'asso (m) *as·soh*

ache *n* il dolore *do·loh·re* □ *vi* fare* male *fah·ray mah·le*

acid *n* l'acido (m) *ah·chee·doh*

acknowledge *vt* (*letter*) accusare ricevuta di *ak·koo·zah·ray ree·che·voo·ta dee*

acne *n* l'acne (f) *ak·ne*

acorn *n* la ghianda *gyan·da*

acquaintance *n* la conoscenza *ko·no·shen·tsa*

acquire *vt* acquistare *ak·kwee·stah·ray*

acquisition *n* l'acquisizione (f) *ak·kwee·zee·tsyoh·ne*

acre *n* l'acro (m) *a·kroh*

across *prep* □ **to walk across the road** attraversare la strada *at·tra·ver·sah·ray la strah·da*; **I saw him from across the road** l'ho visto dall'altra parte della strada *lo vee·sto dal·lal·tra par·te del·la strah·da*; **we drove across France** abbiamo attraversato la Francia in macchina *ab·byah·mo at·tra·ver·sah·to la fran·cha een mak·kee·na*

acrylic *adj* acrilico(a) *a·kree·lee·ko(a)*

act *n* (*of play*) l'atto (m) *at·toh*; (*at circus etc*) il numero *noo·me·roh* □ *vi* (*behave*) comportarsi *kom·por·tar·see* □ *vt* **to act Hamlet** fare* la parte di Amleto *fah·ray la par·te dee am·le·to*; **to act as X** fungere* da X *foon·je·re da X*

acting *adj* supplente *soop·plen·te*

action *n* (*movement*) l'azione (f) *a·tsyoh·ne*; (*act*) l'atto (m) *at·toh*

active *adj* attivo(a) *at·tee·vo(a)*

activity *n* l'attività *at·tee·vee·ta*

actor *n* l'attore (m) *at·toh·re*

actress *n* l'attrice (f) *at·tree·che*

actually *adv* infatti *een·fat·tee*

acute accent *n* l'accento acuto (m) *ach·chen·toh a·koo·to*

adapt *vt* adattare *a·dat·tah·ray*

adapter, adaptor *n* (*electrical*) il raccordo *rak·kor·doh*

add *vt* (*comment*) aggiungere* *aj·joon·je·re*; **add (up)** (*numbers*) sommare *som·mah·ray*

adder *n* (*snake*) la vipera *vee·pe·ra*

addict *n* il/la tossicomane *tos·see·ko·ma·ne*

addition *n* l'addizione (f) *ad·dee·tsyoh·ne*

address *n* l'indirizzo (m) *een·dee·reets·tsoh* □ *vt* (*letter*) indirizzare *een·dee·reets·tsah·ray* T98, F2, S27

adhesive tape *n* (*for wound*) il cerotto *che·rot·toh*

adjourn *vi* rinviare la seduta *reen·vee·ah·ray la se·doo·ta*

adjournment *n* il rinvio *reen·vee·oh*

adjust *vt* aggiustare *aj·joo·stah·ray*

administration *n* l'amministrazione (f) *am·mee·nee·stra·tsyoh·ne*

admire *vt* ammirare *am·mee·rah·ray*

admission n l'entrata (f) *en·trah·ta* L13

admission fee n il prezzo d'ingresso *prets·tsoh deen·gres·soh*

adopt vt adottare *a·dot·tah·ray*

Adriatic (Sea) n l'Adriatico (m) *a·dree·a·tee·koh*

adult n l'adulto (m) *a·dool·toh* □ adj per adulti *payr a·dool·tee*

advance n (money) anticipare *an·tee·chee·pah·ray* □ vi avanzare *a·van·tsah·ray* □ n (loan) l'anticipo (m) *an·tee·chee·poh*; **in advance** in anticipo *een an·tee·chee·poh* M10

advantage n il vantaggio *van·taj·joh*

adventure n l'avventura (f) *av·ven·too·ra*

advertise vt (product) fare* pubblicità a *fah·ray poob·blee·chee·ta* a □ vi to advertise for a secretary fare* un'inserzione per trovare una segretaria *fah·ray oon·een·sayr·tsyoh·ne payr tro·vah·ray oo·na se·gre·tah·rya*

advertisement n la réclame *ray·klam*

advertising n la pubblicità *poob·blee·chee·ta* Bm17

advertising agency n l'agenzia pubblicitaria (f) a *jen·tsee·a poob·blee·chee·tah·rya*

advice n il consiglio *kon·seel·yoh*

advise vt consigliare *kon·seel·yah·ray*; to advise someone to do something consigliare a qualcuno di fare qualcosa *kon·seel·yah·ra·ya a kwal·koo·no dee fah·ray kwal·ko·sa*

aerial n l'antenna (f) *an·tayn·na*

aerosol n la bombola spray *bohm·bo·la spry*

affair n (matter) l'affare (m) *af·fah·re*; affairs gli affari *af·fah·ree*

affect vt influire *een·floo·ee·re*

affection n l'affetto (m) *af·fet·toh*

affectionate adj affettuoso(a) *af·fet·twoh·so(a)*

affiliated company n la filiale *feel·yah·le*

afford vt □ I can't afford it non me lo posso permettere *nohn may lo pos·so payr·mayt·te·re*

afraid adj □ to be afraid of something avere* paura di qualcosa *a·vay·re pa·oo·ra dee kwal·ko·sa*; I'm afraid not temo di no *te·mo de no*; I'm afraid I can't do it mi dispiace non posso farlo *mee dee·spyah·che ma nohn pos·so far·lo*

Africa n l'Africa (f) *a·free·ka*

African adj africano(a) *a·free·kah·no(a)*

after prep, adv dopo *doh·po*; to come after someone/something seguire qualcuno/qualcosa *se·gwee·re kwal·koo·no/kwal·ko·sa*; 4 years after 4 anni dopo *4 an·nee doh·po* □ conj after dopo che *doh·po ke*; after we had left dopo che fummo partiti *doh·po ke foom·mo par·tee·tee*

afternoon n il pomeriggio *po·me·reej·joh*

aftershave (lotion) n il dopobarba *doh·po·bar·ba*

afterward(s) adv dopo *doh·po*

again adv ancora *an·koh·ra*; di nuovo *dee nwo·vo*

against prep contro *kohn·tro*

age n (of person) l'età (f) *e·ta*; (era) l'epoca (f) *e·po·ka*; under age minorenne *mee·no·ren·ne*

agency n (office) l'agenzia (f) *a·jen·tsee·a*

agenda n l'ordine del giorno (m) *ohr·dee·ne del johr·noh*

agent n l'agente (m) *a·jen·te*; the Renault agent il concessionario Renault *kon·ches·syoh·nah·ryoh re·no*

aggressive adj aggressivo(a) *ag·gres·see·vo(a)*

agile adj agile *ah·jee·le*

ago adv □ 4 years ago 4 anni fa *4 an·nee fa*

agony n il dolore atroce *do·loh·re a·troh·che*

agree vt/i □ to agree with somebody essere* d'accordo con qualcuno *es·se·re dak·kor·doh kon kwal·koo·no*; to agree on (price) mettersi* d'accordo su *mayt·ter·see dak·kor·doh soo*; onions don't agree with me le cipolle non mi si confanno *le chee·pohl·le nohn mee see kon·fan·no*

agreement n l'accordo (m) *ak·kor·doh*

agricultural adj agricolo(a) *a·gree·ko·lo(a)*

agriculture n l'agricoltura (f) *a·gree·kol·too·ra*

ahead adv □ to see something ahead vedere* qualcosa in lontananza *ve·day·re kwal·ko·sa een lon·ta·nan·tsa*; to plan ahead fare* dei progetti in anticipo *fah·ray de·ee pro·jet·tee een an·tee·chee·po*; to think ahead pensare al futuro *pen·sah·ray al foo·too·roh* □ prep ahead of the others davanti agli altri *da·van·tee al·yee al·tree*

aim vt (gun etc) puntare *poon·tah·ray*; to aim a gun at someone puntare un fucile contro qualcuno *poon·tah·ray oon foo·chee·le kohn·tro kwal·koo·no* □ vi aim prendere* la mira *pren·de·re la mee·ra* □ n (intention) lo scopo *sko·poh*

air n l'aria (f) *ah·rya*; by air per via aerea *payr vee·a a·e·re·a* □ vt (room) arieggiare *a·ree·ej·jah·ray*; (clothes) sciorinare *sho·ree·nah·ray*

air bed n il materasso pneumatico *ma·te·ras·soh pne·oo·ma·tee·ko*

air bus n l'aerobus (m) *a·e·ro·boos*

air-conditioned adj con aria condizionata *kohn ah·rya kon·dee·tsyoh·nah·ta*

air-conditioning n il condizionamento dell'aria *kon·dee·tsyoh·na·mayn·toh del·lah·rya* A44

aircraft n l'aereo (m) *a·e·re·oh*

air filter n il filtro dell'aria *feel·troh del·lah·rya*

air force n l'aviazione (f) *a·vya·tsyoh·ne*

air freight n il trasporto aereo *tra·spor·toh a·e·re·o*

air letter n la lettera per via aerea *let·te·ra payr vee·a a·e·re·a*

airline n la compagnia aerea *kom·pan·yee·a a·e·re·a*

air mail n □ by air mail per posta aerea *payr po·sta a·e·re·a*

air-mattress n il materasso pneumatico *ma·te·ras·soh pne·oo·ma·tee·ko*

airplane n l'aeroplano (m) *a·e·ro·plah·noh*

airport n l'aeroporto (m) *a·e·ro·por·toh* T36

airtight adj ermetico(a) *er·me·tee·ko(a)*

air travel n il viaggio aereo *vyaj·joh a·e·re·o*

à la carte adv alla carta *al·la kar·ta*

alarm n (signal, apparatus) l'allarme (m) *al·lar·me* □ vt allarmare *al·lar·mah·ray*

alarm (clock) n la sveglia *zvayl·ya*

album n (for photos etc) l'album (m)

al·boom; (record) il longplaying *long·ple·eeng*

alcohol n l'alcol (m) *al·kol* E54

alcoholic adj (drink) alcolico(a) *al·ko·lee·ko(a)* □ n l'alcolizzato(a) (m/f) *al·ko·leedz·dzah·to(a)*

alcove n l'alcova (f) *al·ko·va*

Algeria n l'Algeria (f) *al·je·ree·a*

Algerian adj algerino(a) *al·je·ree·no(a)*

Algiers n Algeri (f) *al·je·ree*

alike adj simile *see·mee·le*

alive adj vivo(a) *vee·vo(a)*

all adj (with singular noun) tutto(a) *toot·toh(a)*; (with plural noun) tutti(e) *toot·tee(·te)*; **all day** tutta la giornata *toot·ta johr·nah·ta*; **all the tables** tutte le tavole *toot·te le tah·vo·le*; **all the bread** tutto il pane *toot·to eel pah·ne*; **all passengers** tutti i passeggeri *toot·tee ee pas·sej·je·ree* □ pron **all** (singular) il tutto *eel toot·toh*; (plural) i tutti *ee toot·tee*; **all you need** tutto ciò di cui ha bisogno *toot·to cho dee koo·ee a bee·zohn·yoh*; **all of them know that...** sanno tutti che... *san·no toot·tee ke*

Allah n Allah (m) *al·la*

allergic to adj allergico(a) a *al·ler·jee·ko(a) a*

allergy n l'allergia (f) *al·ler·jee·a*

alley n il vicolo *vee·ko·loh*

alliance n l'alleanza (f) *al·le·an·tsa*

allocate vt assegnare *as·sen·yah·ray*

allow vt □ **to allow someone to go** permettere* a qualcuno di partire *payr·mayt·te·re a kwal·koo·no dee partire·re*; **we will allow $10** assegneremo $10 *as·sen·ye·re·mo $10*; **allow 10 minutes to get there** calcoli 10 minuti per arrivarci *kal·ko·lee 10 mee·noo·tee payr ar·ree·var·chee*

allowance n (state payment) l'assegno (m) *as·sayn·yoh*

alloy n la lega *lay·ga*

all right adv (yes) bene *be·ne*; **he's all right** (safe, fit) sta bene *sta be·ne*; **he did it all right** (satisfactorily) l'ha fatto bene *la fat·to be·ne*

almond n la mandorla *man·dor·la*

almond paste n la pasta di mandorla *pa·sta dee man·dor·la*

almost adv quasi *kwah·zee*

alone adj solo(a) *soh·lo(a)*

along prep □ **along the street** lungo la strada *loon·go la strah·da*

aloud adv (read) ad alta voce *ad al·ta voh·che*

alphabet n l'alfabeto (m) *al·fa·be·toh*

alpine adj alpino(a) *al·pee·no(a)*

Alps pl le Alpi *al·pee*

already adv già *ja*

also adv anche *an·ke*

altar n l'altare (m) *al·tah·re*

alter vt alterare *al·te·rah·ray*

alternator n (in car) l'alternatore (m) *al·ter·na·toh·re*

although conj benché *ben·ke*

altitude n l'altitudine (f) *al·tee·too·dee·ne*

aluminum n l'alluminio (m) *al·loo·meen·yoh*

always adv sempre *sem·pre*

a.m. adv del mattino *del mat·tee·noh*

am vi □ **I am** sono *soh·no*

amalgamation n la fusione *foo·zyoh·ne*

amateur n il dilettante *dee·let·tan·te*

ambassador n l'ambasciatore (m) *am·ba·sha·toh·re*

amber n (traffic light) il giallo *jal·loh*

ambition n (aim) l'ambizione (f) *am·bee·tsyoh·ne*

ambitious adj ambizioso(a) *am·bee·tsyoh·so(a)*

ambulance n l'ambulanza (f) *am·boo·lan·tsa* I12

amenities pl le comodità *ko·mo·dee·ta*

America n l'America (f) *a·me·ree·ka*

American adj americano(a) *a·me·ree·kah·no(a)*

amethyst n l'ametista (f) *a·me·tee·sta*

among prep fra *fra*

amount n (total) l'importo (m) *eem·por·toh*; **a large amount of X** una grande quantità di X *oo·na gran·de kwan·tee·ta dee X*; **a small amount of X** un po' di X *oon po dee X* □ vi **it amounts to L.4000** ammonta a L.4000 *am·mohn·ta a L4000*

amp n l'ampère (m) *am·pehr*

amplifier n l'amplificatore (m) *am·plee·fee·ka·toh·re*

amuse vt divertire *dee·ver·tee·re*

amusement park n il luna-park *loo·na·park*

an art un(a) *oon(a)*

analysis n l'analisi (f) *a·nah·lee·see*

analyze vt analizzare *a·na·leedz·dzah·ray*

ancestor n l'antenato(a) (m/f) *an·te·nah·to(a)*

anchor n l'ancora (f) *an·ko·ra*

anchovy n l'acciuga (f) *ach·choo·ga*

and conj e *ay*; **better and better** sempre meglio *sem·pre mel·yo*; **to go and buy** andare* a comprare *an·dah·ray a kom·prah·ray*

anemic adj anemico(a) *a·ne·mee·ko(a)*

anesthetic n l'anestetico (m) *a·ne·ste·tee·koh*

angel n l'angelo (m) *an·je·loh*

anger n la collera *kol·le·ra*

angler n il pescatore *pe·ska·toh·re*

angling n la pesca *pay·ska*

angora n (fabric) l'angora (f) *an·go·ra*

angry adj (person) arrabbiato(a) *ar·rab·byah·to(a)*; **to be angry with someone** essere* arrabbiato con qualcuno *es·se·re ar·rab·byah·to kohn kwal·koo·no*

animal n l'animale (m) *a·nee·mah·le*

ankle n la caviglia *ka·veel·ya*

anniversary n l'anniversario (m) *an·nee·ver·sah·ryoh*

announce vt annunziare *an·noon·tsyah·ray*

annoy vt (person) dare* fastidio a *dah·ray fa·stee·dyoh a*; (thing) annoiare *an·no·yah·ray*

annual adj annuale *an·noo·ah·le*

annuity n la rendita vitalizia *ren·dee·ta vee·ta·lee·tsya*

anorak n la giacca a vento *jak·ka a ven·toh*

another adj □ **another beer please!** ancora una birra, per favore! *an·koh·ra oo·na bee·ra payr fa·voh·re*; **I want to see another shirt** vorrei vedere un'altra camicia *vor·re·ee ve·day·re oo·nal·tra ka·mee·cha*

answer n la risposta *ree·spoh·sta* □ vi rispondere* *ree·spohn·de·re*; □ vt **to answer a question** rispondere* a una domanda *ree·spohn·de·re a oo·na do·man·da*; **to answer the phone** rispondere* al telefono *ree·spohn·de·re al te·le·fo·noh*

ant n la formica *for·mee·ka*

Antarctic n l'Antartide (f) *an·tar·tee·de*

antenna n l'antenna (f) *an·tayn·na*

antibiotic n l'antibiotico (m) *an·tee·bee·o·tee·koh*

antifreeze n l'anticongelante (m) *an·tee·kon·je·lan·te*

antihistamine n l'antistaminico (m) *an·tee·sta·mee·nee·koh*

antique n l'oggetto d'antiquariato (m) *oj·jet·toh dan·tee·kwa·ree·ah·toh* S84

antique dealer n l'antiquario (m) *an·tee·kwah·ryoh*

antiseptic n l'antisettico (m) *an·tee·set·tee·koh*

any adj □ give me any book mi dia qualsiasi libro *mee dee·a kwal·see·a·see lee·broh*; we haven't any bread non abbiamo pane *nohn ab·byah·mo pah·ne*; have you any bread? ha del pane? *a del pah·ne*; is there any more soup? c'è ancora minestra? *che an·koh·ra mee·ne·stra* □ **pron** we haven't any non ne abbiamo *nohn nay ab·byah·mo*; can any of you sing? qualcuno di voi sa cantare? *kwal·koo·no dee voy sa kan·tah·ray*

anybody, anyone pron □ can you see anybody? può vedere qualcuno? *pwo ve·day·re kwal·koo·no*; I can't see anybody non vedo nessuno *nohn vay·do nes·soo·no*; anybody at all chiunque *kee·oon·kwe*

anything pron □ can you see anything? può vedere qualcosa? *pwo ve·day·re kwal·ko·sa*; I can't see anything non vedo niente *nohn vay·do nyen·te*; anything at all qualunque cosa *kwa·loon·kwe ko·sa*

anyway adv (none the less) tuttavia *toot·ta·vee·a*

anywhere adv □ I'll take you anywhere you like la porterò dovunque voglia *la por·te·ro do·voon·kwe vol·ya*; I can't see it anywhere non lo vedo in nessun luogo *nohn lo vay·do een nes·soon lwo·goh*

apart adv (separately) a parte *a par·te*

apartment n l'appartamento (m) *ap·par·ta·mayn·toh*

ape n la scimmia *sheem·mya*

aperitif n l'aperitivo (m) *a·pe·ree·tee·voh*

apologize vi scusarsi *skoo·zar·see*

apparently adv apparentemente *ap·pa·ren·te·mayn·te*

appear vi apparire* *ap·pa·ree·re*; he appears to be ill sembra malato *saym·bra ma·lah·to*; it appears that... pare che... *pah·re ke*

appendicitis n l'appendicite (f) *ap·pen·dee·chee·te*

appetite n l'appetito (m) *ap·pe·tee·toh*

appetizer n qualcosa che stimola l'appetito *kwal·ko·sa ke stee·mo·la lap·pe·tee·toh*

applause n gli applausi *ap·plow·zee*

apple n la mela *may·la*

apple tree n il melo *may·loh*

appliance n l'apparecchio (m) *ap·pa·rayk·kyoh*

application n (for job) la domanda *do·man·da*

apply vi □ to apply for a job presentare una domanda d'impiego *pre·zen·tah·ray oo·na do·man·da deem·pye·goh*

appoint vt nominare *no·mee·nah·ray*

appointment n (rendezvous) l'appuntamento (m) *ap·poon·ta·mayn·toh*; (to job) la nomina *no·mee·na* Sn35, Bm9

appreciate vt apprezzare *ap·prets·tsah·*

ray □ vi (in value) aumentare di valore *ow·men·tah·ray de va·loh·re*

apprentice n l'apprendista (m/f) *ap·pren·dee·sta*

approach n l'avvicinarsi *av·vee·chee·nar·see* □ vt to approach a place avvicinarsi ad un luogo *av·vee·chee·nar·see ad oon lwo·goh*

approval n l'approvazione (f) *ap·pro·vah·tsyoh·ne*; on approval in prova *een pro·va*

approve of vt approvare *ap·pro·vah·ray*

approximate adj approssimativo(a) *ap·pros·see·ma·tee·vo(a)*

apricot n l'albicocca (f) *al·bee·kok·ka*

April n aprile (m) *a·pree·le*

apron n il grembiule *grem·byoo·le*

aquarium n l'acquario (m) *ak·kwah·ryoh*

Arab n l'arabo(a) (m/f) *a·ra·bo(a)*

Arabic adj arabo(a) *a·ra·bo(a)* □ n l'arabo (m) *a·ra·bo*

arcade n la galleria *gal·le·ree·a*

arch n l'arco (m) *ar·koh*

architect n l'architetto (m) *ar·kee·tayt·toh*

architecture n l'architettura (f) *ar·kee·tet·too·ra*

Arctic n l'Artico (m) *ar·tee·koh*

are vi □ we are siamo *syah·mo*; you are siete *sye·te*; they are sono *soh·no*

area n (of surface) l'area (f) *ah·re·a*; (region) la regione *re·joh·ne*

Argentina n Argentina (f) *ar·jen·tee·na*

Argentine adj argentino(a) *ar·jen·tee·no(a)*

argue vi (quarrel) litigare *lee·tee·gah·ray*

argument n (quarrel) la lite *lee·te*

arithmetic n l'aritmetica (f) *a·reet·me·tee·ka*

arm n (of person) il braccio *brach·choh* 122

armchair n la poltrona *pol·troh·na*

arms pl le armi *ar·mee*

army n l'esercito (m) *e·zer·chee·toh*

around adv □ to look around guardarsi intorno *gwar·dar·see een·tohr·no*; things lying around cose sparse da tutte le parti *ko·se spar·se da toot·te le par·tee* □ prep to go around the world andare* intorno al mondo *an·dah·ray een·tohr·no al mohn·doh*; around $10 circa $10 *cheer·ka $10*

arrange vt (flowers, furniture) disporre* *dee·spohr·re*; (meeting) fissare *fees·sah·ray*

arrears pl gli arretrati *ar·re·trah·tee*; to be in arrears with a payment essere* in arretrato con un pagamento *es·se·re een ar·re·trah·to kohn oon pa·ga·mayn·toh*

arrest vt arrestare *ar·re·stah·ray*

arrival n l'arrivo (m) *ar·ree·voh*

arrive vi arrivare *ar·ree·vah·ray*

arrow n la freccia *fraych·cha*

art n l'arte (f) *ar·te*

artery n l'arteria (f) *ar·te·ree·a*

art gallery n la galleria d'arte *gal·le·ree·a dar·te*

arthritis n l'artrite (f) *ar·tree·te*

artichoke n il carciofo *kar·cho·foh*; Jerusalem artichoke il topinambur *to·pee·nam·boor*

article n l'articolo (m) *ar·tee·ko·loh*

artificial adj artificiale *ar·tee·fee·chah·le*

artist n l'artista (m/f) *ar·tee·sta*

as conj □ as he was asleep (because)

poiché dormiva *poy·kay dor·mee·va*; (*while*) mentre dormiva *mayn·tre dor·mee·va*; **he arrived as we left** è arrivato mentre stavamo partendo *e ar·ree·vah·to mayn·tre sta·vah·mo par·ten·do*; **do as I say** faccia come le dico io *fach·cha koh·me le dee·ko ee·o*; **as big as** così grande come *ko·see gran·de koh·me*; **as for** this quanto a questo *kwan·to a kway·sto*; **as if, as though** come se *koh·me say*; **as well** (*too*) anche *an·ke*; **as much as** tanto(a) quanto(a) *tan·to(a) kwan·to(a)*

asbestos *n* l'amianto (*m*) *a·myan·toh*

ash *n* (*tree*) il frassino *fras·see·noh*; (*cinders*) la cenere *chay·ne·re*

ashamed *adj* □ **to be ashamed** (**of**) vergognarsi (di) *ver·gon·yar·see (dee)*

ashcan *n* il bidone *bee·doh·ne*

ashore *adv* a terra *a ter·ra*

ashtray *n* il portacenere *por·ta·chay·ne·re* A41

Asia *n* Asia (*f*) *ah·zee·a*

Asian *adj* asiatico(a) *a·zee·a·tee·ko(a)*

ask *vt/i* domandare *do·man·dah·ray*; **to ask a question** fare* una domanda *fah·ray oo·na do·man·da*; **to ask someone the time** chiedere* l'ora a qualcuno *kyay·de·re loh·ra a kwal·koo·no*; **to ask for something** chiedere* qualcosa *kyay·de·re kwal·ko·sa*

asleep *adj* addormentato(a) *ad·dor·men·tah·to(a)*

asparagus *n* l'asparago (*m*) *a·spa·ra·goh*

aspirin *n* l'aspirina (*f*) *a·spee·ree·na*

assemble *vt* (*parts of machine*) montare *mon·tah·ray*

assembly line *n* la catena di montaggio *ka·tay·na dee mon·taj·joh*

asset *n* (*financial*) l'attivo (*m*) *at·tee·voh*

assistant *n* (*in shop*) il/la commesso(a) *kom·mays·so(a)* Bm7

associate *n* il/la socio(a) *so·cho(a)*

association *n* l'associazione (*f*) *as·so·chya·tsyoh·ne*

assorted *adj* assortito(a) *as·sor·tee·to(a)*

assume *vt* (*suppose*) supporre* *soop·pohr·re*

asthma *n* l'asma (*f*) *az·ma*

at *prep* □ **at 4 o'clock** alle 4 *al·le 4*; **at my house** a casa mia *a kah·sa mee·a*; **to throw something at someone** gettare qualcosa a qualcuno *jet·tah·ray kwal·ko·sa a kwal·koo·no*; **not at all** affatto *af·fat·to*; **at once** subito *soo·bee·to*

Athens *n* Atene (*f*) *a·te·ne*

athlete *n* l'atleta (*m/f*) *at·le·ta*

Atlantic Ocean *n* l'Atlantico (*m*) *at·lan·tee·ko*

atlas *n* l'atlante (*m*) *at·lan·te*

attach *vt* attaccare *at·tak·kah·ray*

attack *vt* attaccare *at·tak·kah·ray* □ *n* l'attacco (*m*) *at·tak·koh*

attempt *vt* tentare *ten·tah·ray* □ *n* il tentativo *ten·ta·tee·voh*

attend *vt* (*meeting etc*) assistere* a *as·see·ste·re a*

attic *n* la soffitta *sof·feet·ta*

attitude *n* l'atteggiamento (*m*) *at·tej·ja·mayn·toh*

attorney *n* l'avvocato (*m*) *av·vo·kah·toh*

aubergine *n* la melanzana *me·lan·dzah·na*

auction *n* la vendita all'asta *vayn·dee·ta al·la·sta*

audience *n* (*in theater*) il pubblico *poob·blee·koh*

audio-guide *n* l'audioguida (*f*) *ow·dyo·gwee·da* L3

audio-visual *adj* audiovisivo(a) *ow·dyo·vee·zee·vo(a)*

audit *vt* verificare *ve·ree·fee·kah·ray*

auditor *n* il revisore dei conti *re·vee·zoh·re de·ee kohn·tee*

auditorium *n* la sala *sah·la*

au gratin *adj* au gratin *ō gra·tañ*

August *n* agosto (*m*) *a·goh·sto*

aunt(ie) *n* la zia *tsee·a*

Australia *n* Australia (*f*) *ow·strah·lya*

Australian *adj* australiano(a) *ow·stra·lyah·no(a)*

Austria *n* Austria (*f*) *ow·strya*

Austrian *adj* austriaco(a) *ow·stree·a·ko(a)*

author *n* l'autore (*m*) *ow·toh·re*

automatic *adj* automatico(a) *ow·to·ma·tee·ko(a)* □ *n* (*car*) la macchina automatica *mak·kee·na ow·to·ma·tee·ka*

automatically *adv* automaticamente *ow·to·ma·tee·ka·mayn·te*

automation *n* l'automazione (*f*) *ow·to·ma·tsyoh·ne*

auto(mobile) *n* la macchina *mak·kee·na*

auto show *n* il salone dell'automobile *sa·loh·nay del·low·to·mo·bee·lay*

autumn *n* l'autunno (*m*) *ow·toon·noh*

available *adj* disponibile *dee·spo·nee·bee·le*

avalanche *n* la valanga *va·lan·ga*

avenue *n* il viale *vyah·le*

average *adj* medio(a) *me·dyo(a)* □ *n* la media *me·dya*

aviation *n* l'aviazione (*f*) *a·vya·tsyoh·ne*

avocado *n* l'avocado (*m*) *a·vo·kah·doh*

avoid *vt* evitare *e·vee·tah·ray*

away *adv* □ **away from home** fuori di casa *fwo·ree dee kah·sa*; **he's away for a week** è partito per una settimana *e par·tee·to payr oo·na set·tee·mah·na*; **30 kilometers away** a 30 chilometri *a 30 kee·lo·me·tree*

awful *adj* terribile *ter·ree·bee·le*

ax *n* la scure *skoo·re*

axle *n* l'asse (*m*) *as·se*

B

baby *n* il/la bambino(a) *bam·bee·no(a)* C18

baby buggy, baby carriage *n* la carrozzina per bambini *kar·rots·tsee·na payr bam·bee·nee*

baby-sit *vi* fare* da babysitter *fah·ray da bay·bee·see·ter* C4

baby-sitter *n* la babysitter *bay·bee·see·ter*

baccarat *n* il baccarà *bak·ka·ra*

bachelor *n* lo scapolo *skah·po·loh*

back *n* (*of person*) la schiena *skye·na*; (*of animal*) la groppa *grop·pa*; (*of chair*) lo schienale *skye·nah·le*; (*reverse side*) il rovescio *ro·ve·shoh*; (*of hall, room*) il fondo *fohn·doh*; (*in sports*) il terzino *ter·tsee·noh* □ *adv* (*backwards*) indietro *een·dye·tro*; **to come/go back** tornare *tor·nah·ray* □ *vt* **back** (*support*) assecondare *as·se·kon·dah·ray*; (*financially*) finanziare *fee·nan·tsyah·ray*; (*bet on*) puntare su *poon·tah·ray soo*; **to back the car** fare* marcia indietro *fah·ray mar·cha een·dye·tro*

backache *n* il mal di schiena *mal dee skye·na*

backdate vt (letter) retrodatare re·tro·da·tah·ray

backer n il finanziatore fee·nan·tsya·toh·re

backgammon n la tavola reale tah·vo·la re·ah·le

background n lo sfondo sfohn·doh

backing n il sostegno so·stayn·yoh

backlash n la reazione re·a·tsyoh·ne

backlog n □ backlog of work il lavoro accumulato la·voh·roh ak·koo·moo·lah·to

back pack n lo zaino dzy·noh

backward adj (glance) indietro een·dye·tro; (child) tardivo(a) tar·dee·vo(a)

backwards adv indietro een·dye·tro

bacon n la pancetta pan·chayt·ta

bad adj cattivo(a) kat·tee·vo(a); to go bad (food) guastarsi gwa·star·see; a bad debt un debito insolvibile oon day·bee·toh een·sol·vee·bee·le

badge n il distintivo dee·steen·tee·voh

badly adv (not well) male mah·le; to want something badly desiderare molto qualcosa de·see·de·rah·ray mohl·to kwal·ko·sa

badminton n il volano vo·lah·noh

bag n (of paper) il sacchetto sak·kayt·toh; (paper carrier) il sacco sak·koh; (handbag) la borsa bohr·sa; bags (luggage) i bagagli ba·gal·yee B69, T21f, 78, S25

baggage n i bagagli ba·gal·yee T22

baggage car n il bagagliaio ba·gal·ya·yoh

baggage check n lo scontrino per i bagagli skon·tree·noh payr ee ba·gal·yee

baggage checkroom n il deposito bagagli de·po·zee·toh ba·gal·yee T24, 32

baggage claim n il recapito dei bagagli re·ka·pee·toh de·ee ba·gal·yee

baggage room n il deposito bagagli de·po·zee·toh ba·gal·yee

bail n (for prisoner) la cauzione kow·tsyoh·ne; on bail su cauzione soo kow·tsyoh·ne

bait n (in fishing) l'esca (f) ay·ska

bake vt cuocere* al forno kwo·che·re al fohr·noh

baker n il fornaio for·na·yoh S29

bakery n il panificio pa·nee·fee·choh

balance n l'equilibrio (m) e·kwee·lee·bree·oh; (remainder owed) il saldo sal·doh; balance of power l'equilibrio politico (m) e·kwee·lee·bree·oh po·lee·tee·ko; balance of payments la bilancia dei pagamenti bee·lan·cha de·ee pa·ga·mayn·tee; balance of trade la bilancia commerciale bee·lan·cha kom·mer·chah·le; to lose one's balance perdere* l'equilibrio per·de·re le·kwee·lee·bree·oh □ vt balance bilanciare bee·lan·chah·ray; (accounts) pareggiare pa·rej·jah·ray □ vi pareggiare pa·rej·jah·ray

balance sheet n il bilancio bee·lan·choh

balcony n il balcone bal·koh·ne

bald adj calvo(a) kal·vo(a)

ball n la palla pal·la; (inflated) il pallone pal·loh·ne; (of string, wool) il gomitolo go·mee·to·loh; (dance) il ballo bal·loh

ballet n il balletto bal·layt·toh

balloon n il pallone pal·loh·ne

ballot n lo scrutinio skroo·tee·nyoh

bamboo n il bambù bam·boo

ban vt proibire pro·ee·bee·re □ n la proibizione pro·ee·bee·tsyoh·ne

banana n la banana ba·nah·na

band n (musical) la banda ban·da

bandage n la benda ben·da

bandaid n il cerotto che·rot·toh

bang n (of gun etc) il colpo kohl·poh; (of door) lo sbattere zbat·te·re; (blow) il colpo kohl·poh □ vt (door) sbattere zbat·te·re; to bang one's head battersi la testa bat·ter·see la te·sta □ vi bang (gun etc) esplodere* e·splo·de·re

bangs pl la frangia fran·jah

bank n (of river, lake) la riva ree·va; (finance) la banca ban·ka □ vt (money) depositare de·po·zee·tah·ray □ vi to bank with Smiths avere* un conto con Smiths a·vay·re oon kohn·toh kohn Smiths M28

bank account n il conto bancario kohn·toh ban·kah·ryo M29

bank balance n il saldo bancario sal·doh ban·kah·ryo

bank bill n la tratta trat·ta

bankbook n il libretto di banca lee·brayt·toh de ban·ka

bank charges pl le spese bancarie spay·se ban·kah·rye

banker n il banchiere ban·kye·re

bank loan n il prestito bancario pre·stee·toh ban·kah·ryo

bank manager n il direttore di banca dee·ret·toh·re de ban·ka M31

bank note n la banconota ban·ko·no·ta

bankrupt adj fallito(a) fal·lee·to(a); to go bankrupt fare* fallimento fah·ray fal·lee·mayn·toh

bankruptcy n la bancarotta ban·ka·roht·ta

banner n la bandiera ban·dye·ra

banquet n il banchetto ban·kayt·toh

baptism n il battesimo bat·tay·zee·moh

Baptist adj battista bat·tee·sta

bar n (metal) la sbarra zbar·ra; (counter) il banco ban·koh; (drinking establishment) il bar; bar of soap la saponetta sa·po·nayt·ta; bar of chocolate la tavoletta di cioccolata tah·vo·layt·ta dee chok·ko·lah·ta E54, L51

barbecue n il barbecue bar·bee·kyoo

barbed wire n il filo di ferro spinato fee·loh dee fer·roh spee·nah·to

barber n il barbiere bar·bye·re

bare adj (person, head) nudo(a) noo·do(a); to go barefoot andare* a piedi scalzi an·dah·ray a pye·dee skal·tsee

bargain n (cheap buy) l'occasione (f) ok·ka·zyoh·ne; to make a bargain concludere* un affare kon·kloo·de·re oon af·fah·re

bargaining n (negotiation) la contrattazione kon·trat·ta·tsyoh·ne

barge n la chiatta kyat·ta

bark n (of tree) la corteccia kor·taych·cha; (of dog) il latrato la·trah·toh □ vi abbaiare ab·ba·yah·ray

barmaid n la cameriera al banco ka·me·rye·ra al ban·koh

barman n il barista ba·ree·sta

barn n il granaio gra·na·yoh

barracks pl la caserma ka·ser·ma

barrel n (for beer) il barile ba·ree·le

barrier n (fence) la barriera bar·rye·ra

bartender n il barista ba·ree·sta

base n la base bah·ze □ vt basare ba·zah·ray

baseball n il baseball bays·bol

basement n il seminterrato se·meen·ter·rah·toh

basic adj di base dee bah·ze

basically *adv* fondamentalmente *fon·da·mayn·tal·mayn·te*

basin *n* (*dish*) la scodella *sko·del·la*; (*for washing*) il lavabo *la·vah·boh*

basis *n* la base *bah·ze*

basket *n* il canestro *ka·ne·stroh*

basketball *n* la pallacanestro *pal·la·ka·ne·stroh*

bat *n* (*animal*) il pipistrello *pee·pee·strel·loh*

bath *n* il bagno *ban·yoh*; (*tub*) la vasca da bagno *va·ska da ban·yoh* A4

bathe *vi* bagnarsi *ban·yar·see* □ *vt* (*wound etc*) bagnare *ban·yah·ray*

bathing cap *n* la cuffia da bagno *koof·fya da ban·yoh*

bathing suit *n* il costume da bagno *ko·stoo·me da ban·yoh*

bathroom *n* la stanza da bagno *stan·tsa da ban·yoh*; (*lavatory*) il bagno *ban·yoh* A17

batter *n* (*for frying*) la pastella *pa·stel·la*

battery *n* (*for radio etc*) la pila *pee·la*; (*in car*) la batteria *bat·te·ree·a* T177

battle *n* la battaglia *bat·tal·ya*

bay *n* (*on coast*) la baia *ba·ya*

bazaar *n* il bazar *ba·dzar*

be *vi* essere* *es·se·re*; I am sono *soh·no*; you are è *e*; he is è *e*; we are siamo *syah·mo*; they are sono *soh·no*; how are you? come sta? *koh·me sta*; I am hungry ho fame *o fah·me*; what is that? che cosa è quello? *ke ko·sa e kwayl·lo*; how much is it? quanto costa? *kwan·to ko·sta*; it is hot fa caldo *fa kal·do*; we are going to the beach andiamo alla spiaggia *an·dyah·mo al·la spyaj·ja*; we have been to Paris siamo andati a Parigi *syah·mo an·dah·tee a pa·ree·jee*; he is a doctor è medico *e me·dee·koh*

beach *n* la spiaggia *spyaj·ja* L27

bead *n* la perlina *per·lee·na*

beam *n* (*of wood*) la trave *trah·ve*; (*of light*) il raggio *raj·joh*

beans *pl* i fagioli *fa·jo·lee*

bear *n* l'orso (*m*) *ohr·soh* □ *vt* (*weight*) sorreggere* *sor·rej·je·re*; (*endure*) sopportare *sop·por·tah·ray*

beard *n* la barba *bar·ba*

bearings *pl* (*in car*) i cuscinetti *koo·shee·nayt·tee*; to take one's bearings orientarsi *o·ree·en·tar·see*

beat *vt* (*hit*) colpire *kol·pee·re*; (*defeat*) battere *bat·te·re* □ *vi* (*heart*) battere *bat·te·re*

beautiful *adj* bello(a) *bel·lo(a)*

beauty *n* la bellezza *bel·layts·tsa*

because *conj* perché *payr·kay*; because of a causa di *a kow·za dee*

become *vi* diventare *dee·ven·tah·ray*

bed *n* il letto *let·toh*; in bed a letto *a let·toh*; to go to bed andare* a letto *an·dah·ray a let·toh* A4, I50

bedclothes *pl* le coperte *ko·per·te*

bedding *n* la biancheria da letto *byan·ke·ree·a da let·toh* A68

bedroom *n* la camera *kah·me·ra*

bee *n* l'ape (*f*) *ah·pe*

beech *n* il faggio *faj·joh*

beef *n* la carne di manzo *kar·ne dee man·dzoh*

beer *n* la birra *beer·ra* E55

beet *n* la barbabietola *bar·ba·bye·to·la*

beetle *n* lo scarafaggio *ska·ra·faj·joh*

before *prep* (*in time*) prima di *pree·ma dee*; before noon prima di mezzogiorno *pree·ma dee medz·dzo·johr·noh*; before the king (*in space*) davanti al re *da·van·tee al ray* □ *adv* be-

fore prima *pree·ma*; we've met before ci siamo già conosciuti *chee syah·mo ja ko·no·shoo·tee* □ *conj* before (*time*) che *pree·ma ke*; before I go to bed prima che io vada a letto *pree·ma ke ee·oh vah·da a let·toh*

beg *vt* mendicare *men·dee·kah·ray*

beggar *n* il/la mendicante *men·dee·kan·te*

begin *vt/i* cominciare *ko·meen·chah·ray*

beginner *n* il/la principiante *preen·chee·pyan·te*

behalf *n* □ on behalf of a nome di *a noh·me dee*

behave *vi* comportarsi *kom·por·tar·see*; behave yourself! comportati bene! *kom·por·ta·tee be·ne*

behavior *n* il comportamento *kom·por·ta·mayn·toh*

behind *adv, prep* dietro *dye·tro*; to look behind guardare indietro *gwar·dah·ray een·dye·tro*; to be behind schedule essere* in ritardo *es·se·re een ree·tar·doh*

beige *adj* beige *bayzh*

belief *n* (*faith*) la fede *fay·de*; (*tenet*) la credenza *kre·den·tsa*

believe *vt/i* credere *kray·de·re*; to believe in credere a *kray·de·re a*

bell *n* la campana *kam·pah·na*; (*electric*) il campanello *kam·pa·nel·loh*

bellboy *n* il fattorino d'albergo *fat·to·ree·noh dal·ber·goh*

belong *vi* □ to belong to someone appartenere* a qualcuno *ap·par·te·nay·re a kwal·koo·no*; to belong to a club essere* membro di un club *es·se·re mem·broh dee oon kloob*

belongings *pl* gli effetti personali *ef·fet·tee per·so·nah·lee*

below *adv, prep* sotto *soht·to*

belt *n* (*for waist*) la cintura *cheen·too·ra* S78

beltway *n* la circonvallazione *cheer·kon·val·la·tsyoh·nay*

bench *n* (*seat*) la panca *pan·ka*; (*work table*) il banco *ban·koh*

bend *n* la curva *koor·va* □ *vt* piegare *pye·gah·ray* □ *vi* (*person*) chinarsi *kee·nar·see*; (*road*) curvare *koor·vah·ray* T206

beneath = below

benefit *n* il vantaggio *van·taj·joh*; it's of no benefit (to us) non ci serve *nohn chee ser·ve*

Benelux *n* Benelux (*m*) *be·ne·looks*

berm *n* la corsia di emergenza *kor·see·a dee e·mer·jen·tsa*

berry *n* la bacca *bak·ka*

berth *n* la cuccetta *kooch·chayt·ta*

beside *prep* accanto a *ak·kan·to a*

besides *adv* (*moreover*) inoltre *een·ohl·tre* □ *prep* besides him oltre a lui *ohl·tre a loo·ee*

best *adj* il/la migliore *eel/la meel·yoh·re* □ *n* he's the best è il migliore *e eel meel·yoh·re* □ *adv* he can do it best lo fa meglio lui *lo fa mel·yo loo·ee*

best man *n* il testimone dello sposo *te·stee·mo·ne del·lo spo·zoh*

bet *vt/i* scommettere* *skom·mayt·te·re* □ *n* la scommessa *skom·mays·sa*

better *adj* migliore *meel·yoh·re* □ *adv* he sings better than you canta meglio di te *kan·ta mel·yo dee te*; to get better (*from illness*) migliorare *meel·yo·rah·ray*; they are better off than us (*richer*) sono più ricchi di noi *soh·no pyoo reek·kee dee noy*

between *prep* tra *tra*

beyond prep oltre *ohl·tre*; beyond my reach fuori la mia portata *fwo·ree la mee·a por·tah·ta*; beyond his means fuori la sua portata *fwo·ree la soo·a por·tah·ta*

Bible n la Bibbia *beeb·bya*

bicycle n la bicicletta *bee·chee·klayt·ta*

bid vt (amount) offrire* *of·free·re* □ vi to bid for something fare* un'offerta per qualcosa *fah·ray oo·nof·fer·ta payr kwal·ko·sa* □ n bid l'offerta (f) *of·fer·ta*

bidder n l'offerente (m/f) *of·fe·ren·te*

big adj (person, house) grande *gran·de*; (sum of money) grosso(a) *gros·so(a)*

bikini n il bikini *bee·kee·nee*

bilingual adj bilingue *bee·leen·gwe*

bill n (account) il conto *kohn·toh*; (bank note) la banconota *ban·ko·no·ta* T189, M22, A21, E42

billiards n il biliardo *bee·lyar·doh*

billion n il miliardo *mee·lyar·doh*

bin n (for refuse) la pattumiera *pat·too·mye·ra*

bind vt (tie) legare *le·gah·ray*

binoculars pl n il binocolo *bee·no·ko·loh*

biology n la biologia *bee·o·lo·jee·a*

birch n (tree) la betulla *be·tool·la*

bird n l'uccello (m) *ooch·chel·loh* L41

birth n la nascita *na·shee·ta*

birth certificate n l'atto di nascita (m) *at·toh dee na·shee·ta*

birthday n il compleanno *kom·ple·an·noh*

biscuit n (sweet) il biscotto *bee·skot·toh*; (savory) il cracker *krak·ker*

bishop n il vescovo *vay·sko·voh*

bit n (piece) il pezzo *pets·tsoh*; a bit of un pezzo di *oon pets·tsoh dee*

bite vt mordere* *mor·de·re* □ n (by animal) il morso *mor·soh*; (by insect) la puntura *poon·too·ra*; (of food) il boccone *bok·koh·ne*

bitter adj amaro(a) *a·mah·ro(a)*

black adj nero(a) *nay·ro(a)*; a black coffee un caffè nero *oon kaf·fe nay·ro*

blackberry n la mora *mo·ra*

blackbird n il merlo *mer·loh*

black currant n il ribes *ree·bes*

black eye n l'occhio nero (m) *ok·kyoh nay·ro*

blackjack n il gioco del ventuno *jo·koh del ven·too·no*

black market n la borsa nera *bohr·sa nay·ra*

bladder n la vescica *ve·shee·ka*

blade n (of knife) la lama *lah·ma*

blame vt (reproach) incolpare *een·kol·pah·ray*; to be to blame essere* colpevole *es·se·re kol·pay·vo·le*

blank adj in bianco *een byan·ko*; blank check l'assegno in bianco (m) *as·sayn·yoh een byan·ko*; please leave blank lasciate in bianco per favore *la·shah·te een byan·ko payr fa·voh·re*

blanket n la coperta *ko·per·ta* A41

blast n (explosion) lo scoppio *skop·pyoh*

blaze n (fire) l'incendio (m) *een·chen·dyoh* □ vi ardere* *ar·de·re*; (lights) risplendere *ree·splen·de·re*

blazer n la giacca sportiva *jak·ka spor·tee·va*

bleed vi sanguinare *san·gwee·nah·ray*

blend vt mescolare *me·sko·lah·ray* □ n la miscela *mee·she·la*

bless vt benedire* *be·ne·dee·re*

blind adj (person) cieco(a) *che·ko(a)*

□ n (at window) la tendina *ten·dee·na*

blind alley n il vicolo cieco *vee·ko·loh che·ko*

blind corner n la curva senza visibilità *koor·va sen·tsa vee·zee·bee·lee·ta*

blink vi battere le palpebre *bat·te·re le pal·pe·bre*

blister n (on skin) la vescichetta *ve·shee·kayt·ta*

blizzard n la bufera di neve *boo·fe·ra dee nay·ve*

block n (of stone) il blocco *blok·koh*; 3 blocks away (streets) alla terza strada *al·la ter·tsa strah·da*; apartment block il casamento *ka·sa·mayn·toh* □ vt block bloccare *blok·kah·ray*; block letters lo stampatello *stam·pa·tel·loh*; block booking la prenotazione a gruppo *pre·no·ta·tsyoh·ne a groop·poh*

blockage n l'ostruzione (f) *o·stroo·tsyoh·ne*

blond(e) adj biondo(a) *byohn·do(a)*

blood n il sangue *san·gwe*

blood group n il gruppo sanguigno *groop·poh san·gween·yo* 148, 49

blood poisoning n la setticemia *set·tee·che·mee·a*

blood pressure n la pressione sanguigna *pres·syoh·ne san·gween·ya* 142

bloom n (flower) il fiore *fyoh·re* □ vi fiorire *fyo·ree·re*

blossom n i fiori *fyoh·ree*

blot n la macchia *mak·kya* □ vt (ink) asciugare *a·shoo·gah·ray*

blouse n la camicetta *ka·mee·chayt·ta* S19

blow n (knock) il colpo *kohl·poh* □ vi (wind) soffiare *sof·fyah·ray*; (fuse) saltare *sal·tah·ray* □ vt to blow one's nose soffiarsi il naso *sof·fyar·see eel nah·soh*

blow-dry n l'asciugatura con fon (f) *a·shoo·ga·too·ra kohn eel fon*

blow-out n la foratura *fo·ra·too·ra*

blue adj azzurro(a) *adz·dzoor·ro(a)*

bluebottle n il moscone *mos·koh·ne*

blue chips pl i valori di prima classe *va·loh·ree dee pree·ma klas·se*

blueprint n il progetto *pro·jet·toh*

blunt adj (knife) smussato(a) *zmoos·sah·to(a)*

blush vi arrossire *ar·ros·see·re*

board n (of wood) l'asse (f) *as·se*; (for notices) il tabellone *ta·bel·loh·ne*; (of directors) il consiglio d'amministrazione *kon·seel·yoh dam·mee·nee·stra·tsyoh·ne*; on board (ship, plane) a bordo a *bor·doh* □ vt board (train, bus) salire* su *sa·lee·re soo*; (ship) salire* a bordo di *sa·lee·re a bohr·doh dee*

boarding house n la pensione *pen·syoh·ne*

boarding pass n la carta d'imbarco *kar·ta deem·bar·koh*

boast vi vantarsi *van·tar·see*

boat n la barca *bar·ka* L29

bobby pin n la forcina *for·chee·na*

body n il corpo *kor·poh*; (corpse) il cadavere *ka·dah·ve·re*

bodyguard n (person) la guardia del corpo *gwar·dya del kor·poh*

bog n la palude *pa·loo·de*

boil vi bollire *bol·lee·re* □ vt (water) fare* bollire *fah·ray bol·lee·re* □ n (on skin) il foruncolo *fo·roon·ko·loh*

bold adj audace *ow·dah·che*

bolster n il capezzale *ka·pets·tsah·le*

bolt n il chiavistello *kya·vee·stel·loh*

□ *vt* (*door*, *gate*) chiudere* a chiavistello *kyoo·de·re a kya·vee·stel·loh*

bomb *n* la bomba *bohm·ba*

bone *n* l'osso (*m*) *os·soh*; (*of fish*) la spina *spee·na*

bonfire *n* il falò *fa·lo*

bonus *n* (*on salary*) il premio *pre·myoh*

book *n* il libro *lee·broh* □ *vt* (*seat*) prenotare *pre·no·tah·ray*

boom *n* (*noise*) il rombo *rohm·boh*; (*economic*) il boom *boom* □ *vi* business is booming gli affari vanno a gonfie vele *lyee af·fah·ree van·no a gohn·fye vay·le*

boost *vt* (*sales*) aumentare *ow·men·tah·ray*

boot *n* lo stivale *stee·vah·le*

booth *n* (*telephone*) la cabina *ka·bee·na*

border *n* (*edge*) il bordo *bohr·doh*; (*of country*) la frontiera *fron·tye·ra*

bored *adj* stufo(a) *stoo·fo(a)*

boring *adj* noioso(a) *no·yoh·so(a)*

born *adj* nato(a) *nah·to(a)*; to be born nascere* *na·she·re*

borough *n* il borgo *bohr·goh*

borrow *vt* prendere* in prestito *pren·de·re een pre·stee·toh*; to borrow something from someone prendere* qualcosa in prestito da qualcuno *pren·de·re kwal·ko·sa een pre·stee·toh da kwal·koo·no*

boss *n* il capo *kah·poh*

botanical gardens *pl* il giardino botanico *jar·dee·noh bo·ta·nee·ko*

both *adj* ambedue *am·be·doo·e*; both girls tutte e due le ragazze *toot·te e doo·e le ra·gats·tse* □ **pron** both (of them) tutti(e) e due *toot·tee(·te) e doo·e*

bother *vt* (*annoy*) seccare *sek·kah·ray* □ *vi* please don't bother non si disturbi per favore *nohn see dee·stoor·bee payr fa·voh·re* □ *n* bother (*nuisance*) la seccatura *sek·ka·too·ra*; (*effort*) il fastidio *fa·stee·dyoh*

bottle *n* la bottiglia *bot·teel·ya*; (*baby's*) il biberon *bee·be·ron* E11, C2

bottleneck *n* l'ingorgo (*m*) *een·gohr·goh*

bottle opener *n* l'apribottiglie (*m*) *ah·pree·bot·teel·ye*

bottom *n* il fondo *fohn·doh*; (*of page*, *list*) il piede *pye·de*; (*of person*) il sedere *se·day·re* □ *adj* inferiore *een·fe·ryoh·re*

bounce *vi* (*ball*) rimbalzare *reem·bal·tsah·ray*

bound *adj* □ bound for (*ship*) con destinazione per *kohn de·stee·na·tsyoh·ne payr* □ *n* out of bounds oltre i limiti *ohl·tre ee lee·mee·tee*

boundary *n* il limite *lee·mee·te*

bourbon *n* il whisky americano *wee·skee a·me·ree·kah·no*

boutique *n* la boutique *boo·teek*

bow[1] *vi* inchinarsi *een·kee·nar·see* □ *n* l'inchino (*m*) *een·kee·noh*

bow[2] *n* (*ribbon*) il nodo *no·doh*

bowl *n* (*for food*) la scodella *sko·del·la*; (*for washing*) la bacinella *ba·chee·nel·la*

bow tie *n* la cravatta a farfalla *kra·vat·ta a far·fal·la*

box *n* la scatola *skah·to·la*

boxing *n* il pugilato *poo·jee·lah·toh*

box number *n* la casella postale *ka·sel·la po·stah·le*

box office *n* il botteghino *bot·te·gee·noh*

boy *n* il ragazzo *ra·gats·tsoh*

boycott *vt* boicottare *boy·kot·tah·ray*

boyfriend *n* il ragazzo *ra·gats·tsoh*

bra *n* il reggiseno *rej·jee·say·noh*

bracelet *n* il braccialetto *brach·cha·layt·toh*

bracken *n* la felce *fayl·che*

bracket *n* (*in writing*) la parentesi *pa·ren·te·zee*

brain *n* il cervello *cher·vel·loh*; **brains** (*as food*) il cervello *cher·vel·loh*

braised *adj* stufato(a) *stoo·fah·to(a)*

brake *n* il freno *fray·noh* □ *vi* frenare *fre·nah·ray* T173, 210

brake fluid *n* il fluido per i freni *floo·ee·doh payr ee fray·nee*

branch *n* (*of tree*) il ramo *rah·moh*; (*of store*, *bank etc*) la succursale *sook·koor·sah·le*

brand *n* (*of product*) la marca *mar·ka* S96

brand name *n* la marca *mar·ka*

brandy *n* il brandy *bran·dee* E56

brass *n* l'ottone (*m*) *ot·toh·ne*

brave *adj* coraggioso(a) *ko·raj·joh·so(a)*

bread *n* il pane *pah·ne* E30

break *n* (*pause*) la pausa *pow·za* □ *vt* rompere* *rohm·pe·re*; (*record*) battere *bat·te·re*; to break in (*car*) rodare *ro·dah·ray*; to break one's arm rompersi* il braccio *rohm·per·see eel brach·choh* □ *vi* break rompersi* *rohm·per·see*; to break down (*car*) guastarsi *gwa·star·see* B65, T164

breakdown *n* (*of car*) l'avaria (*f*) *a·va·ree·a*

break even *vi* pareggiare i costi *pa·rej·jah·ray ee ko·stee*

breakfast *n* la colazione *ko·la·tsyoh·ne* A9, 26

breast *n* il seno *say·noh*; (*chest*, *of poultry*) il petto *pet·toh*

breath *n* il fiato *fyah·toh*

breathe *vi* respirare *re·spee·rah·ray*

breeze *n* la brezza *bredz·dza*

brewery *n* la birreria *beer·re·ree·a*

bribe *vt* corrompere* *kor·rohm·pe·re*

brick *n* il mattone *mat·toh·ne*

bride *n* la sposa *spo·za*

bridegroom *n* lo sposo *spo·zoh*

bridge *n* il ponte *pohn·te*; (*game*) il bridge *breej*

bridle *n* la briglia *breel·ya*

brief *adj* breve *bre·ve*

briefcase *n* la borsa *bohr·sa*

briefs *pl* lo slip *zleep*

bright *adj* chiaro(a) *kyah·ro(a)*; (*clever*) intelligente *een·tel·lee·jen·te*

bring *vt* portare *por·tah·ray*; to bring in (*profit*) produrre* *pro·door·re*

Britain *n* Gran Bretagna (*f*) *gran bre·tan·ya*

British *adj* britannico(a) *bree·tan·nee·ko(a)*

broad *adj* largo(a) *lar·go(a)*

broadcast *vt* trasmettere* *tra·zmayt·te·re* □ *n* la trasmissione *tra·zmees·syoh·ne*

broccoli *n* i broccoli *brok·ko·lee*

brochure *n* l'opuscolo (*m*) *o·poo·sko·loh* A6, Bm22

broil *vt* arrostire alla griglia *ar·ro·stee·re al·la greel·ya*

broke *adj* (*penniless*) squattrinato(a) *skwat·tree·nah·to(a)*

broker *n* l'agente (*m*) *a·jen·te*

bronchitis *n* la bronchite *bron·kee·te*

bronze *n* il bronzo *brohn·dzoh*

brooch n la spilla *speel·la* S85
broom n la scopa *skoh·pa*
brother n il fratello *fra·tel·loh*
brother-in-law n il cognato *kon·yah·toh*
brown adj marrone *mar·roh·ne*; (*hair*) castano(a) *ka·stah·no(a)*
bruise n la contusione *kon·too·zyoh·ne*
brush n (*for cleaning*) la spazzola *spats·tso·la*; (*for painting*) il pennello *pen·nel·loh*; (*for hair*) la spazzola per capelli *spats·tso·la payr ka·payl·lee* □ vt spazzolare *spats·tso·lah·ray*
Brussels n Bruxelles (f) *brook·sel*
Brussels sprouts pl i cavolini di Bruxelles *kah·vo·lee·nee dee brook·sel*
bubble n la bollicina *bol·lee·chee·na*
bucket n il secchio *sayk·kyoh*
buckle n la fibbia *feeb·bya*
bud n il bocciolo *boch·cho·loh*
budget n il bilancio preventivo *bee·lan·choh pre·ven·tee·vo*
bug n (*insect*) la cimice *chee·mee·che*
build vt (*house*) costruire* *ko·stroo·ee·re*
building n l'edificio (m) *e·dee·fee·choh* L11
bulb n il bulbo *bool·boh*; (*light*) la lampadina *lam·pa·dee·na*
bulk n □ in bulk (*in large quantities*) all'ingrosso *al·leen·gros·soh*; (*unpackaged*) sfuso(a) *sfoo·zo(a)*; bulk buying l'acquisto all'ingrosso (m) *ak·kwee·stoh al·leen·gros·soh*
bull n il toro *to·roh*
bulldozer n il bulldozer *bool·do·zer*
bullet n la pallottola *pal·lot·to·la*
bulletin n il bollettino *bol·let·tee·noh*
bulletin board n il tabellone *ta·bel·loh·nay*
bullfight n la corrida *kor·ree·da*
bump n (*knock*) l'urto (m) *oor·toh*; (*lump*) il bernoccolo *ber·nok·ko·loh* □ vt urtare *oor·tah·ray*
bumper n (*on car*) il paraurti *pa·ra·oor·tee*
bun n il panino *pa·nee·noh*
bunch n (*of flowers*) il mazzo *mats·tsoh*
bundle n il fascio *fa·shoh*
bungalow n il bungalow
bunk n la cuccetta *kooch·chayt·ta*; bunk beds il letto a castello *let·toh a ka·stel·loh*
buoy n la boa *bo·a*
buoyant adj (*market*) in rialzo *een ree·al·tsoh*
bureau n (*office*) l'ufficio (m) *oof·fee·choh*
burglar n lo scassinatore *skas·see·na·toh·re*
burn vt bruciare *broo·chah·ray*; I've burned my arm mi sono bruciato il braccio *mee soh·no broo·chah·to eel brach·choh*
burst vi scoppiare *skop·pyah·ray* □ vt fare* scoppiare *fah·ray skop·pyah·ray*
bury vt (*person*) seppellire *sep·pel·lee·re*
bus n l'autobus (m) *ow·to·boos*; (*long distance*) il pullman *pool·man* T87f, F15
bush n il cespuglio *che·spool·yoh*
business n (*dealings, work*) gli affari *af·fah·ree*; (*firm*) la ditta *deet·ta*; on business per affari *payr af·fah·ree*; to do business with someone fare* affari con qualcuno *fah·ray af·fah·ree kohn kwal·koo·no* E6, Bm28
business expenses pl le spese di rap-

presentanza *spay·ze dee rap·pre·zen·tan·tsa*
business hours pl le ore d'ufficio *oh·re doof·fee·choh*
businessman n l'uomo d'affari (m) *wo·moh daf·fah·ree*
business trip n il viaggio d'affari *vyaj·joh daf·fah·ree* Bm11
businesswoman n la donna d'affari *don·na daf·fah·ree*
bus service n il servizio autobus *ser·vee·tsyoh ow·to·boos*
bus stop n la fermata autobus *fer·mah·ta ow·to·boos* T94
bust n il busto *boo·stoh*
busy adj occupato(a) *ok·koo·pah·to(a)*; (*place*) animato(a) *a·nee·mah·to(a)*
busy signal n il segnale "occupato" *sen·yah·le ok·koo·pah·to*
but conj ma ma; not this, but that non questo ma quello *nohn kway·sto ma kwayl·lo* □ prep all but him tutti tranne lui *toot·tee tran·ne loo·ee*
butane n il butano *boo·tah·noh*
butcher n il macellaio *ma·chel·la·yoh*; butcher's (*shop*) la macelleria *ma·chel·le·ree·a* S29
butter n il burro *boor·roh* E31, S30
butterfly n la farfalla *far·fal·la*
button n il bottone *bot·toh·ne* Sn76
buy vt comprare *kom·prah·ray*; to buy out (*partner etc*) disinteressare *dee·zeen·te·res·sah·ray* S6
buyer n (*customer*) l'acquirente (m/f) *ak·kwee·ren·te*; (*for shop, factory*) il compratore *kom·pra·toh·re*, la compratrice *kom·pra·tree·che* Bm3
by prep (*next to*) accanto a *ak·kan·to a*; to go by London (*via*) passare via Londra *pas·sah·ray vee·a lohn·dra*; by air per via aerea *payr vee·a a·e·re·a*; by train/car in treno/macchina *een tre·noh/mak·kee·na*; we'll be there by 4 o'clock saremo lí per le 4 *sa·ray·mo lee payr le 4* □ adv a plane flew by è passato un aereo *e pas·sah·to oon a·e·re·oh*
bypass n la circonvallazione *cheer·kon·val·la·tsyoh·ne*

C

cab n (*taxi*) il tassí *tas·see*
cabaret n il cabaret *ka·ba·ray* L42
cabbage n il cavolo *kah·vo·loh*
cabin n (*in ship*) la cabina *ka·bee·na*
cabin cruiser n il cabinato *ka·bee·nah·toh*
cable n il cavo *kah·voh*
cactus n il cacto *kak·toh*
caddie n il caddie *kad·dee*
café n il caffè *kaf·fe*
cafeteria n il ristorante self-service *ree·sto·ran·tay self·sayr·vees*
cage n la gabbia *gab·bya*
cake n la torta *tohr·ta*
calcium n il calcio *kal·choh*
calculate vt calcolare *kal·ko·lah·ray*
calculator n la calcolatrice *kal·ko·la·tree·chay*
calendar n il calendario *ka·len·dah·ree·oh*
calf n il vitello *vee·tel·loh*
call n (*shout*) il grido *gree·doh*; (*on phone*) la chiamata *kya·mah·ta* □ vi (*shout*) gridare *gree·dah·ray* □ vt chiamare *kya·mah·ray*; (*telephone*) telefonare a *te·le·fo·nah·ray a*; call me at 7 a.m. (*in hotel etc*) mi svegli alle 7 di mattina *mee zvayl·yee al·lay*

7 *dee mat·tee·na*; **to be called** chiamarsi *kee·ah·mar·see* Sn11

call girl *n* la ragazza squillo *ra·ga·tsa skwee·loh*

calm *adj* (*sea, day*) calmo(a) *kal·moh(a)*; (*person*) tranquillo(a) *tran·kweel·loh(a)*

calorie *n* la caloria *ka·lo·ree·a*

camel *n* il cammello *kam·mel·loh*

camera *n* la macchina fotografica *mak·kee·na fo·to·gra·fee·ka*; (*TV*) la telecamera *te·le·kah·me·ra* S47f

camp *vi* accamparsi *ak·kam·pahr·see* A80f

campaign *n* la campagna *kam·pan·ya* Bm17

camp-bed *n* la brandina *bran·dee·na*

camping *n* il campeggio *kam·payj·joh*; **to go camping** fare* del campeggio *fah·ray del kam·payj·joh*

camp(ing) site *n* il campeggio *kam·payj·joh* A84

camshaft *n* l'albero a camme (*m*) *al·bay·roh a kam*

can[1] *n* (*container*) il barattolo *ba·rat·to·loh* S33

can[2] *vi* potere* *po·tay·ray*; **I can** posso *pos·soh*; **you can** può *pwo*; **he/she can** (egli/ella) può *ayl·yee/ayl·la pwo*; **we can** possiamo *pos·see·ah·moh*

Canada *n* Canadà (*m*) *ka·na·da*

Canadian *adj* canadese *ka·na·day·say*

canal *n* il canale *ka·nah·lay*

canasta *n* la canasta *ka·na·sta*

cancel *vt* (*reservation*) annullare *an·nool·lah·ray*; (*appointment*) disdire* *dees·dee·re*

cancer *n* il cancro *kan·kroh*

candidate *n* (*for election*) il/la candidato(a) *kan·dee·da·toh(a)*

candle *n* la candela *kan·day·la*

candy *n* la caramella *ka·ra·mel·la*

cane *n* (*walking stick*) il bastone da passeggio *ba·stoh·nay da pas·sayj·joh*

canned *adj* in scatola *een skah·to·la*

cannon *n* il cannone *kan·noh·nay*

canoe *n* la canoa *ka·no·a*

canoeing *n* □ **to go canoeing** fare* della canoa *fah·ray del·la ka·no·a*

can-opener *n* l'apriscatole (*m*) *ah·pree·skah·to·lay*

canteen *n* la mensa *men·sa*

canvas *n* la tela *tay·la*

cap *n* (*hat*) il berretto *ber·rayt·toh*

capable *adj* capace *ka·pah·chay*; **capable of** capace di *ka·pah·chay dee*

cape *n* la cappa *kap·pa*

capital *n* (*city*) la capitale *ka·pee·tah·lay*; (*finance*) il capitale *ka·pee·tah·lay*; **in capitals** in maiuscole *een ma·yoos·ko·lay*; **capital A** A maiuscola *a ma·yoos·ko·la*

capital goods *pl* le materie prime *ma·te·rye pree·may*

capitalism *n* il capitalismo *ka·pee·ta·lee·zmoh*

capitalist *n* il/la capitalista *ka·pee·ta·lee·sta*

capital letter *n* la lettera maiuscola *let·te·ra ma·yoos·ko·la*

capsule *n* (*of medicine*) la capsula *kap·soo·la*

captain *n* il capitano *ka·pee·tah·noh*; (*of plane*) il comandante *ko·man·dan·tay*

capture *vt* catturare *kat·too·rah·ray*

car *n* la macchina *mak·kee·na*; (*of train*) il vagone *va·goh·nay* T108f, A28

carafe *n* la caraffa *ka·raf·fa* E11

caramel *n* il caramello *ka·ra·mel·loh*

carat *n* il carato *ka·ra·toh*

carbon *n* il carbonio *kar·boh·nyoh*

carbon copy *n* la copia carbone *ko·pya kar·boh·nay*

carbon paper *n* la carta carbone *kahr·ta kar·boh·nay*

carburetor *n* il carburatore *kar·boo·ra·toh·ray*

card *n* (*post*) la cartolina *kahr·to·lee·na*; (*playing card*) la carta da gioco *kahr·ta da jo·koh*; **to play cards** giocare a carte *jo·kah·ray a kahr·tay* S91, Bm2, M25

cardboard *n* il cartone *kahr·to·nay*

card game *n* il gioco di carte *jo·koh dee kahr·tay*

cardigan *n* il cardigan *kahr·dee·gan*

card index *n* lo schedario *ske·dah·ree·oh*

care *n* (*carefulness*) la cura *koo·ra* □ *vi* **I don't care** non me ne importa *nohn me ne eem·por·tah*; **to take care of** (*children etc*) curare *koo·rah·ray*

career *n* la carriera *kar·ree·e·ra*

careful *adj* (*cautious*) prudente *proo·den·tay*; **be careful!** attenzione! *at·ten·tsyoh·nay*

care of, c/o *prep* presso *pres·soh*

caretaker *n* il custode *koo·sto·day*

car-ferry *n* il traghetto per auto *tra·gayt·toh payr ow·toh*

cargo *n* il carico *kah·ree·koh*

Caribbean (Sea) *n* il Mar dei Caraibi *mahr de·ee ka·ra·ee·bee*

carnation *n* il garofano *ga·ro·fa·noh*

carnival *n* il carnevale *kahr·ne·vah·lay*

carol *n* il canto di Natale *kan·toh dee na·ta·lay*

carpenter *n* il falegname *fa·len·yah·may*

carpet *n* il tappeto *tap·pay·toh*

carport *n* la tettoia *tet·toh·ya*

carrot *n* la carota *ka·ro·ta*

carry *vt* (*in hands, arms*) portare *por·tah·ray*; (*transport*) trasportare *tra·spor·tah·ray*; **to carry out an order** eseguire un ordine *e·ze·gwee·ray oon ohr·dee·nay*

carryall *n* la borsa *bohr·sa*

carry-out *adj* (*food*) da portar via *da por·tar vee·a*

cart *n* il carrello *kar·rel·loh*

cartel *n* il cartello *kar·tel·loh*

carton *n* (*box*) la scatola di cartone *skah·to·la dee kar·to·nay*; (*of yogurt etc*) la scatola *skah·to·la*

cartoon *n* la vignetta umoristica *veen·yayt·ta oo·mo·ree·stee·ka*; (*animated*) il cartone animato *kahr·to·nay a·nee·mah·toh*

cartridge *n* (*for gun*) la cartuccia *kahr·tooch·cha*; (*for camera*) il rollino *rol·lee·noh*; (*of tape*) la cassetta *kas·sayt·tah*

carve *vt* (*meat*) trinciare *treen·chah·ray*

case *n* la valigia *va·lee·ja*; (*of wine*) la cassetta *kas·sayt·ta*; (*instance*) il caso *kah·zoh*; (*lawsuit*) la causa *kow·za*; **just in case...** nel caso che... *nel kah·zoh kay*; **in case of** in caso di *een kah·zoh dee*; **in any case** ad ogni modo *ad ohn·yee mo·doh*

cash *vt* (*check*) riscuotere* *ree·skwo·te·ray* □ **the cash** i soldi *sol·dee*; **to pay cash for something** pagare qualcosa in contanti *pa·gah·ray kwal·ko·sa een kon·tan·tee*; **cash on delivery** pagamento alla consegna *pa·ga·mayn·toh al·la kon·sayn·ya* M25, L56

cashdesk *n* la cassa *kas·sa*

cash flow *n* il flusso di capitale *floos·soh de ka·pee·tah·lay*

cashier *n* il/la cassiere(a) *kas·sye·ray(a)*

cashmere *n* il cachemire *kash·meer*

casino *n* il casinò *ka·see·noh*

casserole *n* (*food*) lo spezzatino *spets·tsa·tee·noh*; (*dish*) la casseruola *kas·ser·wo·la*

cassette *n* la cassetta *kas·sayt·ta*

cassette-recorder *n* il magnetofono a cassetta *man·ye·to·fo·noh a kas·sayt·ta*

cast *n* (*of play*) gli attori *lyee at·toh·ree*

cast iron *n* la ghisa *gee·za*

castle *n* il castello *ka·stel·loh* F6, L5

castor oil *n* l'olio di ricino (*m*) *ol·yoh dee ree·chee·noh*

casual clothes, casual wear *n* i vestiti sportivi *ves·tee·tee spor·tee·vee*

cat *n* il gatto *gat·toh*

catalog *n* il catalogo *ka·tah·lo·goh* Bm18

catch *vt* (*ball, animal, fish, person*) acchiappare *ak·kyap·pah·ray*; (*train, illness*) prendere* *pren·de·ray*; to catch cold prendere* freddo *pren·de·ray frayd·doh*

cathedral *n* la cattedrale *kat·te·drah·lay* F3

catholic *adj* cattolico(a) *kat·to·lee·koh(a)*

cattle *pl* il bestiame *be·stee·ah·may*

cauliflower *n* il cavolfiore *ka·vol·fyoh·ray*

cause *n* la causa *kow·za* □ *vt* causare *kow·zah·ray*

cave *n* la caverna *ka·ver·na*

caviar(e) *n* il caviale *ka·vee·ah·lay*

cedar *n* il cedro *chay·droh*

ceiling *n* il soffitto *sof·feet·toh*

celebrate *vi* fare* festa *fah·ray fe·sta* □ *vt* festeggiare *fes·tej·jah·ray*

celeriac *n* il sedano rapa *se·da·no rah·pa*

celery *n* il sedano *se·da·noh*

cell *n* (*in prison*) la cella *chel·la*

cellar *n* lo scantinato *skan·tee·nah·toh*

cello *n* il violoncello *vee·o·lon·chel·loh*

cellophane *n* il cellofan *chel·lo·fan*

Celsius *adj* *chel·syoos*

cement *n* il cemento *che·mayn·toh*

cemetery *n* il cimitero *chee·mee·te·roh*

cent *n* il centesimo *chen·te·zee·moh*

centenary *n* il centenario *chen·te·na·ree·oh*

center *n* il centro *chen·troh* F4

centigrade *adj* centigrado *chen·tee·gra·doh*

centiliter *n* il centilitro *chen·tee·lee·troh*

centimeter *n* il centimetro *chen·tee·me·troh*

central *adj* centrale *chen·trah·lay*

central heating *n* il riscaldamento centrale *ree·skal·da·mayn·toh chen·trah·lay* A44

century *n* il secolo *se·ko·loh*

cereal *n* (*breakfast*) il cereale *che·re·ah·lay* A44

ceremony *n* la cerimonia *che·ree·mo·nee·a*

certain *adj* certo(a) *cher·toh(a)*

certainly *adv* certamente *cher·ta·mayn·tay*

certificate *n* il certificato *cher·tee·fee·kah·toh*

certified mail *n* la posta raccomandata *pos·ta rak·ko·man·dah·ta*

certified public accountant *n* il ragioniere diplomato *ra·jo·nye·ray dee·plo·mah·toh*

chain *n* la catena *ka·tay·na*

chain store *n* il negozio a catena *ne·go·tsyoh a ka·tay·na*

chair *n* la sedia *se·dya*; (*armchair*) la poltrona *pol·troh·na*

chair-lift *n* la seggiovia *sej·jo·vee·a*

chairman *n* il presidente *pre·see·den·tay*

chalet *n* lo chalet *sha·le*

chalk *n* il gesso *jes·soh*

Chamber of Commerce *n* la camera di commercio *ka·may·ra dee kom·mer·choh*

champagne *n* lo sciampagna *sham·pan·ya*

champion *n* il campione *kam·pyoh·nay*

chance *n* □ by chance per caso *payr kah·zoh*; he has a good chance of... egli ha delle buone possibilità di... *ay·lyee a del·lay bwo·nay pos·see·bee·lee·ta dee*

chancellor *n* (*in Germany, Austria*) il cancelliere *kan·chel·lye·ray*

change *vt/i* cambiare *kam·bee·ah·ray*; to change one's clothes cambiarsi *kam·bee·ahr·see*; to change trains at Marseilles cambiare treno a Marsiglia *kam·bee·ah·ray tre·noh a Mahr·seel·ya* □ *n* change (*transformation*) il cambiamento *kam·bya·mayn·toh*; (*money*) gli spiccioli *speech·cho·lee*; a change in the weather un cambiamento del tempo *oon kam·bya·mayn·toh del tem·poh* T91, M15, 21f

Channel *n* la Manica *mah·nee·ka*

chapel *n* la cappella *kap·pel·la*

chapter *n* il capitolo *ka·pee·to·loh*

character *n* (*nature*) il carattere *ka·rat·te·ray*

charge *n* (*accusation*) l'accusa (*f*) *ak·koo·za*; to make a charge for something fare* pagare qualcosa *fah·ray pa·gah·ray kwal·ko·sa*; free of charge gratuito(a) *gra·too·ee·toh(a)*; to be in charge of essere* responsabile per *es·se·ray res·pon·sah·bee·lay payr* □ *vt* charge (*money*) fare* pagare *fah·ray pa·gah·ray*; charge it to my account lo addebiti al mio conto *loh ad·de·bee·tee al mee·oh kohn·toh* M3

charm *n* il fascino *fa·shee·noh*

charming *adj* incantevole *een·kan·tay·vo·lay*

chart *n* (*map*) la carta nautica *kar·ta now·tee·ka*; (*diagram, table*) il grafico *gra·fee·koh*

charter *vt* (*plane, bus*) noleggiare *no·lej·jah·ray*

charter flight *n* il volo charter *voh·loh char·ter*

chase *vt* inseguire *een·say·gwee·ray*

chassis *n* il telaio *te·la·yoh*

chauffeur *n* l'autista *ow·tees·ta*

cheap *adj* a buon mercato *a bwon mer·kah·toh* S14, Sn21

cheat *vi* imbrogliare *eem·brol·yah·ray*

check *n* (*banking*) l'assegno (*m*) *as·sayn·yoh*; (*bill*) il conto *kohn·toh*; can I have the check please? il conto per favore *eel kohn·toh payr fa·voh·ray* □ *vt* check controllare *kon·trol·lah·ray*; (*train time etc*) verificare *ve·ree·fee·kah·ray*; to check in (*at hotel*) registrarsi *re·jee·strahr·see*; (*at airport*) presentarsi *pre·zen·tahr·see*; to check out pagare il conto *pa·gah·ray eel kohn·toh* M22f, A23

checkbook *n* il libretto di assegni *lee·brayt·toh dee as·sayn·yee*

check(er)ed adj (patterned) a quadretti a kwa·drayt·tee
checkers pl il gioco della dama jo·koh del·la dah·ma
checking account n il conto corrente kohn·toh kor·ren·tay
checkout n (in store) la cassa kas·sa
checkroom n il deposito bagagli de·po·zee·toh ba·gal·yee
cheek n la guancia gwan·cha; (impudence) la sfacciataggine sfach·cha·taj·jee·nay
cheeky adj sfacciato(a) sfach·chah·toh(a)
cheer vt applaudire ap·plow·dee·ray; **cheers!** cincìn! cheen·cheen
cheese n il formaggio for·maj·joh E26, S30
cheesecake n la torta di ricotta tor·tah dee ree·kot·ta
chef n il capocuoco kah·po·kwo·koh
chemical adj chimico(a) kee·mee·koh(a)
chemist n (pharmacist) il farmacista far·ma·chee·sta; **chemist's shop** la farmacia far·ma·chee·a S40f
chemistry n la chimica kee·mee·ka
cherry n la ciliegia chee·lee·ay·jah; (tree) il ciliegio chee·lee·ay·joh
chess n gli scacchi skak·kee
chest n (of body) il petto pet·toh
chestnut n la castagna ka·stan·ya
chew vt masticare ma·stee·kah·ray
chewing gum n la gomma da masticare gohm·ma da ma·stee·kah·ray
chicken n il pollo pohl·loh
chicken pox n la varicella va·ree·chel·la
chicory n la cicoria chee·ko·ree·a
chief n (boss) il capo kah·poh
child n il/la bambino(a) bam·bee·noh(a) A4, C1, 14f
chili n il chile kee·lay
chill vt (wine, food) raffreddare raf·fred·dah·ray; **to serve something chilled** servire qualcosa freddo sayr·vee·ray kwal·koh·sa frayd·doh
chimney n il camino ka·mee·noh
chin n il mento mayn·toh
china n la porcellana por·chel·lah·na
China n Cina (f) chee·na
Chinese adj cinese chee·nay·say ◻ n (language) il cinese chee·nay·say
chip n (electronics) il chip cheep; (in gambling) il gettone jet·toh·nay
chips pl le patatine pa·ta·tee·nay
chives pl l'erba cipollina (f) er·ba chee·pol·lee·na
chocolate n la cioccolata chok·ko·lah·ta
choice n la scelta shayl·ta
choir n il coro koh·roh
choke n (of car) la valvola dell'aria val·voh·la del·lah·ryah
cholesterol n la colesterina koh·lay·stay·ree·na
choose vt scegliere* shayl·ye·ray
chop vt (food) tritare tree·tah·ray ◻ n pork chop la braciola di maiale bra·cho·la dee ma·yah·lay
chopsticks pl i bastoncini ba·ston·chee·nee
Christian n il/la cristiano(a) kree·stee·ah·noh(a)
Christian name n il nome di battesimo noh·may dee bat·tay·zee·moh
Christmas n Natale (m) na·tah·lay
Christmas card n la cartolina di Natale kahr·to·lee·na dee na·tah·lay
Christmas Day n il giorno di Natale johr·noh dee na·tah·lay

Christmas Eve n la vigilia di Natale vee·jeel·ya dee na·tah·lay
Christmas tree n l'albero di Natale (m) al·be·roh dee na·tah·lay
chrome n il cromo kro·moh
chrysanthemum n il crisantemo kree·zan·te·moh
church n la chiesa kye·za L3, 16f, Sn86
churchyard n il camposanto kam·po·san·toh
cider n il sidro see·droh
cigar n il sigaro see·ga·roh
cigarette n la sigaretta see·ga·rayt·ta S95f
cigarette case n il portasigarette por·ta·see·ga·rayt·tay
cigarette lighter n l'accendino (m) ach·chen·dee·noh S101
cinema n il cinema chee·ne·ma Mc44
cinnamon n la cannella kan·nel·la
circle n il cerchio chayr·kyoh; (in theater) la galleria gal·le·ree·a
circuit n (electric) il circuito cheer·koo·ee·toh
circumstances pl le circostanze cheer·ko·stan·tsay
circus n il circo cheer·koh
city n la città cheet·ta; **city center** il centro della città chen·troh del·la cheet·ta Mc44
city hall n il municipio moo·nee·chee·pee·oh
civilization n la civilizzazione chee·vee·leed·za·tsee·oh·nay
civil servant n il/la funzionario(a) sta·tale foon·tsyo·nah·ree·oh(a) sta·tah·lay
civil service n l'amministrazione statale (f) am·mee·nee·stra·tsyoh·nay sta·tah·lay
civil war n la guerra civile gwer·rah chee·vee·lay
claim vt (lost property, baggage) chiedere* la restituzione di kyay·de·ray la re·stee·too·tsyoh·nay dee
clam n la vongola von·go·la
clap vi applaudire ap·plow·dee·ray
claret n il chiaretto kya·rayt·toh
clasp n la fibbia feeb·bya
class n la classe klas·say; **to travel first class** viaggiare in prima classe vyaj·jah·ray een pree·ma klas·say; **a second class ticket** un biglietto di seconda classe oon beel·yay·toh dee se·kohn·da klas·say
classical adj (music, art) classico(a) klas·see·koh(a)
clause n (in contract) la clausola klow·zo·la
clay n l'argilla (f) ahr·jeel·la
clean adj pulito(a) poo·lee·toh(a) ◻ vt pulire poo·lee·ray; **to have a suit cleaned** fare* pulire un vestito fah·ray poo·lee·ray oon ve·stee·toh
cleaner n (of house etc) la donna delle pulizie don·na del·lay poo·lee·tsee·ay
cleaner's n la tintoria teen·to·ree·a
clear adj (transparent) trasparente tras·pa·ren·tay; (distinct) chiaro(a) kyah·roh(a); (not blocked) libero(a) lee·be·roh(a) ◻ vt sbloccare zblok·kah·ray
clerk n (in office) l'impiegato(a) (m/f) eem·pye·gah·toh(a); (in store) il/la commesso(a) kom·mays·soh(a)
clever adj (person) intelligente een·tel·lee·jen·tay; (plan) ingegnoso(a) een·jen·yoh·soh(a)
client n il/la cliente klee·en·tay
cliff n la scogliera skol·ye·ra
climate n il clima klee·ma

climb *vt* (*tree, wall*) arrampicarsi su *ar·ram·pee·kahr·see·soo*; **to climb over** something scavalcare qualcosa *ska·val·kah·ray kwal·ko·sa*

clinic *n* la clinica *klee·nee·ka*

cloak *n* il mantello *man·tel·loh*

cloakroom *n* il guardaroba *gwar·da·ro·ba*

clock *n* l'orologio (*m*) *o·ro·lo·joh*

close[1] *adj* (*near*) vicino(a) *vee·chee·noh(a)*; (*stuffy*) afoso(a) *a·foh·soh(a)*; **close to** vicino a *vee·chee·noh a*; **close by** vicino *vee·chee·noh* T198

close[2] *vt* chiudere* *kyoo·de·ray* □ *vi* the door closed la porta si chiuse *la por·ta see kyoo·say*; **when do the shops close?** a che ora si chiudono i negozi? *a kay oh·ra see kyoo·do·no ee ne·go·tsee* A29

closed circuit television *n* la televisione a circuito chiuso *te·le·vee·zee·oh·nay a cheer·koo·ee·toh kyoo·soh*

closet *n* l'armadio (*m*) *ahr·mah·dyoh*

cloth *n* (*cleaning*) il panno *pan·noh*

clothes *pl* i vestiti *ves·tee·tee* Sn66, 74

clotheshorse *n* il cavalletto per il bucato *ka·val·layt·toh payr eel boo·kah·toh*

clothesline *n* la corda per stendere il bucato *cor·da payr sten·de·ray eel boo·kah·toh*

clothespin *n* la molletta *mol·layt·ta*

cloud *n* la nuvola *noo·vo·la*

cloudy *adj* nuvoloso(a) *noo·vo·loh·soh(a)*

clove *n* il chiodo di garofano *kyo·doh dee ga·ro·fa·noh*; **clove of garlic** lo spicchio d'aglio *speek·kyoh dal·yoh*

clown *n* il pagliaccio *pal·yach·choh*

club *n* (*society*) il club *kloob*; **clubs** (*in cards*) i fiori *fyoh·ree*

club car *n* il vagone ristorante *va·goh·nay ree·sto·ran·te*

clumsy *adj* (*person*) goffo(a) *gof·foh(a)*

clutch (*of car*) la frizione *free·tsyoh·nay*

coach *n* (*of train*) la vettura *vet·too·ra*; (*bus*) il pullman *pool·man*; (*instructor*) l'allenatore (*m*) *al·le·na·toh·ray*

coal *n* il carbone *kahr·boh·nay*

coarse *adj* (*texture, material*) ruvido(a) *roo·vee·doh(a)*

coast *n* la costa *ko·sta*

coastguard *n* il guardacoste *gwahr·da·ko·stay*

coat *n* il mantello *man·tel·loh*

coat hanger *n* l'attaccapanni (*m*) *at·tak·ka·pan·nee*

cock(erel) *n* il gallo *gal·loh*

cockle *n* il cardio *kahr·dee·oh*

cocktail *n* (*drink*) il cocktail *kok·tail*; **shrimp cocktail** l'antipasto di gamberetti (*m*) *an·tee·pa·stoh dee gam·be·rayt·tee*

cocoa *n* il cacao *ka·kow*

coconut *n* il cocco *kok·koh*

cod *n* il merluzzo *mayr·loots·tsoh*

codeine *n* la codeina *ko·de·ee·na*

coffee *n* il caffè *kaf·fe*; **black coffee** il caffè nero *kaf·fe nay·roh*; **coffee with milk** il caffellatte *kaf·fel·lat·tay* B53, E60f

coffee break *n* la pausa per il caffè *pow·za payr eel kaf·fe*

coffee cup *n* la tazza da caffè *tats·tsa da kaf·fe*

coffeepot *n* la caffettiera *kaf·fet·tye·ra*

coffee table *n* il tavolino da caffè *tah·vo·lee·noh da kaf·fe*

coffin *n* la bara *bah·ra*

cognac *n* il cognac *kon·yak*

coin *n* la moneta *mo·nay·ta*

coincide *vi* coincidere* *koh·een·chee·de·ray*

coincidence *n* la coincidenza *koh·een·chee·den·tsa*

colander *n* il colapasta *koh·la·pa·sta*

cold *adj* freddo(a) *frayd·doh(a)*; **I'm cold** ho freddo *o frayd·doh* □ *n* cold (*illness*) il raffreddore *raf·frayd·doh·ray* E36, S40

coleslaw *n* l'insalata di cavolo (*f*) *een·sa·lah·ta dee kah·vo·loh*

colic *n* la colica *ko·lee·ka*

collaborate *vi* collaborare *kol·la·bo·rah·ray*

collapse *vi* (*person*) accasciarsi *ak·ka·shar·see*

collar *n* il colletto *kol·layt·toh*; (*for dog*) il collare *kol·lah·ray*

colleague *n* il/la collega *kol·le·ga*

collect *vt* (*stamps etc*) collezionare *kol·le·tsyo·nah·ray*; (*donations*) raccogliere* *rak·kol·ye·ray*

collect call *n* la telefonata con la R *te·le·fo·nah·ta kohn la er·re* Sn13

collection *n* (*of mail*) la levata *le·vah·ta*

college *n* il collegio *kol·le·joh*

collide *vi* scontrarsi *skon·trahr·see*

collision *n* lo scontro *skohn·troh*

cologne *n* l'acqua di Colonia (*f*) *ak·kwa dee ko·lon·ya*

color *n* il colore *ko·loh·ray*; **color TV** la televisione a colori *te·le·vee·zyoh·nay a ko·loh·ree*

colored *adj* colorato(a) *ko·loh·ra·to(a)*

comb *n* il pettine *pet·tee·nay* □ *vt* pettinare *pet·tee·nah·ray*

come *vi* (*arrive*) venire* *ve·nee·ray*; **to come in** entrare *en·trah·ray*; **to come off** staccarsi *stak·kahr·see*; **to come out** (*person, sun*) uscire* *oo·shee·ray*; (*stain*) andare* via *an·dah·ray vee·a*; **to come around** (*recover*) riprendere* i sensi *ree·pren·de·ray ee sen·see*

comedian *n* il comico *ko·mee·koh*

comedy *n* la commedia *kom·me·dya*

comfort *n* (*ease*) il conforto *kon·for·toh*

comfortable *adj* comodo(a) *ko·mo·doh(a)*

comforter *n* il piumino *pyoo·mee·noh*

comfort station *n* i gabinetti pubblici *ga·bee·nayt·tee poob·blee·chee*

comic *n* il giornale a fumetti *jor·nah·lay a foo·mayt·tee*

comma *n* la virgola *veer·go·la*

command *n* l'ordine (*m*) *ohr·dee·nay*

comment *n* il commento *kom·mayn·toh*

commerce *n* il commercio *kom·mer·choh*

commercial *adj* commerciale *kom·mer·chah·lay* □ *n* (*ad*) la réclame *ray·klam*

commercialized *adj* (*resort*) commercializzato(a) *kom·mer·cha·leedz·dzah·to(a)*

commission *n* (*sum received*) la commissione *kom·mees·syoh·nay*

commit *vt* (*crime*) commettere* *kom·mayt·te·ray*

committee *n* il comitato *ko·mee·tah·toh*

commodity *n* il prodotto *pro·doht·toh*

common *adj* (*ordinary, frequent*) comune *ko·moo·nay*

Common Market *n* il Mercato Comune *mer·kah·toh ko·moo·nay*

communicate *vi* □ **to communicate**

with someone comunicare con qualcuno *ko·moo·nee·kah·ray kon kwal·koo·noh*

Communist *n* il/la comunista *ko·moo·nee·sta* □ *adj* comunista *ko·moo·nee·sta*

commutation ticket *n* il biglietto di abbonamento *beel·yayt·toh dee ab·bon·a·mayn·toh*

commuter *n* il pendolare *pen·do·lah·ray*

company *n* (*firm*) la ditta *deet·ta* Bm15f

compare *vt* □ **to compare something with something** confrontare qualcosa con qualcosa *kon·fron·tah·ray kwal·ko·sa kohn kwal·ko·sa*

compartment *n* (*on train*) lo scompartimento *skom·pahr·tee·mayn·toh*

compass *n* la bussola *boos·so·la*

compensation *n* il risarcimento *ree·sar·chee·mayn·toh*

competent *adj* competente *kom·pe·ten·tay*

competition *n* la competizione *kom·pe·tee·tsyoh·nay*

competitor *n* il/la concorrente *kon·kor·ren·tay*

complain *vi* lagnarsi *lan·yahr·see*; **to complain about** lamentarsi di *la·men·tahr·see dee*

complaint *n* (*dissatisfaction*) il reclamo *re·klah·moh*

complete *adj* completo(a) *kom·ple·toh(a)* □ *vt* completare *kom·ple·tah·ray*

completely *adv* completamente *kom·ple·ta·mayn·tay*

complex *adj* complicato(a) *kom·plee·kah·toh(a)*

complexion *n* la carnagione *kahr·na·joh·nay*

complicated *adj* complicato(a) *kom·plee·kah·toh(a)*

compliment *n* il complimento *kom·plee·mayn·toh*

component *n* (*for car etc*) il pezzo *pets·tsoh*

composer *n* il compositore *kom·po·zee·toh·ray*

compound interest *n* l'interesse composto (*m*) *een·te·res·se kom·poh·sto*

comprehensive insurance *n* l'assicurazione contro tutti i rischi (*f*) *as·see·koo·ra·tsyoh·nay kohn·troh toot·tee ee ree·skee* T116

computer *n* il computer *kom·pyoo·ta*

computerize *vt* (*system*) automatizzare *ow·to·ma·teedz·dzah·ray*

computer programming *n* la programmazione *pro·gram·ma·tsyoh·nay*

conceited *adj* vanitoso(a) *va·nee·toh·soh(a)*

concern *n* (*anxiety*) l'ansia (*f*) *an·see·a* □ *vt* (*be important to*) interessare *een·te·res·sah·ray*; **that doesn't concern you** ciò non la riguarda *cho nohn la ree·gwahr·da*

concert *n* il concerto *kon·cher·toh* L43

concrete *n* il calcestruzzo *kal·che·stroots·tsoh* □ *adj* in calcestruzzo *een kal·che·stroots·tsoh*

condemn *vt* condannare *kon·dan·nah·ray*

condensed milk *n* il latte condensato *lat·tay kon·den·sah·toh*

condiments *pl* i condimenti *kon·dee·mayn·tee*

condition *n* la condizione *kon·dee·tsyoh·nay*; **on condition that...** a con-

dizione che... *a kon·dee·tsyoh·nay kay*

conditioner *n* (*for hair*) il balsamo *bal·sa·moh* Sn44

conductor *n* (*on bus*) il bigliettaio *beel·yet·ta·yoh*; (*of orchestra*) il direttore *dee·ret·toh·ray*; (*on train*) il capotreno *kah·po·tre·noh*

cone *n* (*for ice cream*) il cono *ko·noh*

confectioner *n* il pasticciere *pa·steech·che·ray*

confectionery *n* i dolciumi *dol·choo·mee*

conference *n* (*meeting*) la riunione *ree·oon·yoh·nay* A37

confess *vt* confessare *kon·fes·sah·ray* □ *vi* confessarsi *kon·fes·sahr·see*; **to confess to something** ammettere* qualcosa *am·met·te·ray kwal·ko·sa*

confession *n* la confessione *kon·fes·syoh·nay* Sn90

confidence *n* (*trust*) la fiducia *fee·doo·cha*; **in confidence** in confidenza *een kon·fee·den·tsa*

confident *adj* fiducioso(a) *fee·doo·choh·so(a)*

confidential *adj* confidenziale *kon·fee·den·tsyah·lay*

confirm *vt* (*reservation etc*) confermare *kon·fer·mah·ray*

confuse *vt* confondere* *kon·fohn·de·ray*; **to confuse one thing with another** confondere* una cosa con un'altra *kon·fohn·de·ray o·na ko·sa kohn oo·nal·tra*

confused *adj* (*muddled*) confuso(a) *kon·foo·zoh(a)*

congratulate *vt* congratularsi con *kon·gra·too·lahr·see kohn*; **to congratulate someone on something** congratularsi con qualcuno per qualcosa *kon·gra·too·lahr·see kohn kwal·koo·noh payr kwal·ko·sa*

congratulations *pl* le felicitazioni *fe·lee·chee·ta·tsyoh·nee*; **congratulations!** felicitazioni! *fe·lee·chee·ta·tsyoh·nee*

conjuror *n* il prestigiatore *pre·stee·ja·toh·re*

connect *vt* (*join*) unire *oo·nee·ray*; **this train connects with the 16:45** questo treno fa coincidenza con quello delle 16.45 *kway·stoh tre·noh fa ko·een·chee·den·tsa kohn kwayl·loh del·lay 16.45*

connection *n* (*train etc*) la coincidenza *ko·een·chee·den·tsa* T8

connoisseur *n* il conoscitore *ko·no·shee·toh·ray*

conscience *n* la coscienza *ko·shen·tsa*

conscious *adj* in sé *een say*

consequence *n* (*result*) la conseguenza *kon·se·gwen·tsa*

conservative *adj* conservatore *kon·sayr·va·toh·ray*, conservatrice *kon·sayr·va·tree·chay*

conservatory *n* (*greenhouse*) la serra *ser·ra*

consider *vt* considerare *kon·see·de·rah·ray*

consist of *vt* consistere* in *kon·see·ste·ray een*

consommé *n* il consommé *kon·som·may*

constipated *adj* stitico(a) *stee·tee·koh(a)*; **to be constipated** stare* stitico(a) *sta·ray stee·tee·koh(a)*

construct *vt* costruire* *ko·stroo·ee·ray*

consul *n* il console *kon·so·lay*

consulate *n* il consolato *kon·so·lah·toh* Sn85

consult vt consultare *kon·sool·tah·ray*

consultant n (doctor) lo/la specialista *spe·cha·lee·sta*; (other specialist) il consulente *kon·soo·len·tay*

consulting room n l'ambulatorio (m) *am·boo·la·to·ree·oh*

consumer n il consumatore *kon·soo·ma·toh·ray*

consumer goods pl i beni di consumo *ee be·nee dee kon·soo·moh*

contact vt mettersi* in contatto con *mayt·ter·see een kon·tat·toh kohn*

contact lenses pl le lenti a contatto *len·tee a kon·tat·toh*

contagious adj contagioso(a) *kon·ta·joh·soh(a)*

contain vt contenere* *kon·te·nay·ray*

container n il recipiente *re·chee·pyen·tay*; (for shipping etc) il container *kon·tay·ner*

contemporary adj (modern) contemporaneo(a) *kon·tem·po·rah·ne·oh(a)*

content(ed) adj contento(a) *kon·ten·toh(a)*

contents pl il contenuto *kon·te·noo·toh*; (table in book) l'indice (m) *een·dee·chay*

contest n (competition) il concorso *kon·kohr·soh*

contestant n il/la concorrente *kon·kor·ren·tay*

continent n il continente *kon·tee·nen·tay*; the Continent l'Europa continentale (f) *ay·oo·ro·pa kon·tee·nen·tah·lay*

continental adj continentale *kon·tee·nen·tah·lay*

continental breakfast n la colazione *ko·la·tsyoh·nay*

continual adj continuo(a) *kon·tee·nwoh(a)*

continue vt/i continuare *kon·tee·noo·ah·ray*; to continue to do continuare a fare *kon·tee·noo·ah·ray a fah·ray*

continuous adj continuo(a) *kon·tee·nwoh(a)*

continuously adv continuamente *kon·tee·noo·a·men·tay*

contraband n il contrabbando *kon·trab·ban·doh*

contraceptive n l'anticoncezionale (m) *an·tee·kon·che·tsyoh·nah·lay*

contract n il contratto *kon·trat·toh*

contractor n l'imprenditore (m) *eem·pren·dee·toh·ray*

contrary n □ on the contrary al contrario *al kon·trah·ree·oh*

contribute vi contribuire *kon·tree·boo·ee·ray*

control vt dominare *do·mee·nah·ray* □ circumstances beyond our control le circostanze che non dipendono da noi *cheer·ko·stan·tsay kay nohn dee·pen·do·no da noi*

controls pl i comandi *ko·man·dee* T120

control tower n la torre di controllo *tohr·ray dee kon·trol·loh*

conurbation n la zona di concentramento *dzoh·na dee kon·chen·tra·men·toh*

convalescence n la convalescenza *kon·va·le·shen·tsa*

convenient adj utile *oo·tee·lay*; convenient to stores vicino(a) ai negozi *vee·chee·noh(a) a·ee ne·go·tsee*

convent n il convento *kon·ven·toh*

conversation n la conversazione *kon·vayr·sa·tsyoh·nay*

convertible n (car) l'automobile decappottabile (f) *ow·to·mo·bee·lay de·kap·pot·tah·bee·lay*

convince vt convincere* *kon·veen·che·ray*

cook vt cucinare *koo·chee·nah·ray* □ vi the meat is cooking la carne si sta cocendo *kahr·nay see sta ko·chen·doh* □ n cook il/la cuoco(a) *kwo·koh(a)*

cooker n la cucina *koo·chee·na*

cookie n il biscotto *bee·skot·toh*

cooking n la cucina *koo·chee·na*

cool adj fresco(a) *fray·skoh(a)*

cooling system n il sistema di raffreddamento *see·stay·ma dee raf·fred·da·men·toh*

co-operate vi collaborare *kol·la·bo·rah·ray*

co-operative n la cooperativa *koh·o·pay·ra·tee·va*

copper n (metal) il rame *rah·may*

copy n la copia *ko·pya* □ vt copiare *ko·pyah·ray* Bm22

copyright n il copyright *ko·pee·rite*

coral n il corallo *ko·ral·loh*

cord n (twine) la corda *kor·da*; (fabric) il velluto a coste *vel·loo·toh a ko·stay*

cordial n il cordiale *kor·dyah·lay*

corduroy n il velluto a coste *vel·loo·toh a ko·stay*

cork n il sughero *soo·ge·roh*; (of bottle) il tappo *tap·poh*

corkscrew n il cavatappi *ka·va·tap·pee*

corn n (cereal crop) il mais *ma·ees*; (on foot) il callo *kal·loh*

corner n (of streets) l'angolo (m) *an·go·loh*; (bend in road) la curva *koor·va* □ vi prendere* la curva *pren·de·ray la koor·va*

cornet n (of ice cream) il cornetto *kor·nayt·toh*

cornflakes pl i fiocchi di granturco *fyok·kee dee gran·toor·koh*

corn-on-the-cob n la pannocchia *pan·nok·kya*

cornstarch n la farina di granturco *fa·ree·na dee gran·toor·koh*

coronation n l'incoronazione (f) *een·ko·ro·na·tsyoh·nay*

corporation n (firm) la società *so·che·ta*; (of town) il consiglio comunale *kon·seel·yoh ko·moo·nah·lay*

corporation tax n la tassa industriale *tas·sa een·doo·stryah·lay*

correct adj (accurate) esatto(a) *e·zat·toh(a)*; (proper) corretto(a) *kor·ret·toh(a)* □ vt correggere* *kor·rej·je·ray*

correction n (alteration) la correzione *kor·re·tsyoh·nay*

correspondence n (mail) la corrispondenza *kor·ree·spon·den·tsa*

correspondence course n il corso per corrispondenza *kohr·soh payr kor·ree·spon·den·tsa*

corridor n il corridoio *kor·ree·doh·yoh*

corrode vt corrodere* *kor·ro·de·ray*

corrugated iron n la lamiera di ferro ondulata *la·mye·ra dee fer·roh on·doo·lah·ta*

corrugated paper n la carta increspata *kahr·ta een·kre·spah·ta*

corrupt adj corrotto(a) *kor·ro·toh(a)*

corruption n la corruzione *kor·roo·tsee·oh·nay*

corset n il corsetto *kor·sayt·toh*

Corsica n Corsica (f) *kor·see·ka*

cosmetics pl i cosmetici *koz·me·tee·chee*

cosmetic surgery n la chirurgia estetica *keer·oor·jee·a e·ste·tee·ka*

cosmopolitan adj cosmopolita *koz·mo·po·lee·ta*

cost n il costo *ko·stoh*; to buy something at cost comprare qualcosa a

prezzo di costo kom·prah·ray kwal·ko·sa a prets·tsoh dee ko·stoh □ vt
cost costare ko·stah·ray S4, Bm23
cost of living n il costo della vita ko·stoh del·la vee·ta
costs pl (of production etc) le spese spay·say
costume n (theatrical) il costume ko·stoo·may
costume jewelry n i gioielli di fantasia joy·yel·lee dee fan·ta·zee·a
cot n la brandina bran·dee·na
cottage n il cottage kot·tij
cottage cheese n il formaggio magro for·maj·joh mah·groh
cotton n (fabric) il cotone ko·toh·nay; (thread) il filo di cotone fee·loh dee ko·toh·nay
cotton batting n l'ovatta (f) o·vat·ta
couch n il divano dee·vah·noh
couchette n la cuccetta koo·chayt·ta
cough n la tosse tohs·say □ vi tossire tos·see·ray S40
cough drops pl le pastiglie per la tosse pa·steel·yay payr la tohs·say
cough medicine n lo sciroppo per la tosse shee·rop·poh payr la tohs·say
could vi □ we could do it lo potremmo fare loh po·trem·moh fah·ray; could I have... potrei avere... po·tre·ee a·vay·ray
council n (of town) il consiglio comunale kon·seel·yoh ko·moo·nah·lay
counselor n l'avvocato (m) av·vo·kah·toh
count vt (objects, people) contare kon·tah·ray □ vi to count up to 10 contare fino a 10 kon·tah·ray fee·no a 10
counter n (in shop) il banco ban·koh; (gambling) il gettone jet·toh·nay
counterfoil n il talloncino tal·lon·chee·noh
country n (land) il paese pa·ay·zay; (not town) la campagna kam·pan·ya; in the country in campagna een kam·pan·ya Mc13
countryside n la campagna kam·pan·ya
county n la contea kon·te·a
coup d'état n il colpo di stato kohl·poh dee stah·toh
coupé n (car) il coupé koo·pay
couple n (persons) la coppia kop·pya; a couple of (a few) un paio di oon pa·yoh dee
coupon n il buono bwo·noh
courage n il coraggio ko·raj·joh
courgettes pl gli zucchini tsook·kee·nee
courier n la guida gwee·da
course n (lessons) il corso kohr·soh; (of meal) il piatto pyat·toh; (for golf) il campo kam·poh; course of treatment il trattamento trat·ta·mayn·toh
court n (law) il tribunale tree·boo·nah·lay; (tennis etc) il campo kam·poh
courtyard n il cortile kor·tee·lay
cousin n il/la cugino(a) koo·jee·noh(a)
cover n (of book) la copertina ko·payr·tee·na; (blanket) la coperta ko·per·ta; (insurance) la protezione pro·te·tsyoh·ne; under separate cover in plico a parte een plee·koh a par·te □ vt cover coprire* ko·pree·ray; (distance) percorrere* payr·kohr·re·ray
cover charge n il prezzo del coperto prets·tsoh del ko·per·toh L54
covering letter n la lettera di accompagnamento layt·te·ra dee ak·kom·pan·ya·mayn·toh
cow n la vacca vak·ka
coward n il vigliacco veel·yak·koh
cowboy n il cow-boy kow·boy

crab n il granchio gran·kyoh
crack n (split) la fessura fes·soo·ra; (noise) lo schiocco skee·ok·koh □ vt to crack a glass incrinare un bicchiere een·kree·nah·ray oon beek·kye·ray □ vi the glass cracked il bicchiere si è incrinato eel beek·kye·ray see e een·kree·nah·toh
cracker n (crisp wafer) il cracker kra·ker; (paper toy) il petardo pe·tahr·doh
cradle n la culla kool·la
craft n l'arte (f) ahr·tay
craftsman n l'artigiano (m) ahr·tee·jah·noh
cramp n il crampo kram·poh
cranberry n il mirtillo meer·teel·loh
crane n (machine) la gru groo
crash n (noise) il fracasso fra·kas·soh; (collision) lo scontro skohn·troh □ vt to crash one's car avere* uno scontro con la macchina a·vay·ray oo·noh skohn·troh kohn la mak·kee·na □ vi to crash into something schiantarsi contro qualcosa skyan·tar·see kohn·tro kwal·ko·sa
crash course n il corso intensivo kohr·soh een·ten·see·voh
crash helmet n il casco kas·koh
crash-landing n l'atterraggio di fortuna (m) at·ter·raj·joh dee for·too·na
crate n la cassa kas·sa
crawfish, crayfish n il gambero gam·be·roh
crawl vi strisciare stree·shah·ray □ n (swimming) il crawl krol
crayon n il pastello pa·stel·loh
crazy adj pazzo(a) pats·tsoh(a)
cream n la panna pan·na; (cosmetic) la crema kre·ma □ adj crema kre·ma
cream cheese n il formaggio cremoso for·maj·joh kre·moh·so
creamy adj (texture) vellutato(a) vel·loo·tah·to(a)
crease n la piega pye·ga
creased adj sgualcito(a) zgwal·chee·toh(a)
create vt creare kray·ah·ray
crèche n il nido d'infanzia nee·doh deen·fan·tsya
credit n il credito kray·dee·toh; on credit a credito a kray·dee·toh; to give somebody credit fare* credito a qualcuno fah·ray kray·dee·toh a kwal·koo·noh □ vt to credit L.5000 to someone's account accreditare L.5000 al conto di qualcuno ak·kre·dee·tah·ray L5000 al kohn·toh dee kwal·koo·noh
credit card n la carta di credito kahr·ta dee kray·dee·toh T163, M13
creditor n il creditore kray·dee·toh·ray, la creditrice kray·dee·tree·chay
credit squeeze n la restrizione del credito re·stree·tsyoh·nay del kray·dee·toh
crème de menthe n la crème de menthe krem duh mont
cress n il crescione kre·shoh·nay
Crete n Creta (f) kray·ta
crew n (of ship, plane) l'equipaggio (m) e·kwee·paj·joh
crib n (baby's) il lettino let·tee·noh C12
cricket n (sport) il cricket kree·ket
crime n il delitto de·leet·toh
criminal adj criminale kree·mee·nah·lay
cripple n lo/la zoppo(a) tsop·poh(a)
crisis n la crisi kree·zee
crisp adj croccante krok·kan·tay

criticize vt criticare *kree·tee·kah·ray*
crockery n le stoviglie *sto·veel·ye*
crocodile n il coccodrillo *kok·koh· dreel·loh*
crocus n il croco *kroh·koh*
croissant n il croissant *krwah·soñ*
crooked adj storto(a) *stor·toh(a)*
crop n (harvest) il raccolto *rak·kol·toh*; (whip) il frustino *froo·stee·noh*
croquet n il croquet *kroh·key*
croquette n la crocchetta *krok·kayt·ta*
cross n la croce *kroh·chay* □ vt (road, sea) attraversare *at·tra·vayr·sah·ray*; to cross out cancellare *kan·chel·lah· ray*
crossing n (voyage) la traversata *tra· vayr·sah·ta*
crossroads n l'incrocio (m) *een·kroh· choh*
crosswalk n l'attraversamento pedonale (m) *at·tra·vayr·sa·mayn·toh pe· do·nah·lay*
croupier n il croupier *kroo·pyay*
crouton n il crostino *kro·stee·noh*
crowd n la folla *fol·la*
crowded adj affollato(a) *af·fol·lah· toh(a)*
crown n la corona *ko·roh·na*
crude adj (oil etc) grezzo(a) *graydz· zoh(a)*
cruel adj crudele *kroo·de·lay*
cruise n la crociera *kro·che·ra*; to go on a cruise fare* una crociera *fah·ray oo·na kro·che·ra*
crumb n la briciola *bree·cho·la*
crush vt schiacciare *skya·chah·ray*
crust n la crosta *kro·sta*
crutch n la gruccia *grooch·cha*
cry vi piangere* *pyan·je·ray* □ il grido *gree·doh*
crystal n (glass) il cristallo *kree·stal·loh*
cube n la zolletta *tsol·layt·ta*
cubicle n la cabina *ka·bee·na*
cucumber n il cetriolo *che·tree·o·loh*
cuddle vt abbracciare *ab·brach·chah· ray*
cuff n (of shirt) il polsino *pol·see·noh*
cuff link n il gemello *je·mel·loh*
cuisine n la cucina *koo·chee·na*
cul-de-sac n il vicolo cieco *vee·ko·loh che·koh*
cultivate vt coltivare *kol·tee·vah·ray*
culture n la cultura *kool·too·ra*
cup n la tazza *tats·tsa*; (trophy) la coppa *kop·pa*
cupboard n l'armadio (m) *ahr·mah· dyoh*
curb n il bordo del marciapiede *bohr· doh del mar·cha·pye·de*
cure vt curare *koo·rah·ray*
curious adj (inquisitive) curioso(a) *koo·ree·oh·soh(a)*; (strange) strano(a) *strah·noh(a)*
curl n il ricciolo *reech·cho·loh*
curler n (for hair) il bigodino *bee·go· dee·noh*
curly adj ricciuto(a) *reech·choo·toh(a)*
currant n l'uva passa (f) *oo·va pas·sa*
currency n la valuta *va·loo·ta*; foreign currency la divisa estera *dee·vee·za e· ste·ra*
current n (of water, air) la corrente *kor·ren·tay*
curry n il curry *kah·ree*
curry powder n la polvere di curry *pohl·ve·ray dee kah·ree*
curtain n la tenda *ten·da*
curve n la curva *koor·va*
cushion n il cuscino *koo·shee·noh*
custard n la crema *kre·ma*
custom n il costume *ko·stoo·may*

customer n il/la cliente *klee·en·tay*
custom-made adj fatto(a) su misura *fat·toh(a) soo mee·zoo·ra*
customs n la dogana *do·gah·na*
customs duty n il dazio *da·tsyoh*
customs officer n il doganiere *do·ga· nye·ray*
cut vt tagliare *tal·yah·ray*; (reduce) ridurre* *ree·door·ray*; (dilute) diluire *dee·loo·ee·ray*; to cut oneself tagliarsi *tal·yahr·see* □ n cut (wound) la ferita *fe·ree·ta*; (of meat) il pezzo *pets·tsoh* Sn36
cute adj (pretty) grazioso(a) *gra·tsyoh· soh(a)*
cutlery n la posateria *po·sah·te·ree·a*
cutlet n la cotoletta *ko·to·layt·ta*
cut-rate adj a prezzo ridotto *a prets· tsoh ree·doht·toh*
cycle vi andare* in bicicletta *an·dah· ray een bee·chee·klayt·ta*
cycling n il ciclismo *chee·klee·zmoh*; to go cycling fare* del ciclismo *fah·ray del chee·klee·zmoh*
cyclist n il/la ciclista *chee·klee·sta*
cylinder n il cilindro *chee·leen·droh*
Cyprus n Cipro (m) *chee·proh*
Czechoslovakia n Cecoslovacchia (f) *che·ko·slo·vak·kya*
Czech(oslovakian) n cecoslovacco(a) *che·ko·slo·vak·koh(a)*

D

dacron n il terilene *te·ree·le·ne*
dad(dy) n il papà *pa·pa*
daffodil n il trombone *trom·boh·ne*
dagger n il pugnale *poon·yah·le*
daily adj quotidiano(a) *kwo·tee·dee· ah·no(a)* □ n (newspaper) il quotidiano *kwo·tee·dee·ah·noh*
dainty adj delicato(a) *de·lee·kah·to(a)*
dairy store n la latteria *lat·te·ree·a*
dam n la diga *dee·ga*
damage n il danno *dan·noh*; damages i danni *dan·nee* □ vt damage danneggiare *dan·nej·jah·ray* Sn48
damp adj umido(a) *oo·mee·do(a)*
dance vi ballare *bal·lah·ray* □ n il ballo *bal·loh* L43
dandruff n la forfora *fohr·fo·ra*
danger n il pericolo *pe·ree·ko·loh*
dangerous adj pericoloso(a) *pe·ree·ko· loh·so(a)*
Danish adj danese *da·nay·se* □ n il danese *da·nay·se*
dare vi □ to dare to do something osare fare qualcosa *o·zah·ray fah·ray kwal·ko·sa*
dark adj buio(a) *boo·yo(a)*; (color) scuro(a) *skoo·ro(a)*; (hair) bruno(a) *broo·no(a)*
darling n caro(a) (m/f) *kah·ro(a)*
darn vt rammendare *ram·men·dah·ray*
dart n (to throw) il dardo *dar·doh*; (on clothes) la pince *pañs*; game of darts il gioco dei dardi *jo·koh de·ee dar· dee*
dash n (in writing) il trattino *trat·tee· noh*
dash(board) n il cruscotto *kroos·kot· toh*
data pl i dati *dah·tee*
data bank, data base n la banca di dati *ban·ka de·ee dah·tee*
data file n l'archivio di dati (m) *ar·kee· vee·oh dee dah·tee*
data processing n l'elaborazione dei dati (f) *e·la·bo·ra·tsyoh·nay de·ee dah·tee*
date n (day) la data *dah·ta*; (appoint-

ment) l'appuntamento (*m*) *ap·poon· ta·mayn·toh*; (*fruit*) il dattero *dat·te· roh*; **what's the date today?** quanti ne abbiamo oggi? *kwan·tee ne ab·byah· mo oj·jee*; **out of date** antiquato(a) *an·tee·kwa·to(a)*

date line *n* la meridiana di cambiamento di data *me·ree·dee·ah·na dee kam·bya·mayn·toh dee dah·ta*

daughter *n* la figlia *feel·ya* C11

daughter-in-law *n* la nuora *nwoh·ra*

dawn *n* l'alba (*f*) *al·ba*

day *n* il giorno *johr·noh*; (*length of time*) la giornata *johr·nah·ta*; **every day** ogni giorno *ohn·yee johr·noh*; **day by day** di giorno in giorno *dee johr·noh een johr·noh*; **the day before** il giorno prima *eel johr·noh pree·ma*; **the next** *or* **following day** l'indomani (*m*) *leen·do·mah·nee* T111

day nursery *n* il nido d'infanzia *nee· doh deen·fan·tsya* C4

dazzle *vt* abbagliare *ab·bal·yah·ray*

dead *adj* (*person*) morto(a) *mor·to(a)*; (*battery*) scaricato(a) *ska·ree·kah· to(a)*; **the line is dead** (*phone*) la linea è bloccata *la lee·ne·a e blok· kah·ta*

dead end *n* il vicolo cieco *vee·ko·loh che·ko*

deaf *adj* sordo(a) *sohr·do(a)*

deal *n* l'affare (*m*) *af·fah·ray* □ *vi* **to deal with a firm** avere* rapporti d'affari con una ditta *a·vay·re rap·por·tee daf·fah·ree kohn oo·na deet·ta*; **to deal with a subject** trattare un argomento *trat·tah·ray oon ar·go·mayn· toh*; **to deal in something** commerciare in qualcosa *kom·mayr·chah·ray een kwal·ko·sa*

dealer *n* il commerciante *kom·mayr· chan·te*; (*cards*) il mazziere *mats· tsye·re*

dear *adj* caro(a) *kah·ro(a)*; **Dear Sir** Egregio Signore *e·gre·joh seen·yoh· ray*; **Dear Madam** Gentile Signora *jen·tee·le seen·yoh·ra*; **Dear Mr. Smith** Egregio Signor Smith *e·gre· joh seen·yohr smith*

death *n* la morte *mor·te*

death certificate *n* il certificato di morte *chayr·tee·fee·kah·toh dee mor·te*

debate *n* il dibattito *dee·bat·tee·toh*

debit *n* l'addebito (*m*) *ad·day·bee·toh* □ *vt* **to debit L.5000 to someone's account** addebitare L.5000 al conto di qualcuno *ad·day·bee·tah·ray L5000 al kohn·toh dee kwal·koo·no*

debt *n* il debito *day·bee·toh*; **to be in debt** avere* dei debiti *a·vay·re de·ee day·bee·tee*

decade *n* il decennio *de·chen·nyoh*

decaffeinated *adj* decaffeinizzato(a) *de·kaf·fe·ee·needz·dzah·to(a)*

decanter *n* la caraffa *ka·raf·fa*

deceive *vt* ingannare *een·gan·nah·ray*

December *n* dicembre (*m*) *dee·chem· bre*

decent *adj* (*moral*) decente *de·chen·te*; (*respectable*) onesto(a) *o·ne·sto(a)*

decide *vi* (*between alternatives*) decidersi* *de·chee·der·see*; **to decide to do something** decidere* di fare qualcosa *de·chee·de·re dee fah·ray kwal· ko·sa*

decimal *adj* decimale *de·chee·mah·le* □ *n* il decimale *de·chee·mah·le*

decimal point *n* la virgola decimale *veer·go·la de·chee·mah·le*

decision *n* la decisione *de·chee·zyoh· nay*

deck *n* (*of ship*) il ponte *pohn·te*; (*of cards*) il mazzo *mats·tsoh*

deckchair *n* la sedia a sdraio *se·dya a zdra·yo* L26

declare *vt* dichiarare *dee·kya·rah·ray*; **nothing to declare** niente da dichiarare *nyen·te da dee·kya·rah·ray*

decorate *vt* (*adorn*) decorare *de·ko· rah·ray*; (*paint*) verniciare *vayr·nee· chah·ray*

decorations *pl* gli addobbi *ad·dob·bee*

decrease *n* il diminuire *dee·mee·noo· ee·re*

deduct *vt* detrarre* *de·trar·re*

deep *adj* (*water, hole*) profondo(a) *pro·fohn·do(a)*; (*voice*) basso(a) *bas· so(a)*

deepfreeze *n* il congelatore *kon·je·la· toh·re*

deer *n* il cervo *cher·voh*

defeat *vt* sconfiggere* *skon·feej·je·re* □ *n* la sconfitta *skon·feet·ta*

defect *n* il difetto *dee·fet·toh*

defective *adj* difettoso(a) *dee·fet·toh· so(a)*

defend *vt* difendere* *dee·fen·de·re*

defense *n* la difesa *dee·fay·sa*

deficit *n* il deficit *de·fee·cheet*

definite *adj* (*distinct*) chiaro(a) *kyah· ro(a)*; (*certain*) certo(a) *cher·to(a)*

definitely *adv* certamente *cher·ta· mayn·tay*

deflation *n* la deflazione *de·fla· tsyoh·ne*

deformed *adj* deforme *de·fohr·me*

defrost *vt* (*food*) disgelare *dee·zje·lah· ray*; (*refrigerator*) sbrinare *zbree· nah·ray*

defroster *n* l'antiappannante (*m*) *an· tee·ap·pan·nan·te*

degree *n* il grado *grah·do*; (*university*) la laurea *low·re·a*

de-ice *vt* sghiacciare *zgyach·chah·ray*

delay *vt* (*hold up*) ritardare *ree·tar· dah·ray*; (*postpone*) rinviare *reen· vee·ah·ray*; **the train has been delayed** il treno ha un ritardo *eel tre·no a oon ree·tar·doh* □ *n* **delay** (*to train, plane*) il ritardo *ree·tar·doh* T83

delegate *vt* delegare *de·le·gah·ray*

delegation *n* la delegazione *de·le·ga· tsyoh·nay*

deliberate *adj* intenzionale *een·ten· tsyoh·nah·le*

deliberately *adv* apposta *ap·po·sta*

delicate *adj* delicato(a) *de·lee·kah· to(a)*

delicatessen *n* la salumeria *sa·loo·me· ree·a*

delicious *adj* delizioso(a) *de·lee·tsyoh· so(a)*

delighted *adj* felicissimo(a) *fe·lee· chees·see·mo(a)*

deliver *vt* (*mail*) distribuire *dee·stree· boo·ee·re*; (*goods*) consegnare *kon· sen·yah·ray*

delivery *n* (*of mail*) la distribuzione *dee·stree·boo·tsyoh·ne*; (*of goods*) la consegna *kon·sayn·ya*

de luxe *adj* di lusso *dee loos·so*

demand *vt* esigere* *e·zee·je·re* □ *n* (*for goods*) la domanda *do·man·da*

demonstrate *vt* (*appliance etc*) mostrare *mo·strah·ray*

demonstration *n* la dimostrazione *dee· mo·stra·tsyoh·ne*; (*political*) la manifestazione *ma·nee·fe·sta·tsyoh·ne*

denim *n* la tela di blue-jeans *tay·la dee bloo·jeens*

Denmark n Danimarca (f) da·nee·mar·ka

dense adj (fog etc) fitto(a) feet·to(a)

dent n l'ammaccatura (f) am·mak·ka·too·ra

dentist n il/la dentista den·tee·sta I54

dentures pl la dentiera den·tye·ra I64

deny vt negare ne·gah·ray

deodorant n il deodorante de·o·do·ran·te

department n (in store) il reparto re·par·toh S11

department store n il grande magazzino gran·de ma·gadz·dzee·noh

departure board n il tabellone delle partenze ta·bel·loh·ne del·le par·ten·tse T38

departure lounge n la sala di partenza sah·la dee par·ten·tsa

depend vi □ it depends dipende dee·pen·de; to depend on dipendere* da dee·pen·de·re da

deposit n (down payment) il deposito de·po·zee·toh; (for key etc) la cauzione kow·tsyoh·ne □ vt (money) depositare de·po·zee·tah·ray M9

depot n la stazione autobus sta·tsyoh·ne ow·to·boos; (trains) lo scalo skah·loh

depressed adj (person) giù di spirito joo dee spee·ree·toh

depth n la profondità pro·fohn·dee·ta

deputy n (second-in-command) il/la vice vee·che

derby n la bombetta bom·bayt·ta

describe vt descrivere* de·skree·ve·re

description n la descrizione de·skree·tsyoh·ne

desert n il deserto de·zer·toh

deserve vt meritare me·ree·tah·ray

design n il disegno dee·sayn·yoh □ vt disegnare dee·sen·yah·ray

designer n il disegnatore dee·sen·ya·toh·re; (of clothes) il/la modellista mo·del·lee·sta

desire n il desiderio de·see·de·ree·oh

desk n (in office) la scrivania skree·va·nee·a; (reception) il ricevimento ree·che·vee·mayn·toh

desperate adj disperato(a) dee·spe·rah·to(a)

despite prep malgrado mal·grah·do

dessert n il dolce dohl·che

dessertspoon n il cucchiaio kook·kee·a·yoh

destination n la destinazione de·stee·na·tsyoh·ne

destroy vt distruggere* dee·strooj·je·re

detached house n la villa veel·la

detail n il particolare par·tee·ko·lah·ray; in detail dettagliatamente det·tal·yah·ta·mayn·tay Bm20

detailed adj dettagliato(a) det·tal·yah·to(a)

detective n l'investigatore (m) een·ve·stee·ga·toh·ray

detergent n il detersivo de·tayr·see·voh

determined adj deciso(a) de·chee·so(a); to be determined to do something essere* deciso a fare qualcosa es·se·re de·chee·so a fah·ray kwal·ko·sa

detour n la deviazione de·vee·a·tsyoh·ne; to make a detour fare* una deviazione fah·ray oo·na de·vee·a·tsyoh·ne T134

devaluation n la svalutazione zva·loo·ta·tsyoh·ne

devalue vt (currency) svalutare zva·loo·tah·ray

develop vi svilupparsi zvee·loop·par·see □ vt (photo) sviluppare zvee·loop·pah·ray

developing country n il paese in via di sviluppo pa·e·ze een vee·a dee zvee·loop·poh

development n (housing) la zona residenziale dzo·na re·see·den·tsyah·le

diabetes n il diabete dee·a·be·te

diabetic n il/la diabetico(a) dee·a·be·tee·ko(a)

diagnosis n la diagnosi dee·an·yo·zee

diagonal adj diagonale dee·a·go·nah·le

diagram n il diagramma dee·a·gram·ma

dial vt (number) comporre* kom·pohr·re

dialect n il dialetto dee·a·let·toh

dial tone n il segnale di linea libera sen·yah·le dee lee·nay·a lee·bay·ra

diameter n il diametro dee·a·me·troh

diamond n il diamante dee·a·man·te; diamonds (cards) i quadri kwa·dree

diaper n il pannolino pan·no·lee·noh C19

diarrhea n la diarrea dee·ar·re·a

diary n l'agenda (f) a·jen·da

dice n i dadi dah·dee

dictate vt (letter) dettare det·tah·ray

dictionary n il dizionario dee·tsyoh·nah·ree·oh

die vi morire* mo·ree·re

diesel n il diesel dee·zel

diesel engine n il motore diesel mo·toh·re dee·zel

diesel fuel n la nafta naf·ta

diet n (slimming) la dieta dee·e·ta; to be on a diet stare* a dieta stah·ray a dee·e·ta

difference n la differenza deef·fe·ren·tsa

different adj differente deef·fe·ren·te; different from diverso(a) da dee·ver·so(a) da

difficult adj difficile deef·fee·chee·le

difficulty n la difficoltà deef·fee·kol·ta

dig vt (ground) vangare van·gah·ray; (hole) scavare ska·vah·ray; to dig up scavare ska·vah·ray

digital adj digitale dee·jee·tah·le

dike n la diga dee·ga

dilute vt diluire de·loo·ee·re

dim adj (light) debole day·bo·le; (room) oscuro(a) o·skoo·ro(a) □ vt (headlights) abbassare ab·bas·sah·ray

dimensions pl le dimensioni dee·men·syoh·nee

dimmer n l'interruttore degli anabbaglianti (m) een·ter·root·toh·re del·yee an·ab·bal·yan·tee

diner n il ristorante self-service ree·sto·ran·te self·sayr·vees

dinghy n il dinghy din·gee; (inflatable) il gommone gom·moh·ne

dining car n il vagone ristorante va·goh·ne ree·sto·ran·te

dining room n la sala da pranzo sah·la da pran·dzoh

dinner n la cena chay·na E6

dinner jacket n lo smoking smo·keeng

dinner party n la cena chay·na

dip vt (into liquid) immergere* eem·mer·je·re

diploma n il diploma dee·plo·ma

diplomat n il diplomatico dee·plo·ma·tee·koh

dipstick n l'asta dell'olio (f) a·sta del·lol·yoh

direct adj diretto(a) dee·ret·to(a) □ adv to fly to Venice direct prendere* un volo diretto per Venezia pren·de·re oon vo·loh *dee·ret·to* payr ve·ne·tsya □ *vt* direct (traffic) dirigere* *dee·ree·je·re*

direction *n* la direzione *dee·re·tsyoh·ne*; **in the direction of** nella direzione di *nel·la dee·re·tsyoh·ne dee*; **directions** (to a place) le indicazioni *een·dee·ka·tsyoh·nee*; **directions for use** le istruzioni per l'uso *ee·stroo·tsyoh·nee payr loo·zoh*

director *n* (of firm) il direttore *dee·ret·toh·re*; (of film) il regista *re·jee·sta* Bm3

directory *n* la guida *gwee·da*; (telephone) l'elenco telefonico (m) *e·len·ko te·le·fo·nee·ko* Sn16

dirt *n* la sporcizia *spor·chee·tsya*

dirty *adj* sporco(a) *spor·ko(a)* A49

disabled *adj* invalido(a) *een·va·lee·do(a)* I2, 3

disadvantage *n* lo svantaggio *zvan·taj·joh*; **at a disadvantage** svantaggiato(a) *zvan·taj·jah·to(a)*

disagree *vi* □ **to disagree with somebody** non essere* d'accordo con qualcuno *nohn es·se·re dak·kor·doh kohn kwal·koo·no*; **eggs disagree with me** le uova mi restano sullo stomaco *le wo·va mee re·sta·no sool·lo sto·ma·koh*

disagreement *n* il dissenso *dees·sen·soh*

disappear *vi* sparire* *spa·ree·re*

disappointed *adj* deluso(a) *de·loo·zo(a)*

disapprove *vi* □ **to disapprove of something** disapprovare qualcosa *dee·zap·pro·vah·ray kwal·ko·sa*

disaster *n* il disastro *dee·za·stroh*

disc brakes *pl* i freni a disco *fray·nee a dee·sko*

discipline *n* la disciplina *dee·shee·plee·na*

disc jockey *n* il disc-jockey *deesk·jok·kee*

disco(thèque) *n* la discoteca *dee·sko·te·ka*

discount *n* lo sconto *skohn·toh*; **at a discount** con uno sconto *kohn oo·no skohn·toh* M5f

discouraged *adj* scoraggiato(a) *sko·raj·jah·to(a)*

discover *vt* scoprire* *sko·pree·re*

discreet *adj* discreto(a) *dee·skray·to(a)*

discrimination *n* (racial etc) la discriminazione *dee·skree·mee·na·tsyoh·ne*

discuss *vt* discutere* *dee·skoo·te·re*

disease *n* la malattia *ma·lat·tee·a*

disguise *n* il travestimento *tra·ve·stee·mayn·toh*; **in disguise** travestito(a) *tra·ve·stee·to(a)*

disgust *n* il disgusto *dee·zgoo·stoh*

disgusted *adj* indignato(a) *een·deen·yah·to(a)*

dish *n* il piatto *pyat·toh* E19

dishcloth *n* lo strofinaccio per i piatti *stro·fee·nach·choh payr ee pyat·tee*

dishonest *adj* disonesto(a) *dee·zo·ne·sto(a)*

dishtowel *n* il canovaccio *ka·no·vach·choh*

dish up *vt* servire *ser·vee·re*

dishwasher *n* la lavastoviglie *la·va·sto·veel·ye*

disinfect *vt* disinfettare *dee·zeen·fet·tah·ray*

disinfectant *n* il disinfettante *dee·zeen·fet·tan·te*

disk *n* il disco *dee·sko*; **slipped disk** l'ernia al disco (f) *er·nee·a al dee·sko*

dislocate *vt* slogare *zlo·gah·ray*

dismiss *vt* (from job) licenziare *lee·chen·tsyah·ray*

disobedient *adj* disubbidiente *dee·zoob·bee·dyen·te*

disobey *vt* disubbidire *dee·zoob·bee·dee·re*

dispatch *vt* spedire *spe·dee·re*

disposable *adj* da gettare via *da jet·tah·ray vee·a*

dispute *vt* (fact) contestare *kon·te·stah·ray* □ *n* la disputa *dee·spoo·ta*; (industrial) il conflitto *kon·fleet·toh*

disqualify *vt* squalificare *skwa·lee·fee·kah·ray*

dissolve *vt* sciogliere* *shol·ye·re* □ *vi* sciogliersi *shol·yer·see*

distance *n* la distanza *dee·stan·tsa*; **in the distance** in lontananza *een lon·ta·nan·tsa*

distant *adj* distante *dee·stan·te*

distilled water *n* l'acqua distillata (f) *ak·kwa dee·steel·lah·ta*

distillery *n* la distilleria *dee·steel·le·ree·a*

distinct *adj* (clear) distinto(a) *dee·steen·to(a)*

distinguish *vt* distinguere* *dee·steen·gwe·re*; **to distinguish something from something** distinguere* qualcosa da qualcosa *dee·steen·gwe·re kwal·ko·sa da kwal·ko·sa*

distract *vt* distrarre* *dee·strar·re*

distress *n* l'angoscia (f) *an·go·sha*; **a ship in distress** una nave in pericolo *oo·na nah·ve een pe·ree·ko·lo*

distributor *n* (in car) il distributore *dee·stree·boo·toh·re*; (commercial) il grossista *gro·sees·ta*

district *n* (of town) il quartiere *kwar·tye·re*; (in country) la regione *re·joh·ne*; (administrative) la circoscrizione *cheer·ko·skree·tsyoh·ne*

disturb *vt* (interrupt) disturbare *dee·stoor·bah·ray*; **do not disturb** pregasi non disturbare *pre·ga·see nohn dee·stoor·bah·ray*

ditch *n* il fossato *fos·sah·toh*

divan *n* il divano *dee·vah·noh*

dive *vi* tuffarsi *toof·far·see* □ *n* il tuffo *toof·foh*

diversify *vt/i* diversificare *dee·ver·see·fee·kah·ray*

divert *vt* deviare *de·vee·ah·ray*

divide *vt* (separate) separare *se·pa·rah·ray*; (apportion) dividere* *dee·vee·de·re*; **to divide 8 by 4** dividere* 8 per 4 *dee·vee·de·re 8 payr 4*

divided highway *n* la carreggiata doppia *kar·rej·jah·ta dop·pya*

dividend *n* il dividendo *dee·vee·den·doh*

divingboard *n* il trampolino *tram·po·lee·noh*

divorce *n* il divorzio *dee·vor·tsyoh*

divorced *adj* divorziato(a) *dee·vor·tsyah·to(a)*

dizzy *adj* (person) preso(a) da vertigine *pray·so(a) da ver·tee·jee·ne*

do *vt/i* fare* *fah·ray*; **will it do?** (be enough) basta così? *ba·sta ko·see*; (be suitable) conviene? *kon·vye·ne*; **you know him, don't you?** lo conosce, non è vero? *lo ko·no·she, nohn e vay·ro*; **he didn't come, did he?** non è venuto, vero? *nohn e ve·noo·to, vay·ro*

dock *n* il bacino *ba·chee·noh*

doctor *n* il medico *me·dee·koh*; **it's Doctor Smith** è il dottor/la dottoressa Smith *e eel dot·tohr/la dot·toh·res·sa Smith* I6

doctor's office *n* il gabinetto medico *ga·bee·nayt·toh me·dee·ko*

document *n* il documento *do·koo·mayn·toh* Bm22, T121

dog *n* il cane *kah·ne*

do-it-yourself *n* il fatelo da voi *fah·te·lo da voy*

doll *n* la bambola *bam·bo·la*

dollar *n* il dollaro *dol·la·roh* M23

dollar bill *n* la banconota di un dollaro *ban·ko·no·ta da oon dol·la·roh*

donate *vt (funds)* donare *do·nah·ray*

donation *n (money)* il dono *doh·noh*

done *adj (cooked)* cotto(a) *kot·to(a)*

donkey *n* l'asino *(m) ah·see·noh*

door *n* la porta *por·ta* A60

doorbell *n* il campanello *kam·pa·nel·loh*

door handle, doorknob *n* la maniglia *ma·neel·ya*

doorman *n (in hotel)* il portiere *por·tye·re*

doormat *n* lo zerbino *dzer·bee·noh*

doorstep *n* il gradino della porta *gra·dee·noh del·la por·ta*

door-to-door salesman *n* il venditore a domicilio *ven·dee·toh·re a do·mee·cheel·yoh*

dormitory *n (room)* il dormitorio *dor·mee·to·ryoh; (of college)* la casa dello studente *kah·sa del·lo stoo·den·te*

dosage *n* il dosaggio *do·zaj·joh*

dose *n* la dose *do·ze*

dot *n* il punto *poon·toh*

dotted line *n* la linea punteggiata *lee·ne·a poon·tej·jah·ta*

double *vt* raddoppiare *rad·dop·pyah·ray* □ *adv* to cost double costare il doppio *ko·stah·ray eel dop·pyoh* □ *adj* double doppio(a) *dop·pyo(a)*; a double whiskey un whisky doppio *wee·skee dop·pyo*

double bed *n* il letto matrimoniale *let·toh ma·tree·mo·nyah·le* A4

double-parking *n* il parcheggio in doppia fila *par·kayj·joh een dop·pya fee·la*

double room *n* la camera matrimoniale *kah·me·ra ma·tree·mo·nyah·le* A4

doubt *n* il dubbio *doob·byoh*; no doubt senza dubbio *sen·tsa doob·byoh*; without (a) doubt senza alcun dubbio *sen·tsa al·koon doob·byoh* □ *vt* doubt dubitare *doo·bee·tah·ray*; I doubt it ne dubito *ne doo·bee·to*

doubtful *adj* incerto(a) *een·cher·to(a)*

dough *n* la pasta *pa·sta*

doughnut *n* il bombolone *bom·bo·loh·ne*

dove *n* la colomba *ko·lohm·ba*

down *n (fluff)* il piumino *pyoo·mee·noh* □ *adv* to come down venire* giú *ve·nee·re joo*; to go down scendere* *shayn·de·re* □ *prep* down giú per *joo payr*

downhill *adv* in discesa *een dee·shay·sa*; to go downhill scendere* *shayn·de·re*

down payment *n* l'acconto *(m) ak·kohn·toh*

downstairs *adv* di sotto *dee soht·to*

downstream *adv* a valle *a val·le*

downtown *adv* in centro *een chen·troh* □ *adj* downtown Chicago il centro di Chicago *chen·troh dee shee·kah·go*

downward(s) *adv* in basso *een bas·so*

doze *vi* sonnecchiare *son·nek·kyah·ray*

dozen *n* la dozzina *dodz·dzee·na*; 4

dozen eggs 4 dozzine di uova *4 dodz·dzee·ne dee wo·va*

drab *adj* scialbo(a) *shal·bo(a)*

draft *n (wind)* la corrente d'aria *kor·ren·te dah·ree·a; (financial)* la cambiale *kam·bee·ah·le; (rough outline)* l'abbozzo *(m) ab·bots·tsoh*

draft beer *n* la birra alla spina *beer·ra al·la spee·na*

draftsman *n* il disegnatore *dee·sen·ya·toh·re*

drag *vt* trascinare *tra·shee·nah·ray*

drain *n* la fogna *foh·nya* □ *vt (land)* prosciugare *pro·shoo·gah·ray; (vegetables)* scolare *sko·lah·ray; (sump, pool)* svuotare *zvwo·tah·ray*

drainboard *n* lo scolapiatti *sko·la·pyat·tee*

drainpipe *n* il tubo di scolo *too·boh dee skoh·loh*

drama *n (art)* il teatro *te·ah·troh*

dramatic *adj* drammatico(a) *dram·ma·tee·ko(a)*

drape *n* la tenda *ten·da*

drastic *adj* drastico(a) *dra·stee·ko(a)*

draw *vt (picture)* disegnare *dee·sen·yah·ray*; to draw out *(money)* ritirare *ree·tee·rah·ray*; to draw up *(document)* redigere* *re·dee·je·re*

drawer *n* il cassetto *kas·sayt·toh*

drawing *n* il disegno *dee·sayn·yoh*

drawing pin *n* la puntina *poon·tee·na*

dread *vt* temere *te·may·ray*

dream *n* il sogno *sohn·yoh* □ *vi* sognare *son·yah·ray*; to dream of or about sognare di *son·yah·ray dee*

dress *n* il vestito *ve·stee·toh* □ *vt (child)* vestire *ve·stee·re* □ *vi (oneself)* vestirsi *ve·steer·see* S56, 58

dress circle *n* la prima galleria *pree·ma gal·le·ree·a*

dressing *n (salad)* il condimento *kon·dee·mayn·toh; (stuffing)* il ripieno *ree·pye·noh*

dressing gown *n* la vestaglia *ve·stal·ya*

dressing table *n* la tavola da toeletta *tah·vo·la da to·e·let·ta*

dried *adj (fruit, beans)* secco(a) *sayk·ko(a)*; dried milk il latte in polvere *lat·te een pohl·ve·re*

drift *vi (boat)* andare* alla deriva *an·dah·ray al·la de·ree·va*

drill *n (tool)* il trapano *tra·pa·noh* □ *vt (hole)* perforare *payr·fo·rah·ray*

drink *vt* bere* *bay·re* □ *n* la bevanda *be·van·da*; have a drink! prenda qualcosa da bere! *pren·da kwal·ko·sa da bay·re* L53, B52

drinking water *n* l'acqua potabile *(f) ak·kwa po·tah·bee·le* A88

drip *n* la goccia *gohch·cha* □ *vi* gocciolare *goch·cho·lah·ray*

drip-dry *vt* lasciare ad asciugarsi *la·shah·ray ad a·shoo·gar·see* □ *adj (shirt etc)* che non si stira *ke nohn see stee·ra*

drive *vt (car etc)* guidare *gwee·dah·ray* □ *vi* andare* in macchina *an·dah·ray een mak·kee·na*; do you drive? sa guidare? *sa gwee·dah·ray* □ *n* drive *(journey)* il viaggio *vee·aj·joh; (driveway)* l'ingresso *(m) een·gres·soh*; to go for a drive fare* un giro in macchina *fah·ray oon jee·roh een mak·kee·na*; left-hand drive la guida a sinistra *gwee·da a se·nee·stra*; front-wheel drive la trazione anteriore *tra·tsyoh·ne an·te·ryoh·re*

driver *n (of car)* il guidatore *gwee·da·toh·re; (of taxi, bus)* il conducente *kon·doo·chen·te*

driver's license *n* la patente di guida *pa·ten·te dee gwee·da* T10

drizzle *n* la pioviggine *pyo·veej·jee·ne*

drop *n* (*of liquid*) la goccia *gohch·cha* □ *vt* (*let fall*) lasciare cadere *la·shah·ray ka·day·re* □ *vi* (*fall*) cadere* *ka·day·re*

drought *n* la siccità *seech·chee·ta*

drown *vt* annegare *an·ne·gah·ray*

drug *n* (*medicine*) il medicinale *me·dee·chee·nah·le*; (*narcotic*) la droga *dro·ga* 144

druggist *n* il/la farmacista *far·ma·chee·sta*

drugstore *n* la farmacia *far·ma·chee·a*

drum *n* il tamburo *tam·boo·roh*

drumstick *n* (*of chicken*) la coscia *ko·sha*

drunk *adj* ubriaco(a) *oo·bree·ah·ko(a)*

dry *adj* secco(a) *sayk·ko(a)* □ *vt* asciugare *a·shoo·gah·ray*

dry-clean *vt* lavare a secco *la·vah·ray a sayk·ko*

dry-cleaner's *n* la tintoria *teen·to·ree·a*

duck *n* l'anatra (*f*) *ah·na·tra*

due *adj* (*owing*) da pagarsi *da pa·gar·see*; **when is the train due?** quando deve arrivare il treno? *kwan·do de·ve ar·ree·vah·ray eel tre·no*

duke *n* il duca *doo·ka*

dull *adj* (*day, weather*) uggioso(a) *ooj·joh·so(a)*; (*boring*) noioso(a) *no·yoh·so(a)*

dumb *adj* muto(a) *moo·to(a)*; (*stupid*) stupido(a) *stoo·pee·do(a)*

dump *n* (*for rubbish*) il luogo di scarico *lwo·go dee skah·ree·ko*

dumping *n* (*of goods*) il dumping *dum·peeng*

dumpling *n* lo gnocco *nyok·ko*

dune *n* la duna *doo·na*

dungarees *pl* la tuta *too·ta*

dungeon *n* la prigione sotterranea *pree·joh·ne sot·ter·rah·ne·a*

durable *adj* (*fabric, article*) resistente *re·see·sten·te*

during *prep* durante *doo·ran·te*

dusk *n* il crepuscolo *kre·poo·sko·lo*

dust *n* la polvere *pohl·ve·re* □ *vt* (*furniture*) spolverare *spol·ve·rah·ray*

dustpan *n* la paletta *pa·layt·ta*

dusty *adj* polveroso(a) *pol·ve·roh·so(a)*

Dutch *adj* olandese *o·lan·day·se* □ *n* l'olandese (*m*) *o·lan·day·se*

duty *n* (*obligation*) il dovere *do·vay·ray*; (*function*) il compito *kohm·pee·to*; (*tax*) il dazio *da·tsyoh*; **on duty** (*doctor*) in servizio *een sayr·vee·tsyoh*; **off duty** fuori servizio *fwo·ree sayr·vee·tsyoh*

duty-free *adj* esente da dogana *e·zen·te da do·gah·na* T41, S10

dye *n* la tinta *teen·ta* □ *vt* tingere* *teen·je·re*

dynamic *adj* (*person*) dinamico(a) *dee·na·mee·ko(a)*

dynamo *n* la dinamo *dee·na·mo*

E

each *adj* ogni *ohn·yee* □ *pron* ciascuno(a) *cha·skoo·no(a)*

eager *adj* desideroso(a) *de·see·de·roh·so(a)*; **to be eager to do something** essere* impaziente di fare qualcosa *es·se·re eem·pa·tsyen·te dee fah·ray kwal·ko·sa*

eagle *n* l'aquila (*f*) *ah·kwee·la*

ear *n* l'orecchio (*m*) *o·rayk·kyoh*

earache *n* il mal d'orecchi *mal do·rayk·kee*; **to have an earache** avere*

mal d'orecchi *a·vay·re mal do·rayk·kee*

earlier *adj* precedente *pre·che·den·te* □ *adv* prima *pree·ma*

early *adj* primo(a) *pree·mo(a)*; **you're early** Lei è in anticipo *lay e een an·tee·chee·poh* □ *adv* early presto *pre·sto*

earn *vt* guadagnare *gwa·dan·yah·ray*

earnings *pl* gli introiti *een·troy·tee*

earplugs *pl* i tappi per gli orecchi *tap·pee payr lyee o·rayk·kee*

earring *n* l'orecchino (*m*) *o·rek·kee·noh*

earth *n* la terra *ter·ra*

earthquake *n* il terremoto *ter·re·mo·toh*

ease *vt* (*pain*) alleviare *al·le·vyah·ray*

easily *adv* facilmente *fah·cheel·mayn·te*

east *n* l'est (*m*) *est*; **the East** l'Oriente (*m*) *o·ree·en·te* □ *adv* east ad est *ad est*

Easter *n* Pasqua (*f*) *pa·skwa*

Easter egg *n* l'uovo di Pasqua (*m*) *wo·voh dee pa·skwa*

eastern *adj* orientale *o·ree·en·tah·le*

East Germany *n* la Germania Orientale *jer·mah·nya o·ree·en·tah·le*

easy *adj* facile *fah·chee·le*

eat *vt* mangiare *man·jah·ray*

eau-de-Cologne *n* l'acqua di Colonia (*f*) *ak·kwa dee ko·lon·ya*

eccentric *adj* eccentrico(a) *ech·chen·tree·ko(a)*

echo *n* l'eco (*m/f*) *e·koh*

éclair *n* il cannolo *kan·no·loh*

economic *adj* economico(a) *e·ko·no·mee·ko(a)*

economical *adj* (*use, method*) economico(a) *e·ko·no·mee·ko(a)*

economics *n* l'economia (*f*) *e·ko·no·mee·a*

economist *n* l'economista (*m/f*) *e·ko·no·mee·sta*

economy *n* (*of country*) l'economia (*f*) *e·ko·no·mee·a*

eczema *n* l'eczema (*m*) *ek·ze·ma*

edge *n* il bordo *bohr·doh*; (*of blade*) il filo *fee·loh*

edition *n* l'edizione (*f*) *e·dee·tsyoh·ne*

educate *vt* istruire *ee·stroo·ee·re*

education *n* l'istruzione (*f*) *ee·stroo·tsyoh·ne*

E.E.C. *n* la C.E.E. *che·e*

eels *pl* le anguille *an·gweel·lay*

effect *n* l'effetto (*m*) *ef·fet·toh*; **to take effect** avere* effetto *a·vay·re ef·fet·toh*

effective *adj* (*remedy etc*) efficace *ef·fee·kah·che*

efficient *adj* efficiente *ef·fee·chen·te*

effort *n* lo sforzo *sfor·tsoh*

e.g. *abbrev* p.es. *payr e·zaym·pyoh*

egg *n* l'uovo (*m*) *wo·voh* S31

egg cup *n* il portauovo *por·ta·wo·voh*

eggplant *n* la melanzana *me·lan·dzah·na*

Egypt *n* Egitto (*m*) *e·jeet·toh*

Egyptian *adj* egiziano(a) *e·jee·tsyah·no(a)*

eiderdown *n* il piumino *pyoo·mee·noh*

eight *num* otto *ot·to*

eighteen *num* diciotto *dee·chot·to*

eighth *adj* ottavo(a) *ot·tah·vo(a)*

eighties *pl* (*decade*) gli anni ottanta *an·nee ot·tan·ta*

eighty *num* ottanta *ot·tan·ta*

either *pron* □ **either of you** o l'uno o l'altro di voi *o loo·noh o lal·troh dee voy*; **which one? - either** quale? - o l'uno o l'altro *kwah·le - o loo·noh o* *lal·troh* □ *adj* on either side a tutti e due i lati *a toot·tee e doo·e ee lah·tee* □ *conj* either ... or ... o ... o o ... o

elaborate *adj* complicato(a) *kom·plee·kah·to(a)*

elastic *n* l'elastico (m) *e·la·stee·koh*

elastic band *n* l'elastico (m) *e·la·stee·koh*

elbow *n* il gomito *goh·mee·toh*

elder *adj* maggiore *maj·joh·re*

eldest *adj* il/la maggiore *maj·joh·re*

elect *vt* eleggere* *e·lej·je·re*

election *n* l'elezione (f) *e·le·tsyoh·ne*

electric(al) *adj* elettrico(a) *e·let·tree·ko(a)*

electric blanket *n* la coperta elettrica *ko·per·ta e·let·tree·ka*

electrician *n* l'elettricista (m) *e·let·tree·chee·sta*

electricity *n* l'elettricità (f) *e·let·tree·chee·ta* A62

electronic *adj* elettronico(a) *e·let·tro·nee·ko(a)*

electronics *n* l'elettronica (f) *e·let·tro·nee·ka*

elegant *adj* elegante *e·le·gan·te*

element *n* l'elemento (m) *e·le·mayn·toh*

elephant *n* l'elefante (m) *e·le·fan·te*

elevator *n* l'ascensore (m) *a·shen·soh·re* A30

eleven *num* undici *oon·dee·chee*

eleventh *adj* undicesimo(a) *oon·dee·che·zee·mo(a)*

elm *n* l'olmo (m) *ohl·moh*

else *adj* □ somewhere else altrove *al·troh·ve*; someone else qualcun altro *kwal·koon al·troh*

embankment *n* il terrapieno *ter·ra·pye·noh*

embargo *n* l'embargo (m) *em·bar·goh*

embark *vi* imbarcarsi *eem·bar·kar·see*

embarrassed *adj* imbarazzato(a) *eem·ba·rats·tsah·to(a)*

embassy *n* l'ambasciata (f) *am·ba·shah·ta*

embrace *vt* abbracciare *ab·brach·chah·ray*

embroidered *adj* ricamato(a) *ree·ka·mah·to(a)*

embroidery *n* il ricamo *ree·kah·moh*

emerald *n* lo smeraldo *zme·ral·doh*

emergency *n* l'emergenza (f) *e·mer·jen·tsa* Ea8

emergency exit *n* l'uscita di sicurezza (f) *oo·shee·ta dee see·koo·rayts·tsa*

emergency landing *n* l'atterraggio di emergenza (m) *at·ter·raj·joh dee e·mer·jen·tsa*

emery board *n* la limetta di carta smerigliata *lee·mayt·ta dee kar·ta zme·reel·yah·ta*

emigrate *vi* emigrare *e·mee·grah·ray*

emotion *n* l'emozione (f) *e·mo·tsyoh·ne*

emotional *adj* (person) impressionabile *eem·pres·syoh·nah·bee·le*

emperor *n* l'imperatore (m) *eem·pe·ra·toh·re*

emphasis *n* l'enfasi (f) *en·fa·zee*; emphasis on something l'enfasi su qualcosa *len·fa·zee soo kwal·ko·sa*

emphasize *vt* sottolineare *sot·to·lee·ne·ah·ray*; (syllable etc) accentuare *ach·chen·too·ah·ray*

empire *n* l'impero *eem·pe·roh*

employ *vt* (worker) impiegare *eem·pye·gah·ray*

employee *n* l'impiegato(a) (m/f) *eem·pye·gah·to(a)*

employer *n* il datore di lavoro *da·toh·re dee la·voh·roh*

employment *n* l'impiego (m) *eem·pye·goh*

empty *adj* vuoto(a) *vwo·to(a)* □ *vt* vuotare *vwo·tah·ray*

enamel *n* lo smalto *zmal·toh*

enclosure *n* (in letter) l'allegato (m) *al·le·gah·toh*

encore *n* il bis *bees*; encore! bis! *bees*

encyclop(a)edia *n* l'enciclopedia (f) *en·chee·klo·pe·dee·a*

end *n* la fine *fee·ne*; (of table) il capo *kah·poh* □ *vt* terminare *ter·mee·nah·ray* □ *vi* finire *fee·nee·re*

endive *n* (smooth) l'indivia (f) *een·dee·vya*; (curly) la cicoria *chee·ko·rya*

endorse *vt* (document) firmare *feer·mah·ray*

enemy *n* il nemico *ne·mee·koh*

energetic *adj* energico(a) *e·ner·jee·ko(a)*

energy *n* l'energia (f) *e·ner·jee·a*

engaged *adj* (betrothed) fidanzato(a) *fee·dan·tsah·to(a)*; (busy) occupato(a) *ok·koo·pah·to(a)*

engagement *n* (betrothal) il fidanzamento *fee·dan·tsa·mayn·toh*

engagement ring *n* l'anello di fidanzamento (m) *a·nel·loh dee fee·dan·tsa·mayn·toh*

engine *n* (motor) il motore *mo·toh·re*; (of train) la locomotiva *lo·ko·mo·tee·va* T178

engineer *n* l'ingegnere (m) *een·jen·ye·re*

England *n* Inghilterra (f) *een·geel·ter·ra*

English *adj* inglese *een·glay·se* □ *n* l'inglese (m) *een·glay·se*; in English in inglese *een·glay·se*

enjoy *vt* (concert, outing) gustare *goo·stah·ray*; to enjoy oneself divertirsi *dee·ver·teer·see*

enjoyment *n* il piacere *pya·chay·re*

enlarge *vt* ingrandire *een·gran·dee·re*

enormous *adj* enorme *e·nor·me*

enough *pron* abbastanza *ab·ba·stan·tsa*; have you enough? ne ha abbastanza? *nay a ab·ba·stan·tsa* □ *adj* enough time/books abbastanza tempo/libri *ab·ba·stan·tsa tem·poh/lee·bree* □ *adv* big enough abbastanza grande *ab·ba·stan·tsa gran·de* S38

ensemble *n* (clothes) l'insieme (m) *een·sye·me*

enter *vt* (room) entrare in *en·trah·ray een* □ *vi* entrare *en·trah·ray*

enterprise *n* l'impresa (f) *eem·pray·sa*

entertain *vt* (amuse) intrattenere* *en·trat·te·nay·re*; (give hospitality) ricevere *ree·chay·ve·re*

entertainment *n* (show) lo spettacolo *spet·ta·ko·loh* L42

enthusiasm *n* l'entusiasmo (m) *en·too·zee·a·zmoh*

enthusiastic *adj* entusiasta *en·too·zee·a·sta*

entrance *n* (way in) l'ingresso (m) *een·gres·soh*

entrance fee *n* il prezzo d'ingresso *prets·tsoh deen·gres·soh*

entrée *n* il primo piatto *pree·mo pyat·toh*

entry *n* (way in) l'ingresso (m) *een·gres·soh*

envelope *n* la busta *boo·sta* S92

envious *adj* invidioso(a) *een·vee·dyoh·so(a)*

environment *n* l'ambiente (m) *am·byen·te*

envy *vt* invidiare *een·vee·dyah·ray* □ n l'invidia (*f*) *een·vee·dya*
epidemic *n* l'epidemia (*f*) *e·pee·de·mee·a*
epilepsy *n* l'epilessia (*f*) *e·pee·les·see·a*
equal *adj* uguale *oo·gwah·le*
equator *n* l'equatore (*m*) *e·kwa·toh·re*
equipment *n* l'equipaggiamento (*m*) *e·kwee·paj·ja·mayn·toh*
equivalent *adj* equivalente *e·kwee·va·len·te*
erase *vt* cancellare *kan·chel·lah·ray*
eraser *n* la gomma per cancellare *gohm·ma payr kan·chel·lah·ray*
ermine *n* (*fur*) la pelliccia di ermellino *pel·leech·cha dee er·mel·lee·noh*
erotic *adj* erotico(a) *e·ro·tee·ko(a)*
errand *n* la commissione *kom·mees·syoh·ne*; **to do** *or* **run an errand** fare* una commissione *fah·ray oo·na kom·mees·syoh·ne*
error *n* l'errore (*m*) *er·roh·re*; **in error** per sbaglio *payr zbal·yoh*
escalator *n* la scala mobile *skah·la mo·bee·le*
escalope *n* la scaloppina *ska·lop·pee·na*
escape *vi* scappare *skap·pah·ray*
escort *vt* accompagnare *ak·kom·pan·yah·ray* □ n l'accompagnatore (*m*) *ak·kom·pan·ya·toh·re*
especially *adv* specialmente *spe·chal·maynt·te*
Esperanto *n* l'esperanto (*m*) *e·spe·ran·toh*
espresso (coffee) *n* l'espresso (*m*) *e·spres·soh* E60
essay *n* il saggio *saj·joh*
essential *adj* (*necessary*) essenziale *es·sen·tsyah·le*
establish *vt* stabilire *sta·bee·lee·re*; (*business*) fondare *fon·dah·ray*
estate *n* (*property*) la tenuta *te·noo·ta*
estimate *vt* stimare *stee·mah·ray* □ n la stima *stee·ma* Bm23
etc *abbrev* ecc *ech·che·te·ra*
ethical *adj* etico(a) *e·tee·ko(a)*
ethnic *adj* etnico(a) *et·nee·ko(a)*
etiquette *n* l'etichetta (*f*) *e·tee·kayt·ta*
Europe *n* Europa (*f*) *e·oo·ro·pa*
European *adj* europeo(a) *e·oo·ro·pe·o(a)*
evaporate *vi* evaporare *e·va·po·rah·ray*
evaporated milk *n* il latte evaporato *lat·te e·va·po·rah·to*
even *adj* (*level*) piano(a) *pyah·no(a)*; (*equally matched*) uguale *oo·gwah·le*; **an even number** un numero pari *oon noo·me·roh pah·ree* □ adv **even** faster ancor più veloce *an·kohr pyoo ve·loh·che*; **even a child could do it** anche un bambino potrebbe farlo *an·ke oon bam·bee·noh po·treb·be far·lo*; **even so** tuttavia *toot·ta·vee·a*
evening *n* la sera *say·ra*; **in the evening** la sera *la say·ra* L45, Mc44
evening dress *n* (*woman's*) l'abito da sera (*m*) *ah·bee·toh da say·ra*; (*man's*) lo smoking *smo·keeng*
evening paper *n* il giornale della sera *johr·nah·le del·la say·ra*
event *n* l'avvenimento (*m*) *av·ve·nee·maynt·toh*
eventually *adv* alla fine *al·la fee·ne*
ever *adv* sempre *sem·pre*; **have you ever been to London?** è mai stato a Londra? *e my stah·to a lohn·dra*; **ever since he...** da quando egli... *da kwan·do eyl·yee*; **he's been there ever since** da allora è sempre lì *da al·loh·ra e sem·pre lee*

every *adj* ogni *ohn·yee*; **every other day** ogni due giorni *ohn·yee doo·e johr·nee*; **every 6th day** ogni sei giorni *ohn·yee se·ee johr·nee*
everybody, everyone *pron* tutti *toot·tee*
everything *pron* tutto *toot·to*
everywhere *adv* dappertutto *dap·per·toot·to*
evidence *n* (*proof*) la prova *pro·va*; (*of witness*) la testimonianza *te·stee·mo·nyan·tsa*
evil *adj* cattivo(a) *kat·tee·vo(a)*
evolution *n* l'evoluzione (*f*) *e·vo·loo·tsyoh·ne*
ex- *pref* ex- *eks*
exact *adj* (*correct*) esatto(a) *e·zat·to(a)*; (*detailed*) preciso(a) *pre·chee·zo(a)*
exactly *adv* precisamente *pre·chee·za·mayn·te*
exaggerate *vt/i* esagerare *e·za·je·rah·ray*
exaggeration *n* l'esagerazione (*f*) *e·za·je·ra·tsyoh·ne*
examination *n* (*exam*) l'esame (*m*) *e·zah·me*; (*inspection*) l'ispezione (*f*) *ee·spe·tsyoh·ne*; (*medical*) la visita *vee·zee·ta*
examine *vt* (*inspect*) ispezionare *ee·spe·tsyoh·nah·ray*
example *n* l'esempio (*m*) *e·zem·pyoh*; **for example** per esempio *payr e·zem·pyoh*
exceed *vt* superare *soo·pe·rah·ray*
excellent *adj* eccellente *ech·chel·len·te*
except (for), except(ing) *prep* tranne *tran·ne*
exception *n* l'eccezione (*f*) *ech·che·tsyoh·ne*
exceptional *adj* eccezionale *ech·che·tsyoh·nah·le*
excess *n* l'eccedenza (*f*) *ech·che·den·tsa*
excess baggage *n* il bagaglio eccedente *ba·gal·yoh ech·che·den·te*
exchange *vt* cambiare *kam·byah·ray*; **to exchange something for something** cambiare qualcosa per qualcos'altro *kam·byah·ray kwal·ko·sa payr kwal·ko·sal·tro* □ n exchange (*between currencies*) il cambio *kam·byoh*; (*telephone*) la centrale *chen·trah·le*
exchange rate *n* il tasso di cambio *tas·soh dee kam·byoh* M23
excise duties *pl* le imposte sul consumo *eem·poh·ste sool kon·soo·moh*
excited *adj* commosso(a) *kom·mos·so(a)*
excitement *n* l'eccitazione (*f*) *ech·chee·ta·tsyoh·ne*
exciting *adj* emozionante *e·mo·tsyoh·nan·te*
exclaim *vi* esclamare *e·skla·mah·ray*
exclude *vt* escludere* *e·skloo·de·re*
exclusive *adj* (*club, shop*) esclusivo(a) *e·skloo·zee·vo(a)*; **exclusive rights** l'esclusiva (*f*) *e·skloo·zee·va*; **exclusive of... ...** non compresa *nohn kom·pray·sa*
excursion *n* la gita *jee·ta*; **to go on an excursion** fare* una gita *fah·ray oo·na jee·ta* L6
excuse *vt* scusare *skoo·zah·ray*; **excuse me** mi scusi *mee skoo·zee* □ n excuse (*pretext*) la scusa *skoo·za*
execute *vt* (*kill*) giustiziare *joo·stee·tsyah·ray*
executive *n* il direttore *dee·ret·toh·re*
exercise *n* l'esercizio (*m*) *e·zer·chee·tsyoh*

exercise book n il quaderno kwa·der· noh

exhaust n (fumes) il gas di scappa· mento gas dee skap·pa·mayn·toh; (pipe) il tubo di scappamento too·bo dee skap·pa·mayn·toh

exhausted adj esausto(a) e·zow·sto(a)

exhibition n la mostra moh·stra

exist vi esistere* e·zee·ste·re

existence n l'esistenza (f) e·zee·sten·tsa

exit n l'uscita (f) oo·shee·ta

exit permit n il permesso di uscita per· mays·soh dee oo·shee·ta

exotic adj esotico(a) e·zo·tee·ko(a)

expand vt (material) dilatare dee·la· tah·ray; (business) sviluppare zvee· loop·pah·ray □ vi (material) dilatarsi dee·la·tar·see; (business) svilupparsi zvee·loop·par·see

expect vt (anticipate) aspettare a·spet· tah·ray; **I expect he'll come sup· pongo che verrà** soop·pohn·go ke ver·ra; **I expect so credo di sì** cre·do dee see; **she's expecting a baby at· tende un bambino** at·ten·de oon bam·bee·noh Bm4

expedition n la spedizione spe·dee· tsyoh·ne

expenditure n le spese spay·se

expense n (cost) la spesa spay·sa; ex· penses le spese spay·se

expensive adj costoso(a) ko·stoh·so(a)

experience n l'esperienza (f) e·spe·ree· en·tsa

experienced adj esperto(a) e·sper·to(a)

experiment n l'esperimento (m) e·spe· ree·mayn·toh

expert n l'esperto (m) e·sper·toh

expire vi scadere* ska·day·re

explain vt spiegare spye·gah·ray

explanation n la spiegazione spye·ga· tsyoh·ne

explode vi esplodere* e·splo·de·re

explore vt esplorare e·splo·rah·ray

explosion n l'esplosione (f) e·splo· zyoh·ne

export n l'esportazione (f) e·spor·ta· tsyoh·ne □ vt esportare e·spor·tah· ray

exporter n l'esportatore (m) e·spor·ta· toh·re

express vt esprimere* e·spree·me·re □ adv **to send something express mandare qualcosa per espresso** man· dah·ray kwal·ko·sa payr e·spres·so

expression n l'espressione (f) e·spres· syoh·ne

express letter n l'espresso (m) e·spres· so

express train n il rapido ra·pee·doh ↑54

expressway n l'autostrada (f) ow·to· strah·da

extension n (building) l'annesso (m) an·nes·so; (phone) il telefono in· terno te·le·fo·noh een·ter·no

exterior adj esterno(a) e·ster·no(a)

external adj esterno(a) e·ster·no(a)

extra adj supplementare soop·ple·men· tah·re; **postage extra più le spese po· stali** pyoo le spay·se po·stah·lee □ adv **extra in più** een pyoo M3, A18

extraordinary adj straordinario(a) stra· or·dee·nah·ree·o(a)

extravagant adj stravagante stra·va· gan·te

extremely adv estremamente e·stre· ma·mayn·te

eye n l'occhio (m) ok·kyoh

eyebrow n il sopracciglio so·prach· cheel·yoh

eyeglasses pl gli occhiali ok·kyah·lee

eyelash n il ciglio cheel·yoh

eyelid n la palpebra pal·pe·bra

eyeliner n l'eye-liner (m) e·ye·line·er

eyeshadow n l'ombretto (m) om·brayt· toh

eyesight n la vista vee·sta

F

fabric n il tessuto tes·soo·toh Sn68

face n il viso vee·zoh

face card n la figura fee·goo·ra

facecloth n la manopola di spugna ma· no·po·la dee spoon·ya

face cream n la crema per il viso kre· ma payr eel vee·zoh

facilities pl i servizi ser·vee·tsee

facing prep di fronte a dee frohn·te a

fact n il fatto fat·toh; **in fact infatti** een·fat·tee

factor n il fattore fat·toh·re

factory n la fabbrica fab·bree·ka

faculty n (university) la facoltà fa· kol·ta

fade vi affievolirsi af·fye·vo·leer·see; (colour) sbiadire zbee·a·dee·re

Fahrenheit adj Fahrenheit fah·ren·hite

fail vi (person) non riuscire* nohn ree· oo·shee·re; (plan) fallire fal·lee·re; (brakes) guastarsi gwa·star·see □ vt (exam) non superare nohn soo·pe· rah·ray □ n **without fail senza fallo** sen·tsa fal·loh

failure n l'insuccesso (m) een·sooch· ches·soh; (person) il/la fallito(a) fal· lee·to(a); (mechanical) l'avaria (f) a· va·ree·a; (of brakes) il guasto gwa· stoh

faint vi svenire* zve·nee·re □ adj (sound etc) debole day·bo·le; **I feel faint mi sento venir meno** mee sen·to ve·neer may·no

fair adj (just) giusto(a) joo·sto(a); (hair) biondo(a) byohn·do(a); (aver· age) discreto(a) dee·skray·to(a) □ adv **to play fair giocare secondo le regole** jo·kah·ray se·kohn·do le re· go·le □ n **fair (commercial) la fiera** fye·ra

fairground n il campo della fiera kam· poh del·la fye·ra

fairly adv (rather) piuttosto pyoot·to· sto

fairy n la fata fah·ta

faith n la fede fay·de

faithfully adv □ **yours faithfully di· stinti saluti** dee·steen·tee sa·loo·tee

fake adj falso(a) fal·so(a)

fall vi (person) cadere* ka·day·re; (prices etc) ribassare ree·bas·sah·ray; **to fall down cadere** ka·day·re; **to fall in love innamorarsi** een·na·mo·rar· see □ n **fall la caduta** ka·doo·ta; (de· crease) la diminuzione dee·mee·noo· tsyoh·ne; (season) l'autunno (m) ow· toon·noh

false adj (name etc) falso(a) fal·so(a); **false teeth la dentiera** den·tye·ra

familiar adj (impertinent) sfacciato(a) sfach·chah·to(a); **to be familiar with something conoscere* bene qualcosa** ko·noh·she·re be·ne kwal·ko·sa

family n la famiglia fa·meel·ya A2

famous adj famoso(a) fa·moh·so(a)

fan n (folding) il ventaglio ven·tal·yoh; (electric) il ventilatore ven·tee·la·toh· re; (in car) la ventola ven·to·la; (sup· porter) il tifoso tee·fo·so

fanbelt n la cinghia della ventola cheen·gya del·la ven·to·la T183

fancy adj di lusso dee·loos·soh

fancy dress n il costume ko·stoo·me

far adv lontano lon·tah·no; (much) di gran lunga dee gran loon·ga; how far is it to…? quanto dista da qui a…? kwan·to dee·sta da kwee a; as far as the station fino alla stazione fee·no al·la sta·tsyoh·ne; as far as I know per quanto io sappia payr kwan·to ee·o sap·pya; the Far East l'Estremo Oriente (m) e·stre·mo o·ryen·te F12

farce n la farsa far·sa

fare n il prezzo del biglietto prets·tsoh del beel·yayt·toh; (in taxi) il prezzo della corsa prets·tsoh del·la kohr·sa

farm n la fattoria fat·to·ree·a

farmer n l'agricoltore (m) a·gree·kol·toh·re

farmhouse n la casa colonica kah·sa ko·lo·nee·ka

farmyard n l'aia (f) a·ya

far-sighted adj presbite prez·bee·te

farther adv piú lontano pyoo lon·tah·no

farthest adv il piú lontano eel pyoo lon·tah·no

fascinating adj affascinante af·fa·shee·nan·te

fashion n la moda mo·da; the latest fashions l'ultima moda lool·tee·ma mo·da

fashionable adj di moda de mo·da

fast adj (speedy) veloce ve·loh·che; (dye) solido(a) so·lee·do(a); my watch is fast il mio orologio va avanti eel mee·o o·ro·lo·joh va a·van·tee □ adv fast velocemente ve·loh·che·mayn·te; to be fast asleep essere profondamente addormentato(a) es·se·re pro·fohn·da·mayn·te ad·dor·men·tah·to(a) T52, 200

fasten vt attaccare at·tak·kah·ray; fasten seat belts allacciate le cinture di sicurezza al·lach·chah·te le cheen·too·re dee see·koo·rayts·tsa

fat adj (person) grasso(a) gras·so(a) □ n il grasso gras·soh

fatal adj fatale fa·tah·le

father n il padre pah·dre

father-in-law n il suocero swo·che·roh

faucet n il rubinetto roo·bee·nayt·toh A31

fault n (defect) il difetto dee·fet·toh; (blame) la colpa kohl·pa; whose fault is it? di chi è la colpa? dee kee e la kohl·pa; it's not my fault non è colpa mia nohn e kohl·pa mee·a

faulty adj difettoso(a) dee·fet·toh·so(a)

favor n il favore fa·voh·re; to do someone a favor fare* un favore a qualcuno fah·ray oon fa·voh·re a kwal·koo·no; I'm not in favor of that idea non sono a favore di quell'idea nohn soh·no a fa·voh·re dee kwayl·lee·de·a

favorite adj favorito(a) fa·vo·ree·to(a)

fawn adj fulvo(a) fool·vo(a)

fear n la paura pa·oo·ra

feasibility n la fattibilità fat·tee·bee·lee·ta

feasibility study n lo studio della fattibilità stoo·dyoh del·la fat·tee·bee·lee·ta

feast n il banchetto ban·kayt·toh

feather n la piuma pyoo·ma

feature film n il lungometraggio loon·go·me·traj·joh

features pl n le fattezze fat·tayts·tse

February n febbraio (m) feb·bra·yoh

federal adj federale fe·de·rah·le

fed up adj stufo(a) stoo·fo(a)

fee n l'onorario (m) o·no·rah·ryoh

feed vt nutrire noo·tree·re □ vi mangiare man·jah·ray

feedback n il feed-back feed·bak

feel vt (touch) toccare tok·kah·ray; I feel that… penso che…. pen·so ke □ vi it feels soft è soffice al tatto e sof·fee·che al tat·toh; I feel hungry ho fame o fah·me; I feel better mi sento meglio mee·sen·to mel·yoh; I feel like a beer gradirei una birra gra·dee·rey oo·na beer·ra

feeling n la sensazione sen·sa·tsee·oh·ne; (emotion) il sentimento sen·tee·men·toh

fellow n il tizio tee·tsyoh; fellow countryman il/la connazionale kon·na·tsyoh·nah·le

felt n (cloth) il feltro fayl·troh

felt-tip pen n il pennarello pen·na·rel·loh

female adj (animal) femmina faym·mee·na; the female sex il sesso femminile eel ses·soh fem·mee·nee·le

feminine adj femminile fem·mee·nee·le

fence n il recinto re·cheen·toh

fender n (on car) il paraurti pa·ra·oor·tee

fern n la felce fayl·che

ferry n (small) il traghetto tra·gayt·toh; (large) la nave-traghetto nah·ve·tra·gayt·toh

fertile adj (land) fertile fer·tee·le

festival n il festival fe·stee·val L4

fetch vt andare* a prendere an·dah·ray a pren·de·re

fête n la festa fe·sta

fever n la febbre feb·bre

few adj poche(i) po·kee(·ke); a few books pochi libri po·kee lee·bree □ pron there are very few ce ne sono pochissimi(e) che nay soh·no po·kees·see·mee(·me); there are quite a few ce ne sono abbastanza che nay soh·no ab·ba·stan·tsa

fiancé(e) n il/la fidanzato(a) fee·dan·tsah·to(a)

fiber n la fibra fee·bra

fiberglass n la lana di vetro lah·na dee vay·troh

fiction n la narrativa nar·ra·tee·va

field n il campo kam·poh

field glasses pl n il binocolo bee·no·ko·loh

fierce adj feroce fe·roh·che

fifteen num quindici kween·dee·chee

fifth adj quinto(a) kween·to(a)

fifty num cinquanta cheen·kwan·ta

fig n il fico fee·koh

fight n il lottare lot·tah·ray □ n il combattimento kom·bat·tee·mayn·toh

figure n (of human) la figura fee·goo·ra; (number) la cifra chee·fra; to have a nice figure essere* ben fatta es·se·re ben fat·ta □ vt figure (suppose) supporre* soop·pohr·re

file n (tool) la lima lee·ma; (dossier) l'archivio (m) ar·kee·vyoh

filing cabinet n l'archivio (m) ar·kee·vyoh

fill vt riempire* ree·em·pee·re; to fill in/out/up riempire* ree·em·pee·re; fill it up! (car) il pieno, per favore! eel pye·noh payr fa·voh·re

fillet n (of meat, fish) il filetto fee·layt·toh

filling adj (food) sostanzioso(a) so·stan·tsyoh·so(a) □ n (in tooth) l'otturazione (f) ot·too·ra·tsyoh·ne I58

filling station n la stazione di servizio sta·tsyoh·ne dee ser·vee·tsyoh F9

film *n* (*movie*) il film *feelm*; (*for camera*) la pellicola *pel·lee·ko·la* L44, S47f

filter *n* il filtro *feel·troh*

filter-tip *adj* (*cigarettes*) con filtro *kohn feel·troh* S95

final *adj* finale *fee·nah·le*

finally *adv* finalmente *fee·nal·mayn·te*

finals *pl* (*sports*) finali *fee·nah·le*

finance *n* la finanza *fee·nan·tsa* □ *vt* finanziare *fee·nan·tsyah·ray*

Finance Minister *n* il Ministro delle Finanze *mee·nee·stroh del·le fee·nan·tse*

financial *adj* finanziario(a) *fee·nan·tsy·ah·ryo(a)*

find *vt* trovare *tro·vah·ray*; **to find out** scoprire* *sko·pree·re*

fine *adj* (*delicate*) fino(a) *fee·no(a)*; (*weather*) bello(a) *bel·lo(a)*; (*that's*) fine! molto bene! *mohl·to be·ne* □ *n* la multa *mool·ta* T196

finger *n* il dito *dee·toh*

finish *vt/i* finire *fee·nee·re*

Finland *n* Finlandia (*f*) *feen·lan·dya*

Finnish *adj* finlandese *feen·lan·day·se* □ il finlandese *feen·lan·day·se*

fire *n* il fuoco *fwo·koh*; (*accident*) l'incendio (*m*) *een·chen·dyoh*; **the house is on fire** la casa è in fiamme *la kah·sa e een fyam·me*; **to set fire to** appiccare il fuoco a *ap·pee·kah·ray eel fwo·koh* □ *vt* **to fire a gun** sparare un colpo di fucile *spa·rah·ray oon kohl·poh dee foo·chee·le*; **to fire someone** (*dismiss*) licenziare qualcuno *lee·chen·tsyah·ray kwal·koo·no* A72, Ea4

fire alarm *n* l'allarme antincendio (*m*) *al·lar·me an·teen·chen·dyoh*

firearm *n* l'arma da fuoco (*f*) *ar·ma da fwo·koh*

fire department *n* i vigili del fuoco *vee·jee·lee del fwo·koh* Ea7

fire engine *n* l'autopompa (*f*) *ow·to·pohm·pa*

fire escape *n* l'uscita di sicurezza (*f*) *oo·shee·ta dee see·koo·rayts·tsa*

fire extinguisher *n* l'estintore (*m*) *e·steen·toh·re*

fireman *n* il pompiere *pom·pye·re*

fireplace *n* il focolare *fo·ko·lah·re*

fire station *n* la caserma dei pompieri *ka·zer·ma dey pom·pye·ree*

fireworks *pl* i fuochi d'artificio *fwo·kee dar·tee·fee·choh*

firm *n* la ditta *deet·ta* □ *adj* (*object, material*) stabile *stah·bee·le*; (*person*) fermo(a) *fayr·mo(a)* Bm15, 17

first *adj* primo(a) *pree·mo(a)* □ *adv* prima *pree·ma* □ *n* **in first** (*gear*) in prima *een pree·ma*; **at first** dapprima *dap·pree·ma*

first aid *n* il pronto soccorso *prohn·to sok·kohr·soh*

first-aid kit *n* la cassetta di pronto soccorso *kas·sayt·ta dee prohn·to sok·kohr·soh*

first-class *adj* (*work etc*) di prima classe *dee pree·ma klas·se*; **to travel first class** viaggiare in prima classe *vyaj·jah·ray een pree·ma klas·se*

first floor *n* il pianterreno *pyan·ter·ray·noh* A5

first name *n* il nome *noh·me*

fir (tree) *n* l'abete (*m*) *a·bay·te*

fiscal *adj* fiscale *fee·skah·le*

fiscal year *n* l'anno fiscale (*m*) *an·noh fee·skah·le*

fish *n* il pesce *pay·she* E28

fishing *n* la pesca *pay·ska*; **to go fishing**

andare* a pesca *an·dah·ray a pay·ska* L35

fishing rod *n* la canna da pesca *kan·na da pay·ska*

fishmonger *n* il pescivendolo *pe·shee·vayn·do·loh*

fist *n* il pugno *poon·yoh*

fit *adj* (*strong, healthy*) in forma *een fohr·ma*; (*suitable*) adatto(a) *a·dat·to(a)* □ *vt/i* **it fits** (me) mi sta bene *mee sta be·ne* □ *n* (*seizure*) l'accesso (*m*) *ach·ches·soh*

five *num* cinque *cheen·kwe*

fix *vt* fissare *fees·sah·ray*; (*mend*) riparare *ree·pa·rah·ray*; (*prepare*) preparare *pre·pa·rah·ray*

fizzy *adj* gassoso(a) *gas·soh·so(a)*

flag *n* la bandiera *ban·dye·ra*

flag stop *n* la fermata facoltativa *fayr·mah·ta fa·kol·ta·tee·va*

flake *n* la scaglia *skal·ya*; (*of snow*) il fiocco *fyok·koh*

flame *n* la fiamma *fyam·ma*

flammable *adj* infiammabile *een·fyam·mah·bee·le*

flan *n* la torta di frutta *tohr·ta dee froot·ta*

flannel *n* (*facecloth*) la manopola di spugna *ma·no·po·la dee spoon·ya*

flap *n* la patta *pat·ta* □ *vi* (*sail*) sventolare *zven·to·lah·ray*

flash *n* il bagliore *bal·yoh·re*; (*on camera*) il flash *flash* □ *vi* (*light*) balenare *ba·le·nah·ray* S55

flashbulb *n* il flash *flash*

flashcube *n* il cubo flash *koo·boh flash*

flashlight *n* la lampadina tascabile *lam·pa·dee·na ta·skah·bee·le*

flask *n* il thermos *ter·mos*

flat *adj* piatto(a) *pyat·to(a)*; (*deflated*) sgonfio(a) *zgohn·fyo(a)*; (*battery*) scarico(a) *skah·ree·ko(a)*; (*beer*) stantio(a) *stan·tee·o(a)*; **B flat** (*music*) il si bemolle *see be·mol·le*; **flat rate** il prezzo fisso *prets·tsoh fees·soh*

flavor *n* il sapore *sa·poh·re*

flea *n* la pulce *pool·che*

flea market *n* il mercato delle pulci *mer·kah·toh del·le pool·chee*

fleet *n* la flotta *flot·ta*; **fleet of vehicles** il parco macchine *par·koh mak·kee·ne*

Flemish *adj* fiammingo(a) *fyam·meen·go(a)* □ il fiammingo *fyam·meen·goh*

flesh *n* la carne *kar·ne*

flexible *adj* flessibile *fles·see·bee·le*

flight *n* il volo *voh·loh*; **flight of steps** la scalinata *ska·lee·nah·ta* T2f, 39, 48

flight attendant *n* l'assistente di volo (*m/f*) *as·sees·ten·te dee voh·loh*

flint *n* (*in lighter*) la pietra focaia *pye·tra fo·ka·ya*

flippers *pl* (*for swimming*) le pinne *peen·ne*

flirt *vi* flirtare *fleer·tah·ray*

float *vi* galleggiare *gal·lej·jah·ray* □ *n* (*for swimming, fishing*) il galleggiante *gal·lej·jan·te*

flock *n* il gregge *grayj·je*

flood *n* l'inondazione (*f*) *een·on·da·tsyoh·ne*

floodlight *n* il riflettore *ree·flet·toh·re*

floodlit *adj* illuminato(a) *eel·loo·mee·nah·to(a)*

floor *n* il pavimento *pa·vee·mayn·toh*; **1st floor** (*Brit*), **2nd floor** (*US*) il primo piano *pree·mo pyah·noh*

floor lamp *n* la lampada a stelo *lam·pa·da a ste·loh*

florist *n* il/la fioraio(a) *fyoh·ra·yo(a)*

flour n la farina *fa·ree·na*

flow vi scorrere* *skohr·re·re*; (traffic) circolare *cheer·ko·lah·ray*

flow chart n l'organigramma (m) or *ga·nee·gram·ma*

flower n il fiore *fyoh·re* L41

flowerbed n l'aiuola (f) *a·yoo·wo·la*

flu n l'influenza (f) *een·floo·en·tsa*

fluent adj □ he speaks fluent French parla francese correntemente *par·la fran·chay·ze kor·ren·te·mayn·te*

fluorescent light n il tubo fluorescente *too·boh floo·o·re·shen·te*

fluoride n il fluoruro *floo·o·roo·roh*

flush vt □ to flush the toilet tirare lo sciacquone *tee·rah·ray lo shak·kwoh·ne*

flute n il flauto *flow·toh*

fly n la mosca *moh·ska* □ vi volare *vo·lah·ray*

flying n il volare *vo·lah·re*

flyover n (road) il cavalcavia *ka·val·ka·vee·a*

foam n la schiuma *skyoo·ma*

focus vt mettere* a fuoco *mayt·te·re a fwo·koh*

fog n la nebbia *nayb·bya*

foggy adj nebbioso(a) *neb·byoh·so(a)*; it's foggy c'è della nebbia *che del·la nayb·bya*

fog light n il proiettore fendinebbia *pro·yet·toh·re fen·dee·nayb·bya*

foil n (for food) la stagnola *stan·yo·la*

fold vt piegare *pye·gah·ray*

folding chair n la sedia pieghevole *se·dya pye·gay·vo·le*

folding table n la tavola pieghevole *tah·vo·la pye·gay·vo·le*

folk dance n il ballo folcloristico *bal·loh fol·klo·ree·stee·ko*

folk song n il canto folcloristico *kan·toh fol·klo·ree·stee·ko*

follow vt/i seguire *se·gwee·re*

following adj seguente *se·gwen·te*

food n il cibo *chee·boh* S11, Mc41

food poisoning n l'intossicazione alimentare (f) *een·tos·see·ka·tsyoh·ne a·lee·men·tah·re*

foot n (of person, measurement) il piede *pye·de*; (of animal) la zampa *tsam·pa*

football n (soccer) il calcio *kal·choh*; (ball) il pallone *pal·loh·ne*

footbrake n il freno a pedale *fre·noh a pe·dah·le*

footpath n il sentiero *sen·tye·roh*

for prep for pay?; to sell something for L.5000 vendere qualcosa per L.5000 *vayn·de·re kwal·ko·sa payr L5000*; to leave for London partire per Londra *par·tee·re payr lohn·dra*; to walk for an hour camminare un'ora *kam·mee·nah·ray oo·noh·ra*; what's the Italian for "dog"? come si dice "dog" in italiano? *koh·me see dee·che dog een ee·ta·lyah·no*; it's warm for March fa caldo per marzo *fa kal·do payr mar·tsoh*

forbid vt vietare *vee·e·tah·ray*; to forbid someone to do something proibire a qualcuno di fare qualcosa *pro·ee·bee·re a kwal·koo·no dee fah·ray kwal·ko·sa*; it is forbidden è vietato(a) *e vee·e·tah·to(a)*

force n (violence) la forza *for·tsa* □ vt (compel) costringere* *ko·streen·je·re*

ford n il guado *gwah·doh*

forecast n il pronostico *pro·no·stee·koh*; (weather) la previsione del tempo *pre·vee·zyoh·ne del tem·poh*

forehead n la fronte *frohn·te*

foreign adj straniero(a) *stran·ye·ro(a)*

foreigner n lo/la straniero(a) *stran·ye·ro(a)* T191

foreign exchange market n il mercato delle valute estere *mer·kah·toh del·le va·loo·te e·ste·re*

foreign policy n la politica estera *po·lee·tee·ka e·ste·ra*

foreman n il caposquadra *kah·po·skwa·dra*

forename n il nome *noh·me*

forest n la foresta *fo·re·sta*

forever adv per sempre *payr sem·pre*

forgery n la falsificazione *fal·see·fee·ka·tsyoh·ne*

forget vt dimenticare *dee·men·tee·kah·ray* B68

forgive vt perdonare *per·do·nah·ray*

fork n la forchetta *for·kayt·ta*; (in road) il bivio *bee·vyoh*

form n la forma *fohr·ma*; (document) il modulo *mo·doo·loh*; in good form in forma *een fohr·ma*

formal adj formale *for·mah·le*

fortnight n una quindicina di giorni *oo·na kween·dee·chee·na dee johr·nee*

fortune n (wealth) la fortuna *for·too·na*

forty num quaranta *kwa·ran·ta*

forward vt (letter) fare* proseguire *fah·ray pro·se·gwee·re*

forward(s) adv avanti *a·van·tee*; the seat is too far forward il sedile è troppo in avanti *eel se·dee·le e trop·po een a·van·tee*

fountain n la fontana *fon·tah·na*; (for drinking) la fontanella *fon·ta·nel·la*

fountain pen n una penna stilografica *payn·na stee·lo·gra·fee·ka*

four num quattro *kwat·troh*

fourteen num quattordici *kwat·tor·dee·chee*

fourth adj quarto(a) *kwar·to(a)*

fox n la volpe *vohl·pe*

fracture n (of arm etc) la frattura *frat·too·ra*

fragile adj fragile *frah·jee·le*

frame n (of picture) la cornice *kor·nee·che*; frames (of eyeglasses) la montatura *mon·ta·too·ra*

France n Francia (f) *fran·cha*; in/to France in Francia *een fran·cha*

free adj libero(a) *lee·be·ro(a)*; (costing nothing) gratuito(a) *gra·too·ee·to(a)* Bm10

freeway n l'autostrada (f) *ow·to·strah·da*

freeze vi gelare *je·lah·ray* □ vt (food) congelare *kon·je·lah·ray*

freezer n il congelatore *kon·je·la·toh·re*

freight n (goods) le merci *mayr·chee*

freight train n il treno merci *tray·noh mayr·chee*

French adj francese *fran·chay·ze* □ n il francese *fran·chay·ze*

french fried potatoes, french fries pl le patatine fritte *pa·ta·tee·ne freet·te*

frequent adj frequente *fre·kwen·te*

fresh adj fresco(a) *fray·sko(a)*; (impudent) insolente *een·so·len·te*

Friday n venerdì (m) *ve·ner·dee*

fridge n il frigo *free·goh*

fried adj fritto(a) *freet·to(a)*

friend n l'amico(a) (m/f) *a·mee·ko(a)*

friendly adj amichevole *a·mee·kay·vo·le*

frighten vt spaventare *spa·ven·tah·ray*

fringe n la frangia *fran·ja*

fritter n la frittella *freet·tel·la*

frog n la rana *rah·na*

frogs legs pl i cosciotti di rana *ko·shot·tee dee rah·na*

from prep da *da*; from London da Londra *da lohn·dra*; from 8 o'clock dalle otto in poi *dal·le ot·to een poy*; water from the faucet l'acqua di rubinetto *ak·kwa dee roo·bee·nayt·toh*

front adj anteriore *an·te·ryoh·re* □ n (foremost part) la parte anteriore *par·te an·te·ryoh·re*; (seaside) in lungomare *loon·go·mah·re*; at the front davanti *da·van·tee*; to sit in front sedersi* davanti *se·dayr·see da·van·tee*

frontier n la frontiera *fron·tye·ra*

front-wheel drive n la trazione anteriore *tra·tsyoh·ne an·te·ryoh·re*

frost n il gelo *je·loh*

frozen adj (food) congelato(a) *kon·je·lah·to(a)*

fruit n la frutta *froot·ta*

fruit salad n la macedonia *ma·che·don·ya*

fry vt friggere* *freej·je·re*

fry(ing) pan n la padella *pa·del·la*

fuel n il carburante *kar·boo·ran·te*

fuel pump n la pompa del carburante *pom·pa del kar·boo·ran·te*

full adj pieno(a) *pye·no(a)*; full of pieno(a) di *pye·no(a) dee*; full up (bus etc) completo(a) *kom·ple·to(a)*

full stop n il punto *poon·toh*

full-time adj, adv a tempo pieno *a tem·po pye·noh*

fun n □ it was great fun è stato molto divertente *e stah·to mohl·to dee·ver·ten·te*

funds pl i fondi *fohn·dee*

funeral n il funerale *foo·ne·rah·le*

funny adj (amusing) divertente *dee·ver·ten·te*; (strange) curioso(a) *koo·ryoh·so(a)*

fur n il pelo *pay·loh*

fur coat n la pelliccia *pel·leech·cha*

furnish vt (room etc) ammobiliare *am·mo·bee·lyah·ray*

furniture n i mobili *mo·bee·lee*

further adv più lontano *pyoo lon·tah·no*

furthest adv il più lontano *eel pyoo lon·tah·no*

fuse n il fusibile *foo·zee·bee·le* T180, A77

fuss n le storie *sto·rye*; to make a fuss fare* delle storie *fah·ray del·le sto·rye*

future n il futuro *foo·too·roh*

G

gadget n il dispositivo *dees·po·see·tee·vo* S15

gain vt (obtain) guadagnare *gwa·dan·yah·ray* □ vi (clock) andare* avanti *an·dah·ray a·van·tee*

gala n la gala *gah·la*

gale n il vento forte *ven·toh for·te*

gallery n la galleria *gal·le·ree·a*; (in theater) il loggione *loj·joh·nay*

gallon n il gallone *gal·loh·nay*

gallop vi galoppare *ga·lop·pah·ray* □ n il galoppo *ga·lop·poh*; to go at a gallop andare* al galoppo *an·dah·ray al ga·lop·poh*

gamble vi giocare *jo·kah·ray*

gambler n il giocatore d'azzardo *jo·ka·toh·ray dadz·dzar·doh*

gambling n il gioco d'azzardo *jo·ko dadz·dzar·doh* L55f

game n il gioco *jo·ko*; (hunting) la cacciagione *kach·cha·joh·nay*; a game of

tennis una partita di tennis *oo·na par·tee·ta dee ten·nees*

gang n la banda *ban·da*

gangster n il gangster *gang·ster*

gangway n (passage) il passaggio *pas·saj·joh*; (bridge) la passerella *pas·se·rel·la*

gap n lo spazio vuoto *spats·yoh vwo·toh*

garage n (for parking) l'autorimessa (f) *ow·toh·ree·mes·sa*; (service station) il garage *ga·raj* T168

garbage n le immondizie *eem·mon·dee·tsee·ay*

garbage can n la pattumiera *pat·too·mye·rah* A71

garden n il giardino *jar·dee·noh*

garden center n il centro per il giardinaggio *chen·troh payr eel jar·dee·naj·joh*

gardener n il giardiniere *jar·dee·nye·ray*

gargle vi fare* gargarismi *fah·ray gar·ga·reez·mee*

garlic n l'aglio (m) *al·yoh*

garlic sausage n il salame all'aglio *sa·lah·may al·lal·yoh*

garment n l'indumento (m) *een·doo·mayn·toh*

gas n il gas *gas*; gas stove la cucina a gas *koo·chee·na a gas*

gasket n la guarnizione *gwar·nee·tsee·oh·nay*

gas(oline) n la benzina *ben·dzee·na* T155

gas station n la stazione di servizio *sta·tsyoh·ne dee ser·vee·tsyoh* F9

gate n (of garden) il cancello *kan·chel·loh*; (of building) la porta *por·ta*

gateau n la torta *tohr·ta*

gather vt (assemble) raccogliere* *rak·kol·ye·ray* □ vi (crowd) radunarsi *ra·doo·nahr·see*

gathered adj arricciato(a) *ar·reech·chah·toh(a)*

gauge n (device) l'indicatore (m) *een·dee·ka·toh·ray*

gauze n la garza *gar·dza*

gay adj (merry) allegro(a) *al·lay·groh(a)*

gear n (equipment) l'equipaggiamento (m) *e·kwee·paj·ja·mayn·toh*; (of car) la marcia *mahr·cha*; in gear innestato(a) *een·ne·stah·toh(a)*; 2nd/3rd gear seconda/terza marcia *se·kon·da/tayr·tsa mahr·cha*; high/low gear quarta/prima marcia *kwar·ta/pree·ma mahr·cha*

gearbox n la scatola del cambio *skah·to·la del kam·byoh*

gearshift n la leva del cambio di marcia *lay·va del kam·byoh dee mahr·cha*

gem n la gemma *jem·ma*

gender n il genere *je·ne·ray*

general adj generale *je·ne·rah·lay* □ n (soldier) il generale *je·ne·rah·lay*; in general in generale *een je·ne·rah·lay*

general delivery adv fermo posta *fayr·mo po·sta* Sn7

general election n le elezioni politiche *e·lets·ee·oh·nee po·lee·tee·kay*

general knowledge n la cultura generale *kool·too·ra je·ne·rah·lay*

generally adv generalmente *je·ne·rahl·mayn·tay*

general practitioner, G.P. n il medico generico *me·dee·koh je·ne·ree·koh*

generation n la generazione *je·ne·ra·tsee·oh·nay*

generator n (electrical) il generatore je·ne·ra·toh·ray

generous adj (person) generoso(a) je·ne·roh·soh(a); (gift) splendido(a) splen·dee·doh(a)

Geneva n Ginevra (f) jee·ne·vra

gentle adj mite mee·tay

gentleman n il signore seen·yoh·ray

genuine adj autentico(a) ow·ten·tee·koh(a)

geography n la geografia jay·oh·gra·fee·a

geology n la geologia jay·oh·loh·jee·a

geometry n la geometria jay·oh·me·tree·a

geranium n il geranio je·rah·nee·oh

germ n il microbo mee·kro·boh

German adj tedesco(a) te·day·skoh(a) □ n il tedesco te·day·skoh

Germany n Germania (f) jer·mah·nya; in/to Germany in Germania een jer·mah·nya

gesture n il gesto jes·toh

get vt (obtain) ottenere* ot·te·nay·ray; (fetch) prendere* pren·de·ray; (receive) ricevere ree·chay·ve·ray; (prepare: food) preparare pray·pa·rah·ray; (catch: illness) prendere* pren·de·ray; to have got(ten) (possess) avere* a·vay·ray; to get tired stancarsi stan·kahr·see; to get ready prepararsi pray·pa·rahr·see; how do we get there? come ci si arriva? koh·may chee se ar·ree·va; to get home arrivare a casa ar·ree·vah·ray a kah·sa; get off the grass non calpestate l'erba! nohn kal·pes·tah·tay ler·ba; to get one's hair cut farsi* tagliare i capelli far·see tal·yah·ray ee ka·pel·lee; to get away (escape) fuggire fooj·jee·ray; how are you getting on? come va? koh·may va; to get onto a road entrare su una strada en·trah·ray soo·oo·na strah·da; to get through (on phone) ottenere* la linea ot·te·nay·ray la lee·nay·a; to get up alzarsi al·tsahr·see

gherkin n il cetriolino che·tree·oh·lee·noh

ghetto n il ghetto get·toh

ghost n il fantasma fan·taz·ma

giant n il gigante jee·gan·tay

gift n il regalo re·gah·loh; (ability) il talento ta·len·toh

gifted adj dotato(a) do·tah·toh(a)

gift token n il buono-regalo bwo·noh·re·gah·loh

gift-wrap vt incartare con carta da regalo een·kahr·tah·ray kon kahr·ta da re·gah·loh

gin n (drink) il gin jeen

ginger n lo zenzero tsen·tse·roh

ginger ale n la bibita allo zenzero bee·bee·ta al·loh tsen·tse·roh

gingerbread n il pan di zenzero pahn dee tsen·tse·roh

gingham n la percallina a quadretti payr·kal·lee·na a kwa·dret·tee

gipsy n lo zingaro tseen·ga·roh

girdle n (corset) il corsetto kor·sayt·toh

girl n (child) la bambina bam·bee·na; (young woman) la ragazza ra·gats·tsa S106

girlfriend n la ragazza ra·gats·tsa

give vt dare* dah·ray; to give a party dare* una festa dah·ray oo·na fes·ta; to give someone something dare* qualcosa a qualcuno dah·ray kwal·koh·sa a kwal·koo·no; to give away regalare ray·ga·lah·ray; to give back restituire re·stee·too·ee·ray; to give in

(yield) cedere che·de·ray; to give up (abandon hope) abbandonare ab·ban·do·nah·ray; to give up smoking smettere* di fumare zmayt·te·ray dee foo·mah·ray; to give way (traffic) dare* la precedenza dah·ray la pre·che·den·tsa

glacé adj glacé gla·say

glad adj felice fe·lee·chay; I was glad to hear... ero lieto di sapere... e·roh lee·yay·toh dee sa·pay·ray

glamorous adj affascinante af·fa·shee·nan·tay

glance n lo sguardo zgwar·doh □ vi to glance at dare* uno sguardo a dah·ray oo·no zgwar·doh a

gland n la ghiandola gee·an·doh·la

glare n (of light) il bagliore bal·yoh·ray

glass n il vetro vay·troh; (tumbler) il bicchiere beek·kye·ray; (glassware) gli articoli di vetro ar·tee·ko·lee dee vay·troh B54, E13

glasses pl gli occhiali ok·kyah·lee B68

glide vi scivolare shee·voh·lah·ray

glider n l'aliante (m) a·lee·an·tay

gliding n (sport) il volo a vela voh·loh a vay·la

global adj globale glo·bah·le

globe n (map) il globo glo·boh

globe artichoke n il carciofo kar·cho·foh

glove n il guanto gwan·toh

glove compartment n il vano portaoggetti vah·noh por·ta·oj·jet·tee

glow vi essere* incandescente es·se·ray een·kan·de·shen·tay

glue n la colla kol·la □ vt incollare een·kol·lah·ray

glycerin(e) n la glicerina glee·che·ree·na

gnat n il moscerino mo·she·ree·noh

go vi andare* an·dah·ray; (leave) partire par·tee·ray; (clock, machine) funzionare foon·tsyoh·nah·ray; to go shopping fare* la spesa fah·ray la spay·sa; to go bad marcire mar·chee·ray; how did it go? come è andato? koh·may e an·dah·toh; the books go here i libri vanno qui ee lee·bree van·noh kwee; it won't go in non ci sta nohn chee sta; all our money's gone è finito tutto il nostro denaro e fee·nee·toh toot·toh eel no·stroh de·nah·roh; I'm going to do it lo faccio io loh fach·choh ee·oh; go ahead! faccia pure! fach·cha poo·ray; to go away partire par·tee·ray; to go back tornare tor·nah·ray; to go down scendere* shayn·de·ray; to go in entrare en·trah·ray; to go out uscire oo·shee·ray; to go out with somebody uscire con qualcuno oo·shee·ray kon kwal·koo·noh; this goes with your dress questo s'intona con il Suo vestito kwes·toh seen·toh·na kon eel soo·oh ves·tee·toh; we will have to go without milk dovremo fare a meno del latte do·vray·moh fah·ray a may·noh del lat·tay

goal n (sport) la rete ray·tay; (aim) lo scopo sko·poh

goat n la capra kah·pra

god n il dio dee·oh; God Dio (m) dee·oh

godfather n il padrino pa·dree·noh

godmother n la madrina ma·dree·na

goggles pl gli occhiali ok·kyah·lee

gold n l'oro (m) o·roh □ adj d'oro do·roh; gold-plated placcato d'oro plak·kah·toh do·roh S88, 89

golden adj dorato(a) do·rah·toh(a)

goldfish n il pesce rosso *pay·she rohs· soh*

golf n il golf *golf* L33

golf ball n la palla da golf *pal·la da golf*

golf club n la mazza da golf *mats·tsa da golf*; (*association*) il club di golf *kloob dee golf*

golf course n il campo di golf *kam·poh dee golf*

golfer n il giocatore di golf *jo·ka·toh· ray dee golf*

good adj buono(a) *bwo·noh(a)*; (*weather*) bello(a) *bel·loh(a)*; (*well-behaved*) educato(a) *e·doo·kah· toh(a)*; **to be good at golf** essere* forte nel golf *es·se·ray for·tay nel golf*; **spinach is good for you** gli spinaci fanno bene alla salute *lyee spee· nah·chee fan·no be·nay al·la sa·loo· tay*; **it'll do you good** le farà bene *lay fa·ra be·nay*; **good morning/afternoon!** buon giorno! *bwon johr·noh*; **good evening!** buona sera! *bwo·na say·ra*; **good night!** buona notte! *bwo·na not·tay*

goodbye excl arrivederci *ar·ree·ve· dayr·chee*

Good Friday n venerdì santo *ve·ner· dee san·toh*

goods pl le merci *mayr·chee*

goose n l'oca (f) *o·ka*

gooseberry n l'uva spina (f) *oo·va spee·na*

gossip vi chiacchierare *kya·kye·rah·ray* □ n (*chatter*) la chiacchiera *kya· kye·ra*

goulash n il gulasch *goo·lash*

gourmet n il buongustaio *bwon·goos· ta·ee·yoh*

govern vt (*country*) governare *go·vayr· nah·ray*

government n il governo *go·vayr·noh*

governor n (*of colony*) il governatore *go·vayr·na·toh·ray*; (*of institution*) il direttore *dee·ret·toh·ray*, la direttrice *dee·ret·tree·chay*

gown n (*dress*) la veste *ves·tay*; (*academic*) la toga *to·ga*

grab vt afferrare *af·fer·rah·ray*

graceful adj grazioso(a) *gra·tsyoh· soh(a)*

grade n il grado *grah·doh*; (*class*) la classe *klas·say*

grade crossing n il passaggio a livello *pas·saj·joh a lee·vel·loh*

grade school n la scuola elementare *skwo·la e·le·men·tah·ray*

gradual adj graduale *gra·dwa·lay*

gradually adv gradualmente *gra·doo· al·men·tay*

graduate n (*from university*) il/la laureato(a) *low·ray·ah·toh(a)* □ vi laurearsi *low·ray·ar·see*

grain n (*cereal crops*) il grano *grah· noh*; (*in wood*) la venatura *vay·na· too·ra*

gram n il grammo *gram·moh*

grammar n la grammatica *gram·ma· tee·ka*; grammar (*book*) il libro di grammatica *lee·broh dee gram·ma· tee·ka*

grand adj magnifico(a) *ma·nyee·fee· koh(a)*

grandchild n il/la nipotino(a) *nee·po· tee·noh(a)*

granddaughter n la nipote *nee·poh·tay*

grandfather n il nonno *non·noh*

grandfather clock n l'orologio a pendolo (m) *o·ro·lo·joh a pen·do·loh*

grandmother n la nonna *non·na*

grand piano n il pianoforte a coda *pya· no·for·tay a koh·da*

Grand Prix n il Gran Premio *gran pre· myoh*

grandson n il nipote *nee·poh·tay*

grant n (*to student*) la borsa di studio *bohr·sa dee stoo·dee·oh*; (*to institution*) la sovvenzione *sov·ven·tsyoh· nay* □ vt (*wish*) accordare *ak·kor· dah·ray*

grapefruit n il pompelmo *pom·pel·moh*

grapefruit juice n il succo di pompelmo *sook·koh dee pom·pel·moh*

grapes pl l'uva (f) *oo·va*

graph n il grafico *gra·fee·koh*

grasp vt (*seize*) afferrare *af·fer·rah·ray*

grass n l'erba (f) *er·ba*

grate n la grata *grah·ta* □ vt (*food*) grattugiare *grat·too·jah·ray*

grateful adj grato(a) *grah·toh(a)*

grater n la grattugia *grat·too·jah*

grave n la tomba *tohm·ba*

grave (accent) n l'accento grave (m) *ach·chen·toh grah·vay*

gravel n la ghiaia *ghee·a·ya*

graveyard n il camposanto *kam·po· san·toh*

gravy n la salsa *sal·sa*

gray adj grigio(a) *gree·joh(a)*

graze n la scalfittura *skal·feet·too·ra* □ vt (*skin*) scalfire *skal·fee·ray*

grease n il grasso *gras·soh*; (*lubricant*) il lubrificante *loo·bree·fee·kan·tay*

greasy adj grasso(a) *gras·soh(a)*

great adj grande *gran·day*; (*excellent*) magnifico(a) *ma·nyee·fee·koh(a)*

Great Britain n Gran Bretagna (f) *gran bre·tan·ya*

Greece n Grecia (f) *gray·cha*

greedy adj goloso(a) *go·loh·soh(a)*

Greek adj greco(a) *gre·koh(a)* □ n il greco *gre·koh*

green adj verde *vayr·day*

green card n la carta verde *kar·ta vayr· day*

greenhouse n la serra *ser·ra*

green salad n l'insalata verde (f) *een· sa·lah·ta vayr·day*

greet vt salutare *sa·loo·tah·ray*

greeting n il saluto *sa·loo·toh*

greeting card n la cartolina *kar·to· lee·na*

grey adj grigio(a) *gree·joh(a)*

grief n il dolore *do·loh·ray*

grill n (*gridiron*) la griglia *greel·ya* □ vt cuocere* ai ferri *kwo·che·ray ai fer· ree*

grillroom n la rosticceria *ro·steech·che· ree·a*

grimace n la smorfia *zmor·fee·a*

grin vi sorridere* *sor·ree·de·re* □ n il sorriso *sor·ree·soh*

grind vt macinare *ma·chee·nah·ray*

grip vt afferrare *af·fer·rah·ray*; n (*case*) la valigetta *va·lee·jayt·ta*

grit n la graniglia *gra·neel·ya*

groan vi gemere *je·me·ray* □ n il gemito *je·mee·toh*

grocer n il droghiere *dro·gye·ray*

groceries pl i generi alimentari *je·ne· ree a·lee·men·tah·ree*

grocery shop n la drogheria *dro·ge· ree·a*

gross n la grossa *gros·sa* □ adj (*before deductions*) lordo(a) *lohr·doh(a)*

gross national product, GNP n il prodotto nazionale lordo *pro·doht·toh na·tsyoh·nah·le lohr·do*

grotesque adj grottesco(a) *grot·tay· skoh(a)*

ground n la terra *ter·ra* □ adj (*coffee*)

macinato(a) *ma·chee·nah·toh(a)*; **ground beef** la carne tritata *kahr·nay tree·tah·ta*

groundcloth n la tela impermeabile *tay·la eem·payr·may·ah·bee·lay*

ground floor n il pianterreno *pyan·ter·ray·noh*

groundnut n l'arachide (f) *a·ra·kee·day*

grounds pl (land) i terreni *ter·ray·nee*; (of coffee) i fondi di caffè *fon·dee dee kaf·fe*

group n il gruppo *groop·poh*

grouse n (bird) il tetraone *te·tra·oh·nay*

grow vi crescere* *kre·she·ray* □ vt (plants) coltivare *kol·tee·vah·ray*; **to grow up** crescere* *kre·she·ray*

growl vi ringhiare *reen·gyah·ray*

grown-up adj adulto(a) *a·dool·toh(a)* □ n l'adulto(a) (m/f) *a·dool·toh(a)*

growth n la crescita *kray·shee·ta*; (in amount etc) l'aumento (m) *ow·men·to*; (anatomical) l'escrescenza (f) *es·kre·shen·tsa*

grumble vi brontolare *bron·to·lah·ray*

grunt vi grugnire *groon·yee·ray*

guarantee n la garanzia *ga·ran·tsee·a* □ vt garantire *ga·ran·tee·ray*

guard n (prisoner) custodire *koo·sto·dee·ray*; (protect) proteggere* *pro·tej·je·ray* □ n (sentry) la sentinella *sen·tee·nel·la*; (soldiers) la guardia *gwar·dya*

guardian n il tutore *too·toh·ray*, la tutrice *too·tree·chay*

guess vt indovinare *een·do·vee·nah·ray* □ vi congetturare *kon·jet·too·rah·ray*

guest n l'ospite (m/f) *o·spee·tay*; (at hotel) il/la cliente *klee·en·tay*

guest-house n la pensione *pen·see·oh·nay*

guest-room n la camera degli ospiti *kah·me·ra del·yee o·spee·tee*

guide n la guida *gwee·da* L10

guidebook n la guida *gwee·da* L3

guide dog n il cane per ciechi *kah·nay payr che·kee*

guided tour n la visita con guida *vee·zee·ta kohn gwee·da* L5

guilt n la colpevolezza *kol·pay·vo·layts·tsa*

guilty adj colpevole *kol·pay·vo·lay*

guinea fowl n la gallina faraona *gal·lee·na fa·ra·oh·na*

guitar n la chitarra *kee·tar·ra*

gum n (of teeth) la gengiva *jen·jee·va*; (chewing gum) la gomma da masticare *gohm·ma da ma·stee·kah·ray* 163

gun n il fucile *foo·chee·lay*

gunman n il bandito *ban·dee·toh*

gust n la raffica *raf·fee·ka*

gusty adj (wind) burrascoso(a) *boor·ras·koh·so(a)*

gym(nasium) n la palestra *pa·le·stra*

gymnastics n la ginnastica *jeen·nas·tee·ka*

gypsy n lo zingaro *tseen·ga·roh*

H

haberdashery n il vestiario maschile *ve·stee·ah·ree·oh ma·skee·le*

habit n l'abitudine (f) *a·bee·too·dee·ne*

haddock n l'eglefino (m) *ay·glay·fee·noh*

Hague (the) n l'Aia (f) *la·ya*

hail n la grandine *gran·dee·ne* □ vi it's hailing grandina *gran·dee·na*

hair n i capelli *ka·payl·lee*; (single strand) il capello *ka·payl·loh* Sn37

hairbrush n la spazzola per capelli *spats·tso·la payr ka·payl·lee*

haircut n (style) il taglio dei capelli *tal·yoh dey ka·payl·lee*; **to have a haircut** farsi* tagliare i capelli *far·see tal·yah·ray se ka·payl·lee*

hairdresser n il parrucchiere *par·rook·kye·re* Sn36f

hair-drier n l'asciugacapelli (m) *a·shoo·ga·ka·payl·lee* Sn43

hairpin n la forcina *for·chee·na*

hairpin curve n la curva a gomito *koor·va a goh·mee·toh*

hair spray n la lacca *lak·ka*

hair-style n l'acconciatura (f) *ak·kon·cha·too·ra*

half n la metà *me·ta*; **half an hour** una mezz'ora *medz·dzoh·ra*; **two and a half** due e mezzo *doo·e ay medz·dzoh*; **to cut something in half** tagliare qualcosa in due *tal·yah·ray kwal·ko·sa een doo·e* □ adj a half dozen una mezza dozzina *oo·na medz·dza dodz·dzee·na*; **three and a half kilometers** tre chilometri e mezzo *tray kee·lo·me·tree ay medz·dzo* □ adv half a metà *a me·ta*; **half open** semiaperto(a) *se·mee·a·per·to(a)*

half-fare n la tariffa ridotta *ta·reef·fa ree·doht·ta*

half-hour n la mezz'ora *medz·dzoh·ra*

half-price adj a metà prezzo *a me·ta prets·tsoh*

half-time n l'intervallo (m) *een·ter·val·loh*

halfway adv a metà strada *a me·ta strah·da*

hall n (entrance) il vestibolo *ve·stee·bo·loh*; (room) la sala *sah·la*

hallmark n il marchio *mar·kyoh*

halve vt (divide in two) dividere* a metà *dee·vee·de·re a me·ta*; (reduce by half) ridurre* alla metà *ree·door·re al·la me·ta*

ham n il prosciutto *pro·shoot·toh* S31

hamburger n l'hamburger (m) *ham·bur·gur*

hammer n il martello *mar·tel·loh*

hammock n l'amaca (f) *a·mah·ka*

hamper n la cesta *chay·sta*

hand n la mano *mah·noh*; (of clock) la lancetta *lan·chayt·ta*; **by hand** a mano *a mah·noh* □ vt **to hand someone something** dare* qualcosa a qualcuno *dah·ray kwal·ko·sa a kwal·koo·no*

handbag n la borsa *bohr·sa*

handbook n il manuale *ma·noo·ah·le*

hand-brake n il freno a mano *fre·noh a mah·noh*

hand cream n la crema per le mani *kre·ma payr le mah·nee*

handcuffs pl le manette *ma·nayt·te*

handicap n lo svantaggio *zvan·taj·joh*; (golf) l'handicap (m) *han·dee·kap*

handkerchief n il fazzoletto *fats·tso·layt·toh*

handle n (of door) la maniglia *ma·neel·ya*; (of cup, knife) il manico *mah·nee·koh*; (for winding) la manovella *ma·no·vel·la* □ vt (touch) toccare *tok·kah·ray*; (deal with) trattare *trat·tah·ray*; **handle with care** fragile *frah·jee·le*

handlebar(s) n il manubrio *ma·noo·bryoh*

hand-luggage *n* il bagaglio a mano *ba·gal·yoh a mah·noh*

handmade *adj* fatto(a) a mano *fat·to(a) a mah·noh* S107

handrail *n* (*on stairs*) il corrimano *kor·ree·mah·noh*

handsome *adj* (*person*) bello(a) *bel·lo(a)*

handy *adj* (*convenient*) pratico(a) *pra·tee·ko(a)*

hang *vt* appendere* *ap·pen·de·re*; (*criminal*) impiccare *eem·peek·kah·ray* □ *vi* pendere *pen·de·re*; **hang on!** (*on phone*) aspetti! *a·spet·tee*; **to hang up** (*phone*) deporre* il ricevitore *de·pohr·re eel ree·che·vee·toh·re*

hangover *n* il mal di testa dopo una sbornia *mal dee te·sta doh·po oo·na zbor·nya*; **to have a hangover** avere* il mal di testa dopo una sbornia *a·vay·re mal dee te·sta doh·po oo·na zbor·nya*

happen *vi* succedere* *sooch·che·de·re*; **what happened to him?** che cosa gli è successo? *ke ko·sa lyee e sooch·ches·so*

happiness *n* la felicità *fe·lee·chee·ta*

happy *adj* contento(a) *kon·tayn·to(a)*

harbor *n* il porto *por·toh*

harbor master *n* il capitano di porto *ka·pee·tah·noh dee por·toh*

hard *adj* (*not soft*) duro(a) *doo·ro(a)*; (*difficult*) difficile *deef·fee·chee·le* □ *adv* (*work*) sodo *so·do*

hard-boiled *adj* sodo(a) *so·do(a)*

hardware *n* le ferramenta *fer·ra·mayn·ta*; (*computing*) il hardware *hard·wer*

hard-wearing *adj* resistente *re·see·sten·te*

hare *n* la lepre *le·pray*

harmful *adj* nocivo(a) *no·chee·vo(a)*

harmless *adj* innocuo(a) *een·no·kwo(a)*

harness *n* i finimenti *fee·nee·mayn·tee*

harp *n* l'arpa (*f*) *ar·pa*

harsh *adj* (*severe*) severo(a) *se·ve·ro(a)*

harvest *n* (*of grain*) il raccolto *rak·kol·toh*; (*of grapes*) la vendemmia *ven·daym·mya* □ *vt* (*grain*) mietere *mye·te·re*; (*grapes*) fare* la vendemmia di *fah·ray la ven·daym·mya dee*

haste *n* la fretta *frayt·ta*

hat *n* il cappello *kap·pel·loh* S12

hatchback *n* (*car*) la macchina a cinque porte *mak·kee·na a cheen·kwe por·te*

hate *vt* odiare *o·dyah·ray*

hatred *n* l'odio (*m*) *o·dyoh*

hat stand *n* l'attaccapanni (*m*) *at·tak·ka·pan·nee*

have *vt* avere* *a·vay·re*; (*meal*) fare* *fah·ray*; **to have a shower** fare* una doccia *fah·ray oo·na dohch·cha*; **to have a drink** prendere* qualcosa da bere *pren·de·re kwal·ko·sa da bay·re*; **she has to do it** deve farlo *de·ve far·lo*; **to have something done** far* fare qualcosa *far fah·ray kwal·ko·sa*

hay *n* il fieno *fye·noh*

hay fever *n* la febbre da fieno *feb·bre da fye·noh* S40

he *pron* egli *ayl·yee*; **here he is!** eccolo! *ek·ko·lo*

head *n* la testa *te·sta*; (*chief*) il capo *kah·poh*

headache *n* il mal di testa *mal dee te·sta*; **to have a headache** avere* il mal di testa *a·vay·re mal dee te·sta* S40

headlight *n* il faro *fah·roh*

headline *n* il titolo *tee·to·loh*

headmaster *n* il preside *pre·see·de*

headmistress *n* il preside *pre·see·de*

head office *n* la sede centrale *se·de chen·trah·le*

head-on *adj* frontale *fron·tah·le*

headphones *pl n* la cuffia *koof·fya*

headrest *n* il poggiatesta *poj·ja·te·sta*

heal *vi* (*wound*) guarire *gwa·ree·re*

health *n* la salute *sa·loo·te*

health foods *pl n* i cibi naturali *chee·bee na·too·rah·lee*

health service *n* il servizio sanitario *ser·vee·tsyoh sa·nee·tah·ryo*

healthy *adj* (*person*) sano(a) *sah·no(a)*

heap *n* il mucchio *mook·kyoh*

hear *vt/i* sentire *sen·tee·re*; **I can't hear (you)** non La sento *nohn la sen·to*

hearing aid *n* l'apparecchio acustico (*m*) *ap·pa·rayk·kyoh a·koo·stee·ko*

heart *n* il cuore *kwo·re*; **by heart** a memoria *a me·mo·ree·a*; **hearts** (*cards*) i cuori *kwo·ree* I1

heart attack *n* l'attacco cardiaco (*m*) *at·tak·koh kar·dee·a·ko*

heartburn *n* il bruciore di stomaco *broo·choh·re dee sto·ma·koh*

hearth *n* il focolare *fo·ko·lah·re*

heat *n* il calore *ka·loh·re*; (*sports*) la batteria *bat·te·ree·a*

heater *n* il riscaldatore *ree·skal·da·toh·re*

heating *n* il riscaldamento *ree·skal·da·mayn·toh* A44f, 66

heavy *adj* pesante *pe·san·te*

hedge *n* la siepe *sye·pe*

heel *n* il tallone *tal·loh·ne*; (*of shoe*) il tacco *tak·koh*

height *n* (*of object*) l'altezza (*f*) *al·tayts·tsa*; (*of person*) la statura *sta·too·ra*

helicopter *n* l'elicottero (*m*) *e·lee·kot·te·roh*

hello *excl* ciao *chow*

helmet *n* il casco *ka·skoh*

help *n* l'aiuto (*m*) *a·yoo·toh*; **help! aiuto!** *a·yoo·toh* □ *vt* help aiutare *a·yoo·tah·ray*; **can you help me?** mi può aiutare? *mee pwo a·yoo·tah·ray*; **help yourself** si serva *see ser·va*; **I can't help it** non posso farci nulla *nohn pos·so far·chee nool·la* B60, T78

helping *n* la porzione *por·tsyoh·ne*

hem *n* l'orlo (*m*) *ohr·loh* Sn76

hemorrhoids *pl* le emorroidi *e·mor·roy·dee*

hen *n* la gallina *gal·lee·na*

her *pron* lei *lay*; **it's her** è lei *e lay*; **give it to her** glielo dia *lye·lo dee·a* □ *adj* her suo *soo·o*, sua *soo·a*, suoi *swoy*, sue *soo·e*; **her brothers** i suoi fratelli *ee swoy fra·tel·lee*; **her sisters** le sue sorelle *le soo·e so·rel·le*

herbs *pl* le erbe *er·be*

here *adv* qui *kwee*; **here's my sister** ecco mia sorella *ek·ko mee·a so·rel·la*; **here she comes** eccola che viene *ek·ko·la ke vye·ne*

hernia *n* l'ernia (*f*) *er·nee·a*

herring *n* l'aringa (*f*) *a·reen·ga*

hers *pron* il/la suo(a) *eel/la soo·o(a)*; (*plural*) i suoi *ee swoy*, le sue *le soo·e*

herself *pron* lei stessa *lay stays·sa*; **she did it herself** l'ha fatto lei stessa *la fat·to lay stays·sa*; **she dressed herself** si è vestita *see e ve·stee·ta*

hesitate *vi* esitare *e·zee·tah·ray*; **to hesitate to do something** esitare a fare qualcosa *e·zee·tah·ray a fah·ray kwal·ko·sa*

hiccup *n* il singhiozzo *seen·gyots·tsoh*; **to have (the) hiccups** avere* il singhiozzo *a·vay·re eel seen·gyots·tsoh*

hide *n* (*leather*) la pelle *pel·le* □ *vt* nascondere* *na·skohn·de·re* □ *vi* nascondersi* *na·skohn·der·see*

hi-fi *adj* ad alta fedeltà *al·al·ta fe·del·ta* □ *n* il sistema hi-fi *see·ste·ma hi·fi*

high *adj* alto(a) *al·to(a)*; (*pitch, voice*) acuto(a) *a·koo·to(a)* □ *adv* in alto *een al·to*; **6 meters high** alto(a) 6 metri *al·to(a) 6 me·tree*

highchair *n* il seggiolone *sej·jo·loh·ne* C3

high-class *adj* di prim'ordine *dee pree·mohr·dee·ne*

higher *adj* piú alto(a) *pyoo al·to(a)*

high-heeled *adj* a tacchi alti *a tak·kee al·tee*

high school *n* il liceo *lee·che·oh*

high-speed *adj* rapido(a) *ra·pee·do(a)*

high tide *n* l'alta marea (*f*) *al·ta ma·re·a*

highway *n* la strada statale *strah·da sta·tah·le*

Highway Code *n* il codice stradale *ko·dee·che stra·dah·le*

hijack *vt* dirottare *dee·rot·tah·ray*

hijacker *n* il dirottatore *dee·rot·ta·toh·re*

hike *n* l'escursione a piedi (*f*) *e·skoor·syoh·ne a pye·dee*

hiking *n* l'escursionismo a piedi (*m*) *e·skoor·syoh·nee·zmoh a pye·dee*; **to go hiking** fare* delle escursioni a piedi *fah·ray del·le e·skoor·syoh·nee a pye·dee*

hill *n* la collina *kol·lee·na*; (*slope*) il pendio *pen·dee·oh*

hilly *adj* collinoso(a) *kol·lee·noh·so(a)*

him *pron* lo *lo*; **it's him** è lui *e loo·ee*; **give it to him** glielo dia *lye·lo dee·a*

himself *pron* lui stesso *loo·ee stays·so*; **he did it himself** l'ha fatto lui stesso *la fat·to loo·ee stays·so*; **he dresses himself** si veste *see ve·ste*

hip *n* l'anca (*f*) *an·ka*

hire *vt* noleggiare *no·lej·jah·ray*; **to hire something out** noleggiare qualcosa *no·lej·jah·ray kwal·ko·sa* T108*f*

his *adj* suo *soo·o*, sua *soo·a*, suoi *swoy*, sue *soo·e*; **his brothers** i suoi fratelli *ee swoy fra·tel·lee*; **his sisters** le sue sorelle *le soo·e so·rel·le* □ *pron* his il/la suo(a) *eel/la soo·o(a)*; (*plural*) i suoi *ee swoy*, le sue *le soo·e*

history *n* la storia *sto·ree·a*

hit *vt* (*with hand*) battere *bat·te·re*; (*with bat*) colpire *kol·pee·re*; (*with car*) urtare *oor·tah·ray* □ *n* (*blow*) il colpo *kohl·poh*

hitchhike *vi* fare* l'autostop *fah·ray low·to·stop*

hitchhiker *n* l'autostoppista (*m/f*) *ow·to·stop·pee·sta*

hobby *n* il passatempo *pas·sa·tem·poh*

hockey *n* l'hockey (*m*) *ho·kee*

hold *vt* tenere* *te·nay·re*; (*contain*) contenere* *kon·te·nay·re*; (*support*) sostenere* *so·ste·nay·re*; **hold him still** lo tenga fermo *lo ten·ga fayr·mo*; **hold on!** (*on phone*) aspetti *a·spet·tee*; **to hold up** (*delay*) trattenere* *trat·te·nay·re*

hole *n* il buco *boo·koh*

holiday *n* (*day*) la festa *fe·sta*; (*period*) le vacanze *va·kan·tse*; **on holiday in** vacanza *een va·kan·tsa*

Holland *n* Olanda (*f*) *o·lan·da*

hollow *adj* cavo(a) *ka·vo(a)*

holy *adj* santo(a) *san·to(a)*

home *n* la casa *kah·sa*; (*institution*) l'asilo (*m*) *a·zee·loh*; **at home** a casa *a*

kah·sa; **to go home** andare* a casa *an·dah·ray a kah·sa*

home address *n* l'indirizzo di casa (*m*) *een·dee·reets·tsoh dee kah·sa*

homesick *adj* □ **to be homesick** provare la nostalgia *pro·vah·ray la no·stal·jee·a*

homework *n* i compiti *kohm·pee·tee*

homogenized *adj* omogeneizzato(a) *o·mo·je·ne·eedz·dzah·to(a)*

honest *adj* onesto(a) *o·ne·sto(a)*

honey *n* il miele *mye·le*

honeymoon *n* la luna di miele *loo·na dee mye·le*; **we're on our honeymoon** siamo in viaggio di nozze *syah·mo een vyaj·joh dee nots·tse*

hood *n* il cappuccio *kap·pooch·choh*; (*of car*) il cofano *ko·fa·noh*

hook *n* l'uncino (*m*) *oon·chee·noh*; (*fishing*) l'amo (*m*) *ah·moh*; **hook and eye** il gancio ed occhiello *gan·choh ad ok·kyel·loh*

hoop *n* il cerchio *chayr·kyoh*

hoot *vi* (*sound horn*) suonare il clacson *swo·nah·ray eel klak·son*

hop *vi* saltare su un piede solo *sal·tah·ray soo oon pye·de soh·lo*

hope *n* la speranza *spe·ran·tsa* □ *vi* sperare *spe·rah·ray*; **I hope so/not** spero di sì/no *spe·ro dee see/no*

horizon *n* l'orizzonte (*m*) *o·reedz·dzohn·te*

horizontal *adj* orizzontale *o·reedz·dzon·tah·le*

horn *n* (*of animal*) il corno *kor·noh*; (*of car*) il clacson *klak·son*

horrible *adj* orribile *or·ree·bee·le*

horror movie *n* il film d'orrore *feelm dor·roh·re*

hors d'œuvre *n* l'antipasto (*m*) *an·tee·pa·stoh*

horse *n* il cavallo *ka·val·loh*

horseback riding *n* l'equitazione (*f*) *e·kwee·ta·tsyoh·ne*; **to go horseback riding** fare* dell'equitazione *fah·ray del·le·kwee·ta·tsyoh·ne*

horse-racing *n* le corse ippiche *kohr·se eep·pee·ke*

hose *n* (*pipe*) il tubo flessibile *too·boh fles·see·bee·le*

hospital *n* l'ospedale (*m*) *o·spe·dah·le* I52, E6

hospitality *n* l'ospitalità (*f*) *o·spee·ta·lee·ta*

host *n* l'ospite (*m*) *o·spee·te*

hostage *n* l'ostaggio (*m*) *o·staj·joh*; **to take someone hostage** prendere* qualcuno come ostaggio *pren·de·re kwal·koo·no koh·me o·staj·joh*

hostel *n* l'ostello (*m*) *o·stel·loh*

hostess *n* l'ospite (*f*) *o·spee·te*

hot *adj* caldo(a) *kal·do(a)*; (*spicy*) piccante *peek·kan·te*

hot dog *n* il hot-dog *hot·dog*

hotel *n* l'albergo (*m*) *al·ber·goh* B59, A6, 29

hotplate *n* la piastra riscaldante *pya·stra ree·skal·dan·te*

hot-water bottle *n* la borsa di acqua calda *bohr·sa dee ak·kwa kal·da*

hour *n* l'ora (*f*) *oh·ra*

hourly *adv* ogni ora *ohn·yee oh·ra*

house *n* la casa *kah·sa*; **on the house** offerto(a) dalla casa *of·fer·to(a) dal·la kah·sa* A56*f*

housecoat *n* la vestaglia *ve·stal·ya*

household *n* la famiglia *fa·meel·ya*

housekeeper *n* la governante *go·ver·nan·te*

housewife *n* la casalinga *ka·sa·leen·ga*

housework n il lavoro domestico *la·voh·roh do·me·stee·ko*

housing n l'alloggio (m) *al·loj·joh*

hovercraft n il hovercraft *ho·ver·kraft*

how adv come *koh·me;* how long? quanto tempo? *kwan·to tem·po;* how long have you been here? da quanto è qui? *da kwan·to e kwee;* how many? quanti(e)? *kwan·tee(·te);* how much? quanto(a)? *kwan·to(a);* how many people? quante persone? *kwan·te per·soh·ne;* how much milk? quanto latte? *kwan·to lat·te*

however conj tuttavia *toot·ta·vee·a*

hug vt abbracciare *ab·brach·chah·ray*

hullo excl ciao *chow*

human adj umano(a) *oo·mah·no(a)*

hump n (on road) il dosso *dos·soh*

hundred num cento *chen·to;* a hundred and one centuno *chen·too·no;* a hundred and two centodue *chen·to·doo·e;* a hundred (and) eighty five centottantacinque *chen·tot·tan·ta·cheen·kwe;* a hundred people cento persone *chen·to per·soh·ne;* hundreds of books centinaia di libri *chen·tee·na·ya dee lee·bree*

hundredth adj centesimo(a) *chen·te·zee·mo(a)*

Hungarian adj ungherese *oon·ge·ray·se* □ n l'ungherese (m) *oon·ge·ray·se*

Hungary n Ungheria (f) *oon·ge·ree·a*

hunger n la fame *fah·me*

hungry adj affamato(a) *af·fa·mah·to(a);* to be hungry avere* fame a·*vay·re fah·me*

hunt vt cacciare *kach·chah·ray*

hurricane n l'uragano (m) *oo·ra·gah·noh*

hurry vi affrettarsi *af·fret·tar·see;* hurry up! faccia presto! *fach·cha pre·sto* □ n to be in a hurry avere* fretta a·*vay·re frayt·ta* B63, Ea10

hurt vi dolere* *do·lay·re;* that hurts! quello fa male! *kwayl·lo fa mah·le;* to hurt oneself farsi* male *far·see mah·le*

husband n il marito *ma·ree·toh* T115, S103

hut n (shed) la capanna *ka·pan·na;* (on mountain) il rifugio *ree·foo·joh*

hygienic adj igienico(a) *ee·je·nee·ko(a)*

hymn n l'inno (m) *een·noh*

hyphen n il trattino *trat·tee·noh*

hysterical adj isterico(a) *ee·ste·ree·ko(a)*

I

I pron io *ee·o*

ice n il ghiaccio *gyach·choh* A90

icebox n la ghiacciaia *gyach·cha·ya*

ice cream n il gelato *je·lah·toh*

ice cube n il cubetto di ghiaccio *koo·bayt·toh dee gyach·choh*

ice hockey n l'hockey su ghiaccio (m) *ho·kee soo gyach·choh*

Iceland n Islanda (f) *ee·slan·da*

icing n (on cake) la glassa *glas·sa*

idea n l'idea (f) *ee·de·a*

ideal adj ideale *ee·de·ah·le*

identical adj identico(a) *ee·den·tee·ko(a)*

identify vt identificare *ee·den·tee·fee·kah·ray*

identity card n la carta d'identità *kar·ta dee·den·tee·ta*

idiot n l'idiota (m/f) *ee·dyo·ta*

if conj se *say*

ignition n (car) l'accensione (f) *ach·chen·syoh·ne*

---

ignition key n la chiave dell'accensione *kyah·ve del·lach·chen·syoh·ne* T182

ignorant adj ignorante *een·yo·ran·te*

ignore vt (person) ignorare *een·yo·rah·ray*

ill adj malato(a) *ma·lah·to(a)*

illegal adj illegale *eel·le·gah·le*

illegitimate adj illegittimo(a) *eel·lay·jeet·tee·moh(a)*

illness n la malattia *ma·lat·tee·a*

illustration n l'illustrazione (f) *eel·loo·stra·tsyoh·ne*

imagination n l'immaginazione (f) *eem·ma·jee·na·tsee·oh·nay*

imagine vt immaginare *eem·ma·jee·nah·ray*

imitate vt imitare *ee·mee·tah·ray*

immediate adj immediato(a) *eem·me·dyah·to(a)*

immediately adv subito *soo·bee·to*

immersion heater n lo scaldabagno *skal·da·ban·yoh*

immigrant n l'immigrante (m/f) *eem·mee·gran·te*

impatient adj impaziente *eem·pa·tsyen·te*

imperfect adj difettoso(a) *dee·fet·toh·so(a)*

impersonal adj impersonale *eem·per·so·nah·le*

import n l'importazione (f) *eem·por·ta·tsyoh·ne* □ vt importare *eem·por·tah·ray*

importance n l'importanza (f) *eem·por·tan·tsa*

important adj importante *eem·por·tan·te*

importer n l'importatore (m) *eem·por·ta·toh·re*

impossible adj impossibile *eem·pos·see·bee·le*

impress vt (win approval) impressionare *eem·pres·syoh·nah·ray*

impression n l'impressione (f) *eem·pres·syoh·ne*

impressive adj impressionante *eem·pres·syoh·nan·te*

improve vt/i migliorare *meel·yo·rah·ray*

improvement n il miglioramento *meel·yo·ra·mayn·toh*

in prep in *een;* put it in the box lo metta nella scatola *lo mayt·ta nel·la skah·to·la;* in May in maggio *een maj·joh;* he did it in 2 days l'ha fatto in 2 giorni *la fat·to een 2 johr·nee;* he'll be back in 2 days tornerà fra 2 giorni *tor·ne·ra fra 2 johr·nee;* in town/France in città/Francia *een cheet·ta/fran·cha;* in Italian in italiano *een ee·ta·lyah·noh* □ adv is he in? è a casa? *e a kah·sa;* the train is in il treno è arrivato *eel tre·noh e ar·ree·vah·to*

incentive n l'incentivo (m) *een·chen·tee·voh*

inch n il pollice *pol·lee·che*

incident n (event) l'avvenimento (m) *av·ve·nee·mayn·toh*

incinerator n l'inceneratore (m) *een·che·ne·ra·toh·re*

include vt includere* *een·kloo·de·re*

including prep compreso(a) *kom·pray·so(a)*

inclusive adj (costs) globale *glo·bah·le;* from 6th to 12th inclusive dal 6 al 12 incluso *dal 6 al 12 een·kloo·zo* □ adv inclusive of tip servizio compreso *ser·vee·tsyoh kom·pray·so*

income n il reddito *red·dee·toh*

income tax n l'imposta sul reddito (f) *eem·poh·sta sool red·dee·toh*

incomplete adj incompleto(a) *een·kom·play·toh(a)*

inconvenient adj poco pratico(a) *po·ko pra·tee·ko(a)*; (time, place) scomodo(a) *sko·mo·do(a)*

incorrect adj sbagliato(a) *zbal·ya·toh(a)*

increase vt/i aumentare *ow·men·tah·ray* □ n (in size) l'accrescimento (m) *ak·kre·shee·mayn·toh*; (in number) l'aumento (m) *ow·mayn·toh*

incredible adj incredibile *een·kre·dee·bee·le*

indecent adj indecente *een·day·chen·tay*

independence n l'indipendenza (f) *een·dee·pen·den·tsa*

independent adj indipendente *een·dee·pen·den·te*

index n l'indice (m) *een·dee·che*

indexed adj (interest rates etc) legato(a) all'indice del costo della vita *le·gah·to(a) al·leen·dee·che del ko·stoh del·la vee·ta*

India n l'India (f) *een·dee·a*

Indian adj indiano(a) *een·dee·ah·no(a)* □ n l'indiano(a) (m/f) *een·dee·ah·no(a)*

indicator n (of car) la freccia *fraych·cha*

indigestible adj indigesto(a) *een·dee·je·sto(a)*

indigestion n l'indigestione (f) *een·dee·je·styoh·ne*

indirect adj (route) indiretto(a) *een·dee·ret·to(a)*

individual adj individuale *een·dee·vee·doo·ah·le*

individually adv singolarmente *seen·go·lar·mayn·te*

indoor adj (games) al coperto *al ko·per·to*

indoors adv (be) in casa *een kah·sa*; (go) dentro *dayn·tro*

industrial adj industriale *een·doo·stree·ah·le*

industry n l'industria (f) *een·doo·stree·a*

inedible adj immangiabile *eem·man·jah·bee·le*

inefficient adj inefficiente *een·ef·fee·chen·te*

inevitable adj inevitabile *een·e·vee·tah·bee·le*

inexpensive adj poco costoso(a) *po·ko ko·stoh·so(a)*

infection n l'infezione (f) *een·fe·tsyoh·ne*

infectious adj infettivo(a) *een·fet·tee·vo(a)*

inferior adj inferiore *een·fe·ryoh·re*

inflammation n l'infiammazione (f) *een·fyam·ma·tsyoh·ne* I27

inflatable adj gonfiabile *gon·fyah·bee·le*

inflate vt gonfiare *gon·fee·ah·re*

inflation n (economic) l'inflazione (f) *een·fla·tsyoh·ne*

influence n l'influenza (f) *een·floo·en·tsa*

inform vt avvisare *av·vee·zah·ray*

informal adj (party) informale *een·for·mah·le*

information n le informazioni *een·for·ma·tsyoh·nee*

information desk/office n l'ufficio informazioni (m) *oof·fee·choh een·for·ma·tsyoh·nee*

ingredients pl gli ingredienti *een·gre·dyen·tee*

inhabit vt abitare in *a·bee·tah·ray een*

inhabitant n l'abitante (m/f) *a·bee·tan·te*

inherit vt ereditare *e·re·dee·tah·ray*

initials pl le iniziali *ee·nee·tsyah·lee*

injection n l'iniezione (f) *een·ye·tsyoh·ne*

injure vt ferire *fe·ree·re*

injured adj ferito(a) *fe·ree·to(a)* I16

injury n la ferita *fe·ree·ta*

ink n l'inchiostro (m) *een·kyo·stroh*

inn n la locanda *lo·kan·da*

innocent adj innocente *een·no·chen·te*

inoculation n la vaccinazione *vach·chee·na·tsyoh·nay*

input n (computing) l'input (m) *een·poot*

insect n l'insetto (m) *een·set·toh* S40

insect repellent n l'insettifugo (m) *een·set·tee·foo·goh*

inside n l'interno (m) *een·ter·noh* □ adj the inside wall la parete interna *la pa·ray·te een·ter·na* □ prep inside the box dentro la scatola *dayn·tro la skah·to·la* □ adv to be/go inside stare*/andare* dentro *stah·ray/an·dah·ray dayn·tro*; to turn something inside out rivoltare qualcosa *ree·vol·tah·ray kwal·ko·sa*

insist vi insistere* *een·see·ste·re*; to insist on something insistere* su qualcosa *een·see·ste·re soo kwal·ko·sa*

insolent adj insolente *een·so·len·te*

inspect vt ispezionare *ee·spe·tsyoh·nah·ray*

inspector n l'ispettore (m) *ee·spet·toh·re*

instalment n la rata *rah·ta* M11

instalment plan n la vendita a rate *vayn·dee·ta a rah·te*

instant adj immediato(a) *eem·me·dyah·to(a)*; instant coffee il caffè solubile *kaf·fe so·loo·bee·le* □ n instant l'istante (m) *ee·stan·te*

instead adv invece *een·vay·che*; instead of invece di *een·vay·che dee*

institute n l'istituto (m) *ee·stee·too·toh*

instructions pl le istruzioni *ee·stroo·tsyoh·nee*

instructor n l'istruttore (m) *ee·stroot·toh·re*

instructress n l'istruttrice (f) *ee·stroot·tree·chay*

instrument n lo strumento *stroo·mayn·toh*

insulin n l'insulina (f) *een·soo·lee·na*

insult n l'insulto (m) *een·sool·toh* □ vt insultare *een·sool·tah·ray*

insurance n l'assicurazione (f) *as·see·koo·ra·tsyoh·ne* T116, 189

insurance company n la compagnia di assicurazione *kom·pan·yee·a dee as·see·koo·ra·tsyoh·ne* T213

insurance policy n la polizza di assicurazione *po·leets·tsa dee as·see·koo·ra·tsyoh·ne*

insure vt assicurare *as·see·koo·rah·ray* □ vi to insure against something assicurarsi contro qualcosa *as·see·koo·rar·see kohn·tro kwal·ko·sa*

insured adj assicurato(a) *as·see·koo·rah·to(a)*

intelligence n l'intelligenza (f) *een·tel·lee·jen·tsa*

intelligent adj intelligente *een·tel·lee·jen·te*

intend vt destinare *de·stee·nah·ray*; to intend to do something avere* l'intenzione di fare qualcosa *a·vay·re* *leen·ten·tsyoh·ne dee fah·ray kwal·ko·sa*

intention *n* l'intenzione (*f*) *een·ten·tsyoh·ne*

interchange *n* (*on roads*) l'incrocio (*m*) *een·kroh·choh*

intercom il citofono *chee·to·foh·noh*

interest *n* l'interesse (*m*) *een·te·res·se*; (*hobby*) il passatempo *pas·sa·tem·poh* □ *vt* interessare *een·te·res·sah·ray*

interested *adj* interessato(a) *een·te·res·sah·to(a)*; **to be interested in** interessarsi a *een·te·res·sar·see a*

interesting *adj* interessante *een·te·res·san·te*

interest rate *n* il tasso d'interesse *tas·soh deen·te·res·se*

interfere *vi* intromettersi* *een·tro·mayt·ter·see*

interior *adj* interiore *een·te·ryoh·re*

intermission *n* (*in performance*) l'intervallo (*m*) *een·ter·val·loh*

internal *adj* interno(a) *een·ter·no(a)*

Internal Revenue *n* il fisco *fee·skoh*

international *adj* internazionale *een·ter·na·tsyoh·nah·le* Sn16

interpret *vt* interpretare *een·ter·pre·tah·ray* □ *vi* fare* da interprete *fah·ray da een·ter·pre·te*

interpreter *n* l'interprete (*m/f*) *een·ter·pre·te*

interrupt *vt/i* interrompere* *een·ter·rohm·pe·re*

intersection *n* (*of roads*) l'incrocio (*m*) *een·kroh·choh*

interview *n* (*for job*) il colloquio *kol·lo·kwee·oh*

into *prep* in *een*

introduce *vt* (*person*) presentare *pre·zen·tah·ray* Mc27

introduction *n* (*in book*) l'introduzione (*f*) *een·tro·doo·tsyoh·ne*; (*social*) la presentazione *pre·zen·ta·tsyoh·ne*

invalid *n* l'invalido (*m*) *een·va·lee·doh*

invent *vt* inventare *een·ven·tah·ray*

invention *n* l'invenzione (*f*) *een·ven·tsyoh·ne*

inventory *n* l'inventario (*m*) *een·ven·tah·ryoh*

invest *vt/i* investire *een·ve·stee·re*

investment *n* l'investimento (*m*) *een·ve·stee·mayn·toh*

investor *n* l'azionista (*m/f*) *a·tsyoh·nee·sta*

invisible *adj* invisibile *een·vee·zee·bee·lay*

invitation *n* l'invito (*m*) *een·vee·toh*

invite *vt* invitare *een·vee·tah·ray*

invoice *n* la fattura *fat·too·ra*

iodine *n* lo iodio *ee·oh·dee·oh*

Iran *n* Iran (*m*) *ee·ran*

Iraq *n* Irak (*m*) *ee·rak*

Ireland *n* Irlanda (*f*) *eer·lan·da*

Irish *adj* irlandese *eer·lan·day·se*

iron *n* (*material, golf club*) il ferro *fer·roh*; (*for clothes*) il ferro da stiro *fer·roh da stee·roh* □ *vt* stirare *stee·rah·ray*

ironmonger *n* il negoziante in ferramenta *ne·go·tsyan·te een fer·ra·mayn·ta*

is *vi* □ **she/he is** è e

island *n* l'isola (*f*) *ee·zo·la*; (*traffic*) il salvagente pedonale *sal·va·jen·te pe·do·nah·le*

Israel *n* Israele (*m*) *ee·zra·e·le*

issue *n* (*matter*) la questione *kwe·styoh·ne*; (*of magazine*) il numero *noo·me·roh*; (*of stocks*) l'emissione (*f*) *e·mees·syoh·ne*

it *pron* □ **it's blue** è azzurro(a) *e adz·dzoor·ro(a)*; **take it** lo/la prenda *lo/la pren·da*; **it's me** sono io *soh·no ee·o*; **it's raining** piove *pyo·ve*; **it's 5 kilometers** sono 5 chilometri *soh·no 5 kee·lo·me·tree*

Italian *adj* italiano(a) *ee·ta·lyah·no(a)* □ *n* l'italiano (*m*) *ee·ta·lyah·noh* Mc28

Italy *n* l'Italia (*f*) *ee·ta·lya*

itch *n* il prurito *proo·ree·toh* □ *vi* prudere* *proo·de·re*

item *n* l'articolo (*m*) *ar·tee·ko·loh*

itemized *adj* (*bill etc*) dettagliato(a) *dayt·tal·ya·toh(a)* T189

its *adj* suo *soo·o*, sua *soo·a*; (*with plural noun*) suoi *swoy*, sue *soo·e*

ivory *n* l'avorio (*m*) *a·vo·ryoh*

J

jack *n* (*for car*) il cric *kreek*; (*cards*) il fante *fan·te*

jacket *n* la giacca *jak·ka*

jail *n* la prigione *pree·joh·nay*; **in jail** in prigione *een pree·joh·nay*

jam *vi* (*machine*) bloccarsi *blok·kar·see* □ *n* la marmellata *mar·mel·lah·ta*; (*in traffic*) l'ingorgo (*m*) *een·gohr·goh*

janitor *n* il portiere *por·tye·re*

January *n* gennaio (*m*) *jen·na·yoh*

Japan *n* il Giappone *jap·poh·ne*

Japanese *adj* giapponese *jap·po·nay·se* □ *n* il giapponese *jap·po·nay·se*

jar *n* il barattolo *ba·rat·to·loh*

jaw *n* la mascella *ma·shel·la*

jazz *n* il jazz *jazz* L43

jealous *adj* geloso(a) *je·loh·so(a)*

jeans *pl* i blue-jeans *bloo·jeens*

jeep *n* la jeep *jeep*

jellyfish *n* la medusa *me·doo·za*

jerkin *n* la giacca a vento *jak·ka a ven·toh*

jersey *n* (*fabric*) il jersey *jer·zee*; (*sweater*) la maglia *mal·ya*

jet *n* (*plane*) l'aviogetto (*m*) *a·vyo·jet·toh*

jetty *n* il pontile *pon·tee·le*

Jew *n* l'ebreo (*m*) *e·bre·oh*

jewel *n* il gioiello *jo·yel·loh*

jeweler *n* il gioielliere *jo·yel·lye·re*

jewelry *n* i gioielli *jo·yel·lee* S84

Jewish *adj* ebreo(a) *e·bre·o(a)*

jigsaw (*puzzle*) *n* il puzzle *puz·zuhl*

jingle *n* (*advertising*) la cantilena *kan·tee·le·na*

job *n* (*employment*) l'impiego (*m*) *eem·pye·goh*; (*task*) il compito *kohm·pee·toh* Mc39

jockey *n* il fantino *fan·tee·noh*

jogging *n* il footing *foo·teeng*; **to go jogging** fare* del footing *fah·ray del foo·teeng*

join *vt* unire *oo·nee·re*; (*club*) diventare socio di *dee·ven·tah·ray so·cho dee*; **do join us** venga pure con noi *ven·ga poo·re kohn noy*

joint *n* (*of body*) la giuntura *joon·too·ra*; (*of meat*) la trancia di carne *tran·cha dee kar·ne*

joint ownership *n* la comproprietà *kom·pro·pree·e·ta*

joint-stock company *n* la società per azioni *so·che·ta payr a·tsyoh·nee*

joke *n* lo scherzo *skayr·tsoh*

joker *n* (*cards*) il jolly *jol·lee*

journalist *n* il/la giornalista *johr·na·lee·sta*

journey *n* il viaggio *vyaj·joh*

joy *n* la gioia *jo·ya*

jubilee n il giubileo *joo·bee·le·oh*

judge n il giudice *joo·dee·che* □ vt giudicare *joo·dee·kah·ray*

judo n il judo *joo·doh*

jug n la brocca *brok·ka*

juice n il succo *sook·koh* E63

jukebox n il juke-box *jook·boks*

July n luglio (m) *lool·yoh*

jumbo jet n il jumbo *joom·boh*

jump vt/i saltare *sal·tah·ray*; to jump (over) a wall saltare un muricciolo *sal·tah·ray oon moo·reech·cho·loh*

jumper n (dress) lo scamiciato *ska·mee·chah·toh*

jumper cables pl i conduttori elettrici *ee kon·doot·toh·ree e·let·tree·chee*

junction n (in road) l'incrocio (m) *een·kroh·choh*; (railway) il raccordo ferroviario *ee·ndoh fer·ro·vee·ah·ree·oh*

June n giugno (m) *joon·yoh*

junior adj (class, pupil) elementare *e·le·men·tah·ray*

junket n la giuncata *joon·kah·ta*

just adv □ just here proprio qui *pro·pree·o kwee*; he's just left è appena partito *e ap·pay·na par·tee·to*; it was just a mistake non era che un errore *nohn e·ra ke oon er·roh·re*; I just managed it ci sono appena riuscito *chee so·no ap·pay·na ree·oo·shee·to*; just above the elbow poco sopra il gomito *po·ko soh·pra eel go·mee·toh*; it only just missed è mancato per poco *e man·kah·to payr po·ko*; he arrived just now è arrivato proprio ora *e ar·ree·vah·to pro·pree·o oh·ra*

justice n la giustizia *joo·stee·tsya*

K

karate n il karatè *ka·rah·te*

kebab n il kebab *ke·bab*

keep n il sostentamento *so·sten·ta·mayn·toh*; to earn one's keep guadagnarsi la vita *gwa·dan·yar·see la vee·ta* □ vt keep (retain) tenere* *te·nay·re*; (feed and clothe) mantenere* *man·te·nay·re*; to keep something till later tenere* qualcosa per più tardi *te·nay·re kwal·ko·sa payr pyoo tar·dee*; to keep something in the refrigerator tenere* qualcosa nel frigo *te·nay·re kwal·ko·sa nel free·goh*; keep the change! tenga il resto! *ten·ga eel re·stoh*; to keep something tidy tenere* qualcosa in ordine *te·nay·re kwal·ko·sa een ohr·dee·ne* □ vi milk doesn't keep very well il latte non si conserva molto bene *eel lat·te nohn see kon·ser·va mohl·to be·ne*

Kenya n Kenia (m) *ken·ya*

kerosene n il cherosene *ke·ro·ze·ne*

ketchup n il ketchup *ke·chup*

kettle n il bollitore *bol·lee·toh·re*

key n la chiave *kyah·ve*; (of piano, typewriter) il tasto *ta·stoh* B68, A41, 60

keyhole n il buco della serratura *boo·koh del·la ser·ra·too·ra*

key ring n il portachiavi *por·ta·kyah·vee*

kick n il calcio *kal·choh* □ vt (person) dare* un calcio a *dah·ray oon kal·choh a*; (ball) calciare *kal·chah·ray*

kid n (leather) il capretto *ka·prayt·toh*

kidnap vt rapire *ra·pee·re*

kidney n (of person) il rene *re·ne*; (to eat) il rognone *ron·yoh·ne*

kidney beans pl i fagioli rossicci *fa·jo·lee ros·seech·chee*

kill vt uccidere* *ooch·chee·de·re*

killer n l'assassino (m) *as·sas·see·noh*

kilo n il chilo *kee·loh* S31

kilogram n il chilogrammo *kee·lo·gram·moh*

kilometer n il chilometro *kee·lo·me·troh*

kilowatt n il chilowatt *kee·lo·vat*

kilt n il kilt *keelt*

kind n (type) il genere *je·ne·re*; a kind of bean una specie di fagiolo *oo·na spe·che dee fa·jo·loh* □ adj kind gentile *jen·tee·le*

king n il re *ray*

kirsch n il kirsch *keersh*

kiss vt baciare *ba·chah·ray*; to kiss (each other) baciarsi *ba·char·see* □ n il bacio *bah·choh*

kitchen n la cucina *koo·chee·na*

kite n l'aquilone (m) *a·kwee·loh·ne*

kleenex n il fazzolettino di carta *fats·tso·let·tee·noh dee kar·ta*

knee n il ginocchio *jee·nok·kyoh*; to sit on someone's knee sedersi* sulle ginocchia di qualcuno *se·dayr·see sool·le jee·nok·kya dee kwal·koo·no*

kneel vi inginocchiarsi *een·jee·nok·kyar·see*; to kneel down mettersi* in ginocchio *mayt·ter·see een jee·nok·kyoh*

knife n il coltello *kol·tel·loh*

knit vt/i lavorare a maglia *la·vo·rah·ray a mal·ya*; to knit a sweater fare* un maglione *fah·ray oon mal·yoh·ne*

knitting needle n il ferro da calza *fer·roh da kal·tsa*

knitwear n la maglieria *mal·ye·ree·a*

knob n (on door) il pomo *poh·moh*; (on radio etc) la manopola *ma·no·po·la*

knock vt colpire *kol·pee·re*; to knock (at) the door bussare alla porta *boos·sah·ray al·la por·ta*; to knock down abbattere *ab·bat·te·re*; to knock out mettere* k.o. *mayt·te·re kappa·oh* □ vi knock (engine) picchiare *peek·kyah·ray*

knot vt annodare *an·no·dah·ray* □ n il nodo *no·doh*; to tie a knot fare* un nodo *fah·ray oon no·doh*

know vt (person) conoscere* *ko·noh·she·re*; (fact, subject) sapere* *sa·pay·re*; to know how to do something sapere* fare qualcosa *sa·pay·re fah·ray kwal·ko·sa*

knowledge n la conoscenza *ko·no·shen·tsa*

knuckle n la nocca *nok·ka*

kohlrabi n il cavolo rapa *kah·vo·loh rah·pa*

kosher adj kasher *kah·sher*

L

label n l'etichetta (f) *e·tee·kayt·ta* □ vt etichettare *e·tee·ket·tah·ray*

labor n la manodopera *mah·no·do·pe·ra*

laboratory n il laboratorio *la·bo·ra·to·ryoh*

laborer n il manovale *ma·no·vah·le*

labor force n la manodopera *mah·no·do·pe·ra*

labor union n il sindacato *seen·da·kah·toh*

lace n il pizzo *peets·tsoh*; (of shoe) il laccio *lach·choh*

ladder n la scala *skah·la*

ladle n il ramaiolo *ra·ma·yo·loh*

lady n la signora *seen·yoh·ra*

lager n la birra chiara *beer·ra kyah·ra*

lake n il lago *lah·goh*

lamb n l'agnello (m) an·yel·loh S37

lambswool n la lana d'agnello lah·na dan·yel·loh

lamp n la lampada lam·pa·da

lamppost n il lampione lam·pyoh·ne

lampshade n il paralume pa·ra·loo·me

land n (opposed to sea) la terra ter·ra; (country) il paese pa·ay·ze; (soil) la terra ter·ra; (property) la proprietà pro·pree·e·ta □ vi (from ship) sbarcare zbar·kah·ray; (plane) atterrare at·ter·rah·ray

landing n (of plane) l'atterraggio (m) at·ter·raj·joh; (on stairs) il pianerottolo pya·ne·rot·to·loh

landing strip n la pista d'atterraggio pee·sta dat·ter·raj·joh

landlady n la padrona pa·droh·na

landlord n il padrone pa·droh·ne

landmark n il punto di riferimento poon·toh dee ree·fe·ree·mayn·toh

landslide n la frana frah·na

lane n (in country) il viottolo vee·ot·to·loh; (in town) il vicolo vee·ko·loh; (of road) la corsia kor·see·a

language n la lingua leen·gwa; (way one speaks) il linguaggio leen·gwaj·joh

language laboratory n il laboratorio linguistico la·bo·ra·to·ryoh leen·gwee·stee·ko

lanolin n la lanolina la·no·lee·na

lap n (of track) il giro jee·roh; (of person) il grembo grem·boh

lard n il lardo lar·doh

larder n la dispensa dee·spen·sa

large adj grande gran·de

laryngitis n la laringite la·reen·jee·te

last adj ultimo(a) ool·tee·mo(a); last night stanotte sta·not·te; last week la settimana scorsa la set·tee·mah·na skohr·sa □ adv last per ultimo payr ool·tee·mo; at last alla fine al·la fee·ne □ vi last durare doo·rah·ray

latch n il saliscendi sa·lee·shayn·dee

late adj (not on time) in ritardo een ree·tar·doh □ adv tardi tar·dee; late in the day tardi tar·dee; the latest news le ultime notizie le ool·tee·me no·tee·tsye; the late king il fu re eel foo re

lately adv recentemente re·chen·te·mayn·te

later adj (date etc) posteriore po·ste·ree·oh·re; (version) più recente pyoo re·chen·te □ adv (to come etc) più tardi pyoo tar·dee

Latin n il latino la·tee·noh □ adj latino(a) la·tee·no(a)

Latin America n l'America Latina (f) a·me·ree·ka la·tee·na

Latin American adj latinoamericano(a) la·tee·no·a·me·ree·kah·no(a)

laugh vi ridere* ree·de·re; to laugh at somebody ridere* di qualcuno ree·de·re dee kwal·koo·no □ n laugh il riso ree·soh

laughter n le risa ree·sa

launch n la motolancia mo·to·lan·cha □ vt (ship) varare va·rah·ray; (product) lanciare lan·chah·ray

laundromat n la lavanderia automatica la·van·de·ree·a ow·to·ma·tee·ka

laundry n (place) la lavanderia la·van·de·ree·a; (clothes) il bucato boo·kah·toh A52, Sn72

lavatory n la toeletta to·e·let·ta

law n la legge layj·je; law and order l'ordine pubblico (m) ohr·dee·ne poob·blee·ko

lawn n (grass) il prato rasato prah·toh ra·sah·to

lawn mower n la falciatrice fal·cha·tree·che

lawn tennis n il tennis su erba ten·nees soo er·ba

lawyer n l'avvocato (m) av·vo·kah·toh Sn83

laxative n il lassativo las·sa·tee·voh

lay vt posare po·sah·ray; to lay the table apparecchiare la tavola ap·pa·rek·kyah·ray la tah·vo·la; to lay the fire preparare il fuoco pre·pa·rah·ray eel fwo·koh; to lay down deporre* de·pohr·re; (wine) mettere* in cantina mayt·te·re een kan·tee·na; to lay off (workers) licenziare lee·chen·tsyah·ray

layer n lo strato strah·toh

lazy adj pigro(a) pee·gro(a)

lead[1] vt condurre* kon·door·re □ vi (in contest) essere* in testa es·se·re een te·sta; this door leads into the garden questa porta dà sul giardino kway·sta por·ta da sool jar·dee·noh □ n lead (electrical) il filo fee·loh; (dog's) il guinzaglio gween·tsal·yoh

lead[2] n il piombo pyohm·boh; (in pencil) la mina mee·na

leaf n la foglia fol·ya

leak n (water) la perdita per·dee·ta; (gas) la fuga foo·ga □ vi fare* acqua fah·ray ak·kwa T179, Sn50

lean adj (meat) magro(a) ma·gro(a) □ vi pendere pen·de·re; to lean against something appoggiarsi a qualcosa ap·poj·jar·see a kwal·ko·sa

learn vt imparare eem·pa·rah·ray

lease n l'affitto (m) af·feet·toh

leash n il guinzaglio gween·tsal·yoh

least adj □ the least money il meno denaro eel may·no de·nah·roh; the least amount la minima quantità la mee·nee·ma kwan·tee·ta □ adv the least expensive il meno caro eel may·no kah·ro □ n he has the least ha il meno a eel may·no; at least almeno al·may·no; not in the least per niente payr nyen·te

leather n il cuoio kwo·yoh

leave n (holiday) il congedo kon·je·doh; on leave in congedo een kon·je·doh □ vi partire par·tee·re □ vt (room) uscire* da oo·shee·re da; (club, school, object, message) lasciare la·shah·ray; leave it to me lasci fare a me la·shee fah·ray a may; to leave out (omit) omettere* o·mayt·te·re

lecture n la conferenza kon·fe·ren·tsa

ledger n il mastro ma·stroh

leek n il porro por·roh

left adv □ there's some cream left ci avanza un po' di panna chee a·van·tsa oon po dee pan·na; to turn left girare a sinistra jee·rah·ray a see·nee·stra □ adj the left side il lato sinistro lah·to see·nee·stro T104

left-handed adj mancino(a) man·chee·no(a)

leg n (of person) la gamba gam·ba; (of animal) la zampa tsam·pa; leg of lamb il cosciotto d'agnello ko·shoht·toh dan·yel·loh; chicken leg la coscia di pollo ko·sha dee pohl·loh I21

legal adj legale le·gah·le

leisure n l'ozio (m) o·tsyoh

leisure center n il circolo ricreativo cheer·ko·loh ree·kre·a·tee·vo

lemon n il limone lee·moh·ne

lemonade n la limonata lee·mo·na·ta

lemon juice *n* il succo di limone *sook·koh dee lee·moh·ne*

lemon sole *n* la sogliola *sol·yo·la*

lemon-squeezer *n* lo spremilimoni *spre·mee·lee·moh·nee*

lend *vt* prestare *pre·stah·ray*

length *n* la lunghezza *loon·gayts·tsa*

lens *n* (*of glasses*) la lente *len·te*; (*of camera*) l'obiettivo (*m*) *o·byet·tee·voh*

lentils *pl* le lenticchie *len·teek·kye*

less *adj* □ less meat meno carne *may·no kar·ne* □ *adv* less quickly meno rapidamente *may·no ra·pee·da·mayn·te* □ *n* he has less ne ha meno *ne a may·no*; less than meno di/che *may·no dee/kay*

lesson *n* la lezione *le·tsyoh·ne*

let *vt* (*allow*) lasciare *la·shah·ray*; (*rent out*) affittare *af·feet·tah·ray*; to let someone do something permettere* a qualcuno di fare qualcosa *payr·mayt·te·re a kwal·koo·no dee fah·ray kwal·ko·sa*; let me in mi lasci entrare *mee la·shee en·trah·ray*; let's go andiamo *an·dyah·mo*; they let him go lo hanno lasciato andare *lo an·no la·shah·to an·dah·ray*; to let (*house etc*) affittasi *af·feet·ta·see*; to let someone down deludere* qualcuno *de·loo·de·re kwal·koo·no*

letter *n* la lettera *let·te·ra* B71, A25, Sn1

letter box *n* la buca per le lettere *boo·ka payr le let·te·re*

lettuce *n* la lattuga *lat·too·ga*

level *n* il livello *lee·vel·loh* □ *adj* (*surface*) piano(a) *pyah·no(a)*; (*horizontal*) orizzontale *o·reedz·dzon·tah·le*

lever *n* la leva *le·va*

Levis *pl* i blue-jeans *bloo·jeens*

liabilities *pl* (*on balance sheet*) il passivo *pas·see·voh*

library *n* la biblioteca *bee·blee·o·te·ka*

Libya *n* Libia (*f*) *lee·bya*

license *n* (*for driving*) la patente di guida *pa·ten·te dee gwee·da*

license plate *n* la targa d'immatricolazione *tar·ga deem·ma·tree·ko·la·tsyoh·ne* T207

lick *vt* leccare *lek·kah·ray*

licorice *n* la liquirizia *lee·kwee·ree·tsya*

lid *n* il coperchio *ko·per·kyoh*

lie *n* (*untruth*) la bugia *boo·jee·a* □ *vi* giacere* *ja·chay·re*; (*tell a lie*) mentire* *men·tee·re*; to lie down sdraiarsi *zdra·yar·see*

Liechtenstein *n* Liechtenstein (*m*) *leekh·ten·shtine*

life *n* la vita *vee·ta*; for life a vita *a vee·ta*

lifebelt *n* la cintura di salvataggio *cheen·too·ra dee sal·va·taj·joh*

lifeboat *n* (*on ship*) la scialuppa di salvataggio *sha·loop·pa dee sal·va·taj·joh*; (*from shore*) il battello di salvataggio *bat·tel·loh dee sal·va·taj·joh*

lifeguard *n* il bagnino *ban·yee·noh*

life insurance *n* l'assicurazione sulla vita (*f*) *as·see·koo·ra·tsyoh·ne sool·la vee·ta*

life jacket *n* la giacca di salvataggio *jak·ka dee sal·va·taj·joh*

life preserver *n* (*belt*) la cintura di salvataggio *cheen·too·ra dee sal·va·taj·joh*; (*jacket*) la giacca di salvataggio *jak·ka dee sal·va·taj·joh*

lift *vt* sollevare *sol·le·vah·ray*

light *vt* (*fire, cigarette*) accendere* *ach·chen·de·re* □ *n* la luce *loo·che*; (*lamp*) la lampada *lam·pa·da*; (*on*

car) il faro *fah·roh*; (*traffic light*) il semaforo *se·mah·fo·roh*; have you got a light? mi fa accendere? *mee fa ach·chen·de·re* □ *adj* light (*bright, pale*) chiaro(a) *kyah·ro(a)*; (*not heavy*) leggero(a) *lej·je·ro(a)*; light music la musica leggera *moo·zee·ka lej·je·ra*; as soon as light allo spuntar del giorno *al·lo spoon·tar del johr·noh*

light bulb *n* la lampadina *lam·pa·dee·na*

lighter *n* l'accendino (*m*) *ach·chen·dee·noh* S101

lighthouse *n* il faro *fah·roh*

light industry *n* l'industria leggera (*f*) *een·doo·strya lej·je·ra*

lighting *n* (*on road*) l'illuminazione (*f*) *eel·loo·mee·na·tsyoh·ne*

light meter *n* il fotometro *fo·to·me·troh*

lightning *n* il lampo *lam·poh*

like *prep* come *koh·me* □ *adj* simile *see·mee·le*; what's it like? com'è? *kohm·e* □ *vt* like piacere* a *pya·chay·re a*; I'd like to go mi piacerebbe andare *mee pyah·che·reb·be an·dah·ray*; I'd like an ice cream gradirei un gelato *gra·dee·re·ee oon je·lah·toh*; what would you like? che cosa vorrebbe? *ke ko·sa vor·reb·be* S20, 21

likely *adj* probabile *pro·bah·bee·le*; he's likely to come è probabile che venga *e pro·bah·bee·le ke ven·ga*

lily *n* il giglio *jeel·yoh*

lime *n* (*fruit*) il cedro *chay·droh*

lime juice *n* il succo di cedro *sook·koh dee chay·droh*

limit *n* il limite *lee·mee·te*

limousine *n* la limousine *lee·moo·zeen*

limp *vi* zoppicare *tsop·pee·kah·ray*

line *n* la linea *lee·ne·a*; (*railway*) il binario *bee·nah·ryoh*; (*telephone*) la linea *lee·ne·a*; (*people waiting*) la coda *koh·da*; to stand in line fare* la coda *fah·ray la koh·da*

linen *n* (*cloth*) il lino *lee·noh*; (*for beds, table*) la biancheria *byan·ke·ree·a*

liner *n* (*ship*) il transatlantico *trans·at·lan·tee·koh*

lining *n* la fodera *fo·de·ra*

linoleum *n* il linoleum *lee·no·le·oom*

lint *n* la garza *gar·dza*

lion *n* il leone *le·oh·ne*

lip *n* il labbro *lab·broh*

lipstick *n* il rossetto *ros·sayt·toh*

liqueur *n* il liquore *lee·kwoh·re* E14

liquid *n* il liquido *lee·kwee·doh* □ *adj* liquido(a) *lee·kwee·do(a)*

liquid assets *pl* la liquidità *lee·kwee·dee·ta*

liquidation *n* la liquidazione *lee·kwee·da·tsyoh·ne*; to go into liquidation andare* in liquidazione *an·dah·ray een lee·kwee·da·tsyoh·ne*

liquor *n* gli alcolici *al·ko·lee·chee*

list *n* l'elenco (*m*) *e·len·koh* □ *vt* elencare *e·len·kah·ray*

listen *vi* ascoltare *a·skol·tah·ray*; to listen to ascoltare *a·skol·tah·ray*

list price *n* il prezzo di catalogo *prets·tsoh dee ka·tah·lo·goh*

liter *n* il litro *lee·troh* T155

literature *n* la letteratura *let·te·ra·too·ra*

little *adj* piccolo(a) *peek·ko·lo(a)* □ *n* a little un po' *oon po*

live¹ *adj* (*alive*) vivo(a) *vee·vo(a)*

live² *vi* vivere* *vee·ve·re*; *(reside)* abitare *a·bee·tah·ray*

lively *adj* vivace *vee·vah·che*

liver *n* il fegato *fay·ga·toh*

living room *n* il salotto *sa·lot·toh*

load *n* il carico *kah·ree·koh* □ *vt* caricare *ka·ree·kah·ray*

loaf (of bread) *n* il pane *pah·ne*

loan *n* il prestito *pre·stee·toh* □ *vt* prestare *pre·stah·ray*

lobby *n* *(entrance)* il vestibolo *ve·stee·bo·loh*

lobster *n* l'aragosta *(f)* *a·ra·goh·sta*

local *adj* locale *lo·kah·le*; the local shops i negozi del quartiere *ee ne·go·tsee del kwar·tye·re*; a local call *(on phone)* una chiamata urbana *oo·na kya·mah·ta oor·bah·na* E10

lock *n* *(on door)* la serratura *ser·ra·too·ra*; *(in canal)* la chiusa *kyoo·sa* □ *vt* chiudere* *a chiave *kyoo·de·re a kyah·ve*; the door's locked la porta è chiusa a chiave *la por·ta e kyoo·sa a kyah·ve* A47

locker *n* l'armadietto *(m)* *ar·mah·dyayt·toh*

lodger *n* l'inquilino(a) *(m/f)* *een·kwee·lee·no(a)*

lodgings *pl* l'alloggio *(m)* *al·loj·joh*

loft *n* la soffitta *sof·feet·ta*

log *n* *(of wood)* il ceppo *chayp·poh*

logbook *n* *(of car)* il libretto di circolazione *lee·brayt·toh dee cheer·ko·la·tsyoh·ne*

lollipop *n* il lecca-lecca *layk·ka·layk·ka*

London *n* Londra *(f)* *lohn·dra*

lonely *adj* *(person)* solitario(a) *so·lee·tah·ryo(a)*

long *adj* lungo(a) *loon·go(a)*; how long is the river? quant'è lungo il fiume? *kwan·te loon·go eel fyoo·me*; 6 meters long lungo(a) 6 metri *loon·go(a) 6 me·tree*; how long is the program? quanto dura il programma? *kwan·to doo·ra eel pro·gram·ma*; 6 months long che dura 6 mesi *ke doo·ra 6 may·see* □ *adv* lungo a lungo *a loon·go*; all day long tutta la giornata *toot·ta la johr·nah·ta*; I shan't be long non prenderò molto tempo *nohn pren·de·ro mohl·to tem·poh*; as long as *(provided that)* purché *poor·kay*

long-distance *adj* *(phone call)* interurbano(a) *een·tayr·oor·bah·no(a)*

long drink *n* il long drink *long dreenk*

long-term *adj* a lunga scadenza *a loon·ga ska·den·tsa*

long wave *n* le onde lunghe *ohn·de loon·ge*

look *n* lo sguardo *zgwar·doh*; *(appearance)* l'aspetto *(m)* *a·spet·toh* □ *vi* guardare *gwar·dah·ray*; *(appear)* sembrare *sem·brah·ray*; to look at guardare *gwar·dah·ray*; to look like rassomigliare *ras·so·meel·yah·ray*; to look after curare *koo·rah·ray*; to look for cercare *cher·kah·ray*; to look forward to non vedere* l'ora di *nohn ve·day·re loh·ra dee*; look out! attenzione! *at·ten·tsyoh·ne*; to look up *(word)* cercare *cher·kah·ray*

loop *n* il cappio *kap·pyoh*

loose *adj* *(knot)* sciolto(a) *shol·to(a)*; *(clothing)* ampio(a) *am·pyo(a)*; *(stone)* fuori posto *fwo·ree poh·stoh*

lose *vt* perdere* *per·de·re*; to lose one's way smarrirsi *zmar·reer·see* □ *vi* lose *(clock, watch)* ritardare *ree·tar·dah·ray* Sn82

loss *n* la perdita *per·dee·ta* Sn79

lot *n* *(at auction)* il lotto *lot·toh*; lots of or a lot of milk molto latte *mohl·to lat·te*; lots of or a lot of people molta gente *mohl·ta jen·te*; a lot better molto meglio *mohl·to mel·yo*

lotion *n* la lozione *lo·tsyoh·ne*

lottery *n* la lotteria *lot·te·ree·a*

loud *adj* *(voice)* forte *for·te*

loudly *adv* fortemente *for·te·mayn·te*

loudspeaker *n* l'altoparlante *(m)* *al·to·par·lan·te*

lounge *n* *(in house)* il salotto *sa·lot·toh*; *(in hotel)* il salone *sa·loh·ne*; *(at airport)* la sala d'aspetto *sah·la da·spet·toh*

love *vt* amare *a·mah·ray*; to love doing something piacere* molto a qualcuno fare qualcosa *pya·chay·re mohl·to a kwal·koo·no fah·ray kwal·ko·sa*; I'd love to go mi piacerebbe andare *mee pyah·che·reb·be an·dah·ray* □ *n* love l'amore *(m)* *a·moh·re*; to fall in love innamorato(a) *een·na·mo·rah·to(a)*; love from *(on letter)* affettuosamente *af·fet·too·oh·sa·mayn·te*

lovely *adj* bello(a) *bel·lo(a)*; we had a lovely time ci siamo divertiti un mondo *chee syah·mo dee·ver·tee·tee oon mohn·doh*

low *adj* basso(a) *bas·so(a)*

Low Countries *pl* i Paesi Bassi *pa·ay·zee bas·see*

lower *adj* inferiore *een·fe·ryoh·re*

low tide *n* la bassa marea *bas·sa ma·re·a*

LP *n* il longplaying *long·ple·eeng*

Ltd *abbrev* S.r.l. *es·se·er·re·el·le*

luck *n* la fortuna *for·too·na*; good luck! buona fortuna! *bwo·na for·too·na*; bad luck la sfortuna *sfor·too·na*

lucky *adj* fortunato(a) *for·too·nah·to(a)*

luggage *n* i bagagli *ba·gal·yee* T21f, A24

luggage cart *n* il carrello per bagagli *kar·rel·loh payr ba·gal·yee* T25

luggage rack *n* il portabagagli *por·ta·ba·gal·yee*

lump *n* *(on skin)* il gonfiore *gon·fyoh·re*; *(in sauce)* il grumo *groo·moh*; lump of sugar la zolletta di zucchero *tsol·layt·ta dee tsook·ke·roh*

lunch *n* il pranzo *pran·dzoh* A26, E6

lunch hour *n* l'ora di pranzo *(f)* *oh·ra dee pran·dzoh*

lung *n* il polmone *pol·moh·ne*

Luxembourg *n* Lussemburgo *(m)* *loos·sem·boor·goh*

luxurious *adj* sontuoso(a) *son·too·oh·so(a)*

luxury *n* il lusso *loos·soh* □ *adj* *(car, hotel)* di lusso *dee loos·soh*

M

macaroni *n* i maccheroni *mak·ke·roh·nee*

machine *n* la macchina *mak·kee·na*

machinery *n* il macchinario *mak·kee·nah·ryoh*

mackerel *n* lo scombro *skohm·broh*

mack(intosh) *n* l'impermeabile *(m)* *eem·payr·may·ah·bee·lay*

mad *adj* *(insane)* pazzo(a) *pats·tsoh(a)*; *(angry)* furioso(a) *foo·ree·oh·soh(a)*

madam *n* signora *(f)* *seen·yoh·ra*

Madeira *n* *(wine)* il madera *ma·de·ra*

made-to-measure *adj* fatto(a) su misura *fat·toh(a) soo mee·zoo·ra*

Madrid *n* Madrid *(f)* *ma·dreed*

magazine *n* *(journal)* la rivista *ree·vee·sta*

magic *n* la magia *ma·jee·a* □ *adj* magico(a) *ma·jee·koh(a)*

magnet *n* la calamita *ka·la·mee·ta*

magnetic tape *n* il nastro magnetico *nas·troh man·ye·tee·koh*

magnificent *adj* magnifico(a) *man·yee·fee·koh(a)*

mahogany *n* il mogano *mo·ga·noh*

maid *n* la domestica *do·me·stee·ka* A67

maiden name *n* il cognome da nubile *kon·yoh·may da noo·bee·lay*

maid service *n* il servizio della domestica *sayr·vee·tsyoh del·la do·mes·tee·ka*

mail *n* la posta *pos·ta* □ *vt* mandare per posta *man·dah·ray payr pos·ta*

mailbox *n* la cassetta della posta *kas·say·ta del·la pos·ta*

mailing list *n* l'elenco di indirizzi (*m*) *e·len·koh dee een·dee·ree·tsee*

mailman *n* il postino *pos·tee·noh*

mail order *n* □ **to buy something by mail order** comprare qualcosa per corrispondenza *kom·prah·ray kwal·ko·sa payr kor·ree·spon·den·tsa*

main *adj* principale *preen·chee·pah·lay* □ *n* **to turn the electricity/water off at the main** chiudere* l'elettricità/l'acqua al contatore *kyoo·de·re le·let·tree·chee·tal/ak·kwa al kon·ta·toh·re*

mainland *n* il continente *kon·tee·nen·tay*

mainly *adv* principalmente *preen·chee·pal·mayn·tay*

maintenance *n* la manutenzione *ma·noo·ten·tsyoh·nay*

major *adj* principale *preen·chee·pah·lay*

majority *n* la maggioranza *maj·jo·ran·tsa*; **elected by a majority of 5** eletto(a) con una maggioranza di 5 voti *e·let·toh(a) kon oo·na maj·jo·ran·tsa dee 5 voh·tee*

make *n* (*of product*) la marca *mahr·ka* □ *vt* fare* *fah·ray*; **to make the beds** rifare* i letti *ree·fah·ray ee let·tee*; **to make someone sad** rattristare qualcuno *rat·tree·stah·ray kwal·koo·noh*; **to make someone do something** far fare* qualcosa a qualcuno *fahr fah·ray kwal·ko·sa a kwal·koo·noh*; **to make do with something** arrangiarsi con qualcosa *ar·ran·jahr·see kon kwal·koh·sa*; **to make (oneself) up** truccarsi *trook·kahr·see*

make-up *n* il trucco *trook·koh*

male *adj* maschio *mask·yo*

mallet *n* il maglio *mal·yo*

malt *n* il malto *mal·toh*

Malta *n* Malta (*f*) *mal·ta*

man *n* l'uomo (*m*) *wo·moh*

manage *vt* (*business*) dirigere* *dee·ree·je·ray*; **can you manage?** ce la fa? *chay la fa*; **to manage to do something** riuscire* a fare qualcosa *ree·oo·shee·ray a fah·ray kwal·ko·sa*

management *n* la direzione *dee·rets·yo·nay*

manager *n* il direttore *dee·ret·toh·ray* M31

manageress *n* la direttrice *dee·ret·tree·chay*

managing director, M.D. *n* il direttore generale *dee·ret·toh·ray je·ne·rah·lay*

manicure *n* la manicure *ma·nee·koo·ray*

manicure set *n* il nécessaire per unghie *nay·ses·sayr payr oon·gye*

man-made *adj* artificiale *ahr·tee·fee·chah·lay*

manner *n* (*way*) il modo *mo·doh*; (*attitude*) l'atteggiamento (*m*) *at·tej·ja·mayn·toh*

manners *pl* le maniere *man·ye·ray*

manpower *n* la manodopera *mah·noh·do·pe·ra*

mansion *n* il palazzo *pa·lats·tsoh*

mantelpiece *n* il caminetto *ka·mee·nayt·toh*

manual *adj* manuale *ma·nwah·lay* □ *n* (*book*) il manuale *ma·nwah·lay*

manufacture *vt* fabbricare *fab·bree·kah·ray*

manufacturer *n* il fabbricante *fab·bree·kan·tay*

manufacturing *n* la fabbricazione *fab·bree·ka·tsyo·nay*

many *pron* molti *mohl·tee* □ *adj* **many books** molti libri *mohl·tee lee·bree*

map *n* (*of country*) la carta geografica *kahr·ta jay·oh·gra·fee·ka*; (*of town*) la pianta *pyan·ta* F7, L3, S94

marble *n* (*material*) il marmo *mahr·moh*; (*ball*) la bilia *beel·ya*

March *n* marzo (*m*) *mahr·tsoh*

march *vi* marciare *mahr·chah·ray* □ *n* la marcia *mahr·cha*

margarine *n* la margarina *mahr·ga·ree·na*

margin *n* (*on page*) il margine *mahr·jee·nay*

marina *n* il porticciolo *por·teech·cho·loh*

marjoram *n* la maggiorana *maj·jo·rah·na*

mark *n* il segno *sen·yo*; (*stain*) la macchia *mak·kya*; (*currency*) il marco *mahr·koh*; (*in school*) il voto *voh·toh* □ *vt* segnare *sen·yah·ray*; (*stain*) macchiare *mak·kyah·ray*

market *n* il mercato *mayr·kah·toh* □ *vt* (*product*) vendere *vayn·de·ray* Bm16

market-day *n* il giorno di mercato *johr·noh dee mayr·kah·toh*

marketing *n* il marketing *mahr·ke·ting*

marketing manager *n* il direttore di marketing *dee·ret·toh·ray dee mahr·ke·ting*

market-place *n* la piazza del mercato *pyats·tsa del mayr·kah·toh*

market research *n* la ricerca di mercato *ree·chayr·ka dee mayr·kah·toh*

market value *n* il valore di mercato *va·loh·ray dee mayr·kah·toh*

marmalade *n* la marmellata d'arance *mahr·mel·lah·tah dar·an·chay*

maroon *adj* bordeaux *bor·doh*

marriage *n* il matrimonio *ma·tree·mon·yoh*

married *adj* sposato(a) *spo·zah·toh(a)*; **they were married yesterday** si sono sposati ieri *see so·noh spo·zah·tee ye·ree* Mc42

marrow *n* (*vegetable*) la zucca *tsook·ka*

marry *vt* sposare *spo·zah·ray* □ *vi* sposarsi *spo·zahr·see*

martini *n* (*Brit*) il Martini *mahr·tee·nee*; (*US*) il gin con Martini *jeen kon mahr·tee·nee*

marvelous *adj* meraviglioso(a) *me·ra·veel·yoh·soh(a)*

marzipan *n* il marzapane *mahr·tsa·pah·nay*

mascara *n* il mascara *mas·ka·ra*

masculine *adj* maschile *mas·kee·lay*

mash *vt* schiacciare *skya·chah·ray*

mashed potatoes *pl* il purè di patate *poo·re dee pa·tah·tay*

mask *n* la maschera *mas·ke·ra* □ *vt* mascherare *mas·ke·rah·ray*

mass *n* (*church*) la messa *mes·sa*; a

mass of blossom una massa di fiori *oo·na mas·sa dee fyo·ri*

massage n il massaggio *mas·saj·joh* □ vt massaggiare *mas·saj·jah·ray*

masseur n il massaggiatore *mas·saj·ja· toh·re*

masseuse n la massaggiatrice *mas·saj· ja·tree·chay*

massive adj massiccio(a) *mas·see· choh(a)*

mass-produce vt fabbricare in serie *fab·bree·kah·ray een ser·ye*

mass production n la produzione in serie *pro·doo·tsyoh·nay een ser·ye*

mast n (ship's) l'albero (m) al·be·roh; (radio) l'antenna trasmittente (f) an· tayn·na tras·meet·ten·tay

master n il maestro *ma·ay·stroh*

master key n il passe-partout *pas·par· too*

masterpiece n il capolavoro *kah·po·la· voh·roh*

mat n la stuoia *stoo·oy·a*; (place mat) il sottopiatto *sot·toh·pyat·toh*; (under a glass) il sottobicchiere *sot·toh·beek· kyie·ray*

match n il fiammifero *fyam·mee·fe· roh*; (sport) la partita *pahr·tee·ta* □ vt intonarsi a *een·to·nahr·see a* S99

matchbox n la scatola di fiammiferi *skah·to·la dee fyam·mee·fe·ree*

material n il materiale *ma·te·ryah·lay*; (fabric) la stoffa *stof·fa* S60

maternity dress n il pré-maman *pray· ma·man*

maternity hospital n la maternità *ma· tayr·nee·ta*

mathematics n la matematica *ma·te· ma·tee·ka*

matter n □ what's the matter? che c'è? *ke che* □ vi it doesn't matter non fa niente *nohn fa nyen·tay*

mattress n il materasso *ma·te·ras·soh*

mature adj (wine) maturo(a) *ma·too· roh(a)*; (cheese) stagionato(a) *sta·jo· nah·toh(a)*

mauve adj malva *mal·va*

maximize vt portare al limite massimo *por·tah·ray al lee·mee·tay mas·see· moh*

maximum n il massimo *mas·see·moh* □ adj massimo(a) *mas·see·moh(a)*

May n maggio (m) *maj·joh*

may vi □ may I come in? posso entrare? *pos·soh en·trah·ray*; it may rain potrà piovere *po·tra pyo·ve·ray*; we may as well go ci varrebbe andare *chee var·reb·bay an·dah·ray*

Mayday n il segnale di soccorso *sen· yah·lay dee sok·kohr·soh*

mayonnaise n la maionese *ma·yo·nay· say*

mayor n il sindaco *seen·da·koh*

me pron mi *mee*; give it to me me lo dia *may loh dee·a*; he gave it to me me lo diede *may loh dye·day*; it's me sono io *so·noh ee·oh*

meal n il pasto *pas·toh* T42, E47

mean adj (miserly) tirchio(a) *teer· kyoh(a)*; (unkind) meschino(a) *mes· kee·noh(a)* □ vt (signify) significare *seen·yee·fee·kah·ray*; to mean to do avere* l'intenzione di fare *a·vayr·ay leen·ten·tsyo·nay dee fah·ray*

meaning n il significato *seen·yee·fee· kah·toh*

means pl i mezzi *medz·dzee*; by means of per mezzo di *payr medz·dzoh dee*

meanwhile adv intanto *een·tan·toh*

measles n il morbillo *mor·beel·loh*

measure vt/i misurare *mee·zoo·rah·ray*

measurements pl le misure *mee·zoo· ray*

meat n la carne *kahr·nay*

mechanic n il meccanico *mek·kan·ee· koh* T167

media pl i mass media *mass mee·dee·a*

median strip n lo spartitraffico *spar· tee·traf·fee·koh*

medical adj medico(a) *me·dee·koh(a)*

medicine n (pills etc) la medicina *me· dee·chee·na*

Mediterranean adj mediterraneo(a) *me·dee·ter·rah·nay·oh(a)*; the Mediterranean (Sea) il Mediterraneo *me·dee·ter·rah·nay·oh*

medium adj medio(a) *me·dee·o(a)*; medium wave le onde medie *ohn·day me·dee·ay*

meet vt (encounter) incontrare *een· kon·trah·ray*; (make acquaintance of) fare* la conoscenza di *fah·ray la kon·o·shen·tsa dee*; (demand) rispondere* a *ree·spon·de·ray a*; I'll meet you at the station (go to get) verrò a prenderla alla stazione *ver· roh a pren·dayr·la al·la sta·tsyoh·nay*

meeting n la riunione *ree·oon·yoh·nay*

melon n il melone *me·loh·nay*

melt vt sciogliersi* *shol·yer·see* □ vt fondere* *john·de·ray*

member n il socio *so·choh* T5, L57

memo(randum) n la nota *no·ta*

memory n la memoria *me·mo·ree·a*; one of my memories un mio ricordo *oon mee·oh ree·kor·doh*

mend vt riparare *ree·pa·rah·ray*

menswear n l'abbigliamento per uomo (m) *ab·beel·ya·mayn·toh payr wo· moh*

mental hospital n l'ospedale psichiatrico (m) *o·spe·dah·lay psee·kee·a· tree·koh*

mentholated adj al mentolo *al men·to· loh*

mention vt menzionare *men·tsyo·nah· ray*; don't mention it non c'è di che! *nohn che dee kay*

menu n il menù *me·noo* E8

merchant n il mercante *mayr·kan·tay*; (shop keeper) il negoziante *ne·go· tsyan·tay*

merge vi fondersi* *fohn·der·see*

merger n la fusione *foo·zyoh·nay*

meringue n la meringa *me·reen·ga*

merry adj gaio(a) *ga·yoh(a)*

merry-go-round n la giostra *jo·stra*

mess n il disordine *dee·zohr·dee·nay*; to make a mess mettere* in disordine *met·te·ray een dee·zohr·dee·nay*; to make a mess of (spoil) rovinare *ro· vee·nah·ray*

message n il messaggio *mes·saj·joh*

messenger n il messaggero *mes·saj·je· roh*

metal n il metallo *me·tal·loh*

meter n il contatore *kon·ta·toh·ray*; (measure) il metro *met·roh*

method n il metodo *me·to·doh*

Methodist n il metodista *me·to·dee·sta*

methylated spirits pl l'alcool denaturato (m) *al·kol day·na·too·rah·toh*

metric adj metrico(a) *met·ree·koh(a)*

Mexican adj messicano(a) *me·see·ka· noh(a)*

Mexico n il Messico (m) *mes·see·koh*

microchip n il microchip *mee·kro·chip*

microcomputer n il microcomputer *mee·kro·kom·poo·tayr*

microfiche n la microscheda *mee·kro· ske·da*

microfilm n il microfilm *mee·kro·feelm*

microphone n il microfono *mee·kro·fo·noh*

microprocessor n il microprocessor *mee·kro·pro·ches·sohr*

microwave oven n il forno a microonde *fohr·noh a mee·kro·ohn·day*

midday n il mezzogiorno *medz·dzo·johr·noh*; **at midday** a mezzogiorno *a medz·dzo·johr·noh*

middle n il mezzo *medz·dzoh*; **right in the middle** nel bel mezzo *nel bel medz·dzoh*; **in the middle of the night** nel cuore della notte *nel kwo·ray del·la not·tay*

middle-aged adj di mezza età *dee medz·dza ay·ta*

middle-class adj borghese *bor·gay·say*

Middle East n il Medio Oriente *med·yoh o·ree·en·tay*

middle management pl i quadri medi *kwa·dree me·dee*

midnight n la mezzanotte *medz·dza·not·tay*; **at midnight** a mezzanotte *a medz·dza·not·tay*

midwife n la levatrice *le·va·tree·chay*

might vi □ **it might rain** potrebbe piovere *po·treb·bay pyo·ve·ray*; **we might as well go** tanto vale che andiamo *tan·toh vah·lay kay an·dya·moh*

migraine n l'emicrania (f) *e·mee·krah·nee·a*

mild adj (weather) mite *mee·tay*; (cigarette) leggero(a) *lej·je·roh(a)*; (taste) dolce *dohl·chay*

mile n il miglio *meel·yoh*

miles per hour, m.p.h. miglia all'ora *meel·ya al·loh·ra*

mileage n ≈ il chilometraggio *kee·lo·me·traj·joh* T113

military adj militare *mee·lee·tah·ray*

milk n il latte *lat·tay* E61, S34

milk chocolate n il cioccolato al latte *chok·ko·lah·toh al lat·tay*

milkman n il lattaio *lat·ta·yoh*

milkshake n il frullato di latte *frool·lah·toh dee lat·tay*

mill n il mulino *moo·lee·noh*; (for coffee) il macinino *ma·chee·nee·noh* □ vt macinare *ma·chee·nah·ray*

milligram n il milligrammo *meel·lee·gram·moh*

milliliter n il millilitro *meel·lee·lee·troh*

millimeter n il millimetro *meel·lee·me·troh*

million num il milione *mee·lee·oh·nay*

millionaire n il milionario *mee·lee·o·nah·ree·oh*

millionth adj milionesimo(a) *mee·lee·o·ne·zee·moh(a)*

mince vt tritare *tree·tah·ray*

mincer n il tritacarne *tree·ta·kahr·nay*

mind n la mente *mayn·tay*; **to change one's mind** cambiare idea *kam·byah·ray ee·de·a*; **to make up one's mind** decidersi *de·chee·der·see* □ vt **I don't mind the heat** non mi dispiace il caldo *nohn mee dee·spyah·chay eel kal·doh*; **I don't mind** non mi importa *nohn mee eem·por·ta*; **never mind** non importa *nohn eem·por·ta*; **do you mind if…?** le spiace se…? *le spyah·chay se*; **mind the step** attenzione allo scalino *at·ten·tsyoh·nay al·loh ska·lee·noh*

mine pron il mio *eel mee·oh*, la mia *la mee·a*; (plural) i miei *ee mee·ay·ee*; le mie *le mee·ay* □ n (for coal etc) la miniera *mee·nye·rah*

miner n il minatore *mee·na·toh·ray*

mineral water n l'acqua minerale (f) *a·kwa mee·ne·rah·lay*

minestrone (soup) n il minestrone *mee·ne·stroh·nay*

minibus n il pullmino *pool·mee·noh*

minicomputer n il minicomputer *mee·nee·kom·poo·ter*

minimum n il minimo *mee·nee·moh* □ adj minimo(a) *mee·nee·moh(a)*

miniskirt n la minigonna *mee·nee·gohn·na*

minister n (in government) il ministro *mee·nee·stroh*; (of religion) il pastore *pa·stoh·ray* S88

ministry n (government) il ministero *mee·nee·ste·roh*

mink n (fur) il visone *vee·zoh·nay*

mink coat n il mantello di visone *man·tel·loh dee vee·zoh·nay*

minor adj (road) secondario(a) *se·kon·dah·ree·oh(a)*; (injury) leggero(a) *lej·je·roh(a)*; **minor operation** l'intervento minore (m) *een·tayr·ven·toh mee·noh·ray*

minority n la minoranza *mee·no·ran·tsa*

mint n (herb) la menta *mayn·ta*; (confectionery) la caramella alla menta *ka·ra·mel·la al·la mayn·ta*

minus prep meno *may·noh*; **at minus 2 degrees** a 2 gradi sotto zero *a 2 grah·dee soht·toh dze·roh*

minute n il minuto *mee·noo·toh*; **just a minute** un momento *oon mo·mayn·toh*

mirror n lo specchio *spek·kyoh* S70

miscarriage n l'aborto (m) *a·bor·toh*

miserable adj infelice *een·fe·lee·chay*

misprint n l'errore di stampa (f) *er·roh·ray dee stam·pa*

Miss n Signorina (f) *seen·yo·ree·na*

miss vt (target) mancare *man·kah·ray*; (train) perdere* *payr·de·ray*; **I miss London** sento la mancanza di Londra *sen·toh la man·kan·tsa dee lohn·dra*; **to miss out** omettere* *oh·mayt·te·ray*

missing adj (object) smarrito(a) *zmar·ree·toh(a)*; (person) disperso(a) *dee·spayr·soh(a)*; **some pages are missing** mancano alcune pagine *man·ka·noh al·koo·nay pah·jee·nay*; **my wallet is missing** è sparito il mio portafoglio *e spa·ree·toh eel mee·oh por·ta·fol·yoh*

mist n la foschia *fo·skee·a*

mistake n lo sbaglio *zbal·yoh*; **by mistake** per sbaglio *payr zbal·yoh*; **to make a mistake** sbagliarsi *zbal·yahr·see* B40, E45

mistress n (lover) l'amante (f) *a·man·tay*

mitt(en) n la manopola *ma·no·po·la*

mix vt mescolare *me·sko·lah·ray*; **to mix up** (confuse) confondere* *kon·fohn·de·ray* □ vi **mix** mescolarsi *me·sko·lahr·see*

mixed adj (co-ed) misto(a) *mee·stoh(a)*; **mixed grill** il misto di carne ai ferri *eel mee·stoh dee kahr·nay a·ee fer·ree*

mixer n il frullatore *frool·la·toh·ray*

mixture n la mescolanza *me·sko·lan·tsa*

moan n il gemito *je·mee·toh* □ vi gemere *je·me·ray*

model n il modello *mo·del·loh*; (mannequin) l'indossatrice (f) *een·dos·sa·tree·chay*; **this year's model** il modello di quest'anno *eel mo·del·loh dee kway·stan·noh*; **a model railroad** una ferrovia in miniatura *oo·na fer·ro·vee·a een meen·nya·too·ra*

modern *adj* moderno(a) *mo·der·noh(a)* S84

modernize *vt* modernizzare *mo·der·needz·dzah·ray*

modest *adj* modesto(a) *mo·de·stoh(a)*

modification *n* la modifica *mo·dee·fee·ka*

modify *vt* modificare *mo·dee·fee·kah·ray*

mohair *n* il mohair *mo·er*

molasses *n* la melassa *me·las·sa*

molecule *n* la molecola *mo·le·ko·la*

moment *n* il momento *mo·mayn·toh*; **at the moment** in questo momento *een kway·stoh mo·mayn·toh*

mom(my) *n* la mamma *mam·ma*

Monaco *n* Monaco (*f*) *mo·na·koh*

monastery *n* il monastero *mo·na·ste·roh*

Monday *n* lunedì (*m*) *loo·ne·dee*

monetary *adj* monetario(a) *mo·ne·tah·ree·oh(a)*

money *n* il denaro *de·nah·roh*; **to make money** fare* soldi *fah·ray sol·dee* M17, 18

money order *n* il vaglia *val·ya*

monitor *n* (*TV*) il monitore *mo·nee·toh·ray*

monk *n* il monaco *mo·na·koh*

monkey *n* la scimmia *sheem·mya*

mono *adj* mono *mo·noh*; **in mono** in mono *een mo·noh*

monopoly *n* il monopolio *mo·no·po·lyo*

monorail *n* la monorotaia *mo·no·ro·ta·ya*

monster *n* il mostro *moh·stroh*

month *n* il mese *may·say*

monthly *adj* mensile *men·see·lay* □ *n* il mensile *men·see·lay*

monument *n* il monumento *mo·noo·mayn·toh*

mood *n* l'umore (*m*) *oo·moh·ray*; **in a good mood** di buon umore *dee bwon oo·moh·ray*

moon *n* la luna *loo·na*

moor *vt* ormeggiare *or·mej·jah·ray*

mop *n* la scopa di cotone *sko·pa dee ko·toh·ne* □ *vt* asciugare *a·shoo·gah·ray*

moped *n* il ciclomotore *chee·klo·mo·toh·ray*

more *adj* ancora di *an·koh·ra dee*; **more cheese** ancora del formaggio *an·koh·ra del for·maj·joh*; **more people** più gente *pyoo jen·tay* □ *pron* **I'd like (some) more** gradirei ancora un po' *gra·dee·ray an·koh·ra oon po* □ *adv* **more dangerous** than più pericoloso che/di *pyoo pe·ree·ko·loh·soh kay/dee*; **more or less** più o meno *pyoo o may·noh*

morning *n* la mattina *mat·tee·na*

Moroccan *adj* marocchino(a) *ma·rok·kee·noh(a)*

Morocco *n* il Marocco *ma·rok·koh*

mortgage *n* l'ipoteca (*f*) *ee·po·te·ka* □ *vt* ipotecare *ee·po·te·kah·ray*

Moscow *n* Mosca (*f*) *moh·ska*

moselle *n* (*wine*) il mosella *mo·zel·la*

mosque *n* la moschea *mo·skay·a*

mosquito *n* la zanzara *dzan·dzah·ra*

mosquito net *n* la zanzariera *dzan·dza·ree·e·ra*

most *adv* □ **the most beautiful** il/la più bello(a) *eel/la pyoo bel·loh(a)* □ *adj* **most people** i più *ee pyoo*; **the most cars** il più grande numero di macchine *eel pyoo gran·day noo·me·roh dee mak·kee·nay* □ *pron* **he has the most** ne ha la maggior parte *nay a la maj·johr pahr·tay*; **at the most** al massimo *al mas·see·moh*; **to make the most of** sfruttare al massimo *sfroot·tah·ray al mas·see·moh*

motel *n* il motel *mo·tel*

moth *n* la falena *fa·le·na*

mother *n* la madre *mah·dray*

mother-in-law *n* la suocera *swo·che·ra*

motion *n* (*movement*) il movimento *mo·vee·mayn·toh*

motor *n* il motore *mo·toh·ray*

motorbike *n* la motocicletta *mo·to·chee·klayt·ta*

motorboat *n* il motoscafo *mo·to·skah·foh* L29

motorcyclist *n* il/la motociclista *mo·to·chee·klee·sta*

motorist *n* l'automobilista (*m/f*) *ow·to·mo·bee·lee·sta*

mount *vt* montare *mon·tah·ray*

mountain *n* la montagna *mon·tan·ya*

mountaineering *n* l'alpinismo (*m*) *al·pee·nee·zmoh*; **to go mountaineering** fare* dell'alpinismo *fah·ray del·lal·pee·nee·zmoh*

mouse *n* il topo *to·poh*

mousse *n* la mousse *moos*

mouth *n* la bocca *bohk·ka*

move *vt* muovere* *mwo·ve·ray* □ *vi* muoversi* *mwo·ver·see*; (*traffic*) circolare *cheer·ko·lah·ray*; (*change residence*) traslocarsi *traz·lo·kahr·see*; **to move in** trasferirsi *tra·sfe·reer·see*; **to move out** cambiare casa *kam·byah·ray kah·sa*

movement *n* il movimento *mo·vee·mayn·toh*

movie *n* il film *feelm*

movie camera *n* la cinepresa *chee·ne·pray·sa*

moving van *n* il camion di traslochi *ka·myon de tra·zlo·kee*

moving walkway *n* il marciapiede a rulli *mar·cha·pye·day a rool·lee*

mow *vt* falciare *fal·chah·ray*

mower *n* la falciatrice *fal·cha·tree·chay*

Mr *n* Signor (*m*) *seen·yohr*

Mrs *n* Signora (*f*) *seen·yoh·ra*

Ms *n* Signorina (*f*) *seen·yo·ree·na*

much *adv* □ **much better** molto meglio *mohl·toh mel·yoh*; **much bigger** molto più grande *mohl·toh pyoo gran·day* □ *adj* **much milk** molto latte *mohl·toh lat·tay* □ *pron* **have you got much?** ne ha molto? *ne a mohl·toh*; **not much** non molto *nohn mohl·toh*

mud *n* il fango *fan·goh*

muddle *n* il pasticcio *pa·steech·choh*; **in a muddle** in disordine *een dee·zohr·dee·nay*

muddy *adj* (*water*) fangoso(a) *fan·goh·soh(a)*; (*clothes*) infangato(a) *een·fan·gah·toh(a)*

mud-flap *n* il paraspruzzi *pa·ra·sproots·tsee*

mudguard *n* il parafango *pa·ra·fan·goh*

muffler *n* (*on car*) la marmitta *mar·meet·ta*

mug *n* la tazza *tats·tsa* □ *vt* assalire* *as·sa·lee·ray*

multilevel *adj* a più piani *a pyoo pyah·nee*

multilingual *adj* multilingue *mool·tee·leen·gway*

multinational *adj* multinazionale *mool·tee·nats·yo·nah·lay*

multiple store *n* il negozio a catena *ne·go·tsyoh a ka·tay·na*

multiplication *n* la moltiplicazione *mol·tee·plee·kats·yoh·nay*

multiply *vt* moltiplicare *mol·tee·plee·kah·ray*; **to multiply 9 by 4** moltiplicare 9 per 4 *mol·tee·plee·kah·ray 9 payr 4*

mumps *n* gli orecchioni *o·rek·kyoh·nee*

Munich *n* Monaco di Baviera (*f*) *mo·na·koh dee Ba·vye·ra*

municipal *adj* municipale *moo·nee·chee·pah·lay*

murder *n* l'omicidio (*m*) *o·mee·chee·dee·oh* □ *vt* assassinare *as·sas·see·nah·ray*

muscle *n* il muscolo *moos·ko·loh*

museum *n* il museo *moo·ze·oh* F10, L3

mushroom *n* il fungo *foon·goh*

music *n* la musica *moo·zee·ka*

musician *n* il/la musicista *moo·zee·chee·sta*

Muslim *adj* musulmano(a) *moo·sool·mah·noh(a)* □ *n* il/la musulmano(a) *moo·sool·mah·noh(a)* S9

mussel *n* la cozza *kots·tsa*

must *vi* □ **I must go** devo andare *de·voh an·dah·ray*; **you must come** deve venire *de·vay ve·nee·ray*

mustard *n* la mostarda *mo·stahr·da*

mutton *n* la carne di montone *kahr·nay dee mon·toh·nay*

my *adj* mio(a) *mee·oh(a)*, miei *mee·ay·ee*, mie *mee·ay*; **my brothers** i miei fratelli *ee mee·ay·ee fra·tel·lee*; **my sisters** le mie sorelle *lay mee·ay so·rel·lay*

myself *pron* io stesso(a) *ee·oh stays·soh(a)*; **I washed myself** mi sono lavato(a) *mee so·noh la·vah·toh(a)*; **I did it myself** l'ho fatto io stesso *loh fat·toh ee·oh stays·soh*

mystery *n* il mistero *mee·ster·oh*

N

nail *n* (*human*) l'unghia (*f*) *oon·gya*; (*metal*) il chiodo *kyo·do* □ *vt* inchiodare *een·kyo·dah·ray*

nailbrush *n* lo spazzolino da unghie *spats·tso·lee·noh da oon·gyay*

nailfile *n* la limetta *lee·mayt·ta*

nail polish *n* lo smalto *zmal·toh*

naked *adj* nudo(a) *noo·doh(a)*

name *n* il nome *noh·may*; **what is your name?** come Si chiama? *koh·may see kya·ma*; **my name is** Paul mi chiamo Paul *mee kya·moh Paul* B16, T212

nap *n* (*sleep*) il sonnellino *son·nel·lee·noh*

napkin *n* (*for table*) il tovagliolo *to·val·yo·loh*

narrow *adj* stretto(a) *strayt·toh(a)*

nasty *adj* cattivo(a) *kat·tee·voh(a)*

nation *n* la nazione *na·tsyoh·nay*

national *adj* nazionale *na·tsyoh·nah·lay*; **national anthem** l'inno nazionale (*m*) *een·noh na·tsyoh·nah·lay*; **national dress** il costume nazionale *ko·stoo·may na·tsyoh·nah·lay*

nationality *n* la nazionalità *na·tsyoh·na·lee·ta*

nationalize *vt* nazionalizzare *na·tsyoh·na·leedz·dzah·ray*

native *adj* nativo(a) *na·tee·voh(a)*

natural *adj* naturale *na·too·rah·lay* S60

naturalized *adj* naturalizzato(a) *na·too·ra·leedz·dzah·toh(a)*

naturally *adv* (*of course*) naturalmente *na·too·ral·mayn·tay*

nature *n* la natura *na·too·ra*; (*type, sort*) il genere *je·ne·ray*

naughty *adj* cattivo(a) *kat·tee·voh(a)*

nausea *n* la nausea *now·ze·a*

nave *n* la navata *na·vah·ta*

navy *n* la marina *ma·ree·na*

navy blue *adj* blu scuro *bloo skoo·roh*

near *adv* vicino *vee·chee·noh* □ *prep* **near (to) the house** vicino alla casa *vee·chee·noh al·la kah·sa*; **near (to) Christmas** sotto Natale *soht·toh na·tah·lay*

nearby *adv* qui vicino *kwee vee·chee·noh*

nearly *adv* quasi *kwah·zee*

nearsighted *adj* miope *mee·o·pe*

neat *adj* ordinato(a) *or·dee·nah·toh(a)*; (*liquor*) liscio(a) *lee·shoh(a)*

necessary *adj* necessario(a) *ne·ches·sah·ree·oh(a)*

neck *n* il collo *kol·loh*

necklace *n* la collana *kol·lah·na*

necktie *n* la cravatta *kra·vat·ta*

need *vt* avere* bisogno di *a·vay·ray bee·zohn·yoh dee*; **I need to go** devo andare *de·voh an·dah·ray*; **you needn't come** non occorre che lei venga *nohn ok·kohr·ray kay le·ee ven·ga* S9

needle *n* l'ago (*m*) *ah·goh*; (*on dial*) la lancetta *lan·chayt·ta*

negative *n* (*of photo*) la negativa *ne·ga·tee·va*

negotiable *adj* negoziabile *ne·go·tsyah·bee·lay*

negotiate *vi* negoziare *ne·go·tsyah·ray*

negotiations *pl* le trattative *trat·ta·tee·vay*

neighbor *n* il/la vicino(a) *vee·chee·noh(a)*

neighborhood *n* il vicinato *vee·chee·nah·toh*

neither *pron* né l'uno né l'altro *nay loo·noh nay lal·troh* □ *adv* **neither ... nor** né .... né *nay ... nay* □ *conj* **I wasn't there and neither was he** io non c'ero e nemmeno lui *ee·o nohn che·ro e nem·may·noh loo·ee*

nephew *n* il nipote *nee·poh·tay*

nerve *n* il nervo *ner·voh*; (*courage*) il coraggio *ko·raj·joh*

nervous *adj* (*person*) nervoso(a) *ner·voh·soh(a)*; **nervous breakdown** l'esaurimento nervoso (*m*) *e·zow·ree·mayn·toh ner·voh·so*

nest *n* il nido *nee·doh*

net *n* la rete *ray·tay* □ *adj* (*income, price*) netto(a) *nayt·toh(a)*; **net weight** il peso netto *pay·soh nayt·toh*

neutral *adj* neutrale *ne·oo·trah·lay* □ *n* (*gear*) in folle *een fol·lay*

never *adv* mai *ma·ee*; **he never comes** egli non viene mai *el·yee nohn vye·nay ma·ee*

new *adj* nuovo(a) *nwo·voh(a)*

news *n* le notizie *no·tee·tsye*

newsdealer *n* il giornalaio *johr·na·la·yoh*

newspaper *n* il giornale *johr·nah·lay* S91

newsstand *n* l'edicola (*f*) *e·dee·ko·la*

New Year's Day *n* il Capodanno *kah·po·dan·noh*

New Year's Eve *n* la vigilia di Capodanno *vee·jeel·ya dee kah·po·dan·noh*

next *adj* (*stop, station, week*) prossimo(a) *pros·se·moh(a)*; **next of kin** il parente stretto *pa·ren·tay strayt·toh*

nice *adj* bello(a) *bel·loh(a)*; (*person*) simpatico(a) *seem·pa·tee·koh(a)*

niece *n* la nipote *nee·poh·tay*

night *n* la notte *not·tay* A8

night club *n* il night-club *nait·kloob* L44

nightgown *n* la camicia da notte *ka·mee·cha da not·tay*

nightmare *n* l'incubo (*m*) *een·koo·boh*

night porter *n* il portiere di notte *por·tye·ray dee not·tay*

night school *n* la scuola serale *skwo·la se·rah·lay*

nil *n* lo zero *dze·roh*

nine *num* nove *no·vay*

nineteen *num* diciannove *dee·chan·no·vay*

ninety *num* novanta *no·van·ta*

ninth *adj* nono(a) *no·noh(a)*

nipple *n* (*on bottle*) la tettarella *tet·ta·rel·la*

no *adv* (*as answer*) no *no*

nobody *pron* nessuno *nes·soo·noh*; I can see nobody non vedo nessuno *nohn vay·do nes·soo·noh*

noise *n* il rumore *roo·moh·ray*; (*loud*) il fragore *fra·goh·ray*

noisy *adj* rumoroso(a) *roo·mo·roh·soh(a)*

nominal *adj* (*fee*) simbolico(a) *seem·bo·lee·koh(a)*

non- *pref* non- *nohn-*

nonalcoholic *adj* analcolico(a) *a·nal·ko·lee·koh(a)*

none *pron* nessuno(a) *nes·soo·noh(a)*

nonsense *n* le sciocchezze *shok·kayts·tse*

nonsmoker *n* (*person*) il non-fumatore *nohn·foo·ma·toh·ray*; (*compartment*) lo scompartimento per non-fumatori *skom·par·tee·mayn·toh payr nohn·foo·ma·toh·ree*

noodles *pl* i taglierini *tal·ye·ree·nee*

noon *n* il mezzogiorno *medz·dzo·johr·noh*

no one *pron* nessuno *nes·soo·noh*; I can see no one non vedo nessuno *nohn vay·do nes·soo·noh*

normal *adj* normale *nor·mah·lay*

normally *adv* (*usually*) normalmente *nor·mal·mayn·tay*

north *n* il nord *nord* □ *adv* a nord *a nord* □ *n* northeast il nord-est *nord·est*; northwest il nord-ovest *nord·o·vest*

North America *n* l'America del Nord (*f*) *a·me·ree·ka del nord*

northern *adj* settentrionale *set·ten·tree·o·nah·lay*

North Pole *n* il Polo Nord *po·loh nord*

North Sea *n* il Mare del Nord *mah·ray del nord*

nose *n* il naso *nah·soh*

nosebleed *n* l'emorragia nasale (*f*) *e·mor·ra·jee·a na·sah·lay*

not *adv* non *nohn*; he did not *or* didn't do it egli non l'ha fatto *el·yee nohn la fat·to*; not at all non affatto *nohn af·fat·to*; (*don't mention it*) non c'è di che *nohn che dee kay*

note *n* (*music*) la nota *no·ta*; (*letter*) il biglietto *beel·yayt·toh*; (*banknote*) la banconota *ban·ko·no·ta* M20, 22

notepaper *n* la carta da lettere *kahr·ta da let·te·ray* A41, S92

nothing *n* niente *nyen·tay*

notice *n* (*poster*) l'avviso (*m*) *av·vee·zoh*; (*sign*) il cartello *kahr·tel·loh* □ *vt* notare *no·tah·ray*

notions *pl* la merceria *mayr·che·ree·a*

nougat *n* il torrone *tor·roh·nay*

nought *n* lo zero *dze·roh*

novel *n* (*book*) il romanzo *ro·man·dzoh*

November *n* novembre (*m*) *no·vem·bre*

now *adv* ora *oh·ra*; now and then, now and again ogni tanto *on·yee tan·to*

nowadays *adv* oggigiorno *oj·jee·johr·noh*

nowhere *adv* in nessun luogo *een nes·soon lwo·goh*

nuclear *adj* (*energy, war*) nucleare *noo·klay·ah·ray*

nude *adj* nudo(a) *noo·doh(a)*

nuisance *n* la seccatura *sek·ka·too·ra*; he's a nuisance egli è una persona noiosa *el·yee e oo·na payr·soh·na no·yoh·sa*; it's a nuisance è un fastidio *e oon fa·stee·dyoh*

null and void *adj* nullo(a) e di nessun effetto *nool·loh(a) e dee nes·soon ef·fet·toh*

numb *adj* (*with cold*) intirizzito(a) *een·tee·reedz·dzee·toh(a)*

number *n* (*figure*) il numero *noo·me·roh* Sn12

nun *n* la monaca *mo·na·ka*

nurse *n* l'infermiera (*f*) *een·fayr·mye·ra* □ *vt* (*patient*) curare *koo·rah·ray*

nursery *n* la camera dei bambini *kah·me·ra dey bam·bee·nee*

nursing home *n* la casa di cura *kah·sa dee koo·ra*

nylon *n* il nailon *nai·lon*

O

oak *n* la quercia *kwer·cha*

oar *n* il remo *re·moh*

oats *pl* l'avena (*f*) *a·vay·na*

obedient *adj* obbediente *ob·be·dyen·te*

obey *vi* ubbidire *oob·bee·dee·re* □ *vt* to obey someone ubbidire a qualcuno *oob·bee·dee·re a kwal·koo·no*

object[1] *n* l'oggetto (*m*) *oj·jet·toh*

object[2] *vi* □ to object to a remark obiettare ad una osservazione *o·byet·tah·ray ad oo·na os·sayr·va·tsyoh·ne*

objective *n* l'obiettivo (*m*) *o·byet·tee·voh*

obligation *n* l'obbligo (*m*) *ob·blee·goh*

oblong *adj* oblungo(a) *o·bloon·go(a)*

obscure *adj* oscuro(a) *o·skoo·ro(a)*

obsession *n* l'ossessione (*f*) *os·ses·syoh·ne*

obstacle *n* l'ostacolo (*m*) *o·sta·ko·loh*

obtain *vt* ottenere* *ot·te·nay·re*

obvious *adj* ovvio(a) *ov·vyo(a)*

obviously *adv* ovviamente *ov·vya·mayn·te*

occasion *n* l'occasione (*f*) *ok·ka·zyoh·ne*; (*special event*) l'avvenimento (*m*) *av·ve·nee·mayn·toh*

occasional *adj* (*event*) casuale *ka·zoo·ah·le*

occasionally *adv* di quando in quando *dee kwan·do een kwan·do*

occupation *n* (*job*) l'impiego (*m*) *eem·pye·goh*

occur *vi* (*happen*) accadere* *ak·ka·day·re*

ocean *n* l'oceano (*m*) *o·che·a·noh*

o'clock *adv* □ 3 o'clock alle tre *al·le tray*; it's 4 o'clock sono le 4 *so·no le 4*

October *n* ottobre (*m*) *ot·toh·bre*

odd *adj* (*number*) dispari *dee·spa·ree*; (*strange*) strano(a) *strah·no(a)*

odds *pl* (*in betting*) la quota *kwo·tah*

odometer *n* il contachilometri *kon·ta·kee·lo·me·tree*

of *prep* di *dee*; a friend of mine un mio amico *oon mee·o a·mee·koh*; 3 of them tre di loro *tray dee loh·ro*; 14th of June il quattordici giugno *eel kwat·tohr·dee·chee joon·yo*; made of stone di pietra *dee pye·tra*

of course *adv* naturalmente *na·too·ral· mayn·te*

off *adj (machine)* fermo(a) *fayr·mo(a)*; *(radio, light)* spento(a) *spen·to(a)*; *(water supply)* chiuso(a) *kyoo·so(a)* □ *adv* a day off un giorno libero *oon johr·noh lee·be·ro*; 3% off sconto del 3% *skohn·toh del 3%*; 6 kilometres off a 6 chilometri *a 6 kee·lo·me·tree* □ *prep* to fall off a wall cadere* da un muro *ka·day·re da oon moo·roh*; off the main road fuori della strada principale *fwo·ree del·la strah·da preen·chee·pah·le*

offend *vt* offendere* *of·fen·de·re*

offer *vt* offrire* *of·free·re*; to offer to do something offrire* di fare qualcosa *of·free·re dee fah·ray kwal·ko·sa* □ *n* offer l'offerta *(f)* *of·fer·ta*

office *n* l'ufficio *(m)* *oof·fee·choh*; *(doctor's)* il gabinetto medico *ga· bee·nayt·toh me·dee·ko* T49

office-block *n* il palazzo di uffici *pa· lats·tsoh dee oof·fee·chee*

office hours *pl* le ore d'ufficio *oh·re doof·fee·choh*

officer *n* (in army etc) l'ufficiale *(m)* *oof·fee·chah·le*; *(police)* l'agente di polizia *(m)* *a·jen·te dee po·lee·tsee·a*

office worker *n* l'impiegato(a) d'ufficio *(m/f)* *eem·pye·gah·to(a) doof·fee· choh*

official *adj* ufficiale *oof·fee·chah·le*

off-season *adj* di bassa stagione *dee bas·sa sta·joh·ne*

offshore *adj (island)* al largo *al lar·go*; offshore sailing la navigazione costiera *na·vee·ga·tsyoh·ne ko·stye·ra*

often *adv* spesso *spays·so*

oil *n* l'olio *(m)* *o·lyoh*; *(petroleum)* il petrolio *pe·tro·lyoh* T158

oil filter *n* il filtro dell'olio *feel·troh del·lol·yoh*

oil pan *n (in car)* la coppa dell'olio *kop·pa del·lol·yoh*

oil-rig *n* la piattaforma petrolifera *pyat· ta·fohr·ma pe·tro·lye·ra*

oil tanker *n* la petroliera *pe·tro·lye·ra*

ointment *n* l'unguento *(m)* *oon·gwen· toh*

O.K., okay *adv (agreement)* va bene *va be·ne*; it's OK va bene *va be·ne*

old *adj* vecchio(a) *vayk·kyo(a)*; how old are you? quanti anni ha? *kwan· tee an·nee a*

old-fashioned *adj* antiquato(a) *an·tee· kwah·to(a)*

olive *n* l'oliva *(f)* *o·lee·va*

olive oil *n* l'olio d'oliva *(m)* *o·lyoh do· lee·va*

omelet *n* la frittata *freet·tah·ta*

on *adj (machine)* in moto *een mo·toh*; *(light, radio)* acceso(a) *ach·chay· so(a)*; *(water supply)* aperto(a) *a· per·to(a)*; when is the movie on? quando è in visione il film? *kwan·do è een vee·zee·oh·ne eel feelm* □ *prep* on su *soo*; on the table sulla tavola *sool·la tah·vo·la*; on the train sul treno *sool tre·noh*; on the wall alla parete *al·la pa·ray·te*; on the left/right a sinistra/destra *a see·nee·stra/ de·stra*; come on Friday venga venerdì *ven·ga ve·ner·dee*; on television alla televisione *al·la te·le·vee·zee· oh·ne*

once *adv* una volta *oo·na vol·ta*; once

more ancora una volta *an·koh·ra oo· na vol·ta*

one *num* uno(a) *oo·no(a)*; one day un giorno *oon johr·noh* □ *pron* which one quale *kwah·le*; the one on the table quello(a) sulla tavola *kwayl· lo(a) sool·la tah·vo·la*; this one questo(a) *kway·sto(a)*; one should... uno dovrebbe... *oo·no do·vreb·be*; one another l'un l'altro *loon lal·tro*

one-armed bandit *n* la macchina mangiasoldi *mak·kee·na man·ja·sol·dee*

one-day excursion *n* il biglietto di andata e ritorno lo stesso giorno *beel· yayt·toh dee an·dah·ta e ree·tohr·noh lo stays·so johr·noh* L6

oneself *pron* se stesso(a) *say stays· so(a)*; to dress oneself vestirsi *ve· steer·see*

one-way street *n* la strada a senso unico *strah·da a sen·soh oo·nee·ko*

one-way ticket *n* il biglietto di solo andata *beel·yayt·toh dee soh·lo an· dah·ta* T57

onion *n* la cipolla *chee·pohl·la*

only *adv* solo *soh·lo*; there are only 4 ce ne sono solo 4 *che ne so·no soh·lo 4* □ *adj* the only woman there l'unica donna là *loo·nee·ka don·na la*; an only child un figlio unico *oon feel· yoh oo·nee·ko*; not only non solo *nohn soh·lo*

onto *prep* su *soo*

OPEC *n* l'OPEC *(f)* *oh·pek*

open *adj* aperto(a) *a·per·to(a)* □ *vt (window etc)* aprire* *a·pree·re* □ *vi (store, bank)* aprire* *a·pree·re*; *(play)* cominciare *ko·meen·chah·ray* L12

open-air *adj* all'aperto *al·la·per·to*

open-plan *adj* senza muri divisori *sen· tsa moo·ree dee·vee·zo·ree*

opera *n* l'opera *(f)* *o·pe·ra*

operate *vt (machine)* fare* funzionare *fah·ray foon·tsyoh·nah·ray*

operation *n* l'operazione *(f)* *o·pe·ra· tsyoh·ne*

operator *n* il/la telefonista *te·le·fo·nee· sta*

opinion *n* l'opinione *(f)* *o·pee·nyoh·ne*; in my opinion a mio parere *a mee·o pa·ray·re*

opportunity *n* l'occasione *(f)* *ok·ka· zee·oh·ne*

opposite *adv* dirimpetto *dee·reem·pet· to*; the house opposite la casa di fronte *la kah·sa dee frohn·te*; the opposite sex l'altro sesso *lal·tro ses·soh* □ *n* opposite il contrario *kon·trah· ryoh* □ *prep* di fronte a *dee frohn·te a*

optician *n* l'ottico *(m)* *ot·tee·koh*

optimistic *adj* ottimista *ot·tee·mee·sta*

option *n* l'opzione *(f)* *op·tsyoh·ne*

or *conj* o *o*

orange *n* l'arancia *(f)* *a·ran·cha* □ *adj* arancione *a·ran·choh·ne*

orangeade *n* l'aranciata *(f)* *a·ran· chah·ta*

orange juice *n* la spremuta d'arancia *spray·moo·ta da·ran·cha*

orchard *n* il frutteto *froot·tay·toh*

orchestra *n* l'orchestra *(f)* *or·ke·stra*; *(in theater)* la platea *pla·te·a*

order *n* l'ordine *(m)* *ohr·dee·ne*; *(for goods)* l'ordinazione *(f)* *ohr·dee·na· tsyoh·ne*; out of order *(machine)* guasto(a) *gwa·sto(a)*; in order to do something per fare qualcosa *payr fah·ray kwal·ko·sa* □ *vt* order *(goods, meal)* ordinare *or·dee·nah· ray*

order-form n il modulo d'ordinazione *mo·doo·loh dor·dee·na·tsyoh·ne*

ordinary adj ordinario(a) *or·dee·nah·ryo(a)*

organ n (instrument) l'organo (m) *or·ga·noh*

organization n l'organizzazione (f) *or·ga·needz·dza·tsyoh·ne*

organize vt organizzare *or·ga·needz·dzah·ray*

oriental adj orientale *o·ree·en·tah·le*

origin n l'origine (f) *o·ree·jee·ne*

original adj originale *o·ree·jee·nah·le* □ n l'originale (m) *o·ree·jee·nah·le*

originally adv (at first) originariamente *o·ree·jee·nah·rya·mayn·te*

ornament n l'ornamento (m) *or·na·mayn·toh*

orphan n l'orfano(a) (m/f) *or·fa·no(a)*

other adj altro(a) *al·tro(a)*; the other day l'altro giorno *lal·tro johr·noh* □ pron the other l'altro(a) *lal·tro(a)* S13, 22

otherwise adv altrimenti *al·tree·mayn·tee*; otherwise engaged occupato(a) con altri impegni *ok·koo·pah·to(a) kohn al·tree eem·pen·yee*

ought vi □ I ought to do it dovrei farlo *do·vree·ee far·lo*; he ought to win dovrebbe vincere *do·vreb·be veen·che·re*; that ought to do quello dovrebbe bastare *kwayl·lo do·vreb·be ba·stah·ray*

ounce n l'oncia (f) *ohn·cha*

our adj nostro(a) *no·stroh(a)*; our brothers/sisters i nostri fratelli/le nostre sorelle *ee no·stree fra·tel·lee/lay no·stray so·rel·lay*

ours pron il nostro *eel no·stroh*, la nostra *la no·stra*; (plural) i nostri *ee no·stree*, le nostre *lay no·stray*

ourselves pron noi stessi *noy stays·see*; we dressed ourselves ci siamo vestiti *chee syah·mo ve·stee·tee*

out adv (not at home) fuori *fwo·ree*; (team, player) eliminato(a) *e·lee·mee·nah·to(a)*; the tide is out la marea è bassa *la ma·re·a e bas·sa*; the sun is out il sole splende *eel soh·le splen·de*; the light is out la luce è spenta *la loo·che e spayn·ta* □ prep out of (outside) fuori di *fwo·ree dee*; to be out of gasoline rimanere* senza benzina *ree·ma·nay·re sen·tsa ben·dzee·na*; made out of wood di legno *dee layn·yoh*; he ran out of the house è uscito di corsa dalla casa *e oo·shee·to dee kohr·sa dal·la kah·sa*

outboard adj fuoribordo *fwo·ree·bohr·doh*

outdoor adj all'aria aperta *al·lah·ree·a a·per·ta*

outdoors adv all'aperto *al·la·per·to*

outfit n (clothes) il completo *kom·ple·toh*

outing n la gita *jee·ta*

outlet n (electric) la presa *pray·sa*

outline n (summary) il sommario *som·mah·ree·oh*

outlook n la prospettiva *pro·spet·tee·va*

out-of-date adj (passport, ticket) scaduto(a) *ska·doo·to(a)*

output n la produzione *pro·doo·tsyoh·ne*

outside n l'esterno (m) *e·ster·noh* □ adj the outside wall il muro esterno *eel moo·roh e·ster·no*; the outside lane (in road) la corsia di sorpasso *la kor·see·a dee sor·pas·soh* □ prep outside the house fuori della

casa *fwo·ree del·la kah·sa* □ adv to be outside stare* fuori *stah·ray fwo·ree*; to go outside uscire* *oo·shee·re*

outsize adj (clothes) di taglia grande *dee tal·ya gran·de*

outskirts pl la periferia *pe·ree·fe·ree·a*

oval adj ovale *o·vah·le*

oven n il forno *fohr·noh*

over adv □ to fall over cadere* *ka·day·ray*; to knock over fare* cadere *fah·ray ka·day·ray*; to turn something over rovesciare qualcosa *ro·ve·shah·ray kwal·ko·sa*; come over here venga qui *ven·ga kwee*; he's over here on holiday è qui in vacanza *e kwee een va·kan·tsa*; the match is over la partita è finita *la par·tee·ta e fee·nee·ta* □ prep to jump over something saltare qualcosa *sal·tah·ray kwal·ko·sa*; it weighs over a kilo pesa più di un chilo *pay·sa pyoo dee oon kee·loh*

overall n la tuta *too·ta*

overalls pl la tuta da lavoro *too·ta da la·voh·roh*

overcoat n il cappotto *kap·pot·toh*

overdose n la dose eccessiva *do·ze ech·ches·see·va*

overdraft n lo scoperto *sko·per·toh*

overdrive n l'overdrive (m) *ôv·ver·draiv*

overexposed adj (photo) sovraesposto(a) *soh·vra·e·spoh·sto(a)*

overhead adj (railway) aereo(a) *a·e·re·o(a)* □ adv in alto *een al·to* □ n le spese generali *spay·se je·ne·rah·lee*

overheat vi (engine) surriscaldarsi *soor·ree·skal·dahr·see*

overnight adj (a stay) per una notte *payr oo·na not·te* □ adv (happen) durante la notte *doo·ran·te la not·te*

overpass n il viadotto *vee·a·doht·toh*

overseas adv oltremare *ol·tre·mah·re* □ adj (market) d'oltremare *dol·tre·mah·re*; (visitor) straniero(a) *stra·nye·ro(a)*

overtime n le ore straordinarie *oh·re stra·or·dee·nah·ree·e*; to work overtime fare* dello straordinario *fah·ray del·lo stra·or·dee·nah·ree·o*

overture n l'ouverture (f) *oo·ver·tôôr*

overweight adj (baggage) in eccedenza *een ech·che·den·tsa*; (person) troppo pesante *trop·po pe·san·te*

owe vt (money) dovere* *do·vay·re*; he owes me $5 mi deve $5 *mee de·ve $5*

own adj proprio(a) *pro·pree·o(a)* □ n he did it on his own l'ha fatto da sé *la fat·to da say* □ vt own (possess) possedere* *pos·se·day·re*

owner n il/la proprietario(a) *pro·pree·e·tah·ree·o(a)*

ownership n la proprietà *pro·pree·e·ta*

oxygen n l'ossigeno (m) *os·see·je·noh*

oyster n l'ostrica (f) *o·stree·ka*

P

pace n il passo *pas·soh*; to keep pace with tenere* il passo di *te·nay·re eel pas·soh dee*

Pacific Ocean n l'Oceano Pacifico (m) *o·che·a·noh pa·chee·fee·ko*

pacifier n la tettarella *tet·ta·rel·la*

pack vt (goods) imballare *eem·bal·lah·ray*; to pack one's suitcase fare* la valigia *fah·ray la va·lee·ja* □ n pack il pacchetto *pak·kayt·toh*; (of cards) il mazzo *mats·tsoh*

package n il pacco *pak·koh*

package deal n l'accordo globale (m) *ak·kor·doh glo·bah·le*

package holiday *n* il viaggio organizzato *vyaj·joh or·ga·needz·dzah·to*
packet *n* il pacchetto *pak·kayt·toh* S32,
95
packing *n* (*material*) l'imballaggio (*m*)
eem·bal·laj·joh
packing case *n* la cassa da imballaggio
kas·sa da eem·bal·laj·joh
pad *n* (*notepaper*) il blocco *blok·koh*
paddle *n* (*oar*) la pagaia *pa·ga·ya*;
(*table tennis etc*) la racchetta *rak·
kayt·ta* □ *vi* sguazzare *zgwats·tsah·
ray*
padlock *n* il lucchetto *look·kayt·toh*
page *n* la pagina *pah·jee·na* □ *vt* fare*
chiamare *fah·ray kya·mah·ray*
pageboy *n* il paggio *paj·joh*
paid *adj* (*vacation*) pagato(a) *pa·gah·
to(a)*
pail *n* il secchio *sayk·kyoh*
pain *n* il dolore *do·loh·re* I28, 29
painful *adj* doloroso(a) *do·lo·roh·so(a)*
painkiller *n* il calmante *kal·man·te*
paint *n* la vernice *ver·nee·che* □ *vt* di-
pingere* *dee·peen·je·re*
painter *n* (*decorator*) il pittore *peet·toh·re*; (*decorator*) il decoratore *de·ko·ra·toh·re*
painting *n* (*picture*) il quadro *kwa·droh*
pair *n* il paio *pa·yoh*; (*of people*) la
coppia *kop·pya*; *pair of shoes* paio di
scarpe *pa·yoh dee skar·pe*; *pair of
scissors* le forbici *for·bee·chee*; *pair
of trousers* i pantaloni *pan·ta·loh·nee*
pajamas *pl* il pigiama *pee·jah·ma*
Pakistan *n* Pakistan (*m*) *pa·kee·stan*
Pakistani *adj* pachistano(a) *pa·kee·
stah·no(a)*
palace *n* il palazzo *pa·lats·tsoh* L12
pale *adj* (*face*) pallido(a) *pal·lee·do(a)*;
(*color*) chiaro(a) *kyah·ro(a)*
Palestine *n* Palestina (*f*) *pa·le·stee·na*
Palestinian *adj* palestinese *pa·le·stee·
nay·se*
palm *n* (*of hand*) il palmo *pal·moh*
palm-tree *n* la palma *pal·ma*
pan *n* (*saucepan*) il tegame *te·gah·me*;
(*frying pan*) la padella *pa·del·la*
pancake *n* la frittella *freet·tel·la*
pane *n* il vetro *vay·troh*
panic *n* il panico *pa·nee·koh*; **in
panic** preso(a) dal panico *pray·so(a)
dal pa·nee·koh* □ *vi* panic allarmarsi
al·lar·mar·see
pant *vi* ansimare *an·see·mah·ray*
panties *pl* le mutandine *moo·tan·
dee·ne*
pantomime *n* lo spettacolo natalizio
per bambini *spet·ta·ko·loh na·ta·lee·
tsyo payr bam·bee·nee*
pants *pl* i pantaloni *pan·ta·loh·nee*;
(*undergarment: men's*) le mutande
moo·tan·de; (*women's*) le mutandine
moo·tan·dee·ne
pant(s) suit *n* il tailleur-pantalone *tye·
yur·pan·ta·loh·ne*
panty hose *n* il collant *kol·lon*
paper *n* la carta *kar·ta*; (*newspaper*) il
giornale *johr·nah·le*; **papers** (*passport etc*) i documenti *do·koo·mayn·
tee* □ *vt* **paper** (*wall*) tappezzare *tap·
pets·tsah·ray*
paperback *n* il libro tascabile *lee·broh
ta·skah·bee·le* S94
paper clip *n* la graffetta *graf·fayt·ta*
paprika *n* la paprica *pa·pree·ka*
par *n* (*golf*) la norma *nor·ma*; (*business*) la pari *pah·ree*; **above par** sopra
la pari *soh·pra la pah·ree*
parachute *n* il paracadute *pa·ra·ka·
doo·te*
parade *n* il corteo *kor·te·oh*

paragraph *n* il paragrafo *pa·ra·gra·foh*
parallel *adj* parallelo(a) *pa·ral·le·lo(a)*
paralyzed *adj* paralizzato(a) *pa·ra·
leedz·dzah·to(a)*
parasol *n* il parasole *pa·ra·soh·le*
parcel *n* il pacco *pak·koh* Sn3
pardon *excl* scusate *skoo·zah·te*;
pardon me?, (I beg your) pardon?
prego? *pre·go*
parents *pl* i genitori *je·nee·toh·ree*
Paris *n* Parigi (*f*) *pa·ree·jee*
park *n* il parco *par·koh* □ *vt* parcheggiare *par·kej·jah·ray* □ *vi* **can I park
here?** posso parcheggiare qui? *pos·so
par·kej·jah·ray kwee* T122?
parka *n* la giacca a vento *jak·ka a ven·
toh*
parking disk *n* il disco orario *dee·skoh
o·rah·ryo*
parking lights *pl* i fanali di posizione
fa·nah·lee dee po·zee·tsyoh·ne
parking lot *n* il parcheggio *par·kayj·
joh* T125, 126
parking meter *n* il parchimetro *par·
kee·me·troh*
parking-ticket *n* la multa per sosta vietata *mool·ta payr so·sta vye·tah·ta*
parliament *n* il parlamento *par·la·
mayn·toh*
Parmesan *n* il parmigiano *par·mee·jah·
noh*
parsley *n* il prezzemolo *prets·tsay·mo·
loh*
parsnip *n* la pastinaca *pa·stee·nah·ka*
part *n* la parte *par·te*; (*of machine*) il
pezzo *pets·tsoh*; (*in hair*) la scriminatura *skree·mee·na·too·ra* □ *vt* (*separate*) separare *se·pa·rah·ray* T187,
Sn40
participate *vi* partecipare *par·te·chee·
pah·ray*
participation *n* la partecipazione *par·
te·chee·pa·tsyoh·ne*
particular *adj* particolare *par·tee·ko·
lah·re*; (*special*) speciale *spe·chah·le*
□ *n* **in particular** in particolare *een
par·tee·ko·lah·re*
particularly *adv* particolarmente *par·
tee·ko·lar·mayn·te*
partition *n* (*wall*) il tramezzo *tra·medz·
dzoh*
partly *adv* in parte *een par·te*
partner *n* (*in business*) il socio *so·
choh*; (*dancing*) il cavaliere *ka·va·
lye·re*, la dama *dah·ma*
partridge *n* la pernice *per·nee·che*
part-time *adj* a tempo parziale *a tem·
poh par·tsyah·le*
party *n* (*celebration*) la festa *fe·sta*;
(*group*) il gruppo *groop·poh*; (*political*) il partito *par·tee·toh* T5f
pass *n* (*permit*) il permesso *per·mays·
soh*; (*in mountains*) il passo *pas·soh*
□ *vt* (*place*) passare *pas·sah·ray*;
(*car*) sorpassare *sor·pas·sah·ray*;
(*exam*) essere* promosso(a) a *es·se·
re pro·mos·so(a) a*; (*time*) trascorrere* *tra·skohr·re·re*; (*hand on: object*)
passare *pas·sah·ray*; **please pass the
sugar** mi passa lo zucchero per favore *mee pas·sa lo tsook·ke·roh payr
fa·voh·re*
passage *n* il passaggio *pas·saj·joh*
passenger *n* il/la passeggero(a) *pas·sej·
je·ro(a)*
passenger seat *n* il sedile del passeggero *se·dee·le del pas·sej·je·roh*
passion *n* la passione *pas·syoh·ne*
passport *n* il passaporto *pas·sa·por·toh*
T11f, Sn82
past *adj* passato(a) *pas·sah·to(a)* □ *n* il

passato *pas·sah·toh* □ *adv* to run past passare correndo *pas·sah·ray kor·ren·do* □ *prep* he ran past me mi ha passato di corsa *mee a pas·sah·to dee kohr·sa*; he's past forty ha oltre quarant'anni *a ohl·tre kwa·ran·tan·nee*

pasta *n* la pasta *pa·sta*

paste *n* (glue) la colla *kol·la*; meat paste l'impasto di carne (*m*) *eem·pa·stoh dee kar·ne*

pasteurized *adj* pastorizzato(a) *pa·sto·reedz·dzah·to(a)*

pastille *n* la pastiglia *pa·steel·ya*

pastry *n* la pasta *pa·sta*

pat *vt* carezzare *ka·rets·tsah·ray*

patch *n* (of material) la pezza *pets·tsa*; (for eye) la benda *ben·da*; (spot) la macchia *mak·kya*

pâté *n* il pâté *pa·tay*

patent *n* il brevetto *bre·vayt·toh*

patent leather *n* il cuoio verniciato *kwo·yoh ver·nee·chah·to*

path *n* il sentiero *sen·tye·roh*

patience *n* la pazienza *pa·tsyen·tsa*

patient *adj* paziente *pa·tsyen·te* □ *n* il/la paziente *pa·tsyen·te*

patio *n* il patio *pa·tyoh*

pattern *n* il disegno *dee·sayn·yoh*; (dressmaking) il patron *pa·tron*; (knitting) le istruzioni *ee·stroo·tsyoh·nee*

pause *n* la pausa *pow·za* □ *vi* fare* una pausa *fah·ray oo·na pow·za*

pavement *n* (sidewalk) il marciapiede *mar·cha·pye·de*; (roadway) il lastricato *la·stree·kah·toh*

paw *n* la zampa *tsam·pa*

pay *n* la paga *pah·ga* □ *vt* pagare *pa·gah·ray*; to pay back (money) rimborsare *reem·bohr·sah·ray*; to pay for pagare *pa·gah·ray*; to pay off (workers) licenziare *lee·chen·tsyah·ray* M9f

payable *adj* pagabile *pa·gah·bee·le*

payee *n* il beneficiario *be·ne·fee·chah·ryoh*

paying guest *n* l'ospite pagante (*m/f*) *o·spee·te pa·gan·te*

payment *n* il pagamento *pa·ga·mayn·toh*

payroll *n* il libro paga *lee·broh pah·ga*

peace *n* la pace *pah·che*; (calm) la calma *kal·ma*

peaceful *adj* tranquillo(a) *tran·kweel·lo(a)*

peach *n* la pesca *pe·ska*

peak *n* (of cap) la visiera *vee·zye·ra*; (of mountain) la cima *chee·ma*

peak hours *pl* le ore di punta *oh·re de poon·ta*

peanut *n* l'arachide (*f*) *a·ra·kee·de*

pear *n* la pera *pay·ra*

pearl *n* la perla *per·la*

peas *pl* i piselli *pee·sel·lee*

pebble *n* il ciottolo *chot·to·loh*

peck *vt* beccare *bek·kah·ray*

peculiar *adj* (strange) strano(a) *strah·no(a)*

pedal *n* il pedale *pe·dah·le*

pedalo *n* il pattino a pedali *pat·tee·noh a pe·dah·lee*

pedestrian *n* il pedone *pe·doh·ne*

pedestrian crossing *n* il passaggio pedonale *pas·saj·joh pe·do·nah·le*

pedestrian precinct *n* l'isola pedonale (*f*) *ee·zo·la pe·do·nah·le*

pediatrician *n* il/la pediatra *pe·dya·tra*

peel *vt* sbucciare *zbooch·chah·ray* □ *vi* (person) spellarsi *spel·lar·see* □ *n* la buccia *booch·cha*

peg *n* il picchetto *peek·kayt·toh*; (for

coat) l'attaccapanni (*m*) *at·tak·ka·pan·nee*

pen *n* la penna *payn·na* S92

pencil *n* la matita *ma·tee·ta*

penetrate *vt* penetrare *pe·ne·trah·ray*

penicillin *n* la penicillina *pe·nee·cheel·lee·na*

penis *n* il pene *pe·ne*

penknife *n* il temperino *tem·pe·ree·noh*

pen pal *n* il/la corrispondente *kor·ree·spon·den·te*

pension *n* la pensione *pen·syoh·ne*

pensioner *n* il/la pensionato(a) *pen·syoh·nah·to(a)*

pension fund *n* la cassa di pensionamento *kas·sa dee pen·syoh·na·mayn·toh*

penthouse *n* l'attico (*m*) *at·tee·koh*

people *pl* la gente *jen·te* Mc18

pepper *n* il pepe *pay·pe*; (capsicum) il peperone *pe·pe·roh·ne*; green/red pepper il peperone verde/rosso *pe·pe·roh·ne vayr·de/rohs·so*

peppermint *n* (confectionery) la caramella di menta *ka·ra·mel·la dee mayn·ta*; (plant) la menta peperita *mayn·ta pe·pe·ree·ta*

pepper pot *n* la pepaiola *pe·pa·yo·la*

peppery *adj* pepato(a) *pe·pah·to(a)*

per *prep* per *payr*; 100 km per hour 100 chilometri all'ora *100 kee·lo·me·tree al·loh·ra*; to earn $25 per hour guadagnare $25 all'ora *gwa·dan·yah·ray $25 eel kee·loh*; $3 per kilo $3 il chilo *$3 eel kee·loh*; per person per persona *payr per·soh·na*; per day al giorno *al johr·noh*; per annum all'anno *al·lan·noh*; 20 per cent 20 per cento *20 payr chen·to*

percentage *n* la percentuale *per·chen·too·ah·le*

percolate *vt* (coffee) filtrare *feel·trah·ray*

percolator *n* la macchinetta per il caffè *mak·kee·nayt·ta payr eel kaf·fe*

perfect *adj* perfetto(a) *per·fet·to(a)*

perform *vi* (business) andare* *an·dah·ray* L47

performance *n* (of actor) l'interpretazione (*f*) *een·ter·pre·ta·tsyoh·ne*; (of play) la rappresentazione *rap·pre·zen·ta·tsyoh·ne*; (of car) il rendimento *ren·dee·mayn·toh* L49, 52

perfume *n* il profumo *pro·foo·moh* S44

perhaps *adv* forse *fohr·se*

period *n* (of time) il periodo *pe·ree·o·doh*; (punctuation) il punto *poon·toh*; (menstruation) le mestruazioni *me·stroo·a·tsyoh·nee* □ *adj* (furniture) antico(a) *an·tee·ko(a)*

perm *n* la permanente *per·ma·nen·te*

permanent *adj* permanente *per·ma·nen·te*

permanently *adv* permanentemente *per·ma·nen·te·mayn·te*

permanent wave *n* la permanente *per·ma·nen·te*

permission *n* il permesso *per·mays·soh*

permit *vt* (something) permettere* *per·mayt·te·re*; to permit someone to do something permettere* a qualcuno di fare qualcosa *per·mayt·te·re a kwal·koo·no dee fah·ray kwal·ko·sa* □ *n* il permit il permesso *per·mays·soh*

Persian *adj* persiano(a) *per·syah·no(a)*

person *n* la persona *per·soh·na*; in person di persona *dee per·soh·na*

personal *adj* personale *per·so·nah·le*; (private) privato(a) *pree·vah·to(a)*

personal assistant, P.A. *n* il/la segretario(a) particolare *se·gre·tah·ryo(a) par·tee·ko·lah·re*

personality *n* la personalità *per·so·na· lee·ta*

personally *adv* personalmente *per·so· nal·mayn·te*

personnel *n* il personale *per·so·nah·le*

personnel department *n* l'ufficio del personale (*m*) *oof·fee·choh del per· so·nah·le*

personnel manager *n* il direttore del personale *dee·ret·toh·re del per·so· nah·le*

person-to-person call *n* la telefonata personale *te·le·fo·nah·ta per·so· nah·le* Sn13

perspire *vi* traspirare *tra·spee·rah·ray*

persuade *vt* persuadere* *per·swa·day· re*; **to persuade someone to do something** persuadere* qualcuno a fare qualcosa *per·swa·day·re kwal·koo·no a fah·ray kwal·ko·sa*

peseta *n* la peseta *pe·say·ta*

pessimistic *adj* pessimista *pes·see·mee· sta*

pet *n* l'animale domestico (*m*) *a·nee· mah·le do·me·stee·ko*

petroleum jelly *n* la vaselina *va·ze· lee·na*

petticoat *n* la sottoveste *soht·to·ve·ste*

pharmacist *n* il/la farmacista *far·ma· chee·sta*

pharmacy *n* la farmacia *far·ma·chee·a*

pheasant *n* il fagiano *fa·jah·noh*

phone *n* il telefono *te·le·fo·noh*; **he's on the phone** sta telefonando *sta te· le·fo·nan·do* □ *vt* **phone** telefonare *te·le·fo·nah·ray* Sn10f

phone-call *n* la telefonata *te·le·fo· nah·ta* Sn13

photo *n* la foto *fo·toh* L14, S51

photocopy *n* la fotocopia *fo·to·ko·pya* □ *vt* fotocopiare *fo·to·ko·pyah·ray* Bm13

photograph *n* la fotografia *fo·to·gra· fee·a* □ *vt* fotografare *fo·to·gra·fah· ray* S52

photographer *n* il fotografo *fo·to·gra· foh*

photography *n* la fotografia *fo·to·gra· fee·a*

phrase *n* la frase *frah·ze*

phrase book *n* il libro di fraseologia *lee·broh dee fra·ze·o·lo·jee·a*

physical *adj* fisico(a) *fee·zee·ko(a)*

physics *n* la fisica *fee·zee·ka*

piano *n* il piano *pyah·noh*

pick *n* (pickaxe) il piccone *peek·koh·ne* □ *vt* (flower) cogliere* *kol·ye·re*; (choose) scegliere* *shayl·ye·re*; **to pick up** (object) raccogliere* *rak·kol· ye·re*; **to pick up a friend** andare* a prendere un amico *an·dah·ray a pren·de·re oon a·mee·koh*

pickaxe *n* il piccone *peek·koh·ne*

picket *n* il picchetto *peek·kayt·toh*

pickles *pl* i sottaceti *sot·ta·chay·tee*

picnic *n* il picnic *peek·neek*; **to go on a picnic** andare* a fare un picnic *an· dah·ray a fah·ray oon peek·neek* L39

picture *n* il quadro *kwa·droh*; (drawing) il disegno *dee·sayn·yoh*; (photo) la foto *fo·toh*; (movie) il film *feelm*

pie *n* la torta *tohr·ta*; (meat) il pasticcio *pa·steech·choh*

piece *n* il pezzo *pets·tsoh*; **piece of furniture** il mobile *mo·bee·le*; **a good piece of work** un buon lavoro *oon bwon la·voh·roh*

piecework *n* il lavoro a cottimo *la·voh· roh a kot·tee·moh*

pier *n* il molo *mo·loh*

pierce *vt* trafiggere* *tra·feej·je·re*

pig *n* il maiale *ma·yah·le*

pigeon *n* il piccione *peech·choh·ne*

pigskin *n* la pelle di cinghiale *pel·le dee cheen·gyah·le*

pilchard *n* la sardella *sar·del·la*

pile *n* il mucchio *mook·kyoh* □ *vt* **pile up** ammucchiare *am·mook· kyah·ray*

pill *n* la pillola *peel·lo·la*; **to be on the pill** prendere* la pillola *pren·de·re la peel·lo·la* I47

pillar *n* il pilastro *pee·la·stroh*

pillow *n* il guanciale *gwan·chah·le* A41

pillowcase, pillowslip *n* la federa *fe· de·ra*

pilot *n* il pilota *pee·lo·ta*

pilot light *n* (gas) l'accenditore (*m*) *ach·chen·dee·toh·re*

pimple *n* la bollicina *bol·lee·chee·na*

pin *n* lo spillo *speel·loh*; (safety pin) lo spillo di sicurezza *speel·loh dee see· koo·rayts·tsa* □ *vt* attaccare con uno spillo *at·tak·kah·ray kohn oo·no speel·loh*

pinball *n* il flipper *fleep·per*

pinch *vt* pizzicare *peets·tsee·kah·ray* □ *n* (of salt etc) il pizzico *peets·tsee· koh*

pine *n* il pino *pee·noh*

pineapple *n* l'ananas (*m*) *a·na·nas*

ping-pong *n* il ping-pong *peeng·pong*

pink *adj* rosa *ro·za*

pint *n* la pinta *peen·ta*

pipe *n* (tube) il tubo *too·boh*; (for smoking) la pipa *pee·pa*; (musical) il piffero *peef·fe·roh*; (bag)pipes la cornamusa *kor·na·moo·za* A76, S97

pipeline *n* l'oleodotto (*m*) *o·le·o·doht· toh*

piston *n* il pistone *pee·stoh·ne*

pit *n* la fossa *fos·sa*

pitch *vt* (tent) piantare *pyan·tah·ray*

pitcher *n* la brocca *brok·ka*

pity *n* la compassione *kom·pas·syoh· ne*; **what a pity!** che peccato! *ke pek· kah·to*

pizza *n* la pizza *peets·tsa*

place *n* il luogo *lwo·goh*; (seat) il posto *poh·stoh*; **in place** a posto *a poh·stoh*; **out of place** (object) fuori posto *fwo· ree poh·stoh*; **come back to our place** venga a casa nostra *ven·ga a kah·sa no·stra* □ *vt* **place** (put) mettere* *mayt·te·re*; (a bet) fare* *fah·ray*; **to place an order with someone** collocare un ordine presso qualcuno *kol· lo·kah·ray oon ohr·dee·ne pres·so kwal·koo·no*

place mat *n* il sottopiatto *soht·to·pyat· toh*

place setting *n* il coperto *ko·per·toh*

plaice *n* la passera *pas·se·ra*

plaid *n* il plaid *plahd*

plain *n* la pianura *pya·noo·ra* □ *adj* (clear) chiaro(a) *kyah·ro(a)*; (simple: cooking etc) semplice *saym·plee·che*; (not patterned) unito(a) *oo·nee· to(a)*; **plain chocolate** il cioccolato scuro *chok·ko·lah·toh skoo·ro*; **plain yogurt** lo iogurt naturale *yo·goort na· too·rah·le*

plait *n* (of hair etc) la treccia *traych· cha*

plan *n* (scheme) il progetto *pro·jet·toh*; (map) la pianta *pyan·ta*; (drawing, design) il disegno *dee·sayn·yoh* □ *vt* progettare *pro·jet·tah·ray*; (make a design) disegnare *dee·sayn·yah·ray*

plane *n* l'aereo (*m*) *a·e·re·oh*; (tree) il

platano *pla·ta·noh*; (*tool*) la pialla *pyal·la*; **by plane** in aereo *een a·e·re·oh* B69

planet *n* il pianeta *pya·nay·ta*

planetarium *n* il planetario *pla·ne·tah·ryoh*

plank *n* la tavola *tah·vo·la*

planning *n* (*economic*) la pianificazione *pya·nee·fee·ka·tsyoh·ne*

plant *n* la pianta *pyan·ta*; (*factory*) lo stabilimento *sta·bee·lee·mayn·toh*; (*equipment*) il macchinario *mak·kee·nah·ryoh* □ *vt* piantare *pyan·tah·ray*

plaster *n* (*for wall*) l'intonaco (*m*) *een·to·na·koh*; **plaster cast** (*for limb*) il gesso *jes·soh*; **plaster of Paris** il gesso *jes·soh*

plastic *n* la plastica *pla·stee·ka* □ *adj* in plastica *een pla·stee·ka*; **plastic surgery** la chirurgia plastica *kee·roor·jee·a pla·stee·ka*

plastic bag *n* il sacco in plastica *sak·koh een pla·stee·ka* S25

plate *n* il piatto *pyat·toh*; (*of glass, metal*) la lastra *la·stra*

plated *adj* □ **gold plated** placcato(a) d'oro *plak·kah·to(a) do·roh*

platform *n* (*in station*) la banchina *ban·kee·na*; (*in hall*) il palco *pal·koh*; (*of oil-rig*) la piattaforma *pyat·ta·fohr·ma* T69, 70

platinum *n* il platino *pla·tee·noh*

play *vt/i* giocare *jo·kah·ray*; **to play football** giocare al calcio *jo·kah·ray al kal·choh*; **to play the violin** suonare il violino *swo·nah·rey eel vee·o·lee·noh*; **to play with** giocare con *jo·kah·ray kohn* □ *n* **play** (*theatrical*) il dramma *dram·ma*

player *n* (*in sport*) il giocatore *jo·ka·toh·re*, la giocatrice *jo·ka·tree·che*

playground *n* il cortile *kor·tee·le* C9

play-group *n* il nido d'infanzia *nee·doh deen·fan·tsya*

playing card *n* la carta da gioco *kar·ta da jo·koh*

playing field *n* il campo da gioco *kam·poh da jo·koh*

playpen *n* il box *boks*

pleasant *adj* gradevole *gra·day·vo·le*; (*person*) simpatico(a) *seem·pa·tee·ko(a)*

please *adv* per favore *payr fa·voh·re*

pleased *adj* contento(a) *kon·ten·to(a)*

pleasure *n* il piacere *pya·chay·re*

pleasure boat *n* il battello da diporto *bat·tel·loh da dee·por·toh*

pleated *adj* pieghettato(a) *pye·get·tah·to(a)*

plenty *n* □ **plenty of milk** molto latte *mohl·to lat·te*; **thank you, that's plenty** grazie, basta cosí *gra·tsye ba·sta ko·see*

plexiglas *n* il plexiglas *plek·see·glas*

pliers *pl* le pinze *peen·tse*

plimsolls *pl* le scarpette da tennis *skar·payt·te da ten·nees*

plot *n* (*of land*) l'appezzamento (*m*) *ap·pets·tsa·mayn·toh*; (*in play*) la trama *trah·ma*

plow *n* l'aratro (*m*) *a·ra·troh*

plug *n* (*for basin etc*) il tappo *tap·poh*; (*electric*) la spina *spee·na*; (*in car*) la candela *kan·day·la* □ *vt* tappare *tap·pah·ray*; **to plug something in** attaccare qualcosa *at·tak·kah·ray kwal·ko·sa*

plum *n* la susina *soo·see·na*

plumber *n* l'idraulico (*m*) *ee·drow·lee·koh*

plump *adj* grassoccio(a) *gras·soch·cho(a)*

plus *prep* piú *pyoo*

plywood *n* il compensato *kom·pen·sah·toh*

p.m. *adv* di sera *dee say·ra*

pneumonia *n* la polmonite *pol·mo·nee·te*

poached *adj* affogato(a) *af·fo·gah·to(a)*

P.O. Box *n* la casella postale *ka·sel·la po·stah·le*

pocket *n* la tasca *ta·ska*

pocketbook *n* il portafogli *por·ta·fol·yee*

pocketknife *n* il temperino *tem·pe·ree·noh*

pocket money *n* il denaro per le piccole spese *de·nah·roh payr le peek·ko·le spay·se*

podiatrist *n* il pedicure *pay·dee·koo·ray*

poem *n* la poesia *po·e·zee·a*

poetry *n* la poesia *po·e·zee·a*

point *vt* (*gun*) puntare *poon·tah·ray* □ *vi* **to point at** or **to something** indicare qualcosa *een·dee·kah·ray kwal·ko·sa*; **to point something out** (*show*) mostrare qualcosa *mo·strah·ray kwal·ko·sa* □ *n* **point** il punto *poon·toh*; (*tip*) la punta *poon·ta*; (*in time*) il momento *mo·mayn·toh*; (*electric outlet*) la presa *pray·sa*; **decimal point** la virgola *veer·go·la*; **3 point 4** 3 virgola 4 3 *veer·go·la 4*; **he answered him point by point** gli ha risposto punto per punto *lyee a ree·spoh·sto poon·toh payr poon·toh*; **what's the point?** a che serve? *a ke ser·ve*

point of view *n* il punto di vista *poon·toh dee vee·sta*

poison *n* il veleno *ve·lay·noh*

poisonous *adj* velenoso(a) *ve·le·noh·so(a)*

poker *n* (*card game*) il poker *po·ker*

Poland *n* Polonia (*f*) *po·lo·nya*

Polaroid *adj* polaroid *po·la·royd*

pole *n* (*wooden*) il palo *pah·loh*

Pole *n* il/la polacco(a) *po·lak·ko(a)*

police *n* la polizia *po·lee·tsee·a* T214, Sn77

police car *n* la macchina della polizia *mak·kee·na del·la po·lee·tsee·a*

policeman *n* il poliziotto *po·lee·tsyot·toh*

police station *n* il commissariato *kom·mees·sa·ryah·toh* Sn78

policewoman *n* la donna poliziotto *don·na po·lee·tsyot·toh*

policy *n* la politica *po·lee·tee·ka*; (*insurance*) la polizza *po·leets·tsa*

polio *n* la polio *po·lyoh*

polish *n* (*for shoes*) il lucido *loo·chee·doh*; (*for floor*) la cera *chay·ra* □ *vt* lucidare *loo·chee·dah·ray*

Polish *adj* polacco(a) *po·lak·ko(a)* □ *n* il polacco *po·lak·koh*

polite *adj* gentile *jen·tee·le*

political *adj* politico(a) *po·lee·tee·ko(a)*

politician *n* l'uomo politico (*m*) *wo·moh po·lee·tee·ko*

politics *n* la politica *po·lee·tee·ka*

pollution *n* l'inquinamento (*m*) *een·kwee·na·mayn·toh*

polo *n* il polo *po·loh*

polo neck *n* il collo alto *kol·loh al·to*

polyester *n* il poliestere *po·lee·e·ste·re*

polyethylene *n* il polietilene *po·lee·e·tee·le·ne*

polyethylene bag *n* il sacchetto di plastica *sak·kay·toh dee pla·stee·ka*

pomegranate *n* la melagrana *me·la·grah·na*
pond *n* (*natural*) lo stagno *stan·yoh*; (*artificial*) il bacino *ba·chee·noh*
pony *n* il pony *poh·nee*
pool *n* (*of rain*) la pozzanghera *pots·tsan·ge·ra*; (*swimming*) la piscina *pee·shee·na*; (*game*) il biliardo *bee·lyar·doh* A11
poor *adj* povero(a) *po·ve·ro(a)*; (*mediocre*) mediocre *me·dee·o·kre*
pop *adj* (*music, art*) pop *pop*
pop concert *n* il concerto pop *kon·cher·toh pop*
popcorn *n* il pop-corn *pop·korn*
pope *n* il papa *pah·pa*
pop group *n* il complesso pop *kom·ples·soh pop*
poplar *n* il pioppo *pyop·poh*
poplin *n* la popeline *po·pe·leen*
popsicle *n* il lecca-lecca *layk·ka·layk·ka*
popular *adj* popolare *po·po·lah·ray*; (*fashionable*) di moda *dee mo·da*
population *n* la popolazione *po·po·la·tsyoh·ne*
porcelain *n* la porcellana *por·chel·lah·na*
porch *n* il portico *por·tee·koh*
pork *n* la carne di maiale *kar·ne dee ma·yah·le* S36
porridge *n* il porridge *po·reej*
port *n* il porto *por·toh*
portable *adj* portatile *por·tah·tee·le*
porter *n* (*for luggage*) il facchino *fak·kee·noh*; (*doorkeeper*) il/la portiere(a) *por·tye·re(a)* T25
portfolio *n* il portafoglio *por·ta·fol·yoh*
porthole *n* l'oblò (*m*) *o·blo*
portion *n* la porzione *por·tsyoh·ne*
Portugal *n* Portogallo (*m*) *por·to·gal·loh*
Portuguese *adj* portoghese *por·to·gay·se* □ *n* il portoghese *por·to·gay·se*
position *n* la posizione *po·zee·tsyoh·ne*; (*place, job*) il posto *il·stoh*
positive *adj* positivo(a) *po·zee·tee·vo(a)*; (*definite*) preciso(a) *pre·chee·zo(a)*
possibility *n* la possibilità *pos·see·bee·lee·ta*
possible *adj* possibile *pos·see·bee·le*
possibly *adv* forse *fohr·se*; to do all one possibly can fare* tutto il possibile *fah·ray toot·to eel pos·see·bee·le*
post *n* (*pole*) il palo *pah·loh*; (*mail*) la posta *po·sta*; by post per posta *payr po·sta* □ *vt* post imbucare *eem·boo·kah·ray* Sn1f
postage *n* le spese postali *spay·se po·stah·lee*
postal *adj* postale *po·stah·le*
postal district *n* il distretto postale *dee·strayt·toh po·stah·le*
postal order *n* il vaglia *val·ya*
post-box *n* la cassetta per le lettere *kas·sayt·ta payr le let·te·re*
postcard *n* la cartolina *kar·to·lee·na* L15, S91, Sn2
post-code *n* il codice postale *ko·dee·che po·stah·le*
postdate *vt* postdatare *post·da·tah·ray*
poster *n* il manifesto *ma·nee·fe·stoh*
postman *n* il postino *po·stee·noh*
post office *n* l'ufficio postale (*m*) *oof·fee·choh po·stah·le*; the Post Office le Poste *po·ste* F8
post-office box *n* la casella postale *ka·sel·la po·stah·le*
postpone *vt* rimandare *ree·man·dah·ray*

pot *n* (*for cooking*) la pentola *payn·to·la*; (*for jam*) il barattolo *ba·rat·to·loh*; (*for plant*) il vaso *vah·zoh*
potato *n* la patata *pa·tah·ta*
pottery *n* la ceramica *che·ra·mee·ka*; (*workshop*) la fabbrica di ceramiche *fab·bree·ka dee che·ra·mee·ke*
pot(ty) *n* il vasino *va·zee·noh*
poultry *n* il pollame *pol·lah·me*
pound *n* (*tea, milk*) la sterlina *ster·lee·na*; (*weight*) la libbra *leeb·bra*
pour *vt* (*tea, milk*) versare *ver·sah·ray* □ *vi* scorrere* *skohr·re·re*
powder *n* la polvere *pohl·ve·re*; (*cosmetic*) la cipria *chee·prya*
powder room *n* la toeletta *to·e·let·ta*
power *n* (*of machine*) la potenza *po·ten·tsa*; (*authority*) il potere *po·tay·re*; (*electricity*) la corrente *kor·ren·te*
powerful *adj* potente *po·ten·te*
P.R. *n* le pubbliche relazioni *poob·blee·ke re·la·tsyoh·nee*
practical *adj* pratico(a) *pra·tee·ko(a)*
practice *vt/i* □ to practice running esercitarsi nel correre *e·zer·chee·tar·see nel kohr·re·re*; to practice the piano esercitarsi al pianoforte *e·zer·chee·tar·see al pya·no·for·te*
Prague *n* Praga (*f*) *prah·ga*
pram *n* il carrozzino *kar·rots·tsee·noh*
prawn *n* il gamberetto *gam·be·rayt·toh*
pray *vi* pregare *pre·gah·ray*
prayer *n* la preghiera *pre·gye·ra*
precinct *n* (*administrative area*) la circoscrizione *cheer·ko·skree·tsyoh·ne*
precious *adj* (*jewel etc*) prezioso(a) *pre·tsyoh·so(a)* S87
precise *adj* preciso(a) *pre·chee·zo(a)*
precision *n* la precisione *pre·chee·zyoh·ne*
predict *vt* predire* *pre·dee·re*
prediction *n* la predizione *pre·dee·tsyoh·ne*
prefer *vt* preferire *pre·fe·ree·re*
preferred stock *n* le azioni privilegiate *a·tsyoh·nee pre·vee·le·jah·te*
pregnant *adj* incinta *een·cheen·ta* I46
prejudice *n* il pregiudizio *pre·joo·dee·tsyoh*
preliminary *adj* preliminare *pre·lee·mee·nah·re*
première *n* la prima *pree·ma*
premises *pl* lo stabile *stah·bee·le*
premium *n* il premio *pre·myoh*
prepaid *adj* prepagato(a) *pre·pa·gah·to(a)*
preparation *n* la preparazione *pre·pa·ra·tsyoh·ne*; **preparations** (*for trip*) i preparativi *pre·pa·ra·tee·vee*
prepare *vt* preparare *pre·pa·rah·ray* □ *vi* he's preparing to leave si prepara a partire *see pre·pah·ra a par·tee·re*
Presbyterian *adj* presbiteriano(a) *pre·zbee·te·ree·ah·no(a)*
prescription *n* la ricetta *ree·chet·ta*
present *adj* presente *pre·zen·te*; the present king il re attuale *eel ray at·twah·le* □ *n* present (*gift*) il regalo *re·gah·loh*; at present in questo momento *een kway·sto mo·mayn·toh* □ *vt* present (*give*) regalare *re·ga·lah·ray* S6, 103
presentation *n* la presentazione *pre·zen·ta·tsyoh·ne*
preserve(s) *n* la marmellata *mar·mel·lah·ta*
president *n* (*of country*) il presidente *pre·see·den·te*; (*of company*) il direttore *dee·ret·toh·re*
press *n* (*newspapers, journalists*) la

stampa *stam·pa*; (*printing machine*) la pressa tipografica *pres·sa tee·po·gra·fee·ka* □ *vt* premere *pre·me·re*; (*iron*) stirare *stee·rah·ray*

press-campaign *n* la campagna giornalistica *kam·pan·ya johr·na·lee·stee·ka*

pressure *n* la pressione *pres·syoh·ne* T159

pressure cooker *n* la pentola a pressione *payn·to·la a pres·syoh·ne*

pressure group *n* il gruppo di pressione *groop·poh dee pres·syoh·ne*

prestige *n* il prestigio *pre·stee·joh*

pretax *adj* (*profit*) lordo(a) *lohr·do(a)*

pretend *vi* fingere* *feen·je·re*; to tend to do something fingere* di fare qualcosa *feen·je·re dee fah·ray kwal·ko·sa*

pretty *adj* (*woman, child*) grazioso(a) *gra·tsyoh·so(a)*; (*dress*) bello(a) *bel·lo(a)*

preview *n* l'anteprima (*f*) *an·te·pree·ma*

previous *adj* precedente *pre·che·den·te*; on the previous day il giorno prima *eel johr·noh pree·ma*

price *n* il prezzo *prets·tsoh* □ *vt* (*goods*) fissare il prezzo di *fees·sah·ray eel prets·tsoh dee* B25

price list *n* il listino prezzi *lee·stee·noh prets·tsee*

price range *n* la gamma di prezzi *gam·ma dee prets·tsee*

prick *vt* pungere* *poon·je·re*

pride *n* l'orgoglio (*m*) *or·gohl·yoh*

priest *n* il prete *pre·te* Sn88

primary *adj* (*education*) primario(a) *pree·mah·ryo(a)*

prime minister, P.M. *n* il primo ministro *pree·mo mee·nee·stroh*

prince *n* il principe *preen·chee·pe*

princess *n* la principessa *preen·chee·pays·sa*

principal *n* (*of school etc*) il/la preside *pre·see·de*

print *vt* (*book, newspaper*) stampare *stam·pah·ray*; (*write in block letters*) scrivere* a stampatello *skree·ve·re a stam·pa·tel·loh* □ *n* la stampa *stam·pa*; (*photographic*) la copia *ko·pya*; out of print esaurito(a) *e·zow·ree·to(a)* S50

printer *n* il tipografo *tee·po·gra·foh*

printout *n* lo stampato *stam·pah·toh*

prison *n* la prigione *pree·joh·ne*; in prison in prigione *een pree·joh·ne*

prisoner *n* il/la prigioniero(a) *pree·joh·nye·ro(a)*

private *adj* privato(a) *pree·vah·to(a)*; (*secluded*) isolato(a) *ee·zo·lah·to(a)*; (*confidential*) confidenziale *kon·fee·den·tsyah·le*; in private in privato *een pree·vah·to* A37, E5

private enterprise *n* l'impresa privata (*f*) *eem·pray·sa pree·vah·ta*

private sector *n* il settore privato *set·toh·re pree·vah·to*

prize *n* il premio *pre·myoh*

probable *adj* probabile *pro·bah·bee·le*

probably *adv* probabilmente *pro·ba·beel·mayn·te*

problem *n* il problema *pro·ble·ma* A69

procedure *n* il procedimento *pro·che·dee·mayn·toh*

process *n* il processo *pro·ches·soh*; (*method*) il procedimento *pro·che·dee·mayn·toh* □ *vt* trattare *trat·tah·ray*; (*application, order*) occuparsi di *ok·koo·par·see dee*

produce *vt* produrre* *pro·door·re*; (*play*) mettere* in scena *mayt·te·re*

een she·na □ *n* (*products*) i prodotti *pro·doht·tee*

producer *n* il produttore *pro·doot·toh·re*; (*of play*) il/la regista *re·jee·sta*

product *n* il prodotto *pro·doht·toh* Bm21

production *n* la produzione *pro·doo·tsyoh·ne*; (*of play*) la rappresentazione *rap·pre·zen·ta·tsyoh·ne*

productivity *n* la produttività *pro·doot·tee·vee·ta*

profession *n* la professione *pro·fes·syoh·ne*

professional *adj* professionale *pro·fes·syoh·nah·le*

professor *n* il professore *pro·fes·soh·re*

profit *n* il profitto *pro·feet·toh*

profitability *n* il rendimento *ren·dee·mayn·toh*

profitable *adj* vantaggioso(a) *van·taj·joh·so(a)*

profiterole *n* la profiterole *pro·fee·te·rohl*

profit-making *adj* a scopo di lucro *a sko·poh dee loo·kroh*

profit margin *n* il margine di profitto *mar·jee·ne dee pro·feet·toh*

profit-sharing *n* la compartecipazione agli utili *kom·par·te·chee·pa·tsyoh·ne al·yee oo·tee·lee*

program *n* il programma *pro·gram·ma* □ *vt* programmare *pro·gram·mah·ray* L50

programmer *n* (*person*) il programmatore *pro·gram·ma·toh·re*, la programmatrice *pro·gram·ma·tree·che*

programming *n* (*computer*) la programmazione *pro·gram·ma·tsyoh·ne*

progress *n* il progresso *pro·gres·soh*; to make progress fare* progressi *fah·ray pro·gres·see*

prohibit *vt* proibire *pro·ee·bee·re*

project *n* (*plan*) il progetto *pro·jet·toh*; (*venture*) l'impresa (*f*) *eem·pray·sa*

projector *n* il proiettore *pro·yet·toh·re*

promenade *n* (*by sea*) il lungomare *loon·go·mah·re*

promise *n* la promessa *pro·mays·sa* □ *vt* promettere* *pro·mayt·te·re*

promote *vt* promuovere* *pro·mwo·ve·re*

promotion *n* la promozione *pro·mo·tsyoh·ne*

pronounce *vt* pronunciare *pro·noon·chah·ray*

pronunciation *n* la pronuncia *pro·noon·cha*

proof *n* la prova *pro·va*; a 70° proof whiskey un whisky di 40 gradi *oon wee·skee dee 40 grah·dee*

proper *adj* (*appropriate*) adatto(a) *a·dat·to(a)*; (*correct*) corretto(a) *kor·ret·to(a)*; (*respectable*) conveniente *kon·ve·nyen·te*

properly *adv* correttamente *kor·ret·ta·mayn·te*

property *n* la proprietà *pro·prye·ta*; (*estate*) il patrimonio *pa·tree·mo·nyoh*

prophylactic *n* (*contraceptive*) il preservativo *pre·ser·va·tee·voh*

proposal *n* (*suggestion*) la proposta *pro·poh·sta*

propose *vt* (*suggest*) proporre* *pro·pohr·re*; to propose a toast to someone brindare a qualcuno *breen·dah·ray a kwal·koo·no*

proposition *n* (*proposal*) la proposta *pro·poh·sta*

prospect *n* la prospettiva *pro·spet·tee·va*

prospectus n il prospetto *pro·spet·toh*

prosperous adj prospero(a) *pro·spe·ro(a)*

protect vt proteggere* *pro·tej·je·re*

protein n la proteina *pro·te·ee·na*

protest n la protesta *pro·te·sta* ☐ vi protestare *pro·te·stah·ray*

Protestant adj protestante *pro·te·stan·te* Sn86

prototype n il prototipo *pro·to·tee·poh*

proud adj oroglioso(a) *or·goh·lyoh·so(a)*; **proud of** fiero(a) di *fye·ro(a) dee*

prove vt provare *pro·vah·ray*

provide vt fornire *for·nee·re*; **to provide someone with something** fornire qualcuno di qualcosa *for·nee·re kwal·koo·no dee kwal·ko·sa* ☐ vi **to provide for someone** provvedere* a qualcuno *prov·ve·day·re a kwal·koo·no*

provided, providing conj purché *poor·kay*; **provided (that)** he comes purché venga *poor·kay ven·ga*

province n (region) la provincia *pro·veen·cha*

provincial adj provinciale *pro·veen·chah·le*

proviso n la condizione *kon·dee·tsyoh·ne*

prune n la prugna secca *proon·ya sayk·ka*

P.S. abbrev P.S. *pee·es·se*

psychiatric adj psichiatrico(a) *psee·kee·a·tree·ko(a)*

psychiatrist n lo/la psichiatra *psee·kee·a·tra*

psychological adj psicologico(a) *psee·ko·lo·jee·ko(a)*

psychologist n lo/la psicologo(a) *psee·ko·lo·go(a)*

psychology n la psicologia *psee·ko·lo·jee·a*

P.T.O. abbrev Vedi retro

pub n il bar *bar*

public adj pubblico(a) *poob·blee·ko(a)* ☐ n il pubblico *poob·blee·koh*; **in public** in pubblico *een poob·blee·koh*

public conveniences pl i gabinetti *ga·bee·nayt·tee*

publicity n la pubblicità *poob·blee·chee·ta*

publicity campaign n la campagna di pubblicità *kam·pan·ya dee poob·blee·chee·ta* Bm17

public relations n le pubbliche relazioni *poob·blee·ke re·la·tsyoh·nee*

public relations officer n l'incaricato delle pubbliche relazioni (m) *een·ka·ree·kah·toh del·le poob·blee·ke re·la·tsyoh·nee*

public school n la scuola statale *skwo·la sta·tah·le*

public sector n il settore pubblico *set·toh·re poob·blee·ko*

publish vt pubblicare *poob·blee·kah·ray*

publisher n l'editore (m) *e·dee·toh·re*, l'editrice (f) *e·dee·tree·che*

pudding n il dolce *dohl·che*

puddle n la pozzanghera *pots·tsan·ge·ra*

pull vt/i tirare *tee·rah·ray*; **to pull something out** cavare qualcosa *ka·vah·ray kwal·ko·sa*; **to pull out of a deal** ritirarsi da un affare *ree·tee·rar·see da oon af·fah·re*; **the car pulled in** la macchina si è accostata *la mak·kee·na see e ak·ko·stah·ta*; **he pulled out to pass the car** fece manovra per superare la macchina *fay·che ma·no·*

vra payr soo·pe·rah·ray la mak·kee·na*; **to pull something off** strappare qualcosa *strap·pah·ray kwal·ko·sa*

pullover n il pullover *pool·lo·ver*

pump n la pompa *pohm·pa* ☐ vt pompare *pohm·pah·ray*

pumpkin n la zucca *tsook·ka*

punch n (blow) il pugno *poon·yoh*; (drink) il ponce *pon·che* ☐ vt (with fist) dare* un pugno a *dah·ray oon poon·yoh a*; (ticket etc) forare *fo·rah·ray*

punctual adj (person) puntuale *poon·too·ah·le*; (train) in orario *een o·rah·ryoh*

puncture n la foratura *fo·ra·too·ra*

punish vt punire *poo·nee·re*

punishment n la punizione *poo·nee·tsyoh·ne*

pupil n l'alunno(a) (m/f) *a·loon·no(a)*

purchase n l'acquisto (m) *ak·kwee·stoh* ☐ vt comprare *kom·prah·ray*

pure adj puro(a) *poo·ro(a)*

purée n il purè *poo·re*

purple adj purpureo(a) *poor·poo·re·o(a)*

purpose n lo scopo *sko·poh*; **on purpose** apposta *ap·po·sta*

purse n (for money) il borsellino *bor·sel·lee·noh*; (lady's bag) la borsa *bohr·sa*

push vt spingere* *speen·je·re*; (button) premere *pre·me·re*; (product) lanciare *lan·chah·ray*; **push it in** lo spinga dentro *lo speen·ga dayn·tro*

put vt mettere* *mayt·te·re*; **to put a question** fare* una domanda *fah·ray oo·na do·man·da*; **to put one's things away** mettere* le cose a posto *mayt·te·re le ko·se a poh·stoh*; **to put back** (replace) rimettere* *ree·mayt·te·re*; **to put down a parcel** deporre* un pacco *de·pohr·re oon pak·koh*; **to put on a dress** indossare un abito *een·dos·sah·ray oon ah·bee·toh*; **to put on the light** accendere* la luce *ach·chen·de·re la loo·che*; **to put on the brakes** frenare *fre·nah·ray*; **to put out the light** spegnere* la luce *spen·ye·re la loo·che*; **he put his hand hallungato la mano** a al·loon·gah·to la mah·noh*; **to put someone through** (on phone) mettere* qualcuno in comunicazione *mayt·te·re kwal·koo·no een ko·moo·nee·ka·tsyoh·ne*; **to put up a notice** affiggere* un avviso *af·feej·je·re oon av·vee·zoh*; **to put up capital** fornire del capitale *for·nee·re del ka·pee·tah·le*

puzzle n il rompicapo *rom·pee·kah·poh*; (jigsaw) il puzzle *pa·zel*

pyramid n la piramide *pee·ra·mee·dee*

Pyrenees pl i Pirenei *pee·re·ne·ee*

Q

quail n la quaglia *kwal·ya*

quaint adj curioso(a) *koo·ryoh·so(a)*

qualification n (diploma etc) il titolo *tee·to·loh*; (restriction) la riserva *ree·ser·va*

qualified adj qualificato(a) *kwa·lee·fee·kah·to(a)*

qualify for vt (grant etc) corrispondere* ai requisiti per *kor·ree·spohn·de·re a ee re·kwee·zee·tee payr*; (in sports) qualificarsi per *kwa·lee·fee·kar·see payr*

quality n la qualità *kwa·lee·ta*; **quality goods** gli articoli di qualità *ar·tee·ko·lee dee kwa·lee·ta*

quantity *n* la quantità *kwan·tee·ta*

quarantine *n* la quarantena *kwa·ran·te·na*

quarrel *n* la lite *lee·te* □ *vi* litigare *lee·tee·gah·ray*

quarry *n* la cava *kah·va*

quart *n* due pinte *doo·e peen·te*

quarter *n* il quarto *kwar·toh*; a quarter of an hour un quarto d'ora *oon kwar·toh doh·ra*; (a) quarter to 4 le 4 meno un quarto *le 4 may·no oon kwar·toh*; (a) quarter past 4 le 4 e un quarto *le 4 e oon kwar·toh*

quartz *n* il quarzo *kwar·tsoh*

quay *n* la banchina *ban·kee·na*

quayside *n* la banchina *ban·kee·na*

queen *n* la regina *re·jee·na*

queer *adj* (strange) strano(a) *strah·no(a)*

question *n* la domanda *do·man·da*; (subject discussed) la questione *kwe·styoh·ne*; to ask a question fare* una domanda *fah·ray oo·na do·man·da*; it's a question of è questione di *e kwe·styoh·ne dee*; out of the question fuori discussione *fwo·ree dee·skoos·syoh·ne*

question mark *n* il punto interrogativo *poon·toh een·ter·ro·ga·tee·vo*

questionnaire *n* il questionario *kwe·styoh·nah·ryoh*

quiche *n* la quiche *keesh*

quick *adj* rapido(a) *ra·pee·do(a)*; be quick! faccia presto! *fach·cha pre·sto*

quickly *adv* rapidamente *ra·pee·da·mayn·te*

quiet *adj* tranquillo(a) *tran·kweel·lo(a)*; be quiet! zitto(a)! *tseet·to(a)* A5

quietly *adv* (speak) piano *pyah·no*; (walk, work) silenziosamente *see·len·tsyoh·sa·mayn·te*

quilt *n* la trapunta *tra·poon·ta*

quit *vt* (leave) abbandonare *ab·ban·do·nah·ray* □ *vi* (give up) rinunciare *ree·noon·chah·ray*

quite *adv* (fairly) piuttosto *pyoot·to·sto*; (absolutely) del tutto *del toot·toh*; quite a few abbastanza *ab·ba·stan·tsa*

quiz *n* il quiz *kweez*

quota *n* (of goods) la quota *kwo·ta*

quotation *n* (passage) la citazione *chee·ta·tsyoh·ne*; (price) la quotazione *kwo·ta·tsyoh·ne*

quote *vt* (passage) citare *chee·tah·ray*; (price) quotare *kwo·tah·ray*

R

rabbi *n* il rabbino *rab·bee·noh*

rabbit *n* il coniglio *ko·neel·yoh*

rabies *n* la rabbia *rab·bya*

race *n* la razza *rats·tsa*; (sport) la corsa *kohr·sa*; the races le corse *kohr·se*

racecourse *n* l'ippodromo (*m*) *eep·po·dro·moh*

racehorse *n* il cavallo da corsa *ka·val·loh da kohr·sa*

race relations *pl* i rapporti interrazziali *rap·por·tee een·tayr·rats·tsyah·lee*

race track *n* la pista *pee·sta*

racial *adj* razziale *rats·tsyah·lay*

rack *n* (for luggage) il portabagagli *por·ta·ba·gal·yee*; (for wine) il portabottiglie *por·ta·bot·teel·yay*; (for dishes) lo scolapiatti *sko·la·pyat·tee*

racket *n* (tennis) la racchetta *rak·kayt·ta*

radar *n* il radar *ra·dar*

radar trap *n* il controllo radar *kon·trol·loh ra·dar*

radial ply *adj* cinturato(a) *cheen·too·rah·to(a)*

radiator *n* il radiatore □ *ra·dya·toh·ray* T179

radio *n* la radio *ra·dyoh*; on the radio alla radio *al·la ra·dyoh*

radish *n* il ravanello *ra·va·nel·loh*

rag *n* lo straccio *strach·choh*

ragged *adj* (clothes) a brandelli *a bran·del·lee*

raid *n* (military) l'attacco (*m*) *at·tak·koh*; (by police) l'irruzione (*f*) *eer·roo·tsyoh·nay*; (by criminals) la razzia *rats·tsee·a*

rail *n* (on stairs) il corrimano *kor·ree·mah·noh*; (on bridge, balcony) la ringhiera *reen·gye·ra*; (for train) le rotaie *ro·ta·ye*; by rail per ferrovia *payr fer·ro·vee·a*

railings *pl* la cancellata *kan·chel·lah·ta*

railroad *n* la ferrovia *fer·ro·vee·a*

railroad station *n* la stazione *sta·tsyoh·nay* T69f

rain *vi* piovere* *pyo·ve·re*; it's raining piove *pyo·ve* Mc8

rainbow *n* l'arcobaleno (*m*) *ar·ko·ba·lay·noh*

raincoat *n* l'impermeabile (*m*) *eem·payr·me·ah·bee·lay*

rainy *adj* piovoso(a) *pyo·voh·so(a)*

raise *vt* sollevare *sol·le·vah·ray*; (price) rialzare *ree·al·tsah·ray*; (family) allevare *al·le·vah·ray* □ *n* l'aumento (*m*) *ow·mayn·toh*

raisins *pl* l'uva passa (*f*) *oo·va pas·sa*

rake *n* il rastrello *ra·strel·loh*

rally *n* (political) la manifestazione *ma·nee·fe·sta·tsyoh·nay*; (sporting) il rally *ral·lee*

ramp *n* (slope) la rampa *ram·pa*; (in garage) l'elevatore (*m*) *e·le·va·toh·ray*; entrance/exit ramp lo svincolo *zveen·ko·loh*

ranch *n* il ranch *ranch*

random *adj* fatto(a) a caso *fat·to(a) a kah·zo*; at random a caso *a kah·zo*

range *n* (variety) la scelta *shayl·ta*; (of mountains) la catena *ka·tay·na*; (of missile) la gittata *jeet·tah·ta* □ *vi* to range from X to Y andare* da X a Y *an·dah·ray da X a Y*

range finder *n* (on camera) il telemetro *te·le·me·troh*

rank *n* (status) il rango *ran·goh*

rare *adj* raro(a) *rah·ro(a)*; (steak) al sangue *al san·gwe*

rash *n* l'eruzione (*f*) *e·roo·tsyoh·nay*

raspberry *n* il lampone *lam·poh·nay*

rat *n* il ratto *rat·toh*

rate *n* (price) la tariffa *ta·reef·fa*; at the rate of al ritmo di *al reet·moh dee*; rate of inflation il tasso d'inflazione *tas·soh deen·fla·tsyoh·ne*; rate of exchange il cambio *kam·byoh* M23, Sn21, Bm26

rates *pl* (local tax) le tasse comunali *tas·se ko·moo·nah·lee*

rather *adv* (quite) piuttosto *pyoot·to·sto*; I'd rather go to the movies preferirei andare al cinema *pre·fe·ree·ray an·dah·ray al chee·ne·ma*

ratio *n* il rapporto *rap·por·toh*

rationalization *n* la razionalizzazione *ra·tsyoh·na·leedz·dza·tsyoh·nay*

rationalize *vt* razionalizzare *ra·tsyoh·na·leedz·dzah·ray*

ravioli *n* i ravioli *ra·vee·o·lee*

raw adj (uncooked) crudo(a) kroo·do(a); (unprocessed) grezzo(a) graydz·dzo(a)

raw material n le materie prime ma·te·ree·e pree·me

ray n il raggio raj·joh

razor n il rasoio ra·soh·yo A42

razor blade n la lametta da barba la·met·ta da bar·ba

reach vt (arrive at) arrivare a ar·ree·vah·ray a; (with hand) raggiungere* raj·joon·je·ray; (contact) contattare kon·tat·tah·ray □ n out of reach fuori portata fwo·ree por·tah·ta; within easy reach of the sea a poca distanza dal mare a po·ka dee·stan·tsa dal mah·re

reaction n la reazione re·a·tsyoh·nay

reactor n il reattore re·at·toh·ray

read vt/i leggere* lej·je·re

readdress vt fare* proseguire fah·ray pro·se·gwee·ray

reading n la lettura let·too·ra

ready adj pronto(a) prohn·to(a); ready to do something pronto(a) a fare qualcosa prohn·to(a) a fah·ray kwal·ko·sa Sn56

ready-cooked adj precotto(a) pre·kot·to(a)

ready-made adj (clothes) confezionato(a) kon·fe·tsyoh·nah·to(a)

ready-to-wear adj prêt-à-porter preh·ta·por·tay

real adj vero(a) vay·roh(a); it's a real problem è un vero problema e oon vay·roh prob·le·ma; in real terms realmente re·al·mayn·tay

real estate n la proprietà fondiaria pro·pree·e·ta fon·dee·ah·ree·a

realize vt rendersi* conto di ren·der·see kohn·toh dee; (assets) realizzare re·a·leedz·dzah·ray

really adv veramente ve·ra·mayn·tay

realtor n l'agente immobiliare (m) a·jen·tay eem·mo·beel·yah·ray

rear adj posteriore po·ste·ryoh·ray □ vt (children, cattle) allevare al·le·vah·ray

rear view mirror n lo specchietto retrovisore spek·kyayt·toh re·tro·vee·zoh·ray

reason n la ragione ra·joh·nay

reasonable adj ragionevole ra·joh·nay·vo·lay

receipt n la ricevuta ree·che·voo·ta; (for parcel) la ricevuta di spedizione ree·che·voo·ta da dee·spe·dee·tsyoh·nay; receipts (income) gli introiti een·tro·ee·tee M14

receive vt (letter) ricevere ree·chay·ve·ray; (guest) accogliere* ak·kol·ye·ray

receiver n (phone) il ricevitore ree·che·vee·toh·ray

recent adj recente re·chen·tay

recently adv recentemente re·chen·te·mayn·tay

reception n il ricevimento ree·che·vee·mayn·toh

reception desk n il ricevimento ree·che·vee·mayn·toh

receptionist n (in hotel) l'addetto(a) al ricevimento (m/f) ad·dayt·to(a) al ree·che·vee·mayn·toh

recession n la recessione re·ches·syoh·nay

recipe n la ricetta ree·chet·ta

recognize vt riconoscere* re·ko·noh·she·ray

recommend vt raccomandare rak·ko·man·dah·ray E10, 17

record n (register) la documentazione

do·koo·men·ta·tsyoh·nay; (file) l'archivio (m) ar·kee·vyoh; (disk) il disco dee·skoh; (in sports) il primato pree·mah·toh □ adj (production, crop etc) record re·kord □ vt registrare re·jee·strah·ray

record-player n il giradischi jee·ra·dee·skee

recover vi (from illness) rimettersi* ree·mayt·ter·see

recruit vt (personnel) assumere* as·soo·me·ray □ n la recluta re·kloo·ta

recruitment n il reclutamento re·kloo·ta·mayn·toh

red adj rosso(a) rohs·so(a)

red currant n il ribes rosso ree·bes rohs·so

red-haired adj dai capelli rossi dai ka·pel·lee rohs·see

redirect n (letter) fare* proseguire fah·ray pro·se·gwee·ray

redistribute vt ridistribuire ree·dee·stree·boo·ee·ray

redistribution n la ridistribuzione ree·dee·stree·boo·tsyoh·nay

red light n (traffic light) la luce rossa loo·che rohs·sa; to go through a red light passare con il rosso pas·sah·ray kohn eel rohs·soh

red light district n il quartiere luce rossa kwar·tyay·ray loo·che rohs·sa

red tape n la burocrazia boo·ro·kra·tsee·a

reduce vt ridurre* ree·door·ray □ vi (lose weight) dimagrire dee·ma·gree·ray

reduction n la riduzione ree·doo·tsyoh·nay; (in price) il ribasso ree·bas·soh; to buy something at a reduction comprare qualcosa a prezzo ridotto kom·prah·ray kwal·ko·sa a prets·tsoh ree·doht·to 13

redundant adj (worker) licenziato(a) lee·chen·tsyah·to(a)

referee n (sports) l'arbitro (m) ar·bee·troh

reference n (mention) la menzione men·tsyoh·nay; (testimonial) le referenze re·fe·ren·tse; his reference to this matter la sua menzione di quest'affare la soo·a men·tsyoh·nay dee kway·staf·fah·ray; with reference to your letter in riferimento alla vostra lettera een ree·fe·ree·mayn·toh al·la vo·stra let·te·ra

refer to vt (allude to) alludere* a al·loo·de·ray a; (consult) consultare kon·sool·tah·ray

refine vt raffinare raf·fee·nah·ray

refinery n la raffineria raf·fee·ne·ree·a

reflect vt riflettere* re·flet·te·ray

reflector n (on cycle, car) il catarifrangente ka·ta·ree·fran·jen·tay

refreshments pl i rinfreschi reen·fray·skee

refrigerator n il frigorifero free·go·ree·fe·roh

refund vt rimborsare reem·bor·sah·ray □ n il rimborso reem·bohr·soh

refusal n il rifiuto ree·fyoo·toh

refuse vt rifiutare ree·fyoo·tah·ray; to refuse to do something rifiutarsi di fare qualcosa ree·fyoo·tar·see da fah·ray kwal·ko·sa

regarding prep per quanto riguarda payr kwan·to ree·gwar·da

regardless of prep senza riguardo a sen·tsa ree·gwar·do a

regatta n la regata re·gah·ta

region n la regione re·joh·nay

register n il registro re·jee·stroh

registered letter n la lettera raccomandata *let·te·ra rak·ko·man·dah·ta* Sn6

registered mail n □ **by registered mail con ricevuta di ritorno** *kohn ree·che·voo·ta dee ree·tohr·noh*

registered trademark n il marchio di fabbrica depositato *mar·kyoh dee fab·bree·ka de·po·zee·tah·to*

regret vt rincrescere* *reen·kray·she·ray*

regular adj regolare *re·go·lah·ray*; (usual) abituale *a·bee·too·ah·le*; (ordinary) normale *nor·mah·le*; (size) normale *nor·mah·le*

regulation n (rule) il regolamento *re·go·la·mayn·toh*

rehearsal n la prova *pro·va*

rein n la briglia *breel·ya*

reject vt respingere* *re·speen·je·ray*; (goods in manufacture) rifiutare *ree·fyoo·tah·ray* □ n l'articolo difettoso (m) *ar·tee·ko·loh dee·fet·toh·so*

relation n il/la parente *pa·ren·te*

relative n il/la parente *pa·ren·te* □ adj relativo(a) *re·la·tee·vo(a)*

relax vi rilassarsi *ree·las·sar·see*

release vt (prisoner) liberare *lee·be·rah·ray*; (book, film) fare* uscire *fah·ray oo·shee·ray*

relevant adj relativo(a) *re·la·tee·vo(a)*; **relevant to** pertinente a *payr·tee·nen·te a*

reliability n (of person) la serietà *se·ree·e·ta*; (of car) l'affidabilità (f) *af·fee·da·bee·lee·ta*

reliable adj (person) fidato(a) *fee·dah·to(a)*; (car) solido(a) *so·lee·do(a)*

relief n (from pain, anxiety) il sollievo *sol·ye·voh*

religion n la religione *re·lee·joh·nay*

religious adj (person) religioso(a) *re·lee·joh·so(a)*

rely on vt (person) contare su *kon·tah·ray soo*

remain vi rimanere* *ree·ma·nay·ray*; (be left over) avanzare *a·van·tsah·ray*

remark n l'osservazione (f) *os·sayr·va·tsyoh·nay*

remarkable adj notevole *no·tay·vo·lay*

remedy n il rimedio *ree·me·dyoh*

remember vt ricordarsi di *ree·kor·dar·see dee*

remind vt ricordare *ree·kor·dah·re*; **to remind someone of something** ricordare qualcosa a qualcuno *ree·kor·dah·ray kwal·ko·sa a kwal·koo·no*

remittance n la rimessa *ree·mays·sa*

remote control n il telecomando *te·le·ko·man·doh*

remove vt spostare *spo·stah·ray*; (stain) togliere* *tol·ye·re*

renew vt (subscription, passport) rinnovare *reen·no·vah·ray*

rent n l'affitto (m) *af·feet·toh* □ vt (house etc) affittare *af·feet·tah·ray*; (car) noleggiare *no·lej·jah·ray* A56f, L29

rental n il noleggio *no·layj·joh* A61

rental car n la macchina noleggiata *mak·kee·na no·lej·jah·ta* T108f

reorder vt (goods) riordinare *ree·or·dee·nah·ray*

reorganization n la riorganizzazione *ree·or·ga·needz·dza·tsyoh·nay*

reorganize vt riorganizzare *ree·or·ga·needz·dzah·ray*

repair vt riparare *ree·pa·rah·ray* T188, Sn46f

repay vt (sum) ripagare *ree·pa·gah·ray*; (person) rimborsare *reem·bor·sah·ray*

repeat vt ripetere *ree·pe·te·ray*

repeat order n l'ordine successivo (m) *ohr·dee·ne soo·ches·see·vo*

repetition n la ripetizione *ree·pe·tee·tsyoh·nay*

replace vt (put back) rimettere* *ree·mayt·te·ray*; (substitute) sostituire *so·stee·too·ee·ray*

replacement n la sostituzione *so·stee·too·tsyoh·nay*

reply vi rispondere* *ree·spohn·de·ray*; **to reply to a question** rispondere* a una domanda *ree·spohn·de·ray a una do·man·da* □ n **reply** la risposta *ree·spoh·sta*

report vt riportare *ree·por·tah·ray* □ n il rapporto *rap·por·toh*; (in press) il servizio *sayr·vee·tsyoh*

reporter n (press) il/la cronista *kro·nee·sta*

represent vt rappresentare *rap·pre·zen·tah·ray*

representative n il/la rappresentante *rap·pre·zen·tan·te* T18, Bm19

republic n la repubblica *re·poob·blee·ka*

republican adj repubblicano(a) *re·poob·blee·kah·no(a)*

reputation n la fama *fah·ma*

request n la richiesta *ree·kye·sta*

require vt (need) avere* bisogno di *a·vay·ray bee·zohn·yoh dee*

requirement n l'esigenza (f) *e·zee·jen·tsa*

reroute vt deviare *de·vee·ah·ray*

resale n □ **not for resale** rivendita proibita *ree·vayn·dee·ta pro·ee·bee·ta*

rescue vt salvare *sal·vah·ray* □ n il salvataggio *sal·va·taj·joh*

research n la ricerca *ree·chayr·ka*

resell vt rivendere *ree·vayn·de·ray*

resemble vt rassomigliare *ras·so·meel·yah·ray*; **he resembles his father** rassomiglia a suo padre *ras·so·meel·ya a soo·o pah·dre*

reservation n (of seats, rooms etc) la prenotazione *pre·no·ta·tsyoh·nay*; (doubt) la riserva *ree·ser·va* A57

reserve vt (seat, room) riservare *ree·ser·vah·ray*; (tickets) prenotare *pre·no·tah·ray* B35, A13, E2

reserves pl le riserve *ree·ser·ve*

residence n la residenza *re·see·den·tsa*

residence permit n il permesso di soggiorno *payr·mays·soh dee soj·johr·noh*

residential adj (area) residenziale *re·see·den·tsyah·le*

resign vt dimettersi* *dee·mayt·ter·see*

resignation n le dimissioni *dee·mees·syoh·nee*

resist vt resistere* *re·see·ste·ray*

resistance n (to illness) la resistenza *re·see·sten·tsa*

resort n il luogo di villeggiatura *lwo·go dee veel·lej·ja·too·ra*; **in the last resort** in ultimo *een ool·tee·mo* □ vi **to resort to** ricorrere* a *ree·kohr·re·ray a*

resources pl le risorse *ree·sohr·se*

respect n il rispetto *ree·spet·toh* □ vt rispettare *ree·spet·tah·ray*

respectable adj rispettabile *ree·spet·tah·bee·lay*

responsibility n la responsabilità *re·spon·sa·bee·lee·ta*; **this is your responsibility** questo è di Sua responsabilità *kway·stoh e dee soo·a re·spon·sa·bee·lee·ta*

responsible adj responsabile *re·spon·sah·bee·lay*; **responsible for** (to

blame) responsabile di re·spon·sah·
bee·lay dee; he's responsible for the
department è lui il responsabile del
dipartimento e loo·ee eel re·spon·
sah·bee·lay del dee·par·tee·mayn·toh

rest *vi* riposarsi ree·po·sar·see □ *n* (re-
pose) il riposo ree·po·soh; all the rest
tutto il resto toot·to eel re·sto

restaurant *n* il ristorante ree·sto·ran·te
B59, E1

restrict *vt* limitare lee·mee·tah·ray

restriction *n* la restrizione re·stree·
tsyoh·nay

restroom *n* la toeletta to·e·let·ta

result *n* il risultato ree·sool·tah·toh

retail *n* la vendita al minuto vayn·dee·
ta al mee·noo·toh; to sell something
retail vendere qualcosa al minuto
vayn·de·re kwal·ko·sa al mee·noo·toh
□ *vt* retail vendere al minuto vayn·
de·re al mee·noo·toh

retailer *n* il dettagliante det·tal·yan·te

retail price *n* il prezzo al minuto prets·
tsoh al mee·noo·toh Bm25

retire *vi* andare* in pensione an·dah·
ray een pen·syoh·nay

retired *adj* in pensione een pen·syoh·
nay

retiree *n* il/la pensionato(a) pen·see·
oh·nah·to(a)

retirement *n* il ritiro ree·tee·ro

retrain *vt* riaddestrare ree·ad·de·strah·
ray □ *vi* riaddestrarsi ree·ad·de·strar·
see

retraining *n* il riaddestramento ree·ad·
de·stra·mayn·toh

retread *n* lo pneumatico rimodellato
pne·oo·ma·tee·koh ree·mo·del·lah·
toh

retrieve *vt* (*data*) ricuperare ree·koo·
pe·rah·ray

retrospect *n* □ in retrospect retrospettivamente re·tro·spet·tee·va·mayn·tay

return *vi* tornare tor·nah·ray □ *vt* (*give
back*) restituire re·stee·too·ee·ray;
(*send back*) rinviare reen·vee·ah·ray
□ *n* (*going/coming back*) il ritorno
ree·tohr·noh; (*profit*) il guadagno
gwa·dan·yoh

rev *vi* (*in engine*) il giro jee·roh □ *vt*
imballare eem·bal·lah·ray

revenue *n* il reddito ree·dee·toh

reverse *n* (*gear*) la retromarcia re·tro·
mar·cha; in reverse (*gear*) in retromarcia een re·tro·mar·cha □ *vt* to reverse the charges telefonare ad onere
del destinatario te·le·fo·nah·ray ad o·
ne·re del de·stee·na·tah·ree·oh

reversed charge call *n* la telefonata
con la R te·le·fo·nah·ta kohn la er·re

review *n* la revisione re·vee·zee·oh·
nay; (*of book etc*) la recensione re·
chen·syoh·nay □ *vt* riesaminare ree·
e·za·mee·nah·ray

revise *vt* (*estimate etc*) rivedere* ree·
ve·day·re; (*school work*) ripassare ree·
pas·sah·ray

revive *vt* (*person*) rianimare ree·a·nee·
mah·ray □ *vi* riprendere* i sensi ree·
pren·de·re ee sen·see

revolution *n* (*political*) la rivoluzione
ree·vo·loo·tsyoh·nay

revue *n* la rivista ree·vee·sta

reward *n* la ricompensa ree·kom·
pen·sa

rheumatism *n* il reumatismo re·oo·ma·
tee·zmoh

Rhine *n* il Reno re·no

Rhine (*wine*) *n* il vino del Reno vee·
noh del re·no

Rhone *n* il Rodano ro·da·no

rhubarb *n* il rabarbaro ra·bar·ba·roh

rhythm *n* il ritmo reet·moh

rib *n* la costola ko·sto·la

ribbon *n* il nastro na·stroh

rice *n* il riso ree·soh

rich *adj* ricco(a) reek·ko(a); (*food*) pesante pe·san·te

ride *n* (*in vehicle*) il percorso payr·
kohr·soh; (*on horse*) la cavalcata ka·
val·kah·ta; to go for a ride (*by car*)
fare* un giro in macchina fa·re
oon jee·roh een mak·kee·na; to give
someone a ride into town dare* un
passaggio in città a qualcuno dah·ray
oon pas·saj·joh een cheet·ta a kwal·
koo·noh; it's only a short ride non è
che un breve percorso nohn e ke oon
bre·ve payr·kohr·soh □ *vt* to ride a
horse cavalcare ka·val·kah·ray; to
ride a bicycle andare* in bicicletta
an·dah·ray een bee·chee·klayt·ta

ridge *n* il giogo joh·goh

ridiculous *adj* ridicolo(a) ree·dee·ko·
lo(a)

riding *n* la cavalcata ka·val·kah·ta; to
go riding cavalcare ka·val·kah·ray
L35

rifle *n* il fucile foo·chee·le

right *adj* (*correct*) corretto(a) kor·rayt·
to(a); (*morally good*) giusto(a) joo·
sto(a); (*not left*) destro(a) de·stro(a);
yes, that's right sí, giusto see joo·sto
□ *adv* to turn right girare a destra
jee·rah·ray a de·stra; right in the
middle proprio nel mezzo pro·pree·o
nel medz·dzoh □ *n* right (*right-hand
side*) la destra de·stra; (*entitlement*) il
diritto dee·reet·toh; on/to the right a
destra a de·stra B34, T104

right-handed *adj* chi usa di preferenza
la mano destra kee oo·za dee pre·fe·
ren·tsa la mah·no de·stra

right of way *n* (*on road*) la precedenza
pre·che·den·tsa

ring *n* (*on finger*) l'anello (*m*) a·nel·
loh; (*circle*) il cerchio chayr·kyoh;
(*wedding ring*) la fede fay·de □ *vt* to
ring the (*door*)bell suonare swo·nah·
ray □ *vi* ring suonare swo·nah·ray;
(*telephone*) squillare skweel·lah·ray
S86

rink *n* la pista di pattinaggio pee·sta
dee pat·tee·naj·joh

rinse *vt* risciacquare ree·shak·kwah·ray
□ *n* (*hair tint*) la tintura teen·too·ra

riot *n* il tumulto too·mool·toh

rip *vt* strappare strap·pah·ray □ *vi*
strapparsi strap·par·see

ripe *adj* (*fruit*) maturo(a) ma·too·
ro(a); (*cheese*) stagionato(a) sta·joh·
nah·to(a)

rise *vi* (*go up*) salire* sa·lee·ray;
(*prices*) aumentare ow·men·tah·ray;
(*person*) alzarsi al·tsar·see; (*sun*) sorgere* sohr·je·re □ *n* (*in prices,
wages*) il rialzo ree·al·tsoh

risk *n* il rischio ree·skyoh □ *vt* rischiare
ree·skyah·ray

risotto *n* il risotto ree·sot·toh

rival *n* il/la rivale ree·vah·le; a rival
firm una ditta concorrente oo·na
deet·ta kon·kor·ren·te

river *n* il fiume fyoo·me

Riviera *n* la Costa Azzurra ko·sta adz·
dzoor·ra

road *n* la strada strah·da T133f, F21

road block *n* la barricata bar·ree·
kah·ta

road map *n* la carta stradale kar·ta
stra·dah·le

road sign *n* il segnale sen·yah·le T143f

road test n la prova su strada *pro·va soo strah·da*

road works pl i lavori stradali *la·voh·ree stra·dah·lee*

roar vi (person) urlare *oor·lah·ray*; (lion) ruggire *rooj·jee·ray*; (engine) rimbombare *reem·bom·bah·ray* □ n (of person) l'urlo (m) *oor·loh*; (of lion) il ruggito *rooj·jee·toh*; (of engine) il rombo *rohm·boh*

roast vt arrostire *ar·ro·stee·ray*; roast meat l'arrosto (m) *ar·ro·stoh*

rob vt (person) derubare *de·roo·bah·ray*; (bank) svaligiare *zva·lee·jah·ray*

robbery n il furto *foor·toh*

robe n (after bath) l'accappatoio (m) *ak·kap·pa·toh·yoh*

robot n il robot *ro·bot*

rock n la roccia *roch·cha*; on the rocks (with ice) con ghiaccio *kohn gyach·choh* □ vt rock cullare *kool·lah·ray*

rocket n il razzo *radz·dzoh*

rock ('n' roll n il rock and roll *rok and rol*

rod n (metallic) la barra *bar·ra*; (fishing) la canna da pesca *kan·na da pay·ska*

roll n il rotolo *ro·to·loh*; (bread) il panino *pa·nee·noh* □ vt (on wheels) fare* rotolare *fah·ray ro·to·lah·ray*; to roll up (newspaper etc) arrotolare *ar·ro·to·lah·ray* □ vi roll rotolare *ro·to·lah·ray*

roller skates pl i pattini a rotelle *pat·tee·nee a ro·tel·le*

rolling pin n il matterello *mat·te·rel·loh*

Roman adj romano(a) *ro·mah·no(a)*; Roman Catholic cattolico(a) *kat·to·lee·ko(a)*

Romania n la Romania *ro·ma·nee·a*

Romanian adj romeno(a) *ro·me·no(a)* □ n (language) il romeno *ro·me·noh*

romantic adj romantico(a) *ro·man·tee·ko(a)*

Rome n Roma (f) *roh·ma*

roof n il tetto *tayt·toh*

roof rack n il portabagagli *por·ta·ba·gal·yee*

room n (in house) la stanza *stan·tsa*; (in hotel) la camera *kah·me·ra*; (space) lo spazio *spa·tsyoh*

room service n il servizio di camera *sayr·vee·tsyoh dee kah·me·ra*

root n la radice *ra·dee·chay*

rope n la corda *kor·da*

rose n la rosa *ro·za*

rosé n il rosé *ro·zay*

rot vi marcire *mar·chee·ray*

rotten adj (wood etc) marcio(a) *mar·cho(a)*

rough n (golf) l'erba lunga (f) *er·ba loon·ga* □ adj (surface) ruvido(a) *roo·vee·do(a)*; (weather) burrascoso(a) *boor·ra·skoh·so(a)*; (sea) agitato(a) *a·jee·tah·to(a)*; (not gentle) violento(a) *vee·o·len·to(a)*; a rough estimate un calcolo approssimativo *oon kal·ko·loh ap·pros·see·ma·tee·vo*

roughly adv rudemente *roo·de·mayn·tay*; (approximately) approssimativamente *ap·pros·see·ma·tee·va·mayn·tay*

roulette n la roulette *roo·let*

round adj rotondo(a) *ro·tohn·do(a)* □ n (circle) il cerchio *chayr·kyoh*; (in competition) la partita *par·tee·ta*; (in boxing) il round *rownd*; (of golf) il giro *jee·roh*; (of talks) la serie *se·ree·e* □ prep intorno a *een·tohr·no a*; to go round the shops fare* un giro dei

negozi *fah·ray oon jee·roh de·ee ne·go·tsee*; it's round the corner è dietro l'angolo *e dye·tro lan·go·loh* □ adv to turn something round girare qualcosa *jee·rah·ray kwal·ko·sa*

round figure/number n la cifra tonda *cheef·ra tohn·da*

round trip n il viaggio di andata e ritorno *vyaj·joh dee an·dah·ta e ree·tohr·noh* T58

round trip (ticket) n il biglietto di andata e ritorno *beel·yayt·toh dee an·dah·ta e ree·tohr·noh*

route n l'itinerario (m) *ee·tee·ne·rah·ryoh* T133, F18

routine n la routine *roo·teen* □ adj comune *ko·moo·ne*

row¹ n la fila *fee·la* □ vi (sport) remare *re·mah·ray*

row² n (noise) lo schiamazzo *skya·mats·tsoh*

rowing n (sport) il canottaggio *ka·not·taj·joh*

royal adj reale *re·ah·le*

R.S.V.P. abbrev R.S.V.P.

rub vt fregare *fre·gah·ray*; to rub out cancellare *kan·chel·lah·ray*

rubber n (material) la gomma *gohm·ma*

rubber band n l'elastico (m) *e·la·stee·koh*

rubbish n i rifiuti *ree·fyoo·tee*; (nonsense) le sciocchezze *shok·kayts·tse*

ruby n il rubino *roo·bee·noh*

rucksack n lo zaino *dzy·noh*

rudder n il timone *tee·moh·nay*

rude adj (person) grossolano(a) *gros·so·lah·no(a)*; (remark) scortese *skor·tay·zay*

rug n il tappetino *tap·pe·tee·noh*

rugby n il rugby *roog·bee*

ruin n la rovina *ro·vee·na* □ vt rovinare *ro·vee·nah·ray*

ruins pl le rovine *ro·vee·ne*

rule n (regulation) la regola *re·go·la*; (for measuring) il regolo *re·go·loh* □ vt governare *go·vayr·nah·ray*

ruler n (leader) il capo *kah·poh*; (for measuring) il regolo *re·go·loh*

rum n il rum *room*

rumble vi rombare *rom·bah·ray* □ n il rombo *rohm·boh*

rump steak n la bistecca di girello *bee·stayk·ka dee jee·rel·loh*

run n (outing) la gita *jee·ta*; (in stocking) la smagliatura *zmal·ya·too·ra* □ vi (person, animal) correre* *kohr·re·re*; (liquid) scorrere* *skohr·re·re*; (machine, engine) funzionare *foon·tsyoh·nah·ray*; the trains run every hour i treni partono ogni ora *ee tre·nee par·to·no ohn·yee oh·ra*; the road runs past the house la strada passa davanti alla casa *la strah·da pas·sa da·van·tee al·la kah·sa*; this car runs on diesel questa macchina funziona a nafta *kway·sta mak·kee·na foon·tsyoh·na a naf·ta*; to run after someone correre* dietro a qualcuno *kohr·re·re dye·tro a kwal·koo·no*; to run away fuggire *fooj·jee·re*; to run down or over (car etc) investire *een·ve·stee·ray*; we've run out of milk siamo rimasti senza latte *syah·mo ree·ma·stee sen·tsa lat·te* □ vt run (a business, country) dirigere* *dee·ree·je·ray*

runner beans pl i fagiolini *fa·jo·lee·nee*

running costs pl il costo di esercizio *ko·stoh dee e·zayr·chee·tsyoh*

runway n la pista *pee·sta*

rural adj rurale *roo·rah·le*

rush vi precipitarsi *pre·chee·pee·tar·see* □ vt (goods) mandare con urgenza *man·dah·ray kohn oor·jen·tsa* □ n la fretta *frayt·ta*; **we had a rush of orders** siamo stati inondati di ordinazioni *syah·mo stah·tee een·on·dah·tee dee or·dee·na·tsyoh·nee*

rush hour n l'ora di punta (f) *oh·ra dee poon·ta*

Russia n Russia (f) *roos·sya*

Russian adj russo(a) *roos·so(a)* □ n (language) il russo *roos·soh*

rust n la ruggine *rooj·jee·ne* □ vi arrugginirsi *ar·rooj·jee·neer·see*

rustproof adj inossidabile *een·os·see·dah·bee·lay*

rusty adj arrugginito(a) *ar·rooj·jee·nee·to(a)*

rutabaga n la rapa *ra·pa*

rye n la segale *say·ga·le*; **rye (whiskey)** il whisky di segale *wee·skee dee say·ga·le*

rye bread n il pane di segale *pa·ne dee say·ga·le*

S

saccharin n la saccarina *sak·ka·ree·na*

sachet n la bustina *boo·stee·na*

sack n il sacco *sak·koh* □ vt (dismiss) licenziare *lee·chen·tsyah·ray*

sad adj triste *tree·ste*

saddle n la sella *sel·la*

safe adj (out of danger) salvo(a) *sal·vo(a)*; (not dangerous) innocuo(a) *een·no·kwo(a)* □ n la cassaforte *kas·sa·for·te* A34

safeguard n la salvaguardia *sal·va·gwar·dya*

safety n la sicurezza *see·koo·rayts·tsa*

safety belt n la cintura di sicurezza *cheen·too·ra dee see·koo·rayts·tsa*

safety pin n lo spillo di sicurezza *speel·loh dee see·koo·rayts·tsa*

sage n (herb) la salvia *sal·vya*

sail n la vela *vay·la* □ vi veleggiare *ve·lej·jah·ray* L30

sailboat n il veliero *ve·lye·roh* L29

sailor n il marinaio *ma·ree·na·yoh*

saint n il/la santo(a) *san·to(a)*

sake n □ **for my sake** per me *payr may*

salad n l'insalata (f) *een·sa·lah·ta* E39

salad dressing n il condimento per l'insalata *kon·dee·mayn·toh payr leen·sa·lah·ta*

salary n lo stipendio *stee·pen·dyoh*

sale n la vendita *vayn·dee·ta*; (cheap prices) i saldi *sal·dee*; **on sale or return** da vendere o rimandare *da vayn·de·re o ree·man·dah·ray* Bm19

sales pl (cheap prices) i saldi *sal·dee*

sales assistant n il/la commesso(a) *kom·mays·so(a)*

salesman n (rep) il commesso viaggiatore *kom·mays·soh vyaj·ja·toh·re*

sales manager n il direttore delle vendite *dee·ret·toh·re del·le vayn·dee·te*

saliva n la saliva *sa·lee·va*

salmon n il salmone *sal·moh·ne*

saloon n (bar) il bar *bar*

salt n il sale *sah·le* S32

salt cellar n la saliera *sa·lye·ra*

salty adj salato(a) *sa·lah·to(a)*

same adj stesso(a) *stays·so(a)*; **the same book as** (similar) lo stesso libro di/che *lo stays·so lee·broh dee/kay* □ pron **all the same** nondimeno *nohn·dee·may·no*; (the) **same again please!** lo stesso, per favore *lo stays·soh payr fa·voh·re*

sample n (of goods) il campione *kam·pyoh·ne* □ vt (wine) degustare *de·goo·stah·ray* Bm21

sanctions pl le sanzioni *san·tsyoh·nee*

sand n la sabbia *sab·bya*

sandal n il sandalo *san·da·loh*

sandbank n il banco di sabbia *ban·koh dee sab·bya*

sandwich n il panino imbottito *pa·nee·noh eem·bot·tee·to*; **a ham sandwich** un panino al prosciutto *oon pa·nee·noh al pro·shoot·toh* E70

sandy adj (beach) sabbioso(a) *sab·byoh·so(a)*

sanitarium n il sanatorio *sa·na·to·ryoh*

sanitary napkin n l'assorbente igienico (m) *as·sor·ben·te ee·je·nee·ko*

sarcastic adj sarcastico(a) *sar·ka·stee·ko(a)*

sardine n la sardina *sar·dee·na*

Sardinia n Sardegna (f) *sar·dayn·ya*

satellite n il satellite *sa·tel·lee·te*

satin n il raso *rah·soh*

satire n (play) la satira *sa·tee·ra*

satisfactory adj soddisfacente *sod·dee·sfa·chen·te*

satisfy vt soddisfare* *sod·dee·sfah·ray*

saturate vt (market) saturare *sa·too·rah·ray*

Saturday n sabato (m) *sah·ba·toh*

sauce n la salsa *sal·sa*

saucepan n la pentola *payn·to·la*

saucer n il piattino *pyat·tee·noh*

sauna n la sauna *sow·na* A11

sausage n la salsiccia *sal·seech·cha*

sausage roll n il rustico con salsicetta *roo·stee·koh kohn sal·see·chayt·ta*

sauté adj saltato(a) *sal·tah·to(a)*

save vt (person) salvare *sal·vah·ray*; (money) risparmiare *ree·spar·myah·ray*

savings account n il conto deposito *kohn·to de·po·zee·toh*

savings and loan association n la società immobiliare *so·che·ta eem·mo·beel·yah·re*

savings bank n la cassa di risparmio *kas·sa dee ree·spar·myoh*

savory adj (not sweet) salato(a) *sa·lah·to(a)*

say vt dire* *dee·re*; **could you say that again?** può ripetere quello? *pwo ree·pe·te·re kwayl·lo*

scab n la crosta *kro·sta*

scald vt scottarsi *skot·tar·see*

scale n la scala *skah·la*; (of fish) la scaglia *skal·ya*; **scale of charges** la tariffa *ta·reef·fa*

scales pl (for weighing) la bilancia *bee·lan·cha*

scallion n lo scalogno *ska·lohn·yoh*

scallop n il pettine *pet·tee·ne*

scalp n il cuoio capelluto *kwo·yoh ka·pel·loo·to*

scampi n gli scampi *skam·pee*

Scandinavia n Scandinavia (f) *skan·dee·nah·vya*

Scandinavian adj scandinavo(a) *skan·dee·nah·vo(a)*

scar n la cicatrice *chee·ka·tree·che*

scarce adj raro(a) *rah·ro(a)*

scarcely adv appena *ap·pay·na*

scared adj □ **to be scared** avere* paura *a·vay·re pa·oo·ra*

scarf n la sciarpa *shar·pa*

scarlet adj scarlatto(a) *skar·lat·to(a)*

scene n la scena *she·na*; (sight) la veduta *ve·doo·ta*

scenery n il paesaggio *pa·e·zaj·joh*

scenic route n l'itinerario turistico (m)

ee·tee·ne·rah·ryoh too·ree·stee·ko
F19

scent *n* (*smell*) l'odore (*m*) *o·doh·re*; (*perfume*) il profumo *pro·foo·moh*
S45

schedule *n* il programma *pro·gram·ma*; (*of trains etc*) l'orario (*m*) *o·rah·ryoh*; **on schedule** (*train*) in orario *een o·rah·ryoh*

scheduled flight *n* il volo di linea *voh·loh dee lee·ne·a*

scheme *n* (*plan*) il progetto *pro·jet·toh*

school *n* la scuola *skwo·la*

science *n* la scienza *shen·tsa*

science fiction *n* la fantascienza *fan·ta·shen·tsa*

scientific *adj* scientifico(a) *shen·tee·fee·ko(a)*

scientist *n* lo/la scienziato(a) *shen·tsyah·to(a)*

scissors *pl* le forbici *for·bee·chee*

scooter *n* lo scooter *skoo·ter*

scope *n* □ **within the scope of** entro le possibilità di *ayn·tro le pos·see·bee·lee·ta dee*

score *n* il punteggio *poon·tayj·joh* □ *vt* (*goal*) segnare *sayn·yah·ray*

Scot *n* lo/la scozzese *skots·tsay·se*

Scotch *n* (*liquor*) il whisky scozzese *wee·skee skots·tsay·se*

Scotch tape *n* il nastro adesivo *na·stroh a·de·zee·vo* S93

Scotland *n* Scozia (*f*) *sko·tsya*

Scottish *adj* scozzese *skots·tsay·se*

scourer *n* la spugnetta abrasiva *spoon·yayt·ta a·bra·zee·va*

scrap *n* (*bit*) il pezzettino *pets·tset·tee·noh*

scrape *vt* strisciare *stree·shah·ray*

scratch *vt* graffiare *graf·fyah·ray*

scream *vi* strillare *streel·lah·ray*

screen *n* (*partition*) il paravento *pa·ra·ven·toh*; (*TV, movie*) lo schermo *skayr·moh*

screw *n* la vite *vee·te*

screwdriver *n* il cacciavite *kach·cha·vee·te*

sculpture *n* la scultura *skool·too·ra* L16

sea *n* il mare *mah·re*; **to go by sea** andare* per mare *an·dah·ray payr mah·re*

seafood *n* i frutti di mare *froot·tee de mah·re*

seafront *n* il lungomare *loon·go·mah·re*

sea level *n* il livello del mare *lee·vel·loh del mah·re*

seam *n* la costura *ko·stoo·ra*

search *vt* perquisire *payr·kwee·zee·re*; **to search for** cercare *cher·kah·ray*

seasick *adj* □ **to be seasick** avere* mal di mare *a·vay·re mal dee mah·re*

seaside *n* il mare *mah·re*; **seaside resort** la stazione balneare *sta·tsyoh·ne bal·ne·ah·re*

season *n* la stagione *sta·joh·ne*; **the vacation season** la stagione di villeggiatura *la sta·joh·ne dee veel·lej·ja·too·ra*; **strawberries are in season** è la stagione delle fragole *e la sta·joh·ne del·le frah·go·le*

seasoning *n* il condimento *kon·dee·mayn·toh*

season ticket *n* l'abbonamento (*m*) *ab·bo·na·mayn·toh*

seat *n* il posto *poh·stoh*; **take a seat** si accomodi *see ak·ko·mo·dee* T9, 44, 62, L45

seat belt *n* la cintura di sicurezza *cheen·too·ra dee see·koo·rayts·tsa*

seaweed *n* le alghe *al·ge*

second *n* (*time*) il secondo *se·kohn·doh* □ *adj* secondo(a) *se·kohn·do(a)*

secondary *adj* (*importance*) secondario(a) *se·kon·dah·ryo(a)*

secondary school *n* la scuola media *skwo·la me·dya*

second-class *adj* di seconda classe *dee se·kohn·da klas·se*

second floor *n* il primo piano *pree·mo pyah·noh*

secondhand *adj* (*car etc*) di seconda mano *dee se·kohn·da mah·noh* S14

secret *adj* segreto(a) *se·gray·to(a)* □ *n* il segreto *se·gray·toh*

secretary *n* il/la segretario(a) *se·gre·tah·ryo(a)* Bm7, 12

secretary of state *n* il Segretario di Stato *se·gre·tah·ryoh dee stah·toh*

sector *n* (*economy*) il settore *set·toh·re*

security *n* (*at airport*) la sicurezza *see·koo·rayts·tsa*; (*for loan*) la cauzione *kow·tsyoh·ne*

sedan *n* (*car*) la berlina *ber·lee·na*

sedative *n* il sedativo *se·da·tee·voh*

see *vt/i* vedere* *ve·day·re*; **to see someone off at the station** accompagnare qualcuno alla stazione *ak·kom·pan·yah·ray kwal·koo·no al·la sta·tsyoh·ne*; **to see someone home** accompagnare qualcuno a casa *ak·kom·pan·yah·ray kwal·koo·no a kah·sa*; **to see to something** occuparsi di qualcosa *ok·koo·par·see dee kwal·ko·sa*

seed *n* il seme *say·me*

seem *vi* sembrare *sem·brah·ray*

seersucker *n* il crespo di cotone *kray·spoh dee ko·toh·ne*

seesaw *n* l'altalena (*f*) *al·ta·lay·na*

seldom *adv* raramente *rah·ra·mayn·te*

selection *n* la scelta *shayl·ta* S44, Bm21

self-contained *adj* (*apartment*) indipendente *een·dee·pen·den·te*

self-employed *adj* autonomo(a) *ow·to·no·mo(a)*

selfish *adj* egoistico(a) *e·go·ee·stee·ko(a)*

self-service *adj* self-service *self·ser·vees*

sell *vt* vendere *vayn·de·re* S7

semifinal *n* la semifinale *se·mee·fee·nah·le*

semiskilled *adj* semispecializzato(a) *se·mee·spe·cha·leedz·dzah·to(a)*

senate *n* (*political*) il senato *se·nah·toh*

senator *n* il senatore *se·na·toh·re*

send *vt* mandare *man·dah·ray*

sender *n* il/la mittente *meet·ten·te*

senior *adj* (*in rank*) superiore *soo·pe·ryoh·re*; (*in age*) maggiore *maj·joh·re*

sense *n* (*feeling*) il senso *sen·soh*; (*common sense*) il senso comune *sen·soh ko·moo·ne*; **sense of humor** la vena d'umorismo *vay·na doo·mo·ree·zmoh*; **to make sense** avere* senso *a·vay·re sen·soh*

sensible *adj* ragionevole *ra·jo·nay·vo·le*

sentence *n* la frase *frah·ze*

separate *adj* separato(a) *se·pa·rah·to(a)*

September *n* settembre (*m*) *set·tem·bre*

serious *adj* serio(a) *se·ryo(a)*

serve *vt* servire *ser·vee·re*

service *n* il servizio *ser·vee·tsyoh*; (*for car*) la revisione *re·vee·zyoh·ne*; (*in church*) l'ufficio (*m*) *oof·fee·choh*

service area *n* l'area di servizio (*f*) *ah·re·a dee ser·vee·tsyoh*

service charge *n* il servizio *ser·vee·tsyoh* M4, E44

service industry n l'industria terziaria (f) *een·doo·stree·a ter·tsyah·rya*

service station n la stazione di servizio *sta·tsyoh·ne dee ser·vee·tsyoh* F9

serviette n il tovagliolo *to·val·yo·loh*

set n (collection) la collezione *kol·le·tsyoh·ne* □ vt (alarm) mettere* *mayt·te·re*; to set the table apparecchiare la tavola *ap·pa·rek·kyah·ray la tah·vo·la*; to have one's hair set.farsi* fare la messa in piega *far·see fah·ray la mays·sa een pye·ga*; to set off or out avviarsi *av·vee·ar·see*

settle vt (argument) regolare *re·go·lah·ray*; (bill) saldare *sal·dah·ray* □ vi (wine) depositare *de·po·zee·tah·ray*; to settle out of court conciliare una causa in via amichevole *kon·chee·lyah·ray oo·na kow·za een vee·a a mee·kay·vo·le*; to settle in installarsi *een·stal·lar·see*

settled adj (weather) stazionario(a) *sta·tsyoh·nah·ryo(a)*

seven num sette *set·te*

seventeen num diciassette *dee·chas·set·te*

seventeenth adj diciassettesimo(a) *dee·chas·set·te·zee·mo(a)*

seventh adj settimo(a) *set·tee·mo(a)*

seventy num settanta *set·tan·ta*

several adj parecchi(ie) *pa·rayk·kee (·kye)* □ pron several of us parecchi di noi *pa·rayk·kee dee noy*

sew vi cucire *koo·chee·re* Sn76

sewing machine n la macchina per cucire *mak·kee·na payr koo·chee·re*

sex n il sesso *ses·soh*

sexual intercourse n i rapporti sessuali *rap·por·tee ses·soo·ah·lee*

sexy adj sexy *sek·see*

shade n l'ombra (f) *ohm·bra*; (for lamp) il paralume *pa·ra·loo·me*

shades pl (sunglasses) gli occhiali da sole *ok·kyah·lee da soh·le*

shadow n l'ombra (f) *ohm·bra*

shake vt agitare *a·jee·tah·ray*; to shake hands with someone stringere* la mano a qualcuno *streen·je·re la mah·noh a kwal·koo·no* □ vi shake tremare *tre·mah·ray*

shall vi □ I shall do it lo farò *lo fa·ro*; shall I do it? lo faccio io? *lo fach·cho ee·o*; shall we come tomorrow? veniamo domani? *ve·nyah·mo do·mah·nee*

shallow adj poco profondo(a) *po·ko pro·fohn·do(a)*

shame n la vergogna *ver·gohn·ya*; what a shame! che peccato! *ke pek·kah·toh*

shampoo n lo sciampo *shahm·poh* Sn41

shandygaff n la birra con limonata *beer·ra kohn lee·mo·nah·ta*

shape n la forma *fohr·ma*

share n (part) la parte *par·te*; (finance) l'azione (f) *a·tsyoh·ne* □ vt (money, room) dividere* *dee·vee·de·re*

shark n il pescecane *pe·she·kah·ne*

sharp adj (knife) affilato(a) *af·fee·lah·to(a)*; (bend) brusco(a) *broo·sko(a)*; (intelligent) sveglio(a) *zvayl·yo(a)*

sharp practice n la prassi disonesta *pras·see dee·zo·ne·sta*

shave vi radersi* *rah·der·see*

shaver n il rasoio elettrico *ra·soh·yoh e·let·tree·ko*

shaving brush n il pennello da barba *pen·nel·loh da bar·ba*

shaving cream n la crema per barba *kre·ma payr bar·ba*

shaving soap n il sapone da barba *sa·poh·ne da bar·ba*

shawl n lo scialle *shal·le*

she pron lei *ley*; here she is eccola *ek·ko·la*

shed n la capanna *ka·pan·na*

sheep n la pecora *pe·ko·ra*

sheepskin n la pelle di montone *pel·le dee mon·toh·ne*

sheer adj (stockings) sottile *sot·tee·le*

sheet n il lenzuolo *len·tswo·loh*; (of paper) il foglio *fol·yoh*

shelf n lo scaffale *skaf·fah·le*

shell n (of egg) il guscio *goo·shoh*; (of fish) la conchiglia *kon·keel·ya*

shellfish n (on menu) i frutti di mare *froot·tee dee mah·re*

shelter n (for waiting under) la tettoia *tet·toh·ya* □ vi (from rain etc) ripararsi *ree·pa·rar·see*

shelve vi (beach) digradare *dee·gra·dah·ray* □ vt (project) rinviare *reen·vyah·ray*

sherbet n la granita *gra·nee·ta*

sheriff n lo sceriffo *she·reef·foh*

sherry n lo sherry *sher·ree*

shift n (change) il cambiamento *kam·bya·mayn·toh*; (of workmen) il turno *toor·noh* □ vt to shift gear cambiare marcia *kam·byah·ray mar·cha*

shin n lo stinco *steen·koh*

shine vi (sun etc) splendere *splen·de·re*; (metal) brillare *breel·lah·ray*

shingles n (illness) l'erpete zoster (m) *er·pe·te zo·ster*

shiny adj splendente *splen·den·te*

ship n la nave *nah·ve* □ vt (goods) spedire *spe·dee·re*

shipbuilding n la costruzione navale *ko·stroo·tsyoh·ne na·vah·le*

shipment n il carico *kah·ree·koh*

shipping agent n l'agente marittimo (m) *a·jen·te ma·reet·tee·mo*

shipping company n la compagnia di navigazione *kom·pan·yee·a dee na·vee·ga·tsyoh·ne*

shipyard n il cantiere navale *kan·tye·re na·vah·le*

shirt n la camicia *ka·mee·cha* S58, Sn65

shiver vi rabbrividire *rab·bree·vee·dee·re*

shock n lo shock *shok*; (electric) la scossa elettrica *skos·sa e·let·tree·ka*

shock absorber n l'ammortizzatore (m) *am·mor·teedz·dza·toh·re*

shoe n la scarpa *skar·pa*; (of brake) il ceppo del freno *chayp·poh del fre·noh* S11, 59, 62

shoelace n la stringa *streen·ga*

shoeshop n il negozio di calzature *ne·go·tsyoh dee kal·tsa·too·re*

shoot vt (injure) sparare *spa·rah·ray*; (kill) uccidere* con un colpo di fucile *ooch·chee·de·re kohn oon kohl·poh dee foo·chee·le* □ vi sparare *spa·rah·ray*

shop n il negozio *ne·go·tsyoh*

shoplifting n il taccheggio *tak·kayj·joh*

shopping n gli acquisti *ak·kwee·stee*; to go shopping fare* la spesa *fah·ray la spay·sa*

shopping bag n la borsa per la spesa *bohr·sa payr la spay·sa*

shopping center n il centro commerciale *chen·troh kom·mer·chah·le*

shop steward n il rappresentante sindacale *rap·pre·zen·tan·te seen·da·kah·le*

shop window n la vetrina *ve·tree·na*

shopworn adj sciupato(a) *shoo·pah·to(a)*

shore n (*of sea*) la spiaggia *spyaj·ja*; (*of lake*) la riva *ree·va*

short adj corto(a) *kohr·to(a)*; (*person*) basso(a) *bas·so(a)*; **to be short of something** essere* a corto di qualcosa *es·se·re a kohr·to dee kwal·ko·sa*; **he gave me short change** non mi ha dato tutto il resto *nohn mee a dah·to toot·to eel re·stoh*

shortage n la carenza *ka·ren·tsa*

shortbread n il biscotto di pasta frolla *bee·skot·toh dee pa·sta frol·la*

shortcut n la scorciatoia *skor·cha·toh·ya* T134

short drink n l'alcolico forte (m) *al·ko·lee·koh for·te*

shorten vt accorciare *ak·kor·chah·ray*

shortfall n la deficienza *de·fee·chen·tsa*

shorthand n la stenografia *ste·no·gra·fee·a*

shorthand typist n lo/la stenodattilografo(a) *ste·no·dat·tee·lo·gra·fo(a)*

short list n la lista dei candidati *lee·sta dey kan·dee·dah·tee*

shortly adv (*soon*) fra poco *fra po·ko*

shorts pl i calzoncini *kal·tson·chee·nee*; (*underwear*) le mutande *moo·tan·de*

short-staffed adj □ **to be short-staffed** avere* una mancanza di personale *a·vay·re oo·na man·kan·tsa dee per·so·nah·le*

short term adj a breve termine *a bre·ve ter·mee·ne*

short wave n le onde corte *ohn·day kohr·tay*

shot n (*from gun*) il colpo *kohl·poh*

should vi □ **we should buy it** dovremmo comprarlo *do·vrem·mo kom·prar·lo*; **I should like a...** gradirei un(a)... *gra·dee·rey oon(a)*

shoulder n la spalla *spal·la*

shout n il grido *gree·doh* □ vi gridare *gree·dah·ray*

shovel n la pala *pah·la*

show n (*exhibition*) la mostra *moh·stra*; (*in theater*) lo spettacolo *spet·ta·ko·loh* □ vt mostrare *mo·strah·ray*; (*movie*) proiettare *pro·yet·tah·ray*; **to show someone out** accompagnare qualcuno alla porta *ak·kom·pan·yah·ray kwal·koo·no al·la por·ta* □ vi **show** (*be visible*) vedersi* *ve·dayr·see* L52

show business n il mondo dello spettacolo *mohn·doh del·lo spet·ta·ko·loh*

shower n (*rain*) l'acquazzone (m) *ak·kwats·tsoh·ne*; (*bath*) la doccia *dohch·cha* A4, 87

showroom n la sala d'esposizione *sah·la de·spo·zee·tsyoh·ne*

shrewd adj astuto(a) *a·stoo·to(a)*

shrimp n il gamberetto *gam·be·rayt·toh*

shrink vi restringersi* *re·streen·jer·see*

shrinkage n la diminuzione *dee·mee·noo·tsyoh·ne*

Shrove Tuesday n martedì grasso (m) *mar·te·dee gras·so*

shrub n l'arbusto (m) *ar·boo·stoh*

shrug vi stringersi* nelle spalle *streen·jer·see nel·le spal·le*

shut vt chiudere* *kyoo·de·re*; **to be shut** (*door*) essere* chiuso(a) *es·se·re kyoo·so(a)* □ vi **shut** (*door, window*) chiudersi* *kyoo·der·see*

shutter n (*on window*) l'imposta (f) *eem·po·sta*; (*in camera*) l'otturatore (m) *ot·too·ra·toh·re*

shuttle (service) n (*airline*) il servizio di spola *ser·vee·tsyoh dee spo·la*

shy adj timido(a) *tee·mee·do(a)*

Sicily n Sicilia (f) *see·chee·lya*

sick adj (*ill*) malato(a) *ma·lah·to(a)*; **to be sick** (*vomit*) vomitare *vo·mee·tah·ray*; **I feel sick** mi sento male *mee sen·to mah·le* T45

sickly adj (*ill*) malaticcio(a) *ma·la·teech·choh(a)*

sickness n (*illness*) la malattia *ma·lat·tee·a*; (*nausea*) la nausea *now·ze·a*

side n il lato *lah·toh*; **the right side** (*of cloth etc*) il diritto *dee·reet·toh*; **the wrong side** il rovescio *ro·ve·shoh*; **this side up** alto *al·to*

sideboard n la credenza *kre·den·tsa*

sidelights pl (*on car*) i fanali di posizione *fa·nah·lee dee po·zee·tsyoh·ne*

side-street n la strada secondaria *strah·da se·kohn·dah·rya*

sidewalk n il marciapiede *mar·cha·pye·de*

siesta n la siesta *sye·sta*

sieve n il setaccio *se·tach·choh* □ vt setacciare *se·tach·chah·ray*

sift vt (*sieve*) setacciare *se·tach·chah·ray*

sigh vi sospirare *so·spee·rah·ray*

sight n □ **to have poor sight** avere* la vista debole *a·vay·re la vee·sta day·bo·le*; **a lovely sight** una bella vista *oo·na bel·la vee·sta*; **to see the sights** visitare le cose interessanti *vee·zee·tah·ray le ko·se een·te·res·san·tee*

sightseeing n il turismo *too·ree·zmoh*

sign n il segno *sayn·yoh*; (*notice*) l'insegna (f) *een·sayn·ya* □ vt (*document*) firmare *feer·mah·ray* T194

signal n il segnale *sen·yah·le* T192

signature n la firma *feer·ma*

signpost n il palo indicatore *pah·loh een·dee·ka·toh·re*

silence n il silenzio *see·len·tsyoh*

silent adj silenzioso(a) *see·len·tsyoh·so(a)*

silk n la seta *say·ta*; **a silk dress** un vestito di seta *oon ve·stee·toh de say·ta*

silly adj stupido(a) *stoo·pee·do(a)*

silver n (*metal*) l'argento (m) *ar·jen·toh*; (*money*) la moneta *mo·nay·ta*; (*ware*) l'argenteria (f) *ar·jen·te·ree·a*; **a silver bracelet** un braccialetto d'argento *oon brach·cha·layt·toh dar·jen·toh* S88, 89

similar adj simile *see·mee·le*; **to be similar to** somigliare a *so·meel·yah·ray a*

simmer vi sobbollire *sob·bol·lee·re*

simple adj semplice *saym·plee·che*

since prep da *da*; **I've been here since 4 o'clock** sono qui dalle 4 *soh·no kwee dal·le 4* □ conj **since we arrived** da quando siamo arrivati *da kwan·do syah·mo ar·ree·vah·te*; **since he's ill** poiché è malato *poy·kay e ma·lah·to*

sincere adj sincero(a) *seen·che·ro(a)*

sincerely adv □ **yours sincerely** cordialmente *kor·dyal·mayn·te*

sing vt/i cantare *kan·tah·ray*

single adj (*not double*) singolo(a) *seen·go·lo(a)*; (*not married: man/woman*) celibe/nubile *che·lee·be/noo·bee·le*; **a single bed** un letto a una piazza *oon let·toh a oo·na pyats·tsa*; **a single room** una camera singola *oo·na kah·me·ra seen·go·la*; **a single ticket** un biglietto semplice *oon beel·yayt·toh saym·plee·che*

sink n (*basin*) l'acquaio (m) *ak·kwa·*

yoh □ *vi* (*in water*) affondare *af·fohn·dah·ray*; (*currency*) calare *ka·lah·ray*

sir *n* Signore (*m*) *seen·yoh·re*

siren *n* la sirena *see·re·na*

sirloin *n* la lombata di manzo *lom·bah·tah dee man·dzoh*

sister *n* la sorella *so·rel·la*

sister-in-law *n* la cognata *kon·yah·ta*

sit *vi* sedersi* *se·dayr·see*; **we were sitting at the table** eravamo seduti alla tavola *e·ra·vah·mo se·doo·tee al·la tah·vo·la*; **to sit down** sedersi* *se·dayr·see*

site *n* (*of building*) il sito *see·toh*

sitting room *n* il salotto *sa·lot·toh*

situation *n* (*place*) l'ubicazione (*f*) *oo·bee·ka·tsyoh·ne*; (*circumstances*) la situazione *see·too·a·tsyoh·ne*

six *num* sei *sey*

sixteen *num* sedici *say·dee·chee*

sixteenth *adj* sedicesimo(a) *say·dee·che·zee·mo(a)*

sixth *adj* sesto(a) *se·sto(a)*

sixty *num* sessanta *ses·san·ta*

size *n* le dimensioni *dee·men·syoh·nee*; (*of clothes*) la taglia *tal·ya*; (*of shoes*) il numero *noo·me·roh* S61, 62

skate *n* (*for ice*) il pattino *pat·tee·noh*; (*fish*) la razza *radz·dza* □ *vi* pattinare *pat·tee·nah·ray*

skateboard *n* lo skateboard *skeyt·bord*

skating rink *n* la pista di pattinaggio *pee·sta dee pat·tee·naj·joh*

sketch *n* (*drawing*) il bozzetto *bots·tsayt·toh* □ *vt* abbozzare *ab·bots·tsah·ray*

skewer *n* lo spiedino *spye·dee·noh*

ski *n* lo sci *shee* □ *vi* sciare *shee·ah·ray* L38

ski boot *n* lo scarpone da sci *skar·poh·ne da shee*

skid *n* lo slittamento *zleet·ta·mayn·toh* □ *vi* slittare *zleet·tah·ray*

skier *n* lo sciatore *shee·a·toh·re*, la sciatrice *shee·a·tree·che*

skiing *n* lo sci *shee*; **to go skiing** fare° dello sci *fah·ray del·lo shee*

ski lift *n* la sciovia *shee·o·vee·a*

skill *n* l'abilità (*f*) *a·bee·lee·ta*

skilled *adj* (*workers*) specializzato(a) *spe·cha·leedz·dzah·to(a)*

skillet *n* la padella *pa·del·la*

skim milk *n* il latte scremato *lat·te skre·mah·to*

skin *n* la pelle *pel·le*

ski pants *pl* i pantaloni da sci *pan·ta·loh·nee da shee*

skirt *n* la gonna *gon·na* Sn65

ski run *n* la pista da sci *pee·sta da shee*

skull *n* il teschio *te·skyoh*

sky *n* il cielo *che·loh*

skyscraper *n* il grattacielo *grat·ta·che·loh*

slack *adj* (*loose*) lento(a) *len·to(a)*; (*business*) fiacco(a) *fyak·ko(a)*

slacks *pl* i calzoni *kal·tsoh·nee*

slam *vt* sbattere *zbat·te·re*

slang *n* il gergo *jer·goh*

slap *vt* schiaffeggiare *skyaf·fej·jah·ray*

slate *n* l'ardesia (*f*) *ar·de·zya*

Slav *n* lo/la slavo(a) *zlah·vo(a)*

slave *n* lo/la schiavo(a) *skyah·vo(a)*

sled(ge) *n* (*toboggan*) la slitta *zleet·ta*

sleep *n* il sonno *sohn·noh* □ *vi* dormire *dor·mee·ra* □ *vt* **the apartment sleeps three** l'appartamento ha tre letti *lap·par·ta·mayn·toh a tray let·tee*

sleeping bag *n* il sacco a pelo *sak·koh a pay·loh*

sleeping car *n* il vagone letto *va·goh·ne let·to* T62

sleeping pill *n* il sonnifero *son·nee·fe·roh*

sleet *n* il nevischio *ne·vee·skyoh*

sleeve *n* la manica *mah·nee·ka*

sleigh *n* la slitta *zleet·ta*

slice *n* la fetta *fayt·ta* □ *vt* affettare *af·fayt·tah·ray* S31

slide *vi* scivolare *shee·vo·lah·ray* □ *n* (*chute*) lo scivolo *shee·vo·loh*; (*photo*) la diapositiva *dee·a·po·zee·tee·va*

slide rule *n* il regolo calcolatore *re·go·loh kal·ko·la·toh·re*

slight *adj* (*small*) leggero(a) *lej·je·ro(a)*

slim *adj* snello(a) *znel·lo(a)*

sling *n* (*for arm*) la benda al collo *ben·da al kol·loh*

slip *vi* (*slide*) scivolare *shee·vo·lah·ray*; (*trip*) inciampare *een·cham·pah·ray* □ *n* (*underskirt*) la sottana *sot·tah·na*; (*of paper*) la scheda *ske·da*

slipper *n* la pantofola *pan·to·fo·la*

slippery *adj* sdrucciolevole *zdrooch·cho·lay·vo·le*

slogan *n* lo slogan *zlo·gan*

slope *n* (*angle*) la pendenza *pen·den·tsa*; (*sloping ground*) il pendio *pen·dee·oh*

slot *n* la fessura *fes·soo·ra*

slot machine *n* il distributore automatico *dee·stree·boo·toh·re ow·to·ma·tee·ko*

slow *adj* lento(a) *len·to(a)*; **my watch is slow** il mio orologio va indietro *eel mee·o o·ro·lo·joh va een·dye·tro* □ *vi* **to slow down** *or* **up** rallentare *ral·len·tah·ray*

slowdown *n* lo sciopero bianco *sho·pe·roh byan·koh*

slump *n* il crollo *krol·loh* □ *vi* crollare *krol·lah·ray*

smack *vt* schiaffeggiare *skyaf·fej·jah·ray* □ *n* lo schiaffo *skyaf·foh*

small *adj* piccolo(a) *peek·ko·lo(a)* A15

smallpox *n* il vaiolo *va·yo·loh*

smart *adj* (*elegant*) elegante *e·le·gan·te*; (*clever*) intelligente *een·tel·lee·jen·te*

smash *vt* frantumare *fran·too·mah·ray*

smell *n* l'odore (*m*) *o·doh·re* □ *vt* sentire *sen·tee·re* □ *vi* **to smell of garlic** sapere° di aglio *sa·pay·re dee al·yoh*

smile *n* il sorriso *sor·ree·soh* □ *vi* sorridere° *sor·ree·de·re*

smock *n* la blusa *bloo·za*

smoke *n* il fumo *foo·moh* □ *vt/i* fumare *foo·mah·ray*; **do you smoke?** lei fuma? *ley foo·ma* Mc25

smoked *adj* (*salmon etc*) affumicato(a) *af·foo·mee·kah·to(a)*

smoker *n* (*person*) il fumatore *foo·ma·toh·re*; (*compartment*) lo scompartimento per fumatori *skom·par·tee·mayn·toh payr foo·ma·toh·ree*

smooth *adj* liscio(a) *lee·sho(a)*

smuggle *vt* contrabbandare *kon·trab·ban·dah·ray*

snack *n* lo spuntino *spoon·tee·noh*

snack bar *n* lo snack-bar *znak·bar*

snail *n* la chiocciola *kyoch·cho·la*

snake *n* il serpente *ser·pen·te*

snap *vi* (*break*) spezzarsi *spets·tsar·see*

snap fastener *n* il bottone automatico *bot·toh·ne ow·to·ma·tee·ko*

snatch *vt* afferrare *af·fer·rah·ray*

sneakers *pl* le scarpette *skar·payt·te*

sneeze *n* lo starnuto *star·noo·toh* □ *vi* starnutire *star·noo·tee·re*

snob *n* lo/la snob *znob*

snobbish adj snobistico(a) *zno·bee·stee·ko(a)*

snooker n il biliardo *beel·yar·doh*

snore vi russare *roos·sah·ray*

snorkel n il tubo di respirazione *too·boh dee re·spee·ra·tsyoh·ne*

snow n la neve *nay·ve* □ vi nevicare *ne·vee·kah·ray*; it's snowing nevica *nay·vee·ka*

snowball n la palla di neve *pal·la dee nay·ve*

snowdrift n il cumulo di neve *koo·moo·loh dee nay·ve*

snowman n il pupazzo di neve *poo·pats·tsoh dee nay·ve*

snowplow n lo spazzaneve *spats·tsa·nay·ve*

snuff n il tabacco da fiuto *ta·bak·koh da fyoo·toh*

so adv □ so pleased that... cosí contento(a) che... *ko·see kon·ten·to(a) ke*; I hope so spero di sí *spe·ro dee see*; so many tanti(e) *tan·tee(·te)*; so much tanto(a) *tan·to(a)* □ conj and so we left e cosí siamo partiti *e ko·see syah·mo par·tee·tee*; so do I anch'io *an·kee·oh*; so is he anche lui *an·ke loo·ee*; he did it so that I would go l'ha fatto perché io andassi *la fat·to payr·kay ee·oh an·das·see*

soak vt (washing) mettere* a mollo *mayt·te·re a mol·loh*

soap n il sapone *sa·poh·ne* A41

soap-flakes pl il sapone in scaglie *sa·poh·ne een skal·ye*

soap powder n il detersivo *de·ter·see·voh*

sober adj (not drunk) non ubriaco(a) *nohn oo·bree·ah·ko(a)*

soccer n il calcio *kal·choh*

social adj sociale *so·chah·le*

socialism n il socialismo *so·cha·lee·zmoh*

socialist n il/la socialista *so·cha·lee·sta* □ adj socialista *so·cha·lee·sta*

social security n la sicurezza sociale *see·koo·rayts·tsa so·chah·le*

social services pl i servizi sociali *ser·vee·tsee so·chah·lee*

social worker n l'assistente sociale (m/f) *as·see·sten·te so·chah·le*

society n la società *so·che·ta*; (association) l'associazione (f) *as·so·cha·tsyoh·ne*

sock n il calzino *kal·tsee·noh*

socket n (electrical) la presa *pray·sa* A42

soda n (chemical) la soda *so·da*; a whiskey and soda un whisky con selz *oon wee·skee kohn selts*

soda water n il selz *selts*

sofa n il divano *dee·vah·noh*

soft adj (not hard) morbido(a) *mor·bee·do(a)*; (not loud) basso(a) *bas·so(a)*; (drink) analcolico(a) *a·nal·ko·lee·ko(a)*

soft-boiled adj □ a soft-boiled egg un uovo à la coque *oon wo·voh a la kok*

software n il software *soft·wayr*

soil n il suolo *swo·loh*

solar adj solare *so·lah·re*

soldier n il soldato *sol·dah·toh*

sold out adj esaurito(a) *e·zow·ree·to(a)*

sole n (of foot) la pianta *pyan·ta*; (of shoe) la suola *swo·la*; (fish) la sogliola *sol·yo·la*

solid adj solido(a) *so·lee·do(a)*; in solid gold in oro massiccio *een o·roh mas·seech·cho*

solution n la soluzione *so·loo·tsyoh·ne*

solve vt (problem) risolvere* *ree·sol·ve·re*

some adj □ some apples alcune mele *al·koo·ne may·le*; some bread del pane *del pah·ne*; some people alcune persone *al·koo·ne per·soh·ne* □ pron some (of it) was left ne avanzava un po' *nay a·van·tsah·va oon po*; some (of them) were... alcuni (di loro) erano... *al·koo·nee (dee loh·ro) e·ra·no*

somebody, someone pron qualcuno *kwal·koo·no*

someplace adv in qualche luogo *een kwal·ke lwo·goh*

something pron qualcosa *kwal·ko·sa*; something bigger qualcosa di piú grande *kwal·ko·sa dee pyoo gran·de*

sometimes adv qualche volta *kwal·ke vol·ta*

somewhere adv in qualche luogo *een kwal·ke lwo·goh*

son n il figlio *feel·yoh* Sn84, C10

son et lumière n lo spettacolo di suoni e luci *spet·ta·ko·loh dee swo·nee e loo·chee*

song n la canzone *kan·tsoh·ne*

son-in-law n il genero *je·ne·roh*

soon adv presto *pre·sto*

sophisticated adj sofisticato(a) *so·fee·stee·kah·to(a)*

sore adj (painful) doloroso(a) *do·lo·roh·so(a)*

sorry adj spiacente *spya·chen·te*; (I'm) sorry mi dispiace *mee dee·spyah·che*

sort n (kind) il genere *je·ne·re*

SOS n l'S.O.S. (m) *es·se·o·es·se*

soufflé n il soufflé *soo·flay*

soul n l'anima (f) *ah·nee·ma*

sound n il suono *swo·noh* □ vi it sounds like a car sembra il rumore di una macchina *saym·bra eel roo·moh·re dee oo·na mak·kee·na* □ vt to sound one's horn suonare il clacson *swo·nah·ray eel klak·son*

sound track n la colonna sonora *ko·lohn·na so·no·ra*

soup n la zuppa *tsoop·pa* E35

sour adj (sharp) acerbo(a) *a·cher·bo(a)*; (milk) acido(a) *ah·chee·do(a)*; sour cream la panna agra *pan·na a·gra*

source n la fonte *fohn·te*

south n il sud *sood* □ adv al sud *al sood* □ n southeast il sud-est *soo·dest*; southwest il sud-ovest *soo·do·vest*

South Africa n il Sud-Africa *soo·da·free·ka*

South African adj sudafricano(a) *soo·da·free·kah·no(a)*

South America n l'America del Sud (f) *a·me·ree·ka del sood*

South American adj sudamericano(a) *soo·da·me·ree·kah·no(a)*

southern adj meridionale *me·ree·dyo·nah·le*

South Pole n il Polo Sud *po·loh sud*

souvenir n il ricordo *ree·kor·doh*

Soviet adj sovietico(a) *so·vye·tee·ko(a)*

Soviet Union n l'Unione Sovietica (f) *oo·nyoh·ne so·vye·tee·ka*

soy beans pl la soia *so·ya*

soy sauce n la salsa di soia *sal·sa so·ya*

spa n la stazione termale *sta·tsyoh·ne ter·mah·le*

space n lo spazio *spa·tsyoh*

spacecraft n l'astronave (f) *a·stro·nah·ve*

spade *n* la vanga *van·ga*; **spades** (*cards*) le picche *peek·ke*

spaghetti *n* gli spaghetti *spa·gayt·tee* E22

Spain *n* Spagna (*f*) *span·ya*

Spaniard *n* lo/la spagnolo(a) *span·yo·lo(a)*

Spanish *adj* spagnolo(a) *span·yo·lo(a)* □ *n* lo spagnolo *span·yo·loh*

spare *adj* □ **spare wheel** la ruota di scorta *rwo·ta dee skor·ta*; **spare time** il tempo libero *tem·poh lee·be·ro* □ *n* **spare** (*part*) il pezzo di ricambio *pets·tsoh dee ree·kam·byoh* T187

spare rib *n* la cotoletta di maiale *ko·to·layt·ta dee ma·yah·le*

spark *n* la scintilla *sheen·teel·la*

sparkle *vi* scintillare *sheen·teel·lah·ray*

sparkling *adj* (*wine*) spumante *spoo·man·te*

spark plug *n* la candela *kan·day·la*

sparrow *n* il passero *pas·se·roh*

spatula *n* la spatola *spa·to·la*

speak *vt/i* parlare *par·lah·ray*; **do you speak English?** parla inglese? *par·la een·glay·se*; **to speak to someone about something** parlare a qualcuno di qualcosa *par·lah·ray a kwal·koo·no dee kwal·ko·sa* B24

speaker *n* (*electrical*) l'altoparlante (*m*) *al·to·par·lan·te*

special *adj* speciale *spe·chah·le*

specialize *vi* specializzarsi *spe·cha·leedz·dzar·see* Bm15

specific *adj* specifico(a) *spe·chee·fee·ko(a)*

specifications *pl* le specificazioni *spe·chee·fee·ka·tsyoh·nee*

specify *vt* specificare *spe·chee·fee·kah·ray*

specimen *n* il campione *kam·pyoh·ne*

speech *n* il modo di parlare *mo·doh dee par·lah·ray*; (*oration*) il discorso *dee·skohr·soh*

speed *n* la velocità *ve·lo·chee·ta* □ *vi* to speed up accelerare *ach·che·le·rah·ray*

speedboat *n* il fuoribordo *fwo·ree·bohr·doh*

speeding *n* (*in car*) l'eccesso di velocità (*m*) *ech·ches·soh dee ve·lo·chee·ta*

speed limit *n* il limite di velocità *lee·mee·te dee ve·lo·chee·ta* T138

speedometer *n* il tachimetro *ta·kee·me·troh*

spell *vt* (*in writing*) scrivere* *skree·ve·re* □ *n* (*period*) il breve periodo *bre·ve pe·ree·o·doh*

spend *vt* (*money*) spendere* *spen·de·re*; (*time*) trascorrere* *tra·skor·re·re*

spice *n* le spezie *spe·tsye*

spicy *adj* piccante *peek·kan·te*

spider *n* il ragno *ran·yoh*

spill *vt* rovesciare *ro·ve·shah·ray* □ *vi* rovesciarsi *ro·ve·shar·see* B67

spin *vi* (*rotate*) girare *jee·rah·ray* □ *vt* (*wool*) filare *fee·lah·ray*

spinach *n* gli spinaci *spe·nah·chee*

spin-dry *vt* asciugare nell'asciugapanni *a·shoo·gah·ray nel·la·shoo·ga·pan·nee*

spine *n* (*backbone*) la spina dorsale *spee·na dor·sah·le*

spirit *n* (*soul*) lo spirito *spee·ree·toh*; **spirits** (*alcohol*) i liquori *lee·kwoh·ree*; **in good spirits** di buon umore *dee bwon oo·moh·re*

spit *vi* sputare *spoo·tah·ray* □ *n* (*for roasting*) lo spiedo *spye·doh*

spite *n* il dispetto *dee·spet·toh*; **in spite of** malgrado *mal·grah·do*

splash *n* il tonfo *tohn·foh* □ *vt* schizzare *skeets·tsah·ray* □ *vi* sguazzare *zgwats·tsah·ray*

splint *n* la stecca *stayk·ka*

splinter *n* (*wood*) la scheggia *skayj·ja*

split *vt* (*tear*) lacerare *la·che·rah·ray*; (*divide, share*) dividere* *dee·vee·de·re* □ *vi* (*tear*) strapparsi *strap·par·see* □ *n* (*tear*) la spaccatura *spak·ka·too·ra*

spoil *vt* (*damage*) danneggiare *dan·nej·jah·ray*; (*child*) viziare *vee·tsyah·ray*

spoiled *adj* (*milk*) acido(a) *ah·chee·do(a)*

spokesman *n* il portavoce *por·ta·voh·che*

sponge *n* la spugna *spoon·ya*; (*cake*) il pan di Spagna *pan dee span·ya*

spoon *n* il cucchiaio *kook·kee·a·yoh*

spoonful *n* la cucchiaiata *kook·kee·a·yah·ta*

sport coat, sport jacket *n* la giacca sportiva *jak·ka spor·tee·va*

sport(s) *n* lo sport *sport* L31, Mc24

sport(s) car *n* la macchina sportiva *mak·kee·na spor·tee·va*

sportswear *n* gli indumenti da sport *een·doo·mayn·tee da sport*

spot *n* (*patch*) la macchia *mak·kya*; (*dot*) il punto *poon·toh*; (*pimple*) la pustola *poo·sto·la*; (*locality*) il luogo *lwo·goh*; **on the spot** sul luogo *sool lwo·goh*

spot check *n* il controllo improvviso *kon·trol·loh eem·prov·vee·zo*

spotlight *n* il riflettore *ree·flet·toh·re*

sprain *n* la distorsione *dee·stor·syoh·ne* □ *vt* to sprain one's ankle slogarsi la caviglia *zlo·gar·see la ka·veel·ya*

spray *n* (*of liquid*) lo spruzzo *sproots·tsoh*; (*container*) la bombola spray *bohm·bo·la spray* □ *vt* (*liquid*) spruzzare *sproots·tsah·ray*

spread *vt* (*butter*) spalmare *spal·mah·ray*; (*news*) diffondere* *deef·fohn·de·re*; (*payments*) rateizzare *ra·te·eedz·dzah·ray*; **to spread something out** spiegare qualcosa *spye·gah·ray kwal·ko·sa*

spring *n* (*season*) la primavera *pree·ma·ve·ra*; (*coil*) la molla *mol·la*; (*of water*) la sorgente *sor·jen·te*

spring onion *n* la cipollina *chee·pol·lee·na*

sprinkle *vt* □ **to sprinkle with water** spruzzare con acqua *sproots·tsah·ray kohn ak·kwa*; **to sprinkle with sugar** cospargere* di zucchero *ko·spar·je·re dee tsook·ke·roh*

sprouts *pl* i cavolini di Bruxelles *kah·vo·lee·nee dee broo·sel*

spy *n* la spia *spee·a*

squall *n* la raffica *raf·fee·ka*

square *n* il quadrato *kwa·drah·toh*; (*in town*) la piazza *pyats·tsa* □ *adj* quadrato(a) *kwa·drah·to(a)*; **a square meter** un metro quadrato *oon me·troh kwa·drah·to*; **3 meters square** 3 metri per 3 *3 me·tree payr 3*

squash *vt* (*crush*) schiacciare *skyach·chah·ray* □ *n* (*sport*) lo squash *skwosh*; (*gourd*) la zucca *tsook·ka*

squeeze *vt* (*lemon*) spremere *spre·me·re*; (*hand*) stringere* *streen·je·re* □ *n* (*financial*) la restrizione economica *re·stree·tsyoh·ne e·ko·no·mee·ka*

squirrel *n* lo scoiattolo *sko·yat·to·loh*

stab *vt* pugnalare *poon·yah·lah·ray*

stable *n* la stalla *stal·la* □ *adj* stabile *stah·bee·le*

stadium *n* lo stadio *sta·dyoh*

staff *n* il personale *per·so·nah·le*

stage *n* (*in theater*) il palcoscenico *pal·ko·she·nee·koh*; (*point*) la tappa *tap·pa*; **in stages** a tappe *a tap·pe*

stain *n* la macchia *mak·kya* □ *vt* macchiare *mak·kyah·ray* Sn67

stained glass window *n* la vetrata dipinta *ve·trah·ta dee·peen·ta*

stainless *adj* (*steel*) inossidabile *een·os·see·dah·bee·le*

stair *n* il gradino *gra·dee·noh*

staircase *n* la scala *skah·la*

stairs *pl* le scale *skah·le* I4

stake *n* (*in gambling*) la posta *po·sta*; **to be at stake** essere* in gioco *es·se·re een jo·koh*

stale *adj* (*bread*) raffermo(a) *raf·fayr·mo(a)*; **the room smells stale** la stanza sa di rinchiuso *la stan·tsa sa dee reen·kyoo·so*

stall *n* (*stand*) la bancarella *ban·ka·rel·la* □ *vi* (*car engine*) fermarsi *fer·mar·see*

stalls *pl* (*in theater*) la platea *pla·te·a* L46

stamp *n* (*postage*) il francobollo *fran·ko·bohl·loh*; (*rubber*) il timbro *teem·broh* □ *vt* (*letter*) affrancare *af·fran·kah·ray*; (*visa*) vistare *vee·stah·ray* Sn2

stand *n* (*stall*) la bancarella *ban·ka·rel·la* □ *vi* stare* in piedi *sta·re een pye·dee*; **to stand up** alzarsi *al·tsar·see* □ *vt* stand (*put*) porre* *pohr·re*; (*bear*) sopportare *sop·por·tah·ray*; **to stand for** (*signify*) significare *seen·yee·fee·kah·ray*; **to stand out** spiccare *speek·kah·ray*

standard *n* il grado *grah·doh* □ *adj* standard *stan·dard*

standard of living *n* il tenore di vita *te·no·re dee vee·ta*

staple *n* la graffetta *graf·fayt·ta*

stapler *n* la cucitrice *koo·chee·tree·che*

star *n* la stella *stayl·la*; (*celebrity*) il/la divo/a *dee·vo(a)*

starch *n* l'amido (*m*) *ah·mee·doh*

stare *vi* fissare *fees·sah·ray*; **to stare at somebody** fissare qualcuno *fees·sah·ray kwal·koo·no*

start *vt/i* cominciare *ko·meen·chah·ray* □ *n* (*beginning*) l'inizio (*m*) *ee·nee·tsyoh*

starter *n* (*in car*) il motorino d'avviamento *mo·to·ree·noh dav·vya·mayn·toh*

starve *vi* morire* di fame *mo·ree·re dee fah·me*

state *vt* dichiarare *dee·kya·rah·ray* □ *n* (*condition*) lo stato *stah·toh*; **the State** lo Stato *stah·toh*; **the States** gli Stati Uniti *stah·tee oo·nee·tee*

statement *n* la dichiarazione *dee·kya·ra·tsyoh·ne*

station *n* la stazione *sta·tsyoh·ne*; (*radio*) la stazione radio *sta·tsyoh·ne ra·dyoh* F13

stationer's (shop) *n* la cartoleria *kar·to·le·ree·a*

stationery *n* la cancelleria *kan·chel·le·ree·a*

station wagon *n* la giardinetta *jar·dee·nayt·ta*

statistic *n* la statistica *sta·tee·stee·ka*

statistical *adj* statistico(a) *sta·tee·stee·ko(a)*

statistics *n* la statistica *sta·tee·stee·ka*

statue *n* la statua *sta·too·a*

stay *n* (*period*) il soggiorno *soj·johr·noh* □ *vi* rimanere* *ree·ma·nay·re*; (*reside*) stare* *stah·ray*; **to stay the**

night pernottare *per·not·tah·ray*; **to stay with friends** alloggiare da amici *al·loj·jah·ray da a·mee·chee*; **to stay in** rimanere* a casa *ree·ma·nay·re a kah·sa*; **to stay up** (*at night*) vegliare *vel·yah·ray* A3, 55

steady *adj* fermo(a) *fayr·mo(a)*; (*pace*) regolare *re·go·lah·re*

steak *n* la bistecca *bee·stayk·ka* E23

steal *vt* rubare *roo·bah·ray*; **to steal something from someone** rubare qualcosa a qualcuno *roo·bah·ray kwal·ko·sa a kwal·koo·no*

steam *n* il vapore *va·poh·re* □ *vt* (*food*) cuocere* a vapore *kwo·che·re a va·poh·re*

steamer *n* (*ship*) il piroscafo *pee·ro·ska·foh*

steel *n* l'acciaio (*m*) *ach·cha·yoh*

steep *adj* ripido(a) *ree·pee·do(a)*

steer *vt* (*car*) guidare *gwee·dah·ray*; (*boat*) governare *go·ver·nah·ray*

steering *n* (*in car*) lo sterzo *ster·tsoh*

steering column *n* la colonna dello sterzo *ko·lohn·na del·lo ster·tsoh*

steering-wheel *n* il volante *vo·lan·te*

stem *n* lo stelo *ste·loh*

stenographer *n* lo/la stenodattilografo(a) *ste·no·dat·tee·lo·gra·fo(a)*

step *n* (*pace*) il passo *pas·soh*; (*stair*) il gradino *gra·dee·noh*; **to take steps to do something** prendere* le misure per fare qualcosa *pren·de·re mee·zoo·re payr fah·ray kwal·ko·sa*

stepbrother *n* il fratellastro *fra·tel·la·stroh*

stepdaughter *n* la figliastra *feel·ya·stra*

stepfather *n* il patrigno *pa·treen·yoh*

stepladder *n* la scala portatile *skah·la por·tah·tee·le*

stepmother *n* la matrigna *ma·treen·ya*

stepsister *n* la sorellastra *so·rel·la·stra*

stepson *n* il figliastro *feel·ya·stroh*

stereo(phonic) *adj* stereofonico(a) *ste·re·o·fo·nee·ko(a)* □ *n* lo stereo *ste·re·oh*

sterile *adj* sterile *ste·ree·le*

sterilize *vt* (*disinfect*) sterilizzare *ste·ree·leedz·dzah·ray*

sterling *n* la sterlina *ster·lee·na*

stew *n* lo stufato *stoo·fah·toh*

steward *n* il cameriere di bordo *ka·me·rye·re dee bohr·doh*; (*at club*) l'intendente (*m*) *een·ten·den·te*

stewardess *n* la hostess *ho·stes*

stick *n* il bastone *ba·stoh·ne* □ *vt* (*with glue etc*) incollare *een·kol·lah·ray*

sticking-plaster *n* il cerotto *che·rot·toh*

sticky *adj* appiccicoso(a) *ap·peech·chee·koh·so(a)*

stiff *adj* rigido(a) *ree·jee·do(a)*; **a stiff neck** il torcicollo *tor·chee·kol·loh*

stiletto heels *pl* i tacchi a spillo *tak·kee a speel·loh*

still *adj* (*motionless*) immobile *eem·mo·bee·le*; (*wine etc*) non gassoso(a) *nohn gas·soh·so(a)* □ *adv* (*up to this time*) ancora *an·koh·ra*; (*nevertheless*) tuttavia *toot·ta·vee·a*

sting *vt/i* pungere* *poon·je·re* □ *n* la puntura *poon·too·ra*

stipulate *vt* stipulare *stee·poo·lah·ray*

stipulation *n* la stipula *stee·poo·la*

stir *vt* rimescolare *ree·me·sko·lah·ray*

stitch *n* (*sewing*) il punto *poon·toh*; (*pain*) la fitta *feet·ta*

stock *vt* (*have in shop*) avere* *a·vay·re* □ *n* (*supply*) la riserva *ree·ser·va*; (*in shop*) lo stock *stok*; (*for soup etc*) il brodo *bro·doh*; **stocks** (*financial*) i titoli *tee·to·lee*; **in stock** in magazzino een ma·gadz·dzee·noh; out of stock esaurito(a) e·zow·ree·to(a)

stockbroker n l'agente di cambio (m) a·jen·te dee kam·byoh

stock exchange n la Borsa bohr·sa

stockholder n l'azionista (m/f) a·tsyoh·nee·sta

stocking n la calza kal·tsa

stock market n la Borsa bohr·sa

stole n (wrap) la stola sto·la

stomach n lo stomaco sto·ma·koh

stomach ache n il mal di stomaco mal dee sto·ma·koh; **I have (a) stomach ache** ho mal di stomaco o mal dee sto·ma·koh S40

stone n la pietra pye·tra; (in fruit) il nocciolo noch·cho·loh

stony adj sassoso(a) sas·soh·so(a)

stool n lo sgabello zga·bel·loh

stop n (bus stop) la fermata fer·mah·ta □ vi fermarsi fer·mar·see; **to stop doing something** smettere* di fare qualcosa zmayt·te·re dee fah·ray kwal·ko·sa □ vt stop fermare fer·mah·ray; **to stop someone doing something** impedire a qualcuno di fare qualcosa eem·pe·dee·re a kwal·koo·no di fah·ray kwal·ko·sa; **to stop a check** bloccare un assegno blok·kah·ray oon as·sayn·yoh 173, 94, 201

stopcock n il rubinetto di arresto roo·bee·nayt·toh dee ar·re·stoh

stoplights pl i fanali dei freni fa·nah·lee dey fre·nee

stopover n (air travel) lo scalo skah·loh

stopper n il tappo tap·poh

stop watch n il cronometro kro·no·me·troh

store vt immagazzinare eem·ma·gadz·dzee·nah·ray □ n (stock) la provvista prov·vee·sta; (shop) il negozio ne·go·tsyoh; (big shop, warehouse) il magazzino ma·gadz·dzee·noh

store room n il magazzino ma·gadz·dzee·noh

storm n la tempesta tem·pe·sta

stormy adj tempestoso(a) tem·pe·stoh·so(a)

story n la storia sto·rya; (of building) il piano pyah·noh

stove n la cucina koo·chee·na A70

straight adj diritto(a) dee·reet·to(a); (drink) liscio(a) lee·sho(a) □ adv (shoot, water etc) diritto dee·reet·to; **to go straight home** andare* direttamente a casa an·dah·ray dee·ret·ta·mayn·te a kah·sa; **straight away** subito soo·bee·to F23

strain vt (tea etc) colare ko·lah·ray; (muscle) stirarsi stee·rar·see

strainer n il colino ko·lee·noh

strange adj (unknown) sconosciuto(a) sko·no·shoo·to(a); (unusual) strano(a) strah·no(a)

stranger n lo/la sconosciuto(a) sko·no·shoo·to(a)

strangle vt strangolare stran·go·lah·ray

strap n la cinghia cheen·gya

strapless adj senza spalline sen·tsa spal·lee·ne

straw n la paglia pal·ya

strawberry n la fragola frah·go·la

streak n la striscia stree·sha

stream n il ruscello roo·shel·loh

streamlined adj (car) aerodinamico(a) a·e·ro·dee·na·mee·ko(a)

street n la via vee·a F27

streetcar n il tram tram

streetlamp n il lampione lam·pyoh·ne

strength n la forza for·tsa; (of girder, rope etc) la resistenza re·see·sten·tsa

strengthen vt rinforzare reen·for·tsah·ray

stress n (emphasis) l'enfasi (f) en·fa·zee; (tension) la tensione ten·syoh·ne

stretch vt (fabric etc) tendere* ten·de·re □ vi stirarsi stee·rar·see

stretcher n la barella ba·rel·la

strict adj severo(a) se·ve·ro(a)

strike vt (hit) colpire kol·pee·re; **to strike a match** accendere* un fiammifero ach·chen·de·re oon fyam·mee·fe·roh; **the clock struck three** l'orologio ha battuto le tre lo·ro·lo·joh a bat·too·to le tray □ vi strike (workers) scioperare sho·pe·rah·ray □ n (industrial) lo sciopero sho·pe·roh; **on strike** in sciopero een sho·pe·roh

strikebound adj paralizzato(a) da uno sciopero pa·ra·leedz·dzah·to(a) da oo·no sho·pe·roh

strike-breaker n il crumiro kroo·mee·roh

striker n lo/la scioperante sho·pe·ran·te

string n lo spago spah·goh; (of instrument) la corda kor·da

string bag n la rete ray·te

strip n (stripe, length) la striscia stree·sha

stripe n la striscia stree·sha

strip-lighting n l'illuminazione al neon (f) eel·loo·mee·na·tsyoh·ne al ne·on

stripper n la spogliarellista spol·ya·rel·lee·sta

striptease n lo spogliarello spol·ya·rel·loh

stroke vt accarezzare ak·ka·rets·tsah·ray □ n (swimming) la bracciata brach·chah·ta; (golf) il colpo kohl·poh; (illness) il colpo apoplettico kohl·poh a·po·plet·tee·koh

stroll n la passeggiata pas·sej·ja·tee·na; **to go for a stroll** fare* quattro passi fah·ray kwat·tro pas·see

stroller n il passeggino pas·sej·jee·noh

strong adj (person) forte for·te; (structure, material) solido(a) so·lee·do(a); **it has a strong smell** ha un odore forte a oon o·doh·re for·te

strongbox n la cassaforte kas·sa·for·te

strongroom n la camera blindata kah·me·ra bleen·dah·ta

structure n la struttura stroot·too·ra; (building) l'edificio (m) e·dee·fee·choh

struggle n la lotta lot·ta □ vi (physically) lottare lot·tah·ray; **to struggle to do something** sforzarsi di fare qualcosa sfor·tsar·see dee fah·ray kwal·ko·sa

stub n (record) la matrice ma·tree·che

stubborn adj testardo(a) te·star·do(a)

stuck adj bloccato(a) blok·kah·to(a)

stud n il chiodo kyo·doh; (for collar) il bottoncino da colletto bot·ton·chee·noh da kol·layt·toh

student n lo studente stoo·den·te, la studentessa stoo·den·tays·sa M5

student driver n il guidatore principiante gwee·da·toh·re preen·chee·pyan·te

studio n lo studio stoo·dyoh

study vt/i studiare stoo·dyah·ray □ n (room) lo studio stoo·dyoh; **to enjoy one's studies** provare piacere negli studi pro·vah·ray pya·chay·re nel·yee stoo·dee

stuff n (things) la roba ro·ba; (substance) la sostanza so·stan·tsa

stuffed adj (cushion etc) imbottito(a) eem·bot·tee·to(a); (chicken) farcito(a) far·chee·to(a)

stuffing n (in chicken etc) il ripieno ree·pye·noh

stuffy adj soffocante sof·fo·kan·te

stun vt stordire stor·dee·re

stupid adj stupido(a) stoo·pee·do(a)

style n lo stile stee·le

stylish adj elegante e·le·gan·te

subcommittee n la sottocommissione soht·to·kom·mees·syoh·ne

subcontract n il subappalto soo·bap·pal·toh

subcontractor n il subappaltatore soo·bap·pal·ta·toh·re

subject n (topic) l'argomento (m) ar·go·mayn·toh; (person) il/la suddito(a) sood·dee·to(a); (in school) la materia ma·te·rya □ adj subject to soggetto(a) a soj·jet·to(a) a

submarine n il sommergibile som·mer·jee·bee·le

submit vt (proposal) sottoporre* soht·to·pohr·re

subordinate adj subordinato(a) soo·bor·dee·nah·to(a) □ n il/la subordinato(a) soo·bor·dee·nah·to(a)

subscriber n l'abbonato(a) (m/f) ab·bo·nah·to(a)

subscribe to vt (periodical) abbonarsi a ab·bo·nar·see a

subscription n (to periodical) l'abbonamento (m) ab·bo·na·mayn·toh; (to club) la quota kwo·ta

subsidiary adj affiliato(a) af·fee·lyah·to(a) □ n (company) la filiale fee·lyah·le

subsidize vt sovvenzionare sov·ven·tsyoh·nah·ray

subsidy n la sovvenzione sov·ven·tsyoh·ne

substance n la sostanza so·stan·tsa

substandard adj inferiore een·fe·ryoh·re

substitute n il sostituto so·stee·too·toh □ vt to substitute something for something else sostituire qualcosa a qualcos'altro so·stee·too·ee·re kwal·ko·sa a kwal·ko·sal·tro

subtitle n (of movie) il sottotitolo soht·to·tee·to·loh

subtle adj sottile sot·tee·le

subtotal n il subtotale soob·to·tah·le

subtract vt sottrarre* soht·trar·re

suburb n il sobborgo sob·bohr·goh; **the suburbs** la periferia pe·ree·fe·ree·a

suburban adj suburbano(a) soo·boor·bah·no(a)

subway n (underground passage) il sottopassaggio soht·to·pas·saj·joh; (railway) la metropolitana me·tro·po·lee·tah·na

succeed vi riuscire* ree·oo·shee·re; **he succeeded in doing it** è riuscito a farlo e ree·oo·shee·to a far·lo

success n il successo sooch·ches·soh

successful adj (venture) che ha buon esito ke a bwon e·zee·toh; (businessman) prospero(a) pro·spe·ro(a)

such adj tale tah·le; **such a lot of** tanto(a) tan·to(a); **such a book** un tale libro oon tah·le lee·broh; **such books** tali libri tah·lee lee·bree; **such kindness** tale gentilezza tah·le jen·tee·layts·tsa

suck vt succhiare sook·kyah·ray

sudden adj improvviso(a) eem·prov·vee·zo(a)

suddenly adv improvvisamente eem·prov·vee·za·mayn·te T203

sue vt citare chee·tah·ray

suede n la pelle scamosciata pel·le ska·mo·shah·ta

suet n la sugna soon·ya

suffer vt/i soffrire* sof·free·re

sugar n lo zucchero tsook·ke·roh S31

sugar bowl n la zuccheriera tsook·ke·rye·ra

suggest vt suggerire sooj·je·ree·re

suggestion n il suggerimento sooj·je·ree·mayn·toh

suicide n il suicidio soo·ee·chee·dyoh

suit n (men's) il completo kom·ple·toh; (women's) il tailleur tay·yur; (cards) il seme say·me; (astronaut, diver) la tuta too·ta □ vt **that hat suits you** quel cappello ti sta bene kwayl kap·pel·loh tee sta be·ne; **does Thursday suit you?** Le conviene giovedì? le kon·vye·ne jo·ve·dee S59

suitable adj adatto(a) a·dat·to(a); (fitting) appropriato(a) ap·pro·pree·ah·to(a) S106

suitcase n la valigia va·lee·ja T30, Sn52

sultanas pl l'uva sultanina (f) oo·va sool·ta·nee·na

sum n (total amount) la somma sohm·ma; (problem) il calcolo kal·ko·loh

summary n il sommario som·mah·ryoh

summer n l'estate (f) e·stah·te

summons n la citazione chee·ta·tsyoh·ne

sum total n la somma totale sohm·ma to·tah·le

sun n il sole soh·le

sunbathe vi fare* un bagno di sole fah·ray oon ban·yoh dee soh·le

sunburn n (painful) la scottatura skot·ta·too·ra S40

sunburned adj abbronzato(a) ab·bron·dzah·to(a); (painfully) scottato(a) skot·tah·to(a)

Sunday n domenica (f) do·me·nee·ka

sun dress n il vestito da spiaggia ve·stee·toh da spyaj·ja S58

sunglasses pl gli occhiali da sole ok·kyah·lee da soh·le S7

sun-hat n il cappello da sole kap·pel·loh da soh·le

sunlamp n la lampada a raggi ultravioletti lam·pa·da a raj·jee ool·tra·vyo·layt·tee

sunny adj soleggiato(a) soh·lej·jah·to(a)

sunrise n il sorgere del sole sohr·je·re del soh·le

sunroof n il tetto mobile tayt·toh mo·bee·le

sunset n il tramonto tra·mohn·toh

sunshade n (over table) l'ombrellone (m) om·brel·loh·ne

sunshine n il sole soh·le

sunstroke n l'insolazione (f) een·so·la·tsyoh·ne

suntan n l'abbronzatura (f) ab·bron·dza·too·ra

sun-tanned adj abbronzato(a) ab·bron·dzah·to(a)

suntan oil n l'olio solare (m) o·lyoh so·lah·re S9

sun visor n (in car) la visiera vee·zye·ra

superannuation n la pensione pen·syoh·ne

superior adj (quality) superiore soo·pe·ryoh·re □ n il superiore soo·pe·ryoh·re

supermarket n il supermercato soo·per·mer·kah·toh

superstition n la superstizione soo·per·
stee·tsyoh·ne
superstore n l'ipermercato (m) ee·per·
mer·kah·toh
supertanker n la superpetroliera soo·
per·pe·tro·lye·ra
supervise vt sorvegliare sor·vel·yah·ray
supervisor n il/la sorvegliante sor·vel·
yan·te
supper n (main meal) la cena chay·na;
(snack) lo spuntino spoon·tee·noh
supply vt (goods) fornire for·nee·re; to
supply someone with something for·
nire qualcosa a qualcuno for·nee·re
kwal·ko·sa a kwal·koo·no □ n supply
(stock) la provvista prov·vee·sta;
supply and demand l'offerta e la do·
manda lof·fer·ta e la do·man·da
support vt (hold up) reggere* rej·je·re;
(financially) mantenere* man·te·nay·
re; (party, view etc) sostenere* so·
ste·nay·re □ n (moral, financial) il
sostegno so·stayn·yoh
suppose vt supporre* soop·pohr·re;
he's supposed to be an engineer lo si
ritiene un ingegnere lo see ree·tye·ne
oon een·jen·ye·re; you're supposed to
do it today dovrebbe farlo oggi do·
vreb·be far·lo oj·jee
suppository n la supposta soop·poh·sta
surcharge n la soprattassa soh·prat·
tas·sa
sure adj (person) sicuro(a) see·koo·
ro(a); (fact) certo(a) cher·to(a); it's
sure to work sicuro che funzionerà
see·koo·ro ke foon·tsyoh·ne·ra; he's
sure to come verrà sicuramente ver·
ra see·koo·ra·mayn·te
surely adv sicuramente see·koo·ra·
mayn·te
surface n la superficie soo·per·fee·che
surface mail n □ to send something
surface mail spedire qualcosa per po·
sta ordinaria spe·dee·re kwal·ko·sa
payr po·sta or·dee·nah·rya
surf board n la tavola da surfing tah·
vo·la da soor·feeng
surfing n il surfing soor·feeng; to go
surfing fare* del surfing fah·ray del
soor·feeng
surgeon n il chirurgo kee·roor·goh
surgery n (operation) la chirurgia kee·
roor·jee·a
surname n il cognome kon·yoh·me
surplus n l'eccedenza (f) ech·che·den·
tsa
surprise vt sorprendere* sor·pren·de·re
□ n la sorpresa sor·pray·sa
surprised adj sorpreso(a) sor·pray·
so(a); surprised at sorpreso(a) da
sor·pray·so(a) da
surround vt circondare cheer·kon·dah·
ray
surroundings pl i dintorni deen·tohr·
nee
survey n (of land) il rilievo ree·lye·voh;
(of building) la perizia pe·ree·tsya
surveyor n (of land) il geometra je·o·
me·tra; (of building) l'ispettore (m)
ee·spet·toh·re
survive vi sopravvivere* soh·prav·vee·
ve·re
suspend vt (worker) sospendere* so·
spen·de·re
suspenders pl le bretelle bre·tel·le
suspension n (on car) la sospensione
so·spen·syoh·ne
swallow vt/i inghiottire een·gyot·tee·re
swamp n la palude pa·loo·de
swan n il cigno cheen·yoh
sway vi (person) barcollare bar·kol·

lah·ray; (building, bridge) oscillare
o·sheel·lah·ray
swear vi (curse) bestemmiare be·stem·
myah·ray; he swears that... giura
che... joo·ra ke
sweat n il sudore soo·doh·re □ vi su·
dare soo·dah·ray
sweater n il pullover pool·lo·ver
sweatshirt n la blusa bloo·zah
Swede n lo/la svedese zve·day·se
swede n la rapa svedese rah·pa zve·
day·se
Sweden n Svezia (f) zve·tsya
Swedish adj svedese zve·day·se □ n lo
svedese zve·day·se
sweep vt (floor) scopare sko·pah·ray
sweet n (candy) la caramella ka·ra·
mel·la □ adj (taste, food) dolce dohl·
che; (smell) fragrante fra·gran·te;
(music) armonioso(a) ar·mo·nyoh·
so(a); (cute, pretty) grazioso(a) gra·
tsyoh·so(a); (kind) carino(a) ka·ree·
no(a)
sweet corn n il granturco dolce gran·
toor·koh dohl·che
sweet potato n la patata dolce pa·tah·
ta dohl·che
swell (up) vi (limb etc) gonfiarsi gon·
fyar·see
swelling n (lump) la tumefazione too·
me·fa·tsyoh·ne I26
swerve vi sbandare zban·dah·ray
swim vi nuotare nwo·tah·ray □ vt to
swim the Channel attraversare la
Manica a nuoto at·tra·ver·sah·ray la
mah·nee·ka a nwo·toh L26
swimming n il nuoto nwo·toh; to go
swimming andare* a nuotare an·dah·
ray a nwo·tah·ray
swimming pool n la piscina pee·
shee·na A11
swimming trunks pl il costume da ba·
gno ko·stoo·me da ban·yoh
swimsuit n il costume da bagno ko·
stoo·me da ban·yoh
swing n l'altalena (f) al·ta·lay·na □ vt/i
dondolare don·do·lah·ray
Swiss adj svizzero(a) zveets·tse·ro(a)
switch n l'interruttore (m) een·ter·root·
toh·re □ vt to switch on accendere*
ach·chen·de·re; to switch off spegne·
re* spen·ye·re B66
switchboard n il centralino chen·tra·
lee·noh
switchboard operator n il/la centralini·
sta chen·tra·lee·nee·sta
Switzerland n Svizzera (f) zveets·tse·ra;
in/to Switzerland in Svizzera een
zveets·tse·ra
swollen adj gonfio(a) gohn·fyo(a)
sword n la spada spah·da
syllable n la sillaba seel·la·ba
syllabus n il programma pro·gram·ma
symbol n il simbolo seem·bo·loh
symmetrical adj simmetrico(a) seem·
me·tree·ko(a)
sympathetic adj comprensivo(a) kom·
pren·see·vo(a)
sympathy n la compassione kom·pas·
syoh·ne
symphony n la sinfonia seen·fo·nee·a
symposium n il simposio seem·po·zyoh
symptom n il sintomo seen·to·moh
synagogue n la sinagoga see·na·go·ga
synchromesh n il cambio sincronizzato
kam·byoh seen·kro·needz·dzah·to
syndicate n il sindacato seen·da·kah·
toh
synthetic adj sintetico(a) seen·te·tee·
ko(a)
Syria n Siria (f) see·rya

Syrian *adj* siriano(a) *see·ryah·no(a)*

syrup *n* lo sciroppo *shee·rop·poh*; (golden) syrup la melassa raffinata *me·las·sa raf·fee·nah·ta*

system *n* il sistema *see·ste·ma*

systematic *adj* sistematico(a) *see·ste·ma·tee·ko(a)*

systems analyst *n* l'analista-programmatore (*m*) *a·na·lee·sta·pro·gram·ma·toh·re*

T

tab *n* l'etichetta (*f*) *e·tee·kayt·ta*

table *n* la tavola *tah·vo·la*; (list) la tabella *ta·bel·la* E2f

tablecloth *n* la tovaglia *to·val·ya*

table-mat *n* il sottopiatto *soht·to·pyat·toh*

tablespoon *n* la cucchiaia *kook·kee·a·ya*; (measure) la cucchiaiata *kook·kee·a·yah·ta*

tablet *n* (medicine) la pastiglia *pa·steel·ya*

table tennis *n* il tennis da tavolo *ten·nees da tah·vo·loh*

tack *n* (nail) la bulletta *bool·layt·ta* □ *vi* (sailing) virare di bordo *vee·rah·ray dee bohr·doh*

tackle *vt* (problem) affrontare *af·fron·tah·ray*; (in sports) placcare *plak·kah·ray* □ *n* (gear) l'attrezzatura (*f*) *at·trets·tsa·too·ra*

tactics *pl* la tattica *tat·tee·ka*

tag *n* l'etichetta (*f*) *e·tee·kayt·ta*

tail *n* la coda *koh·da*

tailcoat *n* la marsina *mar·see·na*

tailgate *n* (of car) il portellone posteriore *por·tel·loh·ne po·ste·ryoh·re*

tailor *n* il sarto *sar·toh*

take *vt* prendere* *pren·de·re*; (win: prize) vincere* *veen·che·re*; he took it from me me lo ha preso *me lo a pray·so*; to take someone to the station portare qualcuno alla stazione *por·tah·ray kwal·koo·no al·la sta·tsyoh·ne*; take this to the post office porti questo alla posta *por·tee kway·sto al·la po·sta*; to take a photo scattare una foto *skat·tah·ray oo·na fo·to*; I'm taking French at school studio il francese a scuola *stoo·dyo eel fran·chay·ze a skwo·la*; to take an exam dare* un esame *dah·ray oon e·zah·me*; it takes a lot of effort/an hour ci vuole un grande sforzo/un'ora *chee vwo·le oon gran·de sfor·tsoh/oo·noh·ra*; to take something away togliere* qualcosa *tol·ye·re kwal·ko·sa*; to take something back (return) restituire qualcosa *re·stee·too·ee·re kwal·ko·sa*; to take off (clothes) togliersi* *tol·yer·see*; (plane) decollare *de·kol·lah·ray*; to take someone out to the theater portare qualcuno a teatro *por·tah·ray kwal·koo·no a te·ah·troh*; to have a tooth taken out farsi* togliere un dente *far·see tol·ye·re oon den·te*; to take over a firm assumere* il controllo di una ditta *as·soo·me·re eel kon·trol·loh dee oo·na deet·ta*; to take up a sport cominciare a praticare uno sport *ko·meen·chah·ray a pra·tee·kah·ray oo·no sport*

take-away *adj* (food) da portar via *da por·tar vee·a*

take-home pay *n* lo stipendio netto *stee·pen·dyoh nayt·to*

takeoff *n* (of plane) il decollo *de·kol·loh*

takeover *n* l'acquisto (*m*) *ak·kwee·stoh*

take-over bid *n* l'offerta di acquisto (*f*) *of·fer·ta dee ak·kwee·stoh*

talc(um powder) *n* il talco *tal·koh*

talent *n* il talento *ta·len·toh*

talk *vi* parlare *par·lah·ray*; to talk to someone about something parlare a qualcuno di qualcosa *par·lah·ra·y a kwal·koo·no dee kwal·ko·sa*; to talk something over discutere* di qualcosa *dee·skoo·te·re dee kwal·ko·sa* □ *vt* to talk nonsense dire* sciocchezze *dee·re shok·kayts·tse* □ *n* talk (conversation) la conversazione *kon·ver·sa·tsyoh·ne*; (lecture) la conferenza *kon·fe·ren·tsa*; (negotiations) le trattative *trat·ta·tee·ve*

tall *adj* alto(a) *al·to(a)*; how tall are you? quanto è alto lei? *kwan·to e al·to ley*

tame *adj* (animal) domestico(a) *do·me·stee·ko(a)*

tan *adj* marrone rossiccio *mar·roh·ne ros·seech·cho* □ *n* (on skin) l'abbronzatura (*f*) *ab·bron·dza·too·ra* □ *vi* (in sun) abbronzarsi *ab·bron·dzar·see*

tangerine *n* il mandarino *man·da·ree·noh*

tangle *vt* aggrovigliare *ag·gro·veel·yah·ray*

tango *n* il tango *tan·goh*

tank *n* (of car) il serbatoio *ser·ba·toh·yoh*; (military) il carro armato *kar·roh ar·mah·to*

tanker *n* (ship) la nave cisterna *nah·ve chee·ster·na*; (truck) il camion cisterna *ka·myon chee·ster·na*

tap *n* (for water) il rubinetto *roo·bee·nayt·toh* □ *vt* colpire leggermente *kol·pee·re lej·jer·mayn·te* A31

tape *n* il nastro *na·stroh*; (magnetic) il nastro magnetico *na·stroh man·ye·tee·ko* □ *vt* (record) registrare *re·jee·strah·ray*

tape measure *n* il metro a nastro *me·troh a na·stroh*

tape record *vt* registrare *re·jee·strah·ray*

tape recorder *n* il magnetofono *man·ye·to·fo·noh*

tap-water *n* l'acqua di rubinetto (*f*) *ak·kwa dee roo·bee·nayt·toh* A31

tar *n* il catrame *ka·trah·me*

target *n* il bersaglio *ber·sal·yoh*; (sales etc) l'obiettivo (*m*) *o·byet·tee·voh*

tariff *n* (list of charges) la tariffa *ta·reef·fa*; (tax) la tariffa doganale *ta·reef·fa do·ga·nah·le*

tarmac *n* il macadam *ma·ka·dam*

tart *n* la crostata *kroh·stah·ta*

tartan *n* il tartan *tar·tan*; a tartan skirt una gonna scozzese *oo·na gohn·na skots·tsay·se*

tartar sauce *n* la salsa tartara *sal·sa tar·ta·ra*

task *n* il compito *kohm·pee·toh*

taste *n* il sapore *sa·poh·re*; in poor/good taste di cattivo/buon gusto *dee kat·tee·vo/bwon goo·stoh* □ *vt* taste gustare *goo·stah·ray*; (try) assaggiare *as·saj·jah·ray*; I can't taste the garlic non sento l'aglio *nohn sen·to lal·yoh* □ *vi* it tastes like fish sa di pesce *sa dee pay·she*

tax *n* (on goods) la tassa *tas·sa*; (on income) l'imposta (*f*) *eem·poh·sta* □ *vt* (goods) imporre* una tassa su *eem·pohr·re oo·na tas·sa soo*; (income) tassare *tas·sah·ray* A9, M4

taxable *adj* imponibile *eem·po·nee·bee·le*

taxation n la tassazione tas·sa·tsyoh·ne

tax-free adj esente da tasse e·zen·te da tas·se

taxi n il tassì tas·see; **to go by taxi** andare* in tassì an·dah·ray een tas·see T96f

taxi stand n il posteggio per tassì po·stayj·joh payr tas·see

tea n il tè te; (meal) la merenda me·ren·da; **mint tea** il tè alla menta te al·la mayn·ta E61

tea bag n la bustina di tè boo·stee·na dee te

tea-break n la pausa per il tè pow·za payr eel te

teach vt insegnare een·sen·yah·ray; **to teach someone something** insegnare qualcosa a qualcuno een·sen·yah·ray kwal·ko·sa a kwal·koo·no

teacher n (secondary school) il professore pro·fes·soh·re, la professoressa pro·fes·sor·res·sa; (primary school) il/la maestro(a) ma·e·stro(a)

teacup n la tazza da tè tats·tsa da te

team n la squadra skwa·dra

teapot n la teiera te·ye·ra

tear¹ n (rip) strappare strap·pah·ray □ n lo strappo strap·poh Sn76

tear² n la lacrima la·kree·ma; **in tears** in lacrime een la·kree·me

tearoom n la sala da tè sah·la da te

teaspoon n il cucchiaino kook·kya·ee·noh

tea strainer n il colino da tè ko·lee·noh da te

teat n (for bottle) la tettarella tet·ta·rel·la

technical adj tecnico(a) tek·nee·ko(a)

technician n il/la tecnico(a) tek·nee·ko(a)

technique n la tecnica tek·nee·ka

technological adj tecnologico(a) tek·no·lo·jee·ko(a)

technology n la tecnologia tek·no·lo·jee·a

tee n (in golf) il tee tee

teenager n l'adolescente (m/f) a·do·le·shen·te

tee shirt n la maglietta mal·yayt·ta

telecommunications pl le telecomunicazioni te·le·ko·moo·ne·ka·tsyoh·nee

telegram n il telegramma te·le·gram·ma Sn3

telegraph vt telegrafare te·le·gra·fah·ray

telephone n il telefono te·le·fo·noh; **to be on the telephone** essere* al telefono es·se·re al te·le·fo·noh; **by telephone** per telefono payr te·le·fo·noh □ vt telephone (person) telefonare a te·le·fo·nah·ray a T166, A35, Sn11

telephone booth n la cabina telefonica ka·bee·na te·le·fo·nee·ka

telephone call n la telefonata te·le·fo·nah·ta Sn11

telephone directory n l'elenco telefonico (m) e·len·koh te·le·fo·nee·ko Sn25

telephone exchange n la centrale telefonica chen·trah·le te·le·fo·nee·ka

telephone number n il numero telefonico noo·me·roh te·le·fo·nee·ko Sn12, 24

telephone operator n il/la telefonista te·le·fo·nee·sta

telephoto lens n il teleobiettivo te·le·o·byet·tee·voh

telescope n il telescopio te·le·sko·pyoh

televise vt teletrasmettere* te·le·tra·zmayt·te·re

television n la televisione te·le·vee·zyoh·ne; (set) il televisore te·le·vee·zoh·re; **on television** alla televisione al·la te·le·vee·zyoh·ne

telex n il telex te·lex; **by telex** per telex payr te·lex □ vt telex mandare un telex a man·dah·ray oon te·lex a A35, Bm14

tell vt (fact, news) dire* dee·re; (story) raccontare rak·kon·tah·ray; **to tell someone something** dire* qualcosa a qualcuno dee·re kwal·ko·sa a kwal·koo·no; **to tell someone to do something** dire* a qualcuno di fare qualcosa dee·re a kwal·koo·no dee fah·ray kwal·ko·sa; **I can't tell the difference** between them non posso distinguere tra di loro nohn pos·so dee·steen·gwe·re tra dee loh·ro

teller n il/la cassiere(a) kas·sye·re(a)

temper n □ **in a bad temper** di cattivo umore dee kat·tee·vo oo·moh·re; **to lose one's temper** andare* in collera an·dah·ray een kol·le·ra

temperature n la temperatura tem·pe·ra·too·ra; **to have a temperature** (fever) avere* la febbre a·vay·re la feb·bre; **to take someone's temperature** prendere* la temperatura a qualcuno pren·de·re la tem·pe·ra·too·ra a kwal·koo·no I31

temple n (building) il tempio tem·pyoh

temporary adj provvisorio(a) prov·vee·zo·ryo(a)

tempt vt tentare ten·tah·ray

ten num dieci dye·chee

tenant n l'inquilino(a) (m/f) een·kwee·lee·no(a)

tend vi □ **to tend to do something** tendere* a fare qualcosa ten·de·re a fah·ray kwal·ko·sa

tender adj tenero(a) te·ne·ro(a) □ vi **to tender for something** fare* un'offerta per qualcosa fah·ray oo·nof·fer·ta payr kwal·ko·sa

tennis n il tennis ten·nees L33

tennis court n il campo da tennis kam·poh da ten·nees

tennis racket n la racchetta da tennis rak·kayt·ta da ten·nees

tense adj teso(a) tay·so(a)

tent n la tenda ten·da A81

tenth adj decimo(a) de·chee·mo(a)

tent pole n il palo da tenda pah·loh da ten·da

tent stake n il picchetto peek·kayt·toh

term n (of school etc) il trimestre tree·me·stre; (word) il termine ter·mee·ne; **during his term of office** durante il suo periodo di carica doo·ran·te eel soo·o pe·ree·o·doh dee kah·ree·ka; **terms** (of contract) le condizioni kon·dee·tsyoh·nee

terminal n (air terminal) il terminal ter·mee·nal; (buses) il capolinea kah·po·lee·ne·a; (electricity, computer) il terminale ter·mee·nah·le

terrace n (of café) la terrazza ter·rats·tsa

terrible adj terribile ter·ree·bee·le

territory n il territorio ter·ree·to·ryoh

terrorism n il terrorismo ter·ro·ree·zmoh

terrorist n il/la terrorista ter·ro·ree·sta

terylene n il terilene te·ree·le·ne

test n la prova pro·va; (medical) la visita vee·zee·ta; (driving test) l'esame di guida (m) e·zah·me dee gwee·da □ vt (product) collaudare kol·low·dah·ray; (sight, hearing) esaminare e·za·mee·nah·ray; (ability) mettere* alla prova mayt·te·re al·la pro·va

test-drive n la prova su strada pro·va soo strah·da □ vt to test-drive a car provare una macchina su strada pro·vah·ray oo·na mak·kee·na soo strah·da

text n il testo te·stoh

textbook n il libro di testo lee·broh dee te·stoh

textiles pl i tessili tes·see·lee

texture n la tessitura tes·see·too·ra

than conj che ke; better than him meglio di lui mel·yo dee loo·ee; more than 10 più di 10 pyoo dee 10

thank vt ringraziare reen·gra·tsyah·ray; thank you grazie gra·tsye; thanks to grazie a gra·tsye a

that adj quel(la) kwayl·(·la); that one quello(a) lí kwayl·lo(a) lee □ pron that quello kwayl·lo; give me that mi dia quello mee dee·a kwayl·lo; that's what I want ecco quello che voglio ek·ko kwayl·lo ke vol·yo; what's that? che cos'è quello? ke ko·se kwayl·lo; who's that? chi è? kee e; that is (to say)... cioè cho·e; the photo that I gave you la foto che Le ho dato la fo·to ke le o dah·to □ conj I hope that... spero che... spe·ro ke

thaw vi (ice) sgelare zje·lah·ray; (frozen food) disgelare dee·zje·lah·ray □ vt (food) fare* disgelare fah·ray dee·zje·lah·ray

the art □ the boy il ragazzo eel ra·gats·tsoh; the woman la donna la don·na; the boys i ragazzi eel ra·gats·tsee; the women le donne le don·ne

theater n il teatro te·ah·troh; to go to the theater andare* a teatro an·dah·ray a te·ah·troh

their adj loro loh·ro; their father il loro padre eel loh·ro pah·dre; their mother la loro madre la loh·ro mah·dre; their brothers/sisters i loro fratelli/le loro sorelle ee loh·ro fra·tel·leelle loh·ro so·rel·le

theirs pron il/la loro eel/la loh·ro; (plural) i/le loro eelle loh·ro

them pron li(le) lee(le); buy them li (le) compri lee (le) kohm·pree; show them the books mostri loro i libri moh·stree loh·ro ee lee·bree; he spoke to them ha parlato loro a par·lah·to loh·ro; it's them! sono loro! soh·no loh·ro

themselves pron □ they wash themselves si lavano see lah·va·no; they did it themselves l'hanno fatto loro stessi(e) lan·no fat·to loh·ro stays see·(·se)

then adv lí che; there is c'è che; there are ci sono chee soh·no; is there anyone there? c'è qualcuno là? che kwal·koo·no la; he went there ci è andato chee e an·dah·to; there he/she is! eccolo(a)! ek·ko·lo(a)

thermometer n il termometro ter·mo·me·troh

Thermos n il termos ter·mos

these adj, pron questi(e) kway·stee (·ste); these are what I want ecco quelli(e) che voglio ek·ko kwayl·lee (·le) ke vol·yo

they pron loro loh·ro; they say that... (people in general) si dice che... see

dee·che ke...; there they are eccoli(e) ek·ko·lee(le)

thick adj spesso(a) spays·so(a); (soup) denso(a) den·so(a); 3 meters thick spesso(a) 3 metri spays·so(a) 3 me·tree

thief n il ladro la·droh Ea2

thin adj (line) sottile sot·tee·le; (person) magro(a) ma·gro(a); (material) fine fee·ne; (liquid) poco denso(a) po·ko den·so(a)

thing n la cosa ko·sa; the best thing would be... la cosa migliore sarebbe... la ko·sa meel·yoh·re sa·reb·be; where are your things? dove sono le Sue cose? doh·ve so·no le soo·e ko·se

think vi pensare pen·sah·ray; to think of something pensare a qualcosa pen·sah·ray a kwal·ko·sa; to think about someone pensare a qualcuno pen·sah·ray a kwal·koo·no; I think so credo di sí kre·do dee see; to think something over riflettere* su qualcosa ree·flet·te·re soo kwal·ko·sa

third adj terzo(a) ter·tso(a) □ n third (gear) la terza (marcia) ter·tsa (mar·cha)

third party insurance n l'assicurazione contro terzi (f) as·see·koo·ra·tsyoh·ne kohn·tro ter·tsee

Third World n il Terzo Mondo ter·tso mohn·doh

thirsty adj assetato(a) as·se·tah·to(a); to be thirsty avere* sete a·vay·re say·te

thirteen num tredici tray·dee·chee

thirteenth adj tredicesimo(a) tre·dee·che·zee·mo(a)

thirtieth adj trentesimo(a) tren·te·zee·mo(a)

thirty num trenta trayn·ta

this adj, pron questo(a) kway·sto(a); this one questo(a) kway·sto(a); this is what I want ecco quello che voglio ek·ko kwayl·lo ke vol·yo

thorough adj (work) coscienzioso(a) ko·shen·tsyoh·zo(a)

those adj quelli(e) kwayl·lee·(·le); those boys quei ragazzi kway ra·gats·tsee; those women quelle donne kwayl·le don·ne □ pron those quelli(e) kwayl·lee·(·e); those are what I want ecco quelli(e) che voglio ek·ko kwayl·lee (·le) ke vol·yo

though conj, adv □ though you may think... sebbene Lei possa pensare... seb·be·ne lay pos·sa pen·sah·ray; he's happy, though è contento, comunque e kon·tayn·to, ko·moon·kwe

thought n il pensiero pen·sye·roh; (idea) l'idea (f) ee·de·a

thousand num mille meel·le

thousandth adj millesimo(a) meel·le·zee·mo(a)

thread n il filo fee·loh

threat n la minaccia mee·nach·cha

threaten vt minacciare mee·nach·chah·ray

three num tre tray

thriller n (film) il thriller threel·ler; (book) il giallo jal·loh

throat n la gola goh·la S40

throttle n (in car) l'acceleratore (m) ach·che·le·ra·toh·re

through prep attraverso at·tra·ver·so; (all) through the year durante tutto l'anno doo·ran·te toot·to lan·noh; Monday through Friday da lunedí a venerdí da loo·ne·dee a ve·ner·dee; I couldn't get through (on phone) non sono riuscito ad ottenere la comunicazione *nohn soh·no ree·oo·shee·to ad ot·te·nay·re la ko·moo·nee·ka·tsyoh·ne*; put me through to Mr X mi passi il Signor X *mee pas·see eel seen·yohr X*; when I'm through with my work quando avrò finito il mio lavoro *kwan·do a·vro fee·nee·to eel mee·o la·voh·roh*

through train *n* il treno diretto *tre·noh dee·ret·to* T74

throw *vt* gettare *jet·tah·ray*; (rider) disarcionare *dee·zar·cho·nah·ray*; to throw a 6 (dice) fare* 6 *fah·ray* 6; to throw away buttare via *boot·tah·ray vee·a*

thumb *n* il pollice *pol·lee·che* □ *vt* to thumb a ride fare* l'autostop *fah·ray low·to·stop*

thumbtack *n* la puntina *poon·tee·na*

thump *n* (noise) il tonfo *tohn·fo*

thunder *n* il tuono *two·noh*

thunderstorm *n* il temporale *tem·po·rah·le*

Thursday *n* giovedí (*m*) *jo·ve·dee*

thus *adv* (in this way) cosí *ko·see*

thyme *n* il timo *tee·moh*

tick *n* (mark) il segno *sayn·yoh* □ *vt* segnare *sen·yah·ray* □ *vi* (clock) fare* tic-tac *fah·ray teek·tak*

ticket *n* il biglietto *beel·yayt·toh*; (label) l'etichetta (*f*) *e·tee·kayt·ta*; (parking) la contravvenzione *kon·trav·ven·tsyoh·ne* T61

ticket office *n* la biglietteria *beel·yet·te·ree·a* T49

tickle *vt* solleticare *sol·le·tee·kah·ray*

tide *n* la marea *ma·re·a*; the tide is in/out c'è alta/bassa marea *che al·ta/bas·sa ma·re·a*

tidy *adj* ordinato(a) *or·dee·nah·to(a)*

tie *n* la cravatta *kra·vat·ta* □ *vt* (string, ribbon) annodare *an·no·dah·ray*; to tie a dog to a post attaccare un cane ad un palo *at·tak·kah·ray oon kah·ne ad oon pah·loh*; to tie up a parcel legare un pacco *le·gah·ray oon pak·koh*; to tie up capital immobilizzare del capitale *eem·mo·bee·leedz·dzah·ray del ka·pee·tah·le*

tie-up *n* (traffic) l'ingorgo (*m*) *een·gohr·goh*

tiger *n* la tigre *tee·gre*

tight *adj* (rope) teso(a) *tay·so(a)*; (clothes) stretto(a) *strayt·to(a)*; (schedule) impegnativo(a) *eem·pen·ya·tee·vo(a)*

tights *pl* il collant *ko·loñ*

tile *n* (on floor, wall) la piastrella *pya·strel·la*; (on roof) la tegola *tay·go·la*

till *prep* fino a *fee·no a* □ *conj* till he comes finché verrà *feen·kay ver·ra* □ *n* till (cash register) la cassa *kas·sa*

time *n* il tempo *tem·poh*; what's the time? che ora è? *ke oh·ra e*; the time is 5 o'clock sono le 5 *soh·no le 5*; the first time la prima volta *la pree·ma vol·ta*; how many times? quante volte? *kwan·te vol·te*; a short/long time poco/molto tempo *po·ko/mohl·to tem·poh*; in times past nei tempi passati *nay tem·pee pas·sah·tee*; to have a good time divertirsi *dee·ver·teer·see*; for the time being per il momento *pair eel mo·mayn·toh*; from time to time di tanto in tanto *dee tan·to een tan·to*; just in time giusto in tempo *joo·sto een tem·poh*; on time puntualmente *poon·too·al·mayn·te* B45, T4, L12, 52

timetable *n* (for trains etc) l'orario (*m*) *o·rah·ryoh* T49

time zone *n* il fuso orario *foo·soh o·rah·ryoh*

tin *n* (substance) lo stagno *stan·yoh*

tin foil *n* la stagnola *stan·yo·la*

tip *n* (end) la punta *poon·ta*; (money given) la mancia *man·cha* □ *vt* (tilt) inclinare *een·klee·nah·ray* M4

tire *n* lo pneumatico *pne·oo·ma·tee·koh* T176

tired *adj* stanco(a) *stan·ko(a)*; I'm tired of it ne sono stufo(a) *nay soh·no stoo·fo(a)*

tissue *n* (handkerchief) il fazzolettino di carta *fats·tso·let·tee·noh dee kar·ta*

tissue paper *n* la velina *ve·lee·na*

title *n* il titolo *tee·to·loh*

T-junction *n* (on road) l'incrocio a T (*m*) *een·kroh·choh a tee*

to *prep* a *a*; to the station alla stazione *al·la sta·tsyoh·ne*; to London a Londra *a lohn·dra*; to France in Francia *een fran·cha*; to school a scuola a *skwo·la*; to town in città *een cheet·ta*; give it to me me lo dia *me lo dee·a*; he wants to leave vuole partire *vwo·le par·tee·re*; I forgot to do... ho dimenticato di fare... *o dee·men·tee·kah·to dee fah·ray*; the key to my room la chiave della mia camera *la kyah·ve del·la mee·a kah·me·ra*

toast *n* il pane tostato *pah·ne to·stah·to*; to propose a toast to someone proporre* un brindisi a qualcuno *pro·pohr·re oon breen·dee·zee a kwal·koo·no*

toaster *n* il tostapane *to·sta·pah·ne*

tobacco *n* il tabacco *ta·bak·koh* S97

tobacconist *n* il/la tabaccaio(a) *ta·bak·ka·yoh(a)*

tobacconist's (shop) *n* la tabaccheria *ta·bak·ke·ree·a*

today *adv* oggi *oj·jee*

toe *n* il dito del piede *dee·toh del pye·de*

toffee *n* la caramella *ka·ra·mel·la*

together *adv* insieme *een·sye·me*

toilet *n* la toeletta *to·e·let·ta* A4, 89

toilet paper *n* la carta igienica *kar·ta ee·je·nee·ka* A51

toiletries *pl* gli articoli da toeletta *ar·tee·ko·lee da to·e·let·ta*

toilet water *n* l'acqua di Colonia (*f*) *ak·kwa dee ko·lon·ya*

token *n* (voucher) il buono *bwo·noh*; (for machine) il gettone *jet·toh·ne* Sn18

toll *n* (on road etc) il pedaggio *pe·daj·joh* T139

toll bridge *n* il ponte a pedaggio *pohn·te a pe·daj·joh*

tomato *n* il pomodoro *po·mo·do·roh* S31

tomorrow *adv* domani *do·mah·nee* T1, A19

ton *n* la tonnellata *ton·nel·lah·ta*

tone *n* il tono *to·noh*

tongue *n* la lingua *leen·gwa*

tonic *n* (medicine) il tonico *to·nee·koh*

tonic water *n* l'acqua tonica (*f*) *ak·kwa to·nee·ka*

tonight *adv* stasera *sta·say·ra*

tonne *n* la tonnellata *ton·nel·lah·ta*

tonsillitis *n* la tonsillite *ton·seel·lee·te*

too *adv* (also) anche *an·ke*; it's too big è troppo grande *e trop·po gran·de*; too much troppo *trop·po*; too many books troppi libri *trop·pee lee·bree*

tool *n* l'arnese (*m*) *ar·nay·se*

tooth *n* il dente *den·te* I57

toothache *n* il mal di denti *mal dee den·tee*; to have a toothache avere· il mal di denti *a·vay·re eel mal dee den·tee*

toothbrush *n* lo spazzolino da denti *spats·tso·lee·noh da den·tee*

toothpaste *n* il dentifricio *den·tee·free·choh*

top *n* (*of mountain, ladder*) la cima *chee·ma*; (*of table*) la superficie *soo·per·fee·che*; (*lid*) il coperchio *ko·per·kyoh*; (*of bottle*) il tappo *tap·poh*; on top of su *soo* □ *adj* top superiore *soo·pe·ryoh·re*; (*in rank*) primo(a) *pree·mo(a)*; (*best*) migliore *meel·yoh·re* L22

top hat *n* il cappello a cilindro *kap·pel·loh a chee·leen·droh*

topic *n* l'argomento (*m*) *ar·go·mayn·toh*

toss *vt* (*salad*) rimescolare *ree·me·sko·lah·ray*; to toss a coin fare· a testa e croce *fah·ray a te·sta e kroh·che*

total *n* il totale *to·tah·le* □ *adj* totale *to·tah·le*

touch *vt* toccare *tok·kah·ray* □ *n* in touch with in contatto con *een kon·tat·toh kohn*

tough *adj* (*meat etc*) duro(a) *doo·ro(a)*; (*material*) resistente *re·see·sten·te*

tour *n* il giro *jee·roh* □ *vt* (*town*) visitare *vee·zee·tah·ray* L5, 7

tourism *n* il turismo *too·ree·zmoh*

tourist *n* il/la turista *too·ree·sta*

tourist class *n* la classe turistica *klas·se too·ree·stee·ka*

tourist office *n* l'ufficio turistico (*m*) *oof·fee·choh too·ree·stee·ko* F5

tourist trade *n* il turismo *too·ree·zmoh*

tow *vt* (*trailer*) rimorchiare *ree·mor·kyah·ray*; in tow a rimorchio *a ree·mor·kyoh* T168

toward(s) *prep* verso *ver·so*; to come towards someone venire· incontro a qualcuno *ve·nee·re een·kohn·tro a kwal·koo·no*; his attitude towards others il suo atteggiamento nei confronti altrui *eel soo·o at·tej·ja·mayn·toh ne·ee kon·frohn·tee al·troo·ee*

tow-bar *n* (*on car*) il gancio per rimorchio *gan·choh payr ree·mor·kyoh*

towel *n* l'asciugamano (*m*) *a·shoo·ga·mah·noh* A41

tower *n* la torre *tohr·re*

town *n* la città *cheet·ta*; to go to town andare· in città *an·dah·ray een cheet·ta* T100, L3, F4

town hall *n* il municipio *moo·nee·chee·pyoh*

tow truck *n* l'autogrú (*f*) *ow·to·groo*

toy *n* il giocattolo *jo·kat·to·loh*

toyshop *n* il negozio di giocattoli *ne·go·tsyoh dee jo·kat·to·lee*

trace *n* (*mark*) la traccia *trach·cha*

track *n* (*of animal*) la traccia *trach·cha*; (*pathway*) il sentiero *sen·tye·roh*; (*on record*) il solco *sohl·koh*; (*for trains*) il binario *bee·nah·ryoh*; (*sports*) la pista *pee·sta*

track suit *n* la tuta *too·ta*

tractor *n* il trattore *trat·toh·re*

trade *n* il commercio *kom·mer·choh*

trade-in *n* □ as a trade-in come pagamento parziale *koh·me pa·ga·mayn·toh par·tsyah·le*

trade mark *n* il marchio di fabbrica *mar·kyoh dee fab·bree·ka*

trade name *n* il marchio depositato *mar·kyoh de·po·zee·tah·toh*

trader *n* il/la commerciante *kom·mer·chan·te*

trade union *n* il sindacato *seen·da·kah·toh*

trading stamp *n* il buono premio *bwo·noh pre·myoh*

tradition *n* la tradizione *tra·dee·tsyoh·ne*

traffic *n* (*cars*) il traffico *traf·fee·koh* T133

traffic circle *n* la rotonda *ro·tohn·da*

traffic jam *n* l'ingorgo stradale (*m*) *een·gohr·goh stra·dah·le*

traffic lights *pl* il semaforo *se·mah·fo·roh*

trailer *n* (*for goods*) il rimorchio *ree·mor·kyoh*; (*home on wheels*) la roulotte *roo·lot*

train *n* il treno *tre·noh*; (*on dress*) lo strascico *stra·shee·koh*; by train in treno *een tre·noh* □ *vt* train (*apprentice*) addestrare *ad·de·strah·ray*; (*dog*) ammaestrare *am·ma·e·strah·ray* □ *vi* (*athlete*) allenarsi *al·le·nar·see*; to train as a teacher abilitarsi all'insegnamento *a·bee·lee·tar·see al·leen·sen·ya·mayn·toh* T2f, 51f

trainee *n* l'apprendista (*m/f*) *ap·pren·dee·sta*

training *n* (*for job*) la formazione *for·ma·tsyoh·ne*; (*for sports*) l'allenamento (*m*) *al·le·na·mayn·toh*

tram(car) *n* il tram *tram*

tramp *n* il/la vagabondo(a) *va·ga·bohn·doh(a)*

tranquilizer *n* il tranquillante *tran·kweel·lan·te*

transaction *n* la transazione *tran·sa·tsyoh·ne*

transatlantic *adj* transatlantico(a) *tran·sat·lan·tee·ko(a)*

transfer *vt* □ to transfer the charges (*on phone*) telefonare con la R *te·le·fo·nah·ray kohn la er·re*

transistor *n* il transistore *tran·see·stoh·re*

transit *n* □ in transit in transito *een tran·see·toh*

transit visa *n* il visto di transito *vee·stoh dee tran·see·toh*

translate *vt* tradurre· *tra·door·re*

translation *n* la traduzione *tra·doo·tsyoh·ne*

transmission *n* (*of car*) la trasmissione *tra·zmees·syoh·ne*

transmitter *n* il trasmettitore *tra·zmet·tee·toh·re*

transparent *adj* trasparente *tra·spa·ren·te*

transport *n* il trasporto *tra·spor·toh* □ *vt* trasportare *tra·spor·tah·ray*

trap *n* la trappola *trap·po·la*

trash *n* le immondizie *eem·mon·dee·tsye*

trash can *n* la pattumiera *pat·too·mye·ra* A71

travel *n* i viaggi *vee·aj·jee* □ *vi* viaggiare *vyaj·jah·ray* □ *vt* (*a distance*) percorrere· *per·kohr·re·re*

travel agency *n* l'agenzia di viaggi (*f*) *a·jen·tsee·a dee vee·aj·jee*

travel agent *n* l'agente di viaggi (*m*) *a·jen·te dee vee·aj·jee*

traveler *n* il viaggiatore *vyaj·ja·toh·re*

traveler's check *n* l'assegno per viaggiatori (*m*) *as·sayn·yoh payr vyaj·ja·toh·ree* M12, 22, A23

tray *n* il vassoio *vas·so·yoh*

treacle *n* la melassa *me·las·sa*

treasure *n* il tesoro *te·zo·roh*

Treasury *n* il Ministero del Tesoro *mee·nee·ste·roh del te·zo·roh*

treat *vt* trattare *trat·tah·ray*; (*medi-*

cally) curare *koo·rah·ray*; **I'll treat you to an ice cream** cone Le offrirò un gelato *lay of·free·ro oon je·lah·toh □ n* **a little treat** un piacere *oon pya·chay·re*

treatment *n* il trattamento *trat·ta·mayn·toh*; (*medical*) la cura *koo·ra*

tree *n* l'albero (*m*) *al·be·roh*

trend *n* (*tendency*) la tendenza *ten·den·tsa*

trial *n* (*test*) la prova *pro·va*; (*in law*) il processo *pro·ches·soh*

triangle *n* il triangolo *tree·an·go·loh*

tribe *n* la tribù *tree·boo*

trick *n* (*clever act*) il trucco *trook·koh*; (*malicious*) l'inganno (*m*) *een·gan·noh*; (*in cards*) la mano *mah·no □ vt* ingannare *een·gan·nah·ray*

trifle *n* (*dessert*) la zuppa inglese *tsoop·pa een·glay·se*

trim *vt* (*hedge*) potare *po·tah·ray*; (*hair*) spuntare *spoon·tah·ray*; (*decorate*) ornare *or·nah·ray*

trip *n* (*journey*) il viaggio *vyaj·joh*; (*excursion*) la gita *jee·ta*; **to go on a trip to the beach** fare* una gita al mare *fah·ray oo·na jee·ta al mah·re □ vi* **trip** (*stumble*) inciampare *een·cham·pah·ray*

tripe *n* la trippa *treep·pa*

tripod *n* il treppiede *trep·pye·de*

trivial *adj* insignificante *een·see·nyee·fee·kan·te*

trolley *n* il carrello *kar·rel·loh*

troop *n* la truppa *troop·pa*

tropical *adj* tropicale *tro·pee·kah·le*

tropics *pl* i tropici *tro·pee·chee*

trot *vi* (*horse*) trottare *trot·tah·ray*

trouble *n* (*problems*) i guai *gwy*; **the troubles in this country** i guai di questo paese *ee gwy dee kway·sto pa·ay·ze*; **to take trouble over something** darsi* pena di fare qualcosa *dar·see pay·na dee fah·ray kwal·ko·sa*; **stomach trouble** i disturbi allo stomaco *dee·stoor·bee al·lo sto·ma·koh*; **engine trouble** il guasto al motore *gwa·stoh al mo·toh·re*; **to be in trouble** essere* nei guai *es·se·re nay gwy* Sn47, T169

trouble-shooter *n* (*political*) il conciliatore *kon·chee·lya·toh·re*; (*technical*) il perito *pe·ree·toh*

trousers *pl* i pantaloni *pan·ta·loh·nee* Sn65

trouser-suit *n* il tailleur-pantalone *tye·yur·pan·ta·loh·ne*

trout *n* la trota *tro·ta*

truck *n* (*vehicle*) il camion *ka·myon*

truckstop *n* il ristorante per camionisti *ree·sto·ran·te payr kam·yo·nee·stee*

true *adj* vero(a) *vay·ro(a)*

truffle *n* (*fungus*) il tartufo *tar·too·foh*

truly *adv □* **yours truly** distinti saluti *dee·steen·tee sa·loo·tee*

trump *n* (*cards*) l'atout (*m*) *a·too □ vi* giocare una briscola *jo·kah·ray oo·na bree·sko·la*

trumpet *n* la tromba *trohm·ba*

trunk *n* (*of tree*) il tronco *trohn·koh*; (*for clothes etc*) il baule *ba·oo·le*; (*in car*) il bagagliaio *ba·gal·yah·yoh*

trust *vt* (*person*) fidarsi di *fee·dar·see dee □ n* (*company*) il trust *trust*

truth *n* la verità *ve·ree·ta*

try *vt* provare *pro·vah·ray*; (*in law*) processare *pro·ches·sah·ray*; **to try to do something** cercare di fare qualcosa *cher·kah·ray dee fah·ray kwal·ko·sa*; **to try on a dress** provare un vestito *pro·vah·ray oon ve·stee·toh*

T-shirt *n* la maglietta *mal·yayt·ta*

tube *n* il tubo *too·boh*

Tuesday *n* martedì (*m*) *mar·te·dee*

tulip *n* il tulipano *too·lee·pah·noh*

tuna fish *n* il tonno *tohn·noh*

tune *n* l'aria (*f*) *a·ree·a □ vt* (*engine*) mettere* a punto *mayt·te·re a poon·toh*; (*instrument*) accordare *ak·kor·dah·ray*

tunic *n* (*of uniform*) la tunica *too·nee·ka*

Tunisia *n* Tunisia (*f*) *too·nee·see·a*

tunnel *n* la galleria *gal·le·ree·a*

turbot *n* il rombo *rohm·boh*

turkey *n* il tacchino *tak·kee·noh*

Turkey *n* Turchia (*f*) *toor·kee·a*

Turkish *adj* turco(a) *toor·ko(a) □ n* il turco *toor·ko*

Turkish coffee *n* il caffè alla turca *kaf·fe al·la toor·ka*

Turkish delight *n* il Turkish delight

turn *n* (*bend in road*) la curva *koor·va*; **it's your turn** tocca a Lei *tok·ka a lay*; **in turn** a vicenda *a vee·chen·da □ vi* turn (*person, car*) girare *jee·rah·ray*; **he turned (around)** si è voltato *see è vol·tah·to*; **to turn back** tornare sui propri passi *tor·nah·ray soo·ee pro·pree pas·see*; **to turn professional** diventare professionista *dee·ven·tah·ray pro·fes·syoh·nee·sta □ vt* **turn** girare *jee·rah·ray*; **to turn on** (*light*) accendere* *ach·chen·de·re*; (*water*) aprire* *a·pree·re*; **to turn off** (*light*) spegnere* *spayn·ye·re*; (*water*) chiudere* *kyoo·de·re*; **to turn down** (*heat*) ridurre* *ree·door·re*; (*volume*) abbassare *ab·bas·sah·ray*; **to turn up** (*heat*) alzare *al·tsah·ray*; (*volume*) aumentare *ow·men·tah·ray*; **to turn something over** rovesciare qualcosa *ro·ve·shah·ray kwal·ko·sa* T104, 205

turnover *n* (*money*) il giro d'affari *jee·roh daf·fah·ree*; (*in goods*) il movimento delle merci *mo·vee·mayn·toh del·le mer·chee*

turnpike *n* l'autostrada a pedaggio (*f*) *ow·to·strah·da a pe·daj·joh*

turn signal *n* la freccia *fraych·cha*

turquoise *adj* color turchese *ko·lohr toor·kay·se*

turtle soup *n* la zuppa di tartaruga *tsoop·pa dee tar·ta·roo·ga*

tutor *n* l'insegnante privato(a) (*m/f*) *een·sen·yan·te pree·vah·to(a)*

tuxedo *n* lo smoking *smo·keeng*

TV *n* la TV *tee·voo*

tweed *n* il tweed *tweed*

tweezers *pl* le pinzette *peen·tsayt·te*

twelfth *adj* dodicesimo(a) *do·dee·che·zee·mo(a)*

twelve *num* dodici *doh·dee·chee*

twenty *num* venti *vayn·tee*

twice *adv* due volte *doo·e vol·te*

twig *n* il ramoscello *ra·mo·shel·loh*

twill *n* la saia *sa·ya*

twin beds *pl* i letti gemelli *let·tee je·mel·lee* A4

twins *pl* i gemelli *je·mel·lee*, le gemelle *je·mel·le*

twist *vt* torcere* *tor·che·re □ vi* (*road*) serpeggiare *ser·pej·jah·ray*

two *num* due *doo·e*

two-piece *n* il completo *kom·ple·toh*

tycoon *n* il magnate *man·yah·te*

type *n* (*sort*) il tipo *tee·poh □ vt* (*letter*) dattiloscrivere* *dat·tee·lo·skree·ve·re*

typewriter *n* la macchina da scrivere *mak·kee·na da skree·ve·re*

typewritten *adj* dattiloscritto(a) *dat·tee·lo·skreet·to(a)*

typical *adj* tipico(a) *tee·pee·ko(a)*

typist *n* il/la dattilografo(a) *dat·tee·lo·gra·fo(a)* Bm12

U

ugly *adj* (object, person) brutto(a) *broot·toh(a)*

ulcer *n* l'ulcera (f) *ool·che·ra*

ultimatum *n* l'ultimatum (m) *ool·tee·mah·toom*

umbrella *n* l'ombrello (m) *om·brel·loh*; (on table) l'ombrellone (m) *om·brel·loh·ne*

umbrella stand *n* il portaombrelli *por·ta·om·brel·lee*

umpire *n* l'arbitro (m) *ahr·bee·troh*

unable *adj* □ to be unable to do something non potere* fare qualcosa *nohn po·tay·re fah·ray kwal·ko·sa*

unanimous *adj* (decision) unanime *oo·nah·nee·may*; we were unanimous eravamo tutti d'accordo *e·ra·vah·mo toot·tee dak·kor·doh*

unarmed *adj* (person) disarmato(a) *dee·zar·mah·toh(a)*

unavoidable *adj* inevitabile *een·e·vee·tah·bee·lay*

unbearable *adj* (pain) insopportabile *een·sop·por·tah·bee·lay*

unbeatable *adj* (offer) imbattibile *eem·bat·tee·bee·lay*

unbiased *adj* imparziale *eem·par·tsee·ah·lay*

unbreakable *adj* infrangibile *een·fran·jee·bee·lay*

uncertain *adj* (fact) incerto(a) *een·cher·toh(a)*

unchanged *adj* immutato(a) *eem·moo·tah·toh(a)*

uncle *n* lo zio *tsee·oh*

uncomfortable *adj* scomodo(a) *sko·mo·doh(a)*

unconditional *adj* (offer) incondizionato(a) *een·kon·dee·tsyoh·nah·toh(a)*

unconscious *adj* privo(a) di sensi *pree·vo(a) dee sen·see*

uncover *vt* scoprire* *sko·pree·ray*

under *prep* sotto *soht·toh*; under a kilometer meno di un chilometro *may·no dee oon kee·lo·me·troh*; under repair in riparazione *een ree·pa·ra·tsyoh·nay*; children under 10 i minori di 10 anni *ee mee·noh·ree dee 10 an·nee*

underclothes *pl* la biancheria intima *byan·ke·ree·a een·tee·ma*

undercooked *adj* insufficientemente cotto(a) *een·soof·fee·chen·te·mayn·tay kot·toh(a)*

underdeveloped *adj* (country) sottosviluppato(a) *soht·to·zvee·loop·pah·toh(a)*

underdone *adj* (steak) al sangue *al san·gwe*; (food in general) insufficientemente cotto(a) *een·soof·fee·chen·te·mayn·tay kot·toh(a)*

underexposed *adj* sottoesposto(a) *soht·to·e·spoh·stoh(a)*

undergraduate *n* lo studente universitario *stoo·den·te oo·nee·vayr·see·tah·ryo*, la studentessa universitaria *stoo·den·tays·sa oo·nee·vayr·see·tah·rya*

underground *adj* (pipe etc) sotterraneo(a) *soht·ter·rah·ne·oh(a)* □ n underground railway la metropolitana *me·tro·po·lee·tah·na*

underline *vt* sottolineare *soht·to·lee·ne·ah·ray*

underneath *prep* sotto *soht·toh* □ adv

it's underneath sta di sotto *sta dee soht·to*

underpaid *adj* mal pagato(a) *mal pa·gah·to(a)*

underpants *pl* le mutande *moo·tan·day*

underpass *n* (for pedestrians) il sottopassaggio *soht·to·pas·saj·joh*; (for cars) la sottovia *soht·to·vee·a*

undershirt *n* la canottiera *ka·not·tye·ra*

understand *vt/i* capire *ka·pee·ray*; we understand that... capiamo che... *ka·pyah·mo ke* B21f

understanding *n* la comprensione *kom·pren·syoh·nay*; (agreement) l'intesa (f) *een·tay·sa*

undertake *vt* intraprendere* *een·tra·pren·de·ray*; to undertake to do impegnarsi a fare *eem·pen·yar·see a fah·ray*

undertaking *n* (enterprise) l'impresa (f) *eem·pray·sa*; (promise) l'impegno (m) *eem·payn·yoh*

undervalue *vt* sottovalutare *soht·to·va·loo·tah·ray*

underwear *n* la biancheria intima *byan·ke·ree·a een·tee·ma*

underwrite *vt* (insurance) assicurare *as·see·koo·rah·ray*; (finance) garantire *ga·ran·tee·ray*

underwriter *n* l'assicuratore (m) *as·see·koo·ra·toh·ray*

undo *vt* slacciare *zlach·chah·ray*

undress *vt* svestire *zve·stee·ray* □ vi spogliarsi *spol·yar·see*

unearned income *n* la rendita *ren·dee·ta*

uneconomic *adj* antieconomico(a) *an·tee·e·ko·no·mee·ko(a)*

uneconomical *adj* non economico(a) *nohn e·ko·no·mee·ko(a)*

unemployed *adj* disoccupato(a) *dee·zok·koo·pah·to(a)*; the unemployed i disoccupati *ee dee·zok·koo·pah·tee*

unemployment *n* la disoccupazione *dee·zok·koo·pa·tsyoh·nay*

UNESCO *n* l'UNESCO (f) *oo·ne·sko*

unfair *adj* ingiusto(a) *een·joo·sto(a)*; (competition) sleale *zle·ah·lay*

unfasten *vt* slacciare *zlach·chah·ray*

unfold *vt* spiegare *spee·e·gah·ray*

unfortunate *adj* (event) sfortunato(a) *sfor·too·nah·to(a)*

unfortunately *adv* sfortunatamente *sfor·too·nah·ta·mayn·tay*

unhappy *adj* infelice *een·fe·lee·chay*

uniform *n* la divisa *dee·vee·za*

unilateral *adj* unilaterale *oo·nee·la·te·rah·lay*

union *n* l'unione (f) *oo·nyoh·nay*; (trade union) il sindacato *seen·da·kah·toh*

unique *adj* unico(a) *oo·nee·ko(a)*

unisex *adj* unisex *oo·nee·sex*

unit *n* (of machinery, furniture) l'elemento (m) *e·le·mayn·toh*; (department, squad) il reparto *re·par·toh*; (of measurement) l'unità (f) *oo·nee·ta*

unite *vt* unire *oo·nee·ray*

United Kingdom, U.K. *n* il Regno Unito *rayn·yoh oo·nee·to*

United Nations Organization, UN, UNO *n* le Nazioni Unite *na·tsyoh·nee oo·nee·tay*

United States (of America), US(A) *n* gli Stati Uniti (d'America) *stah·tee oo·nee·tee (da·me·ree·ka)*

unit price *n* il prezzo unitario *prets·tsoh oo·nee·tah·ree·oh*

universal *adj* universale *oo·nee·vayr·sah·lay*

universe n l'universo (m) oo·nee·ver·soh

university n l'università (f) oo·nee·ver·see·ta

unkind adj (person) scortese skor·tay·zay; (remark) cattivo(a) kat·tee·voh(a)

unknown adj sconosciuto(a) sko·no·shoh·toh(a)

unless conj □ unless we come a meno che noi non veniamo a may·no ke noy nohn ve·nya·mo

unlikely adj improbabile eem·pro·bah·bee·lay

unlimited adj illimitato(a) eel·lee·mee·tah·to(a)

unlined adj (clothes) sfoderato(a) sfo·de·rah·to(a)

unlisted adj che non figura nell'elenco telefonico ke nohn fee·goo·ra nel·le·len·koh te·le·fo·nee·ko

unload vt scaricare ska·ree·kah·ray

unlock vt aprire* (con chiave) a·pree·ray (kohn kyah·ve)

unlucky adj sfortunato(a) sfor·too·nah·to(a)

unnatural adj non naturale nohn na·too·rah·lay

unnecessary adj inutile ee·noo·tee·lay

unofficial adj ufficioso(a) oof·fee·choh·so(a); unofficial strike lo sciopero non ufficiale sho·pe·roh nohn oof·fee·chah·lay

unpack vt (case) disfare* dee·sfah·ray; (clothes) togliere* da una valigia tol·ye·ray da oo·na va·lee·ja

unpaid adj (debt) non pagato(a) nohn pa·gah·to(a)

unpleasant adj sgradevole zgra·day·vo·le

unprofitable adj poco redditizio(a) po·ko red·dee·tee·tsyo(a)

unreasonable adj (demand, price) irragionevole eer·ra·joh·nay·vo·le

unripe adj acerbo(a) a·cher·bo(a)

unsalted adj (butter) non salato(a) nohn sa·lah·to(a)

unscrew vt svitare zvee·tah·ray

unskilled labor n il lavoro manuale la·voh·ro ma·nwah·le

unsuitable adj inadatto(a) een·a·dat·to(a)

untidy adj (room) disordinato(a) dee·zor·dee·nah·to(a); (hair) arruffato(a) ar·roof·fah·to(a)

untie vt slegare zle·gah·ray

until prep fino a fee·no a □ conj until he comes finché egli verrà feen·kay el·yee ver·ra

unusual adj insolito(a) een·so·lee·to(a) S108

unwrap vt disfare* dee·sfah·ray

up prep □ to go up a hill salire* su una collina sa·lee·ray soo oo·na kol·lee·na; up till now finora fee·noh·ra; up to 6 fino a 6 fee·no a 6 □ adv up there lassù las·soo; he isn't up yet (out of bed) egli non si è ancora alzato el·yee nohn see e an·koh·ra al·tsah·to

update vt aggiornare aj·johr·nah·ray

uphill adv in su een soo; to go uphill salire* sa·lee·ray

upkeep n la manutenzione ma·noo·ten·tsyoh·nay

upon prep su soo

upper adj superiore soo·pe·ryoh·re; the upper class la classe alta klas·se al·ta

upset price n il prezzo minimo prets·tsoh mee·nee·mo

upside down adv sottosopra soht·to·

soh·pra; to turn something upside down rovesciare qualcosa ro·ve·shah·ray kwal·ko·sa

upstairs adv di sopra dee soh·pra

upturn n (in business) il rialzo ree·al·tso

upward(s) adv in alto een al·to

urban adj urbano(a) oor·bah·no(a)

urgent adj urgente oor·jen·te

urgently adv urgentemente oor·jen·te·maynt·e

us pron ci chee; noi noy; it's us siamo noi syah·mo noy

use n l'uso (m) oo·zo; in use in uso een oo·zo; it's no use è inutile e ee·noo·tee·lay □ vt use usare oo·zah·ray

used adj (car etc) usato(a) oo·za·toh(a); to get used to abituarsi a a·bee·twar·see a □ vi we used to go a davamo an·da·vah·mo

useful adj utile oo·tee·lay

useless adj inutile ee·noo·tee·lay

U.S.S.R. n l'U.R.S.S. (f) loo·erre·esse·esse

usual adj abituale a·bee·too·ah·le

usually adv di solito dee so·lee·to

U-turn n (in car) l'inversione (f) een·vayr·syoh·nay

V

vacancy n (job) il posto vacante poh·sto va·kan·tay; (in hotel etc) la camera libera kah·me·ra lee·be·ra; no vacancies al completo al kom·ple·toh A12

vacant adj (seat, toilet) libero(a) lee·be·roh(a)

vacation n le vacanze va·kan·tse; on vacation in vacanza een va·kan·tsa Mc19

vacationer n il/la villeggiante veel·lej·jan·te

vaccination n la vaccinazione vach·chee·na·tsyoh·nay

vacuum cleaner n l'aspirapolvere (m) a·spee·ra·pohl·ve·re

vague adj vago(a) va·go(a)

vain adj vanitoso(a) va·nee·toh·so(a); in vain invano een·vah·no

valet n (in hotel) il cameriere ka·me·rye·re

valid adj valido(a) vah·lee·do(a)

valley n la valle val·le

valuable adj di gran valore dee gran va·loh·ray

valuables pl gli oggetti di valore oj·jet·tee dee va·loh·ray

value n il valore va·loh·ray □ vt valutare va·loo·tah·ray

value-added tax n l'imposta sul valore aggiunto (f) eem·po·sta sool va·loh·ray aj·joon·toh M4

valve n la valvola val·vo·la

van n il furgone foor·goh·nay

vandal n il teppista tep·pee·sta

vanilla n la vaniglia va·neel·ya; vanilla ice cream il gelato alla vaniglia je·lah·toh al·la va·neel·ya

variable adj variabile va·ree·ah·bee·lay □ n la variabile va·ree·ah·bee·lay

variation n la variazione va·ree·a·tsyoh·nay

variety n la varietà va·ree·e·ta

variety show n lo spettacolo di varietà spet·ta·ko·lo dee va·ree·e·ta

various adj vario(a) vah·ree·oh(a)

varnish n la vernice vayr·nee·chay

vary vi variare va·ree·ah·ray

vase n il vaso vah·zoh

vaseline n la vaselina va·ze·lee·na

Vatican n il Vaticano va·tee·kah·noh

veal n il vitello vee·tel·loh

vegetables pl gli ortaggi or·taj·jee E25

vegetarian adj vegetariano(a) ve·je·ta·ree·ah·no(a)

vehicle n il veicolo ve·ee·ko·loh

veil n il velo vay·loh

vein n la vena vay·na

velvet n il velluto vel·loo·toh

vending machine n il distributore automatico dee·stree·boo·toh·ray ow·to·ma·tee·ko

vendor n il venditore ven·dee·toh·ray

Venice n Venezia (f) ve·ne·tsya

venison n la carne di cervo kar·nay dee cher·voh

ventilator n il ventilatore ven·tee·la·toh·ray

venture n l'impresa (f) eem·pray·sa

veranda n la veranda ve·ran·da

verbal adj (agreement) verbale vayr·bah·lay

verdict n il verdetto vayr·dayt·toh

verge n l'orlo (m) ohr·loh

vermouth n il vermut ver·moot

version n la versione vayr·syoh·nay

versus prep contro kohn·tro

vertical adj verticale vayr·tee·kah·lay

very adv molto mohl·to; the very last l'ultimissimo lool·tee·mees·see·mo; I like it very much mi piace molto mee pyah·che mohl·to; I haven't very much non ho molto nohn o mohl·to

vest n il panciotto pan·chot·toh

vet(erinary surgeon) n il/la veterinario(a) ve·te·ree·nah·ryoh(a)

veto vt mettere* il veto a mayt·te·ray eel ve·to·h a □ il veto ve·toh

V.H.F. abbrev V.H.F. voo·akka·effe

via prep via vee·a

viaduct n il viadotto vee·a·doht·toh

vicar n il curato koo·rah·toh

vice chairman n il vicepresidente vee·che·pre·see·den·te

vice president n il vicepresidente vee·che·pre·see·den·te

vice versa adv viceversa vee·che·ver·sa

victim n (of accident etc) la vittima veet·tee·ma

victory n la vittoria veet·to·ree·a

video n il video vee·de·oh; on video alla televisione al·la te·le·vee·zyoh·nay

videocassette n la videocassetta vee·de·o·kas·sayt·ta

videocassette recorder n il videoregistratore a cassetta vee·de·o·re·jee·stra·toh·ray a kas·sayt·ta

videotape n il videonastro vee·de·o·na·stroh

Vienna n Vienna (f) vee·en·na

view n la vista vee·sta; (opinion) il parere pa·ray·ray A5

villa n la villa veel·la

village n il paesino pa·e·zee·noh

vinaigrette (sauce) n la salsa vinaigrette sal·sa vee·nay·gret

vine n la vite vee·te

vinegar n l'aceto (m) a·chay·toh

vineyard n la vigna veen·ya

vintage n l'annata (f) an·nah·ta; a vintage wine un vino di qualità oon vee·noh dee kwa·lee·ta

vinyl n il vinile vee·nee·le

violence n la violenza vee·o·len·tsa

violin n il violino vee·o·lee·noh

V.I.P. n il V.I.P. voo·ee·pee

visa, visé n il visto vee·stoh

visible adj visibile vee·zee·bee·lay

visit vt visitare vee·zee·tah·ray □ n la

visita vee·zee·ta; (stay) il soggiorno soj·johr·noh Mc31

visitor n il visitatore vee·zee·ta·toh·ray, la visitatrice vee·zee·ta·tree·chay

visual aids pl i sussidi visivi soos·see·dee vee·zee·vee

vital adj (essential) vitale vee·tah·lay

vitamin n la vitamina vee·ta·mee·na

V-neck n il collo a V kol·loh a vee

vocabulary n il vocabolario vo·ka·bo·lah·ree·oh

vodka n la vodka vod·ka

voice n la voce voh·che

void adj (contract) nullo(a) nool·loh(a)

vol-au-vent n il vol-au-vent vol·ŏ·voñ

volcano n il vulcano vool·kah·noh

volleyball n la pallavolo pal·la·voh·loh

voltage n la tensione ten·syoh·nay

volume n il volume vo·loo·me

vomit vi vomitare vo·mee·tah·ray

vote n il voto voh·to □ vi votare vo·tah·ray

voucher n il buono bwo·noh

W

wading pool n la piscina per bambini pee·shee·na payr bam·bee·nee

wafer n il wafer va·fer

waffle n la cialda chal·da

wag vt (tail) dimenare dee·me·nah·ray

wage, wages n il salario sa·lah·ryoh

wage earner n il salariato sa·la·ree·ah·toh

wage freeze n il blocco dei salari blok·koh de·ee sa·lah·ree

wagon n il carro kar·roh

wagon-lit n il vagone letto va·goh·ne let·toh

waist n la vita vee·ta

wait vi aspettare a·spet·tah·ray; to wait for someone aspettare qualcuno a·spet·tah·ray kwal·koo·no; to keep someone waiting fare* aspettare qualcuno fah·ray a·spet·tah·ray kwal·koo·no

waiter n il cameriere ka·me·rye·re E42

waiting list n la lista d'attesa lee·sta dat·tay·sa

waiting room n (at station) la sala d'aspetto sah·la da·spet·toh

waitress n la cameriera ka·me·rye·ra

wake vt svegliare zvel·yah·ray □ vi to wake up svegliarsi zvel·yar·see

Wales n Galles (m) ga·les

walk vi camminare kam·mee·nah·ray; (for pleasure, exercise) passeggiare pas·sej·jah·ray □ vt to walk 10 km fare* 10 km a piedi fah·ray 10 km a pye·dee □ n walk la passeggiata pas·sej·jah·ta; to go for a walk fare* una passeggiata fah·ray oo·na pas·sej·jah·ta L37

walking n il camminare kam·mee·nah·ray

walking stick n il bastone ba·stoh·ne

walkout n lo sciopero sho·pe·roh

wall n (inside) la parete pa·ray·te; (outside) il muro moo·roh

wallet n il portafogli por·ta·fol·yee Sn81

wallpaper n la carta da parati kar·ta da pa·rah·tee

wall-to-wall carpet(ing) n la mochetta mo·kayt·ta

walnut n la noce noh·che

waltz n il valzer val·tser

wander vi errare er·rah·ray

want vt (wish for) volere* vo·lay·re; (need) avere* bisogno di a·vay·re bee·zohn·yoh dee; to want to do

something volere* fare qualcosa *vo·lay·re fah·ray kwal·ko·sa*

war *n* la guerra *gwer·ra*

ward *n* (*in hospital*) la corsia *kor·see·a*

wardrobe *n* (*furniture*) il guardaroba *gwar·da·ro·ba*

warehouse *n* il magazzino *ma·gadz·dzee·noh*

warm *adj* caldo(a) *kal·do(a)*; it's warm today fa caldo oggi *fa kal·do oj·jee*; I'm warm ho caldo *o kal·do* □ *vt* warm scaldare *skal·dah·ray* Mc10

warn *vt* avvertire *av·vayr·tee·re*

warrant(y) *n* la garanzia *ga·ran·tsee·a*

Warsaw *n* Varsavia (*f*) *var·sah·vya*

wart *n* la verruca *ver·roo·ka*

was *vi* □ I was ero *e·ro*; he was era *e·ra*

wash *vt* lavare *la·vah·ray* □ *vi* to wash (oneself), to wash up lavarsi *la·var·see*

washable *adj* lavabile *la·vah·bee·le* S81

washbasin, washbowl *n* il lavabo *la·vah·boh* A49

washcloth *n* il guanto di spugna *gwan·toh dee spoo·nya*

washing *n* (*clothes*) il bucato *boo·kah·toh*; to do the washing fare* il bucato *fah·ray eel boo·kah·toh* A91

washing machine *n* la lavatrice *la·va·tree·che* A93

washroom *n* la stanza da bagno *stan·tsa da ban·yoh* A89

waste *n* lo spreco *spre·koh*; (*rubbish*) i rifiuti *ree·fyoo·tee* □ *vt* sprecare *spre·kah·ray*; to waste one's time perdere* tempo *per·de·re tem·poh*

waste paper basket *n* il cestino *che·stee·noh*

watch *n* l'orologio (*m*) *o·ro·lo·joh* □ *vt* guardare *gwar·dah·ray*; (*spy on*) sorvegliare *sor·vel·yah·ray* S86

water *n* l'acqua (*f*) *ak·kwa* B67, A31, E66, Mc10

watercress *n* il crescione *kre·shoh·ne*

waterfall *n* la cascata *ka·skah·ta*

water heater *n* lo scaldabagno *skal·da·ban·yoh*

watermelon *n* il cocomero *ko·koh·me·roh*

waterproof *adj* impermeabile *eem·payr·me·ah·bee·le*

water-skiing *n* lo sci nautico *shee now·tee·ko*; to go water-skiing fare* dello sci nautico *fah·ray del·lo shee now·tee·ko* L30

watt *n* il watt *vat*

wave *vi* agitare la mano *a·jee·tah·ray la mah·noh* □ *n* l'onda (*f*) *ohn·da*

wavy *adj* (*hair*) ondulato(a) *on·doo·lah·to(a)*

wax *n* la cera *chay·ra*; (*in ear*) il cerume *che·roo·me*

way *n* (*manner*) il modo *mo·doh*; (in) a different way in un modo diverso *een oon mo·doh dee·ver·so*; which is the way to London? qual'è la strada per Londra? *kwah·le la strah·da payr lohn·dra*; to ask the way to Paris chiedere* la strada per Parigi *kyay·de·re la strah·da payr pa·ree·jee*; it's a long way è lontano *e lon·tah·no*; to be in the way bloccare il passaggio *blok·kah·ray eel pas·saj·joh*; on the way strada facendo *strah·da fa·chen·do*; this way please di qua, per favore *dee kwa payr fa·voh·re*; by the way a proposito *a pro·po·see·to* F1f

we *pron* noi *noy*

weak *adj* (*person*) debole *day·bo·le*; (*tea*) leggero(a) *lej·je·ro(a)*

wealth *n* la ricchezza *reek·kayts·tsa*

wealthy *adj* ricco(a) *reek·ko(a)*

weapon *n* l'arma (*f*) *ar·ma*

wear *vt* (*clothes*) portare *por·tah·ray* □ *vi* (*fabric*) logorarsi *lo·go·rar·see*; to wear something out logorare qualcosa *lo·go·rah·ray kwal·ko·sa*; wear and tear il logoramento *lo·go·ra·mayn·toh*

weather *n* il tempo *tem·poh*

weather forecast *n* le previsioni del tempo *pre·vee·zyoh·nee del tem·poh*

weave *vt* tessere *tes·se·re*

wedding *n* il matrimonio *ma·tree·mo·nyoh*

wedding dress *n* l'abito da sposa (*m*) *ah·bee·toh da spo·za*

wedding present *n* il regalo di nozze *re·gah·loh dee nots·tse*

wedding ring *n* la fede *fay·de*

Wednesday *n* mercoledì (*m*) *mayr·ko·le·dee*

weed *n* l'erbaccia (*f*) *er·bach·cha*

week *n* la settimana *set·tee·mah·na* T112

weekday *n* il giorno feriale *johr·noh fe·ree·ah·le*

weekend *n* il week-end *week·end*

weekly *adv* settimanalmente *set·tee·mah·nal·mayn·te* □ *adj* settimanale *set·tee·ma·nah·le* □ *n* (*periodical*) il settimanale *set·tee·ma·nah·le*

weigh *vt* pesare *pe·sah·ray*

weight *n* (*mass*) il peso *pay·soh*

welcome *adj* benvenuto(a) *ben·ve·noo·to(a)* □ *n* l'accoglienza (*f*) *ak·kol·yen·tsa* □ *vt* accogliere* *ak·kol·ye·re*

weld *vt* saldare *sal·dah·ray*

well *n* (*for water*) il pozzo *pohts·tsoh* □ *adv* bene *be·ne*; to be well stare* bene *stah·ray be·ne*; get well soon si ristabilisca presto *see ree·sta·bee·lee·ska pre·sto*; well! bene! *be·ne*

wellington boot *n* lo stivalone di gomma *stee·va·loh·ne dee gohm·ma*

Welsh *adj* gallese *gal·lay·se* □ *n* il gallese *gal·lay·se*

were *vi* □ you were voi eravate *voy e·ra·vah·te*; we were eravamo *e·ra·vah·mo*; they were erano *e·ra·no*

west *n* l'ovest (*m*) *o·vest*; the West l'Occidente (*m*) *loch·chee·den·te* □ *adv* west all'ovest *al·lo·vest*

western *adj* occidentale *och·chee·den·tah·le* □ *n* (*movie*) il western *wes·tern*

West Germany *n* la Germania Occidentale *jer·mah·nya och·chee·den·tah·le*

wet *adj* (*clothes*) bagnato(a) *ban·yah·to(a)*; (*weather, day*) piovoso(a) *pyo·voh·so(a)*; (*paint*) fresco(a) *fray·sko(a)*; (*climate*) umido(a) *oo·mee·do(a)*; to get wet bagnarsi *ban·yar·see*

whale *n* la balena *ba·lay·na*

wharf *n* la banchina *ban·kee·na*

what *adj* quale *kwa·le*; what book? qual libro? *kwahl lee·broh*; what languages? quali lingue? *kwah·lee leen·gwe* □ *pron* what che *ke*; what's happened? che cos'è successo? *ke ko·se sooch·ches·so*; what do you want? cosa vuole? *ko·sa vwo·le*; I saw what happened ho visto quello che è successo *o vee·sto kwayl·lo ke e sooch·ches·so*; I saw what you did ho visto quello che ha fatto *o vee·sto kwayl·lo ke a fat·to*; what's it called? come si chiama? *koh·me see kyah·ma*; what a mess! (*in room*) che disordine! *ke* *dee·zohr·dee·ne*; **what?** (*please repeat*) come? *koh·me*

wheat *n* il frumento *froo·mayn·toh*

wheel *n* la ruota *rwo·ta*; (*steering wheel*) il volante *vo·lan·te*

wheelbarrow *n* la carriola *kar·ryo·la*

wheelchair *n* la sedia a rotelle *se·dya a ro·tel·le* I5

when *conj* quando *kwan·do*; the day when we... il giorno in cui noi... *eel johr·noh een koo·ee noy*

where *conj* dove *doh·ve*; **where are you from?** di dove è? *dee doh·ve e*

whether *conj* se *say*

which *adj* quale *kwah·le*; **which book?** qual libro? *kwahl leen·broh*; **which languages?** quali lingue? *kwah·lee leen·gwe*; **which one of you?** chi di voi? *kee dee voy* □ *pron* the book, which is long il libro, che è lungo *eel lee·broh ke e loon·go*; the apple which you ate la mela che ha mangiato *la may·la ke a man·jah·to*; I don't know which to take non so quale prendere *nohn so kwah·le pren·de·re*; after which dopo di che *doh·po dee ke*; the chair on which la sedia sulla quale *la se·dya sool·la kwah·le*

while *n* il momento *mo·mayn·toh* □ *conj* mentre *mayn·tre*

whip *n* la frusta *froo·sta* □ *vt* (*cream, eggs*) montare *mon·tah·ray*

whipped cream *n* la panna montata *pan·na mon·tah·ta*

whirlpool *n* il vortice *vor·tee·che*

whirlwind *n* il turbine *toor·bee·ne*

whisk *n* il frullino *frool·lee·noh*

whiskey *n* il whisky *wee·skee*

whisper *vi* sussurrare *soos·soor·rah·ray*

whistle *n* (*sound*) il fischio *fee·skyoh*; (*object*) il fischietto *fee·skyayt·toh* □ *vi* fischiare *fee·skyah·ray*

white *adj* bianco(a) *byan·ko(a)*

whitebait *n* i bianchetti *byan·kayt·tee*

White House *n* la Casa Bianca *kah·sa byan·ka*

whiting *n* il merlano *mayr·lah·noh*

Whitsun *n* la Pentecoste *pen·te·ko·ste*

Whitsunday *n* la Pentecoste *pen·te·ko·ste*

who *pron* chi? *kee*; the man who... l'uomo che... *lwo·moh kay*

whole *adj* (*complete*) intero(a) *een·te·ro(a)*

wholesale *n* la vendita all'ingrosso *vayn·dee·ta al·leen·gros·soh* □ *adj, adv* all'ingrosso *al·leen·gros·soh* Bm25

wholesaler *n* il/la grossista *gros·see·sta*

wholewheat bread *n* il pane integrale *pah·ne een·te·grah·le*

whom *pron* chi? *kee*; the man whom you see l'uomo che vede *lwo·moh ke ve·de*; the boy with whom... il ragazzo con cui... *eel ra·gats·tsoh kohn koo·ee*

whooping cough *n* la pertosse *payr·tohs·se*

whose *adj* □ **whose book is this?** di chi è questo libro? *dee kee e kway·sto lee·broh*; the man, whose son l'uomo, il cui figlio *lwo·moh, eel koo·ee feel·yoh*; I know whose it is io so di chi è *ee·o so dee kee e*

why *adv* perché *payr·kay*

wick *n* (*of cigarette lighter*) lo stoppino *stop·pee·noh*

wicked *adj* malvagio(a) *mal·va·jo(a)*

wicker *n* il vimine *vee·mee·ne*

wide *adj* (*broad*) largo(a) *lar·go(a)*;

(*range*) grande *gran·de*; **4 cm. wide** largo(a) 4 cm. *lar·go(a) 4 cm.*

wide-angle lens *n* l'obiettivo grandangolare (*m*) *o·byet·tee·voh gran·dan·goh·lah·re*

widow *n* la vedova *vay·do·va*

widower *n* il vedovo *vay·do·voh*

width *n* la larghezza *lar·gayts·tsa*

wife *n* la moglie *mohl·ye* T115, A2, S103

wig *n* la parrucca *par·rook·ka*

wild *adj* (*animal, tribe*) selvaggio(a) *sel·vaj·jo(a)*; (*flower*) selvatico(a) *sel·va·tee·ko(a)*

wildlife *n* la fauna *fow·na* L40

will *n* (*testament*) il testamento *te·sta·mayn·toh* □ *vi* he will do it lo farà *lo fa·ra*

willing *adj* □ **willing to do something** disposto(a) a fare qualcosa *dee·spoh·sto(a) a fah·ray kwal·ko·sa*

win *vi* vincere* *veen·che·re* □ *vt* vincere* *veen·che·re*; (*contract*) ottenere* *ot·te·nay·re*

wind[1] *n* (*breeze*) il vento *ven·toh*; (*in stomach*) la flatulenza *fla·too·len·tsa*

wind[2] *vt* avvolgere* *av·vol·je·re*; **to wind a bandage round something** avvolgere* una benda intorno a qualcosa *av·vol·je·re oo·na ben·da een·tohr·no a kwal·ko·sa*; **to wind up a clock** caricare un orologio *ka·ree·kah·ray oon o·ro·lo·joh*

windmill *n* il mulino a vento *moo·lee·noh a ven·toh*

window *n* (*in house*) la finestra *fee·ne·stra*; (*in car, train*) il finestrino *fee·ne·stree·noh*; (*of shop*) la vetrina *ve·tree·na*

window shade *n* la tendina *ten·dee·na*

window shopping *n* il guardare le vetrine *gwar·dah·ray le ve·tree·ne*

windshield *n* il parabrezza *pa·ra·brayts·tsa*

windshield washer *n* il lavacristallo *la·va·kree·stal·loh*

windshield wiper *n* il tergicristallo *ter·jee·kree·stal·loh*

windsurfing *n* il surfing a vela *soor·feeng a vay·la*; **to go windsurfing** fare* il surfing a vela *fah·ray del soor·feeng a vay·la*

windy *adj* (*place*) esposto(a) al vento *e·spo·sto(a) al ven·toh*; **it's windy** tira vento *tee·ra ven·toh*

wine *n* il vino *vee·noh* B54, E10f, S35

wine cellar *n* la cantina *kan·tee·na*

wineglass *n* il bicchiere da vino *beek·kye·re da vee·noh*

wine list *n* la lista dei vini *lee·sta de·ee vee·nee* E9

wine waiter *n* il sommelier *so·muh·lyay*

wing *n* l'ala (*f*) *ah·la*

wink *vi* strizzare l'occhio *streets·tsah·ray lok·kyoh*

winner *n* il vincitore *veen·chee·toh·re*, la vincitrice *veen·chee·tree·che*

winter *n* l'inverno (*m*) *een·ver·noh*

winter sports *pl* gli sport invernali *sport een·ver·nah·lee*

wipe *vt* asciugare *a·shoo·gah·ray*; **to wipe off** cancellare *kan·chel·lah·ray*

wire *n* il filo di ferro *fee·loh dee fer·roh*; (*electrical*) il filo elettrico *fee·loh e·let·tree·ko*; (*telegram*) il telegramma *te·le·gram·ma*

wise *adj* (*person*) saggio(a) *saj·jo(a)*; (*decision*) prudente *proo·den·te*

wish *n* il desiderio *de·see·de·ryoh*; **with best wishes** con i migliori auguri

kohn ee meel·yoh·ree ow·goo·ree □
vt/i I wish I could... vorrei potere...
vor·re·ee po·tay·re; to wish for something desiderare qualcosa *de·see·de·
rah·ray kwal·ko·sa*
witch *n* la strega *stray·ga*
with *prep* con *kohn*; red with anger
rosso(a) di collera *rohs·so(a) dee
kol·le·ra*; filled with water pieno(a)
d'acqua *pye·no(a) dak·kwa*
withdraw *vt* (money) ritirare *ree·tee·
rah·ray*
without *prep* senza *sen·tsa*
witness *n* il testimone *te·stee·mo·ne*
□ *vt* (signature) firmare come testimone *feer·mah·ray koh·me te·stee·
mo·ne* T215
wobble *vi* (chair etc) dondolare *don·
do·lah·ray*
wolf *n* il lupo *loo·poh*
woman *n* la donna *don·na*
womb *n* l'utero (m) *oo·te·roh*
wonder *vi* □ to wonder whether... domandarsi se... *do·man·dar·see say*
wonderful *adj* meraviglioso(a) *me·ra·
veel·yoh·so(a)*
wood *n* (material) il legno *layn·yoh*;
(forest) il bosco *bo·skoh*
wooden *adj* di legno *dee layn·yoh*
wool *n* la lana *lah·na*
woolen *adj* di lana *dee lah·na*
word *n* la parola *pa·ro·la*; word for
word parola per parola *pa·ro·la payr
pa·ro·la*
work *n* il lavoro *la·voh·roh*; (art, literature) l'opera (f) *o·pe·ra* □ *vi* lavorare
la·vo·rah·ray; (clock, mechanism)
funzionare *foon·tsyoh·nah·ray*;
(medicine) agire *a·jee·re*; to work out
(problem) risolvere *ree·sol·ve·re*
A65, Sn55
workday *n* il giorno feriale *johr·noh fe·
ree·ah·le*
worker *n* il lavoratore *la·vo·ra·toh·re*,
la lavoratrice *la·vo·ra·tree·che*
work force *n* la manodopera *mah·no·
do·pe·ra*
working capital *n* il capitale d'esercizio
ka·pee·tah·le de·zer·chee·tsyoh
working-class *adj* operaio(a) *o·pe·ra·
yo(a)*
working hours *pl* le ore di lavoro *oh·re
dee la·voh·roh*
working order *n* □ to be in working
order funzionare *foon·tsyoh·nah·ray*
workman *n* l'operaio (m) *o·pe·ra·yoh*
work of art *n* l'opera d'arte (f) *o·pe·ra
dar·te*
works *pl* (mechanism) il meccanismo
mek·ka·nee·zmoh
workshop *n* l'officina (f) *of·fee·chee·na*
world *n* il mondo *mohn·doh*
world power *n* il potere mondiale *po·
tay·re mon·dee·ah·le*
world war *n* la guerra mondiale *gwer·
ra mon·dee·ah·le*
worm *n* il verme *ver·me*
worn *adj* logoro(a) *loh·go·ro(a)*
worn-out *adj* (object) logoro(a) *loh·go·
ro(a)*; (person) sfinito(a) *sfee·nee·
to(a)*
worried *adj* preoccupato(a) *pre·ok·
koo·pah·to(a)*
worry *n* la preoccupazione *pre·ok·koo·
pa·tsyoh·ne*
worse *adj* □ it's worse (than the other)
è peggiore (dell'altro) *e pej·joh·re
(del·lal·tro)* □ *adv* to do something
worse fare* qualcosa di peggio *fah·
ray kwal·ko·sa dee pej·jo*
worst *adj* □ the worst book il peggiore

libro *eel pej·joh·re lee·broh* □ *adv* he
did it worst l'ha fatto il peggio *la fat·
to eel pej·jo*
worth *adj* □ to be worth $5 valere* $5
va·lay·re $5; L.20000 worth of gas
L.20000 di benzina *L20000 dee ben·
dzee·na*; it's worth it vale la pena
vah·le la pay·na
worthwhile *adj* (activity) che vale la
pena *ke vah·le la pay·na*
would *vi* □ she would come if... ella
verrebbe se... *ayl·la ver·reb·be say*;
would you like a cup of coffee? gradi-
rebbe una tazza di caffè? *gra·dee·
reb·be oo·na tats·tsa dee kaf·fe*
wound *n* (injury) la ferita *fe·ree·ta*
wrap *vt* avvolgere* *av·vol·je·re*; to
wrap up a parcel imballare un pacco
eem·bal·lah·ray oon pak·koh □ *n*
wrap (shawl) lo scialle *shal·le* S23
wrapper *n* (paper) la copertina *ko·per·
tee·na*
wrapping paper *n* la carta d'imballaggio *kar·ta deem·bal·laj·joh*
wreck *n* (ship) il naufragio *now·frah·
joh* □ *vt* fare* naufragare *fah·ray
now·fra·gah·ray*; (plans) rovinare *ro·
vee·nah·ray*
wrench *n* la chiave *kyah·ve*
wrestling *n* la lotta *lot·ta*
wring *vt* (clothes) strizzare *streets·tsah·
ray*
wrinkle *n* la ruga *roo·ga*
wrist *n* il polso *pohl·soh*
write *vt/i* scrivere* *skree·ve·re*; to write
down annotare *an·no·tah·ray*; to
write off a debt cancellare un debito
kan·chel·lah·ray oon de·bee·toh B28
writer *n* lo scrittore *skreet·toh·re*, la
scrittrice *skreet·tree·che*
writing *n* la scrittura *skreet·too·ra*; in
writing per iscritto *payr ee·skreet·to*
writing paper *n* la carta da scrivere
kar·ta da skree·ve·re
wrong *adj* sbagliato(a) *zbal·yah·to(a)*;
you're wrong ha torto *a tor·toh*;
what's wrong? che c'è? *ke che*; to go
wrong (machine) guastarsi *gwa·star·
see*

X

Xerox *n* la xerocopia *kse·ro·ko·pya*
□ *vt* fotocopiare *fo·to·ko·pyah·ray*
X-ray *n* (photo) la radiografia *ra·dyo·
gra·fee·a* □ *vt* radiografare *ra·dyo·
gra·fah·ray*

Y

yacht *n* lo yacht *yot*
yachting *n* lo yachting *yo·teeng*; to go
yachting fare* dello yachting *fah·ray
del·lo yo·teeng*
yard *n* (of building) il cortile *kor·tee·
le*; (measure) la iarda *yar·da*
yawn *vi* sbadigliare *zba·deel·yah·ray*
year *n* l'anno (m) *an·noh*; (as duration) l'annata (f) *an·nah·ta*
yearly *adj* annuale *an·noo·ah·le* □ *adv*
annualmente *an·noo·al·mayn·te*
yeast *n* il lievito *lye·vee·toh*
yellow *adj* giallo(a) *jal·lo(a)*
yes *adv* sì *see*
yesterday *adv* ieri *ye·ree*
yet *adv* ancora *an·koh·ra*
yield *n* il rendimento *ren·dee·mayn·
toh*; (financial) il reddito *red·dee·toh*
□ *vt* (investment) rendere* *ren·de·re*
□ *vi* (to traffic) dare* la precedenza
dah·ray la pre·che·den·tsa

yoga n lo yoga *yo·ga*

yogurt n lo yogurt *yo·goort*

you pron *(familiar form)* tu *too*; *(polite form)* Lei *ley*; *(plural form)* voi *voy*; he's watching you ti/La/vi guarda *tee/la/vee gwar·da*; milk is good for you il latte ti fa bene *eel lat·te tee fa be·ne*

young adj giovane *joh·va·ne*

your adj *(familiar form)* tuo *too·o*, tua *too·a*, tuoi *twoy*, tue *too·e*; *(polite form)* Suo *soo·o*, Sua *soo·a*, Suoi *swoy*, Sue *soo·e*; *(plural form)* vostro *vo·stro*, vostra *vo·stra*, vostri *vo·stree*, vostre *vo·stre*; your sisters le tue/Sue/ vostre sorelle *le too·e/soo·e/vo·stre so·rel·le*

yours pron *(familiar form)* il tuo *eel too·o*, la tua *la too·a*; *(polite form)* il Suo *eel soo·o*, la Sua *la soo·a*; *(plural form)* il vostro *eel vo·stro*, la vostra *la vo·stra*; where are yours? dove sono i tuoi/i Suoi/i vostri? *doh·ve soh·no ee twoy/ee swoy/ee vo·stree*; dove sono le tue/le Sue/le vostre? *doh·ve soh·no le too·e/le soo·e/le vo·stre*; these are yours questi sono tuoi/Suoi/vostri *kway·stee soh·no twoy/ swoy/vo·stree*; queste sono tue/Sue/vostre *kway·ste soh·no too·e/soo·e/vo·stre*

yourself pron *(familiar form)* te stesso(a) *tay stays·so(a)*; *(polite form)* Lei stesso(a) *lay stays·so(a)*; you've hurt yourself Si è fatto male *see e fat·to mah·le*; you did it yourself l'ha fatto Lei stesso(a) *la fat·to lay stays·so(a)*

yourselves pron voi stessi(e) *voy stays·see(·se)*; you've hurt yourselves vi siete fatti male *vee sye·te fat·tee mah·le*; you did it yourselves l'avete fatto voi stessi(e) *la·vay·te fat·to voy stays·see(·se)*

youth n *(period)* la gioventú *jo·ven·too*

youth club n il circolo della gioventú *cheer·ko·loh del·la jo·ven·too*

youth hostel n l'ostello della gioventú *(m)* o·stel·loh del·la jo·ven·too*

Yugoslavia n Iugoslavia *(f)* yoo·go·slah·vya*

Yugoslav(ian) adj iugoslavo(a) *yoo·go·slah·vo(a)*

Z

zebra n la zebra *dze·bra*

zero n lo zero *dze·roh*

zinc n lo zinco *tseen·koh*

zip code n il codice postale *ko·dee·che po·stah·le*

zipper n la cerniera lampo *cher·nye·ra lam·poh* S78, Sn76

zone n la zona *dzo·na*

zoo n lo zoo *dzo*

zoom lens n lo zoom *zoom*

zucchini pl gli zucchini *tsook·kee·nee*

Notes

Notes